BAUDELAIRE AND THE ENGLISH TRADITION

BAUDELAIRE

&

THE ENGLISH TRADITION

PATRICIA CLEMENTS

PRINCETON UNIVERSITY PRESS

PRINCETON, NEW JERSEY

PUBLISHED BY PRINCETON UNIVERSITY PRESS, 41 WILLIAM STREET
PRINCETON, NEW JERSEY 08540

IN THE UNITED KINGDOM: PRINCETON UNIVERSITY PRESS
GUILDFORD, SURREY

LIBRARY OF CONGRESS CATALOGING IN PUBLICATION DATA WILL BE
FOUND ON THE LAST PRINTED PAGE OF THIS BOOK

ISBN 0-691-06649-3

PUBLICATION OF THIS BOOK HAS BEEN AIDED BY A GRANT FROM THE
PAUL MELLON FUND OF PRINCETON UNIVERSITY PRESS

THIS BOOK HAS BEEN COMPOSED IN LINOTRON BASKERVILLE

CLOTHBOUND EDITIONS OF PRINCETON UNIVERSITY PRESS BOOKS
ARE PRINTED ON ACID-FREE PAPER AND BINDING MATERIALS
ARE CHOSEN FOR STRENGTH AND DURABILITY

PRINTED IN THE UNITED STATES OF AMERICA
BY PRINCETON UNIVERSITY PRESS
PRINCETON, NEW JERSEY

for my parents
and for
Meryle & Alder
&

Isobel

CONTENTS

ACKNOWLEDGMENTS

Grateful acknowledgment is made to Mrs. Valerie Eliot and Faber and Faber, London, for permission to quote from T. S. Eliot, *Poems Written in Early Youth* and *Collected Poems 1909-1962*, and *The Waste Land: A Facsimile and Transcript of the Original Draft including the Annotations of Ezra Pound, edited by Valerie Eliot.*

Excerpts from "East Coker" and "Burnt Norton" in *Four Quartets* by T. S. Eliot, copyright 1943 by T. S. Eliot, renewed 1971 by Esme Valerie Eliot. Reprinted by permission of Harcourt Brace Jovanovich. Excerpts from "The Waste Land" in *Collected Poems 1909-1962* by T. S. Eliot, copyright 1936 by Harcourt Brace Jovanovich; 1963, 1964 by T. S. Eliot. Reprinted by permission of the publisher.

Acknowledgment is also made to Farrar, Straus & Giroux for permission to quote from T. S. Eliot, *Poems Written in Early Youth*; to Penguin Books for permission to reprint excerpts from Baudelaire, *Selected Writings on Art & Artists*, trans. P. E. Charvet (Penguin Classics, 1972), copyright P. E. Charvet, 1972; to Basil Blackwell, Oxford, for permission to reprint a drawing from Ludwig Wittgenstein, *Philosophical Investigations* (Oxford 1968); to Rosica Colin, London, for permission to quote from Richard Aldington, *Images* (1919) and *Images* (1910-1915); to Macmillan & Co. for permission to quote passages from Edith Sitwell, *Collected Poems*, copyright 1957, reprinted 1958, 1961, 1965.

I am grateful to the University of Alberta, the Canada Council, and the Social Sciences and Humanities Research Council of Canada for time to write this book; to librarians at the Humanities Research Center at the University of Texas, at the Houghton Collection in Harvard, at the Berg Collection in the New York Public Library, at the British Library, and especially at the Taylorian and Bodleian Libraries in Oxford, for help in the research; to the editors of *The University of Toronto Quarterly* and *Figures in a Ground*, for permission to reprint material which appeared first in those places; and to the Paul Mellon Fund of Princeton University Press for a grant in aid of publication.

I owe thanks also, which it gives me great pleasure to acknowledge, to Wilfred and Sheila Watson, Henry Kreisel, Alison White, and E. J. Rose, my teachers and colleagues, who gave me the study of literature; to Dorothy Bednarowska, who supervised this work when it was a D.Phil. thesis; to John Stokes and Lawrence Markert, who shared their knowledge with me; to my friends and colleagues Philip Knight, Jorge Frascara, and Shirley Neuman, who helped in the finishing of this book; and to Professor W. T. Bandy, who gave a galvanizing encouragement.

This book owes most to Isobel Grundy, who gave it her generous criticism at every stage in its long history, and to Meryle and Alder Clark, who gave it its start.

NOTE REGARDING TRANSLATIONS

Wherever possible, I have used the following translations (and abbreviated as indicated). The footnotes give, in italics, the first word of the French quotation; the translation then follows.

C — Baudelaire, *Selected Writings on Art and Artists*, Translated with an Introduction by P. E. Charvet (London, 1972).

M — Baudelaire, *The Mirror of Art, Critical Studies*, Translated and Edited by Jonathan Mayne (New York, 1956).

B — J.-K. Huysmans, *Against Nature*, A New Translation of *A Rebours* by Robert Baldick (London, 1959, repr. 1973).

BAUDELAIRE AND THE ENGLISH TRADITION

Il est vrai que la grande tradition s'est perdue, et que la nouvelle n'est pas faite.

—Baudelaire
"De l'Héroïsme de la Vie Moderne," *Salon de 1846.*

INTRODUCTION

The most striking feature in an account of Baudelaire's post-humous literary life is that he has by so many poets, novelists, and critics of art and literature been regarded as a progenitor. Most of the important developments in French literature in the generations between the 1860's and the 1920's defined themselves in relation to him, and the act of tracking backwards to a source in his work furnishes a recurrent scene in modern French writing. Huysmans' *A Rebours* provides the best-known instance: its decadent, scholarly, origin-seeking protagonist, Des Esseintes, finds in *Les Fleurs du Mal* the source of all that is expressive, significant, and profound in modern literature. He treats the book with exceptional, almost gothic, reverence, making the object reflect in its physical qualities the distinction of the words it embodies. *His* copy is specially printed (in "les admirables lettres épiscopales de l'ancienne maison Le Clere"), made up in a special format ("large . . . rappelant celui des missels"), specially bound (in "une mirifique et authentique peau de truie choisie entre mille, couleur chair"), and specially decorated ("de dentelles noires au fer froid, miraculeusement assorties par un grand artiste"). In that singular book, which commands a more than merely secular descriptive language, Des Esseintes locates origins: Verlaine, he reflects, derives from its psychological side, Théodore Hannon from its plastic vision, and the whole immense "horizon" of modern literature from its "unforgettable doors."[1]

Other generations of French writers, too, followed the stream of modernism back to its source in Baudelaire, who, for Rim-

les admirables . . . the admirable episcopal type of the old house of Le Clere . . . large format similar to that of a mass-book . . . a mirific and authentic flesh-coloured pigskin, one in a thousand, dotted all over where the bristles had been and blind-tooled in black with designs of marvellous aptness chosen by a great artist (B, 146).

baud, it will be remembered, was "le premier voyant, roi des poètes, *un vrai dieu*," and even after the earliest generations of symbolists had been succeeded by newer poetic powers, Baudelaire retained his mythic status as the originator of the modern. Remy de Gourmont, who carried the symbolist tradition into the twentieth century (and into modern English criticism), wrote in *Le Livre des Masques*, which went through more than a dozen editions, that "Toute la littérature actuelle et surtout celle que l'on appelle symboliste, est baudelairienne, non sans doute par la technique extérieure, mais par la technique interne et spirituelle." The history of the modern, he said, could be told backwards from himself, through Henri de Régnier, to Verlaine and Mallarmé. Then, he wrote, "Par eux, on descend le long de la montagne triste jusqu'en la cité dolente des *Fleurs du Mal*." The end of that recurring descent, that repeated retrospective pilgrimage, is the beginning of modern writing. In accounts of the history of modern French literature, *Les Fleurs du Mal* is a sacred book—and the ironies of that transfiguration are no less apparent now than they were when they were created. But these accounts make of *Les Fleurs du Mal* a remarkably new dispensation, and though, like the first chapter of the first Gospel, they are often characterized by their recitation of *begats*, they lead not, in what Swift designated as the best in the old style of criticism, to "the most Antient of all,"[2] but to a departure, to discovery of what Baudelaire himself had hailed as "l'avènement du *neuf*!"

That Baudelaire should appear so insistently in French writing as the source of the modern is hardly a surprise: he is, after all, an incontestably great, modern, French poet. It was with his works that Gallimard launched its Bibliothèque de la Pléiade.[3] But it is altogether more remarkable that he should appear, no less insistently, as the begetter of the modern in English literature. Yet from the moment his work appeared in England, poets and critics valued it (or feared it) chiefly because of what they saw as its originating power. When Swinburne introduced Baudelaire to English readers in the 1860's, he proposed him

Toute la . . . All present-day literature, and especially the literature we call symbolist, is baudelairean, not, probably, in external technique, but in internal and spiritual technique.
Par eux . . . Through them, we come down the sad mountain to the piteous city of *Les Fleurs du Mal*.
l'avènement . . . the advent of the *new*! (M, 37).

as a model for English poets, suggesting that a carefully culti-
vated, wholly intentional imitation of his work could provide an
escape from what he saw as the narrow confinements of "tra-
dition and the taste of the greater number of readers." When
Eliot wrote on him, long after Swinburne had been, to all ap-
pearances, forgotten, he too proposed him as a model, as "the
greatest exemplar in *modern* poetry in any language, for his verse
and language is the nearest thing to a complete renovation that
we have had." Between Swinburne and Eliot there exist several
generations of English poets, who, like them, nominated Baude-
laire as precursor and implicated him in their attempts at "ren-
ovation."

These English writers, like the French, paid their tribute in
several kinds. Baudelaire's history in English imaginative liter-
ature is initiated by Swinburne's representation, in "Ave atque
Vale," of an act of commemoration, in which he lays an offering
on Baudelaire's grave, and Baudelaire and his book are made
part of the iconography of English literature in sometimes sur-
prising ways. His face—or rather, his death-mask—is the model
for the features of Huxley's fictional Spandrell in *Point Counter
Point*; his features, as they were described by his French contem-
poraries and friends, supply the visual qualities of Pater's "mod-
ern poet" in *Gaston de Latour*; his portrait commands the de-
scriptive attention of J. C. Squire on more than one occasion.
His book, too, is permanently embedded in English poetry and
prose as an icon, "bound in some Nile-green skin that has been
powdered with gilded nenuphars and smoothed with hard
ivory," as in Wilde, or darkening a youthful paradise, "as though
with lines of rain," as in the memoirs of Sacheverell Sitwell.

Since his introduction to English readers and writers,
Baudelaire has also drawn the critical attention of a wide range
of poets, novelists, and critics of literature and culture. There
are essays on his work by, among others, Swinburne, William
Allingham, George Saintsbury, Henry James, Arthur Symons,
Havelock Ellis, Lafcadio Hearn, Richard Aldington, J. C. Squire,
T. S. Eliot, John Middleton Murry, Christopher Isherwood, and
W. H. Auden. His work has attracted less formal or direct critical
comment from William Michael Rossetti, Robert Buchanan, Os-
car Wilde, F. S. Flint, John Gould Fletcher, W. B. Yeats, Edith
Sitwell, D. H. Lawrence, and Lytton Strachey. There are, fur-
thermore, several volumes of the sort of George Moore's *Flowers*

of Passion or of J. C. Squire's *Poems and Baudelaire Flowers*, and translations of his work, which began to appear as early as 1869, mainly of his poetry but also of his prose-poems, art criticism, and letters, abound. Among his translators are Lord Alfred Douglas, Arthur Symons, Edna St. Vincent Millay, John Payne, James Elroy Flecker, Edward Lascelles, T. Sturge Moore, Aleister Crowley, Aldous Huxley, Roy Campbell, and Robert Lowell. The "impact" of Baudelaire—the word is Eliot's—registers everywhere in modern English writing. A list of the major works of the period during which modernism was taking shape would include at least these in which Baudelaire is a distinguishing power and an identifying voice: *Poems and Ballads, First and Second Series, The Renaissance, Gaston de Latour, Intentions, The Picture of Dorian Gray, Salomé, The Symbolist Movement in Literature, Heart of Darkness, Rhythm, Blue Review, Wheels, Des Imagistes, Prufrock and Other Observations, The Waste Land, The Sacred Wood, The Problem of Style, Women in Love, Mrs. Dalloway, Point Counter Point.* A list of lesser works of the time, not prominently part of the canon of high modernism, in which his voice is to be heard, is virtually inexhaustible.

Baudelaire is most powerfully present in modern English literature as a suffused and multiply expressive intellectual and imaginative influence, and the sometimes surprising shapes his influence assumes in works of individual writers comprise the subject matter of this book. But his protean presence is by no means confined to the depths, and it does not have its significance only in individual works. It occupies every level of meaning between the profound and the superficial, provokes every tone between the thoughtful and the hysterical, commands every kind of responsive expression from the intensely personal to the wholly public. Baudelaire glitters at the surface of *Sons and Lovers*, for instance, in its elaboration of the motif of "flowers of passion"; he animates the argumentative texture of *Women in Love*, whose passionately derided "flowers of mud" come to represent one side of the novel's sexual conflict; and, with Conrad, he supplies the underlying shape of *Mrs. Dalloway*, the voyage that leads to a vision of "the horror" and to the inclusion, among the flowers Clarissa goes to buy herself, of "flowers of darkness."

Baudelaire's influence in English literature is no less significant when it is conventional than when it is an element in a powerful originality, though in the latter case it has more value. The "flowers" I have just cited suggest not only his particular value to Lawrence and Woolf, but also the existence in the twentieth century of a convention of Baudelaire allusion. Those phrases summon him into activity in those novels just as surely as Eliot's quotation at the end of "The Burial of the Dead" calls him into duty there, and that fact confirms him as a presence in the English tradition as well as in the works of English writers. By the time Lawrence and Woolf wrote, such flowers as they invoked were already rich with the significance of other English contexts, and when they wrote they amplified the already considerable complexity of Baudelaire allusion in English. All of those "flowers" have more than a single root. Lawrence's "flowers of passion" point backward, to Moore's among others; his "flowers of mud" point forward, to the attack on Baudelaire's sexual attitudes in Huxley's most famous novel. And "the horror" and the "flowers of darkness" in *Mrs. Dalloway* initiate a complex series of connections, since *Heart of Darkness*, of which Woolf makes a powerful revision in this novel, is itself a revision of Baudelaire's "Le Voyage," which, by her reference, Woolf invokes. That poem, whose narrative, like Marlow's, is moved forward by the interrupting and prompting questions of the auditors, begins, like his, in excited contemplation of maps and in description of an urgent, childish aspiration to adventure, and it concludes, as does Marlow, having shown experience to be "une oasis d'horreur dans un désert d'ennui." It is Baudelaire's experience, which, in one sense, Marlow lives through. Woolf's Mrs. Dalloway, the product of her creator's powerful seizing, reshaping, and feminizing of a romantic quest which is located precisely in Conrad and Baudelaire,[4] derives part of her life from him, too. But the communal character of this Baudelaire reference does not stop there. It was, of course, the Conradian "horror" that Eliot intended originally as the epigraph for *The Waste Land*, in which he, too, responds profoundly to Baudelaire's poem. And it was while she was setting the text of *The Waste Land* for the Hogarth Press that Virginia Woolf was hard at work on *The Hours*, as *Mrs. Dalloway* was then called.

By the time the modernists were producing their finest works, then, Baudelaire was solidly canonized, part of a conversation that had become almost wholly English. When Eliot recommended him as the exemplar of modern poetry, Baudelaire was a domesticated influence, an aspect now not chiefly of the relation of English literature to French, but of the English tradition itself. From the moment he was so enthusiastically welcomed by Swinburne, Baudelaire came to English readers and writers as part of their own inheritance—so that Woolf's ambivalent reference includes Conrad's, and Conrad's, as several features of his tale show,[5] depends on his awareness of the currency of Baudelaire in late nineteenth-century English writing. Similarly, Wilde's Baudelaire includes Pater's, even if secretly; Edith Sitwell's includes Symons's; and Eliot's includes Swinburne's, even if antagonistically. The appropriation of Baudelaire by the English tradition is part of what I wish to observe in this study; and the Baudelaire who is my subject is not the poet as in himself he really may have been, but, to use Wilde's words, the "complex, multiform," and steadily changing creation of the English writers.

In French accounts of modern literary history, Baudelaire is an ambivalent figure, an emblem both for discontinuity, a radical rejection of the literature of the past, and for a new continuity, the apostolic descent of the moderns. In English literature, from the outset, the ambivalences attached to his name are multiplied, since what in France was simply rejection of the past was in England proposed also as a departure from the national character of the present. Swinburne intended his Baudelaire to be subversive: he proposed him as an antithesis to a confining English tradition, and, from the beginning, for English poets the identification of Baudelaire as a precursor entailed some remarkable exclusions. By every generation of English "moderns" since Swinburne, Baudelaire has been set in opposition to the English line. Making a "brother" of him, Swinburne turned away from "Tennyson & Cie," as he called them in a letter, and so he initiated a process that would conclude in a conception of the development of modern English poetry as the extraordinarily excluding line from Poe to Valéry. The exchange that is at the center of "Ave atque Vale"—in which the poet closes his hand over the "shut scroll" that is Les Fleurs du Mal, taking it "as if a hand were in my hand to hold," and offers to the "sweet singing elder brother" his own garland—predicts a wholesale cultural "swerve." This imagery enacts precisely the idea of tradition as a "handing down," as Eliot said it was in "Tradition and the Individual Talent," but it names the members of its "communion of song" with no very great respect for an idea of literature as the expression of national genius or of literary descent as a branch of national history. Tracking back, by Baudelaire, to Sappho, "the supreme head of song," Swinburne predicts a view of the tradition as "all of the literature of Europe, from Homer."

To defenders of the ancient, national faith and fatherhood, this Baudelaire of Swinburne was grotesque. Robert Buchanan, who is only the most extreme of several early English commentators on Baudelaire and the dangers he represented, saw him as a "Mephistopheles," as a carrier to the island of a new epidemic of "the Italian disease" in literature, and as the "god-father as it were of the modern fleshly school." That language of orthodoxy—of church and state and patriarchy—rings with rhetorical fullness in the English Baudelaire debate, and it is an indication of his usefulness to English poets. His English *semblables* have always used him to establish an idea of their difference. In what Harold Bloom calls the "Eternity of warfare that is poetic influence," Baudelaire represents an idea of alliance, and this is as true of the generation of Eliot as of the generation of Swinburne. When writers of the early twentieth century laid claim to Baudelaire, asserting their likeness to him, they made him in that same gesture serve the purposes of their own renunciations. When John Middleton Murry, for instance, wrote his first essay on Baudelaire, he complained that Wilde, misapprehending his subject completely, had treated the French poets as a "privately printed book of pornography." When Eliot reviewed Symons's translations, he could, he said, "only protest violently." By the end of the second decade of the twentieth century, Baudelaire had been rehabilitated by the newest generation, the subversive had been canonized, and the poet who had scandalized the Victorians was now seen as a profound moralist. But the transmutation of the nineteenth-century "Mephistopheles" into the twentieth-century " 'Poet and Saint . . .' " had exclusion as one of its purposes. An account of the transformations in the English myth of Baudelaire comprises a history of relations among generations of English poets.

1

SWINBURNE

TRADITION AND THE TASTE OF THE
GREATER NUMBER OF READERS

When Swinburne recognized Baudelaire as his elder "brother," he changed the course of the main current of the English tradition, altering in a most unusual way the ideal order against which the individual English talent must define itself. In this history of Baudelaire's affiliation by English poetry, Swinburne has the importance not merely of a beginner, but of a powerful originator. He opened the long conversation with a statement so enduring that when Eliot came to describe *his* Baudelaire, several generations later, it was to Swinburne he turned as antagonist. If Baudelaire is, as Michel Butor says, the pivot around which European poetry turns to become modern, then in England he shares the pivotal place with Swinburne.[1]

Swinburne's admiration for Baudelaire has commanded attention since soon after publication of *Poems and Ballads*, in 1866, even though the documents that record it officially constitute a slim file. Swinburne left his review of the poems, his only public speech, "Ave atque Vale," admiring comments in his *Blake* and other critical works, and affectionate and respectful remarks in letters to other people. Baudelaire left only signs of gratitude for Swinburne's review: the inscribed copy of *Richard Wagner et Tannhäuser à Paris* that Swinburne prized, a letter the English poet never received, and references to the review in a letter to his mother and in one to Whistler.[2] In addition to these bits there is some much-speculated-on information about "messages and courtesies" passed between the two poets by mutual friends ("the admiration of some years," Swinburne said in a note in his *Blake*, "brought me near him by way of written or transmitted word")[3] and there are some compelling and much-repeated stories: of Swinburne rising at the Royal Literary Fund Dinner for 1866 to declaim in passionate staccato his admiration for a condemned French poet; of the photographer Nadar, charged with delivering Baudelaire's letter to Swinburne, deciding at the last moment to go to Brussels instead, so that the letter lay in a drawer until after both Swinburne and his "poor Baudelaire" had died;[4] of Hutton, the editor of *The Spectator*, detecting Swinburne's attempt to slip past him as modern French writers his own inventions Cossu and Clouet ("Or is it Clouët?" he wrote), whose imitations of Baudelaire, as Enid Starkie said, were "scabrous"; of Swinburne, having been misinformed by the papers, starting to compose his most famous elegy before its subject had died.[5] There is more solid information, and less anecdote, about Swinburne's lifelong admiration for Hugo, which can be examined in their considerable correspondence as well as in Swinburne's fulsome poetic and critical praise of his "beloved Master,"[6] and even his association with Mallarmé is more amply recorded than that with Baudelaire. Yet it is Swinburne's interest in Baudelaire that continues to fascinate.

That is partly because Swinburne's Baudelaire is one of his major achievements. This has not always seemed true, and the slow shifts of comment on his sympathy with the "sweet strange elder singer"[7] are illuminating. They trace his own rise and fall on the waves of official criticism at the same time as they sketch the changing shapes of English attitudes toward Baudelaire during the periods in which poetry became "modern." Swinburne's earliest critics, both his friends and his enemies, rushed to see Baudelaire's "influence" as the cause of his "faults." William Michael Rossetti, writing to defend *Poems and Ballads* from the outrage they had provoked, regretted the traces in them of the French "Mephistopheles," and Robert Buchanan, crusading against the "fleshly" poets, made no attempt to restrain his horror about Swinburne's poems, patronizingly attributing their faults to the same source, which he too recognized easily as "Mephistopheles."[8] The lawyer who represented Buchanan in his 1867 suit against the *Examiner* (a consequence of Swinburne's counterattack) told the court that Swinburne had degraded his poetry "by loading it with a beastly sensualism, and by adopting the indecent garbage of the French Baudelaire," and when Taine met the poet in 1871 he saw him as "un visionnaire malade" whose poems "sont dans le genre de Baudelaire et de Victor Hugo."[9]

But Swinburne's declaration of common cause with Baudelaire came gradually to be seen as evidence of his critical powers. At about the turn of the century, one writer heard "the three names of Baudelaire and Swinburne and Immortality sound as one"; a few years later, another said that Swinburne's accomplishment had been the introduction into England of "something entirely new" in poetry and "the carrying into perfect practice" of Baudelaire's theories; and in 1917, the year *Prufrock* saw print, Arthur Symons praised Swinburne lavishly because his early poem "Cleopatra" was "steeped deep in the spirit of Baudelaire."[10] That same year, Edmund Gosse, recording the major facts about the poets' association, maintained that Swinburne's support of Baudelaire required "high intellectual courage," and the *Mercure de France*, a journal read with respect by the emphatically modern, praised Swinburne's ability to penetrate the romanticism of *Les Fleurs du Mal*, to detect their chosen, masterly simplicity, to identify what in them is profoundly and broadly classical.[11]

Swinburne's admiration for his elder "brother," however, and especially his claim of consanguinity, drew altogether sharper comment from a younger generation of writers, who wanted to dissociate him, with whom they said they had little in common, from Baudelaire, with whom they considered they shared much. Harold Nicolson, who wrote an eminently anti-Victorian *Life* of Swinburne, told the Royal Society of Literature in 1925 that Swinburne was a mere imitator, that comparison between the two poets showed only that "Baudelaire, for all of his sardonic reticence, was profound," while "Swinburne, for all his ebullient brilliance, was superficial." He wrote later that Swinburne was constitutionally incapable of perceiving Baudelaire profoundly: "who could contend," he demanded, "that [the Pre-Raphaelites and Baudelaire] penetrated to his inner consciousness or created any permanent attitude?"[12] John Middleton Murry and T. S. Eliot joined in denial of Swinburne's seriousness. Murry saw him as a posturer: "It is as though some Falstaff hit you in the small

un visionnaire . . . a sick visionary whose poems are in the style of Baudelaire and Victor Hugo.

of the back with a flagon of sack and roared: 'I'm a pervert, I am, my old buck!' " Eliot said that Swinburne's view of Baudelaire was "childish," and he resented what he saw as Swinburne's flamboyant appropriation of the French poet: "*Such rugs and jugs and candle lights!*"[13] By the time Eliot wrote, the pattern of comment on the relationship between the two poets had come full circle and achieved an ironic completeness. Swinburne's elder "brother," having changed by slow degrees from a "Mephistopheles" to a "Poet and Saint," had become the *semblable*, the *frère*, of a new generation; and Swinburne, who had been condemned for his submission to the poet of vice, was now accused of not perceiving Baudelaire's merits, damned for his failure to be influenced *enough*, and blamed for damaging by association the reputation of the poet he had introduced to English readers. In England, Eliot wrote in 1930, it had been Baudelaire's "misfortune to be first and extravagantly advertised by Swinburne."[14]

Swinburne, it is true, did much to discourage belief in his seriousness. He told Gosse, for instance, and Gosse repeated these words on every possible occasion, that he had composed his review of *Les Fleurs du Mal*—in which he said that they had the "languid lurid beauty of close and threatening weather"[15]— in a Turkish bath in Paris, and at the same time as he was composing his measured critical praise of Baudelaire's "perfect and careful poetry" (*CB*) and subscribing faithfully to the articles of his aesthetic, he was confecting the mock salacity of Cossu and Clouet, parodies that could only, if published, have undercut the praise. But Swinburne was serious, and he was self-aware. Baudelaire was for him the most consequential aspect of an exploration of French literature that served his major poetic purposes. The comments of his critics reflect clearly, though in an oblique mirror, not only relations among generations of English poets but also those between national literatures, and they show a steady shifting of the context in which English poets worked. To Rossetti, Baudelaire's mere Frenchness was exotic; to Murry and Eliot, his exemplary modernity was the first and his nationality only the second fact about him. For them, he was "*notre* Baudelaire," and that fact, though they failed to say so, was brought to birth partly by Swinburne.[16]

Like many later poets—Aldington or Sitwell or Pound or Eliot, for instance, who made their search for progenitors a critical theme—Swinburne sought to be influenced, and he said so. He recorded obligation to Arnold, for instance, "as to all other real and noble artists whose influence it was my fortune to feel when most susceptible of influence, and least conscious of it, and most in want."[17] When, later, he met Baudelaire's work, he was no longer unaware either of what he wanted to express or of the fact that the "taste" and the "tradition" of the time denied him freedom to express it. He made no secret of his regard for Baudelaire as a poet and critic from whom English poets could learn: it is apparent in practically everything he wrote about him, whether for private or public consumption. The clarity of its expression is a measure both of his boldness (the antithesis of Pater's careful removal from *The Renaissance* of phrases that might suggest to a hostile public the presence there of the French master of the "fleshly school") and of his critical self-consciousness, the contrary of the "childish" obliviousness to the "real" for which he was dismissed by his early twentieth-century critics. When he defended his own poems against attack, as well as when he wrote on Blake or Shakespeare or Rossetti, Swinburne "turned to" Baudelaire not merely with respect, but with all "confidence" and "reverence."[18] In Baudelaire, he says more than once, his readers will find, more perfectly expressed than in his own work, precisely what he had himself aimed to say. Swinburne's "turning to" Baudelaire predicts the turning away of the whole of modern English literature from some of the confinements of its own tradition, narrowly defined. For Swinburne, as for Eliot, Baudelaire's achievement did not diminish the possibilities for poetry, but enlarged them. From the beginning, Baudelaire appears in England *as influence*. Swinburne made him available, proposed him as a shaping force.

Dozens of English poets, including some who dismissed Swinburne on the least critical and most patronizing of grounds, were glad to take up his suggestion, and so Baudelaire, who in France had seemed to father symbolism, came eventually, by a process that is one of the subjects of this book, to support English poetry against that school. Swinburne's acknowledgment that he used what he read, however, that he really did learn from it, together with his unusual talent for parody, has from the beginning done great damage to his own reputation. Robert Buchanan pounced on it, and ran up the rough structure of an argument against influence. "Imitation," he said, both in his anonymous review of *Poems and Ballads* and in his damaging "Fleshly School" pieces, was proof of "insincerity" and "insincerity" a category of "immorality." He presented this argument, he said, on literary grounds; but later, in "The Monkey and the Microscope," he did not hesitate to use it for personal insult:[19]

> A clever Monkey!—worth a smile!
> How really human is his style;
> How worthy of our admiration
> Is such delicious imitation!

More recently, Swinburne's acknowledgment of influence has been a central point in a claim that he had no serious attitude of his own (no "internal centre," Meredith said)[20] and that his work need therefore compel no serious attention. *"Poems and Ballads* were the effervescence with which a quick and shallow nature responded to a certain influence issuing partly from the Greek and Latin classics, partly from medieval legend, partly from the French literature of the nineteenth century," wrote A. E. Housman. Even critics who defend Swinburne's "individuality" have felt obliged to assert it as a paradox, to see him as an original copier. The "Assimilative or Reproductive in point of literary form," said W. M. Rossetti, is "one of the most curious specialties of Mr. Swinburne's writings"; what is remarkable about his poems is that they are "exceedingly fine pieces of work, exceedingly like their adopted models."[21] Alice Meynell wrote in 1909 that upon Mazzini, Shelley, Gautier, and Baudelaire, Swinburne "sustained, he fattened, he enriched his poetry"; and the introduction to a modern selection of Swinburne's poems perpetuates both the point and the figure: Swinburne's imagination, says Robert Nye, "fed on books, it feasted on other men's wits." It is contrary to our expectations, he says, that "pastiche" should be good poetry, but "in Swinburne it is."[22]

The argument about imitation and influence in Swinburne's case was hotly political, on more than one ground. The issue was not, though it claimed to be, whether Swinburne might imitate other writers and still be thought worthy; it was what other writers Swinburne might without offense imitate. As his early, hostile critics saw, Swinburne intended to induce some shifts in the English tradition, and the argument about his imitation was, in its beginnings, a line of defense for his opponents. The question of imitation remained a strain of debate during the whole period in which modernism was taking shape, working out its

history as the international line from Poe to Valéry. It surfaces
brilliantly in Wilde, who made it a main preoccupation of his
criticism, and who, as the author of a column called "Dinner and
Dishes," made the analogy between feeding the imagination and
feeding the stomach serve the purposes of critical satire. On the
subject of his own imitations, Wilde pleads magnificently guilty,
like Bourget insisting that the book is the great initiator,[23] and
it is impossible to argue that his imitations were blind. Swin-
burne's cultivation of influence, however, has often been the
subject of facile psychologizing. He is, we are told in the familiar
argument, a case of arrested development, a man who, "at a
comparatively early age," became "strangely impervious to any
new idea or any fresh experience."[24] His reading, as a conse-
quence, was a refuge from life, his literary experience necessarily
"unreal," the stuff of his poetry merely imitated. His verse, Eliot
said (perhaps intending to outrage), is "not morbid," "not erotic,"
"not destructive": "These are adjectives which can be applied to
the material, the human feelings, which in Swinburne's case do
not exist."[25] Criticism of Swinburne drowns too often in a light
wash of psychology; a reductive argument about his life becomes
an evasive comment on his work. We are invited to see him as
a poet who was almost entirely unselfconscious, or, at most, as
one whose self-consciousness was merely technical. He could
count, he knew his numbers, but in almost everything else his
work was in one way or another the product of the dark dreams
of his childhood, mere fantasy. Swinburne's attitude toward
Baudelaire, or toward any other writer he admired and learned
from, is seen as evidence of his "two dominant and conflicting
impulses, namely, the impulse towards revolt and the impulse
towards submission."[26] From that point of view, poetic influence
is submission; the art-for-art's-sake theory is revolt (but submis-
sive because borrowed); and Swinburne's essay in *The Spectator*
for 6 September 1862, the first notice in England of *Les Fleurs
du Mal*, a principled, perceptive, elegant essay and a new de-
parture in the history of English poetry, can be shrunk to the
size of a "piece of daring" intended to thrill its writer and "épater
le bourgeois."[27] It is sometimes tempting to see criticism of Swin-
burne's work as the most complete, the ideal gratification of his
masochism.

Swinburne's response to Baudelaire, however, is not the out-
come of an obscure impulse to submission. It issues from his

critical intelligence, from his frequently parodic self-awareness, and from his faculty for satiric diagnosis. He went to school to the French, and to Baudelaire in particular, for powerful reasons. He found in Baudelaire's criticism a "sane and just" view of the imagination and its rights in relation to society and morality, and in his poetry both a "passionate and stately" music (*CB*) and a courageous retrieval for poetry of subjects that were thought scandalous in the prudish 'sixties. He saw, furthermore, the possibility of enlarging by alliance the tradition in which English poets wrote. Of course Swinburne intended to confute a too-narrow "tradition and the taste of the greater number of readers" (*CB*). That is a much more subversive purpose than the mere *épatement des bourgeois*, and it is one on which other writers feasted.

*　　*　　*

Exactly when Swinburne first met the "delicate and careful" (*CB*) work of the poet whose cause he decided to interpret and share remains an attractive mystery. He was still in Oxford in the summer of 1857, a member of the "Old Mortality," enjoying a "considerable ripening of [his] intellectual powers."[28] That was the year in which the Obscene Publications Act was passed in England, and, in Paris, the earliest edition of *Les Fleurs du Mal* published, seized, and subjected to what Swinburne, when he reviewed the book four years later, called "a foolish and shameless prosecution." The court that judged Baudelaire's book found it innocent of blasphemy, but guilty of immorality. It fined the poet 300 francs and condemned six of his poems—"Lesbos," "Les Femmes Damnées," "Le Léthé," "A Celle qui est trop gaie," "Les Bijoux," "Les Métamorphoses du Vampire," all of which treat sexual subjects—on the extremely interesting grounds that they "conduisent nécessairement à l'excitation des sens par un réalisme grossier et offensant pour la pudeur."[29] (Flaubert, charged on the same counts earlier in the year, got off.) Later, about two hundred copies of *Les Fleurs du Mal* that had escaped confiscation before the trial were mutilated, the offending poems cut out of them, and remaindered, "sans qu'on eût pris la peine d'y coordonner la pagination."[30] The second edition, 1861, omit-

conduisent . . . lead necessarily to the excitement of the senses by a realism that is rude and offensive to decency.
sans qu'on . . . without anyone taking the trouble to co-ordinate the pagination.

ted the six offending poems but added thirty-five others (including "Le Voyage"), and the guilty verses, thus separated from the rest, began to lead their own, underground life, turning up first in Brussels in 1866 in an edition intended, according to its acrid advertisement, for the "deux cent soixante lecteurs probables qui figurent—à peu près—... le public littéraire en France, depuis que les bêtes y ont décidément usurpé la parole sur les hommes."[31] That edition, of which, the advertisement said, the author would become aware at the same time as the two hundred and sixty readers, bore the famous frontispiece by Félicien Rops, an imprint which, intending to confuse pursuit, read "Amsterdam," and the title *Les Epaves*. These "waifs" or "strays," as the title denominates them, appeared in several subsequent editions of their own (sometimes in lists of pornographic works), rejoining the rest of Baudelaire's poems only after his death in the *Oeuvres Complètes* of 1868, although even there they appeared illegally and as a separate section. The court did not reverse its judgment until 1949.

Swinburne's judgment of *Les Fleurs du Mal*—that it would not "in the long run fail of its meed of admiration whether here or in France"—has not required reversing. His review of the second edition figures in Claude Pichois's chronology of Baudelaire's life: "*6 septembre* [1862]: Dans *The Spectator*, article plein d'admiration de Swinburne sur *Les Fleurs du Mal*" (xlviii), and it is also one of the only two exceptions in Marcel Ruff's account of the critical blank Baudelaire's poems met during his lifetime. The other was a series of three articles written by Verlaine, who was then twenty-one, for *L'Art* in November and December of 1865.[32] Whenever Swinburne's first encounter with Baudelaire's poems took place, his reading of *Les Fleurs du Mal* when he went to Paris in the spring of 1861 was decisive. They had on him, as later on Eliot, "great impact."[33] He began immediately to keep a scrupulously close watch on Baudelaire's works as they appeared. His fake review of "Clouet" shows just how close: he attempted to publish it in 1862; it includes information from Baudelaire's article on Pétrus Borel, which appeared in Paris in

deux cent . . . the probable two hundred and sixty readers who comprise—more or less—the literary public in France, ever since in that country the animals took over speech from men.

6 septembre . . . 6 September [1862]: In *The Spectator*, enthusiastic article by Swinburne on *Les Fleurs du Mal*.

July 1861.[34] Later, Swinburne's bookseller had what amounted
to a standing order: "And please tell Dulau of Soho Square," he
wrote to a friend, "to send me 'Victor Hugo en Zélande'; he will
not forget of course (knowing this address) to send the next
volume of Baudelaire's works when it appears."[35] Swinburne's
library, sold in 1916, included the trophies of his steady pursuit:
the complete works of 1868, *Les Paradis Artificiels, Opium et Ha-
schisch*, the *Oeuvres Posthumes* of 1887 and 1908, and two copies
of *Les Epaves* (1874), as well as two of the earliest critical works,
Asselineau's *Baudelaire, Sa Vie et Son Oeuvre* (1869) and Fizelière's
and Decaux's bibliography, *Charles Baudelaire* (1868). It also in-
cluded two of Swinburne's personal treasures. One was the pam-
phlet *Richard Wagner et Tannhäuser à Paris*, bearing Baudelaire's
inscription, in pencil: "Mr. Algernon C. Swinburne Bon souvenir
et mille Remerciments, C.B." The other was the copy of the rare
first edition of *Les Fleurs du Mal* that William Michael Rossetti
had given him in 1864, about which Dante Gabriel Rossetti wrote
to Swinburne from Paris: "I tremble for the result of your read-
ing Baudelaire's suppressed poems, the crop of which read I
expect you [*sic*] to be in fine flower, not to say fruit, by the time
I reach London. If so, and these new revelations are to be
printed, too, I warn you that the public will not be able to digest
them." (Rossetti concluded his letter with a tantalizing post-
script: "Baudelaire is away or I should have met him.")[36]

    Swinburne's response to Baudelaire's work was extraordinary.
Between 1861 and 1868, he took full possession of the territory
Baudelaire had made available to him. In his criticism, his poems,
his remarkable attempts at prose fiction, his satires and parodies,
he invented a conversation with his "unbeholden friend" to
which he attributed great significance.[37] Simple enumeration of
the works of his early years in which Baudelaire figures prom-
inently, either explicitly or unnamed, demonstrates the weight
he attached to the conversation he was inventing. In his review
he marked out the boundaries he would defend, aligning Baude-
laire enthusiastically with himself in opposition to nationalistic
or moralizing criticism. In *A Year's Letters*, also written in 1861,
he dramatized his critical position in the steelily aesthetic Lady
Midhurst. Shortly afterward he carried his convictions into

Mr. Algernon . . . Mr. Algernon C. Swinburne Best regards and a thousand
Thanks, C.B.

mocking, conspiratorial attack in his reviews of Cossu and Clouet. During these same years he was composing the *Poems and Ballads* of the First Series, elaborating some of the same subject matter that had caused the French court to send *Les Epaves* into exile and that would soon cause Moxon's to withdraw his own book from circulation, and he was working on his intensely Baudelairean second novel, *Lesbia Brandon*. In 1866, he linked himself publicly with Baudelaire by recommending him, in his speech to the Royal Literary Fund Dinner, for the study of English poets, and by invoking his support in what he called "my defensive and offensive pamphlet—Laus Diabolo," the *Notes on Poems and Reviews*.[38] In 1868 he named Baudelaire as his "brother" in "Ave atque Vale" and called him a "critic of incomparably delicate insight and subtly good sense" in his own major critical work, the study of Blake, which interprets the English poet in terms provided by the French one.[39] Baudelaire exerts powerful pressure on the shapes, subjects, and language of all these works. Later, in *Under the Microscope* (1872), Swinburne cited Baudelaire again as authority for his assertion that a poem's moral is none the worse for being implicit; and in his *Study of Shakespeare* (1880) he turned "Not for the first and probably not for the last time . . . with all confidence as with all reverence . . . to the exquisite critical genius of a long honoured and long lamented fellow-craftsman."[40] For Swinburne, Baudelaire's work was both a central fact and a representative of value. The flower, not to say the fruit, at the thought of which Dante Gabriel Rossetti said he trembled, was chosen.

From the beginning, Swinburne's Baudelaire is a complex construction. Later, sharply opposed views of him would emerge in England—Eliot would see him as a "saint," Yeats as the type of the sensuous man, Murry as an intensely straining moralist, Huxley (after Lawrence) as one of the "grand perverts"—but Swinburne holds a number of those opposing elements together. His careful pointing of the prose in the memorial "notice" he added to his *Blake* emphasizes the balance and opposition of his view:

> . . . no more of fervent yet of perfect verse, no more of subtle yet of sensitive comment, will be granted us at the hands of Charles Baudelaire: that now for ever we must fall back upon what is left us. It is precious enough. We may see again as various a power as was his, may feel again as

fiery a sympathy, may hear again as strange a murmur of revelation, as sad a whisper of knowledge, as mysterious a music of emotion; we shall never find so keen, so delicate, so deep an unison of sense and spirit. What verse he could make, how he loved all fair and felt all strange things, with what infallible taste he knew at once the limit and the licence of his art, all may see at a glance.[41]

Swinburne's imaginative and critical response to Baudelaire embodies that antithesis and variety. In his official criticism he gives an official portrait, balancing the "courage and good sense" (*CB*) of Baudelaire's aesthetic with the moral weight of his poems, the perfection of the treatment with the appropriateness of the challenging subject matter. That criticism goes together with his memorial poem to make up a passionate and careful "study," as he might have called it. In other pieces, however, those not usually entered seriously into the "Swinburne-Baudelaire" file, he makes Baudelaire part of his fascination with dupery and disguise. This darker, mocking drawing presents an acid, masked criticism of a world in which "les bêtes ont décidément usurpé la parole sur les hommes." Because of circumstances or bad luck—Swinburne did not publish *Lesbia Brandon* in his lifetime and his attempt to hoax *The Spectator* failed—his unofficial portrait of Baudelaire did not see public light. It probably saw a good deal of private light, however: Lafourcade suggests that Swinburne might have sent copies of his Cossu and Clouet to Baudelaire himself, and Gosse reports that he liked nothing better than to read to his friends from *Lesbia Brandon*.[42] The Baudelaire who emerges from this privately circulated material is an enlightening grotesque, a confirmation of Swinburne's subversive purpose. What is remarkable is that the satiric or secret works go hand in hand with the others: it was while he was working on his serious review of *Les Fleurs du Mal* that Swinburne stitched up and nailed together his Baudelaire parodies and while he worked on his *Blake* that he pieced bits of Baudelaire's criticism and large chunks of his subject matter into *Lesbia Brandon*. Taken together, the two aspects of his Baudelaire suggest both Swinburne's self-consciousness and his full purpose. Both privately and publicly, he made his "brother" serve his own opposition to critical and moral conventions. What the privately circulated material reveals is how far Swinburne did share with Baudelaire's early English critics a view of the poet as absolutely outside current convention. And while for Robert Buchanan, for instance, that radical difference was horrifying, for Swinburne it was very useful indeed.

The first point in Swinburne's opposition was his internationalism: he diagnosed the cramp Pound was to complain of in London, and, some sixty years before Pound's *New Age* articles prescribed "An Approach to Paris" as the remedy, Swinburne set about achieving it in a many-sided exploration of the literature of "*notre* France," as he called it in a letter to Mallarmé.[43] Like Eliot and more than Arnold, he reached easily into French literature for his defining comparisons; like Eliot he used the French tradition to fence with the English. His natural habit of weaving English culture together with French appears not only in his criticism, though abundantly there, but also in every other aspect of his work. He takes sometimes lavish steps, as in the fake epigraph to "Laus Veneris," to assert the blood connection between his early poems and a French tradition. His novels are actually attempted as works in English that might have been produced in France; they name French ancestors and address problems posed in French novels. His parodies and satires (*La Fille du Policeman, La Soeur de la Reine*, his hoaxing reviews) derive their "humour," as he liked to call it, as well as their bite from the clash of cultural viewpoints, the conflict of national literary conventions. He also was able to ensure that what he wrote on French literature commanded attention in France. Michel Lévy, for instance, hastened to translate and reprint his article on Vacquerie, as having "le double intérêt d'être d'un écrivain illustre et de montrer comment les écrivains français sont appréciés en Angleterre."[44] Swinburne wrote delightedly to Dante Gabriel Rossetti in 1869 that "The Rappel has reprinted from the Courier de l'Europe an excellent version of my article on l'Homme Qui Rit . . . describing the article as 'du à la plume du premier poète actuel de l'Angleterre.' (Pendez-vous MM. Tennyson et Cie!)"[45] And Swinburne kept the good opinion of literary Frenchmen: Maupassant wrote a preface to the translation of *Poems and Ballads* of 1891; Francis Vielé-Griffin translated *Laus Veneris* for a separate edition in 1923.[46] To dismiss Swinburne's

le double . . . the double interest of being by a famous writer and of showing how French writers are appreciated in England.

du à la plume . . . 'from the pen of the greatest living poet in England.' (Hang yourselves, Messers Tennyson and Co!).

interest in French literature as merely "the knowledgeable pose of the English aristocrat" is seriously to miss the point.[47]

When Eliot wrote the most famous essay of his early years, he could without straining credulity say that "the tradition" included "the whole of the literature of Europe." How unlikely that would have seemed when Swinburne wrote his early famous essay on Baudelaire, or when he made his only public speech, is worth remembering. It appears in some of the other speeches at the Royal Literary Fund Dinner at which Swinburne asserted his point about the value of "mutual and reciprocal" influence between France and England.[48] In the toast to which Swinburne replied, to the "Historical and Imaginative Literature of England," George Stovin Venables indicated how little English literature might require alliance with any other: it had never been excelled or even equalled, he said, and "at this moment," England was one of "only two countries in the world which have any imaginative literature whatever." In Italy, Venables reported, "literature is absolutely dead or asleep. In Spain, literature has been dead for centuries," and in Germany there was not a single poet. The English, he said, should be careful not to take their literature for granted. And while Venables cautioned against complacency, Sir Willoughby Jones, who proposed the toast to the Church of England, reminded his audience of the special connections between the national literature and the national morality. "There is no doubt," he said, "that the tone of English literature is eminently Church of England; and I will venture to say that the plays of Shakespeare are as good sound Church of England books as any in the English language. . . . Why do I say that these plays are sound Church of England books? Because the chief lesson they teach us is this. They hold up to our admiration the four qualities of gentleness, forbearance, moderation and truth; and I believe those four qualities are eminently characteristic of the Church of England." Venables introduced Swinburne as the right person to reply to the toast to English literature, not only because he was "thoroughly imbued with the knowledge and with the traditions of the best school," but also because he had written "a grand English poem." On the very eve of the publication of *Poems and Ballads*, Swinburne was given a heavy charge: "I am sure," Venables said, "that he will feel that as, at present, the representative of the future in English poetry, he has a great responsibility upon him and a noble task to accomplish."

Swinburne made his major point plainly in his reply. The poets of France and England, he said, drew on a unified tradition. "He who has best praised Shakespeare," he said of Hugo, "is hitherto the sole successor of Shakespeare." Like Eliot later, he asserted the value of "cross-breeding" in poetry,[49] like him using the horticultural metaphor: "In the imaginative literature of the present day," he said, "I at least can discern no more promising sign than the constant and tenacious influence of England upon France, of France upon England. This mutual and reciprocal influence, valuable as it is and fruitful as it must be, is partially, but is not wholly, a new thing." It was in the context of that unified tradition that he set his estimate of Baudelaire as "one of the most exquisite, most delicate, and most perfect poets of the century—perfect in sound, in colour, in taste of metre, and in tone of emotion" and recommended him, together with Hugo, as an "influence."

Swinburne was certain he shared his belief in the value of "mutual influence" with Baudelaire, who, he said in his speech, "has devoted half his time to the translation and introduction of English writers among the French—not without fruit and not without cost." That is the first claim of his review, which praises Baudelaire's work on English and American writers as evidence of his more than national conception of his art. When Swinburne wrote, in a letter, that he had had "the honour to be coupled with Baudelaire as a fellow labourer,"[50] he meant not only as a fellow-poet, but also as a fellow-critic whose purpose was to break the national mold, to enable, as Valéry observed in 1924, "la poésie française [sortir] enfin des frontières de la nation."[51] Baudelaire's relationship to Poe was his model: he was certain that the "long, arduous and faithful labour of his brother-poet and translator" was responsible for Poe's fame.[52] Long afterward he wrote to Mallarmé that his forthcoming study of Blake's poems for the *République des Lettres* "peut-être ne seraient pas sans intérêt pour les poètes français," and that "depuis que nous avons perdu Baudelaire il n'y a que vous qui pourriez dignement

la poésie . . . French poetry finally to go beyond the borders of the nation.
depuis que . . . since we have lost Baudelaire, only you could worthily undertake this glorious task with which I hardly dare entrust myself.

entreprendre cette tâche glorieuse dont j'ose à peine me charger."[53] In becoming for some French journals "le premier poète actuel de l'Angleterre" and an authoritative reporter on English views on French writers, Swinburne enacted what he saw as Baudelaire's international vision, reopening the borders long before most modernist writers attempted by conscious (and inherited) cosmopolitanism to escape the confinements of national tradition.

Swinburne's speech to the Royal Literary Fund sharpens to after-dinner directness a point he had already made five years before in his more densely argued review of *Les Fleurs du Mal*. The review, which careless retrospect has often seen as merely a conventional repetition of the slogans of art for art's sake, is measured, reasonable, and penetrating, by far the most important English reaction to Baudelaire in the nineteenth century and the only fully serious one until George Saintsbury's, thirteen years later.[54] It is also the first statement of the major critical discoveries of Swinburne's career, the genesis of his attempt to track to their sources the "laws" of his art. And it is a significant moment in the history of English criticism, since it heralds three major assertions of modern literature: that the "brotherhood" of poets is international; that poetry and imaginative prose have the right to deal with unorthodox or unusual psychological and sexual subject matter; that the language of criticism stands in need of revision. The review is remarkable for yet another fact: when he wrote it, Swinburne worked, perhaps for the first but certainly not for the last time, with his Baudelaire in front of him. He modelled both his analysis and his praise precisely on what Baudelaire himself had written in his own *Notes Nouvelles Sur Edgar Poe*. (Those *Notes* came to be immensely influential: they provide the critical center of Swinburne's own *Blake* and the foundation of Conrad's "Preface" to *Nigger of the Narcissus*, for instance.) The historical irony in Swinburne's use of them is unavoidable: what Eliot saw as "extravagant" advertisement turns Baudelaire's own criticism to praise of his own poems.

Swinburne opens his review onto a wide perspective, suggesting at the outset that a power of more than national appeal distinguishes the best poetry. He goes on, however, to claim that conditions are no less adverse to poetry in France than in England: there, as here, he says, taking the "thin-spun classical work" of Théodore de Banville as an example, poetry is starved by the soil in which it attempts to grow, restrained by a wrong-headed and tyrannical criticism. When a poet arises who, unlike Banville, has the power to oppose the restrictions of current critical orthodoxy, that is an event of importance not merely in one country but wherever poetry attempts to flourish. From the beginning, Swinburne joins his art-for-art's-sake arguments to his case for internationalism. When Baudelaire wrote to thank him for the review, of which Swinburne had sent him a copy, he acknowledged the point. Wagner, he said, thanking him for the *Tannhäuser* pamphlet, had told him that he could never have believed that a French poet could so perfectly have understood German music. "N'étant pas exclusivement patriote," Baudelaire wrote, he took that as a compliment. He went on to fold Swinburne into an exclusive company: "Permettez-moi, à mon tour, de vous dire: *'Je n'aurais jamais cru qu'un littérateur anglais pût si bien pénétrer la beauté française, les intentions françaises et la prosodie française.'* Mais après la lecture des vers imprimés dans le même numéro . . . et pénétrés d'un sentiment à la fois si réel et si subtil, je n'ai plus été étonné du tout; il n'y a que les poètes pour bien comprendre les poètes."[55]

Swinburne's review makes Baudelaire's criticism central, attributing the perfection of his poetry to the rightness and rigor of his critical conception: Baudelaire's first publications, his essays on art, show "such admirable judgment, vigour of thought and style, and appreciative devotion to the subject, that the worth of his own future work in art might have been foretold even then." Of course, Baudelaire's *Notes* give just such a prominence to Poe's critical views. In America, he says, exploiting the international comparison, there are plenty of "pédants qui valent bien les nôtres pour rappeler sans cesse l'artiste à la beauté antique, pour questionner un poète ou un romancier sur la moralité de son but et la qualité de ses intentions" (II, 320). Poe's distinction,

N'étant . . . Not being exclusively patriotic myself.
Permettez-moi . . . Allow me, in turn, to say to you: 'I would never have believed that an English man of letters could so clearly understand French beauty, French intentions and French prosody.' But after reading the poetry printed in the same number . . . expressing feelings at once so real and so subtle, I was no longer at all surprised; only poets can properly understand poets.
pédants . . . pedants at least the equal of our own at ceaselessly calling artists back to antique beauty, at cross-questioning a poet or a novelist on the morality of his aims and the quality of his intentions (C,189-90).

however—"Car il ne fut jamais dupe!" (II, 321)—was to have refused to subscribe to error:

Un semblable milieu social engendre nécessairement des erreurs littéraires correspondantes. C'est contre ces erreurs que Poe a réagi aussi souvent qu'il a pu et de toute sa force. Nous ne devons donc pas nous étonner que les écrivains américains, tout en reconnaissant sa puissance singulière comme poète et comme conteur, aient toujours voulu infirmer sa valeur comme critique. Dans un pays où l'idée de l'utilité, la plus hostile du monde à l'idée de beauté, prime et domine toute chose, le parfait critique sera le plus *honorable*, c'est-à-dire celui dont les tendances et les désirs se rapprocheront le plus des tendances et des désirs de son public . . . celui qui cherchera dans un livre de poésie les moyens de perfectionner la conscience. Naturellement, il deviendra d'autant moins soucieux des beautés réelles, positives, de la poésie; il sera d'autant moins choqué des imperfections et même des fautes dans l'exécution. (II, 328)

That paragraph provides the design for Swinburne:

French poetry of the present date, taken at its highest, is not less effectually hampered by tradition and the taste of the greater number of readers than our own is. A French poet is expected to believe in philanthropy, and break off on occasion in the middle of his proper work to lend a shove forward to some theory of progress. The critical students there, as well as here, judging by the books they praise and the advice they proffer, seem to have pretty well forgotten

Car il . . . For dupe he never was! (C, 191).
Un semblable . . . A social environment of this order is bound to produce corresponding literary errors. It is these errors that Poe battled against, as often as he could, and with all his might. We must therefore be in no way surprised that American writers, whilst recognizing his remarkable power as poet and storyteller, have always tended to challenge his value as a critic. In a country where the utilitarian idea, the most hostile in the world to the idea of beauty, takes first place and dominates all other considerations, the perfect critic will be the most 'respectable,' that is to say, the critic whose instinctive attitudes and desires will come closest to the attitudes and desires of his readers; the one who, confusing faculties and types of production, will ascribe to them all one single purpose; the one who will seek in a book of poetry a means of perfecting the conscience. Naturally he will, to that extent, become less attentive to the real positive beauties of poetry; he will, to that extent, be less shocked by the blemishes and even the vices of form (C, 198).

that a poet's business is presumably to write good verses, and by no means to redeem the age and remould society. No other form of art is so pestered with this impotent appetite for meddling in quite extraneous matters; but the mass of readers seem actually to think that a poem is the better for containing a moral lesson or assisting in a tangible and material good work. The courage and sense of a man who at such a time ventures to profess and act on the conviction that the art of poetry has absolutely nothing to do with didactic matter at all, are proof enough of the wise and serious manner in which he is likely to handle the materials of his art. From a critic who has put forward the sane and just view of this matter with a consistent eloquence, one may well expect to get as perfect and careful poetry as he can give.

Yet despite the "hérésie de l'enseignement" and although "aucun poème ne sera si grand, si noble, si véritablement digne du nom du poème, que celui qui aura été écrit uniquement pour le plaisir d'écrire un poème" (II, 333), neither Baudelaire nor Swinburne proposes criticism for criticism's sake. Each makes the art-for-art's-sake arguments serve the purposes of social criticism, and each presents his heroic proponent of aesthetic independence (Poe for Baudelaire, Baudelaire for Swinburne) as a social critic, in pitched opposition to positions derived from what Baudelaire detested as the philosophy of progress. Baudelaire saw Poe's social mockery and his critical brilliance as vitally connected: he is great in his metaphysical subtlety, in the beauty of his conceptions and in the rigor of his analysis; but he is no less great in his quality as *caricature, jongleur, farceur* (II, 321). Swinburne's Blake demonstrates the connection, too, in, for instance, what seems almost like "a scrap saved from some tattered chorus of Aristophanes, or caught up by Rabelais as the fragment of a litany at the shrine of the *Dive Bouteille*."[56]

To the charge that Baudelaire's poems were immoral, then, Swinburne replied firmly that they were well made: while the

hérésie . . . the heresy of didacticism (C, 203).
aucun poème . . . no poem will be as great, as noble, so truly worthy of the name 'poem' as the one written for no purpose other than the pleasure of writing a poem (C, 203).
caricature . . . caricature, trickster, joker.

answer baffled some of his readers, he saw it as a refusal, like
Poe's, to subscribe to error. Aiming to shift aesthetic judgment
from subject to treatment, he offers Baudelaire's least conven-
tional subjects for approval on grounds of their art. Of "Une
Charogne," here introduced to English readers, he writes:
"Thus, even of the loathsomest bodily putrescence and decay he
can make some noble use; pluck out its meaning and secret, even
its beauty, in a certain way, from actual carrion." Of "Les Litanies
de Satan," he says: "it is one of the noblest lyrics ever written,"
"every verse has the vibration in it of naturally sound and pure
metal." He presses the case for the formal perfection of Baude-
laire's work: his "mastery of the sonnet-form," he writes, "is
worth remarking as a test of his natural bias towards such forms
of verse as are most nearly capable of perfection"; and it is his
"supreme excellence of words" that enables him to "grapple with
and fitly render the effects of such material." That sharp sepa-
ration of "mere material," as Pater would call it in his "Giorgione"
essay, and art (a separation that is far more extremely expressed
in Eliot's remark about "the material, the human feelings, which
in Swinburne's case do not exist") aims to protect poetry from
moralizing zeal, of course, but it also initiates a revision of critical
language. Having put poetry beyond the reach of non-aesthetic
criticism by making judgment of its subject matter "extraneous,"
Swinburne pushes his "aesthetic" position still further (preceding
Pater's *anders-streben* in the process) and commends Baudelaire's
poems for the forces they borrow from the other arts. He calls
Les Fleurs du Mal a "complicated tune of poems" and admires its
painterly qualities: its "quality of *drawing*. . . recalls the exquisite
power . . . of great French artists now living. His studies are
admirable for truth and grace; his figure-painting has the ease
and strength, the trained skill, and beautiful gentle justice of
manner, which come out in such pictures as the *Source* of Ingres,
or that other splendid study by Flandrin, of a curled-up naked
figure under full soft hot light, now exhibiting here." (The tone
of the *salon* is not out of place in this review; and the "quality
of drawing" is relevant to the striking "study" that opens *Lesbia
Brandon*.) Swinburne turns Baudelaire's poetry into a landscape-
painting of his own—it has "thick shadow of cloud about it, and
fire of molten light"—and he uses the same terms to insist on
subordinating its morality to its art. The "moral side of the book
is not thrust forward in the foolish and repulsive manner of a

half-taught artist," he says, "the background, as we called it, is not out of drawing."

Those grounds for the evaluation of poetry, which by their assertion of dramatic distance between artist and subject open an argument that would emerge in 1919 as the "impersonality" theory, would not of course have dismayed Pound, who saw form as "the test of a man's sincerity" and wrote that while Keats had got so far as to see that poetry "need not be the pack-mule of philosophy," Swinburne had "recognized poetry as an art"; but they did trouble the editor of *The Spectator*, who wrote to Swinburne that he found his ideas "a little unintelligible." "What is Poetry and Art?" he asked. "Are they all 'flowers'? Are they all to be judged by smell and sight? . . . You write as if Art and Poetry consisted of pictorial qualities. Can you hold to anything so narrow?"[57] The answer to the question was no, as Hutton really should have known from Swinburne's discussion of the morality of *Les Fleurs du Mal*, but the aesthetic Swinburne was adopting—and so laying down in print for the first time in English some of the basic positions of modernism—made the formal quality of a work its justification, the proper center of attention for both poet and critic. Poe, Baudelaire had written in his *Notes Nouvelles*,

> était avant tout sensible à la perfection du plan et à la cor-
> rection de l'exécution; démontant les oeuvres littéraires
> comme des pièces mécaniques défectueuses (pour le but
> qu'elles voulaient atteindre), notant soigneusement les vices
> de fabrication; et quand il passait au détail de l'oeuvre, à
> son expression plastique, au style en un mot, épluchant, sans
> omission, les fautes de prosodie, les erreurs grammaticales
> et toute cette masse de scories, qui, chez les écrivains non
> artistes, souillent les meilleures intentions et déforment les
> conceptions les plus nobles. (II, 328)

était avant . . . Above all, he was sensitive to the degree of perfection in the structure, and to formal correction. He would take literary works to pieces like a defective mechanism (defective, that is, in relation to its avowed aims), noting carefully the faults in manufacture; and, when he came to examine a work in detail, in its plastic form or, in a word, its style, he would, without omitting anything, sift the errors of prosody, the grammatical mistakes, and all that mass of surface scum which, in writers who are not artists, spoils the best intentions and distorts the most noble conceptions (C, 198-99).

Description of poetry in the language of painting was already
a familiar characteristic of Baudelaire's criticism by the time he
compared Poe to Delacroix, finding poetry in the painting and
color in the prose. When Swinburne writes of Baudelaire's poems
that the background is not out of drawing, he recalls specifically
what the French poet had written about the American: in Poe's
tales, "les fonds et les accessoires y sont appropriés au sentiment
des personnages" (II, 317). For Swinburne, as for Baudelaire
before and Pater after, the comparisons of the arts—or, rather,
the critical transpositions—and the conceit of the *anders-streben*
seemed, paradoxically, to emphasize what in poetry was poetry
and "not another thing."[58] The painting analogy in Swinburne,
like the idea of abstraction in Pater, displaces value from subject
to treatment. Like James and after Baudelaire, Swinburne insists
that the poet must have his *donnés*: "The main charm of the book
is, upon the whole, that nothing is wrongly given, nothing ca-
pable of being re-written or improved on its own ground. Con-
cede the starting point and you cannot have a better runner."
That argument is part of Swinburne's program for realliance:
only poets can understand poets (soon Eliot would say that only
poets can understand poetry) and only the language of the arts
is appropriate to describe an art. This of course gives English
poets more in common with French poets than with some English
readers, and poetry more in common with painting than with
philosophy. Swinburne was launching an offensive on the lan-
guage of criticism. The following passage from his *Blake*, which
has sometimes drawn the attention of critics for the borrowed
synaesthesia of its conclusion, is most interesting for the problem
it sets as a frame for the borrowing:[59]

> There is something too rough and hard, too faint and
> formless, in any critical language yet devised, to pay tribute
> with the proper grace and sufficiency to the best works of
> the lyrical art. One can say, indeed, that some of these ear-
> liest songs of Blake's have the scent and sound of Elizabethan
> times upon them . . . but when we have to drop comparison
> and cease looking back or forward for verses to match with
> these, we shall hardly find words to suit our sense of their
> beauty. . . . They have a fragrance of sound, a melody of

les fonds . . . The backgrounds and the accessories are always appropriate to
the feelings of the characters (C, 186).

colour, in a time when the best verses produced had merely
the arid perfume of powder, the twang of dry wood, and
adjusted strings; when here the painting was laid on in
patches, and there the music meted out by precedent; colour
and sound never mixed together into the perfect scheme of
poetry.

Swinburne offers those lateral steps across the boundaries of the
arts as a revision to critical language: that is part of his first lesson
from Baudelaire.

Swinburne's article on *Les Fleurs de Mal* takes a moderate view
of their morality. He would advance his art-for-art's-sake ar-
guments with more of the spirit of battle in his *Blake*, but even
there he has none of the extremeness of Gautier, for whom "Rien
de ce qui est beau n'est indispensable à la vie" and, conversely,
"En général, dès qu'une chose devient utile, elle cesse d'être
belle."[60] Indeed in his *Blake* Swinburne contradicts that view
directly, maintaining that "if the art of verse is not indispensable
and indestructible, the sooner it is put out of the way the better."[61]
His Baudelaire review aims at balance on the moral question:
"There is not one of these poems that could have been written
in a time when it was not the fashion to dig for moral motives
and conscious reasons," he says, or "which has not a distinct and
vivid background of morality to it." He does not argue that the
poems are without moral effect, only that their morality is a
quality of the art and not of the material, a consequence of
execution rather than didactic intention. "If any reader could
extract from any poem a positive spiritual medicine," he writes,
"if he could swallow a sonnet like a moral prescription—then
clearly the poet supplying these intellectual drugs would be a
bad artist; indeed, no real artist, but a huckster and vendor of
miscellaneous wares. But those who will look for them may find
moralities in plenty behind every poem of M. Baudelaire's." That
balanced position, basic both to Swinburne's reading of *Les Fleurs
du Mal* and to his own work, takes him some distance from
Gautier, for whom even such a whiff of utility was too strong,
but it reflects precisely Swinburne's source, in which the follow-

Rien de . . . Nothing that is beautiful is indispensable to life.
En général . . . In general, as soon as a thing becomes useful it ceases to be
beautiful.

ing lines succeed directly the passage on the *hérésie de l'enseigne-ment* to which Swinburne refers in his *Blake*:

Je ne veux pas dire que la poésie n'ennoblisse pas les moeurs,—qu'on me comprenne bien,—que son résultat final ne soit pas d'élever l'homme au-dessus du niveau des intérêts vulgaires; ce serait évidemment une absurdité. Je dis que si le poète a poursuivi un but moral, il a diminué sa force poétique; et il n'est pas imprudent de parier que son oeuvre sera mauvaise. La poésie ne peut pas, sous peine de mort ou de défaillance, s'assimiler à la science ou à la morale; elle n'a pas la Vérité pour objet, elle n'a qu'Elle-même. Les modes de démonstration de vérité sont autres et sont ailleurs. La Vérité n'a rien à faire avec les chansons. (II, 333)

Swinburne had those *Notes* very much in mind when he wrote in his *Blake* that the "contingent result" of good art and noble writing was "that the spirit and mind of men then living will receive on some points a certain exaltation and insight," and he had still not forgotten them when he said in his *Study of Shakespeare* that "A discovery of some importance has recently been proclaimed as with blare of vociferous trumpets and flutter of triumphal flags; no less a discovery than this—that a singer must be tested by his song."[62]

It is not for its attempt at balance in an argument about morality and the independence of poetry that Swinburne's review of Baudelaire is usually remembered, however, but for its presentation of the "perfect artist" as the type of the decadent poet. The poet has, Swinburne writes, a natural attraction to "sad and strange things—the weariness of pain and the bitterness of pleasure—the perverse happiness and wayward sorrows of exceptional people." He is drawn "Not [to] the luxuries of pleasure in their first simple form, but [to] the sharp and cruel enjoyments of pain, the acrid relish of suffering felt or inflicted, the sides

Je ne veux . . . Let there be no misunderstanding: I do not mean to say that poetry does not ennoble manners—that its final result is not to raise man above the level of squalid interests; that would clearly be absurd. What I am saying is that, if the poet has pursued a moral aim, he will have diminished his poetic power; nor will it be incautious to bet that his work is bad. Poetry cannot, except at the price of death or decay, assume the mantle of science or morality; the pursuit of truth is not its aim, it has nothing outside itself. The modes of demonstration of truth are other, and elsewhere. Truth has nothing to do with song (C, 204).

on which nature looks unnatural." Swinburne sees in "Une Mar-
tyre" the "hideous violence wrought by a shameless and senseless
love" and a "poetry of strange disease and sin" clothed in "glo-
rious style and decorative language." The poems, he writes, have
"altogether a feline style of beauty—subtle, luxurious, with
sheathed claws"; their style is "sensuous and weighty; the sights
seen are steeped most often in sad light and sullen colour." The
"Litanies de Satan" are the book's "key-note" because "here it
seems as if all failure and sorrow on earth, and all the cast-out
things of the world—ruined bodies and souls diseased—made
their appeal, in default of help, to Him in whom all sorrow and
all failure were incarnate."

That description supplies Swinburne with direction for his
own poetry and prose—it is his examination of the very subject
matter he defends in *Notes on Poems and Reviews*—and it also
provides a pattern for English descriptions of Baudelaire's work.
Trimmed from the context of Swinburne's argument, the de-
scription could be knit without seam into Gautier's 1868 preface
to *Les Fleurs du Mal*, since there, too, the poems are offered as
the product of "the last hours of civilization" and made to ex-
emplify a theory of literary decadence. Swinburne's later readers
would find in his review, as in Gautier's preface, a source for
the sensational and conventional "baudelairism" against which
still later readers would rebel. There is historical irony in that
sequence, too, however, since Swinburne's description of the
decadent poet, like Gautier's preface, is again drawing specifi-
cally on what Baudelaire had written on Poe. The *Notes Nouvelles*,
to which Swinburne is so widely indebted, both in the review
and in the *Blake*, opens with an acid defense of "*Littérature de
décadence!*" In the dying agonies of the setting sun, Baudelaire
says, "*certains esprits poétiques*" can find new delights. Poe is
one such, a nervous, perverse poet ("*Genus irritable vatum!*"),
whose poems, as Baudelaire had noted in his first study of him,
focus on sick or diseased subjects. They have "des fonds violâtres
et verdâtres où se révèlent la phosphorescence de la pourriture
et la senteur de l'orage"; they show women "toutes lumineuses

certains . . . some poetic minds.
des fonds . . . lurid backgrounds of mingled purple and green, which reveal
the phosphorescence of decay and the smell of the storm.
toutes . . . bathed in light, feverish, dying of mysterious maladies.

et malades, mourant de maux bizarres"; they present "l'amour du grotesque . . . l'amour de l'horrible" (II, 317-18). Most importantly, Baudelaire writes, "nous noterons que cet auteur, produit d'un siècle infatué de lui-même, enfant d'une nation plus infatuée d'elle-même qu'aucune autre, a vu clairement, a imperturbablement affirmé la méchanceté naturelle de l'Homme" (II, 322). That perception lies behind Poe's psychology, as Baudelaire sees it, and it probably also prompts Swinburne's identification of "Les Litanies de Satan" as the "key-note" of the *Fleurs*. What Poe saw, and what pits him against the facile optimism of his time and his place, is that there is in man

une force mystérieuse dont la philosophie moderne ne veut pas tenir compte; et cependant, sans cette force innommée, sans ce penchant primordial, une foule d'actions humaines resteront inexpliquées, inexplicables. Ces actions n'ont d'attrait que *parce que* elles sont mauvaises, dangereuses; elles possèdent l'attirance du gouffre. Cette force primitive, irrésistible, est la Perversité naturelle, qui fait que l'homme est sans cesse et à la fois homicide et suicide, assassin et bourreau;—car, ajoute-t-il, avec une subtilité remarquablement satanique, l'impossibilité de trouver un motif raisonnable suffisant pour certaines actions mauvaises et périlleuses, pourrait nous conduire à les considérer comme le résultat des suggestions du Diable. . . . (II, 322-23)

For Baudelaire, Poe and the idea of decadence constituted a strong antithesis to the philosophy of progress. The language of Swinburne's description of *Les Fleurs du Mal* makes all the

l'amour . . . the love of the grotesque . . . the love of the horrible (C, 186-87).

nous noterons . . . let us take careful note that this author, the product of a self-infatuated age, the child of a nation more full of its own importance than any other, has seen clearly, has calmly proclaimed the natural wickedness of man (C, 192).

une force . . . a mysterious force that modern philosophy refuses to take into account; and yet without this unmentioned force, without this primeval tendency, a vast number of human actions will remain unexplained, inexplicable. These actions exercise a pull only because they are bad, dangerous; they have the lure of the abyss. This primitive, irresistible force is the natural perversity that results in man's being constantly, and at one and the same time, homicidal and suicidal, murderer and executioner; for, he adds, with a remarkably satanic subtlety, in the absence of an adequate, reasonable motive to account for certain evil and dangerous actions, we might be led to put them down to the promptings of the Devil . . . (C, 192).

"failure and sorrow" of that book as moral a contradiction as
Poe's. Baudelaire could hardly have hoped for a more sympa-
thetic introduction abroad.

Swinburne worked on *William Blake, A Critical Essay*, from Oc-
tober 1862 to February 1867. During those years, he composed
it "little by little," expanding it, as he says in the dedication to
William Michael Rossetti, from a "slight study" to an "elaborate
essay." He wrote it "in the leisure of months, and in the intervals
of my natural work"; it absorbed him for such a long time be-
cause "I found so much unsaid, so much unseen, that a question
soon rose before me of simple alternatives: to do nothing, or to
do much."[63] The book, Swinburne's most complex and deliberate
articulation of his aesthetic, is an intensely personal document,
"invaluable," as its best recent critic says, not for the study of
Blake but for the study of Swinburne.[64] In his slow wrestling
with the "unsaid" and the "unseen," Swinburne worked out, in
the forum of a practical critical argument, the consequences of
his attempt to make a unified tradition of the literatures of
France and England. His *Blake* sees an English poet in terms
Swinburne had only recently learned. It aims to do for the Eng-
lish poet what Baudelaire had done for Poe—to justify his unor-
thodox, irregular, non-conformist achievement by an unclut-
tered aesthetic reasoning, and in that justification to attack
narrow orthodoxy, stunted metaphysics, and shrinking conform-
ity in literary criticism—and it makes Baudelaire's "unsurpass-
able" study of Poe the rock on which it builds.[65] Swinburne kept
Baudelaire as vividly present to his critical imagination when he
wrote this "critical essay" as Blake himself: he had published his
review of *Les Fleurs du Mal* in the month before he started work
on the *Blake*, and he began, though prematurely, to write "Ave
atque Vale" only three months after he sent the *Blake* to the
publisher.[66] By all of its important threads—its thematic preoc-
cupations, its critical propositions, its carefully elaborated figu-
rative language—*William Blake* is connected to Swinburne's read-
ing of Baudelaire and to the other things he wrote on him.

Swinburne unveils his critical purpose at the outset by de-
scribing Blake as beyond the range of every category of nor-
mative judgment. In a time of reason and categorical argument,
he was "possessed" of fervent, furious belief: "among sane men
who had disproved most things and proved the rest, here was
an evident madman who believed a thing, one may say, only

insomuch as it was incapable of proof" (56). Blake subscribed
to no artistic conventions, since "What was best to other men,
and in effect excellent of its kind, was to him worst," and no
convention could contain him, since "we can hardly imagine a
time or scheme of things in which he could have lived and
worked without some interval of revolt" (55). Swinburne pre-
sents him as an absolute outsider, the perfect case by which to
test the power of criticism, since, by the standards Swinburne
had already called "extraneous," Blake would have to be seen as
unhealthy, irrational, and immoral. This Blake presents a prob-
lem in critical judgment, the question of whether poetry can be
judged as poetry and not another thing. The subject of Swin-
burne's "essay" is his chief instrument of critical exploration.

That critical reversal, by which the example escapes the cat-
egory to show that categorization is inadequate, gives Swin-
burne's argument about Blake much in common with his ar-
gument about Baudelaire. If Blake had "little enough of
recognition or regard from the world" (53), so had Baudelaire,
who must wait for the "long run" for his "meed of admiration"
(*CB*). Criticism lumbers behind. But the judgment of a poet is
a different matter, and here, as in his review of Baudelaire's
poems, Swinburne distinguishes sharply between official criti-
cism and a description and judgment of poetry as poetry. In
fact, he makes such a distinction a kind of pre-condition of his
book by placing these words, which he borrows from *Richard
Wagner et Tannhäuser à Paris*, at the head of its first chapter:[67]

> Tous les grands poëtes deviennent naturellement, fatale-
> ment, critiques. Je plains les poëtes que guide le seul instinct;
> je les crois incomplets. Dans la vie spirituelle des premiers,
> une crise se fait infailliblement, où ils veulent raisonner leur
> art, découvrir les lois obscures en vertu desquelles ils ont
> produit, et tirer de cette étude une série de préceptes dont
> le but divin est l'infaillibilité dans la production poétique. Il

Tous les grands . . . all great poets naturally, inevitably become critics. I feel
sorry for poets guided by their instincts alone; I regard them as incomplete. In
the spiritual life of great poets, a crisis is bound to occur that leads them to
examine their art critically, to seek the mysterious laws that guided them, the
idea being to draw from this study a series of precepts whose divine aim is
infallibility in the poetic process. For a critic to become a poet would be mirac-
ulous, whereas for a poet not to have a critic within him is impossible (C, 340).

serait prodigieux qu'un critique devînt poëte, et il est im-
possible qu'un poëte ne contienne pas un critique.

—CHARLES BAUDELAIRE.

Swinburne's attribution, in small capitals, makes visually im-
pressive what unfolds in his text, the relation in his mind of the
English poet and the French, and the quotation itself acknowl-
edges the foundation of his critical purpose.

Baudelaire, of course, is central to the important aesthetic
passage, which, in the opening pages of the second chapter,
presents Swinburne's most famous, boldest, and most buttressed
exposition of his views on the independence of art.[68] It brings
together the principal strands in his "essay" and it unfolds the
critical program by which he proposes to judge Blake's and every
other poet's work. It is here that Swinburne cries, "Art for art's
sake first of all, and afterwards we may suppose all the rest shall
be added to her," drawing largely for the remarks with which
he surrounds that cry from Baudelaire's *Notes Nouvelles Sur Edgar
Poe*,[69] and attributing those views to Blake. Far from denying his
source or submerging it for the purpose of keeping his text
unallied, Swinburne draws attention to it in more than one way.
In the center of an argument announced with a quotation from
Baudelaire, Swinburne quotes him again: "A living critic of in-
comparably delicate insight and subtly good sense, himself 'im-
peccable' as an artist, calls this 'the heresy of instruction' (*l'hérésie
de l'enseignement*): one might call it, for the sake of a shorter and
more summary name, the great moral heresy."[70] The reference
to Baudelaire—gratuitous, since, as Swinburne knew perfectly
well, the *hérésie de l'enseignement* had first been named by Poe, in
"The Poetic Principle"—is complemented by a laudatory note
(the "notice" of Baudelaire's life).[71] Swinburne firmly associates
Baudelaire, "by way of exposition rather than excursion," with
"the real point of view taken during life by Blake, and necessary
to be taken by those who would appreciate his labours and pur-
poses." They were, Swinburne says, "to readjust all questions of
[faith or principle] by the light of art and law of imagination—
to reduce all outlying provinces, and bring them under govern-
ment of his own central empire—the 'fourfold spiritual city' of
his vision" (140). That critical center of *William Blake*, the defense
of the imagination and its rights in relation to science and mo-
rality, brings together the three dominant voices of this work.

Swinburne compounds his acknowledgment of Baudelaire with his biographical note, written when, his book in press, he heard of Baudelaire's "mortal illness." The note is personal to a high degree, acknowledging "the admiration of some years," which it offers as an excuse to repeat "the immortal words which too often return upon our lips 'Ergo in perpetuum, frater, ave atque vale!'" That reference makes significant connection with Swinburne's poem in which, as in the *Blake*, he insists on his brotherhood with "the illustrious poet, the faultless critic, the fearless artist" (138).

While he is occupied chiefly by an idea of critical justice (which involves recognition of the imagination as the "reine des facultés"), Swinburne expands his argument to suggest, as in both his Royal Literary Fund Dinner speech and his review of Baudelaire, that cramped critical standards have dangerously narrowed the English tradition. His *Blake* ends on that note:

> "Let us now praise famous men, and our fathers who were before us." Those who refuse them that are none of their sons; and among all these "famous men, and our fathers," no names seem to demand our praise so loudly as theirs who while alive had to dispense with the thanksgiving of men. To them doubtless, it may be said, this is now more than ever indifferent: but to us it had better not be so. (346)

The unacknowledged fathers are likely to be those who have refused to gratify tradition, as it now stands, and the taste of the greater number; but "those to whom the higher ways of work are not sealed ways" will be glad to praise them. "A more noble memory is hardly left us," Swinburne writes, than Blake's, "and it is not for his sake that we should contend to do him honour." The health of the present depends upon the truth of its estimate of the past; the great unorthodox predecessors must not be forgotten. Like Pater's, Swinburne's modernism expresses itself in a revaluation and retriangulation of the past.

Swinburne expresses his revisionary purpose in an elaborately drawn-out religious metaphor. Blake, he announces at the beginning of the essay, "was born and baptized into the church of rebels" (55). The rebellion announced there presents the test case for criticism; but the steadily elaborated metaphor leads Swinburne into description of an antithetical tradition, a paradoxically anarchical hierarchy to set against the establishment, and his religious metaphor connects his comments on Blake with what he had written elsewhere on Baudelaire. The following passage appears in the first chapter of the *Blake*:

> It is in fact only by innate and irrational perception that we can apprehend and enjoy the supreme works of verse and colour; these, as Blake indicates with a noble accuracy, are not things of the understanding; otherwise, we may add, the whole human world would appreciate them alike or nearly alike, and the high and subtle luxuries of exceptional temperaments would be made the daily bread of the poor and hungry; the *vinum daemonum* which now the few only can digest safely and relish ardently would be found medicinal instead of poisonous, palatable instead of loathsome, by the run of eaters and drinkers; all specialties of spiritual office would be abolished, and the whole congregation would communicate in both kinds. All the more, meantime, because this "bread of sweet thought and wine of delight" is not broken or shed for all, but for a few only—because the sacramental elements of art and poetry are in no wise given for the sustenance or the salvation of men in general, but reserved mainly for the sublime profit and intense pleasure of an elect body or church—all the more on that account should the ministering official be careful that the paten and chalice be found wanting in no one possible grace of work or perfection of material. (85-86)

That *vinum daemonum* has a place in "Ave atque Vale," too. In the poem Swinburne addresses Baudelaire: the "lord of light" appears only rarely among us, he says, but

> Thy lips indeed he touched with bitter wine,
> And nourished them indeed with bitter bread;
> Yet surely from his hand thy soul's food came,
> The fire that scarred thy spirit at his flame
> Was lighted, and thine hungering heart he fed
> Who feeds our hearts with fame.

The "communion of song" of "Ave atque Vale" celebrates what David G. Riede has called the "apostolic succession of poets."[72] So does the communion in *William Blake, A Critical Essay*. In his elegy and his major work of criticism, Swinburne identifies a vital tradition of poetry which stands in opposition to the one sanctioned by official criticism, and in both he names Baudelaire as at once the partner of his enterprise and his nearest ancestor in the challenging line of fathers and sons.

* * *

Swinburne, of course, had no intention of writing the kind of criticism utilitarians would value as "le plus *honorable*." Even before he began to construct his criticism to a design he found in Baudelaire, he had played at the kind of mockery Baudelaire admired in Poe, setting himself in a gleefully satiric relationship to his readers. Swinburne would not have known about Baudelaire's insatiable desire, as he wrote in a letter to his mother, to insult France, nor of his temptation to preface the second edition of *Les Fleurs du Mal* with "une violente bouffonnerie," but he would very early have learned that Baudelaire thought of Poe as "un Ilote qui veut faire rougir son maître."[73] Love of satire gave the two another point of similarity, since Swinburne had corrective blushing in mind when he wrote his own *canards*, in which he aimed, with the paradoxical clarity of disguise, to gull hypocritical criticism.

Swinburne's ironic voice is familiar from his earliest criticism. In his undergraduate "review" of *The Monomaniac's Tragedy*, for instance, a high-minded and reader-protecting reviewer deplores the fact that "Ernest Wheldrake," the poet (author of *Eve, a Mystery*) and his publisher have reviewed themselves under a false name: "These gentlemen may consider the occupation of literary forgery as remarkably humorous and amusing; but we can tell them that all honourable men will be revolted by such a flagrant instance of dishonesty." The moral infraction, says the reviewer, swollen with purpose, is far more grave than a mere question of "literary merit or demerit."[74] That "Wheldrake" tone invades the series of articles on French literature that Swinburne wrote for *The Spectator* in 1861 and 1862 (which includes the review of *Les Fleurs du Mal*). A kind of Trabb's boy at the heels of inflated criticism, it culminates in the fake reviews of his robot writers, Félicien Cossu and Ernest Clouet.[75] Swinburne began to insinuate his inventions into existence as early as May 1862, when he referred in a footnote to the "*Recueil de Chants Bretons*, edited

une . . . a violent clowning.
un Ilote . . . a helot who wants to make his master blush.

by Félicien Cossu, première série (no more published), p. 89,
Paris, 1858," and he continued what Cecil Y. Lang calls his "cam-
paign of authentication" in the first three of his articles on *Les
Misérables*.[76] The reviews he wrote of the works of this manu-
factured pair are themselves a parody of everything else he wrote
in the series, particularly of his essay on Baudelaire. Cossu and
Clouet are intimately related by a variant of the international
brotherhood. (*La Fille du Policeman*, Lang points out, parodied
specific French texts, and some of the plumage of the present
hoaxes is plucked with a nice exactitude from Hugo.)[77] Cossu
and Clouet, however, derive from the author of *Les Fleurs du
Mal*, who was probably the "coxswain in this service [of moral
rebellion], one of a French squadron given overmuch to cruising
in dangerous waters among sharp straits and shoals." Some of
Cossu's poems and Clouet's themes guy the very poems Swin-
burne had cited in his review, seizing upon Baudelaire's most
"offending" subjects—the satanism and blasphemy, the psycho-
logical and sexual studies—to parade them before a reviewer
who adopts, one by one, as by comic inevitability, precisely the
positions most fiercely ridiculed by proponents of art for art's
sake.

The hoaxes reveal an apparently violent contradiction of at-
titudes on Swinburne's part, since they subject the "perfect poet"
of the review to grotesque caricature. The refrain from "L'In-
vitation au Voyage," for instance—

> Là, tout n'est qu'ordre et beauté,
> Luxe, calme et volupté

—becomes, in the revision Swinburne made for Cossu, "Tout
est superbe, infâme, épouvantable et sale." The "sharp perfect
finale," as Swinburne called it when he quoted it in his review,
of "A Une Passante"—

> Dont le regard m'a fait soudainement renaître,
> Ne te verrai-je plus que dans l'éternité?

—is travestied as

Là, tout . . . Everything there is harmony and beauty, luxury, tranquillity, and
delight (S, 107).
Tout est . . . Everything is arrogant, infamous, appalling and foul.
Dont le . . . Whose glance brought me suddenly to life again in a second birth,
shall I never see you again, except in eternity? (S, 221).

Ah! réponds, cadavre implacable,
Larve inutile de l'amour,
Que de son poids le Temps accable,
Nous reconnaîtrons-nous un jour?

Whole sections of Cossu's garishly urban verses caricature Baudelaire's vocabulary and vision, and the review of Clouet contains a sketch of Pétrus Borel (or Champavert le Lycanthrope) based on an article Baudelaire had published in the *Revue fantaisiste* a few months earlier.[78] In the Clouet review, Swinburne reshapes for satire the theme of the "Litanies de Satan": Clouet's aim, he says, is "To justify the ways of Satan to man"—"Sin is his mental snuff."

The reviewer's inflated distaste for these offensive verses is exemplary. From one poem—"upon the whole the most shamefully wicked production we have ever perused"—he dares not quote a single verse. The work he reviews, he says, should be "a warning sign of the unimaginable excess to which the corruption of French literature is now carried": none of it "is fit to be read aloud in the hearing of Englishwomen." The Cossu review concludes with an appeal to the innocence of its readers:

Accusations are often put forward, at home and abroad, against the restrictions imposed by a possibly exaggerated sense of decency on the English literature of the present day. We have seen what are the results of a wholly unfettered licence; base effeminacy of feeling, sordid degradation of intellect, loathsome impurity of expression, in a word every kind of filth and foolery which a shameless prurience can beget on a morbid imagination. Surely, whatever our shortcomings may be, we may at least congratulate ourselves that no English writer could for an instant dream of putting forth such a book as the poems of M. Félicien Cossu.

(Pendez-vous MM Venables et Cie!)

Swinburne concocted his hoaxes, by classic formula, for two audiences. He intended the dupes to settle complacently at least briefly into the reviewer's inflated moralism and to succumb only gradually to the discomfort that is evident in Hutton's letter on the subject of "flowers," "smell and sight." And he expected the

Ah! réponds . . . Ah! reply, implacable corpse, Useless phantom of love, Which Time crushes with his weight, Will we meet again one day?

knowing audience, the intimates of his parodic address, to de-
light both in the cuts he was inflicting on moralistic criticism and
in the *entre nous* admission, a kind of literary nudge or wink,
that the subjects of the parodies really were offensive. Since the
hoaxes were detected, the audience of dupes did not materialize;
but if, as Lafourcade suspected, Swinburne sent his parodies to
Baudelaire, they may have reached an important member of the
select audience, one who had admired Poe as a *jongleur* and
expressed the view that, "En matière des caricatures, les Anglais
sont des ultra" (II, 566). That possibility adds sense to Swin-
burne's remark that Cossu's book, "though as yet we believe
unnoticed by English critics, has enjoyed a success not wholly
unequivocal with at least a portion of the French public." The
reviews, if they reached him, could hardly have given Baudelaire
an unmixed delight, since the price of their successful mockery
of the attitudes that had sent his poems into exile was a brutal
reduction of material he had treated seriously, but he would
have recognized their tone immediately.

Swinburne's hoaxes leave no doubt that he saw Baudelaire as
the ally of his attack on the prohibition of sexual subjects. They
make him the model for outrage. The Clouet article, finishing
in what Lang calls "a piece of bravura,"[79] describes Clouet's ideal,
"l'homme-phallus," in terms that call up Baudelaire's dandy and
"Une Charogne." Furthermore, these hoaxes make Baudelaire—
in relation to *The Spectator* audience—the secret patron of that
purpose. The secrecy gave Swinburne much pleasure: "In every
age there is a certain quantity of moral force secretly at work,"
he writes in the Clouet article, "busied with whatever of skill and
energy may be at hand to further it, in counteracting the tend-
encies of the time." In a pirouette of self-mockery, he deplores
his own counter-tradition, making Clouet imitate "Les Phares,"
the poem in which Baudelaire calls art a "divine opium" and
celebrates great artists of the past. "Under the head of *Les Eclai-
reurs*," Swinburne writes, "our friend has thought fit to class some
of the most unmentionable names in literary history. He anoints
with a rancid oil of consecration the heads of men too infamous
for open reference."

Both the secrecy and the grotesqueness of Swinburne's fake
reviews are significant elements of his response to Baudelaire.
They unmask his purpose, and suggest how the arguments of

En matière . . . When it comes to caricature, the English are extremists (C, 234).

his serious criticism were strategic, a necessary, balancing, aesthetic hypocrisy. His Cossu review implies that a "possibly exaggerated sense of decency" in criticism engenders a possibly exaggerated revolt in literature. The idea of the connection between prurience and purity provides the machinery of his unfinished *La Soeur de la Reine,* in which Queen Victoria, radically revised into a coquette, is brought face to face with her long-hidden sister, Kitty, who conducts a hectic and eclectic sexual life. In a farce in which sexual hypocrisy is the subject, the recognition scene is the object. Kitty is brought before the Queen:[80]

> LA REINE—Mais, au nom de Dieu! qu'est-ce donc que cette femme?
> SIR PEEL (*faisant un pas en avant*)—C'est une fille publique!
> LA DUCHESSE (*se relevant*)—C'est la soeur de votre reine! Saluez, milords!
> SIR PEEL (*montrant du doigt* LORD JOHN RUSSELL, *anéanti*)— C'est la maîtresse de cet homme!
> LE LORD MAYOR (*Il relève* KITTY *et lui passe son bras autour de la taille*)—C'est ma femme!

The necessary pairs of Swinburne's satire are almost worthy of Wilde's. Kitty is one of the accompanying Other Victorians; Cossu's poetry is the spontaneous product of a too-pure criticism. "Nothing is so favourable to the undergrowth of real indecency as this overshadowing foliage of fictions, this artificial network of proprieties," Swinburne wrote later, in an argument that might have been Lawrence's.[81] His hoaxes and satires, passed among his friends, constituted the admission to a highly select audience that while one literary argument might be about the perfection of form, that was certainly not the only issue.

*   *   *

Swinburne's novels recast as creative experiment what his criticism had been proposing. They show to what degree his own work unified the two traditions; they embody his attempt to

La Reine . . . THE QUEEN: But in God's name! Who is this woman?
SIR PEEL (*taking a step forward*)—She's a prostitute!
THE DUCHESS (*getting up*)—She's the sister of your queen! Bow, my lords!
SIR PEEL (*pointing at* LORD JOHN RUSSELL, *dumbfounded*)—She's the mistress of this man!
THE LORD MAYOR (*He raises* KITTY *to her feet and puts his arm around her waist*)— She's my wife!

subdue in realistic prose the psychological, social, and sexual subject matter he had veiled in the vagueness of verse; and they allegorize his own hostile relation to current proprieties. The novels are impressive, the first because of its polished surface, the second, whose surface is jagged, because of its analytical depth. Both issue from the period of Swinburne's greatest interest in Baudelaire: although it could not find a publisher until 1877, *A Year's Letters* was written in 1862; and although its publication was delayed until 1952, *Lesbia Brandon* (a title not given by its author) was begun in 1864 and probably almost entirely assembled by 1867, the year of "Ave atque Vale."[82] The relation of the two novels to one another suggests the deepening hold on Swinburne's imagination of what he had seen as Baudelaire's enterprise.

The novels lay their literary roots bare for inspection. Swinburne's masters in *A Year's Letters* include, as the text makes insistently clear, Balzac and Laclos: these suggest the genre, the "realism," and the analysis. *Lesbia Brandon* derives from these same sources and, as Randolph Hughes points out in his generously documented edition, from Latouche's *Fragoletta* and Gautier's "golden book of spirit and sense," as Swinburne was himself to call it in his "Sonnet (With a Copy of *Mademoiselle de Maupin*)."[83] *Lesbia Brandon* makes its debt to Balzac more explicit than does the first novel, opening with a luxuriantly pictorial description of the eyes of Lady Wariston which are, we are told, like those of Balzac's "Georgian girl" in *La Fille aux Yeux d'Or*. Both novels take pains to ensure that some, at least, of their sources will be recognized: like Beardsley's drawings of *Salomé* at her toilette, they display the lettered titles of their formative texts. But of course that careful accounting for lineage ("fraternité ou cousinage," as Baudelaire might have put it) depends on the existence of Swinburne's smaller audience: this is an address to the knowing. In the first novel Swinburne dramatizes (in Lady Midhurst) a critical position from his Baudelaire review. In the second he explores as realistically as he found possible the material he had attributed to Baudelaire, and, from time to time, he makes Mr. Linley speak in Baudelaire's words.

The two novels work from similarly imaged beginnings to similar conflicts. The first fact about both, as most of their critics observe, is their presentation of a closed, remote, stifling world. The closeness of the societies is in itself an intense prohibition, and each novel sets its characters in conflict by opposing to the social rules about sex what Lady Midhurst, who inhabits both novels, calls "the natural sense of liking."[84] The likings in both are unorthodox and are effortlessly defeated by society, but their treatment in the two novels is almost directly opposed. *A Year's Letters* maintains a resolutely social tone: the epistolary form necessarily distances passion in reporting it, and the dark ironies accumulate beneath a surface they never shatter. "Le dénouement," says Lady Midhurst, who takes that line and many another from Balzac, "C'est qu'il n'y a pas de dénouement" (156). Summarizing the novel's events for her niece, she puts it this way: "Joli ménage! one might have said at first sight—knowing [the situation], and *not* knowing what Englishwomen are here well known to be. And here we are at the last chapter with no harm done us yet. You end as a model wife, she as a model mother; you wind up your part with a suitor to dismiss, she hers with a baby to bring up. All is just as it was, as far as we all go" (157). But in the unfinished *Lesbia Brandon*, where Swinburne reaches more boldly into analysis of those "sides on which nature looks unnatural," the characters whose "studies" surround those of Herbert, the autobiographical protagonist, die voluntary deaths, physical or spiritual, and the protagonist himself is condemned to a spiritual chill, a specifically sexual alienation.

These novels, Swinburne's prose comedy and tragedy of the passions, draw very differently upon their Baudelaire material. Lady Midhurst, who towers over *A Year's Letters*, is a character constructed chiefly of aesthetic theory, a spokeswoman for the aestheticizing of experience in the best art-for-art manner. She repeatedly compares the stuff of English life to the shapes of French novels, to Balzac's in particular. She is consistently preoccupied by style—that keeps her head cool when the emotional temperature rises—and she is always on the side of art. "Avoid all folly; accept no traditions," she writes to her granddaughter, "take no sentiment on trust. Here is a bit of social comedy in which you happen to have a part to play; act as well as you can, and in the style now received on the English boards. Above all, don't indulge in tragedy out of season" (64). That she should be formed of aesthetics, a "realistic" character derived from an impeccably literary ancestry, provides Swinburne with a recurrent

Le dénouement . . . The denouement is that there is no denouement.

joke: "Upon my word," she says, after summarizing the events surrounding her as a plot to rival Feydeau, "I think it an idea which might bear splendid fruit in the hands of a great realistic novelist: I see my natural profession now, but I fear too late" (154).

That embodied aestheticism, "fruit" of Swinburne's reading in French literature, gives *A Year's Letters* its vitality. It is pitched against a background of conventional Victorian virtues, carefully sketched in an authorially voiced "Prologue": of "social reform," philanthropy, domestic virtue, and "the incessant titillations of charity and of that complacency with which virtuous people look back on days well spent" (7). To Lady Midhurst's dissonance with this program Swinburne keys his satire: "You know my lifelong abhorrence of the rampant Briton, female or male"; she writes to her niece, "and my perfect disbelief in the peculiar virtue of the English hearth and home" (155). When Swinburne published the novel, fifteen years after writing it, he signalled its satire in a prefatory letter from "publisher" to "author" and in a few other emphatic passages, such as the following on Mr. Cheyne's philanthropic zeal:

> Had fate or date allowed it,—but stern chronology forbade,—he would assuredly have figured as president, as member, or at least as correspondent of the Society for the Suppression of Anatomy, the Society for the Suppression of Sex, or the Ladies' Society for the Propagation of Contagious Disease (Unlimited). But these remarkable associations, with all their potential benefits to be conferred on purblind and perverse humanity, were as yet unprofitably dormant in the sluggish womb of time. (168-69)

When Swinburne added that, he had already slipped into the habit of "enormous panegyric or superlative damnation"[85] that he had avoided in his early years. The added prefatory letter attributes Lady Midhurst's abhorrence of the rampant Briton to her diet of French literature. Advising the pseudonymous "Mrs. Horace Manners" to suppress her book, the publisher says, "A long sojourn in France, it appears to me, has vitiated your principles and confused your judgment. Whatever may be the case abroad, you must know that in England marriages are usually prosperous; that among us divorces are unknown, and infidelities incomprehensible. The wives and mothers of England are exempt, through some inscrutable but infallible law of nature, from the errors to which women in other countries . . . are but too fatally liable" (3). In *A Year's Letters*, Swinburne throws his art-for-art's-sake views into a critical relation to the manners and morals of the time: he makes Lady Midhurst's aesthetics support his own sexual politics.

Lesbia Brandon's connections with Baudelaire are primarily those of literary criticism, which, as in the first novel, provides a hostile or antithetical view of the book's society. They are often very precise: for example, a conversation about Balzac in chapter three borrows specifically from what Baudelaire had written about him. (In his *Study of Shakespeare*, Swinburne borrowed the passage again, adopting for his own critical purposes, and translating in a note, Baudelaire's distinction between "unimaginative realism and imaginative reality."[86]) In *Lesbia Brandon* critical views of the passage are distributed more or less equally between Lady Midhurst and Mr. Linley, in a conversation crucially positioned, which has as its most obvious purpose the shattering of the provincial circle. Lady Midhurst and Mr. Linley are "worldly"; they first appear as occupants of a railway carriage on their way to Ensdon, the remote country location of much of the action. There, as literary and moral sophisticates among the rustic and innocent, they reject provincial literary orthodoxies—they name Balzac as superior to the greatest, though unnamed, English novelist—and sweep aside provincial moral proprieties. They raise a nicely managed comic panic both by what they say and by the language in which they say much of it. "Why are you talking French at both ends of the room?" (65) queries their bewildered host, and when Mr. Linley talks punningly of "de satanés genoux! ne pas lire satinés," he produces a crisis of paternal protectiveness in one Sir John Fieldfare whose son follows the conversation with "an evident and ominous relish, which . . . gave small promise of that muscular morality and sinewy sanctity preached and extolled by performers in the writing-school of Christian gymnastics." In his "exquisite agony of virtue," Sir John cries out, "Lord Wariston, what are we to think of the crops?" (59).

But in *Lesbia Brandon* Swinburne aimed at more "fulgurant harmony" than he had produced in *A Year's Letters*, and the shift

de satanés . . . devilish knees! *not* satin-like ones.

of interest from Lady Midhurst to Mr. Linley reflects his darker
intention. She, we are told on more than one occasion, "likes
innocence" (58); he, the "sage" or "philosopher," represents a
dark and secret knowledge, for which Swinburne allows him to
usurp the center of *Lesbia Brandon*. He knows about literature,
of course, as the conversation about Balzac indicates, and also
about "the sides on which nature seems unnatural" (*CB*). He is
a repository of identifying secrets and an initiating priest of the
sexual rituals. He first appears at the novel's moment of tran-
sition, when the protagonist moves from boyhood in first ap-
prehending the association of pain and pleasure. It is no accident
that reading Balzac is said to be like "eating the fruit of knowl-
edge" (70), nor that Mr. Linley, "glittering with venom so as to
look swollen and burnished like a chafing snake" (48), should
preside over the acquisition of bitter knowledge. The moment
of discovery in the carefully structured third chapter is of a kind
familiar to readers of *Marius the Epicurean* and *Gaston de Latour*
and *Dorian Gray*, although it is more boldly presented than in
Pater and more psychologically analytical than in Wilde.

Swinburne saw his second novel as experimental: a "hybrid
book," a "scheme of mixed verse and prose—a sort of étude à
la Balzac *plus* the poetry."[87] Its poetry must be understood to
include more than the verses Swinburne wrote for it. It is seri-
ously an attempt to combine the analysis of real experience (the
human feelings, which in Swinburne's case did exist) with pow-
erfully organized allegory. *Lesbia Brandon* is Swinburne's account
of the dissociation of sexual sensibility, and in spite of its unfin-
ished state its pattern is apparent. Its central action, the devel-
opment of Herbert Seyton, moves from a natural, pagan unity
of soul and sense to a bleak spiritual aridity and sexual alienation
that are the products of that unity broken. The secondary ac-
tions—the sexual histories of Lady Wariston, Lesbia Brandon,
Charles Denham—repeat the pattern. These sexual tragedies
together comprise a dark tale to set beside the dominant Vic-
torian sexual mythology, the view that discussion of sexual mat-
ters is in England both superfluous and impertinent, as anyone
can tell by observing that the English papers carry "no reports,
no trials, no debates" on them (*AYL*, 3).

Swinburne makes his subject clear at the outset and underlines
it at the end. The novel opens with an intensely physical de-
scription of Lady Wariston's very spiritual eyes and a reference

to Balzac as "the greatest analyst of spirit and flesh that ever
lived" (1). It ends (in a dénouement derived from *La Fanfarlo*,
Baudelaire's prose fiction) by embodying those separated entities
in two bracketed characters, Attilio Mariani, the patriot, and
Leonora Harley, the prostitute, in whom "the two extremes of
nature may be confronted with each other, in their likeness and
after their kind; soul almost without body, and body almost
without soul: neither man nor woman complete in their own
way" (168). (In the note in his *Blake*, it will be remembered,
Swinburne said of Baudelaire, "we shall never find so keen, so
delicate, so deep an unison of sense and spirit.")

Herbert Seyton begins in a protected environment. Ensdon is
"A green moist place . . . sparing rather than lavish of natural
fruit and flower, but with well-grown trees and deep-walled gar-
dens to the back of it" (7). There, the boy "lived and grew on
like an animal or a fruit" (8) and became "a small satisfied pagan"
(11):

> The nature of things had room to work in him, for the chief
> places in his mind were not preoccupied by intrusive and
> unhealthy guests wheeled in and kept up by machinery of
> teaching and preaching. There was matter in him fit to
> mould into form and impregnate with colours: and upon
> this life and nature were at work, having leisure and liberty
> to take their time. (11)

These walled gardens, however, are not sufficient protection
against the world, and while Mr. Linley and Lady Midhurst hold
forth on the knowledge that is gained by reading Balzac, Seyton
is brutally and unjustly flogged for a naturally prompted diso-
bedience. The flogging brings not only pain but also erotic com-
fort from his sister, and so the association of pain and pleasure
and prohibition. That is the crystallizing event in Seyton's de-
velopment, of which his subsequent unrequited love for Lesbia
Brandon is only a repetition, and by the time the novel ends he
is wholly alienated. He has, we are told, "senses deadened and
a hardening skin." "Inaction and inadequacy oppressed his con-
science, and a profitless repugnance against things that were: he
held on to his daily life with loose and empty hands, and looked
out over it with tired unhopeful eyes" (157). Seyton's sexual chill
is dramatized in his repulsion of the prostitute, Leonora Harley.

In all this Linley has a central, if not an active, role. He is a

commanding presence in the chapter that records the boy's crys-
tallizing erotic deflection. He it is who leaves Seyton with Leonora
Harley, saying "in the wheeziest of false notes," "C'est l'amour,
l'amour, l'amour" (117); he sees himself as a kind of artificial
father-figure to Seyton, who closely resembles his dead son. "I
believe in likenesses, and that they go deep," he says. "I shall
write a treatise some day on their meaning. It is significant of
something, I am convinced, when two faces without a vein of
kindred blood in them are so alike" (118-19). He is a parental
version of the double to Seyton, who grows from likeness to
Linley's son, to likeness to Linley himself, whose "whole face
bore the seal of heavy sorrow and a fatal fatigue; as though
restrained self-contempt and habitual weariness of habit were
too strong for the endurance of a tough and supple nature" (45).

Randolph Hughes has observed that Linley has "Baudelairean
attitudes" and pointed out some of the means by which Swin-
burne associates the two. Hughes does not press these facts to
their meaning, however, which is more than incidental. Linley's
connections with Baudelaire demonstrate the quality of the
brotherhood Swinburne would claim in "Ave atque Vale." He is
not, like Huxley's Spandrell, modelled directly upon Baudelaire
the man. He is a composite character, associated certainly with
de Sade and possibly with Lord Houghton.[88] But he dispenses
large doses of Baudelaire which are central to the design of a
work both autobiographical and allegorical.

Hughes mentions the Baudelairean provenance of Linley's
anti-nature speech to Lady Wariston, which identifies him as a
dandy. It also establishes his place in the book's analysis of spirit
and sense. Lady Wariston responds to it by asking whether he
has ever written "moral essays." "I thought of it once," he replies,
"but a friend suggested the addition of a syllable to the adjective,
and of course I refrained" (120). What he has said is:

> I fear sometimes that nature is a democrat. Beauty you see
> is an exception; and exception means rebellion against a
> rule, infringement of a law. That is why people who go in
> for beauty pure and plain—poets and painters and all the
> tail trash of the arts, besides all men who believe in life—
> are all born aristocrats on the moral side. Nature, I do think,
> if she had her own way, would grow nothing but turnips;
> only the force that fights her, for which we have no name,

now and then revolts; and the dull soil here and there rebels
into a rose. (119-20)

Linley states and restates this basic proposition in practically
every one of his conversations, and recurrently emphasizes the
difference from Lady Midhurst, whose aesthetic, by comparison,
is more positively disposed toward natural beauty. In their open-
ing conversation, for instance, about Lady Wariston's beauty, she
exclaims: "Her eyes! de l'or fondu, de l'or bruni; one must go
to Balzac to see such eyes." "It's a pity her hair will take no sort
of dye," he replies (48). He takes the same anti-nature attitude,
indexed by allusion to Baudelaire's comments on cosmetics,
when Lord Wariston praises Lady Midhurst's beauty. "A qui le
dîtes-vous?" Linley replies. "I never cared much for white and
red. Art's above nature in that respect, with King Lear's leave;
if you know how to lay it on, and where, and when" (58).

Linley's actions carry his preference for the artificial into the
moral sphere: he arranges, partly for the pleasure of detached
observation, the passions of the three important characters. His
game is in each case the same: he pits cold consciousness against
passion, supplies a destructive knowledge. He urges Lady War-
iston forward in her relationship with Denham; he introduces
Seyton to Leonora Harley, proffering lust for unrequited love;
he undeceives Denham about his parentage and so makes his
passion, and his life, impossible. Baudelaire supplies Swinburne
with his alienating agent, one of the poles of the book's argument
about the dissociation of sexual sensibility.

In his review of *Les Fleurs du Mal*, Swinburne identified their
subjects as "Not the luxuries of pleasure in their first simple
form, but the sharp and cruel enjoyments of pain, the acrid
relish of suffering felt or inflicted, the sides on which nature
looks unnatural," as "sad and strange things—the weariness of
pain and the bitterness of pleasure—the perverse happiness and
wayward sorrows of exceptional people." Those are of course
the subjects of *Lesbia Brandon*. That Swinburne associated them
specifically and directly with Baudelaire is made clear in the
terms of his description of Denham, in whose eyes, he writes,
there is "hatred" and "desire" and "Something too of wayward
and hopeless pleasure" (31). Denham, like Lady Wariston and

de l'or . . . cast gold, burnished gold.
A qui . . . Who are you saying this to?

Lesbia Brandon and Herbert Seyton, belongs to the group of
self-torturers to whom Baudelaire gave voice in "L'Héautoni-
morouménos," the character who sees himself as both the wound
and the knife, the cheek and the slap, the limbs and the wheel,
the victim and the hangman. In this novel, Swinburne is less
interested in comic or satiric observation (like that of the dinner-
party scene of the third chapter) than in unseen emotional de-
velopments. Denham's sadism grows invisibly from the frustra-
tion of his love for Lady Wariston:

> But the hidden disease in spirit and heart struck inwards,
> and daily deeper: it pierced him through the flesh to his
> mind. Silent desire curdled and hardened into poisonous
> forms; love became acrid in him and crusted with a bitter
> stagnant scum of fancies ranker than weeds. Under the mask
> or under the rose he was passing through quiet stages of
> perversion. He could not act out his sin and be rid of it; he
> held it as though in his hand night and day till it burnt his
> palm to the bone. (20)

Swinburne is attempting to deal in prose fiction with the phe-
nomenon Baudelaire spoke of in Poe, that of "la Perversité na-
turelle, qui fait que l'homme est sans cesse et à la fois homicide
et suicide, assassin et bourreau." That subject matter makes Swin-
burne a great deal more "modern" than his public audience
could have been, and, if Randolph Hughes is right, than some
members of his private audience, who maneuvered to keep the
novel out of print.[89] These characters, in whose illegal or unor-
thodox passions Swinburne strove to represent realistically a
Tannhäuser for the prudish sixties, are made terribly, painfully,
conscious of their conflicts. "Curiously he seemed to contemplate
himself with a quiet scientific wonder," Swinburne writes of Den-
ham, "to feel the pulses of his fever, to examine and approve or
condemn the play played out on the inner stage of his mind"
(38). "Conscious of herself to the core of her sensitive and fervent
nature," he writes of Lady Wariston, "she crucified her soul grad-
ually, driving as it were through hands and feet the nails of self-
knowledge, submitting her spirit as it bled and quivered to a
horrible vivisection, till she saw every nerve naked and felt every

---

la Perversité . . . The natural perversity that results in man's being constantly,
and at one and the same time, homicidal and suicidal, murderer and executioner
(C, 192).

drop of blood drawn from the several wounds" (133). Lesbia Brandon, "poetess and pagan," is conscious to the end: "I'm dying upwards," she says to Seyton, "My head is as clear as my voice" (159). *Lesbia Brandon* keeps before us, as Swinburne says Baudelaire's "Femmes Damnées" do, "an infinite perverse refinement, an infinite reverse aspiration, 'the end of which things is death.' "90 This subject matter and this Baudelairean presence also characterize, of course, *Poems and Ballads*. But the novels avoid the mossiness of the poems, their "wordy obscurity," as Edmund Wilson said, who also wished that "the obstacles he met" had not prevented Swinburne from making "his full contribution to English fiction."91

*　　*　　*

It was neither his public praise, however, nor his privately circulated caricature and novels, that caused Swinburne's name to "sound as one" with those of Baudelaire and Immortality. The welding began in the heat of public and critical reaction to *Poems and Ballads, First Series* and was completed when he published "Ave atque Vale." The elegy brings together the strands in his appreciation of Baudelaire: it addresses the dead poet in a language that is both personal and impersonal, both private and public; it pays its tribute in a densely woven texture of allusion by which Swinburne identifies both his own tradition and his chosen "community of song"; and it lays down for future generations of English readers of Baudelaire a powerful description of him as the type of the decadent poet.

What chiefly distinguishes "Ave atque Vale" from Swinburne's other elegiac verses is its tone: while they can be sometimes merely formal and fervid, this elegy is careful and personal. Its decisive stroke is its epigraph, the lines from "La servante au grand coeur dont vous étiez jalouse," a sonnet in which Baudelaire figures in homely terms the sorrows of the dead and urges upon family and friends the simple obligation of caring for the "eternal bed." The lines supply "Ave atque Vale" with its expressly personal note, with its movingly simple intimate imagery of unclasped and clasped hands, and with what Swinburne called in a letter a "tone of deeper thought or emotion than was called forth by the death of Gautier."92 All this is put together with a formal, classical act of remembrance. The opening lines, because they are a reply to Baudelaire's injunction, "Nous devrions quand même lui porter quelques fleurs," raise conventional emblem to personal statement and give a distant sense of dialogue. Swinburne holds the intimate and the formal in balance from the beginning: the poet both places his garland on the tomb of a brother with whom he has shared time and makes a libation to a poet with whom he shares eternity; while the mortal laments the death of a fellow-laborer, the "God of all suns and songs" bends to place the laurel and the "most high Muses" weep.

The epigraph also adds layers of nuance to the flower imagery which is, as critics have shown, the chief organizing device of the poem. In none of Swinburne's memorial verses is the conventional elegiac imagery of gardens more appropriately elaborated or effectively transformed. Here it is not only a direct response to Baudelaire's suggestion that one ought to carry flowers to the dead, but also a tribute in extended imagery to the book of poems Swinburne commemorates. Baudelaire's title stands as the central conceit of Swinburne's elegy, the frame over which he lays the allusions that gather steadily, stanza by stanza. The fact that Baudelaire called his poems "flowers" imposes upon the literary sense of gardens and garlands an exceptional force and gives a kind of literal sense to Swinburne's suggestion that the living gardener will complete the harvest of his departed colleague; the seasonal imagery of autumn and harvest easily contains both the Swinburnean emphasis on cyclical movement and the Baudelairean themes of the implacable destructiveness of time and retribution. Swinburne's choice of epigraph, and his reiterated insistence that the imagery of his poem is shared with his subject, brilliantly personalize what might otherwise have remained merely stylized.

The flower imagery of "Ave atque Vale" shares the double character of the poem's address. Swinburne describes both an exotic, poisonous, unearthly garden and "seedlands" of "honey and spice," "roses and ivy and wild vine." He takes pains to associate Baudelaire with the former—with what might be described as artificial, over-complex, excessively paradoxical. His poem both begins and ends with an emphasized contrast between natural and Baudelairean fruits of the earth. Swinburne declines

---

Nous devrions . . . we really ought to take her some flowers (S, 10).

to offer the dead poet "quiet sea-flower moulded by the sea, / Or simplest growth of meadow-sweet or sorrel," imagining that he would be better honored by a more striking garland of "Half-faded fiery blossoms, pale with heat / And full of bitter summer," products of a "fervid languid" climate and "mightier skies."

Thou sawest, in thine old singing season, brother,
  Secrets and sorrows unbeheld of us:
  Fierce loves, and lovely leaf-buds poisonous,
Bare to thy subtler eye, but for none other
  Blowing by night in some unbreathed-in clime;
  The hidden harvest of luxurious time,
Sin without shape, and pleasure without speech;
  And where strange dreams in a tumultuous sleep
  Make the shut eyes of stricken spirits weep;
And with each face thou sawest the shadow on each,
  Seeing as men sow men reap.

In the penultimate stanza Swinburne pushes the image of perverse growth still further:

Out of the mystic and the mournful garden
  Where all day through thine hands in barren braid
  Wove the sick flowers of secrecy and shade,
Green buds of sorrow and sin, and remnants grey,
  Sweet-smelling, pale with poison, sanguine-hearted,
  Passions that sprang from sleep and thoughts that started,
Shall death not bring us all as thee one day
  Among the days departed?

That garden is not entirely unfamiliar in Swinburne's poems, in which "rare rank flowers" are more common than one of those adjectives suggests, but it is decidedly unlike the others he planted in his memorial verses. For "Barry Cornwall," for instance, he imagined "a white rose thornless that grows in the garden of time," and for Gautier, of whom "Il semblait qu'en passant son pied semât des roses," he saw "the whole soul of the sun in spring."[93] In "Ave atque Vale," however, the sun is setting; and Baudelaire stands alone in Swinburne's poems as the "gardener of strange flowers," the fully decadent poet.

Il semblait . . . It seemed that in passing his foot seeded roses.

To those dichotomies—of intimate and distant address, of sim-
ple, natural flowers and complex, artificial ones—it is necessary
to add another. "Ave atque Vale" addresses the question of the
significance of a poet's life and work: it inquires into the kind
of loss that is represented by his death and the kind of gain that
is represented by his poems, moving from the "unclasped hand
of unbeholden friend" to a recognition that the "shut scroll" that
is left can fill the void, "As though a hand were in my hand to
hold." Swinburne engages two dimensions of time. One is that
occupied by the "elected poetic company," the "unbroken con-
tinuity [of poetry] from generation to generation," in which he
declares Baudelaire's place, and his own. It is a version—far more
resonant and detailed—of his "unified tradition," an assertion
that one of his communities is "the whole of the literature of
Europe from Homer"[94] (although Swinburne here associates
Baudelaire's poetry with Sappho, "the supreme head of song").
The other, mortal side of the temporal dichotomy, named under
the cover of allusion, is no less a declaration of poetic community.

In the same year as Swinburne published "Ave atque Vale,"
Théophile Gautier's extremely influential preface to the defin-
itive edition of Baudelaire's works appeared in Paris. Gautier's
preface, like Swinburne's poem, sets forth Baudelaire's work in
the extreme colors of decay. The imagery of the following pas-
sage, for instance, is remarkably like that in "Ave atque Vale":

> . . . il a su trouver ces nuances morbidement riches de la
> pourriture plus ou moins avancée, ces tons de nacre et de
> burgau qui glacent les eaux stagnantes, ces roses de phthisie,
> ces blancs de chlorose, ces jaunes fielleux de bile extravasée,
> ces gris plombés de brouillard pestilentiel, ces verts empoi-
> sonnés et métalliques puant l'arséniate de cuivre . . . et toute
> cette gamme de couleurs exaspérées poussées au degré le
> plus intense, qui correspondent à l'automne, au coucher du

. . . *il a su* . . . he knew how to find those shades that are morbidly rich with
more or less advanced decay, these tones of pearl and mother-of-pearl like ice
over stagnant waters, these consumptive pinks, these chlorotic whites, these
splenetic whites of extravasated bile, these greys leaded with pestilential fog,
these poisoned and metallic greens, reeking of copper arsenate . . . and that
whole range of exaggerated colors, pushed to their most intense, which corre-
spond to autumn, to sunset, to the over-ripeness of fruit, and to the last hour
of civilizations.

soleil, à la maturité extrême des fruits, et à la dernière heure des civilisations.

"Son bouquet," Gautier writes in his preface, "se compose de fleurs étranges, aux couleurs métalliques, au parfum vertigineux, dont le calice, au lieu de rosée, contient d'âcres larmes ou des gouttes d'aqua-tofana."[95] Swinburne's "strange flowers," his "Green buds of sorrow and sin, and remnants grey, / Sweet-smelling, pale with poison, sanguine-hearted," are there too.

It would be pleasing to think that the setting sun of "Ave atque Vale" had inspired Gautier and so made Swinburne one of the voices in the most consequential piece of Baudelaire criticism ever written, and it is tempting, since Swinburne's poem preceded Gautier's preface into print by a few weeks. But the raw chronology suggests a false hypothesis, because in his preface Gautier is borrowing from himself. In August 1862 his introduction to seven poems of Baudelaire had appeared in Eugène Crépet's prestigious anthology, Les Poètes Français; and in September 1867 Le Moniteur Universel had printed his obituary notice of Baudelaire.[96] His preface to the 1868 edition of Les Fleurs du Mal takes important material from both of these earlier essays and so cannot be directly associated with Swinburne's poem.

What Swinburne may have taken from Gautier's earlier pieces, however, is another question. There is every reason to believe that Swinburne would have taken the trouble to lay his hands on everything written about Baudelaire by Gautier, whom he had admired "from boyhood almost." When Gautier's earlier pieces were published, Swinburne's interest in Baudelaire was especially keen. In 1862, he was fresh from his important encounter with Les Fleurs du Mal, about to see his review of the book in print, and working on other material related to his reading of Baudelaire. In 1866 and 1867, he was at work on his memorial poem and about to publish in his Blake his "notice" of Baudelaire's life. He needed, as he said in a letter to George Powell, more information "than has appeared in the English papers."[97] Gautier's essays would have held for him the greatest possible interest, and Gautier's earliest essay includes the following passage:

Son bouquet . . . His bouquet is made up of strange flowers, with metallic colors, with dizzying perfumes, whose calyx contains bitter tears or drops of aqua-tofana instead of dew.

On lit dans les contes de Nathaniel Hawthorne la descrip-
tion d'un jardin singulier où un botaniste toxicologue a réuni
la flore des plantes vénéneuses. Ces plantes aux feuillages
bizarrement découpés, d'un vert noir ou minéralement glau-
que, comme si le sulfate de cuivre les teignait, ont une beauté
sinistre et formidable. On les sent dangereuses malgré leur
charme; elles ont dans leur attitude hautaine, provocante
ou perfide, la conscience d'un pouvoir immense ou d'une
séduction irrésistible. De leur fleurs férocement bariolées et
tigrées, d'un pourpre semblable à du sang figé ou d'un blanc
chlorotique, s'exhalent des parfums âcres, pénétrants, ver-
tigineux; dans leurs calices empoisonnés la rosée se change
en aqua-tofana, et il ne voltige autour d'elles que des can-
tharides cuirassées d'or vert, ou des mouches d'un bleu d'a-
cier dont la piqûre donne le charbon. L'euphorbe, l'aconit,
la jusquiame, la cigüe, la belladone y mèlent leurs froids
virus aux ardents poisons des tropiques et de l'Inde. . . .[98]

It is most unlikely that Swinburne saw that before writing his
own review of *Les Fleurs du Mal*, but very likely indeed that he
saw it in time to weave it into the dense tissue of external ref-
erence that makes up "Ave atque Vale." Gautier's comment on
Baudelaire's significant title sounds the note of Swinburne's
poem, too: it shows "que l'auteur ne s'est pas amusé à cueillir
des vergiss-mein-nicht au bord des sources et à faire de banales
variations sur ces vieux thèmes de l'amour et du printemps."
Not "quiet sea-flower" or "simplest growth of meadow-sweet."
In his obituary, Gautier said that the comparison of *Les Fleurs*

On lit dans . . . We read in the stories of Nathaniel Hawthorne the description
of an unusual garden in which a botanist-toxicologist gathered together the flora
of poisonous plants. These plants, with their strangely cut foliage—black green
or minerally glaucous, as if tainted by copper sulfate—have a sinister and pow-
erful beauty. You feel them dangerous in spite of their charm; they have in their
haughty, provocative, or perfidious attitude an awareness of immense power or
irresistible seductiveness. From their fiercely streaked and spotted flowers, pur-
ple like congealed blood or chlorotic white, exhale bitter, penetrating, dizzying
perfumes; in their poisoned calyxes dew is transformed to aqua-tofana, and the
only creatures flying around them are cantharides, armoured in green gold, or
steel-blue flies whose bite infects with anthrax. In this garden, wart-wort, wolf's-
bane, hemlock, and belladonna mix their cold venom with the fiery poisons of
the tropics and of India. . . .

que l'auteur . . . that the author did not amuse himself gathering forget-me-
nots at the edges of springs and making banal variations on the old themes of
love and springtime.

du Mal to Hawthorne's poisonous garden had pleased Baude-
laire. In making Gautier's description part of his range of al-
lusion, Swinburne included in his contemporary brotherhood of
song the poet Baudelaire had called "impeccable." The thin
flame of "Ave atque Vale" runs down the ages, tracing the ap-
ostolic succession of poets, but it also runs round the horizon of
the present, utterly unimpeded by national boundaries. In "Ave
atque Vale," as in everything else he wrote about Baudelaire,
Swinburne identifies by cross-reference and allusion and by the
devices of intimate specific reference a poetic community that
he saw as opposition to that of "Tennyson & Cⁱᵉ."

*　　*　　*

For Swinburne "Ave atque Vale" really was a farewell: it ended
the period of his most productive interest in Baudelaire. For
literary history, however, it was part of a beginning, an early and
commanding formulation of a recurrent figure—that of the in-
ternational brotherhood—which would eventually come to dom-
inate versions of the history of modernism, as in Eliot's derivation
of his own work from the line back through Valéry to Poe. It
also gave serious confirmation to what the uproar over *Poems
and Ballads* had suggested: that Swinburne boasted a powerful
confederate in Baudelaire, whose name was a key element in
public debate over the right of English poetry to deal with un-
approved subjects.

The "quaint . . . reception" and "singular . . . fortune" of Swin-
burne's collection gradually established the context for the first
generation of English appreciation of Baudelaire.[99] The first and
second waves of critics, however, had not found out the name
of their target. John Morley attacked *Poems and Ballads* for sen-
suality, immorality, and irresponsibility; Robert Buchanan for
"uncleanness" and "rank blasphemy"; the *London Review* for "in-
sane extravagance of passion" and "raging blasphemy."[100] Bu-
chanan did detect a general foreign flavor, and the *London Re-
view*, deducing that Swinburne had "familiarized himself with
the worst circles of Parisian life, and drenched himself in the
worst creations of Parisian literature," found his writing "so alien
to the spirit of our country that it can obtain no root in the
national soil." But no one saw Baudelaire in Swinburne, even in
the new outrage that followed John Camden Hotten's reissue of
Poems and Ballads. (Robert Buchanan, though, was still hot on

the scent of the "immorality of modern French writers of the
avowedly immoral school.")[101]

It was Swinburne who first identified himself with Baudelaire,
in *Notes on Poems and Reviews*.[102] There, using arguments he had
made in his review of *Les Fleurs du Mal*, and referring to seven
of his new poems (a collection to match *Les Épaves*), he defended
himself against the very charges Baudelaire had faced in court.
He asserts that a poet must obey "the simple laws of his art" (32),
that lyric poetry must be seen dramatically, and that when the
poet has "handled" or transformed his materials the poem must
be read symbolically. To that lesson in aesthetics he adds an
attack. His poems *are* moral, he says: if his critics think them
immoral, that moral constriction of criticism raises the funda-
mental question "whether or not the first and last requisite of
art is to give no offence" (29) or whether poetry will be permitted
to deal with "the full life of man and the whole nature of things"
(30). In the context of this unencumbered argument for freedom
Swinburne invokes the support of two other poets: Sappho—
whose "remaining verses are the supreme success, the final
achievement, of the poetic art" (21)—and Baudelaire, the same
two poets who in "Ave atque Vale" were to stand as the past and
present models of his art. Swinburne associates himself with
Baudelaire in connection with the Tannhäuser story, recounting
how after completing "Laus Veneris" he

> received from the hands of its author the admirable pam-
> phlet of Charles Baudelaire on Wagner's *Tannhäuser*. If any
> one desires to see, expressed in better words than I can
> command, the conception of the mediaeval Venus which it
> was my aim to put into verse, let him turn to the magnificent
> passage in which M. Baudelaire describes the fallen Goddess,
> grown diabolic among ages that would not accept her as
> divine. (26)

Swinburne also concurs, he says, "with the great musician and
his great panegyrist" in judging the Tannhäuser story to be no
tale of "light loves and harmless errors," but the "noble and
significant" representation of spiritual conflict (27). Swinburne
here explicitly allies himself with Baudelaire, the only living poet
he names, in attack on the "anti-sexual moralists,"[103] and he
declares his longing for the day when "England has again such

a school of poetry . . . as she has had at least twice before, or as France has now" (32).

When William Michael Rossetti, who saw Swinburne's *Notes* through the press, wrote of him, he developed the idea of the international connection. He related Swinburne to no more than two living poets, or more probably only one, not English and "probably almost unknown to English readers," author of

> "Les Fleurs du Mal," to which the least commendable parts of the "Poems and Ballads" seem to bear a considerable affinity: we must therefore class Baudelaire's influence upon Swinburne as a bad though not an uncongenial one. The French poet is a sort of poetic Mephistopheles: if Göthe's fiend had been more human-natured and imaginative, he would have been not unlike Baudelaire, who sees the facts of the world to much the same effect as Mephistopheles, only with a poetic colouring, and expresses them in terms which are vivid and moving, instead of withering and dry. If he does not quite say, after Milton's Satan, "Evil, be thou my good," he does at least say, "Evil, be thou my inspiration"; and, being a man of powerful mind, and a very real poetic gift, he succeeds in ringing the changes upon this bad tocsin to some purpose. With squeamishness, whether applied to the criticism of a Baudelaire, a Swinburne, or any other man of genius, we have no sympathy; but, as to approval, we must, with Newman Noggs's barber, "draw the line somewhere," and we draw it before Baudelaire. There is good artistic as well as moral warrant for such a decision. A book like the "Fleurs du Mal" cannot be "in good keeping" in an enlarged sense: it may be in keeping one part of it with another, but not with a complete, healthy, or true view of actualities; and, being thus both partial and perverse, it must of necessity also be violent.[104]

Such an admission from Rossetti, who wrote to defend Swinburne, was almost an invitation to the "critical tribe," as Swinburne called it, to close in.[105] While the first judgment of Baudelaire's poems in England had put some perplexing questions into the mind of the editor of *The Spectator*, the second, after placing Baudelaire in the ranks of the major devils, derived its position from the first principles of Newman Noggs's barber.

Baudelaire's name did not appear in the English journals again (though it had of course appeared in Swinburne's *Blake*) until after publication of his *Oeuvres Complètes* of 1868. That edition was hard to ignore—it was prefaced by Gautier's long memoir and critical commentary and followed by an appendix, gathered by Asselineau and Banville, of critical comment (by Edouard Thierry, F. Dulamon, J. Barbey d'Aurevilly, Charles Asselineau, and letters by Sainte-Beuve, de Custine, and Emile Deschamps).[106] *Fraser's Magazine*, however, which was edited by James Anthony Froude, whom Swinburne hated, was the only English journal to find it worthy of notice in the year of its first publication. It printed an anonymous review, "A Poet of the Lower French Empire," in December, 1869.[107] The reviewer, William Allingham, later thought of his essay as one of his important pieces: he included it among only six essays in his three-volume *Varieties in Prose*, 1893, as dealing with issues that were "not of passing, but of permanent importance," and he remembered the essay with some satisfaction in a diary entry he made in August, 1884. "Tennyson read Baudelaire's *Fleurs du Mal*," he wrote, "and thought him 'a kind of moralist,' though his subjects, he allowed, are shocking. I could not agree (and had, I think, studied Baudelaire more closely); he seems to me to take pleasure in seeing evil committed, and also in seeing evil-doers punished—a devil rather than a moralist."[108]

Allingham presents Baudelaire as a "name that has lately become of note in French poetic literature" who is now ripe for evaluation both because his whole work is now available ("except a few [poems] suppressed by the censorship as too bad for the not very squeamish taste of the French public") and because he is dead. The review is the first in England to relay material from Gautier's preface, on which it depends heavily, and is therefore biographically informative, but to Gautier's already excited account it adds a steadily discrediting slant. It condemns the poet for "sensuousness," "materialism," and "cruelty" (which it identifies as a " 'note' of the New Diabolic School"), and it refers to him repeatedly as "morbid," "unwholesome," or "unhealthy." His subject matter is derived from "his amours and subsequent disgusts" or "the hideousness of disease, death, putrefaction," and his imagery abounds "in serpents, corpses, vampires, grave-worms, nightmares, demons." The reviewer acknowledges Baudelaire as a distinguished stylist and a lover of beauty, but he ascribes the style to imitation, and finds the beauty to be "a

Parisian kind of *beau* . . . wholly material and sensual, yet with
exquisite and fastidious manners, and always more or less *factice*."
This art, it says, amounts to mere artifice: Baudelaire has, in
fact, "little inventiveness" and "not a particle of imagination in
the highest sense of that word, of that great and healthy faculty
(including all others) whereby man has wide and profound vi-
sions of truth." The effect of the review is to trivialize Baude-
laire's life and his art: "Harmonie du Soir," for instance, is said
to be presented in an image "not tragic but *butcherly*." Allingham
neither perceives the morality of *Les Fleurs du Mal* nor appre-
ciates their poetic power. He quotes, from the critical material
which this edition appends to *Les Fleurs du Mal*, but only for the
purpose of discovering superficial or apparent contradictions.
The life that may have been a "puzzling phenomenon" at the
time, he says, is now "no mystery":

> A young Parisian, handsome, clever, and with some money
> to spend, seeks pleasure as his aim; tries vulgar sensuality,
> which disgusts his taste; and aims at a refined and artistic
> voluptuousness, but even this proves unsatisfying; every
> path leads him to the black gulf of ennui.

Mock-sympathy produces no gain in complexity:

> I find in myself a taste for *le beau*, for flowers, and perfumes,
> and pictures, and wine, and fair women; I can't get them,
> enough of them, for I am not rich; I do get them, and they
> sting me; in either case, Damn the Nature of Things!

Allingham's review gives the first paraphrase in English of Gau-
tier's description of the young Baudelaire, and takes up, though
briefly, his contrast with the ravaged poet of forty-six. The con-
trast (which makes his review a distant relative of *Dorian Gray*)
provides Allingham with his conclusion: "He at least points out
with unmistakable clearness the practical unwisdom of a certain
way of thinking about life."

Allingham does not mention any English poet, but he hints at
Swinburne twice. In his swift passage over the critical material
in the 1868 *Fleurs du Mal*, he mentions Asselineau's question, "Is
all our literature now-a-days to be written for schoolgirls?" The
question, he says, has "lately been decocted into an English re-
view article." And, concluding his review on a merciful note,
Allingham nevertheless raises the matter of Baudelaire's influ-

ence: the French poet is "immeasurably above those, whether
his direct imitators or others, who write foul and blasphemous
cleverness from the sting of vanity, as the most telling way to
exhibit themselves and make a strong and immediate sensation."
Swinburne's defense of *Poems and Ballads* had "decocted" the
question, and his poems themselves brought him within the
sweep of Allingham's closing judgment.

In the year of Allingham's review, Baudelaire's name appeared
for the first time in an English book title. John Camden Hotten,
now Swinburne's publisher, issued the first separately published
translations, those of Richard Herne Shepherd: *Translations from
Charles Baudelaire, With a Few Original Poems*. Although advertised
in such a way as to confirm the title's implication that it is mainly
translations, the book actually consists almost entirely of the sub-
ordinately billed "original poems." Only three of Baudelaire's
poems appear—"A Carcass," "Lesbos," and "Wandering and
Weeping" ("Moesta et Errabunda")—and it prints these under
the epigraph, *"Eritis sicut Dii, scientes bonum et malum"* (so linking
Baudelaire again with "Göthe's fiend," as Rossetti called him).
Hotten's advertisements for the book, which print Baudelaire's
name in large, bold capitals, and Shepherd's far more modestly,
list it together with *Notes on Poems and Reviews* and William Mi-
chael Rossetti's *Criticism*. For Hotten, the connections between
Baudelaire and Swinburne were already established and ex-
ploitable.

The year 1870 produced "On Reading Baudelaire's 'Fleurs
du Mal,' " the second English poetical response to him, in a
pseudonymously published volume of *Poems* by "Julio."[109] This
was Joseph Sykes, a confirmed Francophile, who had lived for
years in Paris, and who had written on French history and lit-
erature, though not otherwise on Baudelaire. The poem, which
does not command attention by its intrinsic value, suggests that
Swinburne's elegy had already begun to accumulate imitations:
the view "Julio" takes is not Swinburnean, but it reflects clearly
what at this early stage had already become the conventional
one on Baudelaire. Taking a stoutly moral line, like Allingham
chastening with pity, it identifies the themes of *Les Fleurs du Mal*
as corruption, passion, and artifice; and it makes its moral point
through Swinburne's counterpointed imagery of natural and
unnatural growth, attaching "venal love," "Ennui, satiety" and
"foulest thought and action" to flowers that are positively hellish:

Circle of lust, 'tis e'er the same,
    In narrow round the changes ring—
Languid desire that melts the frame,
    Spasmodic passion's panther-spring.

And worse than these, the fell desire
    To labour in the cause of ill—
Where flowers of evil glow like fire,
    In circles ever wid'ning still.

Like other early English readers of Baudelaire, "Julio" perceives him as morally and aesthetically dangerous: his artificial flowers, ignited perhaps by the heat of the decadent sun, threaten to destroy "healthy" art:

The conflagration spreads around,
    And charred remains its progress show—
A patch of desolated ground,
    On which no healthy plants can grow.

"Julio" makes it clear that he is defending the best traditions in life and art, setting these in antithesis to the Dantesque flaming circles:

Yet near the forest glade extends,
    Birds, too, are singing in the trees,
And vegetation's richness blends
    And wafts its odours on the breeze.

All is not bad, as some would say;
    Near evil's haunts bright virtue lives—
And mighty Nature's sovereign sway
    Her treasured store of blessings gives.

"Julio's" poem makes no mention of Swinburne, but its fire-flowers and its fear of general conflagration suggest him.

Baudelaire appeared once more in the English journals before the explosion of personal hostilities that fused his name with Swinburne's. William Stigand reviewed the "definitive edition" of his works, now reprinted, in *Belgravia* for October 1871.[110] More widely informed than Allingham's, his review draws not only on the material printed in this edition but also on Baudelaire's own criticism and Asselineau's biographical essay. It moves

from examination of several of the poems to consideration of
Baudelaire's life, and it concludes by addressing general issues
of which it sees Baudelaire as illustrative. Stigand quotes from
and sometimes translates into English prose a number of the
Fleurs du Mal—"Elévation," "Bénédiction," "L'Examen de Mi-
nuit," "La Béatrice," "Le Voyage"—and he singles out for special
attention "Préface," as "Au Lecteur" was called in this edition,
in which he finds "savage coarseness" of language which indicates
the "gloomy character" of the book as a whole. He touches on
Baudelaire's affinity with Poe, on his membership in the Club
des Hachischins, on his dandyism, on the trial of *Les Fleurs du
Mal*. He relays the "portrait" of the young poet (repeating, as
does Allingham, Gautier's remark that Baudelaire often "avan-
çait quelque axiome sataniquement monstrueux ou soutenait
avec un sang-froid de glace quelque théorie d'une extravagance
mathématique"), and he suggests the possibility that Baudelaire's
end may have been "brought about by the perversion of his
genius, his arrogant and isolated manner of intellectual life, and
his contempt for all sane appetites, desires, and passions." He,
too, identifies Baudelaire with Milton's Satan (he "endeavoured
to erect the aphorism, 'Evil, be thou my good,' into a principle
of art"), and he considers him open to the charge "that he has
with premeditation taken more loathsome forms of corruption
and vice as matter meet for song than ever were so employed
before, and that he has raised in their behalf diabolic chants of
adoration, sometimes mingled with hate, in which he appears to
resign himself wholly and in ghastly delight to the domination
of evil." Stigand finds Baudelaire guilty as charged, and he or-
ganizes his analysis polemically. He enters the lists to debate a
general question—"Is a moral end to be left out of sight alto-
gether in writing and criticising a poet's work?"—and to oppose
specific enemies, "the champions of art for art's sake." Stigand
identifies these champions unhesitatingly as "Baudelaire and his
admirers," who "have of late years made more noise in England
than in his own country." He names no member of an English
school of Baudelaireans, but, like "Julio," he fears an influence.

It was left to Robert Buchanan to piece these clues together
and to identify Baudelaire as the "final and most tremendous
development" of a phenomenon that threatened to end the Eng-
lish tradition as he saw it. But even Buchanan came slowly to
that certainty; his pamphlet *The Fleshly School of Poetry and Other*

Phenomena of the Day had a long gestation. He began to work out his prejudices in his early review of *Poems and Ballads*, and developed them through his "Immorality in Authorship" and "Fleshly School" articles to their final state in the *Fleshly School* pamphlet of 1872.[111] When he reviewed Swinburne's poems, Buchanan detected a not wholly English inspiration, but rested his contempt on class grounds rather than on national ones: the poems, he said, "bear some evidence of having been inspired in Holywell Street, composed on the Parade at Brighton, and touched up in the Jardin Mabile." A little over a month later, when he wrote on "Immorality in Authorship," he had more precisely fixed his grounds of attack: modern books convey "false impressions concerning modern life in general, and especially with regard to the relations between the sexes." The essay appears at moments to be an inquiry into the possibility of morality in French literature, and it observes in England "a class of writers who are directly under French influence, yet manage dexterously enough to deceive many of our Catos."

While the villain in Buchanan's critical drama was assuming a more distinctly French face, the hero of the conflict was also emerging steadily into light. Tennyson was the English genius: Buchanan would oppose him to the "modern French writers of the 'immoral' school." Without its idea of Tennyson's English genius, which did not require defining, Buchanan's argument might have appeared to be begging the question even more completely:

> In reading books it is easy to notice broad unrealities and indecencies, but very difficult indeed to recognise the poison coated with clean white diction. Mr. Tennyson might write a poem tomorrow which would be essentially immoral, and yet very hard to detect. In point of fact, being a man of genius, he would not do so, but if the thing were done, not many would be awake to it. It requires an occult judgment nowadays to find out immoral books.

Tennyson became yet more useful to Buchanan in "The Fleshly School of Poetry." He had, Buchanan claimed, already domesticated the article's subject matter: in "Vivien," he "indicated the bounds of sensualism in art"; in "Maud," he "afforded distinct precedent for the hysteric tone and overloaded style which is now so familiar to readers of Mr. Swinburne." But the "fleshli-

ness" of "Vivien" only became "unwholesome" in the work of
Rossetti and Swinburne, where it lacked a "moral or intellectual
quality to temper and control it." The "fleshly gentlemen" had

> bound themselves by solemn league and covenant to extol
> fleshliness as the distinct and supreme end of poetic and
> pictorial art; to aver that poetic expression is greater than
> poetic thought, and by inference that the body is greater
> than the soul, and sound superior to sense; and that the
> poet, properly to develop his poetic faculty, must be an
> intellectual hermaphrodite, to whom the very facts of day
> and night are lost in a whirl of aesthetic terminology.

Buchanan intended to show here, as in his later pamphlet, that
he opposed not simply body but unrestrained body; the sexual
insult of the passage (this debate is distinguished by its charges
and counter-charges of "effeminacy") was intentional.

In *The Fleshly School* pamphlet Buchanan inflated the article's
scheme for moral evaluation of literature into a historical design.
He aimed to provide a context for examination of "a phenom-
enon so strange and striking that to a superstitious mind it might
seem a portent, and so hideous that it converts this great city of
civilisation into a great Sodom or Gomorrah waiting for doom."
The English tradition, he wrote, began when Chaucer, "the
morning star of the modern school," purged what was base from
his Italian sources, kept what was noble, and "prepared a breezier
and healthier poetic form of his own." The great Elizabethan
dramatists, "following in Chaucer's footsteps," produced "an
unequalled gallery of human faces and souls," and so made "the
golden dawn of our poetry." "Just when light seemed fullest,"
however, "time and season were miraculously altered, and a pe-
riod arrived, an overclouding of the sun, a portentous darkness,
wherein few could tell whether it was night or day." The darkness
began, Buchanan explains, "as a fever-cloud generated first in
Italy and then blown westward; finally, after sucking up all that
was most unwholesome from the soil of France, to fix itself on
England." He produces a temperature chart of English literary
history: the "Italian disease," he shows, "raged and devastated
art, literature, and society." After generations of waste, "Words-
worth came, and English literature was saved." But the disease
has been given an odious, potent rebirth: "The Scrofulous School
of Literature had been distinguishing itself for many a long year
in Paris," Buchanan wrote, "but it reached its final and most

tremendous development in Charles Baudelaire,—a writer to whom I must now direct the reader's attention."

Buchanan's "attention" is a damaging thing: writing, he says, with Gautier's memoir in front of him, he finds Baudelaire "a poor, attenuated miserable scarecrow of humanity," "that most unsympathetic of all beings, a cold sensualist," a "true child of Mephistopheles." Baudelaire began life, we are told, with an "already singular disposition" and his "limited" reading developed that into a "true literary monstrosity." His translations of Poe are evidence of the "morbid nature of his tastes" and for his poems he "sought out the most morbid themes." "Charles Baudelaire," Buchanan wrote, "lived and died a slave to his own devil; every line he wrote was slave's work; every picture he ever painted was in one hue—the dark blood-tint of his own shame." The horror resides, however, not mainly in what the poet was, but in his effect in England. He is the symbol and the source of current "Sensualism," the "phenomenon" that is central to Buchanan's inquiry.

> [Sensualism] is on the French booksellers' counters, authenticated by the signature of the author of the "Visite de Noces." It is here, there, and everywhere, in art, literature, life, just as surely as it is in the "Fleurs de Mal" [*sic*], the Marquis de Sade's "Justine," or the "Monk" of Lewis. It appeals to all tastes, to all dispositions, to all ages. If the querulous man of letters has his "Baudelaire," the pimpled clerk has his *Day's Doings*, and the dissipated artisan his *Day and Night*.

Buchanan had taken a while to settle: when he first published the "Fleshly School" article, he had written that last point differently. "English society of one kind purchases the *Day's Doings*," he said. "English society of another kind goes into ecstasy over Solomon's pictures—pretty pieces of morality such as 'Love dying by the breath of Lust.' " Since then it had become apparent that Simeon Solomon could not in the same way as Baudelaire represent a threat to the English tradition. "And yet it is this man," Buchanan went on,

> this dandy of the Brothel, this Brummel of the stews, this fifth-rate *littérateur*, who, adopting to a certain extent the self-explanatory and querulous system of the Italian school of poets, and carefully avoiding the higher issues of that

noble school of which Hugo is the living head, has been
chosen (by no angel certainly) to be the god-father as it were
of the modern Fleshly School, and thus to fill the select salon
of English literature with a perfume to which the smell of
Mrs. Aphra Behn's books is savoury, and that of Catullus'
"lepidum novum libellum" absolutely delicious.

Buchanan then turns to Swinburne, whose poems are dangerous
carriers of infection. "All that is worst in Mr. Swinburne," he
writes, "belongs to Baudelaire. . . . Pitiful! that any sane man,
least of all any English poet, should think this dunghill worthy
of importation!"

Though somewhat marred by lengthy passages of gleefully
returned invective, Swinburne's response to Buchanan, in *Under
the Microscope*, is swift, direct, and steady.[112] To Buchanan's racial
and sexual fury, Swinburne replies with argument, maintaining
his view that the morality of a poem is the consequence of its
treatment and not a quality of its subject matter. He illustrates
his position by taking up Buchanan's comments on Tennyson's
"Vivien" on the one hand, and on Baudelaire's "Femmes Dam-
nées" on the other. Swinburne offers Tennyson's poem, which
Buchanan had nominated as the most innocuous treatment of
erotic matter, as immoral: it is obscene, he says, its Vivien "un-
speakably repulsive" (60), because, in attempting to render his
Arthurian material morally acceptable, the poet has made a gross
error in aesthetic judgment. "Wishing to make his central figure
the noble and perfect symbol of an ideal man, he has removed
not merely the excuse but the explanation of the fatal and tragic
loves of Launcelot and Guenevere" (57). That, in Swinburne's
opinion, is a deformation of the "design," and its consequence
is that "the moral tone of the Arthurian story has been on the
whole lowered and degraded" (56-57). Swinburne's position here
is the one he adopted in 1861: "Je ne veux pas dire que la poésie
n'ennoblisse pas les moeurs. . . . Je dis que, si le poète a poursuivi
un but moral, il a diminué sa force poétique."

Swinburne's contrary example, that of a poem whose effect is
moral though its subject matter is morally unconventional, is
"Femmes Damnées," a poem Buchanan had perceived as a hid-
eous influence on Swinburne's "Anactoria," and dubbed

> the most horrid poem ever written by man, a poem un-
> matched for simple hideousness even in Rome during the
> decadence—a piece worthy to be spoken by Ascyltos in Pe-

tronius Arbiter. . . . The interlocutors in this piece are two
women, who have just been guilty of the vilest act conceiv-
able in human debauchery, but the theme and the treatment
are too loathsome for description.

Against this Swinburne musters the converse of the argument
he applied to Tennyson. " 'Smiling saucily,' " he writes, Vivien
"is simply a subject for the police-court," "a common harlot."
The subjects of Baudelaire's poem are altogether larger, "wor-
thier of hell-fire," and "that side of their passion which would
render them amenable to the notice of the nearest station is not
what is kept before us throughout that condemned poem." They
are handled tragically: their "infinite perverse refinement," "in-
finite reverse aspiration," points them toward an unending
"Dantesque cycle and agony of changeless change." The poem
has, Swinburne writes, insisting on "aesthetic" description, "a
lyric close of bitter tempest and deep wide music of lost souls,
not inaptly described by M. Asselineau as a 'fulgurant' harmony
after the fashion of Beethoven" (60).

What Swinburne says of "Femmes Damnées" is consistent with
everything else he said about the morality of Baudelaire's work.
Baudelaire's world—like that of the medieval preacher, he wrote
in the review—stands in hostile antithesis to the pale decorum
of moralizing critics, a reproof to facile optimism and to a crit-
icism that cannot distinguish morality from social convention or
estimate moral significance.

Swinburne's position is, ironically, exactly the one Eliot at-
tacked him for not taking. "Swinburne knew nothing about Evil,
or Vice, or Sin," Eliot wrote; but he defined his own Baudelaire
in points Swinburne had already made. "The worst that can be
said of most of our malefactors, from statesmen to thieves," Eliot
said in 1930, "is that they are not men enough to be damned.
Baudelaire was man enough for damnation," since he perceived
that

what distinguishes the relations of man and woman from
the copulation of beasts is the knowledge of Good and Evil
. . . he was at least able to understand that the sexual act as
evil is more dignified, less boring, than as the natural "life-
giving," cheery automatism of the modern world. For
Baudelaire, sexual operation is at least something not anal-
ogous to Kreuschen Salts.

So far as we are human, what we do must be either evil
or good; so far as we do evil or good, we are human. . . .[113]

But this praise echoes Swinburne, who said that Baudelaire's
Christianity was

more than half of it mere repulsion from the philanthropic
optimism of sciolists in whose eyes the whole aim or mission
of things is to make the human spirit finally comfortable.
Contempt of such facile free-thinking, still more easy than
free, took in him at times the form of apparent reversion
to cast creeds; as though the spirit should seek a fiery refuge
in the good old hell of the faithful from the watery new
paradise of liberal theosophy and ultimate amiability of all
things.[114]

Swinburne saw Baudelaire's "justification," his "dignity," in two
areas: in the perfection of his art and in his sense of moral
significance. In 1881 he still held to his opinion, "that the per-
vading note of spiritual tragedy in the brooding verse of
Baudelaire dignifies and justifies at all points his treatment of
his darkest and strangest subjects."[115]

The Fleshly School controversy sealed the connection between
Swinburne and Baudelaire. While Swinburne's defense, in *Under
the Microscope*, was principled and intelligent, Buchanan's attack
was widely influential. C. K. Hyder speculates that it may have
been the cause of Swinburne's failure to reprint his Baudelaire
review, and he relays Harriet Jay's report that many famous
people, including Cardinal Manning, sent Buchanan messages
of support.[116] Mr. Justice Archibald, who heard Buchanan's suit
in 1876 against *The Examiner*, said during the course of that trial
that Swinburne's worst faults resulted from Baudelaire's influ-
ence (so, sixteen years after Swinburne had deplored the "foolish
and shameless prosecution" of *Les Fleurs du Mal*, bringing the
"brothers" together before the law). The Reverend W. H. Wylie,
commenting on the trial in *The Christian World*, thought that

Had they perceived the truth, Mr. Swinburne and his
friends would have been grateful to Mr. Buchanan for the
advice he gave them. He told them to abandon blasphemy
and the sensual vein of Baudelaire. . . . This excellent advice,
instead of being gratefully received, was spurned; and any
one who desires to see the unholy wrath which it provoked
in the breast of Mr. Swinburne has only to turn to the pam-

phlet, "Under the Microscope," in which he replied to Mr. Buchanan, screaming like a whole menagerie of monkeys, and pouring forth such torrents of invective as, fortunately, have few parallels in the range of English literature.[117]

In truth, these "torrents of invective" included Swinburne's careful defense of "Femmes Damnées" as opposed to "Vivien" and his insistent espousal of a tradition that included all the literature of Europe, from Sappho; Buchanan's "advice" was that Swinburne should "burn all his French books."

It is of course ironic that later writers should have reached the view that Swinburne damaged Baudelaire's reputation by association. Some of Swinburne's early critics—W. M. Rossetti, for instance—feared damage by association, but damage to Swinburne. In 1875, a review of *Essays and Studies*, signed "E.W.G.," marvelled over the incongruity between the healthy English critic and his sickly first subject for criticism:

> It was curious that this bitter and sterile book, full of the beauty of desolation, the mirages of a life destroyed, should have been chosen as the theme on which to flesh that maiden criticism which should soon find its highest delight in glorifying all that is most exalted, masculine, and vital in the poetry of past and present times. It must have been his perversity and rebellion that attracted to the feeble and sickly genius of Baudelaire the fraternal affection of the young Englishman, and his resistance to all tame and sentimental conventionalities what condoned in Mr. Swinburne's eyes the utter want of real healthiness of purpose or originality of intellect.[118]

A defender of Swinburne wrote in 1896 that he had "once professed the 'art for art' heresy of Baudelaire," but that "his maturity has brought a strong and wise development of patriotism."[119] When, in 1917, Edmund Gosse came to write his *Life* of Swinburne, the climate had undergone a major change: Swinburne's admiration for the French poet, he said, was a mark of his "high intellectual courage."[120]

*   *   *

Swinburne's interpretation of Baudelaire is admirably complete. He maintained his complex view of the "sweet strange elder" against reductive fury, insisting that Baudelaire must be seen as a poet, a critic, a moralist. Though he used him in his battles over critical conventions, making him an originator of the opposition tradition, Swinburne never reduced Baudelaire to a simple symbol of revolt. Furthermore, when he took up the major issues in modern literary debate, and attached Baudelaire's name to them or argued them in terms borrowed from Baudelaire, he made *Les Fleurs du Mal* and *L'Art Romantique* and *Curiosités Esthétiques* part of the essential bibliography of modernism. Some of his quotations from Baudelaire—the passage with which he headed his *Blake*, for instance—spin themselves out into long threads in the fabric of English response to Baudelaire. His *Study of Shakespeare* suggests the ways in which even the finest threads of his reading remained distinguishably in the whole. There Swinburne adopts for his own critical purposes Baudelaire's distinction between "unimaginative realism and imaginative reality," giving in a note his own translation of the passage in Baudelaire's essay on Gautier from which it is taken. His translation was to provide the (unacknowledged) critical point of Wilde's review "Balzac in English," and to appear again (this time with acknowledgment) in Arthur Symons's *The Symbolist Movement in Literature*.[121] Its post-Swinburnean life carried it along a tradition that Swinburne did much to establish.

PATER

ALLUSION, ALLEGORY, AND
AESTHETIC COMMUNITY

Pater's major allegorical works, which are what he said Morris's poems were not, "a disguised reflex of modern sentiment," all attach a special, originating, importance to French literature.[1] The "Preface" to *The Renaissance* takes pains to justify the inclusion in that "series" of the essays on French subjects with insistence that the Renaissance itself began and ended in France and that its essential spirit came from the French middle ages. *Marius the Epicurean* reaches out of its time to link Flavian's Euphuism to the concern for language that characterizes the "modern French romanticists."[2] *Gaston de Latour* presents Ronsard, the focus of its aesthetic debates, as the type of the modern poet. Pater devoted a significant proportion of his relatively small critical writing on modern literature to French writers, too—to Feuillet, Lemaître, Amiel, Flaubert, Fabre, Augustin Filon—and, like Swinburne, he frequently took French works to be the best illustrations of his critical points. In the "Essay on Style," for instance, he turns as naturally for his examples to Stendhal and Hugo as to Wordsworth and Blake, and, especially in what he wrote up to about 1877, he cites the French romantics frequently as representative of the modern school. He borrowed widely in French literature from Oxford libraries,[3] and, when his friends or acquaintances remembered him, they did not neglect to mention his interest in French literature. William Sharp recalled that his library was composed largely of "Greek and Latin classics, German and French works on aesthetics, and the treasures of French and English imaginative literature," William Rothenstein that when he visited Pater to draw him, "He questioned me closely about Mallarmé and Verlaine, Huysmans and de Gon-

court, and the younger French writers," and George Moore that
Pater wrote to tell him "how much he admired my appreciations
of the modern French poets."[4] Pater's internationalism, of which
his interest in French literature is only a part, so struck John
Morley that he welcomed *The Renaissance* as reuniting English
thought with that of Europe.[5]

Yet, in spite of this consistent attention to French literature,
Pater sought to preserve an ambiguous attitude toward it. In
work published later in his life, he frequently dissociated his
interests from those of the French moderns. He praised Le-
maître, for instance, for "an entire freedom from the dubious
interests of almost all French fiction"; writing on Mérimée, he
referred to "much we may think of dubious significance in later
French literature"; he linked Gautier to an adolescent preoc-
cupation with "the luxury of disgust"; and, reviewing Arthur
Symons's poetry, he commented on the presence in it of the
"very modern notes" of "Parisian grotesques" and "sickly gaslight
and artificial flowers"—with an absence of approval that is clear
though certainly ironic, given the large bouquet of strange flow-
ers in Pater's own early essays.[6] Part of Pater's attitude was stiffly
proper: he sent to Lady Dorothy Nevill a "volume of French
Stories," which "might lie, as people say, on the drawing-room
table but for their soiled outside, which I must ask you kindly
to excuse."[7]

Pater's public ambivalence toward modern French literature
is sharply reflected in his use of Baudelaire: just *there*, as he
might have said, his mixed manner of interest and denial finds
its most important subject. In this chapter I propose to examine
both his profound indebtedness to Baudelaire's criticism—his
plundering from the *Curiosités Esthétiques* and *L'Art Romantique* is
one of the best cases we have of what Richard Ellmann calls an
"authoritative larceny"[8]—and the means by which, certainly con-
sciously and perhaps with a satisfied sense of irony, he aimed to
deflect discovery. Both the theft and its concealment cast some
light on Pater's stylistic practice, and both are significant facts in
an account of Baudelaire's presence in English literature. While
Swinburne associated Baudelaire publicly with his protest against
restrictions on literature and so made him notorious, Pater wove
him silently into the texture of his prose, and so gave his views,
and sometimes his voice, a powerful currency in England.

For a long time Pater's careful deflections kept his debt to

Baudelaire undiscovered. His earliest critics—J. A. Symonds, for instance, or Arthur Symons—did not hesitate to compare his work to Baudelaire's, on grounds of shared subjects or similar purposes;[9] but the attempts of later, academic critics to uncover documentary proof of a more than general or merely accidental similarity between the two writers frequently met with frustration. Several of Pater's critics suspected that he had used Baudelaire—Enid Starkie, René Wellek, Sir Kenneth Clark and (in his first book) G. D. Monsman among them—but none was more than tentative.[10] Enid Starkie concluded that Pater did not know much about Baudelaire, and Sir Kenneth Clark was unable to find "solid evidence" that Pater had read any of Baudelaire's criticism. Ruth C. Child's early examination of Pater's aesthetic draws an oddly negative conclusion from evidence that positively suggests Pater's early familiarity with Baudelaire.[11] When Pater began to write, she says, "the term 'art for art's sake' was a derogatory catchword in England, calling to mind ivory towers, stinging kisses, and *Fleurs du Mal*":

> With such ideas in the air about him, it is not surprising that the young Pater should show himself an enthusiast for "art for art's sake." Not only was he personally acquainted with Swinburne, but he also knew well a group including John Payne, Arthur O'Shaughnessy, and Simeon Solomon, all of whom professed to belong to the art for art's sake school. Furthermore, he read a good deal of modern French literature, which was filled with references to the battle of *l'art pour l'art*. Particularly he must have come across the art for art's sake theory in the works of Gautier. It does not seem likely that Flaubert and Baudelaire played any considerable part in developing his critical theories.

But the essay on "Style" alone gives evidence of the importance Pater attached to Flaubert, whom he calls his "French guide"; and the indications that he may have known Baudelaire exist not only in his evident familiarity with Swinburne's work, but also in the facts that Payne's *Intaglios* (1871) had focussed sharply on "strange poison-flowers," and that Swinburne had explicitly compared Solomon to Baudelaire in his article on "A Vision of Love."[12]

It was Germain d'Hangest who, in his substantial study of Pater's life and works, first uncovered proof that Pater had read

Baudelaire's criticism. He noticed an important plagiarism in "The School of Giorgione," and he suspected that Pater was in other respects very close to Baudelaire. But d'Hangest deals primarily with other questions and so he does not pursue this one: "reconnaître chez Lessing une source aux idées de Pater," he writes, "ou la trouver, beaucoup plus près de lui chez Baudelaire, ne constitue pas à nos yeux l'essentiel, tant il nous apparaît certain qu'avant toute chose, c'est encore ici un tempérament qui s'exprime." For most of Pater's critics, however, Baudelaire's influence has been "shadowy," "difficult to establish with anything like comfortable precision," and it has seemed, as to John Conlon, "more *fantôme* than *phare*."[13] Since d'Hangest's early work, some of Pater's newer critics have gathered more evidence of his debt: Gerald Monsman speculates provocatively and penetratingly on the question in his most recent book on Pater; Donald Hill assembles a good deal of solid evidence in his edition of *The Renaissance*; and Billie Andrew Inman proposes some points of contact between the two writers in *Walter Pater's Reading*.[14] The fragments are beginning to come together. There is documentary evidence of another kind, too, of Pater's familiarity with Baudelaire's work, in his papers at Harvard University: on one of the slips in the collection, he compares what he calls the "4th Port" and "one of Baudelaire's crit[ms]."[15]

Such "solid evidence" as there is, however, has had to be won against the will of the subject. In some ways, Pater is the precursor for Possum. Baudelaire is no less a force in his work than in Swinburne's, probably more; but he is a force carefully and cunningly hidden. Pater did not in the long run neglect to acknowledge the master of much of his critical thought, but he took the greatest care to ensure that his acknowledgment would be apparent only to very few of his readers. Swinburne's rough and satiric separation of his private from his public audience has its analogue in Pater's careful layering of his texts. In him, allusion and the manipulation of what is often literally a sub-text are masterful: they are carefully and consciously cultivated defenses and delicately controlled instruments of meaning. It is well, reading Pater, to remember what he admired in Browning,

---

reconnaître . . . to recognize in Lessing a source of Pater's ideas, or to find it, much closer to him, in Baudelaire, is not in our view essential, so clear does it seem to us that here, more than anywhere, is the expression of temperament.

a "cobweb of allusions," "double and treble reflexions of the mind
upon itself," "an artificial light . . . constructed and broken over
the chosen situation."[16] What is fascinating about Pater's Baude-
laire is not only that he is the silent source of much that became
dominant in modern literature, but also that he is given and
withdrawn in Pater's prose by a series of masterful clues and
concealments. Another manuscript slip among Pater's papers at
Harvard identifies both a purpose and an intention: it reads, "—
for scholars, the raffinés, the select few—."[17]

From the beginning, Pater's style is highly allusive. It is always
made for the appreciation of a "select few": indeed, the existence
of a "select few" is from the beginning one of his subjects. His
style depends, therefore, on an element of exclusion: in him,
the including gesture of allusion comes together with an unu-
sually marked manner of rejection. After publication of *The Ren-
aissance*, that "drastic" cultural act by which he "effectually set at
naught the authority of the theory of art which hitherto had the
highest sanction among the enlightened,"[18] Pater had to contend
with both particular and general outrage, with reprisals from
his Oxford colleagues—John Wordsworth, for instance, and Jow-
ett, whose opposition to his election to university office is well
known—as well as with wholesale derision—the caricatured ver-
sions of his views in Mallock's Mr. Rose, for instance, who ap-
peared in 1876, or in the composite aesthete in *Patience*. Careful
from the beginning, Pater became notoriously cautious after
publication of *The Renaissance*, and especially after 1877: he si-
lenced his "Conclusion" altogether in that year, and, after *The
Renaissance*, much of his work is tailored as explanation and
justification. (Several of his unpublished manuscripts are part of
this labor of self-defense.)

In his revisions Pater worked to conceal any possibly danger-
ous sources or affinities of his thought, compelled, as David
Newsome shows, by Jowett's threat of scandalous exposure of
his emotional life to restrain his aesthetic enthusiasms.[19] While
he could say to Arthur Symons that he admired Baudelaire's
prose "immensely," and to A. C. Benson that " 'I admire Poe's
originality and imagination . . . but I cannot read him in the
original. He is so rough; I read him in Baudelaire's transla-
tion,' "[20] he could hardly be expected to leave a public acknowl-
edgment of his debt to the French poet who, in the year before
The Renaissance appeared, had been identified by Robert Bu-

chanan as the "godfather as it were of the modern Fleshly School" and defended by Swinburne as author of the "Femmes Damnées." In the case of Baudelaire, Pater was even more than ordinarily cautious: he took minute pains, whose very littleness is a measure of the danger he must have felt, to exclude from what he wrote anything that might have suggested to a hostile reader that he was allied with the author of *Les Fleurs du Mal.* When he finally did allow Baudelaire's name to stand in his work, though even then only with the coolest ambivalence, times seemed safer: he was himself no longer at the mercy of Oxford, and Oscar Wilde was referring easily, admiringly, and frequently to Baudelaire in his articles in the *Pall Mall Gazette.* Pater's long silence and self-censorship, however, did not prevent him from filleting Baudelaire carefully into his texts, acknowledging by echo and allusion his profound intellectual indebtedness. The echoes, of course, did not need to be made audible to everyone.

Both Pater's concern for a select audience and his ambivalent reference to Baudelaire are aspects of his preoccupation with intellectual and artistic community. He is fascinated by what he calls "our modern idea, or platitude, of the *Zeit-geist*";[21] and while it is the chief duty of his aesthetic critic to distinguish the individualizing quality in an artist's work, he must also detect the ways in which individuals are knitted to one another by shared qualities of sensibility and perception. He found the Renaissance itself attractive, he says, because it issues from a moment in which artists and philosophers "do not live in isolation, but breathe a common air, and catch light and heat from each other's thoughts" (xiii). Through his fictionalized Ronsard, Pater is at pains to point out to the young Gaston de Latour that the awakening of his spirit to poetry is not the product of one author alone but of several together, not of a star, but of a constellation. His unpublished essay on English literature begins by outlining the antithetical possibilities for criticism—a close psychological examination of the individual writer on the one hand, and an "ascription" or "reference" of the "special quality" of the individual writer or book to "some general phase of evolution" on the other—but it is satisfied only by a synthesis of these: "We possess a ph^y of lit. so far as we detect in the individ. writer & his wrk a sym. of wh. he is perhaps unconscious with contemporary writers, with workers of other kinds, with those characteristic and general moods of the age he lived in."[22] Pater delights in tracking the "chain of secret influences" (109) that is the structure of aesthetic expression, both in the direct line of descent and in the network of lateral connections. *The Renaissance* is fascinated by critical moments of transition, or exchange, both of the kind in which Verrocchio, ceding his place, "turned away as one stunned . . . from the bright animated angel of Leonardo's hand" (94) and of that in which the competition for the commission of *The Battle of the Standard* brought together three luminous names: "Michelangelo was twenty-seven years old; Lionardo more than fifty; and Raphaelle, then nineteen years old, visiting Florence for the first time, came and watched them as they worked" (120). The confluence of cultures, the conjunctions of disciplines, the contact and clash of personal viewpoints—from which intellectual movements issue and which give for a moment the illusion of freedom, while inventive adjustment refashions convention—these supply Pater with his central subject.

One of the "raffinés" for whom Pater wove the intricacies of his textual reference was certainly Swinburne. Whatever the facts about their personal acquaintance,[23] it is incontestable that the two were closely familiar with one another's work and conscious of sharing their materials. That scholars have for so long agreed to remain in doubt about their familiarity with one another may well be another consequence of Pater's cultivated side-stepping. Swinburne's remark in a letter to John Morley, however, that he admired and enjoyed Pater's work "so heartily that I am somewhat shy of saying how much," is well known. So is Pater's acknowledgment (which, allowing for the exaggerations of courtesy, is true): his early essays in the *Fortnightly*, he said, owed "their inspiration entirely to the example of [Swinburne's] work in the same line."[24] All but one of the essays in *The Renaissance* succeeded publication of *Poems and Ballads, Notes on Poems and Reviews*, and *William Blake*, and those works left their imprint clearly on what Pater wrote. Their evident effect in the essays of *The Renaissance* confirms the impression left by the one letter Pater is known to have written to Swinburne, that their shared interest in the most modern French literature was a point of contact between them. Pater here thanks Swinburne for sending his "beautiful French verses on Gautier" and "The English Sonnet" (which Lawrence Evans identifies as "Ode" and "Sonnet, with a copy of *Mademoiselle de Maupin*").[25]

The Renaissance, of course, as a document of the modern "rev-

olutionist" spirit, which Pater admired from the time he read
his early essay to the Old Mortality, is intimately related to Swin-
burne's early writing. Its central theme—the "outbreak of the
human spirit" expressed in "the care for physical beauty, the
worship of the body, the breaking down of those limits which
the religious system of the middle age imposed on the heart and
the imagination," or what Pater calls the "antinomianism" (xi-
xii) of the period—is the animating theme of *Poems and Ballads*
and of the *Notes* that were written to defend them. Both Pater
and Swinburne embody their revolt against limitation in an ad-
miration of complexity. His subject, Pater says in *The Renaissance*,
is "complex, many-sided" (xi), just as Swinburne's is "many-
faced, multifarious";[26] his typical hero, like Swinburne's ago-
nized protagonists, looks in two directions at once. He admires
Pico della Mirandola for his quixotic attempt to "reconcile forms
of sentiment which at first sight seem incompatible, to adjust the
various products of the human mind to each other in one many-
sided type of intellectual culture" (18). His Tannhäuser, Abelard,
Winckelmann—like Gaston and Marius, but unlike Denys L'Au-
xerrois and Sebastian Van Storck, in whom Pater figures the
purified opposites—struggle to unite two mutually excluding
ideals.

The first essay in the series, to which Pater attaches great
importance in the "Preface," demonstrates the blood relation of
his work and Swinburne's. Its Aucassin, Tannhäuser, and Venus
are all figures through whom Swinburne had already expressed
the conflicts of his own time. In the early story of Aucassin and
Nicolette, Pater saw a literature concerned with "a spirit of free-
dom, in which law has passed away" (16). Aucassin's preference
for hell in the company of scholars, actors, and horsemen to
heaven in the company of priests, he said, embodies the most
attractive element of the Renaissance, "this rebellious element,
this sinister claim for liberty of heart and thought" (16). Swin-
burne had brought that same speech of Aucassin to bear upon
his own passionate defense of the liberty of art. In the passage
of his *Blake* that leads up to his art-for-art's-sake cry, he cited
the Albigensian "Aucassin" and called on his readers to observe
how the poets of the Renaissance age, "with their eager nascent
worship of beautiful form and external nature, dealt with es-
tablished opinion and the incarnate moralities of church or
household."[27] Pater makes his Tannhäuser significant and ex-

emplary like Swinburne's—he "prefigures the character of the Renaissance, that movement in which, in various ways, the human mind wins for itself a new kingdom of feeling and sensation and thought."[28] He casts his Venus, too, in an inherited mold. For Swinburne, in the *Notes on Poems and Reviews*, she is a "fallen goddess," a "queen of evil, the lady of lust, [who] will endure no rival but God";[29] for Pater, she represents a movement "beyond the bounds of the primitive Christian ideal . . . a strange idolatry, a strange rival religion," an embodiment of "this rebellious and antinomian element, the recognition of which has made the delineation of the middle age by the writers of the Romantic school in France, by Victor Hugo for instance, in 'Notre Dame de Paris,' so suggestive and exciting" (15).

Swinburne's *Blake* makes the Albigensian "Aucassin" one of three strong supports for his own position: his *credo* invokes Aucassin, Blake, and Baudelaire. When, in his *Notes on Poems and Reviews*, he describes what conflicts he had planned for his Tannhäuser and what powerful and noble evil for his Venus, he calls on Baudelaire and Wagner. Those would not have been inaudible references to Pater. Some "artistic conceptions" of the middle ages, says Pater's essay on Michelangelo's poetry, "became almost conventional, handed on from artist to artist." A pictorial element, a legend, or even a book, could acquire an independent existence, "so that no single workman could claim it as his own" (83): the Tannhäuser legend was an example of such independent existence. Associating his own Venus and Tannhäuser generally with "the Romantic school in France" and particularly with Hugo, Pater could not possibly have been unaware that he linked himself in the chain that included Swinburne and Wagner and Baudelaire.

Pater identified his community, even though he did not identify himself, in his earliest publication, his review of William Morris's poems.[30] That essay, whose tailpiece became the "Conclusion" to *The Renaissance*, suggests not only the argument of Swinburne's *Blake* on the subject of art for art's sake, but also some of its cadences. Like Swinburne, Pater is concerned here to put philosophy and religion in their place: "The service of philosophy, and of religion and culture as well, to the human spirit, is to startle it into a sharp and eager observation" (210). The object of wisest attention is "the poetic passion, the desire of beauty, the love of art for art's sake . . . for art comes to you professing frankly to give nothing but the highest quality to your moments as they pass, and simply for those moments' sake" (213). Those words were written by June, 1868,[31] six months after publication of Swinburne's *Blake*, which goes so clearly into the same territory, denying, on the one hand, that art can ever be the "handmaid of religion, exponent of duty, servant of fact, or pioneer of morality," and asserting, on the other, that the "contingent result of having good art about you and living in a time of noble writing or painting may no doubt be this; that the spirit and mind of men then living will receive on some points a certain exaltation and insight caught from the influence of such forms and colours of verse or painting."[32] Pater's review leaves no doubt of his sympathy with those remarks, which have a significant context in Swinburne's *Blake*: they precede his naming of Baudelaire as the opponent of the *hérésie de l'enseignement*. (Pater's *Renaissance* epigraph, too—*Ye shall be as the wings of the dove*—suggests the "exaltation" of Swinburne, which, in turn, is related to the "enlèvement de l'âme" of Baudelaire's *Notes* on Poe.)

Pater and Swinburne share much more ground than this. The import of these similarities is specific: they connect Pater's work with Swinburne's at precisely the points at which Swinburne proclaims his fraternal alliance with Baudelaire. Although he does not say so directly, Pater certainly knew it, and when, twenty years after Swinburne's *William Blake* and "Ave atque Vale," he published his own tribute to Baudelaire, the "Modernity" chapter of *Gaston de Latour*, he made Swinburne the partner of his praise.

*   *   *

Pater mentions Baudelaire explicitly in only two of his works, and he alludes to him clearly in one other—all long after Swinburne and even after Saintsbury had declared him a valuable influence and each time in a manner designed to evade particular attention.[33] In his 1876 essay on "Romanticism" he names Baudelaire, along with Hugo, Gautier, and Mürger, as a representative of the modern French school; in his 1890 lecture on Mérimée he names him as an example of "the mental story of the nineteenth century"; and in the "Modernity" chapter of *Gaston de Latour*, 1888, while he does not actually name him, he refers to " 'flowers of evil.' "[34] When he makes those references, Pater is stone-faced: in the essay and the lecture he offers Baudelaire's name as merely one example among others; in the historical romance he appears almost to condemn what he names in Baudelaire's own words. Those references, however, flower into meaning when they are examined in their contexts. The "Mérimée" lecture and *Gaston de Latour* demonstrate with an unusual clarity Pater's art of complex, conscious, and sustained allusion, or what he called in his Mérimée lecture the "machinery" of a "rooted habit of intellectual reserve."[35] (I shall consider the "Romanticism" essay, which is a different case, later on.)

In *Gaston de Latour* Pater evokes Baudelaire just when he forces his young protagonist to a crisis of conscience. Gaston has been brought to a moral reversal by what he calls "the worship of physical beauty." It is Pater's favorite subject, transition, the moment at which convention is challenged by change and one ethical system set into an as yet undetermined contest with another. *The Renaissance* essays take the heroic view of such a time of inexorable social and philosophical change. Leonardo, Michelangelo, and the rest flower anomalously from unstable conditions, asserting by their very existence a kind of triumph over the evolutionary necessities. In *Gaston*, however, Pater renders the crisis tenderly, from a naive point of view: Gaston might be one of the "young men" for whose safety Pater withdrew the "Conclusion" from the second edition of *The Renaissance*. Beauty and religion seem to him to be in destructive conflict:

And therewith came the consciousness, no longer of mere bad neighbourship between what was old and new in his life, but of incompatibility between two rival claimants upon him, of two ideals. Might that new religion be a religion not altogether of goodness, a profane religion, in spite of its poetic fervours? There were "flowers of evil," among the rest. It came in part, avowedly, as a kind of consecration of evil, and seemed to give it the beauty of holiness. Rather, good and evil were distinctions inapplicable in proportion as these new interests made themselves felt. For a moment, amid casuistical questions as to one's indefeasible right to liberty of heart, he saw himself, somewhat wearily, very far gone from the choice, the consecration, of his boyhood. If he could but be rid of that altogether! Or if that would but speak with irresistible decision and effect! Was there per-

haps somewhere, in some penetrative mind in this age of
novelties, some scheme of truth, some science about men
and things, which might harmonise for him his earlier and
later preference, "the sacred and profane loves," or, failing
that, establish, to his pacification, the exclusive supremacy
of the latter?

Gaston here faces the recurring conflict of Pater's works: it
appears in his Marius, Tannhäuser, and Abelard; it animates
the opposed emotional predilections of "A Child in the House"
and "An English Poet"; and it dramatizes the tensions which, at
the end of his career, Pater saw as central to the philosophy of
Plato. It is (and he described it in all of the following terms) the
conflict between the concrete and the abstract, the particular and
the general, the real and the ideal, the sensory and the intellec-
tual. Gaston is brought to this essential conflict by poetry, by the
gift from his friend "Jasmin, poetic Jasmin" of the *Odes* of Ron-
sard, whose close attention to the temporal and the sensory sat-
isfies a need his earlier idealism had ignored. The chapter neatly
allegorizes the concerns of the age in which it was written, re-
taining their lucidness and intensity, but displacing them in Pa-
ter's typical manner to a remote time and place. Ronsard's "mo-
dernity," which includes "flowers of evil," overturns Gaston's
single-minded devotion to the "sacred loves" and plunges him
into the equivalent of Marius's, and Dorian Gray's, *nuit blanche*.

Pater makes Ronsard's general allegorical function transpar-
ent, both in the title of his chapter and in his theory-laden prose:
Ronsard is the type of the modern poet. His *Odes* perform for
Gaston "what it is the function of contemporary poetry to effect
anew for sensitive youth in each succeeding generation," showing
him that contemporary poetry can be vividly distinct from the
"poetry of mere literature." The chapter dramatizes Pater's cen-
tral critical proposition, that of aesthetic relativity. He writes:

It was the power of "modernity," as renewed in every
successive age for genial youth, protesting, defiant of all
sanction in these matters, that the true "classic" must be of
the present, the force and patience of present time. He had
felt after the thing, and here it was,—the one irresistible
poetry there had ever been, with the magic word spoken in
due time, transforming his own age and the world about
him, presenting its every-day touch, the very trick one knew

it by, as an additional grace, asserting the latent poetic rights of the transitory, the fugitive, the contingent.

What Pater takes no steps to reveal, however, in a chapter in which he evokes Baudelaire's poems only, apparently, to dismiss them, is that the brief he gives to Ronsard and the words in which he describes it are copied directly from Baudelaire—from, in fact, the chapter of his essay on Constantin Guys, *Le Peintre de la Vie Moderne*, which is "La Modernité": "La modernité, c'est le transitoire, le fugitif, le contingent, la moitié de l'art dont l'autre moitié est l'éternel et immuable," Baudelaire writes. "Cet élément transitoire, fugitif, dont les métamorphoses sont si fréquentes, vous n'avez pas le droit de le mépriser ou de vous en passer" (II, 695). The "latent poetic rights" that Pater's chapter is written to defend derive from him.

Pater's attribution to his fictionalized Ronsard of words taken directly from Baudelaire shifts the terms in which his "Modernity" chapter must be read. Associating Baudelaire with Ronsard, in a chapter whose purpose is to dramatize the idea that every age has its "modernity," Pater makes him "the new hero or demi-god of poetry," and the substitution fractures the fictional surface of this unfinished romance and disturbs its placid relation to the allegorical depths. When Ronsard is understood generally as the type of the modern poet, Pater's allegory is comfortably general, and no particular literary politics are implied; when this type is connected by specific textual links to Baudelaire, however, the allegory is transformed into particularity at several points and heated by the history of a quite specific debate, in which Pater had been a participant. Pater inscribes Baudelaire at two levels of this text, at the level of argument (since it is his conception of modernity that is put forward in *Gaston de Latour*) and at the level of allegorized reality. His trick is both to steal and to acknowledge and to keep both actions carefully veiled from all but the select few among his readers. His reference to "flowers of evil" at the end of the chapter is stoutly ambivalent, at once a lure and a deflection: it admits the existence of a disapproving view of Baudelaire without confess-

La modernité . . . Modernity is the transient, the fleeting, the contingent; it is one half of art, the other being the eternal and the immovable (C, 403).
Cet élément . . . You have no right to despise this transitory fleeting element, the metamorphoses of which are so frequent, nor to dispense with it (C, 403).

ing either its own closeness to him or its own vulnerability to
disapproval. But for the *raffinés* it identifies Pater's own aesthetic
community, and this "Modernity" chapter joins "Ave atque Vale"
as a tribute to the author of the *Flowers of Evil*, who, like Ronsard,
had been a "leader" in a "great poetic battle." Swinburne's *vinum
daemonum* is drunk here again.

The ideas of Pater's chapter lie on its surface. In these pages
he outlines an aesthetic of reconciliation, a rapprochement of
the transitory and the eternal, the actual and the permanent.
The aesthetic he attributes to Ronsard is, of course, his own, but
here it is shown in its proximity to its source, since the charac-
teristics of Ronsard's poetry as Gaston sees them and Pater de-
scribes them are those of Guys's painting as Baudelaire had
described that. This program for modernity is derived from that
one, this idealized Ronsard a direct descendant of that idealized
Guys.

The first point in Ronsard's "modernity" is its aggressive claim
for the validity of modern subjects. "Elderly people, Virgil in
hand," Gaston thinks, might lament the deterioration of the age
and think it "unfit for poetic uses," but youth must protest that
"after all said, the sun in the air, and in its own veins, was still
found to be hot, still begetting, upon both alike, flower and fruit;
nay! visibly new flowers, and fruit richer than ever." Gaston's
modern subjects are closely related to Pater's philosophical an-
titheses. What he demands is "a poetry as veritable, as intimately
near, as corporeal, as the new faces of the hour, the flowers of
the actual season," and that is what Ronsard's *Odes* give him—
"no dubious or generalised form" of flower or bird, but "the
exact pressure of the jay at the window," the "exact natural num-
ber" of petals of the flower, the "precise texture" of "such objects
as wine, fruit, the plume in the cap, the ring on the finger," and
"real people, in their real, delightful attire." This modernity has
much in common with a later one, which it helped to breed, but
its first links are elsewhere. "Il y a eu une modernité pour chaque
peintre ancien," Baudelaire writes, in what is more than simply

Il y a eu . . . There was a form of modernity for every painter of the past; the
majority of the fine portraits that remain to us from former times are clothed
in the dress of their own day. They are perfectly harmonious works because the
dress, the hairstyle, and even the gesture, the expression and the smile (each
age has its carriage, its expression and its smile) form a whole, full of vitality (C,
403).

a restatement of his view that beauty is relative, "la plupart des beaux portraits qui nous restent des temps antérieurs sont revêtus des costumes de leur époque. Ils sont parfaitement harmonieux, parce que le costume, la coiffure et même le geste, le regard et le sourire (chaque époque a son port, son regard, et son sourire) forment un tout d'une complète vitalité." If you suppress this "élément transitoire, fugitif," he says, "vous tombez forcément dans le vide d'une beauté abstraite et indéfinissable, comme celle de l'unique femme avant le premier péché" (II, 695). A painter who relies too heavily on the past, he says, "perd la mémoire du présent; il abdique la valeur et les privilèges fournis par la circonstance; car presque toute notre originalité vient de l'estampille que le *temps* imprime à nos sensations" (II, 696). Because Guys is "dirigé par la nature, tyrannisé par la circonstance" (II, 697), he can "dégager de la mode ce qu'elle peut contenir de poétique dans l'historique," "tirer l'éternel du transitoire" (II, 694). Those paradoxes also describe Ronsard's *Odes* as Gaston sees them.

For Pater, as for Baudelaire, the antitheses of thought—"conséquence fatale de la dualité de l'homme" (II, 685-86)—can be disarmed by art, by the pressure imagination exerts on the specifics of sensory experience. Ronsard can make "the visible . . . more visible than ever before"; when he writes of it, "something more [comes] into the rose than its own natural blush." When Guys hunches over his table, "les choses renaissent sur le papier, naturelles et plus que naturelles, belles et plus que belles" (II, 693-94). The intensified visibility of Ronsard's verse exists "just because soul had come to its surface"; the intensified naturalness and beauty of Guys's painting come from the fact that "la fan-

élément . . . this transitory fleeting element . . . you inevitably fall into the emptiness of an abstract and indefinable beauty, like that of the one and only woman of the time before the Fall (C, 403).

perd la mémoire . . . no longer [has] the present in his mind's eye; he throws away the value and the privileges afforded by circumstance; for nearly all our originality comes from the stamp that time impresses upon our sensibility (C, 405).

dirigé . . . guided by nature, tyrannized over by circumstance (C, 406).

dégager . . . extract from fashion the poetry that resides in its historical envelope . . . distil the eternal from the transitory (C, 402).

conséquence . . . an inevitable consequence of the duality of man (C, 393).

les choses . . . And things seen are born again on the paper, natural and more than natural, beautiful and better than beautiful (C, 402).

la fantasmagorie . . . The weird pageant has been distilled from nature (C, 402).

tasmagorie a été extraite de la nature" (II, 694). Both artists are magicians, possessed of a power of transformation:

> Here was a poetry which boldly assumed the dress, the words, the habits, the very trick, of contemporary life, and turned them into gold. It took possession of the lily in one's hand, and projecting it into a visionary distance, shed upon the body of the flower the soul of its beauty. Things were become at once more deeply sensuous and more deeply ideal.

Baudelaire's "Projet d'Epilogue," with its moving alchemical image ("Tu m'as donné ta boue et j'en ai fait de l'or") was not published until 1887, the year Pater began work on *Gaston*, but his central, transforming magician-artist had made several appearances before that. Guys represents him—"Tous les matériaux dont la mémoire s'est encombrée se classent, se rangent, s'harmonisent et subissent cette idéalisation forcée qui est le résultat d'une perception *enfantine*, c'est-à-dire d'une perception aiguë, magique à force d'ingénuité!" (II, 694). So, too, does Baudelaire's Gautier, whose style, together with his intuitive knowledge of *correspondances*, enabled him

> sans cesse, sans fatigue comme sans faute, définir l'attitude mystérieuse que les objets de la création tiennent devant le regard de l'homme. . . . Manier savamment une langue, c'est pratiquer une espèce de sorcellerie évocatoire. C'est alors que la couleur parle, comme une voix profonde et vibrante; que les monuments se dressent et font saillie sur l'espace profond; que les animaux et les plantes, représentants du

Tu m'as . . . You gave me your mud and I've turned it into gold (S, 232).

Tous les . . . All the materials, stored higgledy-piggledy by memory, are classified, ordered, harmonized, and undergo that deliberate idealization, which is the product of a childlike perceptiveness, in other words a perceptiveness that is acute and magical by its very ingenuousness (C, 402).

sans cesse . . . unceasingly, tirelessly, faultlessly, define the mysterious attitude that all created objects present as men look at them. There is, in words, in the Word itself, something sacred that forbids our turning them into a game of chance. Handling a language with skill is to practise a kind of evocative witchcraft. Then does colour speak, like a deep and vibrant voice, then do monuments stand out, erect, against the unplumbed depths of space, then do animals and plants, the representatives of ugliness and evil, make their meaningful grimaces, then does scent provoke its corresponding thoughts and memories, and passion murmur or roar its unchanging language (C, 272).

laid et du mal, articulent leur grimace non équivoque; que le parfum provoque la pensée et le souvenir correspondants; que la passion murmure ou rugit son langage éternellement semblable. (II, 117-18)

The "thaumaturgic power," the "witchery," the "magic" of Ronsard's poems as Gaston sees them owe much to that "espèce de sorcellerie." Ronsard's work is "the magic word spoken in due time," the poet himself a "wizard." It is because his poetry is personal, Gaston thinks, that

> visible, audible, sensible things glowed so brightly, why there was such luxury in sounds, words, rhythms, of the new light come on the world, of that wonderful freshness. With a masterly appliance of what was near and familiar, or again in the way of bold innovation, he found new words for perennially new things, and the novel accent awakened long-slumbering associations. Never before had words, single words, meant so much. . . . The physical beauty of humanity lent itself to every object, animate or inanimate, to the very hours and lapses and changes of time itself. An almost burdensome fulness of expression haunted the gestures, the very dress, the personal ornaments, of the poeple on the highway.

Because of its magic, Pater writes, the school of Ronsard, "to the liveliest spirits of that time . . . seemed nothing less than 'impeccable,' after the manner of the great sacred products of the past." Swinburne, of course, had said in his *Blake* that Baudelaire was "himself 'impeccable' as an artist"; and Baudelaire, it will be remembered, had dedicated *Les Fleurs du Mal* "Au Poète Impeccable / Au parfait Magicien ès Lettres Françaises . . . Théophile Gautier. . . ."

So far, it is clear that by the conscious displacement of allegory Pater makes Baudelaire the hero of *his* modernity, and I have been arguing that the aesthetic he attributes to his Ronsard is lifted almost bodily from Baudelaire. This is the modernist aesthetic of Baudelaire's *correspondances*. (Later I shall argue that Pater's theft here is merely a repetition and dramatization of his own earlier plundering.) There are two other aspects of this

---

Au Poète . . . To the Impeccable Poet, to the Perfect Magician of French Literature.

remarkable chapter to examine. One is its quality of what might
be called choral speech: here Pater joins his praise by an echoing
imagery and by other devices to a series of tributes to Baudelaire,
including Swinburne's. The other is its quality of portraiture: in
this "Modernity" chapter, Pater sketches a physical likeness of
Baudelaire, and he makes this not merely imaginary portrait
part of his identification of the aesthetic community of his own
youth. I shall treat these two themes together.

Pater sets these screened allusions and borrowings in the con-
text of an emphasized and allegorically important garden im-
agery that is reminiscent in some particular ways of Swinburne's
"Ave atque Vale" depiction of Baudelaire as a "gardener of
strange flowers." Gaston moves through the *Val de Loire* on what
becomes a pilgrimage to Ronsard's priory. During the journey
he advances from carefree, curious youth to his crisis of con-
science, and the imagery reflects his two states of mind. He and
his friends first appear in their intellectual "springtide," riding
"under the rows of miraculous white thorn-blossom, and
through the green billows," aware of "the scent and colour of
the field-flowers, the amorous business of the birds, the flush
and re-fledging of the black earth itself." As he travels toward
the Priory, however, Gaston is changed by his reading. The "juice
in the flowers, when Ronsard named them, was like wine or
blood," and the "new faculty, [the] privileged apprehension,"
which the poetry gives him, erodes his peace of mind. Because
of his "new imaginative culture," "the most familiar details of
nature, its daily routine of light and darkness, beset him now
with a kind of troubled and troubling eloquence. The rain, the
first streak of dawn, the very sullenness of the sky, had a power,
only to be described by saying that they seemed to be *moral* facts."
Gaston's natural garden has become, like Baudelaire's "temple,"
eloquent with detail, and the book itself—Ronsard's *Odes*, the
cause of Gaston's intensified vision—"like nothing so much as a
jonquil, in its golden-green binding and yellow edges and per-
fume of the place where it had lain—sweet, but with something
of the sickliness of all spring flowers since the days of Proser-
pine." When Gaston finally discovers the author of his crisis, the
"eminent man of letters, who had been always an enthusiastic
gardener, though busy just now not with choice flowers but with
salutary kitchen-stuff," he finds him "in the high espaliered gar-
den-wall . . . visible through the open doors, a gaunt figure,

hook-nosed, like a wizard, at work with the spade." His face is "all nerve, distressed nerve."

Other details in the chapter confirm Baudelaire as the recipient and Swinburne as one of the partners of Pater's praise. The important point that for Ronsard the theory of poetry always accompanied its practice echoes the first point in both Gautier's and Swinburne's essays on Baudelaire in 1862, as well as in *William Blake*. Pater makes Ronsard forty-six when Gaston finds him. That was the age at which Baudelaire died, and when Gaston looks at the aging poet, he sees that "the unaffected melancholy of his later life was already gathering. The dead!—he was coming to be on their side." In a passage of praise that has already staked common ground with "Ave atque Vale," that is a fascinating and suggestively elegiac comment. The line taken by Ronsard's enemies, furthermore, "satirists literary and religious," who "falsely made a priest of him, a priest who should have sacrificed a goat to pagan Bacchus," raises the issue on which Buchanan and the others attacked and Swinburne defended Baudelaire. But, most importantly, behind the whole psychological and dramatic action of this chapter there lies an only barely suppressed and subversive religious metaphor. Ronsard *is* a priest, though only a lay priest, and Pater's young men both share with him a "long, sad, Lenten office" and take wine with him in "the poet's workroom," "a strange kind of private sanctuary," lined with portraits of the other poets in the Pleiad. It is after that communion, in which the rituals and language of religion are made to serve in the worship of art, that Gaston experiences his crisis of conflict between " 'the sacred and the profane loves,' " thinking not merely of beauty but of the "worship of physical beauty"—"a religion." The "communion" of this chapter is like the one Swinburne described in his *Blake*, in which " 'this bread of sweet thought and wine of delight' is not broken or shed for all, but for a few only."[36]

All of those elements—a pattern of opposition between a natural and a darkened floral imagery, an admiration for poetic "wizardry," and the transformed, aestheticized eucharist—connect Pater's chapter to Swinburne's elegy. But Swinburne is not the only partner in this praise: Pater's cobweb of allusion is more intricately spun than that. He gives a prominent place to a physical account of the poet who is his subject, and he describes him both aging, as when Gaston finds him in his priory, and young, as in the heyday of the Pleiad. By that juxtaposition of the two faces of his representative modern poet Pater places his tribute in a recognizable line. Retrospective tributes to Baudelaire, as Ellen Moers points out, by Asselineau, Nadar, Cousin, Banville, Champfleury, and, most importantly, by Gautier "turned away from the tragic spectacle of his last years to recall the young poet of the early eighteen-forties. In place of the haggard face with deep lines around the mouth, thinning hair and haunted eyes (the face of the Carjat and Nadar photographs from the 'sixties, which have become the permanent image of Baudelaire), they saw the strikingly handsome head of a young man in his early twenties."[37] That contrast, as Allingham's and Stigand's attacks in *Fraser's Magazine* and *Belgravia* attest, became familiar in England, too. (In them, as elsewhere, it springs from Gautier's preface to the *Fleurs du Mal*.) When he makes Gaston gaze at the portrait of the young poet, Pater joins his "Modernity" chapter, under the cover of his allegory, to those other retrospective tributes. The youthful portrait is his device for "remembering"; with the garden imagery, it makes this chapter of *Gaston de Latour* dense with specific allusion.

It is possible, though it cannot be certain, that when he described the portrait of the young Ronsard, Pater had before him the then most famous likeness of Baudelaire not young. "In spite of his pretension to the Epicurean conquest of a kingly indifference of mind, the portrait of twenty years ago," he writes, "betrayed, not less than the living face with its roving, astonished eyes, the haggard soul of a haggard generation." That description sounds remarkably like the picture carried into wide circulation (together with Gautier's preface) by the third edition, the often reprinted "édition définitive" of *Les Fleurs du Mal*. It is an engraving by Adrien Nargeot after a late photograph by Carjat, in which, according to the *Figaro* in 1893, "le grand poète apparaît plutôt comme un galérien inquiétant que comme un paisible collectionneur de flores perverses."[38] That troubling icon, perhaps known already to Pater, was later much studied by English writers.

The portrait of Ronsard, however, which Gaston takes as representative of a generation, is not the only one in the poet's

le grand poète . . . the great poet looked more like a frightening convict than a peaceful collector of perverse flora.

sanctuary. There are several "pictured faces on the walls, in their frames of reeded ebony or jewelled filigree." Some are of the companions of the poet's youth. The gallery causes Gaston to reflect on the general or communal nature of the poetic rebirth that has surprised him. This new poetry, he thinks, "was the product not of one or more individual writers, but . . . a general direction of men's minds," and he recalls Ronsard's remark that "the actual authorship belonged not so much to a star as to a constellation, like that hazy Pleiad he had pointed out in the sky." Pater's hidden Baudelaire is linked by the picture gallery and the meditation with a community: he is the leader in the poetic battle, but profoundly connected to the others. "A social instinct was involved in the matter," Gaston reflects, "and loyalty to an intellectual *movement.*"

The tactics Pater employed two years later in his lecture on Mérimée, of course, are very different from those of *Gaston de Latour.* For one thing, the latter had autobiography among its purposes; for another, it was intended for readers of *Macmillan's Magazine* in the privacy of their own armchairs. By contrast, "Mérimée," which was delivered in Oxford on 17 November 1890 and in London a week later, is appropriately public, its tone immaculately critical, its address not in the least allegorical.[39] Yet in respect of its treatment of Baudelaire, whom it names, the lecture has some significant features in common with the romance.

When Pater names Baudelaire he has a generalizing purpose: just as Ronsard's face had seemed to Gaston to represent the age in which he lived, Baudelaire seems to Pater, along with Mérimée, to exemplify the intellectual development of the nineteenth century. He is a "central type of disillusion." Furthermore, just as the "flowers of evil" lie on the surface of Gaston's thoughts as an apparent rebuke to what they evoke, Pater's reference to Baudelaire in "Mérimée" is soberly reproving. He presents him, with Hugo, as a paradigm of the psychology of art for art's sake. The piece does not mention art for art's sake, but the passage to which I am referring describes autotelic activity. This, Pater suggests, is "fanaticism." The passage contends that the art of the nineteenth century bears the marks of "Kant's negations":

. . . imprisoned now in the narrow cell of its own subjective experience, the action of a powerful nature will be intense, but exclusive and peculiar. It will come to art, or science, to the experience of life itself, not as to portions of human nature's daily food, but as to something that must be by the circumstances of the case exceptional; almost as men turn in despair to gambling or narcotics, and in a little while the narcotic, the game of chance or skill, is valued for its own sake. The vocation of the artist, of the student of life or books, will be realized with something—say! of fanaticism, as an end in itself, unrelated, unassociated. The science he turns to will be a science of crudest fact; the passion extravagant, a passionate love of passion, varied through all the exotic phases of French fiction as inaugurated by Balzac; the art exaggerated, in matter or form, or both, as in Hugo or Baudelaire. The development of these conditions is the mental story of the nineteenth century, especially as exemplified in France.

Baudelaire makes no further appearance in the lecture, and Pater's unsuspecting listeners were left to suppose that his usefulness to it is no more than that of one example among others of a general intellectual shift. The tone could hardly be more analytically distant.

But in "Mérimée," as in *Gaston*, Pater lays his unelaborated naming over a detailed textual dependence. His lecture takes its pattern and the terms of its discussion from *L'Oeuvre et la Vie de Delacroix*, a work of Baudelaire's to which he had already paid scrupulous attention.[40] Baudelaire attributes that passionate love of passion to Guys, in *Le Peintre de la Vie Moderne*, which Pater had been reading recently; and in the Delacroix essay he joins it to his major theme, the matter of the personal and the impersonal in art.[41] He aims, he says, to discover "de quelle *spécialité* la Providence avait chargé Eugène Delacroix dans le développement historique de la Peinture" (II, 743); and he considers that only a myopic intelligence hides behind "le mot vague et obscur du *réalisme*," since, while Nature is a dictionary, no one would consider a dictionary to be a "*composition*, dans le sens

---

de quelle . . . what speciality Providence had entrusted to Eugène Delacroix in the historical development of painting (C, 359).
le mot . . . that vague and obscure word *realism* (C, 363).
composition . . . composition in the poetic sense of the word (C, 364).

poétique du mot" (II, 747). He advances a view of the painter's
genius as essentially double, uniting emotional heat and technical
cold: in this respect like Guys, Delacroix "était passionnément
amoureux de la passion, et froidement déterminé à chercher les
moyens d'exprimer la passion de la manière la plus visible" (II,
746). One of his great preoccupations, Baudelaire says, was to
"dissimuler les colères de son coeur et de n'avoir pas l'air d'un
homme de génie" (II, 758).

In its general subject, its critical agenda, and its conclusions,
Pater's essay returns an image of Baudelaire's Delacroix design.
"Personality *versus* impersonality in art:—how much or how little
of one's self one may put into one's work: whether anything at
all of it: whether one *can* put there anything else": that is Pater's
general subject. To discover in Mérimée his "markedly peculiar
quality of literary beauty": that is Pater's critical agenda. "Serv-
iceable as the basis of a precautionary maxim towards the con-
duct of our own work, self-effacement, or impersonality, in lit-
erary or artistic creation, is, perhaps, after all, as little possible
as strict realism": that is Pater's conclusion. The picture it en-
closes is as like Baudelaire's as is the frame. Both Delacroix and
Mérimée are presented as versions of the dandy, who cultivate
a perfectly disciplined style for the treatment of violent subject
matter—"désolation, massacres, incendies . . . l'éternelle et in-
corrigible barbarie de l'homme" or "bloodshed," "bloody re-
venges," "natural wildness"—and both work from a dark vision,
of "l'inguérissable amertume" (II, 760) or of the "hollow ring of
fundamental nothingness." Pater finds in Mérimée the double-
ness of Delacroix, who, in Baudelaire's words, combined "beau-
coup du *sauvage*" with " beaucoup de l'homme du monde" (II,
758): "There is the formula of Mérimée!" Pater writes, "the
enthusiastic amateur of rude, crude, naked force in men and
women wherever it could be found; himself carrying ever, as a

était . . . passionately in love with passion, and coldly determined to seek the
means of expressing passion in the most visible manner (C, 363).

dissimuler . . . conceal the waves of anger welling up in his heart, and to appear
not to be a man of genius (C, 376).

désolation . . . desolation, massacres, fire . . . the everlasting and incorrigible
barbarity of man (C, 378).

l'inguérissable . . . incurable sense of bitterness (C, 378).

beaucoup . . . much of the *savage* . . . much of the man of the world (M, 324).

mask, the conventional attire of the modern world." Finally, the likeness of the two critical studies may stem from Baudelaire's suggestion that Delacroix and Mérimée could be "legitimately" compared: "C'était la même froideur apparente, légèrement affectée, le même manteau de glace recouvrant une pudique sensibilité et une ardente passion pour le bien et pour le beau; c'était, sous la même hypocrisie d'égoïsme, le même dévouement aux amis secrets et aux idées de prédilection" (II, 757-58).

But Pater's Mérimée is in one respect conceived as the reverse image of Baudelaire's Delacroix, who had "un génie essentiellement personnel" (II, 744). Whereas Delacroix's special contribution to universal beauty is "l'invisible," "l'impalpable, c'est le rêve, c'est les nerfs, c'est l'âme" (II, 744), Mérimée, "gifted . . . with pure *mind*, with the quality which secures flawless literary structure, had, on the other hand, nothing of what we call *soul* in literature." This Delacroix and this Mérimée represent what Pater would call a case of "Personality *versus* impersonality in art."

I am not arguing that Pater's prose is burdened by unconscious memories of his reading of Baudelaire, nor that he was wrestling blindly with the precursor, but that he was perfectly well aware of what he was doing. His cool naming permits his uninformed reader to infer a conventional attitude on his part toward a poet who had become the focus for much moral, aesthetic, and national passion. To that reader, Baudelaire himself would appear to be merely exemplary in "Mérimée," and the very title of his book—"the flowers of evil" (significantly uncapitalized and translated into English)—merely shorthand for a debate about morals and art in *Gaston*, both simply "slides" in Pater's detached examination of literary phenomena. But the informed reader is invited to detect a wholly different attitude toward the banned poet. Like Swinburne, Pater wrote for audiences whose interests were sharply opposed, and he designed his strategy of "complex association" to take into account both the tight circle of Oxford

C'était . . . He had the same apparent coldness, slightly affected, the same icy mantle covering modest sensitiveness and an ardent passion for what is good and beautiful; under the same simulated egoism was to be found the same devotion to personal friends and dearly-held ideas (C, 375).

un génie . . . an essentially personal genius.

l'invisible . . . the invisible, the impalpable, reverie, the nerves, the soul (C, 360).

and the inner circle of a revolutionary artistic community. This art of allusion and allegory is keenly self-conscious and intensely aware of its controlled address to "amis secrets" and "idées de prédilection." It is emblematized in *Gaston de Latour* in the relation of the poet's "workshop" to the priory at large: "a strange kind of private sanctuary, amid these rude conventual buildings." Pater's use of Baudelaire and his oddly uninformative acknowledgment embody his awareness of "the politics of cultural systems." Had Stern Chronology not forbidden, Pater might have paraphrased Stephen Daedalus as Michael Holquist does: "silence is not mandatory, exile may be overcome, as long as cunning reigns."[42]

Pater's concealments are related to his evident admiration for the self-denying "G[uys]" of *Le Peintre de la Vie Moderne*, and for the "superb self-effacement" of Mérimée. In his lecture Pater is as much preoccupied by secrecy as by impersonality, and by masks as much as by self-effacement. He is fascinated by Mérimée's *The Lyre*, which is made up of "pretended Illyrian compositions," and the terms he uses show that his fascination is directly relevant to his own work. Mérimée's book was a counterfeit, but Pater does not call it that. He calls it a series of

prose translations, the reader was to understand, of more or less ancient popular ballads; *la Guzla*, he called the volume, *The Lyre*, as we might say; only that the instrument of the Illyrian minstrel had but one string. Artistic deception, a trick of which there is something in the historic romance as such, . . . was always welcome to Mérimée; it was part of the machinery of his rooted habit of intellectual reserve.

Pater's own historical romance, *Gaston de Latour*, which he had just failed to finish, gave him more than a detached interest in artistic deception—it was a means of defeating the censor.

Pater made his apparently neutral references to Baudelaire at a most unusual moment in his career, when, because of revisions and new editions, both his early and his late work was occupying his mind. In 1888 the third edition of *The Renaissance* restored, with revisions, the "Conclusion" (given in the first edition but dropped from the second) and included for the first time "The School of Giorgione" (perhaps originally intended for the first edition but separately printed in October, 1877, in *The Fortnightly*

Review).[43] The same year saw the serial appearance of *Gaston de Latour* in *Macmillan's Magazine* from June to October. In 1889 Pater included in the first edition of *Appreciations* revised versions of both his 1876 article on "Romanticism" (which contains the one *explicit* reference to Baudelaire that remains to be discussed) and his unsigned 1868 essay on "Poems by William Morris" (from which he had also quarried the "Conclusion" to *The Renaissance*). In 1890, he lectured on Mérimée.

That Baudelaire should have been in Pater's mind when he was concentrating on early work is not surprising, since in much of it Baudelaire is vigorously present. What is surprising is that what Pater gave with one hand, he seems to have taken away with the other. In the same years as he named Baudelaire once openly and once implicitly, he expunged one explicit and other implicit references to him. "Romanticism," 1876, gave Baudelaire as an example, with others, of the romantic movement in France, whose "play is hardly yet over." In 1889 the version of it that Pater printed in *Appreciations* as "Postscript" substituted Hugo's name for Baudelaire's. Pater's revisions to the other pieces are related to that excision. He was concerned, he said, in the case of the "Conclusion," to "bring it closer to my original meaning."[44] The widely noted fact, however, is that he revised that inflammatory work entirely in the direction of caution. The same is true of the revisions to the related "Poems of William Morris," perhaps his most provocative work. He left no trace in his revision, for instance, of his early, daring, and unsigned speculation that "when the simple belief in them has faded away, the most cherished sacred writings may . . . for the first time exercise their highest influence as the most delicate amorous poetry in the world." Some of his revisions are actually misleading: the early assertion that "religion shades into sensuous love, and sensuous love into religion" is transformed in its revision to "religion, monastic religion at any rate, has its sensuous side, a dangerously sensuous side."[45]

When the revisions affect the "meaning" of the "Conclusion," it is almost always by a similar *withdrawal* of meaning. In the fourth edition of *The Renaissance*, 1893, Pater removed the phrase "art for art's sake" with the obvious purpose of dissociating his "Conclusion" from a school now known by its name and identified to a wide audience with Gautier and Baudelaire and Swinburne. It was the identifying tag he obliterated: he left the sense—that art is valuable in and for itself—scattered up and down his series of essays. In the third edition he had already made another change which is of special interest in this context. The passage had at first read:

> While all melts under our feet, we may well catch at any exquisite passion, or any contribution to knowledge that seems, by a lifted horizon, to set the spirit free for a moment, or any stirring of the senses, strange dyes, strange flowers, and curious odours, or the work of the artist's hands or the face of one's friend.

In 1888 Pater altered the punctuation and substituted "strange colours" for "strange flowers." The alteration is feeble, since it produces a merely verbal doubling of the sense already present in "strange dyes," but it does remove the Baudelairean flowers from their most prominent location. It was the "Conclusion," of course, that threatened the moral health of a generation of young men; and it was in the "Conclusion" that Pater drew his moral, making his first, strong "hypothesis," as he called it in his last published work, "of some close connexion between what may be called the aesthetic qualities of the world about us and the formation of moral character."[46] Although Pater took the "strange flowers" out of his "Conclusion," he left them to flourish in the body of *The Renaissance*. There is the "strange flower" of mythology in "Pica Della Mirandola" (36), the "strangeness, something of the blossoming of the aloe" (62) in "Michelangelo," and the "strange blossoms and fruits hitherto unknown" of Leonardo's temperament (110).

Pater's suppression is another significant withdrawal: "strange flowers" is the same kind of identifying shorthand as "flowers of evil." But while he kept his approval veiled in *Gaston de Latour*, and buried, for the satisfaction of his own conscience as well as for the delighting of his sense of irony, an elaborate allegory of indebtedness, Pater had made his enthusiasm apparent in the "Conclusion." Like his subsequent suppression of "art for art's sake," suppression of this enthusiasm extinguishes the suggestion of alliance. But the suggestion certainly was there, and Pater put it there, not later than 23 June 1868, when alliance was what he wanted to suggest. Swinburne's *Blake* had appeared in January of that year, and so had "Ave atque Vale," the one attaching Baudelaire's name to an assertion that art is for art's sake, the other presenting the poet as cultivator of an elaborate imagery of strange flowers. Pater had Baudelaire in mind when he wrote his phrase and again when he deleted it.

That tag is not the only reason for believing that Pater had Baudelaire firmly in his possession by 1868. The Morris review, which was to become the "Conclusion," develops a typically Baudelairean antithesis: Morris's poetry moves, Pater writes, "from dreamlight to daylight." Pater sees Morris's poems as representing two different operations of the senses, treating the early poems as an opium dream, the later as the recovery of the senses from such unnatural dreaming. When he discusses *The Defence of Guinevere*, Pater gives his conceit historical dimensions: "That whole religion of the middle age was but a beautiful disease or disorder of the senses"; he writes, "and a religion which is a disorder of the senses must always be subject to illusions. Reverie, illusion, delirium; they are the three stages of a fatal descent both in the religion and the loves of the middle age." In one of Morris's poems, "the frost of Christmas night on the chapel stones acts as a strong narcotic"; in another, "delirium reaches its height." The essay, which refers openly to De Quincey, and connects "the impression of this delirium" with Hugo, alludes only very quietly to Baudelaire, to his *Paradis Artificiels*. Morris's poetry, which stands in relation to the medieval poetry it draws on as an abstraction from an abstraction, is, Pater says, "literally an artificial or 'earthly paradise.' " The conceit which the quiet allusion introduces, however, divides Morris's art into poems of "mere soul" and those of a "better daylight, but earthly, open only to the senses" and so carries the whole antithetical structure of the essay and presents the polar values of Pater's criticism.

To pursue Baudelaire hide-and-seek through these narrow passages and to detect him where Pater preferred to keep him hidden is a far from trivial exercise, both because it demonstrates the reign of cunning in Pater's work and because *The Renaissance*, where Baudelaire's name does not appear, is the major channel to England of his ideas on art. Here more than anywhere his critical propositions are domesticated and given a central place in the development of modernism in English poetry. *The Renaissance*, which lays down the orthodoxies of high modernism, is in its most important theoretical passages and in some of its most characteristic procedures a compound larceny. Pater transferred, from Baudelaire's account to his own, essential material for his presentation of the aesthetic critic, the constituent elements of aesthetic criticism itself, an idea of abstraction in art, a theory of the relationships of the arts to one another, a repertoire of metaphorical relations, and a conception of modernity. *The Renaissance* establishes a thick network of connections with *Curiosités Esthétiques* and *L'Art Romantique*. Baudelaire stands behind this book as powerfully as behind the "Modernity" chapter of *Gaston de Latour*, and in a deeper silence, since here Pater keeps his accounts very privately indeed.

The most important theoretical passages of *The Renaissance* occur in the "Preface," in which Pater outlines the principles and procedures of "aesthetic criticism"; in the "Conclusion," where he defends the claims of art as against those of philosophy and science; in the "Giorgione" essay, where he advances what he calls a "whole system of . . . art-casuistries"; in the early essay on Winckelmann, where he first draws his distinction between the eternal and the transitory elements in art; and in the essay on Leonardo, where, under the mask of antiquarian criticism, he describes the characteristics of an essentially modern art.

Pater opens and closes the "aesthetic criticism" section of the "Preface" with an assertion that since beauty is relative, the attempt to find a "universal formula" for it is useless and wrongheaded. The aesthetic critic must concentrate his attention on the object before him, but not precisely in the way Arnold proposed, since he must recognize that his original data are his sensations. He must first feel those intensely, and then attempt to account for them in terms of the qualities of the object. His judging function will be to distinguish the intense and individual moments from the "common" moments in an artist's work and to note the points at which the special or defining quality is present. This criticism is concerned with two identifications: that of the object, which will reflect the mind of the artist, and that of the critic himself.

The idea of relativity, on which Pater's critical position is based and which he takes to be the essentially "modern" spirit, was by no means new in the "Preface." He explores it in the earliest of his published essays. In the one on Coleridge he attributes its development as a philosophical idea to "the influence of the sciences of observation," whose method ("continual analysis of facts of rough and general observation into groups of facts more precise and minute") is relevant to the "moral world [which] is ever in contact with the physical." The relative spirit, he says, "has invaded moral philosophy from the ground of the inductive sciences," and its consequences in the moral world include "a new analysis of the relations of body and mind, good and evil, freedom and necessity. Hard and abstract moralities are yielding to a more exact estimate of the subtlety and complexity of our life."[47] Pater's long essay on Winckelmann draws a sharp contrast between the "unperplexed, emphatic outlines of Hellenic humanism" (204) and a complex modern art which must recognize the "intricacy, the universality of natural law, even in the moral order" (205). Those two essays, together with the one on Morris, present three versions of Pater's persistent conflict with the ideal: Coleridge, he says, spent a sad life in a "struggle against the application of the relative spirit to moral and religious questions"; Winckelmann appears in rapt contemplation of an "absolute form" no longer possible in art; Morris's poems divide, as though by "revolt," between dreamlight and daylight, "mere soul" and the senses.

What is new to Pater in some of his later essays and in the "Preface," then, is not an idea of relativity, even of beauty's relativity, but the systematic derivation from that idea of a program for criticism. He aims to put at the service of criticism what he calls the "faculty for truth," "a power of distinguishing and fixing delicate and fugitive detail,"[48] and he outlines a critical activity whose object, the very opposite of Coleridge's attempt to apprehend the absolute and get it acknowledged, will be to apprehend, acknowledge, and fix the transitory. Furthermore, Pater's "aesthetic criticism," as it is outlined in the "Preface," prepares for an effect of the "Conclusion" that was not present in the Morris essay. When, in the "Preface" and the "Conclusion," and from time to time in the essays they surround, Pater detaches himself as a critic from the object of his contemplation and speaks directly to his reader, he isolates a key figure in the literature of the transition and of the modern period. Stepping out of his historically distanced allegory of art to speak in his own time, Pater makes the "aesthetic critic" himself the center of important activity, the point at which the forces unite in the instant of appreciation. To that dramatized figure Pater attaches the powerful defense of the arts with which *The Renaissance* concludes.

Both the critical program and the dramatized figure of the aesthetic critic come to Pater from his reading of Baudelaire. The borrowing is wholesale.

The idea of relativity is Baudelaire's point of departure, too, as he announces in the first chapter of his *Salon de 1846*, "A Quoi Bon la Critique?"[49] It is the function of criticism, as of art, he writes, to attend to "des destinées particulières" (II, 418): "Chaque siècle, chaque peuple [a] possédé l'expression de sa beauté et de sa morale" (II, 419). Every day, he says, he sees "un certain nombre de Kalmouks, d'Osages, d'Indiens, de Chinois et de Grecs antiques" pass under his window, and he observes that "Chaque individu est une harmonie" (II, 456). He returns to the point brilliantly in *L'Exposition Universelle* of 1855, which, again, he opens with a discussion of critical method. This time he sketches the antithetical possibilities for criticism: systematic (he also calls this pedantic, academic, pedagogical) and independent, dramatized in two commanding figures, "l'insensé doctrinaire du Beau" and "un homme du monde, intelligent." He transports these to a distant country, to test what he calls their "cosmopolitanism" (which he sees as a facet of imagination) by depriving them of familiar conventions. Under these circumstances, he says, "L'insensé doctrinaire du Beau déraisonnerait, sans doute; enfermé dans l'aveuglante forteresse de son système, il blasphémerait la vie et la nature" (II, 577). The other, however, the "intelligent," unimprisoned by systems, would be freely curious and open to new sensory riches. Baudelaire blesses him by describing in lush and racy language his response to color, form, movement, smell: "tout ce monde d'harmonies nouvelles entrera

des . . . individual destinies.
Chaque siècle . . . Since every century, every people has achieved the expression of its own beauty and system of moral values (C, 51).
un certain . . . a number of Kalmucks, red-skins, Indians, Chinese and ancient Greeks.
Chaque individu . . . Each individual is a harmony (C, 78).
L'insensé . . . The witless doctrinaire of beauty would babble nonsense, no doubt; imprisoned in the blinding fortress of his system, he would blaspheme against life and nature (C, 117).
tout . . . this whole world of new harmonies will slowly enter into him, penetrate him patiently like the steam of a scented bath house; all these unknown springs of life will be added to his own; some thousands of ideas and sensations will enrich his mortal's dictionary (C, 117).

lentement en lui, le pénétrera patiemment, comme la vapeur d'une étuve aromatisée; toute cete vitalité inconnue sera ajoutée à sa vitalité propre; quelques milliers d'idées et de sensations enrichiront son dictionnaire de mortel" (II, 577). The contrast leads him to a marvellously tart statement of his critical position:

> J'ai essayé plus d'une fois, comme tous mes amis, de m'enfermer dans un système pour y prêcher à mon aise. Mais un système est une espèce de damnation qui nous pousse à une abjuration perpétuelle; il en faut toujours inventer un autre, et cette fatigue est un cruel châtiment. Et toujours mon système était beau, vaste, spacieux, commode, propre et lisse surtout; du moins il me paraissait tel. Et toujours un produit spontané, inattendu, de la vitalité universelle venait donner un démenti à ma science enfantine et vieillotte, fille déplorable de l'utopie. J'avais beau déplacer ou étendre le criterium, il était toujours en retard sur l'homme universel, et courait sans cesse après le beau multiforme et versicolore, qui se meut dans les spirales infinies de la vie. (II, 577-78)

Because his systems condemned him ceaselessly to the humiliation of new conversions, he says, he gave them up altogether: "Pour échapper à l'horreur de ces apostasies philosophiques, je me suis orgueilleusement résigné à la modestie: je me suis contenté de sentir; je suis revenu chercher un asile dans l'impeccable naïveté" (II, 578).

That "impeccable naïveté," or aesthetic protestantism, gives Baudelaire's criticism its sense of excitement. In fact, as he said in a letter, his critical works are "reliés entre eux par une pensée

J'ai essayé . . . Like all my friends I have tried more than once to lock myself inside a system, so as to be able to pontificate as I liked. But a system is a kind of damnation that condemns us to perpetual backsliding; we are always having to invent another, and this form of fatigue is a cruel punishment. And every time, my system was beautiful, big, spacious, convenient, tidy and polished above all; at least so it seemed to me. And every time, some spontaneous unexpected product of universal vitality would come and give the lie to my puerile and old-fashioned wisdom, much-to-be-deplored daughter of Utopia. In vain did I shift or extend the criterion, it could not keep up with universal man and it was for ever chasing multiform and multicoloured beauty, which dwells in the infinite spirals of life (C, 117-18).

Pour échapper . . . To escape from the horror of these philosophic apostasies, I arrogantly resigned myself to modesty; I became content to feel; I came back and sought sanctuary in impeccable naïveté (C, 118).

reliés . . . unified by unique and systematic thought.

unique et systématique," but their system is derived from a collection of "naive" starts. His critical method, as Margaret Gilman observes, is always the same: his point of departure is description of the experience itself, which, subsequently, he translates, analyzes, and generalizes from.[50] His insistence that he is not an expert always amounts to an assertion that he is not, like the *professeurs-jurés* he scorns in *L'Exposition Universelle*, packed with preconceptions. Here, he proclaims himself "ignorant"; in the *Salon de 1859*, he says that he has simply responded to an invitation to record his "rapide promenade philosophique à travers les peintures" (II, 608); in *Les Paradis Artificiels*, he begins with comic aggression, ironically contrasting the textbook definition of wine with some of the experiences it can produce (I, 377). Even the essay on laughter begins with a refusal—"Je ne veux pas écrire un traité de la caricature; je veux simplement faire part au lecteur de quelques réflexions qui me sont venues souvent au sujet de ce genre singulier" (II, 525). In the Wagner pamphlet, Baudelaire isolates the figure who is at the center of *L'Art Romantique*:

> . . . qu'il me soit permis, dans cette appréciation, de parler souvent en mon nom personnel. Ce *Je*, accusé justement d'impertinence dans beaucoup de cas, implique cependant une grande modestie; il enferme l'écrivain dans les limites les plus strictes de la sincérité. (II, 779)

Those refusals are fine strategy: they require the reader to believe nothing at the outset except that he is addressed (though gradually they draw him into the text by identification), and they require the critic to go to the aesthetic confrontation unarmed with systems.

The nakedness of the aesthetic encounter is crucial in Baudelaire, both to the artist confronting the ceaseless metamorphoses of nature and to the critic facing the endless variety of "le beau universel." Both—since Baudelaire endows his critic with the

rapide . . . brisk philosophic walk round the exhibition (C, 285).
Je ne veux . . . I do not propose to write a treatise on caricature; all I want to do is to impart to the reader a few reflections that have often occurred to me on this strange genre (C, 140).
qu'il me . . . and may I, in the course of the following appreciation, be allowed to speak often in my own name. That 'I,' justly taxed with impertinence in many cases, implies, however, a high degree of modesty; it imprisons the writer within the strictest limits of sincerity (C, 325).

qualities of the artist—join to their intellectual independence two
other essential qualities, strong temperament and abnormally
acute sensory perception. Baudelaire's critic, like his artist, aims
by freshness of perception, to recreate "nos plus matinales
impressions." The best, like Guys, will have a power of "l'enfance
retrouvée à volonté" (II, 690)—that is, a disciplined power of
sensory perception. Guys's work, it will be remembered, is "le
résultat d'une perception enfantine, c'est-à-dire, d'une perception
aiguë" (II, 694).

Since "Le beau est toujours bizarre"—and the bizarre no merely
accidental quality of beauty, but "son immatriculation, sa ca-
ractéristique" (II, 578)—an openness to new manifestations of
"le beau universel" is indispensable to this critic. In art the con-
verse of strange, new beauty is inconceivable: "un beau banal!"
But in criticism "les règles utopiques conçues dans un petit tem-
ple scientifique quelconque de la planète" (II, 579) threaten the
life of art itself. Baudelaire's culinary comparison is serious:

Cette dose de bizarrerie qui constitue et définit l'indivi-
dualité, sans laquelle il n'y a pas de beau, joue dans l'art
(que l'exactitude de cette comparaison en fasse pardonner
la trivialité) le rôle du goût ou de l'assaisonnement dans les
mets, les mets ne différant les uns des autres, abstraction
faite de leur utilité ou de la quantité de substance nutritive
qu'ils contiennent, que par l'idée qu'ils révèlent à la langue.
(II, 579)

After "le beau," the most frequently repeated word in L'Exposition
Universelle is "la variété." That is the first quality of the world

nos plus . . . our youngest, our morning impressions (C, 398).
l'enfance . . . childhood recaptured at will (C, 398).
le résultat . . . the product of a childlike perceptiveness, in other words a per-
ceptiveness that is acute . . . (C, 402).
Le beau . . . Beauty always has an element of strangeness (C, 119).
son immatriculation . . . It is its hallmark, its special characteristic (C, 119).
les règles . . . utopian rules, excogitated in some little temple or other of learning
somewhere on the planet (C, 119).
Cette dose . . . This element of strangeness which constitutes and defines in-
dividuality, without which there is no beauty, plays in art (and may the precision
of this comparison excuse its triviality) the role of taste or flavouring in cookery;
if the individual usefulness or the degree of nutritious value they contain be
excepted, viands differ from each other only by the idea they reveal to the
tongue (C, 119).

faced by this critic. "Je m'appliquerai donc, dans la glorieuse analyse de cette belle Exposition, si variée dans ses éléments, si inquiétante par sa variété, si déroutante pour la pédagogie, à me dégager de toute espèce de pédanterie." Others, he says, will speak of technical or academic matters: "O vanité! je préfère parler au nom du sentiment, de la morale et du plaisir" (II, 579). Exposed individually in his own pronoun, this critic will aim to discover the essential individuality of the artist whose work he examines: "la critique doit chercher plutôt à pénétrer intimement le tempérament de chaque artiste et les mobiles qui le font agir qu'à analyser, à raconter chaque oeuvre minutieusement" (II, 583). He will seek the defining quality of each artist, "la clef du caractère de M.G." (II, 690), the "faculté principale" of Gautier (II, 117), the "spécialité" of Delacroix (II, 743). Discovery of that identifying quality is the counterpart of his assertion of his own critical identity, the Je. It, too, is presented in antithesis to systematic criticism: "Je crois, monsieur," Baudelaire writes in the long essay on Delacroix, "que l'important ici est simplement de chercher la qualité caractéristique du génie de Delacroix et d'essayer de la définir" (II, 743). "Simplement" is part of the strategy. It remains, he writes in the essay on Wagner (taking up again the play on "taste"), "à chercher et à vérifier par quelle qualité propre, personelle, [un artiste] se distingue des autres. Un artiste, un homme vraiment digne de ce grand nom, doit posséder quelque chose d'essentiellement *sui generis*, par la grâce de quoi il est *lui* et non un autre. A ce point de vue, les artistes peuvent être comparés à des saveurs variées . . ." (II, 806).

Je m'appliquerai . . . I shall therefore strive, in this glorious chance I have of analysing this superb exhibition, so full of variety in its elements, so disturbing by its variety, so baffling for pedagogues, to avoid all kinds of pedantry (C, 119).

O vanité . . . O Vanity! I prefer to speak in the name of feeling, of morality and pleasure (C, 119-120).

la critique . . . criticism's task must be to try and explore to its innermost depths each artist's temperament and the motives that inspire him, rather than to analyse or describe every painting minutely (C, 124).

la clef . . . the key to the character of M. G. (C, 397).

Je crois . . . To my mind, sir, the important thing here is simply to look for the characteristic quality of Delacroix's genius and to try and define it (C, 359).

à chercher . . . we then need to seek and assess the peculiar personal qualities that distinguish him from others. An artist, a man really worthy of that great name, must surely have in him something essentially *sui generis*, by the grace of which he is himself and not someone else. From this point of view, artists may be compared to a miscellany of flavours (C, 354).

Baudelaire hides the breadth of his critical purpose in an iron-
ically modest language—"J'espère que quelques personnes, sa-
vantes sans pédantisme, trouveront mon *ignorance* de bon goût"
(II, 579)—but that apparently carefree sheltering in impeccable
naïveté expands the responsibilities of the critic far beyond the
narrowly technical or academic. This criticism, speaking in the
name of morality, feeling, and pleasure, answers questions of
value. It also isolates the critic: the exemplary *homme du monde*
is likely to be one of "ces voyageurs solitaires qui ont vécu pen-
dant des années au fond des bois, au milieu des vertigineuses
prairies, sans autre compagnon que leur fusil, contemplant, dis-
séquant, écrivant" (II, 576). The landscape is in pointed contrast
to the little temple of scientific criticism; this critic, like the poet-
hero of *Le Voyage*, or like the painter of modern life, is a questing
solitary. Guys sits up alone while the city sleeps, in his dark
solitude calling back to light the flashing particulars of experi-
ence: "Et les choses renaissent sur le papier" (II, 693).

His powers of perception carry Baudelaire's critic to the in-
tersection point: he confronts variety in its particularity, unaided
by systems (which would in any case be outstripped by the speed
of the world), but he is obliged to transform all of that urgent
change and dazzling variety into something both static and ac-
cessible to others. He is by definition committed to two worlds:
"un rêveur dont l'espirit est tourné à la généralisation, aussi bien
qu'aux détails" (II, 575). Because he is "locked up within the
blinding fortress of his system" the *professeur-juré* cannot make
connections and transitions between the two; because he is a
man of the world, open to it, Baudelaire's exemplary critical
traveller can, by adding new experiences to his "dictionnaire de
mortel," learn to play on "l'immense clavier des *correspondances*"
(II, 577). The imagery is important here, too: language and
music liberate, extend into space (the dictionary and the key-
board), and make connections. In this criticism, sensation and

J'espère . . . I hope that some people, learned without pedantry, will find my
'ignorance' in good taste (C, 120).

ces voyageurs . . . lone travellers who have lived for years in forest depths or
in vast prairie solitudes, their gun as sole companion, contemplating, analysing,
writing (C, 116).

Et les choses . . . And things seen are born again on the paper (C, 402).

un rêveur . . . a dreamer given to generalizations as well as to the study of detail
(C, 115).

l'immense . . . the vast keyboard of nature's correspondences (C, 117).

significance cannot be prised apart; flavors come attached to ideas. Faced with "un échantillon de la beauté universelle," Baudelaire's critic must connect the two elements of beauty: so that the new object can be understood, he must "opère en lui-même une transformation qui tient du mystère," and he must, "par un phénomène de la volonté agissant sur l'imagination, . . . apprenne de lui-même à participer au milieu qui a donné nais-sance à cette floraison insolite" (II, 576). The function of this critic is always the same: in the essay on Wagner, having pre-sented himself as the "critic ingénu" who merely records "ses propres impressions," Baudelaire writes: "Je résolus de m'in-former du pourquoi, et de transformer ma volupté en connais-sance" (II, 786). This criticism is strictly analogous to art itself: to his power of childish perception, Guys adds "l'esprit analy-tique qui lui permet d'ordonner la somme de matériaux invo-lontairement amassée" (II, 690); from the rush of particular experience he extracts "la fantasmagorie" (II, 694). Both the critic and the artist of Baudelaire's design are fully engaged in the two, balancing elements of beauty. This is an argument against solipsism.

Baudelaire's critical scheme constitutes a powerful defense of art—and, like Swinburne, he perceives the threat to art's life to be criticism itself. The utopian prescriptions of a scientific temple are as dangerous as the *hérésie de l'enseignement*—and they issue from the same parentage. Baudelaire devotes the *Exposition Uni-verselle*, like the *Notes Nouvelles Sur Edgar Poe*, to an attack on the philosophy of progress and its material conception of history. Against criticism derived from such false premises, as he sees them, he pits his resolutely amateur *Je*. This *Je*, speaking in the name of feeling, pleasure, and morality, stands against a reduc-tive scientism, asserting the humane value of art. His most fa-mous statement of his position occurs in the opening section of

un échantillon . . . a sample of universal beauty (C, 116).
opère . . . must bring about within himself a transformation, which is something of a mystery, and, by a phenomenon of will-power acting on his imagination . . . learn by his own effort to share in the life of the society that has given birth to this unexpected bloom (C, 116).
Je résolus . . . I determined to discover the why and the wherefore, and thus to exchange my sensuous pleasure for knowledge (C, 333).
l'esprit analytique . . . the analytical mind that enables it to bring order into the sum of experience (C, 398).

the *Salon* of 1846. It is the passage with which Swinburne heads *William Blake*.

> Je crois sincèrement que la meilleure critique est celle qui est amusante et poétique; non pas celle-ci, froide et algébrique, qui, sous prétexte de tout expliquer, n'a ni haine ni amour, et se dépouille volontairement de toute espèce de tempérament; mais,—un beau tableau étant la nature réfléchie par un artiste,—celle qui sera ce tableau réfléchi par un esprit intelligent et sensible. Ainsi le meilleur compte rendu d'un tableau pourra être un sonnet ou une élégie. (II, 418)

Pater adopts every point, and some of the language, of this critical argument. The "Preface" makes his critical principles explicit, standing, like the opening chapter of the *Salon de 1846*, as an answer to the question, "A Quoi Bon la Critique?" Pater begins by dismissing abstract aesthetics in favor of personal speech. His "aesthetic critic," remembering both that "beauty exists in many forms" and that the definition of beauty "becomes unmeaning and useless in proportion to its abstractness," will depend not on a system but on a susceptibility. He must possess, not the "correct abstract definition of beauty for the intellect, but a certain kind of temperament, the power of being deeply moved by the presence of beautiful objects." He will also regard all objects, and not merely works of art, as capable of producing "pleasurable sensations, each of a more or less unique kind," and he will aim, as both the "Preface" and the "Conclusion" make clear, to sharpen his capacity to experience them strongly. He will ask, as the important questions about such objects, "What effect does it really produce on me? Does it give me pleasure? . . . How is my nature modified by its presence, and under its influence?" Freed from abstractions, this critic will place himself in direct relationship to the object of contemplation: "one must realise such primary data for oneself, or not at all." And when

Je crois . . . I sincerely believe that the best criticism is the criticism that is entertaining and poetic; not a cold analytical type of criticism, which, claiming to explain everything, is devoid of hatred and love, and deliberately rids itself of any trace of feeling, but, since a fine painting is nature reflected by an artist, the best critical study, I repeat, will be the one that is that painting reflected by an intelligent and sensitive mind. Thus the best accounts of a picture may well be a sonnet or an elegy (C, 50).

he has fully experienced, or "realised," his impressions, he will
also aim to transform his experience into knowledge: "This in-
fluence he feels and wishes to explain, analysing it, and reducing
it to its elements." This reduction to elements makes the sense
of actual taste suggest the kind of individuality that is present
in works of art: "To him, the picture, the landscape, the engaging
personality in life or in a book, *La Gioconda*, the hills of Carrera,
Pico of Mirandula, are valuable for their virtues, as we say in
speaking of a herb, a wine, a gem; for the property each has of
affecting one with a special, unique, impression of pleasure."
The principle of difference, the uniqueness of individual ex-
periences, is the basis of this critic's effort, and the more he
"realises" of these unique and particular impressions, the wider
will become his repertoire: "Education grows in proportion as
one's susceptibility to these impressions increases in depth and
variety." What he has to do, his function, is as familiar as the
rest: "to distinguish, analyse, and separate from its adjuncts, the
virtue by which a picture, a landscape, a fair personality in life
or in a book, produces this special impression of beauty or pleas-
ure, to indicate what the source of the impression is, and under
what conditions it is experienced."

Pater conceived his "Conclusion" as a defense of the claims of
art in relation to those of philosophy and science. The larger
part of it is a summary of what modern philosophy can tell us
about life. The last section, however, answers another question,
which also appears in the transition paragraph of the Morris
essay. There Pater attributes it to a critical reader, who asks,
since

> The modern world is in possession of truths; what but a
> passing smile can it have for a kind of poetry which, assum-
> ing artistic beauty of form to be an end in itself, passes by
> those truths and the living interests which are connected
> with them, to spend a thousand cares in telling once more
> these pagan fables as if it had but to choose between a more
> and a less beautiful shadow?[51]

The answer Pater gives is that in the cultivation, discrimination,
and analysis of impressions, and in the explanatory accounting
for them in terms of the "influence" that has produced them,
we can experience a liberation from the prison of the self. "Fail-
ure," he wrote unhesitatingly in the Morris article, "is to form

habits; for habit is relative to a stereotyped world; meantime it is only the roughness of the eye that makes any two things, persons, situations—seem alike."⁵² What the "exquisite passion" or the "contribution to knowledge" can do, even if only for a moment, is "by a lifted horizon to set the spirit free." The "solitary prisoner" of this "Conclusion" is liberated by a passionate attention to the world, with its "strange dyes, strange flowers and curious odours." This, too, is an argument against solipsism.

The terms of Pater's defense of art and aesthetic criticism are strikingly Baudelairean: the fortress and the freedom, as well as the relation to the whole argument of the idea of the essential novelty of beauty, which can call the mind out of its prison. Pater's final contrast, in the antepenultimate and penultimate paragraphs of the "Conclusion," between the life of "sharp and eager observation" and "facile orthodoxy," brings together the elements of Baudelaire's central, dramatic contrast of the *homme du monde* and the *l'insensé doctrinaire du Beau*, a contrast to which, as we shall see later, he returns in his last work, *On Plato and Platonism*. His catalogue of possible objects of intense attention comes close to those collected by Baudelaire's man of the world in his new unknown country and added to his earthly dictionary: curiously shaped buildings, disquieting vegetation, unexpected human attitudes, unfamiliar perfumes, and "ces fleurs mystérieuses dont la couleur profonde entre dans l'oeil despotiquement, pendant que leur forme taquine le regard" (II, 577). In Pater, as in Baudelaire, those "strange flowers" imply a whole aesthetic.

When Pater gathered his essays together for publication as a book, his "Conclusion" was ready to hand, and went from the Morris essay to *The Renaissance* with very little change. The "Preface," however, remained to be written: Pater was still at work on it, as his letters show, in November of 1872, three months before *The Renaissance* was finally published.⁵³ It added at the last stage of his book's construction both his explicit statement of critical principles, therefore, and his final, most prominent dramatization of his "aesthetic critic." But neither of these was new to him when he wrote his "Preface": they long predate 1872. His ideas on aesthetic criticism are scattered up and down the "series" of essays in *The Renaissance*, as an element of its structure. The idea of the formula, or "special characteristic" of each artist, for instance, appears in the essays on Botticelli, Leonardo, and du

Bellay; beauty's relativity in those on Pico, Giorgione, and Winck-
elmann, as well as in the "Conclusion"; the duty of the aesthetic
critic in those on Botticelli, Leonardo, and Giorgione. The "Pref-
ace" and the "Conclusion," then, are by no means detached in
their preoccupations, or in their reliance on Baudelaire, from
the body of the book. Pater was as actively interested in Baude-
laire's criticism in the years during which he composed the var-
ious *Renaissance* essays as he was in 1868 and 1872, when he
wrote its terminal pieces. The chronology of its essays is therefore
irrelevant to my argument: all of them, including, as I shall
attempt to show, the earliest, are rooted in Pater's consciousness
of his attachment to what Swinburne had defined as an alter-
native tradition supported by the French poet. Some of them
are attached to Baudelaire's criticism by clear and specific bor-
rowings, some by common principle and shared critical sensi-
bility. I shall examine three of the essays: "The School of Gior-
gione," in which Pater makes his most consequential theoretical
remarks; "Winckelmann," in which he adds to an Hegelian view
of the history of art his view of the vitality of the modern; and
"Leonardo," in which he abandons the purposes of history and
embodies in that Renaissance figure an idea of modernity that
is clearly derived from his own time.

"The School of Giorgione," probably the last of *The Renaissance*
essays to be written[54]—and the most influential, although absent
from the first edition—includes in its famous point about the
Anders-streben a crucial and, since d'Hangest, much-noted bor-
rowing from Baudelaire.[55] The plagiarism is fascinating, both
because it supplies a vital step in Pater's argument (without it,
all art could *not* aspire to the condition of music) and because,
like the quotation in *Gaston de Latour*, it is both carefully masked
and only part of a larger, unnoted reliance on its source. The
unacknowledged quotation, however, is most usefully examined
in its place in Pater's argument.

The importance of "The School of Giorgione" rests, not on
its practical criticism, but on its theoretical opening remarks,
which carried a great deal of weight among Pater's followers.
Arthur Symons, for instance, said that here "Pater came perhaps
nearer to a complete or final disentangling of the meanings and
functions of the arts than any writer on aesthetics has yet done,"
and Oscar Wilde took the major points of the "Giorgione" essay
for his favorite critical themes.[56] (The essay has hardly dated

yet, as the "Overture" to Claude Lévi-Strauss's *The Raw and the Cooked* indicates.)[57] Its opening pages, which are connected to the practical examination of the school of Giorgione only by an almost mechanical repetition of their main point, address two issues: the separateness of the arts (and the way in which the mode of each derives from the sensory material appropriate to it) and the ways in which they cross over to produce what he calls a "poetical" effect. Later aesthetic theorists would see in the first point the basis for a defense of abstract art and in the second the early description of what was later more universally titled the "aesthetic emotion."

"The School of Giorgione"[58] is an essential text of literary and aesthetic modernism, but it reflects the conditions of its creation more clearly than some of Pater's critical writing, and, though its issue links it to the modernists, its sources connect it profoundly to Pater's own contemporaries. Like the "Conclusion," it declares its place in the literature of art for art's sake. Its purpose is to defend "the sensuous element in art, and with it almost everything in art that is essentially artistic," to note "the element of song in the singing," and, therefore, to displace subject matter from a position of prominence in the judgment of works of art. It disavows any interest in the exact relation of beauty to preconceived truth, and it argues both that "the mere matter of a poem . . . should be nothing without the form . . . that this form . . . should become an end in itself" and that it is only by a purified attention to his material that an artist can convey any other effect. Those purposes and the terms in which he expresses them link Pater's "Giorgione" essay both with his own "Preface" and "Conclusion" as part of his assertion of the absolute value of art, and with Swinburne's defenses of form as "the one adorable thing in the world."[59] It is telling that Pater should turn for illustration of some theoretical points not only to the apparent subjects of his essay, but to two other artists who had attracted Swinburne's critical attention: to Legros, who figures in "Notes on Some Pictures of 1868," and to Blake in his lyrics. Like Swinburne's *Blake*, "The School of Giorgione" confirms the centrality of art for art's sake in the development of literary modernism.

But the claim that art is an end in itself undergoes some extremely fruitful rephrasing and development in Pater's essay. To the familiar assertion that the singer must attend to the song and the critic to the singing, Pater adds three sharpened focuses. He argues that each art has "its own special mode of reaching the imagination"; that "in its primary aspect" each art is abstract, that is, merely sensory; that the arts are related to one another by their ability to produce a "poetical" effect. These points carry the invasion of Baudelaire's critical ideas deep into English territory.

Pater emphasizes the apparent paradox of his position, prefacing his claim that the arts *can* reinforce one another with a repeated assertion that their modes are sharply distinct. The painter, he says, must attend to the "essential pictorial qualities" of his work, the drawing and the coloring. If these delight the appropriate sense, then "by this delight only [can they] be the medium of whatever poetry or science may lie beyond it in the intention of the composer." The same argument, slightly adjusted, applies to poetry, so that "lyrical poetry, just because in it you are least able to detach the matter from the form," is "at least artistically, the highest and most complete form of poetry." In both poetry and painting, the perfection of form is closely connected with "a certain suppression or vagueness of mere subject," so that a riverside in France is superior for artistic purposes to one in Switzerland, the "mere topography" counting for less in it. The Venetian school, Pater claims, masters the difficult landscape of its place by retaining only "certain abstracted elements" of it, "presenting us with the spirit or essence only of a certain sort of landscape, a country of the pure reason or half-imaginative memory." By such reasoning, music is the "true type or measure of consummate art" because it has *no* subject matter, as Pater seems to have conceived of it. By such reasoning, furthermore, though Pater does not say this, music ought most perfectly to embody the aesthetic paradox: its apparent sensuous purity ought to make it the most "poetical" of the arts.

The central paradox, by which an art intensely concentrated on the sensory matter appropriate to it will be capable of producing general or "poetic" effects, is supplied in Pater's argument by the *Anders-streben*:

> . . . it is noticeable that, in its special mode of handling its
> given material, each art may be observed to pass into the
> condition of some other art, by what German critics term

an *Anders-streben*, a partial alienation from is own limitations, by which the arts are able, not indeed to supply the place of each other, but reciprocally to lend each other new forces.

When he wrote that, d'Hangest says, Pater had *L'Art Romantique* in front of him, since the defining sentence is Baudelaire's: "C'est, du reste, un des diagnostics de l'état spirituel de notre siècle que les arts aspirent, sinon à se suppléer l'un l'autre, du moins à se prêter réciproquement des forces nouvelles."[60] The sentence is part of Baudelaire's description of the special quality of Delacroix: he has produced the invisible, the impalpable, dreams, nerves, *soul* with "la perfection d'un peintre consommé, avec la rigueur d'un littérateur subtil, avec l'éloquence d'un musicien passionné," and because of that he is "le plus *suggestif* de tous les peintres, celui dont les oeuvres . . . font le plus penser, et rappellent à la mémoire le plus de sentiments et de pensées poétiques" (II, 744-45). Pater's presentation of the point bears traces of imperfect translation: it would be more usual to render *forces* as "strengths." And it is strikingly misleading: to attribute to "German critics" an idea that is copied directly from a French one, and to give a German title to the phenomenon he defines, is exceptionally evasive. This is a treasure Pater wanted to bury deeply. There are, apparently, no such "German critics": "Neither Goethe nor Hegel uses the term, and I have not been able to find it in the vocabulary of any other German writers," says Donald Hill.[61] The *Anders-streben*, or other-striving, of Pater's essay is an astonishingly successful concealment, a version in German of Baudelaire's verb, "*aspirer*." Pater's borrowing, furthermore, has left its marks not only in the lines d'Hangest recognized, but also in Pater's most famous dictum ("All art constantly *aspires* towards the condition of music") and in the major propositions of his essay.

Baudelaire's idea of the reciprocal relations among the arts is part of his system of *correspondances*, as he makes clear in his essay on Wagner. There, as d'Hangest notes, he quotes Wagner

C'est . . . It is one element in the diagnosis of the spiritual climate of our age, be it added, that the arts strive, if not to substitute for one another, at least to lend each other new power and strength, by the help of their own (C, 361).

la perfection . . . the perfection of a consummate painter, with the rigour of a subtle writer, the eloquence of a passionate musician . . . the most suggestive of all painters, the one whose works . . . give the most food for thought, and recall to the mind the greatest sum of poetic feelings and thought (C, 361).

on the limitations of the arts and on the idea that "l'oeuvre la plus complète du poète devrait être celle qui, dans son dernier achèvement, serait une parfaite musique."[62] Pater may well have drawn on that work, too, in composition of "The School of Giorgione": he certainly knew it. In it Baudelaire quotes the reactions to Wagner's music of Liszt and Berlioz in order to demonstrate that "la véritable musique suggère des idées analogues dans des cerveaux différents." He goes on to quote from his own sonnet "Correspondances," and to claim that what really would be surprising would be "que le son *ne pût pas* suggérer la couleur, que les couleurs *ne pussent pas* donner l'idée d'une mélodie, et que le son et la couleur fussent impropres à traduire des idées" (II, 784). It is because of the crossover of sensory effects that the arts can reciprocally lend one another new powers; and that same system lies undescribed behind the misleadingly titled *Anders-streben*. Concentration on the material—on, say, line and color—is the key: only the most concentrated sound will suggest color. But it is by means of Baudelaire's *correspondances* that, in Pater's words, "some of the most delightful music seems to be always approaching to figure, to pictorial definition," that architecture aims at the condition of a picture, sculpture aspires toward color, "all the arts in common aspiring towards the principle of music." The *Anders-streben* might well have been titled (with more historical accuracy and with greater clarity) *correspondances*. It is the fruitful paradox of that system of *correspondances* that motivates Pater's advance into abstraction, too: the paradox that makes matter turn to "spirit" or the "sensuous matter" of an art to "poetry." Pater opens his argument (which is an extension of the aesthetic critic's program) by describing two common, antithetical, false critical opinions: that all art is merely the expression of "the same fixed quantity of imaginative thought" and its sensuous matter therefore of indifferent importance; and that in art "all is mere technical acquirement in delineation or touch." What Pater calls the "true pictorial charm" consists of neither of these extremes, each of which depends too

l'oeuvre . . . the most complete work of any poet ought to be the one that in its ultimate form was perfect music (C, 339).

la véritable . . . true music suggests similar ideas in different minds (C, 330).

que le son . . . that sound could not suggest colour, that colours could not give the idea of melody, and that both sound and colour together were unsuitable as media for ideas (C, 330).

singly on the "pure intelligence," but of a conception of color and drawing as the sensuous matter of painting, which make their appeal under the direction of the "peculiar pictorial temperament or constitution" of the artist. This synthetic pictorial quality "lies between" those two extremes, and it appeals to the synthesizing faculty that Pater, borrowing Arnold's term, calls the "imaginative reason." The essentially pictorial qualities make their appeal to the senses:

> This *drawing*, then—the arabesque traced in the air by Tintoret's flying figures, by Titian's forest branches; this colouring—the magic conditions of light and hue in the atmosphere of Titian's *Lace-girl*, or Rubens's *Descent from the Cross*—these essential pictorial qualities, must first of all delight the sense, delight it as directly and sensuously as a fragment of Venetian glass, and by this delight only be the medium of whatever poetry or science may lie beyond it in the intention of the composer. In its primary aspect, a great picture has no more definite message for us than an accidental play of sunlight and shadow for a moment, on one's wall or floor, is itself indeed a space of such falling light, caught as the colours are caught in an Eastern carpet, but refined upon, and dealt with more subtly and exquisitely than by nature itself.

That passage has led Sir Kenneth Clark, and others, to think that Pater arrived independently at an idea of abstraction in painting. But his debt is clear, in its details as in its outline. Baudelaire outlines the idea in the work from which Pater has already quoted: "La ligne et la couleur font penser et rêver toutes les deux; les plaisirs qui en dérivent sont d'une nature différente, mais parfaitement égale et absolument indépendante du sujet du tableau." This pleasure, which he calls "primitif," can be perceived in a painting placed at sufficient distance for the appeal of subject to be lost. "Et l'analyse du sujet, quand vous vous approchez, n'enlèvera rien et n'ajoutera rien à ce plaisir primitif." He reverses the example:

> *La ligne* . . . Both line and colour arouse thought and induce reverie; the pleasures that flow from these are different in kind, but perfectly equal and absolutely independent of the subject of the picture (C, 370).
> *Et l'analyse* . . . Nor will the act of analysing the subject when you come closer take anything away from this initial pleasure, or add anything to it (C, 370).

Une figure bien dessinée vous pénètre d'un plaisir tout à fait étranger au sujet. Voluptueuse ou terrible, cette figure ne doit son charme qu'à l'arabesque qu'elle découpe dans l'espace. Les membres d'un martyr qu'on écorche, le corps d'une nymphe pâmée, s'ils sont savamment dessinés, comportent un genre de plaisir dans les éléments duquel le sujet n'entre pour rien; si pour vous il en est autrement, je serai forcé de croire que vous êtes un bourreau ou un libertin. (II, 753)

Baudelaire's arabesque in space is also Pater's; his claim that line and color produce "ce plaisir primitif" becomes Pater's assertion that the pictorial qualities must first delight the sense; his contrast, for the sake of showing no essential difference, of the swooning nymph and the flayed martyr, is Pater's similarly mounted contrast between the *Lace-girl* and the *Descent from the Cross*, as well as the source of his remark about the colors in the carpet. This first appearance in England of the idea of abstraction is not after all independently achieved.[63]

In spite of its first title, *Studies in the History of the Renaissance*, Pater's book is everywhere preoccupied by the present in which it was written. Its "aesthetic critic" is a decidedly modern figure, presented emphatically as such: modern consciousness, Pater declares, springs from conditions discovered by modern science; it is sharply distinct from the consciousness of any past; aesthetic criticism is its expression. But *this* aesthetic critic supplies his view of the modern in his examination of various pasts: he shares the present moment with the reader, and together the two look back over a landscape of artistic achievement, reaching into the darkness in what became the typical modernist critical gesture, to retrieve the best and make it *new*. The past is of interest chiefly for its relation to the present, however, and the "great masters," Pater writes, are, most often,

typical standards, revealing instances of the laws by which certain aesthetic effects are produced. The old masters in-

Une figure . . . A well drawn figure inspires in you a pleasure that is quite foreign to the subject. Be it voluptuous or frightening, this figure owes its charm exclusively to the pattern it describes in space. The limbs of a martyr being flayed alive, or the body of a nymph in a swoon, provided they are skilfully drawn, offer a species of pleasure in which the nature of the subject counts for nothing; if it were otherwise for you, you would oblige me to write you down as a torturer or an amorist (C, 370).

deed are simpler; their characteristics are written larger, and are easier to read, than their analogues in all the mixed confused productions of the modern mind. But when once one has succeeded in defining for oneself those characteristics and the law of their combination, one has acquired a standard or measure which helps us to put in its right place many a vagrant genius, many an unclassified talent, many precious though imperfect products. (88)

And while Pater examines the old masters for their value as "analogues" of the present, he also organizes his essays to point to one end, which is always present. The penultimate essay, on Joachim Du Bellay, carries the Renaissance to its conclusion in France, with the Pleiad and Ronsard (and so to the starting-point of *Gaston de Latour*), and the last, "Winckelmann," brings Pater's meditation on the history of the development of the arts wholly up to date, moving from consideration of the Greeks, through the Middle Ages and the Renaissance, to Winckelmann and Goethe and "one at the end" of the chain of "circumstance" (206).

"Winckelmann" addresses two aesthetic matters, both implicit in what I have already quoted from the essay on Michelangelo's poetry: the relation to one another of the two "elements" of art and the nature of each. This essay, on the historical development of art, depends heavily on Hegel, whose views it appropriates on a large scale; but for what makes it contemporary, its address to current conditions, it depends on Baudelaire, whose approval of modern art fuels Pater's "sharp repudiation" of Hegel's judgment that " 'the form of art has ceased to be the supreme need of the spirit.' "[64] While it is Hegel who furnishes Pater's view of the historical development and of the relation of the arts to one another, it is Baudelaire who supplies his valuation of modernity and so permits the last essay in this "historical" series to end, on the note of the *Salons* of 1845 and 1846, with a call for recognition of the heroism of modern life.

Like the "Modernity" chapter of *Gaston de Latour*, "Winckelmann" contends with the question of aesthetic relativity and identifies the two constituent elements of beauty as "permanence" and "change." On that separation it constructs its argument. The "element of permanence" in art, Pater says, is "a standard of taste" derived from a specific period in Greek history, represented most perfectly in Greek sculpture, and "maintained in a purely intellectual tradition" (170). The best works of succeeding generations, he says, take their place in that tradition, forming "a series of elevated points, taking each from each the reflexion of a strange light."[65] He illustrates his point in his famous and fascinating reference to Raphael's Vatican frescoes: one commemorates "the tradition of the Catholic religion," showing "the great personages of Christian history, with the Sacrament in the midst"; another shows what he calls "a very different company," that of "the classical tradition, the orthodoxy of taste," the ancient and Renaissance poets grouped round Apollo, whose spirit (as in "Ave atque Vale") has descended on them (168). "Winckelmann's intellectual history authenticates the claims of this tradition in human culture." But while Pater's subject is entirely and ardently Hellenist, his essay is not. To the art that celebrates the "element of permanence" he opposes another, the modern tradition, in which the "element of change" predominates. In the sculpture that best embodies the classical ideal, what is "all-important" is "not the special situation, but the type, the general character of the subject to be delineated" (188). In modern, romantic art, by contrast, of which painting and poetry are most representative, the all-important is "the choice and development of some special situation, which lifts or glorifies a character in itself not poetical." Browning's "poetry of situations" supplies Pater with his example: what he does is "to employ the most cunning detail, to complicate and refine upon thought and passion a thousand-fold" (187), aiming not at simplicity, generality, and breadth, but at complexity, passion, and particularity. While Hellenic art "purges away" "all that is accidental, all that distracts from the simple effect upon us of the supreme types of humanity, all traces in them of the commonness of the world" (189), the art of the moderns aims to produce "a single moment of passion thrown into relief" (187) by the devices of complexity.

Though Pater finds Winckelmann "supreme" in insight into the first kind of art, he finds him limited in his response to the other:

> Living in a world of exquisite but abstract and colourless form, he could hardly have conceived of the subtle and penetrative, but somewhat grotesque art of the modern world. What would he have thought of Gilliatt, or of the

bleeding mouth of Fantine in that first part of "Les Misé-
rables," penetrated as it is with a sense of beauty as lively
and transparent as that of a Greek? (197)

Pater requires an aesthetic capable of dealing "confidently and
serenely with life, conflict, evil" (197); here, in the essay of 1866,
as in the unfinished romance of 1888, he turns away from an
abstract, colorless art to one which combines both contending
"elements" of beauty. Goethe supplies the exemplary union "of
the Romantic spirit, its adventure, its variety, its deep subjectivity,
with Hellenism, its transparency, its rationality, its desire of
beauty—that marriage of Faust and Helena, of which the art of
the nineteenth century is the child" (201). In Browning's work,
Pater writes, a little world of passion is balanced on a needle's
point; his gift is shown by the way in which he accepts a character
in itself of no special interest and "throws it into some situation,
apprehends it in some delicate pause of life, in which for a
moment it becomes ideal" (187). The two elements of Pater's
modern art, his preference of it to the classical, his synthesis of
the particular and the ideal, and the question by which he eval-
uates Winckelmann for the modern world all echo Baudelaire:
"que ferait, que dirait, un Winckelmann moderne," Baudelaire
asks in the *Exposition Universelle*, "en face d'un produit chinois,
produit étrange, bizarre, contourné dans sa forme, intense par
sa couleur, et quelquefois délicat jusqu'à l'évanouissement?" (II,
576). His *Salon* of 1846 concludes in address to the very question
of Pater's famous "Hellenist" piece. "Il est vrai que la grande
tradition s'est perdue," he writes, "et que la nouvelle n'est pas
faite" (II, 493). But the great tradition, he says, is only the "idéa-
lisation ordinaire et accoutumée de la vie ancienne" (II, 493),
the eternalization of what was once particular, and since every
beauty includes the two elements, we also have our beauty: "Le

que ferait . . . what, I say, would a modern Winckelmann do, what would he
say, at the sight of a Chinese product, a strange product, weird, contorted in
shape, intense in colour, and sometimes delicate to the point of fading away?
(C, 116).
Il est vrai . . . It is true that the great tradition is lost and that the new one is
as yet unformed (C, 104).
idéalisation . . . the ordinary and customary process of idealizing life in antiquity
(C, 104).
Le spectacle . . . Scenes of high life and of the thousands of uprooted lives that
haunt the underworld of a great city . . . are there to show us that we have only
to open our eyes to see and know the heroism of our day (C, 106).

spectacle de la vie élégante et des milliers d'existences flottantes qui circulent dans les souterrains d'une grande ville . . . nous prouvent que nous n'avons qu'à ouvrir les yeux pour connaître notre héroïsme" (II, 495). "Le merveilleux nous enveloppe et nous abreuve comme l'atmosphère; mais nous ne le voyons pas" (II, 496). Turning to Balzac as his example, Baudelaire concludes his comments on "the heroism of modern life": "Car les héros de l'*Iliade* ne vont qu'à votre cheville, ô Vautrin, ô Rastignac, ô Birotteau . . . et vous, ô Honoré de Balzac, vous le plus héroïque, le plus singulier, le plus romantique et le plus poétique parmi tous les personnages que vous avez tirés de votre sein!" (II, 496).

Pater's interpretation of Leonardo da Vinci takes its terms from the art against which he balances the classical tradition of orthodox taste. Like all his *Renaissance* subjects, Leonardo is made typical: he represents one side of "what is called 'the modern spirit,' with its realism, its appeal to experience" (102). The essay keeps the idea of modernity at the forefront: Leonardo is said to have anticipated modern scientific ideas, mechanics, German aesthetics; his Mona Lisa, culminating the historical dislocation, "might stand," Pater says, as "the symbol of the modern idea" (119). In 1876 (some seven years after first publishing his "Leonardo" essay in *The Fortnightly Review* and three after collecting it in *The Renaissance*), when he came to describe "Romanticism" in an article for *Macmillan's Magazine*, Pater made clear how strongly Leonardo represented for him the modern impulse. He transferred to his new essay the central formula of the old, making the words in which he had described the special quality of Leonardo now describe the romantic spirit itself. Leonardo, he said in *The Renaissance*, was a genius "composed, in almost equal parts, of curiosity and the desire of beauty." These were the two "elementary forces" in him, "curiosity often in conflict with the desire of beauty, but generating, in union with it, a type of subtle and curious grace." In the essay on "Romanticism," he said: "It is the addition of strangeness to beauty that constitutes the romantic character in art; and the desire of beauty

---

Le merveilleux . . . The marvellous envelops and saturates us like the atmosphere; but we fail to see it (C, 107).

Car les héros . . . For the heroes of the *Iliad* do not so much as reach up to your ankles, oh! Vautrin, oh! Rastignac, oh! Birotteau . . . and you, oh! Honoré de Balzac, you the most heroic and the most remarkable, the most romantic and the most poetical of all the characters you have drawn from your heart (C, 107).

being a fixed element in every artistic organization, it is the addition of curiosity to this desire of beauty that constitutes the romantic temper."[66]

Pater writes in "Romanticism" that the romantic spirit, with which he has identified Leonardo (but only to readers of *The Renaissance*, since he does not name him here), is not confined to any particular period in history. It is "an enduring principle in the artistic temperament," perceptible in the Middle Ages and "even in Sophocles," but it is not always present in the same measure. The characteristics of Leonardo's art are those of "outbreaks of this spirit," which come naturally "when, in men's desires towards art and poetry, curiosity may be noticed to take the lead; when men come to art and poetry, with a deep thirst for intellectual excitement, after a long *ennui*." In this essay Pater is concerned with the forward edge of romanticism, which he finds in modern France: "neither Germany, with its Goethe and Tieck, nor England, with its Byron and Scott, is nearly so representative of the romantic temper as France, with Mürger, and Gautier and Victor Hugo." Indeed, in France the "play" of the romantic movement "is hardly yet over."

The "Romanticism" essay makes curiosity and strangeness its principal points: curiosity over-balancing the desire of beauty marks out the romantic artist; strangeness over-balancing order marks out romantic art. The desire of the romantic artist, Pater writes, is "towards a beauty born of unlikely elements, by a profound alchemy, by a difficult initiation, by the charm which wrings it even out of terrible things." He finds in the modern French writers a positive value for "the intense, the exceptional"; he observes that their art is often distorted by the strength of passion, distinguished by "something of a terrible grotesque, of the *macabre* . . . though always combined with perfect literary execution." (Of this last, he gives Gautier's *Morte Amoureuse* and, not for the first time, Hugo's Gilliatt as examples.) The flowers of the romantic movement are not entirely natural: they are "ripened not by quiet, everyday sunshine, but by the lightning, which, tearing open the hill-side, brought the seeds hidden there to a sudden, mysterious blossoming."

Pater's romanticism essay is oddly eclectic: it canvasses much that he had already written, for an unusual summary of his thought. It is also unusually open in its expression of admiration and affinity. Pater makes it clear both that he admires the most

recent expression of romanticism that he finds in the modern
French writers and that his own criticism is congruent with that
of some modern French critics. He quotes from Sainte-Beuve,
and he cites Stendhal.[67] It is here, too, that he makes his most
explicit references to Baudelaire, using his name alternately with
Hugo's in a list of participants in "that modern romanticism, the
French romanticism." He praises his writing on "the whole pa-
thetic philosophy of children's toys," cites him as a "lover of
animals" and a "charming" writer about them, and names him
as one whose work attains unity of the Leonardan sort. The last
reference is the most interesting:

> ... what in the eighteenth century is but an exceptional
> phenomenon, breaking through its fair reserve and discre-
> tion only at rare intervals, is the habitual guise of the nine-
> teenth, breaking through it perpetually, with a feverishness,
> an incomprehensible straining and excitement, which all
> experience to some degree, but yearning also, in the genuine
> children of the romantic school, to be *énergique, frais, et dispos*,
> for those qualities of energy, freshness, comely order; and
> often, in Mürger, in Gautier, in Charles Baudelaire, for
> instance, with singular felicity attaining them.

Here, as elsewhere in Pater, Baudelaire is representative. His
name, not only spoken but spoken in full, suggests an unusual
emphasis.

The connections between "Leonardo da Vinci" and "Roman-
ticism" are obvious; and it is useful to return to the earlier essay
from a reading of the later. In the light cast by "Romanticism,"
Leonardo appears not only a representative romantic and mod-
ern, but the representative of a particular modernity and a spe-
cial romanticism. He is of the party of Swinburne and his Blake,
of Gautier and of Baudelaire. What is theoretical in "The School
of Giorgione," for instance, he enacts: in his *Saint John* (which,
Pater says, reminds him of Gautier, who was reminded by the
same painting of Heine), "We recognise one of those symbolical
inventions in which the ostensible subject is used, not as matter
for definite pictorial realisation, but as the starting-point of a
train of sentiment, subtle and vague as a piece of music" (112).
Leonardo's artistic control incarnates the ideal of Pater's and
Swinburne's criticism: "No one ever ruled over his subject more
entirely than Lionardo, or bent it more dexterously to purely

artistic ends" (112). He is devoted to art for its own sake, clearly
not a moralist or pragmatist in his work: "Other artists have been
as careless of present or future applause, in self-forgetfulness,
or because they set moral or political ends above the ends of art;
but in him this solitary culture of beauty seems to have hung
upon a kind of self-love, and a carelessness in the work of art
of all but art itself" (110). He broods over "the correspondences
which exist between the different orders of living things, through
which, to eyes opened, they interpret each other" (96). He has,
like the Gautier Pater cites both in "Romanticism" and in *Marius
the Epicurean*, a "fascination of corruption" (98) and as for the
formula itself—"curiosity and the desire of beauty"—that links
Pater directly to Baudelaire. More importantly in the present
context, he is a gardener of strange flowers: "Out of the secret
places of a unique temperament he brought strange blossoms
and fruits hitherto unknown; and for him, the novel impression
conveyed, the exquisite effect woven, counted as an end in it-
self—a perfect end" (110-11).

Pater's Leonardo, then, is connected by "a chain of secret
influences" (109) to Baudelaire. Once again Pater forges a series
of identifying textual links, and joins Leonardo, whose repre-
sentative modernity gives him much in common with the Ron-
sard of *Gaston de Latour*, to a familiar "fraternité ou cousinage"
(II, 743). By 1869, when he wrote his essay on Leonardo, he
had already folded Baudelaire quietly into his review of Morris's
poems and so had established what would become a pattern of
private reference in his work; and the Leonardo essay, in which
he granted himself full artistic license for the first time, is closely
connected to Swinburne's "Notes on Some Pictures of 1868" and
his "Notes on Some Old Masters in Florence."[68] The essay is
fascinated both by a theme of secrecy and by a vision of the artist
working "for a few only, perhaps chiefly for himself." It estab-
lishes a rhythmic repetition in its emphasis on disguise: in both
nature and art, as they are represented here, surface and sub-
surface are in conflict. Leonardo is pictured brooding over na-
ture, "tracking the sources of expression to their subtlest re-
treats," seeking "the hidden virtues of plants and crystals" (96)
or explaining "the obscure light of the unilluminated part of the
moon" (103). His works, too, require subtle tracking: "though
he handles sacred subjects continually, he is the most profane
of painters" (112). He uses the incidents of sacred story "not for

their own sake, or as mere subjects for pictorial realisation, but as a symbolical language for fancies all his own" (116). The figure, Pater writes, "is often merely the pretext for a kind of work which carries one quite out of the range of its conventional associations" (112). His Saint John the Baptist, Pater observes, following Gautier, is strikingly like his *Bacchus*, recognizable by his "treacherous smile" as "something far beyond the outward gesture or circumstance" (112). His Mona Lisa is by no means merely the portrait of *La Gioconda*, but a representative beauty "wrought out from within upon the flesh, the deposit, little cell by cell, of strange thoughts and fantastic reveries and exquisite passions" (118). She is, like the Saint John, an "embodiment."

The aesthetic of evocation, which Pater both defends and uses in this essay, is clearly Baudelairean. His description of Delacroix—as "le plus *suggestif* de tous les peintres, celui dont les oeuvres . . . font le plus penser, et rappellent à la mémoire le plus de sentiments et de pensées poétiques déjà connus, mais qu'on croyait enfouis pour toujours dans la nuit du passé" (II, 745)—looks like an agenda for the famous Mona Lisa passage of Pater's essay—which, transforming him from "a critic, according to the received meaning of that term,"[69] into a critic who asked first of all, "What is this picture to *me?*"—might have rested on Baudelaire's famous passage about the "best criticism," which Pater echoed much later in his essay on Amiel.[70]

"Leonardo" does not name Baudelaire as its ancestor, as "Romanticism" does; nor does it take any text of his as a pattern; nor does it incorporate any specific borrowings that I am aware of. This essay about suggestion, however, is everywhere suggestive, and nowhere more than in its closing lines. Here Pater wonders how the artist who had spent his last years as a wanderer, "who had been always so desirous of beauty, but desired it always in such precise and definite forms, as hands or flowers or hair, looked forward now into the vague land, and experienced the last curiosity" (122). Surely, for the *raffinés*, this is allusion—to the last lines of Charles Baudelaire's "Le Voyage."

* * *

The more than intrinsic interest in Pater's use of Baudelaire is, ironically, partly a consequence of his secrecy. Baudelaire's critical ideas and much of his critical language slid silently into the current of English literature and criticism unidentified by some of the very writers who, following Pater, necessarily followed him also. The aesthetic criticism of *The Renaissance*, the theoretical argument of "The School of Giorgione," the establishment in England of a school of "evocative" or "suggestive" criticism— those things involve him as the silent partner in Pater's authority. There remains, however, one other aspect of Pater's thought which draws Baudelaire comfortably into the history of English literature: the practical aesthetic that Pater derived from his metaphysical position. It is congruent in every major point with Baudelaire's doctrine of *correspondances*. I have discussed the synaesthesia aspect of this doctrine above, in connection with "The School of Giorgione": now I shall consider another aspect—its bearing on the relation of the inward and the outward, the perceiver and the perceived—in relation to the whole range of Pater's works, but chiefly to his last, *Plato and Platonism*.

Pater's historical importance, like Baudelaire's own, issues partly from the sustained double emphasis of his criticism. On the one hand, he insists on the facts, the sensory stimuli, the sensuous matter of art, so that he seems in critical retrospect to have strong connections with the early modernists—the Imagists, Pound, early Eliot, for instance—for whom a hawk was always and only a hawk and in whose work the object must occupy the fovea. But even as he demands sensory attentiveness, Pater always insists that it can produce an "escape" from mere sensation to a "spiritual" or "poetical" effect, so that he seems, to a critical retrospect triangulated differently from the first, to be the earliest English writer seriously to explore the critical implications of symbolist inwardness—Swinburne, having taken it up briefly, nevertheless devoted his main effort to his poetry—and to herald not only the intricately echoing verse of Eliot's later years but also the regressive reflexiveness of a still later generation of writers.[71] In Pater's work those antitheses hold together: in subsequent writers, they break apart into what Hugh Kenner calls "the poetic of the cave, the post-symbolist signification of ineffabilities" on the one hand, and what Samuel Hynes, after Pound, calls "the prose tradition" on the other.[72]

From the beginning, no question occupies Pater more than the relation of the type to the individual. His consistent attention to the question of universals—"as we know, one of the constant problems of logic"[73]—unifies his work: his "portraits," his criticism, his philosophy, his allegorical fictions. *Plato and Platonism*,

1893, echoes strikingly and almost precisely the question with which *he* began, twenty-five years earlier. "But let us accept the challenge," Pater had written in his Morris review, "let us see what modern philosophy, when it is sincere, really does say about human life and the truth we can attain in it, and the relation of this to the desire of beauty."[74] That challenge, of course, introduces what became the "Conclusion." In his last published work Pater rephrased the matter: "And holding still to the concrete, the particular, to the visible or sensuous, if you will, last as first," he writes, "thinking of that as essentially the one vital and lively thing, really worth our while in a short life, we may recognise sincerely what generalisation and abstraction have done or may do . . . for the particular gem or flower . . . [for] a mind in search, precisely, of a concrete and intuitive knowledge such as that" (142).

Pater's response to his own questions about the abstract and the concrete, the general and the particular, in 1893 as in 1868, is, like the "wholesale scepticism of Hume or Mill . . . an appeal from the preconceptions of the understanding to the authority of the senses" (24). If Coleridge's career was, as Pater says, a part of the "long pleading of German culture for things 'behind the veil,' "[75] his own was a long, consistent defense of the "latent poetic rights" of the things before the senses. The whole of *The Renaissance* exists to draw aesthetic conclusions from his rejection of the idea that intellection is epistemologically superior to sensation; the whole of *Plato and Platonism* exists to justify the validity of such aesthetic conclusions as he had drawn in *The Renaissance*. In the early review as in the late work on Plato, Pater rejects categorically "the sort of knowledge, if knowledge it is to be called, which corresponds to . . . 'Pure Being.' " It is, he says, only definable as " 'Pure Nothing,' that colourless, formless, impalpable, existence" (25).

Still, Pater's preoccupation with the hard, the concrete, and the particular is only one side of his idea of balance, a correction of "exaggerated inwardness" or "vagueness, a want of definition."[76] The artistic ideals represented in his essays are always double: the ideal art he describes in "Winckelmann," for instance, is "in no sense a symbol, a suggestion of anything beyond its own victorious fairness. The mind begins and ends with the finite image, yet loses no part of the spiritual motive . . . [which] saturates and is identical with it" (178). The triumph of Michelangelo's sculpture lies in its combination of inward and outward, and in its preservation of the individual. Those qualities distinguish it from some Greek sculpture, which is led, Pater says, "to seek the type in the individual, to purge from the individual all that belongs only to the individual, all the accidents, feelings, actions of a special moment" (55). The essays in *The Renaissance* enact the doubleness of Pater's view, presenting what there is of "*genus* and *species* and *differentia*" (142) together with what there is of "strangeness" and individuality—and, since the evolutionary law requires both duplication and difference, Pater's botanical metaphor (a presence in his work from the time of the "exotic flowers" of the Morris review) is by no means merely decorative.

That insistently double emphasis provides the scaffolding for Pater's aesthetic: for him the aesthetic act, critical or creative, is the connection of the two orders, the means of bringing the particular and the general into significant, meaning-multiplying relationship. Ronsard's achievement, to take the most poetical, is to have made the visible "more visible than ever before, just because soul had come to its surface"; Pater's own is to have discovered in the great individuals of the past the "typical standards, or revealing instances of the laws by which certain aesthetic effects are produced." His discussion of Plato's theory of ideas focuses sharply on the acts of transition and connection. The "modern view" of the nature of universals, he says, holds that there is a "general consciousness, a permanent common sense, independent indeed of each one of us, but with which we are, each one of us, in communication. It is in that, those common or general ideas really reside." Into those "common or general names," Pater says, "one's individual experience, little by little, drop by drop, conveys their full meaning or content." It is by "locating the particular in the general, mediating between general and particular, between our individual experience and the common experience of our kind [that] we come to understand each other, and to assist each other's thoughts, as in a common mental atmosphere, an 'intellectual world,' as Plato calls it" (137-38).

The most moving passage in all of Pater, to my mind, is his parable of the seashell in *Plato and Platonism*. It exposes with undefended simplicity the ways in which, for Pater, the orders of mind bear on experience in time. Pater the allegorizer takes up again the contrast between abstract, general knowledge and concrete, particular experience, considering what may be the differences between a "naturalist who deals with things through ideas" and "the layman (so to call him)." Pater sends the layman to school. He who formerly perceived nothing more than a bright seashell on the shore will, after study, see how "converse with the general" can enhance perception of the concrete:

By its juxtaposition and co-ordination with what is ever more and more not *it*, by the contrast of its very imperfection, at this point or that, with its own proper and perfect type, this concrete and particular thing has, in fact, been enriched by the whole colour and expression of the whole circumjacent world, concentrated upon, or as it were at focus in, it. By a kind of short-hand now, and as if in a single moment of vision, all that, which only a long experience, moving patiently from part to part, could exhaust, its manifold alliance with the entire world of nature, is legible upon it, as it lies there in one's hand. (143-44)

Last, as first, Pater does not abandon the visible, and his discussion of Plato's "theory of ideas"—"itself, indeed, not so much a doctrine or theory, as a way of regarding and speaking of general terms"—dramatizes the same elements as went into the making of the aesthetic critic of *The Renaissance*.

Pater's view of the connecting function of art serves the same purposes as does the doctrine of correspondences. That "répertoire de toute métaphore" (II, 117), "magasin d'images" (II, 750), or "immense analogie universelle" (II, 575), serves, like the "general knowledge" of which Pater writes in *Plato and Platonism*, to provide contexts for the findings of the senses, to unite temporal sensory impressions to the common store. The doctrine applies to aesthetic issues the structure of Pater's own thought: the exemplary man of the world in Baudelaire's *Exposition Universelle*, it will be remembered, focuses upon the experience of the moment, but he is rich with memory and best able to understand what is before him because he can "courir avec agilité sur l'immense clavier des *correspondances!*" (II, 577). For Pater,

répertoire . . . that repository of metaphor (C, 272) . . . storehouse of images and signs (C, 366) . . . immense universal analogy (C, 115).
courir avec . . . run nimbly up and down the vast keyboard of nature's correspondences! (C, 117).

as for Baudelaire, the doctrine appeals as a means of multiplying the meaning of experience in time. What Baudelaire represents metaphorically as the "dictionary" of nature, or the "keyboard" of correspondences, Pater offers in his last work as a system of scientific classification. The function of the two schemes is the same: they exist to multiply consciousness of the particular by yoking it to the general. The germ of "the mythic method"—as it appears in the elaborate explanatory *Vision* of Yeats, the great chart of *Ulysses*, or even the notes to *The Waste Land*—lies here. The heroic action of *Four Quartets*, whose delineation of pattern is constantly reshaped by what is "Quick now, here, now," has a supporting intellectual root in Pater's desire to see "this concrete and particular thing . . . enriched by the whole colour and expression of the whole circumjacent world."

Pater does not write directly about Baudelaire's doctrine of *correspondances*, from which the symbolist movement departs; but his Leonardo adheres to a system of analogy that goes by that title, and his 1874 essay "On Wordsworth" identifies, as "a large element in the complexion of modern poetry," an "intimate consciousness of the expression of natural things, which weighs, listens, penetrates, where the earlier mind passed roughly by." Such a consciousness, he says, the perception of a soul in inanimate things, has been "remarked as a fact in mental history again and again. It reveals itself in many forms; but is strongest and most attractive in what is strongest and most attractive in modern literature."[77] It is latently connected with "those pantheistic theories which locate an intelligent soul in material things, and have largely exercised men's minds in some modern systems of philosophy," but Pater links it specifically to the line of French writers he had named as the best representatives of the modern. It is exemplified, he says, by "writers as unlike each other as Senancour and Théophile Gautier: as a singular chapter in the history of the human mind, its growth might be traced from Rousseau to Chateaubriand, from Chateaubriand to Victor Hugo."[78] In describing Wordsworth's ability to "see into the life of things" Pater's language evokes Baudelaire's "Correspondances" sonnet: "every natural object seemed to possess more or less of a moral or spiritual life, to be capable of a companionship with man, full of expression, of inexplicable affinities and delicacies of intercourse."[79] When Pater writes of this aspect of modern literature, he adopts its conventional partly mystical language, but his own view admits the mystical language only as metaphor. Such a conviction—of souls in things—is possible "only in a temperament exceptionally susceptible," like Words-worth's, "to the impressions of eye and ear," and it is, "in its essence, a kind of sensuousness."[80] In "A Child in the House" Pater attributes both the philosophy and the fancy to his auto-biographical subject:

> In later years he came upon philosophies which occupied him much in the estimate of the proportion of the sensuous and the ideal elements in human knowledge, the relative parts they bear in it; and, in his intellectual scheme, was led to assign very little to the abstract thought, and much to its sensible vehicle or occasion. Such metaphysical speculation did but reinforce what was instinctive in his way of receiving the world, and for him, everywhere, that sensible vehicle or occasion became, perhaps only too surely, the necessary con-comitant of any perception of things, real enough to be of weight or reckoning, in his house of thought. There were times when he could think of the necessity he was under of associating all thoughts to touch and sight, as a sympathetic link between himself and actual, feeling, living objects. . . .[81]

That "sympathetic link" is the object both of Baudelaire's *cor-respondances* (which enabled Gautier, it will be recalled, to "définir l'attitude mystérieuse que les objets de la création tiennent de-vant le regard de l'homme") and of Pater's "metaphysical spec-ulation."

I have been concerned in this chapter to show how deeply, specifically, and consciously indebted Pater was to Baudelaire, to whose work he alludes frequently throughout his career but whose name he systematically suppresses or withholds. Such withholding is entirely consistent both with Pater's conception of style and with his usual practice. His comments on style revert frequently to an idea of suppression, defining the exact touch as omission or withdrawal: " 'The artist,' says Schiller, 'may be known rather by what he *omits*,' " Pater observes in "Style," "and in literature, too, the true artist may be best recognised by his tact of omission."[82] The essay on Mérimée dwells on "literary deception" and on the "machinery" of "intellectual reserve"; *Plato and Platonism*, concluding boldly with praise of Plato as an artist, compiles a series of examples of admirable restraint. In "the stringent, short-hand art of Thucydides at his best," Pater finds "the half as so much more than the whole." About Pindar, "his analogue in verse," Pater writes: "Think of the amount of attention he must have looked for, in those who were, not to read, but to sing him, or to listen while he was sung, and to understand. With those fine, sharp-cut gems or chasings of his, so sparely set, how much he leaves for a well-drilled intelligence to supply in the way of connecting thought." In Plato himself, Pater admires an "intellectual astringency" that enhances "the sense of power in one's self, and its effect upon others, by a certain crafty reserve in its exercise, after the manner of a true expert." It is his own justification that Pater proffers at the conclusion of *Plato and Platonism*, commending, with a certain crafty reserve and a Pindaric dependence on his reader, the "dry light" of Heraclitus, or the *siccum lumen* of Bacon.[83]

Pater's unusually dense and precise covert allusion is in part the product of his obvious pleasure in the multiplication of meanings and the complex textures of prose: "words, too, must embroider, be twisted and spun, like silk or golden hair," he writes.[84] But it is also, clearly, a product of his "tact of omission" and a response to the conditions in which he wrote. His sexual unorthodoxy made him especially vulnerable to the power politics of Victorian aesthetic debate: "No wonder Pater avoided scandal like the plague," writes R. M. Seiler. "He had only to remember the fate that befell his contemporary, J. A. Symonds, who had to give up his fellowship (in 1862) after a number of his letters and poems were circulated among his colleagues."[85] For any scandal-avoiding writer in the prudish sixties and seventies, an alliance with Baudelaire, whom Swinburne had named as a father of the revolution and defended for his treatment of sexual subjects, would have been daring; for one both especially vulnerable and living in an especially enclosed political system, such an alliance would have been genuinely dangerous. After 1877, when Jowett threatened him with exposure unless he suppressed his "antinomian" arguments, Pater concealed a great deal. His subterranean references to Baudelaire, however, his detailed textual dependence and careful allegorical representation of the real forces in his imagination, together constitute a stubborn steadfastness, and they have given him the last word.

Pater is an essential base for modernism in English literature: he was, as Yeats wrote, of "revolutionary importance." The quite remarkable similarity of his thought to that of some early twentieth-century writers is readily apparent: he supplied material, as Gerald Monsman has shown, to Virginia Woolf, Joyce, Pound, Eliot, and others.[86] The position he strikes in relation to the object before the senses is, in the context of this study, of greatest importance. With Joyce's earliest Stephen, Pater rejects the "temper which sees no fit abode here for its ideals and chooses therefore to behold them under insensible figures" and whose art lacks "the gravity of solid bodies."[87] His assertion that the "faculty for truth is a power of distinguishing and fixing delicate and fugitive details" suggests the qualities dominant in Pound's "image," "that which presents an intellectual and emotional complex in an instant of time."[88] The Imagist "Rules" suggest him in every point:

1. Direct treatment of the "thing," whether subjective or objective.
2. To use absolutely no word that did not contribute to the presentation.
3. As regarding rhythm: to compose in sequence of the musical phrase, not in sequence of a metronome.[89]

The "Rules" turn Pater's doctrines into a specific work-sheet. His claim, in "Style," that "all art does but consist in the removal of surplusage, from the last finish of the gem-engraver blowing away the last particle of invisible dust, back to the earliest divination of the finished work to be, lying somewhere, according to Michelangelo's fancy, in the rough-hewn block of stone," predicts the care for concision of Hulme's *Notes on Language and Style*.[90] His fusion of "spirit" and "matter" (as in his commendation of Plato as an artist in whose work "the material and the spiritual are blent and fused together" [122]) predicts precisely the attempt at synthesis of Imagist aesthetics and foretells the view taken by Murry in *The Problem of Style*. In his conception of modern poetry as obliged to deal with the transitory, the fugitive, the contingent, but capable at the same time of shedding upon that detail "the soul of its beauty," Pater sets Baudelaire at the center, not only of his own work, but also of the current of English literature in the late nineteenth and early twentieth centuries. When Baudelaire came to be seen by writers in the early twentieth century as an exemplary *modern* poet, quite distinct from the generation of Swinburne and Pater and Wilde, that was at least partly because Pater had joined him anonymously to the issues of modernism.

3

OSCAR WILDE

THE TRUE BROTHERHOOD OF THE ARTS

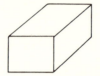

—Ludwig Wittgenstein,
Philosophical Investigations

Wilde's position in the development of modern poetics is as reversible as the lines in Wittgenstein's celebrated drawing or as the identities of some of his own heroes. His criticism can seem either merely eclectic, a noisy summary of current aesthetic ideas, or "the basis for many critical propositions . . . which we like to attribute to more ponderous names,"[1] his work either a cluster of period themes or a rich legacy to Yeats, Joyce, Edith Sitwell, Aldington, Eliot and the others. His Baudelaire shares in that historical doubleness. Wilde made Baudelaire a model for his outraging paradoxes and, as Robert Sherard says, for his unwillingness to suffer fools, and he yoked him to a style of life and art intended at once to provoke and to baffle hostile reaction. In that, his Baudelaire is a recognizable cliché of the decadence. But Wilde also made Baudelaire a defining figure in his critical and imaginative lexicon and the ideal of his sorrowful isolation, and he found in his work, as Basil Hallward might have put it, an image of his own soul. In that, his Baudelaire is part of a powerful originality that belongs both to Wilde and to the decadent movement, and at the same time he is a prominent feature in the immediate background of modernism in English literature.

In Wilde an ever-present reversibility of meaning is the most compelling critical issue. It is the dominant feature of his style—paradox carries both the creation and the destruction of meaning along the same circuit (and so paradoxes are, as Vivian tells Cyril, dangerous things)[2]—and it is the crucial point in his critical argument. Wittgenstein drew his shifting rectangle to illustrate the effect of interpretation on perception: "Each time the text supplies the interpretation of the illustration," he says. "But we can also see the illustration now as one thing now as another.—So we interpret it, and *see* it as we *interpret* it."[3] Wilde put both life and art under the same rule years before Wittgenstein wrote that: both art (as it is talked about in his criticism) and life (as it is represented in his fiction and in his plays) are constantly under the threat of doubling, of turning inside-out or becoming their opposites. That is Wilde's *Truth of Masks*. "A Truth in art is that whose contradictory is also true," he writes.[4] Wilde made the instability of meaning his steady focus. "Things are because we see them," he wrote in "The Decay of Lying," "and what we see, and how we see it, depends on the Arts that have influenced us."[5] That idea, itself the steady bedrock of Wilde's criticism as of his art, is essential in an attempt to discover the significance in his work of Baudelaire, both for the obvious reason that Baudelaire was one of the "influences" shaping Wilde's sight and for the less obvious ways in which Wilde, putting Baudelaire under the pressure of his own texts, made his significance shift. Wilde's Baudelaire is as double as the Wittgenstein drawing, present as one thing to the first sight and another to the second; and he is an index to the connection between cliché and innovation, imitation and originality, influence and mockery.

Wilde is daringly, ostentatiously, and most entertainingly, derivative. What Pater suppressed, Wilde allowed to float to the surface. He dishes up Baudelaire as an element of his style, peppering his work with quotations, borrowings, echoes. Sometimes he quotes epigrammatic lines: " 'The heart contains passion but the imagination alone contains poetry,' says Charles Baudelaire."[6] Sometimes he simply steals: "Dandyism is the assertion of the absolute modernity of Beauty."[7] Often he distorts, wittily:

A man can live for three days without bread, but no man can live for one day without poetry, was an aphorism of

Baudelaire's: you can live without pictures and music, but you can't live without eating, says the author of "Dinner and Dishes." . . . Who indeed, in these degenerate days, would hesitate between an ode and an omelette, a sonnet and a salmi?[8]

In *Impressions of America*, Wilde "civilizes" the most chilling phrase of Baudelaire's "Le Voyage"—"une oasis d'horreur dans un désert d'ennui"—to describe American girls as "little oases of pretty unreasonableness in a vast desert of practical common-sense."[9] In a note on Whistler, he calls the *Salon de 1846* Baudelaire's "charming article on the artistic value of frock coats," and in his comments on costume in Shakespeare's plays, he borrows from it again.[10] Baudelaire makes dozens of brief appearances, often anonymously, often not, in Wilde's work. Some of these are specific, like the "swans . . . lying asleep on the smooth surface of the polished lake, like white feathers fallen upon a mirror of black steel," of "The Portrait of Mr. W. H."; and some, like the "unknown land full of strange flowers and subtle perfumes, a land of which it is joy of all joys to dream, a land where all things are perfect and poisonous," merely heavily suggestive.[11] Individually, Wilde's allusions may appear to have no special interest, since, if he collected bits from Baudelaire, he collected them also from Flaubert and Gautier and, as Oliver Elton said when he persuaded the Oxford Union to refuse the gift of Wilde's poems, sixty more. Those poems, Harold Bloom observes, attributing to Wilde the very definition of the anxiety of influence, "anthologize the whole of English High Romanticism."[12]

Taken together, however, as an element of his style, as part of his artifice, Wilde's invocations have a great deal of interest. The pattern of his Baudelaire allusions emerges from the instances I have just cited. His *formula* combines ostentatious (even if anonymous) and apparently light-hearted reference, the delay of echo, and a dark doubling of meaning. The "degeneracy" of "Dinner and Dishes," for instance: it makes a tidy reversal, dipping suddenly from a breezy snub addressed to the high decadence of mid-nineteenth-century art to explode a paunchy middle-class preoccupation with menus. It balances the poet against the "author of 'Dinner and Dishes,'" and poetry, pictures, and music against sausages and eggs. The silent, obvious reference in *Impressions of America*, which waits on the reader's recognition of the line, reverses the tone of the text altogether, pairing Wilde's drawing-room superficiality with Baudelaire's inescapable disgust, and the later aesthetic tour of America with the earlier appeal to Death, the Old Captain, to plunge "au fond du gouffre . . . pour trouver du *nouveau!*" (I, 134). The *Salon de 1846*, furthermore, while it does mention the "charm" of the frock coat, "cet habit tant victimé" gives it quite different associations as "le symbole d'un deuil perpétuel" (II, 494).

When Wilde alludes to Baudelaire, he often features his name prominently, as part of the plumage; but he folds the sense of the allusion and its effect into an unruly satire, a threat of disorder lying darkly below the immaculately organized surface. Even while he appears to be taming Baudelaire for readers of the *Pall Mall Gazette*, taking down a peg or two that pretentious satanist, Wilde keeps him subversive. Baudelaire is a trouble to the very surface he occupies, standing like "some foul parody, some infamous, ignoble satire" in relation to it.[13] Wilde makes him serve the not always compatible purposes in his work of both surface and symbol.

By the time Wilde wrote, Swinburne's Baudelairean countertradition was flourishing. "Il y a aujourd'hui plus de vingt-cinq ans," Wilde wrote in 1891 to Edmond de Goncourt, "M. Swinburne a publié ses *Poèmes et Ballades*, une des oeuvres qui ont marqué le plus profondément dans notre littérature une ère nouvelle."[14] George Moore had joined the movement as early as 1878, with his *Flowers of Passion*, which proclaimed their allegiance to poetry and death in the gilded figure of a lyre and a skull on their cover—and, by the time Wilde wrote his important works, already had abandoned it.[15] When Beardsley drew the first version of Salomé's *Toilette*, he showed *Les Fleurs du Mal* on her bookshelf.[16] Wilde joined himself early to that tradition, as to his "true brotherhood." While he was at Oxford, he contributed to "A Terminal Magazine of Oxford Poetry" that was called, like Baudelaire's exiled verses, *Waifs and Strays*, and in 1885 he wrote to H. C. Marillier, "I wonder are you all Wordsworthians still at Cambridge, or do you love Keats, and Poe, and Baude-

---

cet habit . . . this much abused frock-coat . . . the mark of perpetual mourning (C, 105).

Il y a . . . More than twenty-five years ago, Mr Swinburne published his *Poems and Ballads*, one of the works which have most profoundly marked a new era in our literature.

laire? I hope so."¹⁷ The first remarkable fact about the Baudelaire
who appears at the surface of Wilde's work, however, is that it
is part of an inheritance. Wilde joins him to a small circle in-
cluding Swinburne and Pater and himself. His terms of praise
describe the circle: *Poems and Ballads*, he said, were "very perfect
and very poisonous poetry"; *The Renaissance* was "the very flower
of decadence"; and Baudelaire was "the most perfect and the
most poisonous of all modern French poets." Those are the very
qualities Wilde attributed to his own work. Of *Dorian Gray* he
said, "It is poisonous if you like, but you cannot deny that it is
also perfect, and perfection is what we artists aim at."¹⁸ Wilde's
praise was neither flippant nor ill-considered, though it pre-
tended to be, and though his shorthand may require decom-
pacting. For him, "perfection" was achieved individualism, and
that is a phenomenon of both aesthetic and social significance.
It represents both the triumph of the modern, as Pater had
described it in his Baudelairean "Winckelmann" essay, and
Wilde's wholehearted adoption of an aesthetic based on the no-
tion that, as he still believed in *De Profundis*, "Modern life is
complex and relative."¹⁹ When he calls the beauty of individuality
"perfection," he subverts critical convention by what is for him
a merely habitual infiltration: while in other critics "perfection"
might be thought a quality of classical art and related to the
representation of types or universals, in Wilde it is made to
describe its own conventional antithesis. Wilde's coupling of
"perfection" and "poison" as terms of praise is, therefore, a kind
of paradox, even though the sources of its contradiction, remote
from the surface, form part of the systematic reversal of the
commonplace that constitutes the critical thought. The major
point here, however, is merely that when Wilde calls Swinburne
and Pater and Baudelaire "perfect," he joins them together un-
der the terms of their own aesthetic. He also joins them together
as a rebellious clan: since the world hates individualism, and
since art is individualism, they are united as a "disturbing and
disintegrating force."²⁰

   Wilde's affinity with Baudelaire, then, is inseparable from his
sense of identity with Swinburne and Pater. It is of course part
of his more general attachment to French writers: he told Robert
Sherard that Flaubert and Gautier and Baudelaire, though gen-
erally thought to be dead, continued actively to be his admirers,
all keenly *interested* in what he wrote.²¹ Part of what he saw in

Baudelaire, however, was what his English masters had taught him to see. The following passage, which first appeared in Wilde's review "Balzac in English" and then later in "The Decay of Lying," demonstrates one of the kinds of association he made:

> The distinction between such a book as M. Zola's "L'Assommoir" and such a book as Balzac's "Illusions Perdues" is the distinction between unimaginative realism and imaginative reality. "All Balzac's characters," said Baudelaire, "are gifted with the same ardour of life that animated himself. All his fictions are as deeply coloured as dreams. Every mind is a weapon loaded to the muzzle with will. . . ."

The quotation, as Wilde says, is from Baudelaire. But the translation and the critical comment, as Wilde does not say, are from Swinburne's *Study of Shakespeare*. "Nothing," Swinburne says of what Baudelaire had written, "could more aptly and perfectly illustrate the distinction indicated in my text between unimaginative realism and imaginative reality."[22]

Such a conflation of voices is not unusual in Wilde's prose, which is, like his lyrics, anthological. Although to speak in the words someone else wrote might not be "sincere," it could be, according to Wilde, "a method by which we can multiply our personalities." He said that first in "The Critic as Artist," as part of Gilbert's argument that "To arrive at what one really believes, one must speak through lips different from one's own." The claim concludes a brilliant and derivative critical argument. He made it again in *Dorian Gray*, attributing it to a narrator revealed, surprisingly, as "I," in the chapter that is dominated by "the yellow book."[23] Wilde's description of Baudelaire's poems, in "The Critic as Artist," is an example of such multiplication. It speaks Wilde's matter but not in Wilde's voice. In the first part of the critical dialogue, Gilbert had quoted Pater's description of the Mona Lisa (going on, it is worth adding, to describe his response to *Tannhäuser*). In the second part he describes *Les Fleurs du Mal*:

> Close to your hand lies a little volume, bound in some Nile-green skin that has been powdered with gilded nenuphars and smoothed with hard ivory. It is the book that Gautier loved, it is Baudelaire's masterpiece. Open it at that sad madrigal that begins

"Que m'importe que tu sois sage?
Sois belle! et sois triste!"

and you will find yourself worshipping sorrow as you have never worshipped joy. Pass on to the poem on the man who tortures himself, let its subtle music steal into your brain and colour your thoughts, and you will become for a moment what he was who wrote it; nay, not for a moment only, but for many barren moonlit nights and sunless sterile days will a despair that is not your own make its dwelling within you, and the misery of another gnaw your heart away. Read the whole book, suffer it to tell even one of its secrets to your soul, and your soul will grow eager to know more, and will feed upon poisonous honey, and seek to repent of strange crimes of which it is guiltless, and to make atonement for terrible pleasures that it has never known. And then, when you are tired of these flowers of evil, turn to the flowers that grow in the garden of Perdita. . . .[24]

What Wilde sees here and the way he sees it come from Pater. He broods over the *Fleurs du Mal* as by pattern: the book is an emblem for a modern, sorrowful beauty "into which the soul with all its maladies has passed"; it evokes "strange thoughts and fantastic reveries and exquisite passions." The words I have just quoted are Pater's, though they might have been Wilde's. It is Leonardo's Lady Lisa who shapes this interpretation of Baudelaire and the eloquent, swooning description of sorrow and sterility, poison and secrecy, honey and strange crimes. Even the concluding contrast, with its antithesis between a troubled, complex modernity and a simple, pastoral beauty, derives from her.

Wilde's description of *Les Fleurs du Mal* exemplifies his importance to this study. On the one hand, he acts as a superior sponge, gathering and distributing themes, summarizing and proliferating influences. That is the consequence of the anthological style that he regarded as a "method": the true critic, Gilbert says, "will realize himself in many forms, and by a thousand different ways, and will ever be curious of new sensations and fresh points of view," and he will certainly not "be the slave of his own opinions."[25] In the exercise of his true critical liberty,

Que m'importe . . . Why should I care if you're as good as gold? Be beautiful, and be sad (S, 70).

Wilde emphasizes the points at which Swinburne and Pater had drawn Baudelaire into the English tradition, and he makes these points plain for all to see. On the other hand, he attaches to Baudelaire one of the deepest impulses of his own imagination, setting at the focus of his vision the figure he singles out from the Baudelairean host in his description of *Les Fleurs du Mal.* "L'Héautontimorouménos," the man who tortures himself, and who, in Baudelaire's poem, is "the wound and the knife . . . the blow and the cheek, the limbs and the rack, the victim and the torturer,"[26] is a defining figure in Wilde's work, the expression here, as in Baudelaire's poem, of a mind shaken and mauled by voracious Irony. In what follows, I want first to examine the ways in which Wilde joins himself to the Baudelaire tradition in English literature by making his critical views glitter at the surface of his own prose and then to consider the ways in which he joins Baudelaire's self-torturer to his own work as an element of a deeply personal expression.

The fact of Wilde's debt to Pater is well known; its extent continues to surprise. Both are relevant here. In 1877, Wilde expressed his admiration for Ruskin, Swinburne, Morris, Symonds, and Pater and for the "revival of culture and love of beauty" he thought they had achieved.[27] By 1882 he had made the revival his own, and he praised the *jeunes guerriers du drapeau romantique* "who are seeking along with me to continue and to perfect the English Renaissance."[28] He appropriated Pater's theories along with his emblem: his 1882 lecture on "The English Renaissance" and his preface to Rennell Rodd's poems outline Paterian ideas that remained central to his criticism throughout his career. In language and figures that are shamelessly Pater's, he embraced the idea that art is abstract, independent of its subject matter: "Nor," he writes, "in its primary aspect, has a painting, for instance, any more spiritual message or meaning for us than a blue tile from the wall of Damascus, or a Hitzen vase." What is to be sought for in painting, he says, comes "from the subject never, but from the pictorial charm only—the scheme and symphony of the colour, the satisfying beauty of the design." He admires Whistler and Moore, "the effect of their work being like the effect given to us by music; for music is the art in which form and matter are always one—the art whose subject cannot be separated from the method of its expression." He sketches out his later view of creative criticism: Rodd's poems "cannot be described in terms of intellectual criticism," but "in terms of the other arts, and by reference to them."[29] From the beginning of his career to the major critical essays of *Intentions*, Wilde proffers Pater's ideas in words that are often Pater's own.

In the context of this study, however, what is most interesting about Wilde's much publicized debt to Pater is that a number of his borrowings from Baudelaire belong to his larger account. The idea of a creative criticism, for instance, the Baudelairean keystone of Pater's theory and method: that provides Wilde with a witty title for "The Critic as Artist" and with the central paradox of *Intentions*: that the "highest Criticism . . . is more creative than creation, and the primary aim of the critic is to see the object as in itself it really is not." In his account of the "true" criticism, Gilbert quotes Pater's description of the Mona Lisa. What would Leonardo have said to all that?

> He would probably have answered that he had contem-
> plated none of these things, but had concerned himself sim-
> ply with certain arrangements of lines and masses, and with
> new and curious colour-harmonies of blue and green. And
> it is for this very reason that the criticism which I have
> quoted is criticism of the highest kind. It treats the work of
> art simply as a starting-point for a new creation.[30]

In calling that "criticism of the highest kind," Wilde joins his comment, certainly consciously, to Baudelaire and Swinburne and Pater. All of the most important characteristics of Wilde's "true" criticism come from the same sources: the critic's relation to the work of art, which is analogous to the artist's relation to the world; the assertion that criticism is "itself an art . . . is really creative in the highest sense of the word . . . is, in fact, both creative and independent"; the claim that "without the critical faculty, there is no artistic creation at all worthy of the name."[31] Those points, it is true, are modern: when he makes them, as Richard Ellmann observes, Wilde "sounds like T. S. Eliot ad-monishing Matthew Arnold" or "like an ancestral Northrop Frye or Roland Barthes."[32] But they come to Wilde from Swinburne and Pater and Baudelaire, and it is no slander to Wilde to point out how much his pre-modernist substance was composed of that late-nineteenth-century nourishment.

The figure who takes his "rapid philosophical walks" through the galleries in Baudelaire's *Salons*, who provides some of the method and much of the impetus to Swinburne's *Blake*, and who becomes the dramatized point of view in Pater's "Preface" and "Conclusion," emerges in Wilde's work as a series of fully dramatized characters. In Wilde's critical dialogues and in *Dorian Gray*, art absorbs criticism in the most literal sense—by making it part of the fiction. His fictionalized "true critic," however, is immediately recognizable as a direct descendant in the line I have described. Like Lord Henry Wotton, he originates in *The Renaissance*—"that book which has had such a strange influence over my life"[33]—and he appears early in Wilde's work. In his lecture on "The English Renaissance of Art," Wilde sketches him in language that is only too familiar. There are two kinds of men, he says, men of action and "men to whom the end of life is thought":

> As regards the latter, who seek for experience itself and not for the fruits of experience, who must burn always with one of the passions of this fiery-coloured world, who find life interesting not for its secret but for its situations, for its pulsations and not for its purpose; the passion for beauty engendered by the decorative arts will be to them more satisfying than any political or religious enthusiasm, any enthusiasm for humanity, any ecstasy or sorrow for love. For art comes to one professing primarily to give nothing but the highest quality to one's moments, and for those moments' sake.[34]

Despite the early date of this, its consanguinity with the later criticism is fully apparent. The later "true critic" of *Intentions* is a much smoother blend, but he is the same spirit. He will "always be sincere in his devotion to the principle of beauty, but he will seek for beauty in every age and in each school, and will never suffer himself to be limited to any settled custom of thought, or stereotyped mode of looking at things."[35] He will be distinguished not by his critical theory but by his temperament; he will consider that his sole aim is to chronicle his own impressions, that the "highest Criticism" will be "the purest form of personal impression," and so on.[36] Even when Wilde claims to go beyond what Pater wrote, he can be seen to be digging out what is implicit there. In "The Decay of Lying," for instance, he writes: "Art never expresses anything but itself. This is the principle of my new aesthetics; and it is this, more than that vital connection

between form and substance, on which Mr. Pater dwells, that
makes music the type of all the arts."37 The departure from Pater,
though Wilde claims one, is not easily discerned in those sen-
tences. These "new aesthetics" were composed of material drawn
from "the only critic of the century whose opinion [he] set
high,"38 and what he drew from him is often precisely what Pater
had taken from Baudelaire.

There is every reason to believe that Wilde saw through the
camouflage to Pater's reliance on Baudelaire. He knew what the
sacred texts were, and he put them together in some extraor-
dinary ways. The following, dazzlingly derivative, comment on
the question of the unity of the arts demonstrates the style of
his compounding:

> And health in art—what is that? It has nothing to do with
> a sane criticism of life. There is more health in Baudelaire
> than there is in [Kingsley]. Health is the artist's recognition
> of the limitations of the form in which he works. It is the
> honour and the homage which he gives to the material he
> uses—whether it be language with its glories, or marble or
> pigment with their glories—knowing that the true broth-
> erhood of the arts consists not in their borrowing one an-
> other's method, but in their producing, each of them by its
> own individual means, each of them by keeping its objective
> limits, the same unique artistic delight. The delight is like
> that given to us by music—for music is the art in which form
> and matter are always one, the art whose subject cannot be
> separated from the method of its expression, the art which
> most completely realises the artistic ideal, and is the con-
> dition to which all the other arts are constantly aspiring.39

There, Wilde makes Baudelaire supply an ideal which he de-
scribes in Pater's words; but, what is more, he discusses the very
matter Pater had taken, word for word, from Baudelaire.40 He
prompts the same question—did he know *exactly* what he was
doing?—in the following passage from "The English Renais-
sance," where, again, he mounts a display of mixed Pater and
Baudelaire:

> I call it our English Renaissance because it is indeed a sort
> of new birth of the spirit of man, like the great Italian Ren-
> aissance of the fifteenth century, in its desire for a more
> gracious and comely way of life, its passion for physical

beauty, its exclusive attention to form, its seeking for new
subjects for poetry, new forms of art, new intellectual and
imaginative enjoyments: and I call it our romantic move-
ment because it is our most recent expression of beauty.[41]

Wilde found in Pater's essay on the French Stories the "many-
sided" movement which was characterized by "the love of the
things of the intellect and the imagination for their own sake,
the desire for a more liberal and comely way of conceiving life
. . . [the] desire to seek first one and then another means of
intellectual or imaginative enjoyment . . . to divine new sources
of it, new experiences, new subjects of poetry, new forms of art."
He discovered the "care for physical beauty, the worship of the
body" in Pater's "Preface."[42] From Baudelaire he took the phrase
which finishes his passage, "Pour moi, le romantisme est l'expres-
sion la plus récente, la plus actuelle du beau" (II, 420). What in
later Wilde was a method for the multiplication of personality
may have been in the earlier a method for the manufacture of
texts.

To say that Wilde's conception of criticism owes most of its
matter to Pater may seem to attribute to the master the whole
significance of the disciple, since almost everything in Wilde can
be seen as an element of his criticism. But that would be to reckon
without the manner (and so to neglect the importance both of
Wilde's "new aesthetics" and of "that vital connection between
form and substance, on which Mr. Pater dwells"). In Wilde, it is
true, the view of what criticism is entails the view of what art
should be. But Wilde transmuted his critical ideas to form. His
chief critical emphasis, on the instability of interpretation and
on the alterations in meaning that can be produced by sudden
switches to "fresh points of view," is a centrally creative fact in
his work, distinguishing it sharply from that of his master—in
whose prose the surface, though complicated by secrecy and
suggestion, is never unstable—and connecting it, by the steady
operation of irony, to the reflexive writers of the twentieth cen-
tury. Wilde's work predicts the uncertain epistemology of much
current writing, the perpetually shifting figure-ground relations
of the plays of Stoppard and Gray, for instance, or the insistently
inverting narrative strategies of contemporary novelists.

The "voracious Irony" in Wilde, his constant threat to reverse

Pour moi . . . For me, romanticism is the most recent, the most up-to-date
expression of beauty (C, 52).

or dismantle his meaning, provides the tension and so the excitement in his critical dialogues, both of which declare his "brotherhood." Cyril and Vivian, Ernest and Gilbert, race almost without drawing breath through the orthodoxies on the most important aesthetic questions—the relation of art and life, and the relation of art and criticism—standing them systematically on their heads. The dialogues are impelled by the "true rhythmical life of words and the fine freedom and richness of effect that such rhythmical life produces" that Wilde thought distinguished his work from Pater's.[43] But he also thought that "one can recognize the liar by his rich rhythmic utterance";[44] and it is that persistently threatening contradiction, as much as the telltale rhythm, that gives Wilde's words their high-wire-act excitement. The critical arguments of both "The Decay of Lying" and "The Critic as Artist" are as much like Wittgenstein's inverting box as is "The Portrait of Mr. W. H." The inversions of both reach past Pater to their sources in Baudelaire.

Wilde announces the Baudelaire connection of his essay on "Decay" in Vivian's first response to the innocent Cyril. (The title, too, is a reversal, since Wilde argues that "the true decadence" occurs when "Life gets the upper hand, and drives Art out into the wilderness.")[45] This dialogue, which considers the "proper place" of Nature and the value of realism, opens with a pointed attack on the Victorian orthodoxies. What Vivian observes in Nature are her "lack of design, her curious crudities, her extraordinary monotony, her absolutely unfinished condition." The idea of her rich variety is only a myth: the variety with which she has been credited exists not in her, but "in the imagination, or fancy, or cultivated blindness of the man who looks at her." "Art," Vivian says, in the dialogue's first, transparent adaptation of Baudelaire, "is our spirited protest, our gallant attempt to teach Nature her proper place."[46] The adapted phrase, as has been noted, is from the *Salon* of 1846: "la première affaire d'un artiste est de substituer l'homme à la nature et de protester contre elle" (II, 473). The antithesis it provides—between art and nature—is the axis of Wilde's critical argument, both here and in "The Critic as Artist." He made it crucial to *Dorian Gray* and *Salomé*, too, and clung to it in prison, writing to Robert Ross, "If I spend my future life reading Baudelaire in a

la première . . . an artist's first job is to substitute man for nature and to protest against her (C, 91).

café, I shall be leading a more natural life than if I take to a hedger's work or plant cacao in mud-swamps."[47] Just as Baudelairean as that antithesis itself is the attribution of sexual characteristics to either side of it. The "gallantry" of Wilde's aesthetic links him again to Baudelaire, whose "Eloge du Maquillage" (a chapter of *Le Peintre de la Vie Moderne*) furnishes him, as well as Mr. Linley, with some of the *mots* he liked most. This major text of modernist poetics makes a strong and witty statement about nature, an attack on the "general blindness" of the Enlightenment:

La plupart des erreurs relatives au beau naissent de la fausse conception du XVIIIe siècle relative à la morale. La nature fut prise dans ce temps-là comme base, source et type de tout bien et de tout beau possibles. La négation du péché originel ne fut pas pour peu de chose dans l'aveuglement général de cette époque. Si toutefois nous consentons à en référer simplement au fait visible . . . nous verrons que la nature n'enseigne rien, ou presque rien, c'est-à-dire qu'elle *contraint* l'homme à dormir, à boire, à manger, et à se garantir, tant bien que mal, contre les hostilités de l'atmosphère. C'est elle aussi qui pousse l'homme à tuer son semblable, à le manger, à le séquestrer, à le torturer; car, sitôt que nous sortons de l'ordre des nécessités et des besoins

La plupart . . . Most wrong ideas about beauty derive from the false notion the eighteenth century had about ethics. In those days, nature was taken as a basis, source and prototype of all possible forms of good and beauty. The rejection of original sin is in no small measure responsible for the general blindness of those days. If, however, we are prepared merely to consult the facts . . . we can see at once that nature teaches nothing or nearly nothing; in other words, it compels man to sleep, drink, eat and to protect himself as best he can against the inclemencies of the weather. It is nature too that drives man to kill his fellowman, to eat him, to imprison and torture him; for as soon as we move from the order of necessities and needs to that of luxury and pleasures, we see that nature can do nothing but counsel crime. It is this so-called infallible nature that has produced parricide and cannibalism, and a thousand other abominations, which modesty and nice feeling alike prevent our mentioning. It is philosophy (I am referring to the right kind), it is religion that enjoins upon us to succour our poor and enfeebled parents. Nature (which is nothing but the inner voice of self-interest) tells us to knock them on the head. Review, analyse everything that is natural, all the actions and desires of absolutely natural man: you will find nothing that is not horrible. Everything that is beautiful and noble is the product of reason and calculation. Crime, which the human animal took a fancy to in his mother's womb, is by origin natural. Virtue, on the other hand, is *artificial*, supernatural. . . . Evil is done without effort, *naturally*, it is the working of fate; good is always the product of an art (C, 425).

pour entrer dans celui du luxe et des plaisirs, nous voyons
que la nature ne peut conseiller que le crime. C'est cette
infaillible nature qui a créé le parricide et l'anthropophagie,
et mille autres abominations que la pudeur et la délicatesse
nous empêchent de nommer. C'est la philosophie (je parle
de la bonne), c'est la religion qui nous ordonne de nourrir
des parents pauvres et infirmes. La nature (qui n'est pas
autre chose que la voix de notre intérêt) nous commande
de les assommer. Passez en revue, analysez tout ce qui est
naturel, toutes les actions et les désirs du pur homme na-
turel, vous ne trouverez rien que d'affreux. Tout ce qui est
beau et noble est le résultat de la raison et du calcul. Le
crime, dont l'animal humain a puisé le goût dans le ventre
de sa mère, est originellement naturel. La vertu, au con-
traire, est *artificielle*, surnaturelle . . . Le mal se fait sans ef-
fort, *naturellement*, par fatalité; le bien est toujours le produit
d'un art. (II, 715-16)

That weighty prelude commends "la haute spiritualité de la
toilette." To justify his preference for the artificial over the nat-
ural, Baudelaire lays bare the single base of his ethic and his
aesthetic: "le bien est toujours le produit d'un art." That view of
nature underlies his conception of the dandy.[48] What is good is
artificial and the artificial is what the will and the imagination
create. To see those faculties as instruments of compensation for
other, natural, faculties, is, on the one hand, to see human beings
as divided and alienated (and solitude is the most prominent
characteristic of Baudelaire's dandy). But his dandy is, on the
other hand, a figure for the integrity of action: since every act
is submitted to the scrutiny of the will and the imagination, it is
at once moral and aesthetic. The dandy, physically, morally, and
socially the result of his own unaided creation, who must live
day and night as though in front of a mirror, embodies the
morality that Baudelaire derives from his view of nature. He
invents, performs, and judges his own actions: "Le dandysme,
qui est une institution en dehors des lois, a des lois rigoureuses"

Le dandysme . . . Dandyism, which is an institution outside the law, has a rigorous
code of laws (C, 419). . . . a kind of cult of the ego . . . the symbol of the aristocratic
superiority of his mind . . . but a dandy can never be a vulgar man. . . . If he
were to commit a crime, he might perhaps be socially damned, but if the crime
came from some trivial cause, the disgrace would be irreparable (C, 420).

(II, 709). The dandy practises "une espèce de culte de soi-même," and an interest in dress is only "un symbole de la supériorité aristocratique de son esprit" (II, 710). He is "l'homme supérieur" (I, 689), by definition incapable of being commonplace: "Mais un dandy ne peut jamais être un homme vulgaire. S'il commettait un crime, il ne serait pas déchu peut-être; mais si ce crime naissait d'une source triviale, le déshonneur serait irréparable" (II, 710-11).

Dandyism's "rigorous laws" entail a number of judgments of value. The dandy, for instance, has a good deal in common with the criminals and the rebels of Baudelaire's poems, the "race de Caïn," for instance, or "Don Juan aux Enfers." Those figures create their uncommonness: "Saint Pierre a renié Jésus . . . il a bien fait!" (I, 122). Artificially produced sensation is good (*les paradis artificiels*); woman, on the other hand, is not good, and Baudelaire's misogyny is staggering:

> La femme est le contraire du Dandy.
> Donc elle doit faire horreur.
> La femme a faim et elle veut manger. Soif, et elle
>   veut boire.
> Elle est en rut et elle veut être foutue.
> Le beau mérite!
> La femme est *naturelle*, c'est-à-dire, abominable.
> Aussi est-elle toujours vulgaire, c'est-à-dire le
>   contraire du Dandy. (I, 677)

The imagination itself, the *reine des facultés* (her implied sex notwithstanding), is an artificializer: the heart contains passion, Baudelaire writes in the line Wilde quotes, but the imagination alone contains poetry.[49] Realism, for Baudelaire, has an undoubtedly dangerous character: the "natural poet," he says, is almost a "monster." "Le goût exclusif du Vrai . . . opprime ici et étouffe le goût du Beau." It is an element of progress, of "la domination progressive de la matière" (II, 616). The public re-

---

La femme . . . Woman is the contrary of the Dandy. Therefore she must be repulsive. She is hungry and she wants to eat. Thirsty, and she wants to drink. She is in heat and she wants to be screwed. And that's all she's good for. Woman is *natural*, therefore abominable. Thus she is always vulgar, that is to say the contrary of the Dandy.

Le goût . . . Our exclusive taste for the true . . . oppresses and smothers the taste for the beautiful . . . the progressive domination of matter (C, 294).

quires progress, admires realism, and contributes to the debasement of art:

> De jour en jour l'art diminue le respect de lui-même, se prosterne devant la réalité extérieure, et le peintre devient de plus en plus enclin à peindre, non pas ce qu'il rêve, mais ce qu'il voit. Cependant, *c'est un bonheur de rêver.* . . . (II, 619)

Baudelaire names two kinds of artist, the realist or, as he prefers to call him, the positivist, who says, "Je veux représenter les choses telles qu'elles sont, ou bien qu'elles seraient, en supposant que je n'existe pas" and the *imaginatif*, who says, "Je veux illuminer les choses avec mon esprit et en projeter le reflet sur les autres esprits" (II, 627). Since nature contains neither color nor line (II, 752), the attempt to mirror nature is something other than art. Art imposes its order.

Baudelaire's view of nature and the perverse reasonableness of his justification of the artificial feeds Wilde's wit and his style. The mistake of modern "coloured" women, Lord Henry tells Dorian, is that "They paint in order to try and look young. Our grandmothers painted in order to try and talk brilliantly. *Rouge* and *esprit* used to go together."[50] They also nourish the argument of *Intentions*. Wilde's paradoxes—"The nineteenth century, as we know it, is largely an invention of Balzac," for instance[51]—are backed by a weight of argument similar to that preceding Baudelaire's praise of cosmetics, and they are achieved by an always-reasonable trivializing of the argument like that in the "Eloge." Wilde pushes this argument even further: while Baudelaire condemns nature for her amoralities, Wilde rejects her for her social imperfections. Wilde's nature is uncomfortable and unconscious, indifferent and unappreciative, the enemy of creation:

> Whenever I am walking in the park here, I always feel that I am no more to her than the cattle that browse on the slope, or the burdock that blooms in the ditch. Nothing is more evident than that Nature hates Mind. Thinking is the most

De jour . . . More and more, as each day goes by, art is losing in self-respect, is prostrating itself before external reality, and the painter is becoming more and more inclined to paint, not what he dreams, but what he sees. And yet *it is a happiness to dream* . . . (C, 297).

Je veux . . . I want to represent things as they are, or as they would be on the assumption that I did not exist. . . . I want to illuminate things with my mind and cast its reflection on other minds (C, 307).

unhealthy thing in the world, and people die of it just as they die of any other disease.[52]

Nature is undesigned, unintelligent, uninteresting, and so, since "the object of Art is not simple truth but complex beauty," as a method "realism is a complete failure."[53] Furthermore, it is dangerous: "if something cannot be done to check, or at least to modify, our monstrous worship of facts, Art will become sterile, and Beauty will pass away from the land,"[54] says Vivian in a phrase that echoes Baudelaire's remark about "Le goût exclusif du Vrai." Art, says Wilde, "takes life as part of her rough material, recreates it, and refashions it in fresh forms, is absolutely indifferent to fact, invents, imagines, dreams, and keeps between herself and reality the impenetrable barrier of beautiful style, of decorative or ideal treatment."[55]

"The Critic as Artist," which moves Wilde's artificializing aesthetic a step further, opens, as "The Decay of Lying" does, with an adaptation of the *Salon de 1846*, whose first section is titled, "A Quoi Bon la Critique?" "But, seriously speaking," Ernest says to Gilbert, "what is the use of art-criticism?"[56] Wilde constructs his dialogue on the ground of Baudelaire's, and Pater's, answers. The best criticism, Baudelaire writes in his *Salon*, "est celle qui est amusante et poétique," and, since a beautiful painting is "la nature réfléchie par un artiste," the best criticism will be "ce tableau réfléchi par un esprit intelligent et sensible" and the best "compte rendu d'un tableau pourra être un sonnet ou une élégie" (II, 418). To that proposition, Wilde applies "the logic of the imagination," and while the questions and answers of the dialogue come from Baudelaire, via Pater as well as directly, the imitated argument is in constant danger of inverting. As Ernest says, Gilbert treats the world as a "crystal ball": "You hold it in your hand, and reverse it to please a wilful fancy."[57] Wilde's self-referential argument is a wholly independent dream, and his critical strategy here, as in his use of the word "perfection," above, is infiltration. He simply attaches to "criticism" a definition that had belonged to "art." Everything in his argument is related, as by corollary, to the proposition that it is in criticism that creativity has its best life. Once the proposition is proved, Wilde's argument can dash to its conclusions; that denied, however, nothing would work. Asserting it, Wilde needs only a *mot* to deal

est celle . . . translated above, p. 114.

with the vexed question of the unity of the arts. Since the critic, as he says in the "Preface" to *Dorian Gray*, is "he who can translate into another manner or a new material his impression of beautiful things," he will simply swallow all the arts: he "reproduces the work that he criticises in a mode that is never imitative . . . and, by transforming each art into literature, solves once for all the problem of Art's unity."[58] The possibility of "translation" of one art into another is simply a derivation from the main assertion. So is Wilde's ranking of painterly virtues: like Pater in "The School of Giorgione," he notes the proper separateness of the arts—"the domain of the painter is . . . widely different from that of the poet," Gilbert says—and, like both Pater and Baudelaire, he concludes that pictures taking literary or historical subjects are "too intelligible" and "rank with illustrations." That is because the best art is evocative, of course. But for Wilde, evocative art is best because it stimulates the critic's creativity, causing him to "brood and dream and fancy," and Wilde's critic is attracted most to works "that possess the subtle quality of suggestion, and seem to tell one that even from them there is an escape into a wider world."[59]

At times, Wilde pushes his sources into parody. The "true critic," as he is reborn here, has some of the qualities of caricature, since, as Wilde would not rush to deny, he has been moved beyond a self-scrutiny that is an attempt to account for the effects of the world to a doctrinaire self-centeredness. This argument, of course, makes art stand in relation to criticism as Lord Arthur Savile's "crime" stands in relation to his future—as the logically necessary outcome of mistaken premises. To believe Wilde now, we must believe not only that Balzac invented the nineteenth century and that Whistler took modern London out of his side, but also that symbolism leapt into being to satisfy the need of Wilde's true critic to brood. (When Ernest protested in this same line, Gilbert, that "critical spirit," replied, "The one duty we owe to history is to rewrite it.")[60]

In any case, Wilde's critic, though for reasons not exactly like Baudelaire's, prefers precisely the kind of art Baudelaire had defined and praised. It is not necessary to refer to the later symbolists, nor even to Huysmans, to find Wilde's aesthetic principles expressed in a critical prose he knew well enough to quote from. His Pateresque critical points are firmly and consciously rooted in Baudelaire, and, while the idea of "suggestion" may have come to him *via* "Leonardo da Vinci," or "The School of Giorgione," it came to him *from L'Art Romantique*. Baudelaire, as I have mentioned in my discussion of Pater's borrowings, writes that he often evaluates a painting "uniquement par la somme d'idées ou de rêveries qu'il apportera dans mon esprit," and in a passage I have already quoted from what Gautier called his most remarkable pages of criticism, he admires Delacroix as the most suggestive of painters, whose work stimulates the poetic thought and the affective memory of its appreciator. Wilde makes those texts his own, and in "The Critic as Artist," where he uses them best, he makes an inexplicit acknowledgment of them by evoking what Baudelaire had written on *Tannhäuser*. Baudelaire's essay, it will be remembered, outlines his idea of criticism as "translation," comparing his version of Wagner to Berlioz's and Liszt's for the purpose of demonstrating both that in the arts there is always "une lacune complétée par l'imagination de l'auditeur" (II, 782) and that "la véritable musique suggère des idées analogues dans des cerveaux différents" (II, 784). It is, he says, "le propre des oeuvres vraiment artistiques d'être une source inépuisable de suggestions" (II, 794). Wilde's dreamy acknowledgment illustrates Baudelaire's critical propositions by using Baudelaire's example. He gathers the various perspectives into one voice, but he submits *Tannhäuser*, as Baudelaire had done, to a series of imaginative transformations or "translations":

> Sometimes, when I listen to the overture to *Tannhäuser*, I seem indeed to see that comely knight treading delicately on the flower-strewn grass, and to hear the voice of Venus calling to him from the caverned hill. But at other times it speaks to me of a thousand different things, of myself, it may be, and my own life, or of the lives of others whom one has loved and grown weary of loving, or of the passions that man has known, or of the passions that man has not known, and so has sought for. To-night it may fill one with that ΕΡΩΣ ΤΩΝ ΑΔΥΝΑΤΩΝ, that *Amour de l'Impossible*, which

uniquement . . . solely by the sum of ideas or dreams that it brings to my mind.
une lacune . . . a gap, bridged by the imagination of the hearer (C, 328).
la véritable . . . true music suggests similar ideas in different minds (C, 330).
le propre . . . the peculiar mark of really artistic works to be an inexhaustible source of ideas (C, 341).

falls like a madness on many who think they live securely
and out of reach of harm, so that they sicken suddenly with
the poison of unlimited desire, and, in the infinite pursuit
of what they may not obtain, grow faint and swoon or stum-
ble. To-morrow, like the music of which Aristotle and Plato
tell us, the noble Dorian music of the Greek, it may perform
the office of a physician, and give us an anodyne against
pain, and heal the spirit that is wounded, and "bring the
soul into harmony with all right things."[61]

That passage follows directly on Gilbert's remarks about Pater's
Mona Lisa. The juxtaposition is telling.

Wilde's critical argument leans heavily in the direction of com-
plete subjectivity, of course: that is the point of his most arresting
critical reversal—"the primary aim of the critic is to see the object
as in itself it really is not." His emphatic "suggestiveness" is the
major force in his argument for the independence of both art
and criticism: by it he both joins Pater's opposition to Arnold
and goes beyond it to exempt both art and criticism from social,
moral, or mimetic duty. In the critical dialogues Wilde's "sugges-
tiveness" is often less a defining quality of art than an escape-
clause for the critical argument, a mere assertion of criticism's
freedom from any responsibility at all. It is witty but circular,
opposing contradiction by simple denial. Since art to be art must
suggest, Wilde seems to say, why art of course will suggest. The
crystal ball in Gilbert's hands, complete, intact, and separate,
aptly represents the argumentative circle. But Wilde's position
perfectly exemplifies his historical doubleness: his "suggestive-
ness," which is entirely compatible with the inward drift of "the
French school of *Symbolistes*," as he calls them in *Dorian Gray*,[62]
is firmly rooted in the pre-symbolist balances. While the subjec-
tivity of *Intentions* gives Wilde a place near the end of the de-
velopmental line that Eliot drew from Poe to Valéry, its justifying
texts connect it solidly to the beginning. The voices speaking
over Wilde's illustrations of the method he commends—Pater's
in the description of the *Mona Lisa* and Baudelaire's in the de-
scription of *Tannhäuser*—are made to support a degree of in-
wardness to which they would not themselves have subscribed.

Wilde supports his late symbolist "suggestion" by invoking a
familiar metaphysical dualism. The critical dialogues, like *Dorian
Gray*, announce his preference for an art that is neither singly

realistic nor singly idealistic, but a fusion of those antitheses, and he attaches that aesthetic preference to a repeated assertion about the relation of spirit and sense. In *Dorian Gray* the matter is central—it is the book's subject—but in the critical dialogues the metaphysical speculations seem to be merely obligatory, part of the identifying decoration of the argument. The aesthetic of "suggestiveness," however, emerges from familiar considerations:

> This is the reason why music is the perfect type of art. Music can never reveal its ultimate secret. This, also, is the explanation of the value of limitations in art. The sculptor gladly surrenders imitative colour, and the painter the actual dimensions of form, because by such renunciations they are able to avoid too definite a presentation of the Real, which would be mere imitation, and too definite a realization of the Ideal, which would be too purely intellectual.[63]

That is, of course, one of Baudelaire's main arguments—"Trop particulariser," he writes, "ou trop généraliser empêchent également le souvenir" (II, 455)—and Pater's presence in Wilde's remarks is equally obvious.

Wilde's critical reversals depend on the important paradox he took from Pater, that art must seem to have no matter at all, or at the very least that its effect must be separate from its content, at the same time as it must be concrete and specific. That contradictory requirement justifies both his Pateresque search for a resolving middle ground in the conflict between spirit and senses, and his romance of individualism. The argument may lack passionate conviction in the critical dialogues, but it keeps Wilde identifiably in the line of Pater, as is its purpose:

> Who, as Mr. Pater suggests somewhere, would exchange the curve of a single rose-leaf for that formless intangible Being which Plato rates so high? What to us is the Illumination of Philo, the Abyss of Eckhart, the Vision of Böhme, the monstrous Heaven itself that was revealed to Swedenborg's blinded eyes? Such things are less than the yellow trumpet of one daffodil of the field, far less than the meanest of the visible arts; for, just as Nature is matter struggling into mind,

Trop particulariser . . . Too much attention to detail or too much generalization alike interfere with memory . . . (C, 77).

so Art is mind expressing itself under the conditions of
matter, and thus, even in the lowliest of her manifestations,
she speaks to both sense and soul alike. To the aesthetic
temperament the vague is always repellent. The Greeks
were a nation of artists, because they were spared the sense
of the infinite. Like Aristotle, like Goethe after he had read
Kant, we desire the concrete, and nothing but the concrete
can satisfy us.[64]

In *Dorian Gray*, however, where Wilde dramatizes that same
Pateresque question, it does engage his serious and even pas-
sionate attention. That book owes as much or more to *Marius
the Epicurean* and *Gaston de Latour* as to *A Rebours*, and what it
owes to each of them is heavily Baudelairean as well. Lord Henry
Wotton gives a new incarnation to Pater's (now Wilde's) "aesthetic
critic" (as several writers on Wilde have noted), and, until the
murder of Basil Hallward, Dorian himself moves through the
dilemmas of Pater's allegorical heroes. Like Marius, he probes
the questions of existence, undergoes a *nuit blanche* that brings
him *almost* to Catholicism, and comes, finally, to the "Conclu-
sion" of *The Renaissance* in almost the very words in which Pater
wrote it:

> [the new Hedonism] was to have its service of the intellect,
> certainly; yet, it was never to accept any theory or system
> that would involve the sacrifice of any mode of passionate
> experience. Its aim, indeed, was to be experience itself, and
> not the fruits of experience, sweet or bitter as they might
> be. Of the asceticism that deadens the senses, as of the vulgar
> profligacy that dulls them, it was to know nothing.[65]

Even though Wilde pushes them almost to the point of parody,
the symbols and the pattern of Dorian's development are basi-
cally those of Gaston or Marius. Wilde intensifies them by ex-
aggerating them and by making the Eden story shine through
them. Dorian, the very picture of innocence, is tempted by the
"aesthetic" Lord Henry in the garden of Basil Hallward; the
temptation reveals Dorian to himself; after that self-knowledge
he can have no peace. In a retrospective moment, after reading
the "yellow book," Dorian renews his loyalty to Lord Henry's
Hedonism, in the service of which he attempts to discover pre-
cisely what Gaston, affected by Ronsard, must discover for his

salvation: "He sought to elaborate some new scheme of life that would have its reasoned philosophy and its ordered principles, and find in the spiritualizing of the senses its highest realization" (130).

But chapter eleven, in which Wilde brings Dorian to his imitated crisis of conscience, is also where he details his protagonist's attempts to emulate the "young Parisian" (125) of the "yellow book." It is to the "yellow book" that Wilde duly attributes what in the novel he calls Dorian's poisoning (146). The "yellow book" is central, both literally and figuratively, to both Wilde's novel and Dorian Gray's life, and it serves several of the complicated purposes of Wilde's design. In the first place, it is presented as the antithesis not merely to realism but to reality. Wilde places his description of its style side by side with an especially chilling example of realistic reporting, the *St. James's Gazette* account of the inquest into the death of Sibyl Vane. When he read it, Dorian "frowned, and, tearing the paper in two, went across the room and flung the pieces away. How ugly it all was! And how horribly real ugliness made things!" (124). Wilde lays his description of the "yellow book" beside that: "The style in which it was written was that curious jewelled style," he writes, "vivid and obscure at once, full of *argot* and of archaisms, of technical expressions and of elaborate paraphrases, that characterizes the work of some of the finest artists of the French school of *Symbolistes*" (125). That is decidedly not "ugly," decidedly not "real." Then, the book is also a satisfying item in Wilde's system of reversals: it effects Dorian's second loss of innocence, which occurs not in a garden but in a library, and not by means of forbidden fruit but by means of "metaphors as monstrous as orchids, and as subtle in colour" (125). Finally, the "yellow book" supplies a large slice of the life of Dorian Gray, who meets it just after Sybil Vane's death and does not emerge from his passionate imitation of its protagonist until just before the murder of Basil Hallward. "For years," chapter eleven begins, "Dorian Gray could not free himself from the influence of this book" (126). The detailed account of Dorian's imitation of the "young Parisian" is a kind of displaced aesthetic autobiography suspending the action of Wilde's novel. This book within a book is an exceptionally useful narrative trick by which Wilde is able at once to expand upon the spiritual development of his protagonist and to suspend the dramatic account of his life of action. Gilbert's question (which is, incidentally, his introduction to the description of *Les Fleurs du Mal*)—"are there not books that can make us live more in one single hour than life can make us live in a score of shameful years?"—is answered here.[66]

The "yellow book" is usually identified as *A Rebours*: there is no doubt that Huysmans's Des Esseintes contributes to the making of "the young Parisian," and I shall discuss him in this light below. But, as Rodney Shewan has pointed out, Wilde wrote in a letter that "The book that poisoned, or made perfect, Dorian Gray does not exist; it is a fancy of mine merely."[67] This is self-evidently not entirely true—Des Esseintes is evidence to the contrary—but what Wilde had in mind for the "yellow book," as Isobel Murray has shown, was something altogether more composite than a simple imitation of *A Rebours*.[68] In this chapter Wilde elaborates two important ideas: that insincerity is "merely a method by which we can multiply our personalities" and that "one had ancestors in literature, as well as in one's own race." The chapter, which solves a problem in fiction by tucking away several of the difficult years of Dorian's life, is also more like Wilde's critical writing than anything else in this idea-burdened story. In it Dorian enacts the principles of "The Decay of Lying" and "The Critic as Artist," even as Wilde's narrative echoes their phrases. The comment about insincerity, for instance, comes from "The Critic as Artist": Dorian, Wilde says, "used to wonder at the shallow psychology of those who conceive the Ego in man as a thing simple, permanent, reliable, and of one essence. To him, man was a being with myriad lives and myriad sensations, a complex multiform creature that bore within itself strange legacies of thought and passion" (143). The comment, which is related to Dorian's *Darwinismus* fling, leads to his speculations about his own heredity: he peruses his own family past with a genetically deciphering eye, recognizing in this or that predecessor this or that quality in himself. Similarly, he imagines "the young Parisian" as "a kind of prefiguring type of himself" (127) in literature, and he manages to discover bits of himself in various characters of historical literature.

Those reflections, on the "complex multiform" character of the Ego, on psychological heredity, and on intellectual inheritance, are relevant to the construction of chapter eleven and to Wilde's conception, or "fancy," of the corrupting book. The chapter is made up of shored fragments: Dorian is personality, multiplied; and the "yellow book" is itself anthological, composed of the texts comprising Wilde's own tradition. While the aesthetic occupations of the "yellow book," and its curious collections of information—about stones or musical instruments or perfumes—are, as Isobel Murray shows, collected from an accidental range of sources, "from books [Wilde] had reviewed and enjoyed," its focus is clear. It is an index to some of the texts in which Wilde's own literary and personal preoccupations are to be found defined. It functions as a kind of missal for Dorian's "worship of the senses" (130).

Although chapter eleven is constructed on a Darwinian frame, Dorian's perusal of his past is presented aesthetically: "He loved to stroll through the gaunt cold picture-gallery of his country house," Wilde writes, "and look at the various portraits of those whose blood flowed in his veins" (143). The picture gallery gives Wilde a fine joke—the *picture* of Dorian Gray has ancestors, too, and in this novel pictures breed pictures and books breed books—but the action also makes Dorian a critic of art, and it joins him to a recognizable and distinguished company of gallery strollers. His critical action, furthermore, like Pater's and like Wilde's in his dialogues, is appropriation. When Dorian confronts these pictures he wants precisely to know, what is this picture to *me*? "Was it young Herbert's life that he sometimes led?" he wonders. "Had some strange poisonous germ crept from body to body till it had reached his own?" (143). Lines of descent are the subject of this chapter, in which Dorian reaches back over the past to recover the identifying elements of the present. It is an act of self-analysis, and it shows Dorian to be compound, familiar. The art gallery of his country house cannot fail to recall the pictures on the walls of Ronsard's study, and it has some of the same functions. Wilde makes the physical descent of Dorian Gray parallel an idea of his mental descent. "Yet one had ancestors in literature," he writes, "as well as in one's own race, nearer perhaps in type and temperament, many of them, and certainly with an influence of which one was more absolutely conscious" (144). These, too, are parts of the "complex multiform creature." Dorian's identification with figures of the past, "the awful and beautiful forms of those whom Vice and Blood and Weariness had made monstrous or mad" (145), even though it is an identification at secondhand ("an abstraction from an abstraction," as Pater might have said), is a mockery of the idea of tradition: it might have found a place in Swinburne's Clouet poem about "Les Eclaireurs." Wilde's own tradition, however, separate from Dorian's, is also clearly one of the collections in chapter eleven.

The "yellow book" chapter focuses on the relation between the spirit and the senses. Wilde treats that, too, as a reversal, since it is "the worship of the senses" to which Dorian devotes himself, and the phrase provides some of the dramatic action of the chapter. Dorian's pleasures include attending Mass and miming pious behavior, and, later, indulging his "passion . . . for ecclesiastical vestments" (139). His "worship of the senses," however, is chiefly literary, and by paradox it results in his domination by a book and is expressed in voices derived from literature. The enactment of Dorian's sensual adventures is shadowy and minimal.

Pater is the paramount force in Wilde's treatment of the "senses" through literature (Lord Henry's "new Hedonism" comes from him),[69] but he is joined here by other familiar voices. The very mention of "the worship of the senses" evokes Gautier, whose *Mademoiselle de Maupin* Swinburne had praised as the "golden book of spirit and sense," and who is duly present in the roll call of chapter eleven, a representative with Dorian of those for whom " 'the visible world existed' " (129). Huysmans is important because of Des Esseintes' program for dislocating his senses to produce unusual mental or spiritual states. Baudelaire is present here, too, called into the company by allusion. Wilde's use of *Tannhäuser* evokes him: Dorian, he writes, wearied of his fantastic musical instruments, "would sit in his box at the Opera, either alone or with Lord Henry, listening in rapt pleasure to 'Tannhäuser,' and seeing in the prelude to that great work of art a presentation of the tragedy of his own soul" (135). Rodney Shewan, who hears an allusion to Swinburne in those lines, speculates that Wilde was thinking of him "as much as, if not more than" Wagner.[70] In his *Notes on Poems and Reviews*, to which Shewan refers, Swinburne names Baudelaire as the better maker, more able than he is himself to express his conception of the antique Venus. Wilde very likely had Baudelaire in mind, too, since it is he who, in the pamphlet Wilde knew very well (see above, pp. 159-60, hears in the prelude to *Tannhäuser* the tragic confrontation of spirit and sense. The opera, he writes, "re-

représente . . . represents the struggle between the two principles that have

présente la lutte des deux principes qui ont choisi le coeur humain pour principal champ de bataille, c'est-à-dire de la chair avec l'esprit, de l'enfer avec le ciel, de Satan avec Dieu. Et cette dualité est représentée tout de suite, par l'ouverture, avec une incomparable habileté" (II, 794). In Baudelaire's own prose work *La Fanfarlo* (which, like *Dorian Gray*, is about nature and artifice), Samuel Cramer, the poet-protagonist, burns two candles, one in front of a volume of Swedenborg and the other in front of "un de ces livres honteux dont la lecture n'est profitable qu'aux esprits possédés d'un gout immodéré de la vérité" (I, 555). *Tannhäuser*, Baudelaire writes, represents "l'idée mère, la dualité psychique constituant le drame" (II, 797): "Tout cerveau bien conformé porte en lui deux infinis, le ciel et l'enfer, et dans toute image de l'un de ces infinis il reconnaît subitement la moitié de lui-même" (II, 795).

Since Wilde's chapter eleven collects various key viewpoints on the relation of the spirit and the senses—from Pater, Huysmans, Gautier, Wagner, Baudelaire—it is no surprise to find that it incorporates specific reference to dandyism. "Fashion," Wilde writes, "by which what is really fantastic becomes for a moment universal, and Dandyism, which, in its own way, is an attempt to assert the absolute modernity of beauty, had, of course, their fascination for him." This comment is distilled from *Le Peintre de La Vie Moderne* and adapted from the *Salon* of 1846. Although Dorian begins with mere *fopperie*, far removed from the daring renunciations of Baudelaire's ideal, he goes on to serious, elaborately artificial dandyism. He creates himself, works on the material of his soul, sketches his life into a visible pattern, and lives, as Baudelaire prescribes, in front of a mirror. The idea central to Baudelaire's dandyism—that one makes one's mask with the perfect control of an artist—provides the rule in Wilde's world by which one can be Ernest in town and Jack in the country, and it also supports his darker theme of the double, of hidden or utterly reversible identity. In *Dorian Gray*, Wilde gives the idea the forceful literalness of Dorian's portrait.

---

chosen the human heart as their main battle-ground, the flesh and the spirit, hell and heaven, Satan and God. And this duality is immediately indicated by the overture with incomparable skill (C, 341).

un de ces . . . one of those shameful books the reading of which is profitable only to minds possessed of an immoderate taste for the truth . . . Every well-ordered brain has within it two infinities, heaven and hell; and in any image of one of these it suddenly recognizes the half of itself (C, 342).

The "yellow book" chapter of *Dorian Gray* is connected to Baudelaire by further threads which run through *A Rebours*. In that work Des Esseintes, too, has a book that he treats as a missal, a guide to the religion of art: it is the works of Baudelaire. Des Esseintes turns to it first in perusing his collection of modern works: he had had it printed, we are told, in "les admirables lettres épiscopales de l'ancienne maison Le Clere," and in "un large format rappelant celui des missels, sur un feutre très léger du Japon, spongieux, doux comme une moelle de sureau et imperceptiblement teinté, dans sa blancheur laiteuse, d'un peu de rose." His copy is printed in the "noir velouté d'encre de Chine," and it has been "vêtue en dehors et recouverte en dedans d'une mirifique et authentique peau de truie choisie entre mille, couleur chair, toute piquetée à la place de ses poils et ornée de dentelles noires au fer froid, miraculeusement assorties par un grand artiste." (Dorian Gray, it will be remembered, "procured from Paris no less than nine large-paper copies of the first edition [of his 'yellow book'], and had them bound in different colours, so that they might suit his various moods and changing fancies" (126-27).

Des Esseintes' admiration for Baudelaire is "sans borne." While other literary analyses of humanity had rested content with "spéculations mauvaises ou bonnes, classifiées par l'Eglise," with "la simple investigation, l'ordinaire surveillance d'un botaniste qui suit de près le développement prévu, de floraisons normales plantées dans la naturelle terre," Baudelaire had gone below the surface and beyond the limits. He had descended "jusqu'au fond de l'inépuisable mine, s'était engagé à travers des galeries abandonnées ou inconnues, avait abouti à ces districts

les admirables . . . the admirable episcopal type of the old house of Le Clere, in a large format similar to that of a mass-book, on a very light Japanese felt, a bibulous paper as soft as elder-pith, its milky whiteness faintly tinged with pink. . . . a velvety China-ink black . . . dressed outside and lined inside with a mirific and authentic flesh-coloured pigskin, one in a thousand, dotted all over where the bristles had been and blind-tooled in black with designs of marvellous aptness chosen by a great artist (B, 146).

sans . . . knew no bounds (B, 146).

spéculations . . . speculations, good or bad, classified by the Church . . . the humdrum researches of a botanist who watches closely the expected development of ordinary flora planted in common or garden soil (B, 146).

jusqu'au . . . to the bottom of the inexhaustible mine, had picked his way along abandoned or unexplored galleries, and had finally reached those districts of the soul where the monstrous vegetations of the sick mind flourish (B, 146).

de l'âme où se ramifient les végétations monstrueuses de la pen-
sée."[71] As decadent poet *par excellence*, he had "révélé la psy-
chologie morbide de l'esprit qui a atteint l'octobre de ses sen-
sations; raconté les symptômes des âmes requises par la douleur,
privilégiées par le spleen; montré la carie grandissante des
impressions," and traced "toutes les phases de ce lamentable
automne, regardant la créature humaine."[72] He was able to see
more deeply than others into pain and evil: "A une époque où
la littérature attribuait presque exclusivement la douleur de vivre
aux malchances d'un amour méconnu ou aux jalousies de l'a-
dultère, il avait négligé ces maladies infantiles et sondé ces plaies
plus incurables, plus vivaces, plus profondes, qui sont creusées
par la satiété, la désillusion, le mépris, dans les âmes en ruine
que le présent torture, que le passé répugne, que l'avenir effraye
et désespère." *A Rebours* derives from Baudelaire an aesthetic of
evil which Wilde re-attaches to him, by allusion, in the last lines
of chapter eleven: "Dorian Gray had been poisoned by a book.
There were moments when he looked on evil simply as a mode
through which he could realize his conception of the beautiful"
(146-47). ("That an artist will find beauty in ugliness, *le beau dans
l'horrible*," Wilde wrote in "Mr. Whistler's Ten O'Clock," "is now
a commonplace of the schools, the argot of the atelier," so at-
taching Baudelaire's phrase from *Le Peintre de la Vie Moderne* [II,
722] to a much less weighty context than chapter eleven of *Dorian
Gray*.)[73]

There is one more important feature of family resemblance
between *Dorian Gray* and *A Rebours* that bears on Baudelaire.
Like Dorian, Des Esseintes is concerned, more than with any
other literary matter, with a selective tradition. When he makes
a critical examination of modern French literature, he concludes
that its masters are Baudelaire, Flaubert, de Goncourt, and Zola.

révélé la psychologie . . . laid bare the morbid psychology of the mind that has
reached the October of its sensations, and had listed the symptoms of souls
visited by sorrow, singled out by spleen; he had shown how blight affects the
emotions . . . every phase of this lamentable autumn, watching the human crea-
ture (B, 147).

A une époque . . . In a period when literature attributed man's unhappiness
almost exclusively to the misfortunes of unrequited love or the jealousies en-
gendered by adulterous love, he had ignored these childish ailments and sounded
instead those deeper, deadlier, longer-lasting wounds that are inflicted by satiety,
disillusion, and contempt upon souls tortured by the present, disgusted by the
past, terrified and dismayed by the future (B, 147-48).

These four, he writes, had "le mieux interné et le mieux pétri" his own spirit.[74] Among the four, Baudelaire has a special place as the precursor. Modern poetry—that is, *good* modern poetry—derives from him. Huysmans' concern for "antécédents" is explicit: Verlaine, he writes, "dérivait, sans croisement, de Baudelaire, surtout par le côté psychologique, par la nuance captieuse de la pensée, par la docte quintessence du sentiment," and Théodore Hannon "descendait du maître, surtout par le côté plastique, par la vision extérieure des êtres et des choses."[75] Only those poets, and Mallarmé, held any attraction for Des Esseintes, who came gradually to think of Hugo as sad and deaf, of Leconte de Lisle as unsatisfying, static, and cold, and even of Gautier as superficial, "constamment borné à réverbérer, avec une impersonnelle netteté, des alentours." He would, Huysmans writes, have exchanged all of their "tours de force" for one new and characteristic work by Baudelaire, "car décidément celui-là était à peu près le seul dont les vers continssent, sous leur splendide écorce, une balsamique et nutritive moelle!"[76]

Having found the moderns inadequate, Des Esseintes turns to Poe, underlining the connection between him and Baudelaire. The action is the one Eliot performs in *From Poe to Valéry*: this Baudelaire of *A Rebours*, like the later one, stands at the center. He opens an immense horizon, "inoubliables portes": his doctrine of correspondences provides the theory for some of Des Esseintes' more remarkable sensory disorientations; his psychological investigations are the model for significant literary truth; his style is the single nutritive marrow. All of that is significant context for *The Picture of Dorian Gray*. Baudelaire is present both by allusion and by analogue in Wilde's yellow book chapter, and,

le mieux . . . had captured and moulded Des Esseintes' imagination more than any others (B, 184).

dérivait . . . was directly descended from Baudelaire, without any cross-breeding, especially in his psychology, in the sophistical slant of his thought, in the skilled distillation of his feeling (B, 188).

descendait . . . his kinship with the master could be seen chiefly in the plastic side of his poetry, in his external view of people and things (B, 189).

constamment . . . always confined himself to sending back the image of his surroundings with impersonal precision (B, 189).

car . . . for the latter was without a doubt almost the only author whose verses, underneath their splendid shell, contained a balsamic and nutritious kernel (B, 190).

in this book of mirrors, Dorian's mimicking of Des Esseintes is a reflection of Des Esseintes' adoration of Baudelaire. The "yellow book" of Wilde's mere "fancy" draws lavishly on a study of Baudelaire as the grand progenitor.

Like everything else in his work, Wilde's Baudelaire is double, an aspect of both surface and symbol. He embellishes the surface of Wilde's works as part of their critical argument, providing, in *Le Peintre de la Vie Moderne*, in the *Tannhäuser* pamphlet, and the remarks on criticism, the means of Wilde's most important critical reversals. When Wilde finds Nature wanting and Style entirely fulfilling, as when he calls criticism the highest creation, he is deriving his argument from Baudelaire and making his own positions a kind of exacerbation of Baudelaire's. Those critical points come to him by the mediation of Swinburne and Pater, and he indicates his awareness that he is speaking as a member of the brotherhood. He joins a piece of Baudelaire to a bit of Swinburne, describes *Les Fleurs du Mal* in a voice he learned from Pater, or supports his argument about nature by referring to Baudelaire on Balzac and by quoting Swinburne's translation of Baudelaire. His procedure for the multiplication of personality, his conflation of voices, reaches an extreme in chapter eleven of *Dorian Gray*, where he piles up images of ancestry, joining his picture gallery to the parade of ancient Vices and to the composite "yellow book," and collecting together the genetic literary inheritance of his time. When Wilde, as Yeats said, passed on phrases as though they were a "password, sign or countersign,"[77] he was indicating not his "provincial" but his ideologically cosmopolitan character, as part of the tradition of which Baudelaire was, as Huysmans said, "maître."

But Wilde found in Baudelaire more than the series of passwords that he positioned so carefully in the surface of his texts and more, even, than the critical ideas he sharpened into the paradoxes of *Intentions*. In "L'Héautontimorouménos," the self-executioner, he found a figure to express the tense and terrible doubleness of his own imagination. This figure, whom Wilde singles out for comment in his description of *Les Fleurs du Mal*, is related by antithesis to the dandy: like him, he results from what Baudelaire calls the tragic duality of man, but while the dandy contends with the duality by an exercise of will, imposing on his mind and body the immaculate order of intention and concentrating himself on his own surface, the self-torturer crumbles the will, undermines intention, and deprives action of significance. He suggests the instability of surfaces, the impossibility of singleness, and the insufficiency of intelligence. He is "un faux accord / Dans la divine symphonie, / Grâce à la vorace Ironie / Qui me secoue et qui me mord." That "voracious Irony" is inescapable—"Elle est dans ma voix, la criarde! / C'est tout mon sang, ce poison noir!"—and it makes the self-torturer the helpless victim of his own solipsism:

> Je suis la plaie et le couteau!
> Je suis le soufflet et la joue!
> Je suis les membres et la roue,
> Et la victime et le bourreau!
>
> Je suis de mon coeur le vampire,
> —Un de ces grands abandonnés
> Au rire éternel condamnés,
> Et qui ne peuvent plus sourire!
> (I, 78-79)

His self-absorption makes him cruel: he inflicts pain "sans colère, / Et sans haine," to produce feeling.

Wilde first imitated this figure, as Enid Starkie noted, in "Humanitad," which appeared in *Poems* (1881) and which laments the broken unity of body and spirit and the shattered harmony of all "separate existences" with "one supreme whole."[78] The poem is written against Wordsworth, from whom it takes some of its terms, and it allegorizes the failure of the English romantic tradition. "There was a time when any common bird / Could make me sing in unison," Wilde writes, "a time / When all the strings of boyish life were stirred / To quick response or more melodious rhyme / By every forest idyll." But that time has passed, he says, and he has taken "discontent to be [his] paramour" and tainted nature's wine with "the salt poison of his own

un faux . . . a dissonant chord in the divine symphony, thanks to the insatiable irony that mauls and savages me. That spitfire is in my voice, all my blood has turned into her black poison.

Je suis . . . I am both the wound and the knife, both the blow and the cheek, the limbs and the rack, the victim and the torturer. I am my own heart's vampire, one of the thoroughly abandoned, condemned to eternal laughter, but who can never smile again (S, 159-60).

sans . . . without anger and without hate (S, 159).

despair." He asserts that meaning has drained away from both nature and learning, and records a retreat from the world to the mirror. The imagery in which he defines the new alienation strikingly foreshadows *The Picture of Dorian Gray*. The figure in whom he embodied it first, however, is the self-executioner: *he* represents the new age, in which "the grace, the bloom of things has flown" and in which soul and body no longer "blend in mystic symphonies." In the following lines Wilde superimposes "L'Héautontimorouménos" over the image of the suffering Christ:

But we have left those gentle haunts to pass
    With weary feet to the new Calvary,
Where we behold, as one who in a glass
    Sees his own face, self-slain Humanity,
And in the dumb reproach of that sad gaze
Learn what an awful phantom the red hand of man can raise.

O smitten mouth! O forehead crowned with thorn!
    O chalice of all common miseries!
Thou for our sakes that loved thee not has borne
    An agony of endless centuries,
And we were vain and ignorant nor knew
That when we stabbed thy heart it was our own real hearts
    we slew.

Being ourselves the sowers and the seeds,
    The night that covers and the lights that fade,
The spear that pierces and the side that bleeds,
    The lips betraying and the life betrayed;
The deep hath calm: the moon hath rest: but we
Lords of the natural world are yet our own dread enemy.

"Suffering," Wilde wrote in *De Profundis*, in which Baudelaire's name appears several times, "is the means by which we exist, because it is the only means by which we become conscious of existing."[79] For him Baudelaire was the poet of suffering and of the observation of suffering. In both "The Critic as Artist" and *De Profundis* he brackets Baudelaire's name with Dante's, and while the comparison was by this time common, Wilde meant it personally. The story about Charles Condor (who, drunk, plunged a pin up to its head into the muscle of his arm and then of his leg) and Wilde (who responded only with the observation,

"How interested Baudelaire would have been!") is probably not a fiction.[80]

That divided figure, the sufferer and the observer (a figure, therefore, for Christ), appears again and again in Wilde's work, but nowhere more vividly than in *Dorian Gray*, whose three main characters make up Wilde's analysis of tragically divided humanity. For Basil Hallward, it will be remembered, Dorian represents an ideal of unity, the very fusion whose loss is the subject of "Humanitad," and in which spirit and sense exist "symphonically." "Unconsciously he defines for me the lines of a fresh school," Hallward tells Lord Henry, "a school that is to have in it all the passion of the romantic spirit, all the perfection of the spirit that is Greek. The harmony of soul and body—how much that is! We in our madness have separated the two, and have invented a realism that is vulgar, an ideality that is void" (10). Hallward speaks there for Wilde, as well as for Gilbert, who wished to "avoid too definite a presentation of the Real, which would be mere imitation, and too definite a realization of the Ideal, which would be too purely intellectual"; but the "fresh school" he defines and examines takes its terms from the century, from Pater and Baudelaire and Wagner, whose works, Baudelaire wrote, "bien qu'ils révèlent un goût sincère et une parfaite intelligence de la beauté classique, participent aussi, dans une forte dose, de l'esprit romantique."

The picture of Dorian Gray tests Hallward's ideal; when it fails, he dies. When he sees the changed portrait—and expresses his "horror"—he becomes a "sick man." Dorian presses him in a bit of dialogue that issues as directly from "aesthetic" thought as anything in "The Critic as Artist":

> "Can't you see your ideal in it?" said Dorian, bitterly.
> "My ideal, as you call it . . ."
> "As you called it."
> "There was nothing evil in it, nothing shameful. You were to me such an ideal as I shall never meet again. This is the face of a satyr."
> "It is the face of my soul."
> "Christ! What a thing I must have worshipped! It has the eyes of a devil."
> "Each of us has Heaven and Hell in him, Basil," cried Dorian, with a wild gesture of despair. (157)

It is Basil Hallward, not Sibyl Vane, who embodies the idealistic proposition of *Dorian Gray*: his desire for the union of soul and body and for the fusion of aesthetic types is, as readers of Pater know, mere nostalgia, an aspiration after antiquity. When the portrait begins to conduct its own life, Wilde splits the fusion into an antithesis, leaving Dorian to wear the static, classically "perfect" portrait while the painted portrait registers the romantic "perfecting" of Dorian's individuality. Dorian's doubling presents the classical and romantic antithesis—very wittily indeed, giving us one of each to look at.[81] In *A Drama in Muslin*, which appeared in 1886, George Moore conducted a similarly ideological experiment, embodying the classical and the romantic as Pater had defined them in "Winckelmann," in the "beautiful" sister, Olive, and the "intelligent" sister, Alice. "But in the beauty of perfect proportions no soul exists," Moore writes, moving from description of Olive to an account of Alice, "the soul asserts itself in certain bodily imperfections of form, which, when understood, become irresistible charms." For Moore, as for Wilde, the "classical" was not adequate to the time; while Alice "had not a feature that was either regular or attractive," her face "was one of interest to the critical observer."[82]

The "colour element" of Wilde's changing—or perfecting— portrait is sin, of course, but since, in the aesthetic Wilde espouses, sin is primarily individuality, a departure from perfection, it is not necessary to suppose that Wilde has any literally satanic purpose in the dialogue I have just quoted.[83] His purpose is aesthetic: the art of the Greeks, Pater said in "Winckelmann," did not take sufficient account of "life, conflict, evil"; the art of the romantics, however, with its "strange flowers," did just that. Wilde is at pains to attach Dorian to that imagery of strange flowers. "His nature had developed like a flower," he writes, "had borne blossoms of scarlet flame" (54-55). The passage in which Dorian discovers the pleasures of self-scrutiny makes the flower imagery prominent, too:

> This portrait would be to him the most magical of mirrors. As it had revealed to him his own body, so it would reveal to him his own soul. And when winter came upon it, he would still be standing where spring trembles on the verge of summer. . . . Not one blossom of his loveliness would ever fade. Not one pulse of his life would ever weaken. Like the

gods of the Greeks, he would be strong, and fleet, and joy-
ous. (106)

But while the visible Dorian will be classically Greek, the portrait
will take its color from corruption, blooming as a flower of evil:
"The surface seemed to be quite undisturbed," Hallward dis-
covers, "and as he had left it. It was from within, apparently,
that the foulness and horror had come" (157). Lionel Johnson's
Latin poem, written to thank Wilde for a copy of *Dorian Gray*,
takes up the imagery:

> Avidly he loves strange loves,
> Savage with beauty
> Plucks strange flowers:
> The more his soul is darkened
> His face displays its brightness more,
> False, but how radiantly so![84]

Wilde details the effects of the failed ideal in his other two
characters, and his analysis of them embodies the novel's con-
nections with the tradition I have been discussing. Both Dorian
Gray and Lord Henry Wotton are crippled by self-consciousness:
both are pre-figured by "L'Héautontimorouménos"; both are
antecedents of Prufrock. Dorian's portrait, "the most magical of
mirrors," is the instrument of the obsessive self-inspection he
enacts on every visit to the old schoolroom, and it permits him
to become, literally, the self-executioner. Lord Henry's doubling,
less dramatically and less imagistically presented, is no less sig-
nificant. Wilde makes him into a self-scrutinizing scientist whose
topic of investigation is "Soul and body, body and soul." "To
become the spectator of one's own life," Dorian quotes him as
saying, "is to escape the suffering of life" (110). He begins as
the observer of himself, and he goes on to become the chilly
investigator of what he calls the "psychology" of others. He ob-
serves Dorian chiefly—his major function in the novel—but he
does so because of his attitude toward himself: "It often hap-
pened that when we thought we were experimenting on others
we were really experimenting on ourselves," Wilde writes (59).

Lord Henry and Dorian, both doubled creatures, have some
connection with Gautier's preface to the definitive edition of *Les
Fleurs du Mal*.[85] Lord Henry, the spectator of his own life, follows
a program remarkably like the one Gautier describes:

... il ne vit plus; il est le spectateur de la vie. Toute sensation lui devient motif d'analyse. Involontairement il se dédouble et, faute d'autre sujet, devient l'espion de lui-même. S'il manque de cadavre, il s'étend sur la dalle de marbre noir, et, par un prodige fréquent en littérature, il enfonce le scalpel dans son propre coeur. . . . A ce jeu longtemps soutenu, les nerfs s'irritent, le cerveau s'enflamme, la sensibilité s'exacerbe; et la névrose arrive avec ses inquiétudes bizarres, ses insomnies hallucinées, ses souffrances indéfinissables, ses caprices morbides, ses dépravations fantasques, ses engouements et ses répugnances sans motif, ses énergies folles et ses prostrations énervées, sa recherche d'excitants et son dégoût pour toute nourriture saine.[86]

Lord Henry is a similar scientist: taking up the same medical metaphor, Wilde makes the surgeon feel the effects of his own experiment:

He had been always enthralled by the methods of natural science, but the ordinary subject-matter of that science had seemed to him trivial and of no import. And so he had begun by vivisecting himself, as he had ended by vivisecting others. Human life—that appeared to him the one thing worth investigating. Compared to it there was nothing else of any value. It was true that as one watched life in its curious crucible of pain and pleasure, one could not wear over one's face a mask of glass, nor keep the sulphurous fumes from troubling the brain and making the imagination turbid with monstrous fancies and misshapen dreams. There were poisons so subtle that to know their properties one had to sicken of them. There were maladies so strange that one had to pass through them if one sought to understand their nature. (56-57)

... il ne vit ... he no longer lives; he is the spectator of life. All sensation becomes for him an incentive to analysis. Involuntarily he splits into two and, wanting another subject, becomes a spy on himself. If he lacks a cadaver, he lays himself out on the black marble slab, and by a feat frequent in literature, he plunges the scalpel into his own heart. ... Kept at this game for a long time, his nerves become irritated, his brain fevered, his sensibility exasperated; and nervous disorder ensues, with its strange worries, its hallucinatory sleeplessness, its undefinable anguishes, its morbid humours, its bizarre depravities, its motiveless infatuations and aversions, its mad energies and irritable prostrations, its search for stimulants and its disgust for all healthy nourishment.

The poisons and the mask of glass also appear in Gautier's defense of *Les Fleurs du Mal* as a book devoted to "la peinture des dépravations et des perversités modernes": some readers behave as though you are a poisoner if you describe the toxic pharmacy of the Borgias, he says, and some as though you can only read *Les Fleurs du Mal* wearing a mask of glass.[87]

Dorian's connection to the famous preface has to do with its literary portraiture. Gautier begins with two "portraits" of the young poet and then moves, in the pattern Ellen Moers noticed, to depiction of the poet old.[88] The first description of Baudelaire young is Gautier's own: it has in common with the early portrait of Dorian Gray its visual emphasis and its emphatic idealization. Gautier makes explicit the painterly quality of his description: the lips, he says, are "voluptueuses et ironiques comme les lèvres des figures peintes par Léonard de Vinci."[89] Then he quotes Banville, who is describing the portrait of Baudelaire by Emile Deroy:

> O rare exemple d'un visage réellement divin, réunissant toutes les chances, toutes les forces et les séductions les plus irrésistibles! Le sourcil est pur, allongé, d'un grand arc adouci, et couvre une paupière orientale, chaude, vivement colorée; l'oeil, long, noir, profond, d'une flamme sans égale, caressant et impérieux, embrasse, interroge et réfléchit tout ce qui l'entoure; le nez, gracieux, ironique. . . . La bouche est arquée et affinée déjà par l'esprit, mais à ce moment pourprée encore et d'une belle chair qui fait songer à la splendeur des fruits. Le menton est arrondi, mais d'un relief

la peinture . . . the painting of modern depravities and perversities.

voluptueuses . . . voluptuous and ironic like the lips of figures painted by Leonardo da Vinci.

O rare . . . Oh rare example of a really divine face, combining the best of all fortunate qualities, all types of strength and the most irresistible attractiveness. His eyebrow is pure, elongated, a wide soft arch, and it covers a warm, vividly colored oriental lid; his eye, long, dark, deep, with an unequalled spark, caressing and imperious, embraces, questions, and reflects everything that surrounds it; his nose, gracious, ironical. . . . His mouth is curved and already refined by his mind, but at this moment still dark red, its beautiful flesh recalling the splendour of fruit. His chin is round, but proudly carried, as powerful as Balzac's. The whole face is warmly, darkly pale, but beneath the pallor appear the pink tones of rich beautiful blood; a youthful beard, ideal, that of a young god, decorates it; his forehead, high, wide, magnificently drawn, is adorned by dark, thick and charming hair which, naturally waved and curled like that of Paganini, falls on the neck of an Achilles or an Antinous!

hautain, puissant comme celui de Balzac. Tout ce visage est d'une pâleur chaude, brune, sous laquelle apparaissent les tons roses d'un sang riche et beau; une barbe enfantine, idéale, de jeune dieu, la décore; le front, haut, large, magnifiquement dessiné, s'orne d'une noire, épaisse et charmante chevelure qui, naturellement ondulée et bouclée comme celle de Paganini, tombe sur un col d'Achille ou d'Antinoüs!

The portrait, Gautier warns, should not be taken too literally, since it is a "double idealization." The contrast in Gautier's preface is his own description of the poet old: it indicates a heavy penalty for early indulgence. In it Baudelaire is seen as aged before his time, paying the price for his beauty, his haschisch, his curiosity. That round, strong face is now "amaigrie et comme spiritualisée," the eyes are wide open, the lips mysteriously shut, appearing to keep sarcastic secrets. "Aux nuances jadis vermeilles des joues se mêlaient des tons jaunes de hâle ou de fatigue."[90] As in *Dorian Gray*, everything tends to debilitation.

When he was young, Wilde thought Gautier the "most subtle of all modern critics, most fascinating of all modern poets."[91] He is certain to have seen Gautier's essay; certain, furthermore, to have read, and with great care, *Gaston de Latour*; and very likely to have been familiar with the double portraiture in reminiscences of Baudelaire. It may be that these are implicated not only in the psychology of *Dorian Gray*, but also in its key dramatic device.

*   *   *

When he drew the first version of the "Toilette" for *Salomé*, Beardsley put *Les Fleurs du Mal* on the shelf under her cosmetic table, and he lettered the spine so that the title would be legible. The gesture is appropriate in two ways, one obvious, one not. The poems constituted an obvious part of Wilde's literary context, and they went into the making of Salomé: their presence on the shelf is an acknowledgment. Beardsley's drawing was suppressed because of its suggestiveness, and when he redrew Salomé fully clothed for the new "Toilette" he removed *Les Fleurs*

amaigrie . . . thin, as though spiritualized.
Aux nuances . . . With the formerly ruddy shades of the cheeks were mixed the yellow tones of suntan or exhaustion.

du Mal from her library. Beardsley's suppression notwithstanding, the early presence of Baudelaire's poems on Salomé's bookshelf is another indication of the insouciance with which Wilde attached himself to Baudelaire.[92] What Pater needed to bury, carefully, Wilde left available for inspection: his allusions to Baudelaire are not seriously secret and his thefts not very earnestly concealed. In his progress from Pater to Wilde, Baudelaire floated to the surface. The fact has meaning: between Pater and Eliot the habit of allusion changes utterly. Pater alludes for secrecy, in such a manner as to conceal the allusion from all but the select audience; Eliot alludes for quite other reasons, and he often attaches his allusions to explanatory comments. Between Pater and Eliot, allusion and echo become important formal facts. Wilde—whose habit of composition was to piece bits together but to make them appear to be one thing—is midway between.

Beardsley's inclusion of *Les Fleurs du Mal* in the drawing of Salomé's toilette also constitutes a joke: it was in Baudelaire that Wilde—and not only he—found a text claiming that cosmetics were an instrument of art and justifying "la haute spiritualité de la toilette." It is perfectly appropriate, and witty, to show Baudelaire's book under a table laden with cosmetic powers and in a drawing in which Salomé is nude. But the joke, like so many of Wilde's own, has a grim sub-surface: it was in Baudelaire's praise of cosmetics that Wilde discovered an equation of artificiality, dandyism, and good, on the one hand; and of nature, woman, and evil, on the other. When Salomé strips away veil after veil, she reveals, as Christopher Nassaar has argued, human nature:[93] but more than this it is female nature, the abominable, as it was for Baudelaire. Salomé unveiled stands in relation to her cosmetic, gilded, and veiled self as the altered portrait stands in relation to the portrait Basil Hallward painted, as "some foul parody, some infamous, ignoble satire." In this play Wilde's antithesis—the cosmetic, artificial woman and the natural, *abominable* woman—takes its terms from the texts that provided the argument (and also the sexual attributes of both art and nature) for "The Decay of Lying."

*   *   *

Wilde was, as he said in *De Profundis*, "a man who stood in symbolic relations to the art and culture of [his] age."[94] He became in England the very cliché of decadence, and he set out definitively the themes that would be written into literary history as those of the *fin-de-siècle*. When he took up Pater, he gave Baudelaire's ideas a wide currency; when he went directly to Baudelaire's works and cut from them, to use Rodney Shewan's metaphor, some of his best epigrams, he gave Baudelaire's name a glittering prominence.[95] Wilde wore Baudelaire everywhere— in what he wrote, in what he drank, in what he said. Arthur Symons records his famous remark to Beardsley, for instance: " 'Absinthe is to all other drinks what Aubrey's drawings are to other pictures: it stands alone: it is like nothing else: it shimmers like southern twilight in opalescent colouring: it has about it the seduction of strange sins. It is just like your drawings, Aubrey; it gets on one's nerves and is cruel. Baudelaire called his poems *Fleurs du Mal*, and I shall call your drawings *Fleurs du Péché*— flowers of Sin.' "[96] William Rothenstein wrote that Wilde wore a red waistcoat to honor Gautier, and Sherard that the same stylish and flamboyant imitativeness "prompted him at least to dally with the poisons that crushed Baudelaire into an inert, voiceless, if sentient mass; and as he had borrowed from Balzac his monkish cowl, from Victor Hugo the form of his paper, so from Baudelaire he took absinthe."[97]

That "romance of art," as Wilde called the relationship between Basil Hallward and Dorian Gray (12), helped to fix the image of Baudelaire. Almost all of Wilde's early memoirists are fascinated by his admiration for Baudelaire. Robert Sherard saw the influence of that "morbid" poet in "The Sphinx" and "The Harlot's House."[98] L.-F. Choisy noted that "Baudelaire a fourni la description de l'animal aux yeux fixes bordés d'or, au sourire subtil et à l'apparence langoureuse."[99] Edward Shanks wrote that "The Sphinx" could not have been written but for Baudelaire and Swinburne, and Holbrook Jackson thought that "The Harlot's House" and "The Sphinx" were "decadent in the sense that Baudelaire was decadent, from whom they inherit almost everything save the English in which they are framed."[100] To Frances Winwar "The Sphinx" seemed "chimerical, sensuous, perverted, evil—a *fleur du mal* transplanted to that innocent vale where the English poet saw only a host of golden daffodils."[101] Frances Winwar was right: Baudelaire had superseded Wordsworth.

Later poets, too, saw Wilde in "symbolic relations" to the time; and they repudiated him. Both Richard Aldington and W. H. Auden lamented the fact that he was taken as a spokesman for much better poets, made by the events of his life into the rep-

resentative of Art. His poems, Aldington points out, sold only
about 1,000 copies during his lifetime; but between 1911 and
1914 his *Selected Poems* "had a great vogue, passing through eight
impressions, of which the first two alone accounted for 30,000
copies."[102] As Aldington's own poetry shows, Wilde's verse was
influential. But Wilde, Aldington writes, "gave the British Phil-
istine his most resounding triumph and at a stroke undid the
patient work of two generations. . . . It may be said of him that
he contributed to prolong the barbarity of nations."[103] Auden
thought, too, that "in England and America, the Wilde scandal
had a disastrous influence, not upon writers and artists them-
selves but upon the attitude of the general public toward the
arts, since it allowed the philistine man to identify himself with
the decent man."[104] When Max Nordau published his giant pam-
phlet *Degeneration*, he dedicated it to Caesare Lombroso, turned
the clichés of science to literary analysis and evaluation, and gave
massive support to British, and for that matter to European,
philistinism. "Degenerates," he wrote, "are not always criminals,
prostitutes, anarchists, and pronounced lunatics; they are often
authors and artists." He certainly took Wilde as a spokesman:

> the doctrine of the 'AEesthetes' affirms, with the Parnas-
> sians, that the work of art is its own aim; with the Diabolists,
> that it need not be moral—nay, were better to be immoral;
> with the Decadents, that it is to avoid, and be diametrically
> opposed to, the natural and the true; and with all these
> schools of the ego-mania of degeneration, that art is the
> highest of all human functions.
>
> Here is the place to demonstrate the absurdity of these
> propositions.

Nordau traced the sickness which Wilde exemplified to France,
to the Parnassians, to Hugo, to Gautier, and, finally, to Baude-
laire: "We must stop there awhile," he says, "for Baudelaire is—
even more than Gautier—the intellectual chief and model of the
Parnassians, and his influence dominates the present generation
of French poets and authors, and a portion also of English poets
and authors, to an omnipotent degree."[105] When Wilde, that
"lord of language," became "a pariah and an outcast," he kept
Baudelaire in his company.[106]

André Gide's memoir of Wilde embodies the identification of
him and Baudelaire in its very form, perhaps not consciously.

Gide does not mention Baudelaire or any memoir of him, but he opens the second chapter of his *Oscar Wilde* with an antithesis between the poet old and the poet young. "Those who came into contact with Wilde only toward the end of his life have a poor notion, from the weakened and broken being whom the prison returned to us, of the prodigious being he was at first." But that sentence initiates a pattern we have seen before, and Gide moves on to details of a familiar kind: "It was in '91 that I met him for the first time. . . . He was rich; he was tall; he was handsome; laden with good fortune and honours. Some compared him to an Asiatic Bacchus; others to some Roman emperor; others to Apollo himself—and the fact is that he was radiant."[107]

Wilde himself, of course, had invited identification with Baudelaire at every stage of his career, and there is a sad appropriateness in his fascination by Baudelaire's suffering. "I do not think that a day passed on which we did not speak, and long, of these unhappy poets," Sherard writes, of the French tragic generation. "The very horror of their fates seemed to heighten for us the splendour of their genius, to call for our greater admiration and enthusiasm."[108] After his own humiliation, Wilde saw Baudelaire as a pattern for his exile: *De Profundis* identifies Wilde's mistakes with the noble errors of his heroes in art, and presents Baudelaire as a voice of the time, a symbol of the bitter victory of art:

> When Marsyas was "torn from the scabbard of his limbs" . . . he had no more song, the Greeks said. Apollo had been victor. The lyre had vanquished the reed. But perhaps the Greeks were mistaken. I hear in much modern Art the cry of Marsyas. It is bitter in Baudelaire, sweet and plaintive in Lamartine, mystic in Verlaine.

But in that self-justifying and self-condemning letter Wilde also makes Baudelaire a personal voice, quoting the last lines of "Un Voyage à Cythère":

> O Seigneur, donnez-moi la force et le courage
> De contempler mon corps et mon coeur sans dégoût.[109]

For Wilde, as for Baudelaire, those feelings were real.

O Seigneur . . . O heavenly Father, give me strength and courage to contemplate my heart and body without disgust! (S, 100).

4

SYMONS

THE GREAT PROBLEM:
TRUTH TO LIFE AND TRUTH TO ART

Arthur Symons's poetry can seem little more than a late skirmish in the art-for-art's-sake cause. Attacked on familiar grounds, he produced familiar defenses. When *London Nights* "was received by the English press with a singular unanimity of abuse," Symons placed himself in the line of Gautier and Swinburne: "I contend on behalf of the liberty of art."[1] "However you may try to convince yourself to the contrary," he said in 1896, "a work of art can be judged only from two standpoints: the standpoint from which its art is measured entirely by its morality, and the standpoint from which its morality is measured entirely by its art."[2] In France he reflected "that such a reception of a work of art would have been possible in no country but England,"[3] and to defense of art against moral tyranny he added Wilde-like praise of the artificial, saying that he could not of course expect what was much good to be much appreciated: art was beyond the capacity of the bourgeois.[4] All of this, added to his later delight in what he called "perverse" subjects, leads one critic to see his work as "conspicuously decadent," a fine example for teaching about the 'nineties.[5]

That summary encourages a significant blindness both about Symons and about the 'nineties: he is an innovator whose writing deserves to be seen as more than a handy illustration of collective obsessions. For him, the art-for-art's-sake argument had important new value and prepared for major achievements in early twentieth-century literature. He addressed the argument directly to the same moralistic assumptions as did his predecessors and contemporaries, but he carried it beyond those into attack on aesthetic assumptions. He took it for granted that the problem of "the good" had been dispatched and that poetry was no longer obliged to reflect the community's moral views; he turned his attention to the characteristically modern problem of knowing how to know "the true" and to redrafting the definition of "the beautiful." The direction in which he took the argument is consequential:

> There is no necessary difference in artistic value between a good poem about a flower in the hedge and a good poem about the scent in a sachet. I am always charmed to read beautiful poems about nature in the country. Only, personally, I prefer town to country. . . .[6]

Here, the substance of Wilde's paradoxes justifies the advance of Symons's poetry into urban territory. While Wilde, following Huysmans, took from Baudelaire the art of going deep, of making the invisible visible, Symons took from him the hints that are present in all of his calls to modernity—at the end of the *Salon* of 1846 or in *Le Peintre de la Vie Moderne*—and turned his attention both on himself and on the world, so that one result of Baudelaire's argument against nature is poetry about cosmetics and another is poetry about the life of great cities. In England, the predominance of that element in the great works of twentieth-century literature was prepared for partly by Symons. He is the first poet in England seriously to seize for poetry a subject matter already domesticated by the novel, but abandoned by poetry during the course of the eighteenth century, and the first to perceive in Baudelaire the techniques of a new poetic realism. His insistence that "modern" poetry must deal with "modern" subjects and his by no means insignificant attempts to discover means for treating those subjects comprise his most important poetic achievements. "Any attempt to extend the subject-matter of art is extremely distasteful to the public," Wilde wrote, "and yet the vitality and progress of art depend in a large measure on the continual expansion of subject-matter."[7] In his verse of the late 'eighties and early 'nineties, Symons prefigures the problems of, among others, the Imagists in the 1910's, and he clears the way for Eliot and Joyce.

Symons's career falls into three sharply distinct stages, and each gives him a place in this study. In the first—his best— Symons aims to define "modernity" in his criticism and to achieve it in his verse. This period, which produced both a wide-ranging critical review of contemporary literature in French and English and a good deal of poetry, ended with a spectacular departure, *The Symbolist Movement in Literature*, in which Symons recants his earlier poetic convictions. Then, in the second period, between *The Symbolist Movement* and his mental breakdown in 1908, Symons virtually abandoned poetry, setting himself instead the task of rendering the "modern" in flexible, fluid, and sensuous prose. Finally, in the long period following his breakdown, Symons wrote copiously—both poetry and prose—but not always coherently. All three of these stages of Symons's development entrench Baudelaire more deeply in the history of English poetry. In the first, when he was attempting to define "modernity" (and doing so in terms which quite precisely predict later writers), Symons treated Baudelaire both critically and poetically as an inexhaustible source of insight on the task of the arts in the modern world. In the second he made him the model for the kind of prose he now thought the right—perhaps the only possible—medium for modernity. And in the third he wrote incessantly about him: essay after essay, whatever its announced "subject," turns to him as the center of most intense interest. In this last stage, however, Symons's poetic interest narrows to obsession, and his Baudelaire becomes a grotesque, the Satanic figure who earned for Symons the sharp reproof of the new generation.

It was in the first part of his career that Symons affected most the course of English poetry. Up to about *The Symbolist Movement in Literature*, he devoted himself to becoming "modern." His "Notes and Impressions" on English writers, his first collection of critical essays, show his steady preoccupation. They are exploratory and tentative, aiming to discover both what modernity is and how it can be achieved:

> To be modern in poetry, to represent really oneself and one's surroundings, the world as it is to-day, to be modern and yet poetical, is, perhaps, the most difficult, as it is certainly the most interesting, of all artistic achievements.[8]

What made modernity difficult, Symons said, was that it bound the poet to two mutually excluding devotions, one to art and one to life. The old amity of the beautiful and the true had been shattered: while ideas of truth had changed, ideas of the beautiful remained the same. "Oneself and one's surroundings" were not fit embodiments of the old beauty. Like the Imagists, Symons felt pressed to devise conventions under which the two loyalties of the poet could be compatible. The simple art-for-art's-sake argument of Gautier and his followers was merely evasive, and for Symons evasion was no longer a possibility. Moreau's paintings, for instance (one of which is implicated in the inward horror of Salomé and Des Esseintes), seemed sheerly escapist:

> To such painters as [Burne-Jones and Moreau], beauty and the modern world are in open and inevitable war; life is a thing to be escaped from, not turned to one's purpose; let us paint pictures, they say, pictures of pictures.
>
> But to another, just now more acceptable, school of painters, the modern world is a thing to struggle with, to conquer in fair fight, to compel to one's purpose, no matter at what cost.[9]

Symons's "modernism" prescribed both a subject and a method, and both seemed to him to condemn poetry to a realism that would make independent art extremely hard to achieve. He described the conflict in a paragraph on James Thomson. (It might have been Aldington on Flint.)

> He was ahead of the fashion in aiming at what we now call modernity; his work is, in a certain sense, more modern than that of any other considerable writer in verse. But in regard to his actual success in so difficult an endeavour, it is not quite easy to define the precise measure of attainment. The great problem presented itself to him, as it does to every writer: how to be real, true to life, and yet poetic, true to art. Thomson never quite mastered the problem: how few have ever mastered it! More than most, he cared for the trivial details, the casual accidents, of 'Sundays out,' and shop-girls' dancing-halls; and he tried to get the full value out of these things by a certain crudity in his transference of them to the canvas. . . . For the real modernity we must turn to Degas; we find it in the new employment of a masterly and really classic art in the interpretation of just such actual things; the very race-horses, if you will, but how differently seen, and with what careful and expressive subtlety rendered! Thomson did much: he at all events caught the life at the moment of its movement; he was intensely vivid, amusing, and true to the lesser and more obvious truths of

Nature. But he did not realize that to be modern is of all
achievements the most difficult, that it requires the most
perfect command of oneself and one's material, consum-
mate art; and that here, more than elsewhere, a flaw, a lapse,
is fatal alike to the illusion and to the distinction of success.

This is a decisive statement: it suggests Symons's technical course
for one thing—his appropriation from painting of methods for
poetry—and it describes his early ideal (which is not unlike Basil
Hallward's), "the new employment of a masterly and really classic
art in the interpretation of just such actual things." His essay
concludes with a tidy summary of his demanding objective: "A
new subject, an individual treatment, a form which retains all
that is helpful in tradition, while admitting all that is valuable in
experiment; that, I think, is modernity becoming classical."[10]
    The two essential subjects of modernism as Symons saw it,
taking up the balance Wilde had abandoned, were "oneself and
one's surroundings": "sensation and nerves" and London. He
admired even the "foiled endeavours" of Thomas Gordon Hake
because his attempts to render sensation represented "a new kind
of poetry, in which science becomes an instrument in the creation
of a new, curious kind of beauty, the beauty, one might almost
say, of pathology." That poetry of pathology was, Symons said
elsewhere, "personal romance, the romance of oneself: just what
nine-tenths of the world never discover at all, even for private
use" and it is "made out of personal sensations, verse which is
half physiological."[11] At the same time, he admired Laforgue for
his triumph over the modern world, for the fact that "he sees,
not only as an imposition, but as a conquest, the possibilities for
art which come from the sickly modern being, with his clothes,
his nerves: the mere fact that he flowers from the soil of his
epoch."[12] *Modern Love* seemed exemplary to him because it
"[deals] modernly with what is essentially modern love—love in
its actual surroundings, in London, in Paris, with all that com-
plexity of self-analysis, of curious consideration, with which we
are so fatally dowered, at the end of this reflective irresolute
century."[13] And while Meredith and some of his followers
triumphed over the difficulties of rendering "oneself," W. H.
Henley made a conquest of the splendid material of "one's sur-
roundings": his poems

may be taken as a sort of manifesto on behalf of what is
surely a somewhat new art, the art of modernity in verse.

In the *London Voluntaries*, for instance, what a sense of the poetry of cities, that rarer than pastoral poetry, the romance of what lies beneath our eyes, in the humanity of streets, if we have but the vision and the point of view! Here, at last, is a poet who can so enlarge the limits of his verse as to take in London. And I think that might be the test of poetry which professes to be modern: its capacity for dealing with London, with what one sees or might see there, indoors and out.

In "Modernity in Verse" Symons casts about for an English example of the modern poet. A poet may choose the right subjects, yet fail to devise a manner for dealing with them: had Whitman "only possessed the art, as he possessed . . . the soul of poetry, it is possible that in him we should have found the typical modern poet"; Thomson "was a man of genius who never found the right utterance, but his endeavour was in the right direction." Browning gives hints of modernism in his "smaller and finer" poems; Meredith's *Modern Love* "almost realizes an ideal"; and Coventry Patmore "has achieved wonders." Henley alone among English poets has devised a music for modern verse: he has had "a wholesome but perilous discontent with the conventions of language and of verse," and what he has

> brought into the language of poetry is a certain freshness, a daring straightforwardness and pungency of epithet, very refreshing in its contrast with the traditional limpness and timidity of the respectable verses of the day. . . . with these unaccustomed words and tones Mr. Henley does certainly succeed in flashing the picture, the impression upon us, in realizing the intangible, in saying new things in a new and fascinating manner.[14]

Those points outline Symons's early inquiry into what would make "the modern world possible for art,"[15] and they articulate a problem that would compel the best attention of his successors, of Joyce, of Woolf, of Eliot in both his poetry and plays, and of the Imagists—the "great problem," as Symons encapsulated it, of "how to be real, true to life, and yet poetic, true to art." They also voice a fear lest in the modern world art may not be possible at all and a conviction that to achieve it would be a "triumph." In Symons, the problems of the nineteenth century are in transition: the language in which he expresses them, like the terms

in which he sees them, link him firmly with a generation to come
and dissociate him sharply from one that had passed. And, since
in his description of the possibilities that do exist for art in the
modern world he borrows solidly from Baudelaire, whose art he
saw as triumphant, Symons's critical labor has as one of its effects
the carrying forward of Baudelaire to the twentieth century in
English poetry. This Baudelaire of the fourth generation is,
again, new.

It is important to distinguish between the earlier Symons and
the later, between Symons as he worked out the problems of his
"modernity" and Eliot's Symons, who seemed a melodramatic
hangover from an indulgent and over-wrought decadence. For
this later Symons, Baudelaire became a kind of patron devil, but
while he was actually working out his own aesthetic, Symons saw
Baudelaire as the inventor of modern poetry, as the discoverer
of new sources of a beauty reconcilable with truth. A letter of
June 1889 refers to his "careful study of Baudelaire and James
Thomson," evidently texts for his study in modernity, and he
saw Baudelaire as the originator of the "poetry of pathology"
that he admired in Hake. "Essentially modern poetry may be
said to have begun in France," he wrote, "with Baudelaire." What
Baudelaire "invented" was a "perverse, self-scrutinizing, trou-
bled art of sensation and nerves."[16] That is of course the new
beauty of "The Decadent Movement":

> If what we call the classic is indeed the supreme art—those
> qualities of perfect simplicity, perfect sanity, perfect pro-
> portion, the supreme qualities—then this representative lit-
> erature of today, interesting, beautiful, novel as it is, is really
> a new and beautiful and interesting disease.[17]

That disease is a version of Pater's idea of the particular. Just
as Pater opposes the concrete to the abstract, the particular to
the general, Symons sets the "diseased" against the traditionally
perfect. Of course he does not intend his label as a condemna-
tion: "Healthy we cannot call [this new literature], and healthy
it does not wish to be considered."[18] "Strangeness" and "disease"
are the qualities of individuality, of what Wilde indeed called
"perfection." Symons thought that it was "one of the modern
discoveries that 'the dignity of the subject' is a figure of speech,
and a misleading one," and, quoting Baudelaire, he praised
Whistler for acting on that discovery, for adjusting his idea of

"the beautiful" to the subjects before him, to "fashionable women, drawing on their gloves in the simplest of daily attitudes, [to] children, standing in the middle of the floor as a child stands to be looked at, [to] men in black coats." What Whistler sought in those subjects was " 'l'étrangeté, qui est le condiment indispensable de toute beauté.' "[19] The addition of strangeness to beauty which (after Baudelaire and Pater and Wilde) Symons said was a characteristic of romantic and modern art, gave the sexual, psychological, self-analytical subjects of his modernism their theoretical justification.

Symons justified his other subject, "one's surroundings," partly on grounds of its variety and richness—to "haunt the strange corners of cities," he said, "to know all the useless, and improper, and amusing people who are alone very much worth knowing, . . . it is such things as these that make for poetry"[20]—and partly on grounds of its artificiality. "A city is no part of nature," he wrote. In London, he found "a peculiar interest in another part of what is artificial, properly artificial."[21] For that subject, too, Symons found a pattern in Baudelaire, who he said was, after Villon, the Poet of Paris.[22]

Symons was neither the only nor the first English poet of his century to take the city as his subject or to link it with Baudelaire. Swinburne's Cossu and Clouet comprise an ironic acknowledgment that this was Baudelaire's subject. In *Marius* Pater hints that he, too, saw the direction that poetry would take—"Life in modern London even, in the heavy glow of summer, is stuff sufficient for the fresh imagination of a youth to build its 'palace of art' of"—and in his review of Symons's *Days and Nights* he welcomes the modern subject matter that made "the rich poetic vintage of our time . . . run clear at last."[23] Wilde, who saw the aestheticized city as part of the artificiality of his art, modelled some of his descriptions of London on *Le Spleen de Paris*, and the inward gaze of Dorian Gray is counterpointed by glimpses of London, which stand against the spiritual mirror as a reminder that the visible world really does exist, after all. But Symons differs radically from these: Swinburne took the city as matter for parody but not for his serious verse; Pater always distanced his modernity in allegory; Wilde made it only a peripheral element of the artifice. For a time, Symons chose this modernism as his exclusive preoccupation, casting himself, as literally as it is possible for a poet to do, as *Le Peintre de la Vie Moderne*:

> I tried to do in verse something of what Degas had done in painting. I was conscious of transgressing no law of art in taking that scarcely touched material for new uses. Here, at least, was a *décor* which appealed to me, and which seemed to me full of strangeness, beauty, and significance.[24]

Degas, Symons said, actually *was* "the painter of modern life"; he achieved "the real modernity."[25] When he made Degas his model, Symons enacted with a rigorous literalness a program derived from Baudelaire's essay on Guys. What Pater had domesticated in English criticism, Symons appropriated for English poetry and prose.

His first three volumes of poems, *Days and Nights* (1889), *Silhouettes* (1892), and *London Nights* (1895), are emblazoned with his aggressive modernism. In them, especially in the first, Symons tackles the problems his criticism defines. *Days and Nights* everywhere declares its allegiances: its dedication invokes Pater ("In all gratitude and admiration"); its defensive epigraph summons Meredith's *Modern Love* ("These things are life: / And life, they say, is worthy of the Muse"); its contents include translations from Leconte de Lisle and Villiers de l'Isle-Adam; its poems expose their roots in Gautier and Swinburne. Some of its titles— "A Café-Singer," "The Opium-Smoker," "The Street-Singer"— identify its themes, some suggest the Impressionist painters, and others keep the French language as a persistent presence in the book, sometimes solid (as in "Scènes de la Vie de Bohème") and sometimes ghostly (as in "The Abandoned"). One poem, "The Temptation of Saint Anthony," is said to be "After a Design by Félicien Rops."[26] But in spite of that accumulation of identifying ancestors, *Days and Nights* is an innovating, admirable book, an attempt to exemplify the "modernism" that preoccupies Symons's criticism. It aims, as its title makes perfectly clear, to keep the antitheses balanced: it will deal with both daylight and darkness, surface and symbol.

Its "Prologue," Symons's manifesto poem, takes up the theme from Meredith, sweeping away what it sees as the husks of an old classicism and charging the new art to turn for its subjects to real, transient life. It sketches the old beauty and the new as two "queens" or "goddesses," and the change in modern poetry as a shift in rule and religion. The goddess of the old order is chilly and remote, all pure form and transcendence:

> Brooding aloft, she reigns a lonely queen,
>> Nor aught of earth nor aught of man would know,
> Impassible, inexorably serene,
>> Cold as the morning on her hills of snow.

Her successor, who rules over *Days and Nights*, is all immanence, an emblem for the human art Symons describes in his essay on Thomson. She is a goddess of balances, the aesthetic of "oneself and one's surroundings," the resolution to a series of pointed antitheses:

> She stands amidst the tumult, and is calm;
>> She reads the heart self-closed against the light;
> She probes an ancient wound, yet brings no balm;
>> She is ruthless, yet she doeth all things right.
>
> She looks on princes in their palaces,
>> She peers upon the prisoner in his cell;
> She sees the saint who prays to God, she sees
>> The way of those that go down quick to hell.
> . . . .
> All serve alike her purpose; she requires
>> The very life-blood of humanity;
> All that the soul concerns, the heart desires,
>> She marks, she garners in her memory.

The old art, Symons says, "from the empty shrine is fled"

>> but go where cities pour
> Their turbid human stream through street and mart,
> A dark stream flowing onward evermore
> Down to an unknown ocean;—there is Art.

This first manifesto poem looks forward to the "dark human stream" that is one side of Conrad's subject in *The Secret Agent*, to the "processions" and "vans" of *Mrs. Dalloway*, to the wanderings of *Ulysses*, and to the crowd flowing over London Bridge in *The Waste Land*. But it comes directly from *Les Fleurs du Mal*. Both its frigid, banished muse and her replacement originate in the alexandrines of "La Beauté" (which went into the making of Wilde's "Sphinx," too), and its companion poem, "Hymne à la

Beauté."²⁷ In the first Baudelaire's goddess of chilly form describes herself:

> Je trône dans l'azur comme un sphinx incompris;
> J'unis un coeur de neige à la blancheur des cygnes;
> Je hais le mouvement qui déplace les lignes,
> Et jamais je ne pleure et jamais je ne ris. (I, 21)

In the other, the poet addresses a more universal and altogether more familiar Goddess:

> Viens-tu du ciel profond ou sors-tu de l'abîme,
> O Beauté? ton regard, infernal et divin,
> Verse confusément le bienfait et le crime,
> Et l'on peut pour cela te comparer au vin. (I, 24)

Symons's new muse descends from her position "aloft" to return a human warmth to art, to shatter monumental stasis, and to restore movement and fluidity to form. It is a brief taken from the Poet of Paris, who gives to his artist the catholicity of the sun:

> Quand, ainsi qu'un poète, il descend dans les villes,
> Il ennoblit le sort des choses les plus viles,
> Et S'introduit en roi, sans bruit et sans valets,
> Dans tous les hôpitaux et dans tous les palais. (I, 83)

What follows Symons's Baudelairean manifesto poem in *Days and Nights* is his search for a "new stock of imagery" of "contemporary life,"²⁸ a means of organizing such material, and an ethical dimension in which to see it.

Symons's first books of verse—in this respect a striking prediction of early Imagist work—waver uncertainly between "modern" and "traditional" themes. In *Days and Nights*, poems which analyze painful states of mind or sketch street visions or touch on violent passions or intentionally damnable braveries, alternate

---

Je trône . . . I reign in the azure like a sphinx, beyond all understanding; my heart of snow matches my swan's whiteness; movement I hate, that disturbs the ideal line, and never do I weep, nor ever smile (S, 27).

Viens-tu . . . O Beauty, do you come from the deep heavens, or do you rise from the bottomless pit? Your gaze, daemonic and divine, deals out good deeds and crime together, and in this you resemble wine (S, 222).

Quand . . . When, like a poet, he comes down into cities, he ennobles the lot of even the meanest things, and, like a monarch, silent and unattended, he enters workhouses and palaces (S, 14).

with poems such as "Wood-Notes: A Pastoral Interlude." In *Sil-houettes*, "Maquillage" and "The Blind Beggar" and "The Absinthe Drinker" co-exist with such a poem as "Pattie," in which "Cool comely country Pattie, grown / A daisy where the daisies grow," gains the moral and aesthetic preference over "courtly city dames, / Pale languid-scented hot-house growth." The poet conceives of these two kinds of verse as opposites, but the tensions in the "modern" are as evident as the platitudinous tone of the "traditional."

The "modernity" of *Days and Nights* expresses itself most obviously in its claim of a new subject matter, but it is no less present in Symons's attempt to discover a means of treating that. Some of the poems in the volume give the impression, as Symons's biographer remarks of his work at this stage, "of an inferior Browning," but they also show the poet resisting the procedures of his earliest literary hero. The fascinating poem, "An Interruption in Court,"[29] demonstrates the inventive stress. Its organization comes from Browning's monologues (though it is not itself a monologue) and the strains in its fabric come from the inadequacy of such organization to Symons's purpose. Its subject matter is *almost* that of Symons's more characteristic impressionistic work. The poem observes a moment in the "real life" of "ordinary" people: it opens with the direct speech of an old man who rises suddenly in a crowded courtroom, claiming that the woman who is charged (we are left to guess with what) is his missing daughter and pleading with the court to recognize what he is certain is a mistake. An unnamed observer, whose position relative to the old man is, we are asked to assume, identical with our own, takes up the narrative: "Now while the old man spoke, I watched the girl." The old man is heard, but not listened to, his daughter is not pardoned, and the waters of the "dark stream" close over both of them.

This poem shares its fundamental idea with Baudelaire's prose poems (which were later to affect Symons's work profoundly): the city tosses up to the sight of the *flâneur*, almost as though for his consumption, the spectacle of detached and lonely people whose characters he must imagine into existence and whose loneliness implies that he, too, floats detached on those same waters. The idea depends upon a sentimental irony: the "I" who is proffered as observer is in fact the poem's subject, and it is his feeling that the poem invites us to share. "An Interruption in Court"

asks the reader to feel, not the desperation and bewilderment
of the old man or the shame and defensive coldness of the
daughter, but the sense of irony, frustrated sympathy, and cu-
riosity of the observer. This is not so Browningesque a poem as
might first appear: although it opens with dramatic presentation
(in which the old man speaks to the court), it moves to narrative
(in which the poet speaks to us), so displacing the observed by
the observer and substituting the analyzed self for the watched
world.

"An Interruption in Court" embodies Symons's early critical
preoccupations, both in its subject matter and in its technique.
The tale it tells is familiar from D. G. Rossetti's *Found*, and like
that painting it allegorizes the development of modern beauty:
the ideal expectation of innocence which belongs to the old man
has been replaced in his daughter by a bitter knowing, and mod-
ern beauty has been relocated in relation to society and the
institutions of power. It is no accident that Symons casts the new
beauty here as a woman (as he does in his manifesto poems), no
accident either that the woman is fallen, carnal, judged, and
condemned. The allegory the poem repeats is familiar from its
past—this is the modern art of *The Renaissance*—and it would
reappear in the poem's future.

Symons enacts in the technique of his poem the change he
dramatizes in its represented action. Modern art, passing from
one generation to another, was also about to pass from the ear
to the eye, and Symons's central technical shift performs that
change. The position of the "I" in this kind of poem is crucial—
it must function as "eye"—and Symons insists on this:

> I've seen it, and I saw this.
>   Still, I say,
> The old man talked.

To be successful this poem had to place the speaker on the first
plane of observation from the outset: the single unity had to be
that of the observing "I." Moving as he does from his dramatic
order, Symons disrupts the work, and it fails. But the ruptures
in its fabric are of considerable interest: his departure from the
dramatic is the shift from ear to eye, from organization by rhet-
oric to organization by visual perception: "Now while the old
man spoke, I watched the girl," he writes, so fracturing the sin-
gleness of speech, forcing the reader to be open to more than

one point of view, and casting the observer/poet into the role he occupies in Symons's later work, that of unifier and decoder of experience ("déchiffreur," as Baudelaire says). That change in mode (from the speaking old man to the watching poet), which is this poem's failure, dramatizes an important shift. "Interpersonal relationships in big cities are distinguished by a marked preponderance of the activity of the eye over the activity of the ear," wrote Walter Benjamin.[30] The poetry of the modern city, as we have come to know it, depends on the shift to the eye, and on the seer, the *flâneur* whose eye consumes the "real world," detects its secret meanings, and orders it in art. (This *flâneur* is a brother of the critic of the *salon*, though his aesthetic stroll, his philosophical promenade, makes the street its gallery.)

Like some of his successors, Symons saw that structure was the problem of modern art. He looked to *Modern Love* for instruction on the quite specific technical matters he was attempting to deal with in such poems as "An Interruption in Court." In an essay on Blunt, he writes:

> In the *Love Sonnets* there is no narrative; the little, charming, prosaic facts that creep in from time to time are but delightful accidents; what we have is the essential poetry of the emotions, of faintly indicated situations, in which the emotions had crystallised. In *Modern Love* there is a narrative; but it is told in "tragic hints," no more. The situation is flashed upon you as by the flash of lightning—then darkness, and then again a flash. The poem stands alone in the literature of its time; moving by "tragic hints" to the cadence of an irony that achieves quite a new expression in verse, it gives voice, in that acid, stinging, bitter-sweet style . . . to all that is new. . . .[31]

Information by tragic hints characterizes the best visual art of the time, according to Symons, and the most important poetry aims at a similar effect:

> It is the aim of Whistler, as of so much modern art, to be taken at a hint, divined at a gesture, or by telepathy. Mallarmé, suppressing syntax and punctuation, the essential links of things, sometimes fails in his incantation, and brings before us things homeless and unattached in middle air.

Verlaine subtilises words in a song to a mere breathing of music.[32]

The problem in poetry, as in painting, is this: what relationship the detail will bear to the whole. In the Browning-formed poems of his early volumes, Symons made the detail a step in a causal sequence. He moved from this to an impressionism which gave the details of his verse only the connections with one another that are implied by the frame. He became aware of the organizing power of the implied perceiver, as some of the pastels in *Silhouettes* illustrate. "On the Beach," for instance, suggests by the terseness of its line that it is a catalogue of sensations made coherent only by the "I" who feels them:

> Night, a grey sky, a ghostly sea,
> The soft beginning of the rain:
> Black on the horizon, sails that wane
> Into the distance mistily.
>
> The tide is rising; I can hear. . . .

In *Days and Nights* the contrast in technique appears in "The Street-Singer," which follows directly on "An Interruption in Court." This poem composes its character not from action but from "faintly indicated" visual characteristics. The "I" is suppressed entirely, and the poem, which is put together of details whose relationship to one another is not described, is as scrupulously impersonal a rendering as the "Preludes" of Eliot.

While he was considering these problems, Symons was writing verse which was (as he said of Swinburne's "Cleopatra") "steeped deep in the spirit of Baudelaire."[33] His poems are full of specific reminiscences and borrowings. His "Blind Beggar" comes directly from "Les Aveugles,"[34] "The Old Women" from "Les Petites Vielles,"[35] "The Wanderers" from "Le Voyage."[36] "To One in Alienation, II" reworks the poem which was later to fascinate J. C. Squire, "Une nuit que j'étais près d'une affreuse juive" (II, 34).[37] Symons's borrowings are far too numerous to list, and they do not merit individual attention, but together they do constitute a major characteristic of his style, and they make it perfectly clear that in the period before he wrote *The Symbolist Movement in Literature, Les Fleurs du Mal* were much in his mind. They exemplified for him the "subtleties, delicate perversities, exquisite complexities of irony [which are] essentially modern."[38]

But Symons was preparing to recant. The manifesto poem to

Knave of Hearts, which was published in 1913, but which included poems written between 1894 and 1908, marks the other end of the period begun by the "Prologue" to *Days and Nights*. This sequence (unfortunately and ideologically titled, "The Brother of a Weed") describes the poet's past:

I have delighted in all visible things
And built the world of my imaginings
Out of the splendour of the day and night,
And I have never wondered that my sight
Should serve me for my pleasure. . . .

It confesses the inadequacy of that past ("And I have been of all men loneliest"), and it turns in a radically new direction. "I will get down from my sick throne," Symons writes, "where I / Dreamed that the seasons of the earth and sky, / The leash of months and stars, were mine to lead." Explicitly rejecting his earlier subjects, Symons announces that he will turn his attention to the humblest objects of the natural landscape. He went into the streets, he says now, only because "I feared myself and sought / In the crowd's hurry a pause / And sanctuary from thought." Now, he writes, "my tired pilgrim feet / Have no more need to roam." *Images of Good and Evil*, which was published the same year as *The Symbolist Movement*, indicates the poetic effects of Symons's *volte-face*. There is no trace in it of the "new, beautiful and interesting" disease of particularity, and its language, powerfully influenced by Yeats, is remote: "Beloved, there is a sorrow in the world," Symons chants, "Too aged to remember its own birth." Retreating from his earlier attempt to be "true to life" and "true to art," he embraces the mildest symbolist themes: "Let me hear music," he writes, "for I am not sad, / But half in love with sadness. To dream so, / And dream, and so forget the dream, and so / Dream I am dreaming!39 Symons had been drawn into what he had seen as the inevitable and open warfare between beauty and the modern world, and he had suffered decisive defeat. The collapse of his poetic, evident in these two volumes of verse, produced, ironically, the only work for which he is much remembered, *The Symbolist Movement in Literature*.

* * *

Pater provides one focus of aesthetic thought in the latter part of the nineteenth century. In *The Symbolist Movement*, his most important work, Symons, who was Pater's disciple as well as his

friend, provides an opposite. He began his career with the pur-
pose and method of Pater. When he was twenty he wrote that
he sought to model his prose style on that of Pater, "the most
exquisite critic of our day." In his essay on "The Decadent Move-
ment in Literature" (1893), he called Pater's prose "the most
beautiful English prose which is now being written."[40] His first
collection of critical essays rejects "critics to whom art means a
theory, a belief, a science" and "this limiting of oneself to a school,
a doctrine, a costume";[41] the introduction to *Plays, Acting, and
Music* (1903) expresses a wish to be "as little abstract as possible,
and to study first principles, not so much as they exist in the
brain of the theorist, but as they may be discovered, alive and
in effective action, in every achieved form of art."[42] He thought
that the "aim of criticism [was] to distinguish what is essential in
the work of a writer; and in order to do this, its first business
must be to find out where he is different from other writers."[43]
In his book on the *Romantic Movement* (1909) he wrote that

> To distinguish poetry, then, where it exists, to consider it
> in its essence, apart from the accidents of the age in which
> it came into being, to define its qualities in itself; that is the
> business of the true critic or student. And in order to do
> this he must . . . clear his mind of all limiting formulas . . .
> disregard all schools or movements as other than convenient
> and interchangeable labels.[44]

Here, too, Pater remains a key. In him, Baudelaire supports
an intense realism, an idea of the proper value of the object and
a respect for the materials of each art. The modern poet in *Gaston
de Latour* renders intensely what he sees, and transforms the
predominant material into a luminous whole which, paradoxi-
cally, seems to include "soul" precisely because it is a faithful
accounting for body. Symons's own early work is the product of
that same pressure toward the concrete, the particular, the sen-
suous: his impressionism is a form of psychological realism. "Mo-
dernity in Verse" is art bound to the particular, and Degas is a
model for modern poetry precisely because he paints "the very
race-horses" he sees. In that, Symons opts for a realism of the
kind implied by Pater's criticism, one that "connects itself with
the empirical character of our science, our philosophic faith in
the concrete, the particular."[45] But *The Symbolist Movement in Lit-
erature* (1899) is a reversal: there Symons argues that the one

hope in life consists in being able to shut the eyes and ears and develop an inward vision. Nothing could more completely oppose Pater, who wondered archly, it will be remembered, whether knowledge gained from the inward eye could properly be called knowledge. *The Symbolist Movement* stands in relationship to *The Renaissance*, as to Symons's own earlier work, as a kind of lunar representation of their solar values. This, Symons's one incontestably influential and popular work,[46] is an eccentric product in his career, entirely compatible neither with what he had written before nor with what he was to write afterwards.

The Symbolist Movement is of consequence not only in the study of modern poetry—it "modernized" T. S. Eliot and John Gould Fletcher, provided Edward Thomas with material for his study of Maeterlinck, and made its way into the notebooks of Thomas Hardy[47]—but also in the study of Baudelaire and English literature, since in its earliest version it left him out. Describing the Symbolist poets, Symons instanced Baudelaire only as their distant relative. He "repaired" his omission in the 1919 edition of his book—but his later version had nothing like the same informing themes as the earlier, as is shown by its inclusion of an essay on Gautier. *The Symbolist Movement*, in the form in which it gave to the French Symbolists "a glamour previously reserved for the English romantic poets,"[48] not only left Baudelaire off the list, but also excluded him explicitly from the Symbolist company. It made its exclusion, furthermore, on the extremely interesting grounds that he was too much a realist. In the early version, Baudelaire—with Flaubert, the de Goncourts, Taine, Zola, Leconte de Lisle—became merely an "offshoot of Romanticism," a participant in

> the age of Science, the age of material things; and words, with that facile elasticity which there is in them, did miracles in the exact representation of everything that visibly existed, exactly as it existed.[49]

Although by the time Eliot reviewed his translations of Baudelaire (1925),[50] Symons seemed to believe that Baudelaire and Verlaine were alike (a belief Eliot took pains to show he did not share), when he first considered the two poets together he saw them as very different indeed.

The Symbolist Movement affected the course of Baudelaire's influence and reputation in England in another, less obvious way.

In Pater's work Baudelaire enforced a quite specific view of modernism (and supplied some of its essential characteristics); but *The Symbolist Movement* outlined an aesthetic sharply opposed to Pater's. When its 1919 edition finally enrolled Baudelaire in the Symbolist list, it attached his name to an aesthetic pointedly opposed not only to the one his work had first supported in England, but also to the position with which its first version had associated him.

Symons's wavering over Baudelaire, in *The Symbolist Movement*, is symptomatic. The contrast and conflict between the aesthetic he outlined here—which was, as Richard Ellmann says, supported by rumors from Ireland[51]—and the one that is represented by the whole work of Pater is the central conflict in English verse of the modern period. The positions of Pater and Symons presented the Imagists with two alternatives, and when many writers of the early twentieth century moved to reject the aesthetic of orthodox symbolism they returned to the aesthetic of Pater. But the two alternatives are curiously connected, and Symons, in presenting his antithesis to Pater, modelled his book so closely on *The Renaissance* as to produce a kind of inverse imitation.

In January 1898, Symons wrote to Edmund Gosse that his *Studies in Two Literatures* had lacked architecture—a fault, he said, "I am particularly anxious not to repeat."[52] The same year, he began to put together *The Symbolist Movement*, a work he had had in mind since 1896, when Smithers announced it in the same number of the *Savoy* that contained an admiring Symons article on Pater.[53] The second collection of essays has a quite different shape from the first. The *Studies in Two Literatures* is composed of four sections—on Elizabethan drama, on contemporary writers, on English writers, on French writers—held together only by the personality of the critic. *The Symbolist Movement*, on the other hand, has a coherent shape and a striking thematic unity achieved not merely by the fact that Symons calls all of his subjects "symbolists" but by the frequent, almost rhythmic, reference to what he describes as the fundamental aesthetic of the movement. The shape of the work is familiar: it consists of eight essays bounded by a generalizing introduction and conclusion. This is the shape of *The Renaissance*, which served as a model for both the architecture and the texture. In the *Savoy* article on Pater, Symons said that *The Renaissance* was "the most beautiful book of prose in our literature," and that the "merit which, more than any other, distinguishes Pater's prose, though it is not the merit most on the surface, is the attention to, the perfection of, the *ensemble*."[54] Like *The Renaissance*, Symons's book achieves its unity by presenting its essays as illustrations of a general principle or a larger "movement of the human spirit"; like *The Renaissance*, it creates a sense of drama by presenting the artists it discusses as revolutionaries in the battle not merely for the liberty to write books or create works of art about specific subjects but for the liberty to feel the whole range of human emotion; like *The Renaissance*, it exploits the variety of its eight sections by adopting a biographical approach to its material, so that the personalities of Verlaine or Leonardo are made as illustrative as their works; and, finally, like *The Renaissance*, it draws general ethical and even religious conclusions from the evidence of art.

The Symbolist Movement, as Barbara Charlesworth writes, is "a public lecture" on French Symbolism: it is intended to instruct.[55] But the work also addresses Pater's aesthetics, and it mounts on them a specific and systematic attack, whose chief strategy is a grand dissonance, the play of a steady and discordant echo. Symons conceived of his book as a revolution in aesthetics, and his style embodies that conception in its tricks of contradiction. He writes, for example, in what is clearly an intentional somersault over the Gautier catchword dear to Pater and others, that the Symbolist movement provides "a literature in which the visible world is no longer a reality, and the unseen world no longer a dream."[56] His conclusion is, just as directly, a trick with Pater's "Conclusion" to *The Renaissance*, as these juxtaposed pieces show:[57]

PATER:
[the inward world of thought is] the race of the midstream, a drift of momentary acts of sight and passion and thought. . . . impressions unstable, flickering, inconsistent, which burn and are extinguished with our consciousness of them. . . . Every one of those impressions is the impression of the individual in his isolation. . . .

SYMONS:
Knowing so much less than nothing, for we are entrapped in smiling and many-coloured appearances, our life may seem to be but a little space of leisure, in which it will be the necessary business of each of us to speculate on what is so rapidly becoming the past and so rapidly becoming the

future, that scarcely existing present which is after all our
only possession. Yet, . . .

PATER:

To such a tremulous wisp constantly reforming itself on the
stream, to a single sharp impression, with a sense in it, a
relic more or less fleeting, of such moments gone by, what
is *real* in our life fines itself down. It is with the movement,
the passage and dissolution of impressions, images, sensa-
tions, that analysis leaves off,—that continual vanishing
away, that strange perpetual weaving and unweaving of our-
selves.

SYMONS:

. . . as the present passes from us, hardly to be enjoyed
except as memory or as hope, and only with an at best partial
recognition of the uncertainty or inutility of both, it is with
a kind of terror that we wake up, every now and then, to
the whole knowledge of our ignorance, and to some per-
ception of where it is leading us.

PATER:

Failure is to form habits. . . . Not to discriminate every mo-
ment some passionate attitude in those about us, and in the
brilliance of their gifts some tragic dividing of forces on
their ways is, on this short day of frost and sun, to sleep
before evening. . . . What we have to do is to be for ever
curiously testing new opinions and courting new impres-
sions, never acquiescing in a facile orthodoxy. . . .

SYMONS:

To live through a single day with that overpowering con-
sciousness of our real position, which, in the moments in
which alone it mercifully comes, is like blinding light or the
thrust of a flaming sword, would drive any man out of his
senses. It is our hesitations, the excuses of our hearts, the
compromises of our intelligence, which save us. We can for-
get so much, we can bear suspense with so fortunate an
evasion of its real issues; we are so admirably finite.

PATER:

For our one chance is in expanding that interval, in getting
as many pulsations as possible into the given time.

SYMONS:

Our only chance, in this world, of a complete happiness, lies in the measure of our success in shutting the eyes of the mind, and deadening its sense of hearing, and dulling the keenness of its apprehension of the unknown.

For Symons, the moment of awareness is not a "gem-like flame" as it is to Pater, but "a blinding light or the thrust of a flaming sword," a violence and a horror of disorder. In his conclusion Pater's imagery is pressed into a foreign service:

as we realise the identity of a poem, a prayer, or a kiss, in that spiritual universe which we are weaving for ourselves, each out of a thread of the great fabric; as we realise the infinite insignificance of action, its immense distance from the current of life; as we realise the delight of feeling ourselves carried onward by forces which it is our wisdom to obey; it is at least with a certain relief that we turn to an ancient doctrine, so much the more likely to be true because it has so much the air of a dream.

In this drift of *The Symbolist Movement*, Yeats obviously counts for a good deal, as he does in Symons's verse of about the same time, but the text of the "Conclusion" also reveals intensely personal reasons for Symons's shift in outlook.[58] The book is not, as one critic sees it, a reasonable culmination of Symons's critical formation up to that date.[59] In its formal debt to Pater and in the fact that it makes a large statement about the French writers to whom Symons had been devoting his attention, it is the outcome of earlier interests; but in its aesthetic, in *what* it says, it is a sudden departure from the themes of his former criticism and the goals of his poetry. Munro writes that, exhausted "by a life dedicated to the gratification of the senses, Symons sought transcendence, and the surest way to heaven was up a Symbolist Parnassus."[60] What is certain is that, exhausted by the attempt to render poetically the transitory information of the senses, Symons abandoned his Pateresque modernism and sought refuge and security in an "ancient doctrine." Pater's work, Yeats said, "taught us to walk upon a rope, tightly stretched through the serene air, and we were left to keep our feet upon a swaying rope in a storm." Symons saved himself with the "revolt against exteriority, against rhetoric, against a materialistic tradition,"[61] the reverse image of Pater's "outbreak of the human spirit" which was characterized by a search after "the pleasures of the senses and the imagination," a "care for beauty," and "worship of the body."[62]

The Symbolist Movement, Symons says in his "Introduction," is about "a kind of religion, with all the duties and responsibilities of the sacred ritual," but he deals with the "practical aesthetics" of Symbolism. That is the doctrine of correspondences, which, he says, "we owe to the fortunate accident of madness" in Gérard de Nerval.[63] Symons's description of the aesthetic turns on two points: that the poet evokes rather than states, and that he is aware of the analogies in the world. Symons writes that in Nerval's sonnets,

> . . . for the first time in French, words are used as the ingredients of an evocation, as themselves not merely colour and sound, but symbol. Here are words which create an atmosphere by the actual suggestive quality of their syllables, as, according to the theory of Mallarmé, they should do; as, in the recent attempts of the Symbolists, writer after writer has endeavoured to lure them into doing. Persuaded, as Gérard was, of the sensitive unity of all nature, he was able to trace resemblances where others saw only divergences. . . . His genius . . . consisted in a power of materialising vision, whatever is most volatile and unseizable in vision, and without losing the sense of mystery, or that quality which gives its charm to the intangible.

Symons quotes a passage from *Le Rêve et la Vie,* in which Nerval writes that

> All things live, all things are in motion, all things correspond; the magnetic rays emanating from myself or others traverse without obstacle the infinite chain of created things: a transparent network covers the world, whose loose threads communicate more and more closely with the planets and the stars.

Symons calls this a mystic doctrine, connected with Pythagoras, Hermes, Boehme, and Swedenborg. He goes on to quote the whole of Nerval's "Vers Dorés," a sonnet, he says, which also "seems to state a doctrine."[64] The doctrine is what Symons takes to be the basis of Symbolism, and it is what supplies unity to his book, as well as, he hopes, to the world: "It is sometimes permitted to us to hope that our convention [of symbolism] is indeed the reflection rather than merely the sign of that unseen reality." It is part of the doctrine of Villiers: "The ideal, to Villiers, being the real, spiritual beauty being the essential beauty, and material beauty its reflection, or its revelation, it is with a sort of fury that he attacks the materialising forces of the world." Mallarmé is its high priest, orchestrating in his verse " 'all the correspondences of the universe, the supreme Music.' "[65]

What is peculiar about Symons's presentation of his "practical aesthetics" is its failure to mention Baudelaire. Symons uses Baudelaire's word (it is also Swedenborg's) to name the phenomenon described by Nerval, and he cannot have failed to note the striking similarity between his description of *correspondances* and Nerval's. Later, in his 1910 work on Rossetti, he associated the doctrine with Baudelaire, citing one of Baudelaire's own sources—"Hoffmann, in his 'Kreisleriana,' anticipates something of what modern poets, Baudelaire, Mallarmé, Rossetti, have sought to find in the mysterious correspondence of the universe"[66]—and going on to quote the passage which is repeated in Baudelaire's sonnet. In *The Symbolist Movement*, however, he enumerates a line of enquirers which excludes Baudelaire. "Did he himself realise all that he had done," he writes of Nerval, "or was it left for Mallarmé to theorise upon what Gérard had but divined?"[67]

It seems unlikely—impossible—that Symons did not at this date know Baudelaire's sonnet. For one thing, his verse shows detailed familiarity with Baudelaire's poems, and for another he could hardly have sifted through the work of the French Symbolists without knowing that they, at least, held Baudelaire's poem to be the source of their doctrine. Furthermore, his essay on Balzac (written in 1899 and included in the 1919 version of *The Symbolist Movement*) both refers to and adopts Baudelaire's view of Balzac; and the essay on Mallarmé probably quotes from Baudelaire's pamphlet on Wagner. (Symons writes that Mallarmé "attains Wagner's ideal, that 'the most complete work of the poet should be that which, in its final achievement, becomes a perfect music.' " Baudelaire renders Wagner's ideal, "l'oeuvre la plus complète du poète devrait être celle qui, dans son dernier achèvement, serait une parfaite musique.")[68] Even in the introduction to *The Symbolist Movement*, Symons shows his familiarity with

Baudelaire's essay on Théophile Gautier. "Nothing, not even conventional virtue," he says, "is so provincial as conventional vice; and the desire to 'bewilder the middle-classes' is itself middle-class."[69] "Récriminer, faire de l'opposition, et même réclamer la justice, n'est-ce pas *s'emphilistiner* quelque peu? On oublie à chaque instant qu'injurier une foule, c'est s'encanailler soi-même," Baudelaire writes (II, 106-7). Symons's *Symbolist Movement* makes its reliance on Baudelaire abundantly clear; its account of Nerval's language, for instance, is evidently modelled on his remarks on *correspondances* in the essay on Gautier (quoted above, p. 108). Such borrowings emphasize the oddness of Symons's omission of Baudelaire from the list of the select company and of his failure to cite him (as the French Symbolists themselves did) as one of the sources of their doctrine. The omission, which attracted Ruth Temple's attention,[70] is a dimension of Symons's striking reversal: Baudelaire, who had provided him with a stance and a strategy for modernism in poetry, now must have seemed to be far too deeply implicated in the aesthetic he was rejecting. Those earlier Baudelairean models for the analysis of oneself and one's surroundings must now have seemed to Symons to be precisely antithetical to the new spiritualism, as he saw it, of the Symbolists.

The doctrine of correspondences provides Symons with a simply schematized dualism. In his discussion of Verlaine, he writes of "that particular unity which consists in a dualism, in the division of forces between the longing after what is evil and the adoration of what is good; or rather, in the antagonism of spirit and flesh."[71] But Symons fails to see that one of the most important points in that system of analogies is that matter and spirit imply one another, and he opts with Villiers and the Symbolists for pure spirit. Villiers' Catholicism, he says, is a flag "under which it was possible to fight on behalf of the spirit, against that materialism which is always, in one way or another, atheist."[72] Villiers' "last word," he says, is "faith; faith against the evidence of the senses, against the negations of materialistic science, against the monstrous paradox of progress."[73] Confronted by the apparent paradox of an unreal visible world and a real unseen world, Symons's Symbolists enlist for the unseen. Villiers is

Récriminer . . . Recriminating and indulging in opposition, and even demanding justice, is there not in all that a certain degree of "philistinization"? How easily we forget that to hurl insults at a crowd puts us ourselves amongst the rabble (C, 260).

the "Don Quixote of idealism . . . life, to him, was the dream, and the spiritual world the reality";[74] Verlaine "was a man certainly, 'for whom the visible world existed,' but for whom it existed always as a vision. He absorbed it through all his senses, as the true mystic absorbs the divine beauty."[75] *The Symbolist Movement* is dominated by the sadly humbled frame of mind Symons expressed in the prefatory letter to Yeats, in which he regrets that he is "so meshed about with the variable and too clinging appearances of things, so weak before the delightfulness of earthly circumstance."

In *Spiritual Adventures* (1905), Symons gives two provocatively contrasting imaginary portraits. One, "The Death of Peter Waydelin," describes a painter of modern life, who insists that "A man must be of his time, else why try to put his time on the canvas?"[76] and who finds his subjects in the artificial life of London:

I have never cared for anything but London, or in London for anything but here, or the Hampstead Road, or about the Docks. I never really chose the music-halls or the public-houses; they chose me. I made the music-halls my clubs; I lived in them, for the mere delight of the thing; I liked the glitter, false, barbarous, intoxicating, the violent animality of the whole spectacle, with its imbecile words, faces, gestures, the very heat and odour, like some concentrated odour of the human crowd, the irritant music, the audience! I went there, as I went to public-houses, as I walked about the streets at night, as I kept company with vagabonds, because there was a craving in me that I could not quiet. I fitted in theories with my facts; and that is how I came to paint my pictures.

But Waydelin's art costs him his life and his story exists to illustrate the principle that "Much of our bad painting comes from respectable people thinking that they can soil their hands with paint and not let the dye sink into their innermost selves." In the other portrait, "Christian Trevalga," Symons shows an artist who, increasingly isolated, finally retreats into madness. His papers include one on which this is written:

It has been revealed to me that there is but one art, but many languages through which men speak it. . . . Music comes nearer than any other of the human languages to the sound of these angelic voices. But painting is also a language, and sculpture, and poetry; only these have more of the atmosphere of the earth about them, and are not so clear. I have heard pictures which spoke to me melodiously, and I have listened to the faultless rhythm of statues. . . .

Those two figures present the absolute opposites of Symons's mind. Peter Waydelin, for whom the visible world exists, sinks to a pitiable death; Christian Trevalga climbs to a visionary isolation.[77]

*   *   *

The Symbolist Movement springs from an aberrant moment in Symons's career—by 1903 he was proclaiming again, "I am one of those for whom the visible world exists, very actively"[78]—but it signals a new departure in his work. About the time he was writing it, Symons turned away from poetry. Lhombreaud reports that in 1901, 1902, and 1903 he composed only thirty poems, by comparison with the 125 he wrote between 1896 and 1898.[79] His essay on Balzac (1899) suggests why: in Dante's time, Symons says,

> poetry could still represent an age and yet be poetry. But to-day poetry can no longer represent more than the soul of things; it has taken refuge from the terrible improvements of civilisation in a divine seclusion, where it sings, disregarding the many voices of the street. Prose comes offering its infinite capacity for detail; and it is by the infinity of its detail that the novel, as Balzac created it, has become the modern epic.[80]

That passage restates Symons's view of "the great problem," confirms his sense of defeat in his attempt to lay hold of "the poetry of cities [which] waits for us in London,"[81] and predicts the new direction of his work. It also reflects the advice Pater gave him in 1888. "I think the present age an unfavorable one for poets," Pater had written, "at least in England . . . I should say, make prose your principal *métier*, as a man of letters."[82] After his false start into mysticism, Symons was coming back to his "religion of the eyes."[83] Now, however, he was leaving poetry behind him; he would celebrate his "religion" in prose.

Symons published his translation of Baudelaire's *Poems in Prose* in 1905. He prefaced it with his verse translation of one of the projected "Epilogues" for *Les Fleurs du Mal*:

> With heart at rest I climbed the citadel's
> Steep height, and saw the city as from a tower,
> Hospital, brothel, prison, and such hells,
>
> Where evil comes up softly like a flower.
> Thou knowest, O Satan, patron of my pain,
> Not for vain tears I went up at that hour;
>
> But, like an old sad faithful lecher, fain
> To drink delight of that enormous trull
> Whose hellish beauty makes me young again.
>
> Whether thou sleep, with heavy vapours full,
> Sodden with day, or, new apparelled, stand
> In gold-laced veils of evening beautiful,
>
> I love thee, infamous city! Harlots and
> Hunted have pleasures of their own to give,
> The vulgar herd can never understand.

Like some of Symons's other renderings of Baudelaire, this translation evades precisely what it appears to admire, that is, the directness of the original diction, preferring instead to poeticize the fleshly, and so it loses not only Baudelaire's effective contrast in kinds of language, but also his bracing anti-aestheticism. But the translation, which enumerates the preoccupations of Symons's own work, stands at the head of his translation as an epilogue to his own attempts to render the city in verse and as a prologue to his new work in prose. In 1907, he published an article on Baudelaire which gives as much attention to his prose as to his poetry. Baudelaire's achievement, Symons writes, was to produce "one book of verse (out of which all French poetry has come since his time), one book of prose in which prose becomes a fine art, some criticism which is the sanest, subtlest, and surest which his generation produced, and a translation which is better than a marvellous original."[84] The "sane, subtle and sure" criticism (the terms are Swinburnean) was much in Symons's mind in the years after he wrote *The Symbolist Movement*. From about the turn of the century to 1908, when he had his nervous breakdown, his criticism alludes to Baudelaire with the same enthusiasm with which it mentions Pater. He cites Baude-

laire's comments on Balzac as the inventor of the modern epic
and he borrows the passage about Balzac's imaginative realism;
he compares Rodin to Baudelaire, seeing the "Femmes Dam-
nées" in the *Gates of Hell*; he quotes Baudelaire on the relation-
ship of the artist to the Philistine; he relays Baudelaire's com-
ments on Whistler and Poe. His essay on Wagner draws
extensively from Baudelaire, "whose equity of conscience in mat-
ters of art was flawless," he says, and whose *Richard Wagner et
Tannhäuser à Paris* was "the first and last word on many of the
problems of Wagner's work."[85] *Studies in Seven Arts* (1906) makes
Pater and Baudelaire its joint supports. Symons, publishing
everywhere, confirmed Baudelaire's aesthetic authority in Eng-
land.

Baudelaire also spurred Symons to new initiatives in his cre-
ative prose in the years after *The Symbolist Movement*. Now that
he had identified prose as the medium of modernity, he made
Le Spleen de Paris and *Petits Poèmes en Prose* his model. He quoted
the following lines from Baudelaire's prefatory letter to *Le Spleen
de Paris* frequently (in both his translation of the prose poems,
for instance, and in his later translation of Baudelaire's *Letters to
His Mother*) and with affection:

> Quel est celui de nous qui n'a pas, dans ses jours d'ambi-
> tion, rêvé le miracle d'une prose poétique, musicale sans
> rhythme et sans rime, assez souple et assez heurtée pour
> s'adapter aux mouvements lyriques de l'âme, aux ondula-
> tions de la rêverie, aux soubresauts de la conscience? (I, 275)

The ideal prose, he says, is born "surtout de la fréquentation
des villes énormes" and it has the qualities of its subject: "Enlevez
une vertèbre, et les deux morceaux de cette tortueuse fantaisie
se rejoindront sans peine. Hachez-la en nombreux fragments,
et vous verrez que chacun peut exister à part" (I, 275). Such
fluidity had been one of Symons's aims from the outset: the prose
ideal is his true antithesis to the banished goddess of *Days and*

Quel . . . Which one of us has not, in his ambitious days, dreamed the miracle
of a poetic prose, musical without rhythm or rhyme, supple and swift enough
to adapt to the lyrical movements of the soul, to the waves of dream, to the
sudden leaps of consciousness?

surtout . . . especially in frequenting enormous cities. . . . Take out a vertebrae,
the two pieces of this winding fantasy rejoin easily. Hack it into numerous
fragments, and you will see that each one can exist by itself.

Nights, the prose poem his true resolution of the conflict between the aesthetic rigidities of verse and the demanding flux of life. For Symons, the prose poem was a natural outcome: in Baudelaire's work in the kind, Symons said in the preface to his translation, "the art is not more novel, precise and perfect than the quality of thought and of emotion." In the years following publication of *The Symbolist Movement in Literature*, which had persuaded Symons finally that poetry belonged in "divine seclusion" and he as artist in the fallen flux, cities became more and more his subject and prose more and more his medium.

In 1903 Symons published *Cities*, his own first attempt to render the "souls and temperaments" of great cities in the supple prose he admired.[86] A year later, he published "The Death of Peter Waydelin," which appropriates for his artist-protagonist the subjects Symons had attempted to domesticate in his verse: " 'And if beauty is not the visible spirit of all that infamous flesh,' " Waydelin says, " 'when I have sabred it like that along my canvas, with all my hatred and all my admiration of its foolish energy, I am at least unable to conjecture where beauty has gone to live in the world.' "[87] The imaginary portrait "Esther Kahn" opens with a tentative evocation of the atmosphere of "one of those dark, evil-smelling streets with strange corners which lie about the Docks."[88] Symons came more and more to see himself as the prose poet of cities. In *London, A Book of Aspects*, he tried to do for London what he thought Baudelaire and Gautier and Nerval had done for Paris, and he associated his purpose explicitly with *Le Spleen de Paris*: "Baudelaire's phrase, 'a bath of multitude,' seemed to have been made for me," he writes. For him the crowd was, he said, a new sensation, an "artificial paradise."[89] The phrase, which supplies Symons's purpose, is from "Les Foules," a prose poem describing the "singulière ivresse de cette universelle communion" of crowds. "Il n'est pas donné à chacun de prendre un bain de multitude," Baudelaire writes, "jouir de la foule est un art" (I, 291). And if Symons's subject and medium are provided by Baudelaire, so, often, are the precise aspects of his London. The book opens, for instance, with an echo from "Le Cygne": "London was once habitable, in spite

---

singulière . . . peculiar drunkenness of this universal communion. . . . It is not given to everyone to plunge into the multitude; to take pleasure in the crowd is an art.

of itself. The machines have killed it. The old, habitable London exists no longer." "Paris change," Baudelaire had written, "Le vieux Paris n'est plus."[90] Symons's description of the Edgeware Road summons the landscape of "Le Vieux Saltimbanque," in which "Tout n'était que lumière, poussière, cris, joie, tumulte; les uns dépensaient, les autres gagnaient, les uns et les autres également joyeux."[91] The mysterious winter afternoon in London takes its character from Baudelaire's crepuscular Paris.

A Book of Aspects, like Le Spleen de Paris, is held together by its central roving figure, and he is motivated not only by the singular drunkenness of this "universal communion," but also by "la passion du voyage" (I, 291). He moves from scene to scene, from landscape to landscape, over what in his verse Symons called "a dark unknown ocean." Such roving became Symons's central subject, and although he did not make himself the poet of London, he did become one of the inventors of the modern romance of cities. His Colour Studies in Paris, for instance, gives the essential topography of mythologized modernism—the Boulevard Saint-Michel, the Café d'Harcourt, the Quartier Latin, the Luxembourg Gardens, Montmartre—and peoples it with phantom fathers, Baudelaire, Verlaine, Mallarmé, Moréas, and others. What began for Symons as the attempt to compel city life into verse in London Nights took him, as a reporter of dreams, not only to Paris and London, but to Rome, Venice, Naples, Seville, Prague, Moscow, Budapest, Belgrade, Sofia, Constantinople, and it issued in a series of books on the cities of Europe in which the dramatis personae are the roving poet with his lustful eye and the "enormous trull" who was beguiling whatever her name. The constant ghostly companion of Symons's walks was Baudelaire. He is potentially present at every turn: "As I drank my vermouth at the Café Perrin in the Grande Rue," Symons writes, in Wanderings, "I saw pass and repass me a beautiful and almost diabolical Creole girl, who was—apart from the colour—the image of Baudelaire's Jeanne Duval." Symons made Baudelaire's images his own. Lhombreaud reports that he took more than thirty photographs of Baudelaire's various residences in Paris, and in "Unspiritual Adventures in Paris," which was one chapter in Wanderings, Symons describes the pattern for his walks:

Paris . . . Paris changes; the old Paris is no longer.
Tout . . . Everything was only light, dust, shouts, joy, tumult; some spent, others earned, both equally happy.

Like a damned soul (to use one of his imaginary images) he
wanders at night, an actual *noctambule*, alone or with Villiers,
Gautier, in remote quarters. The houses of prostitution tor-
ment him, the sight of hospitals, of gambling-houses, the
miserable creatures one comes on in certain quarters, and
the fantastic glitter of lamplight. All this he needs (as I, for
instance, need; as Verlaine needed), a kind of intense cu-
riosity, of excitement, in one's frequentation of these streets,
which comes over me, as if one had taken opium.[92]

*   *   *

Most of Symons's critical writing on Baudelaire falls into the
third phase of his interest in him, and it is curiously detached
from his earlier work. While he was struggling with an idea of
"modernity," Symons used Baudelaire a great deal and wrote on
him only a little. Later, he published much on him and developed
the view that provoked Eliot and others among *les jeunes* to out-
rage.

Symons's criticism on Baudelaire seems to aspire to the con-
dition of the prose poem, as Baudelaire described it. His works
feed into one another in variously sliced segments, fattening in
1920 to the book-length *Charles Baudelaire, A Study*, which, in
turn, nourishes subsequent introductions and commentaries. In
1918 Symons published two articles on Baudelaire; another fol-
lowed in 1919.[93] The revised version of *The Symbolist Movement*
included his 1907 article, and in the same year (1929) he pub-
lished *Lesbia and Other Poems*, which includes a section called
"Intermezzo (To the Memory of Charles Baudelaire)." In 1925
his translations of *Les Fleurs du Mal, Petits Poèmes en Prose* and
Les Paradis Artificiels appeared, and in 1928 his translation of
Baudelaire's *Letters to His Mother, 1833-1866. Jezebel Mort* (1931),
whose dust-jacket claimed that Symons's insight had been "un-
rivalled since Baudelaire wrote *Les Fleurs du Mal*," included three
poems in honor of Baudelaire ("Beauty," "Baudelaire in Hell,"
"The Ghosts"). Almost everything Symons published during
these years gives evidence of a growing obsession. *From Toulouse-
Lautrec to Rodin* (1929), like the introductions to Villiers' *Claire
Lenoir* (1925) and Pierre Louys' *The Woman and the Puppet* (1935),
cites Baudelaire on the slightest provocation.

While in his early work Symons had made Baudelaire his po-
etic double, his identification now was intensely personal. His

unpublished papers suggest what alliance he felt with what he now saw as Baudelaire's Satanic genius. Lhombreaud quotes an incoherent but illuminating poem which was among Symons's papers: "As Baudelaire did and the perfume thereof / Like him I sometimes paid the price / Of what is called a certain sacrifice . . . ," Symons writes. ". . . caught in sins' own snare / Of Satan we had both vitality / And the lust of the flesh and also the tragedy / Of Love's despair and his flesh had been fed." An unpublished paper on "Sex and Aversion" demonstrates the same point: "Neither friend nor foe had the least reason for interfering with any act of mine with any spoken word," Symons wrote, "whether my life was moral or immoral, depraved or degraded, insolent or isolated." That, he said, "remained as literally my own secret, as Baudelaire's, who having cultivated his hysteria—as I was supposed to have cultivated my own hysteria —with all the casuistry of a confessor, did actually become a confessor of sins, who had never told the whole truth."[94] The last lines of that passage are lifted bodily from Symons's 1907 essay on Baudelaire.

Symons's late work makes Baudelaire a grotesque, a lover of bodily corruption, and a passionate "Satanist." His *Charles Baudelaire, A Study*, which appeared in 1920, gathers together pieces he had already written and produces, with ample reference to Gautier's 1868 preface, a late portrait of the decadent poet. It was an anachronism: in that year and the next John Middleton Murry published his articles in the *Athenaeum* and *The Times Literary Supplement*, proclaiming Baudelaire "strong, masculine, deliberate, classical," declaring the "perversity" of his work to be "the least important, the least relevant, and, to the unbiased reader, the least noticeable of its qualities."[95] The classically modern poet Symons had sought was taking shape in the essays of a new generation. His own critical work, however, anagramatized the Mephistophelean figure of the past. In 1929 he wrote that Baudelaire's genius was "tainted with Satanism, with diabolical insinuations."[96]

Symons died in 1944. He was by no means only a poet of the 'nineties: most of his books were published after the turn of the century; his poetry was read at The Poetry Bookshop; Eliot took him on as a critical antagonist in *The Sacred Wood*. He is genuinely a figure of the transition. When his library was sold in 1945 it included a first edition of *Les Fleurs du Mal*, with the manuscript of "Une Charogne," and Baudelaire's *Théophile Gautier*, with an unpublished autograph letter.[97] In *Charles Baudelaire, A Study*, he said that he had in front of him two copies of *Les Épaves*, one inscribed from Malassis to Rossetti, "pour remplir les intentions de l'auteur." He also had, he said,

> a book that Swinburne showed me, that he had richly bound in Paris, and that I bought at the sale of his library on June 19th: *Richard Wagner et Tannhäuser à Paris*. Par Charles Baudelaire. Paris, 1861; with, written in pencil, on the page before the title-page, these words:
>
> > "*A Mr. Algernon C. Swinburne. Bon Souvenir et mille Remerciements. C.B.*"[98]

EDITH SITWELL & SOME OTHERS

DEPARTURES FROM DECADENCE

> Il y a des noms qui deviennent proverbes et adjectifs.
> Quand un petit journal veut, en 1859, exprimer tout le
> dégoût et le mépris que lui inspire une poésie ou un
> roman d'un caractère sombre et outré, il lance le mot:
> *Pétrus Borel!* et tout est dit. Le jugement est prononcé,
> l'auteur est foudroyé.
>
> —Baudelaire, "Pétrus Borel" (II, 153)

In 1917 Camille Mauclair, a poet admired by some of the Im-
agists, wrote with relief that it was at last possible to look clearly
at Baudelaire. Until then, he maintained, evaluation of Baude-
laire's work had been rendered impossible by the phenomenon,
as much sociological as literary, of "baudelairism":

> Sous le nom de "baudelairisme"—que j'emploierai toujours
> en ce livre dans un sens péjoratif—nous avons dû subir
> l'exposé indigné [*sic*] et la condamnation pharisaïque d'un
> état psychologique falsifié, caricaturé. La moindre facétie

Il y a des . . . There are some names that become proverbs and adjectives.
When, in 1859, a little newspaper wants to express all the disgust and scorn
inspired in it by a dark and extreme poetry or novel, it tosses out the word:
Pétrus Borel! and everything is said. The judgement is pronounced, the author
is thunderstruck.

Sous le nom . . . Under the name of "baudelairism"—which I will always use in
this book in a pejorative sense—we have had to put up with the vile description
and sanctimonious condemnation of a falsified and caricatured psychological
state. The least paradoxical wittiness, taken literally, became a count of indict-
ment. And yet this state was less confirmed by the poet's avowed detractors,
moralists or Trissotins, than by a troop of poeticules believing that they inherit
his genius when they imitate his disorder, understanding nothing of the classic
art of Baudelaire, and dressing up with his name and his example the most
unendurable satanic and macabre rhapsodies.

paradoxale, prise à la lettre, devint un chef d'accusation.
Cet état fut encore moins affirmé par les détracteurs avoués,
moralistes ou trissotins, que par une troupe de poétereaux
croyant hériter du génie en imitant son désordre, ne com-
prenant rien à l'art classique de Baudelaire, et couvrant de
son nom et de son exemple les plus insupportables rapsodies
sataniques et macabres.

But now, Mauclair writes, "Il n'y a plus de baudelairisme. Le
mot, si laid, est démodé comme la chose. Il y a Baudelaire."[1]
That was fifty years after Baudelaire's death and sixty years after
publication of *Les Fleurs du Mal*.

"Baudelairism" in England is a slippery subject. "When once
a name passes into the category of symbols," George Saintsbury
wrote as early as 1875 in his essay on Baudelaire, "it is useless
to expect careful and candid appreciation of its owner's works,
except in the case of a very few persons of exceptionally critical
habits or powers."[2] Baudelaire's name had passed into this cat-
egory by the time Swinburne wrote his parodies, even before his
work had been much reviewed in England: Hotten's advertise-
ments for Shepherd's translations, Julio's warning verses, Bu-
chanan's outrage, and Allingham's moral distress all make that
clear. It has to some extent stayed there ever since. "Baudelair-
ism" is assumed to have existed in England as a category of
"decadence." Osbert Burdett, for instance, wrote that the "char-
acter of the literature and art of the Beardsley period was largely
the product of French influence," of Gautier, Baudelaire, Flau-
bert, and Zola, and he attributed "the formula of the whole *Yellow
Book* school" to ideas about art for art's sake that he said were
Baudelaire's.[3] Derek Stanford wrote that his anthology of the
poetry of the 'nineties had as one of its purposes the fishing up
of good poems from the sea of "Baudelaire in English": A.J.A.
Symons's *Anthology of 'Nineties' Verse* (1928), he thought, had given
too many poems in which Baudelaire's sensationalism and sa-
tanism, "reflected and distorted through the wrappings of Vic-
torian rhetoric," produced a "turgidity of language" and much
"over-heated thought and feeling."[4] Whether or not there was
anything like a "school" of "baudelairism" in England, there was
widespread admiration and imitation of the violent elements in

Il n'y a . . . There is no more baudelairism. The word is as out of style as the
thing. There is Baudelaire.

his work and of a "stock of imagery" quite different from the
one Eliot praised in 1930, and the term can usefully designate
this. It carries, as in Mauclair, a pejorative sense: looking at
poems that contribute to this phenomenon, *nous sommes*, as
Baudelaire might have said, *dans l'hôpital de la poésie*.[5]

Mauclair's comment on the freeing of Baudelaire from
"baudelairism," however, measures the desire of some early
twentieth-century writers to link him to modernism: it does not
measure the recovery from what Mauclair describes as a disease.
In the first two decades of this century, "baudelairism" became
very unfashionable indeed, but "rhapsodies sataniques et ma-
cabres" continued to be written in imitation of Baudelaire. Be-
tween the beginning of the century and *The Waste Land*, Baude-
laire's reputation underwent a wholesale revision. During those
years, he ceased to be seen as a romantic, an achieved Individ-
ualist, as Wilde saw him, or a decadent, useful in violent revo-
lution, and began to seem a strong moralist, or even a man
"essentially a Christian, born out of his due time, and a classicist,
born out of his due time," as Eliot wrote, who is "near to Dante
and not without a sympathy with Tertullian."[6] The desire to
relocate Baudelaire in the twentieth century—not merely to re-
vise an estimate of his art or to redescribe its character, but to
assert that he should have been born in our time rather than
his own—is an index to the relations of one generation of English
poets with another. It is a part of a process of dissociation very
like the one Swinburne had launched in the first place. To the
early modernists, the late nineteenth-century poets seemed in-
sincere and out of touch even with the realities of which they
themselves had required a more authentic treatment in poetry.
Evil and sex as they were presented by the late Victorian liber-
tarians were not acceptable to modernists. Baudelaire required
re-reading. Lytton Strachey, for instance, who had elsewhere
contributed importantly to the twentieth-century reaction, wrote
in 1912 that "the spirit" of Baudelaire's work "belongs rather to
the succeeding epoch than to his own," even though its form is
"closely related to his contemporaries."[7]

The shift in Baudelaire's reputation, however, was mixed and
erratic—it was in 1918 that Arthur Symons wrote in *The English
Review*, "Baudelaire's genius is satanical; he has in a sense the
vision of Satan. He sees in the past the lusts of the Borgias, the
sins and vices of the Renaissance; the rare virtues that flourish

like flowers and weeds, in brothels and garrets. He sees the vanity of the world with finer modern tastes than Solomon; for his imagination is abnormal, and divinely normal." In *A Vision* Yeats cast Baudelaire as the archetype of "the sensuous man," as a representative (with Beardsley and Dowson) of Phase Thirteen of the moon, "the only phase where entire sensuality is possible." That phase occupies the position directly across the wheel from the twenty-seventh, that of the Saint, and it is of "great importance," Yeats writes, because "only here can be achieved in perfection that in the *antithetical* life which corresponds to sanctity in the *primary*: not self-denial but expression for expression's sake."[8]

The departure of "baudelairism," which could be seen as the passage of the poet across the axis of the Great Wheel to the position of the Saint, was slow and uncertain. Some of the very writers who insisted on displacing Baudelaire from his own century to the present one, who intended to shake him free of his association with the English 'nineties, produced, at the same time, narrowly conventional imitations of his work. What the modernists often said about the nineteenth-century Baudelaireans—that they made sport of what he took seriously and trivialized what in him was profound—is as true of some of the avant-gardists of the early part of this century, in whose works Baudelaire's name, together with a well-worn imagery and an exhausted subject matter, nevertheless supported an effort to find the *new*.

Although it was imitative, the "baudelairism" of the second decade of this century was not merely affected. Later in her career Edith Sitwell could write with disdain of the flippant internationalism of the " 'Oh, la! la! Moosoor' school of verse" and of Austin Dobson's frenchifying,[9] and in his fifties J. C. Squire could smile complacently at the memory of his youthful attraction to "the grimmest literature I could find"[10]—for Squire that was *Les Fleurs du Mal*. But when Sitwell began her career using Baudelaire and Rimbaud as models, she felt that she was striking a blow against conventional morality in poetry, and in 1909, when Squire published his first book, he linked himself intentionally with John Lane, Arthur Symons, and the "Naughty Nineties," which still seemed to him to represent "something new in England." Squire's shifting responses tidily demonstrate one line of development of attitudes toward Baudelaire in this century. His first response—his most famous, even though he attempted to suppress it—was that first book, *Poems and Baudelaire Flowers*. Then, when he was well established as a literary power in London, "Solomon Eagle" of *The London Mercury*, Squire seized the opportunity of the publication of Symons's *Baudelaire* (1920) to print his mature views on the French poet. And, finally, when he wrote his memoirs, *The Honeysuckle and the Bee*, in 1937, he looked back and reshaped his earliest literary passion.

Squire's *Baudelaire Flowers*, which are opposed by their very title to the later, less exotic *Honeysuckle* and *Bee*, consist of thirty-eight translations: commendably direct and undecorated versions which draw on a wide range of Baudelaire's subjects. Squire does translate "Une Charogne" and one of the "Femmes Damnées," but it is his own verse that embodies his earliest "baudelairism." His "Other Poems" are often about a "fierce splendour/ Of lust" ("The rapture is over / The passion for pressure is spent, / And, lover by lover, / We lie in a languid content"); they sometimes attempt to agitate an imagery of corruption and decay ("The worms hold silent riot, / They burrow rotting skin and flesh, / Eagerly writhing through"); and sometimes they declare fraternity with the world beyond the Channel ("We who have but begun," he writes in "To the Continental Socialists," We who as yet are few, / Send out our hearts to you / Whose cause and ours is one . . . O Brothers").[11] For the young Squire, Baudelaire was the patron of a familiar revolt.

When Squire reviewed Symons's *Charles Baudelaire, A Study*, however, eleven years later, he drew a sharp distinction between the critic and his subject: "the reader who likes the flavour of a bygone fashion," he writes, "may derive some entertainment from the delightful obstinacy with which Mr. Symons maintains his desperately detached attitude towards the seven sins and the seven thousand diseases."[12] Symons, he said, was a left-over: "He, whatever may happen to the rest of the world, is not going to be thrown off his balance by consideration of morals and hygiene. He sings the old tune which has strayed on from the days of Gautier's 'Moi je fais émaux et camées!' How charming a perversion! How beautifully *stated* a brutality! How harmonious a blasphemy!" In 1920, art for art's sake and the decorations of decadence were out of style, and Squire, like some of his contemporaries, aimed to distinguish Baudelaire from the "swarm" of his decadent disciples. His influence, Squire writes, is im-

mense: "His disciples have come to him one by one in the solitude
of their own chambers, but those who bear his marks are found
in all civilised countries, and have included many of the most
conspicuous men of their age." But Baudelaire stands alone. To
his decadent imitators, Squire says, one wants to say, "Stop this
nonsense," or "Take some healthy exercise," but "Baudelaire
cannot be dismissed like that."

Fifty years after his death he still speaks in the portrait
printed in the common edition of his poems. We see those
dark liquid penetrating eyes looking out from under the
contemplative forehead, the wide shut mouth, the pouting
under lip. There is pride in it that tells us we are to expect,
in conversation, no confessional flow, no appeal for pity;
nothing but courteous, precise, ironic sentences, acute brief
analyses, observations slightly tinged with a bitter humour.
But the soul in reserve is evident in the fixed, ardent, mel-
ancholy look. He suffered and he was strong. When he died
of general paralysis, locked up in a body without speech,
his condition was an image of his whole life. He was always
a prisoner beyond reach of human contact, and the lips in
his portrait seem to say that wherever he may find himself
he will be the same on earth or in interstellar space, in
heaven or in hell, a wanderer, a solitary and an alien. There
was power in him, the power of a great personality; but his
strength was strangely manifested. There is a story by him-
self with a hero whose impotence was "so vast" that it was
"epic."

When Squire came back to the subject of Baudelaire in his
memoirs, he cast his early experience as myth; he was the in-
nocent youth; Les Fleurs du Mal was the potential liberator or
corrupter. He had discovered the poems while he was at school,
he recalls, in the edition with "the spell-binding portrait of him
in a smock, the head slightly bowed, the great melancholy eyes
looking straight at one above the wide sensuous mouth, and
Gautier's ample introduction." He read them because Baude-
laire's "material was very unlike that of the approved poets with
whom I was familiar and who were fit to be studied in schools,"
and he read them surreptitiously: "I used, after lights were out,
to steal down from the dormitory to my study in a dressing-
gown to translate him, carefully drawing the curtains so that no

chink of light shone across the lawn." But the older Squire is
equally carefully disparaging: "I left school thirty years ago and
still meet superior youths who think they have discovered Baude-
laire for the first time in the Croydon Free Library or the Oxford
Union." And he notes that he was not, really, influenced: "My
own natural imaginings were not in the least like Baudelaire's
(he haunted me but he did not infect me), but most young writers
go through intellectual measles of some sorts." (His father-in-
law, too, required assurance on that point: not realizing that
some of the poems were translations, Squire says, he expressed
the hope "that they did not record actual experiences of my
own.") Healthy it cannot be called, Arthur Symons had written
admiringly about decadent literature, and healthy it does not
wish to be considered—but "intellectual measles" it might have
wished to avoid. What the elder, patronizing Squire remembers,
however, was the decadence of decadence, the domestication of
revolt, the transformation into mere spots of Gautier's "roses de
phthisie."

   Although the older Squire represented his early attention to
Les Fleurs du Mal as merely a side of his adolescence, he had
been twenty-five when he published his collection. In *The Hon-
eysuckle and the Bee*, furthermore, he remembers only his "in-
dustrious versions" of "The Giantess," "The Carrion," and "the
poem about the repulsive Jewess," whose fascination he attri-
butes to their "strange mixture . . . of realism and romance." But
although they were withdrawn shortly after publication, some
of Squire's translations (which were published as a section of his
book entitled "Blossoms of Evil") have had a longer afterlife
than most of his work. They comprise a major part of James
Laver's edition of *The Flowers of Evil, Translated into English by
Various Hands*, which first appeared, illustrated by Jacob Epstein,
in 1940, and again, illustrated by Pièrre-Yves Trémois, in 1971.[13]
The older Squire, however, who continued, he said, to admire
Baudelaire's "marble purity" of style and his "firm ring of music,"
nevertheless borrowed Henry James's figure to condemn him as
one who "stood in the mud and looked at the stars."[14]

   When Squire launched *The London Mercury* in 1919, he took
pains to dissociate it from the *Mercure de France,* and he wrote
in its second number that he did "not intend to devote to the
study of foreign authors space that might more profitably be

given to the examination of a dead or living man who has written in our own tongue." The title of his journal, said Squire, "derived directly from the Mercuries which were the earliest products of the English periodical Press."[15] Squire's retrenchment was not an isolated gesture: even *Blast* had blasted France, and even Richard Aldington had approved of its "effort to look at art from an Anglo-Saxon point of view instead of from a borrowed foreign standpoint."[16] The "native tradition" had begun to reassert its claims even as the modernists were gathering. Part of the early twentieth-century reaction to the decadence was a desire to shake free of the French, and the war supported a new nationalism. Over the long term, the reaction against the cultural invasion had the effect of re-moralizing the terms of critical debate; over the short term, it produced large-scale self-contradiction, and most of the modernists moved toward maturity, in which they expressed near contempt for the writers of the 'nineties, by way of imitation, or criticism, or both, of their immediate predecessors.

Aldous Huxley is a case in point. He read Baudelaire early, and identified closely with his poetic purposes. In 1914, when he was twenty, he wrote in a letter that "One always feels so queer in the middle of the night, dreadfully melancholy, and fierce, and sentimental, and bored. Everything seems to be so grim and one feels at times like Baudelaire when he says:

> L'ennui, fruit de la morne incuriosité,
> Prend les proportions de l'Immortalité."

Huxley may seem to have been tailoring his feelings to fit a reach-me-down vocabulary, and he goes on to say, self-consciously, "Wonderful stuff French poetry—I once tried to write some myself";[17] but the lines he quotes in that early letter stayed with him. They appear again in his essay on "Accidie" and in his 1929 essay on Baudelaire, and one or other of Baudelaire's spleen poems surfaces frequently in his widely ranging criticism.[18] Some of his own French poetry appeared in *Wheels*, where Edith Sitwell kept the European connections alive, and it was anonymously reviewed by Eliot, in *The Athenaeum*, who called it "a private

L'ennui . . . boredom, the fruit of sullen indifference, takes on the proportions of immortality (S, 175).

exercise, like a set of upper-form hexameters."[19] Huxley also gave Baudelaire a significant place in his work: he translated him in *Cicadas and Other Poems* (1931), gave a fictional portrait of him in *Point Counter Point*, wrote an essay on him for his collection of psychological studies, *Do What You Will*, and represented him substantially in his anthology, *Texts and Pretexts* (1932). It is in the novel that Huxley turns Baudelaire to greatest effect, since there, as Ruth Temple first noticed,[20] he makes Spandrell out of materials supplied by Baudelaire's life and art. Here, Baudelaire is borne out of his due time by the devices of the imagination and made part of a complex and polemical twentieth-century action. Among the many things dramatized in *Point Counter Point* is Baudelaire's continuing power in English literature.

Spandrell is Huxley's first account of Baudelaire. His second appeared later, in *Do What You Will*, but the two are made from the same fabric, and Huxley had done the same reading in preparation for both. He draws in the essay as in the novel on Gautier's preface; and his interpretation relies heavily on François Porché, whose life of Baudelaire he recommended to Robert Nichols in January 1927. "What a hellish life," he said, "—inwardly predestined to hellishness by the man's own character."[21] Huxley also read—but after he had finished the novel—Valéry's preface to *Les Fleurs du Mal*, which seems to have supported his own view of Baudelaire as the representative "modern" poet. In *Do What You Will* he quotes Valéry's observation that Baudelaire's poetry is "la poésie même de la modernité" and derives from it a not very satisfactory answer to his final question, why Baudelaire, in spite of the hellishness, should be so widely admired in Huxley's own time. (*Ennui* is a modern condition, he says: we recognize ourselves in Baudelaire.) Huxley's two "transfigurations" of Baudelaire—to use the word he applied to Mallarmé's translation of Poe's "The Raven"[22]—are the culmination, though certainly not the end, of his long interest, and they stand as a repudiation of his earlier admiration. Both the fictional portrait and the essay are intensely hostile to their subject; and both present Baudelaire, with a marked absence of discrimination, as a "pervert." Each, of course, forms part of a work whose dominant note is antagonism, and in each Huxley manages at once to condemn "perversion" and to advocate "multiplicity" and the abandonment of moral and psychological absolutes.

Spandrell provides a catalogue to the features of "baudelair-
ism" as it was perceived by some of the early twentieth-century
reformers. He is at one level a kind of lowest common denom-
inator Baudelaire, put together of bits and pieces from the re-
ceived view. Huxley makes him a cold sensualist, a sadist, a per-
vert, a diabolist, a false monk, an ascetic. He gives him a highly
developed sense of smell, an adoration of music, a fascination
with hell and evil, an obsession with death, a careful program
of "deliberately cultivated" indulgences, and an overwhelming,
and finally triumphant, ennui. All of these characteristics are
borrowed, not invented: what Huxley was able to take from life
in the case of the other characters in this *roman à clef*, he took,
in the case of Baudelaire, from memoirs and from Baudelaire's
writings. He equips Spandrell with Baudelaire's relationship to
his mother and stepfather, with his financial circumstances, and,
Derek Scale observes, the facial features of Baudelaire's death
mask:[23] "It was a gaunt face. Cheekbone and jaw showed in hard
outline through the tight skin. The grey eyes were deeply set.
In the cadaverous mask only the mouth was fleshy—a wide
mouth, with lips that stood out from the skin like two thick
weals."[24]

He constructs his conversation, his environment, and his men-
tal experience from a vocabulary and an imagery that are lifted
from his subject's own work. He draws lavishly from the "Spleen"
poems, for instance, which had fascinated him from his youth.[25]
When Spandrell is on the scene, there is likely to be rain "sliding
incessantly down the dirty glass of the windows" (305) or "sooty
cobwebs [dangling] from the ceiling" (248) or a damp so pene-
trating as to ensure that "the fungi and the mildew were sprout-
ing even in his soul" (297). The spiritual vegetation is the product
of Spandrell's state of mind, of course: he "really like[s] hating
and being bored." "The rain fell and fell; the mushrooms
sprouted in his very heart and he deliberately cultivated them"
(304). Spandrell, Huxley makes us aware, had "a slimy growth
within him," and he "lay in bed, or sat in his dismal room, or
leaned against the counter in a public house" to watch it with
his "inward eyes" (297). The paralysis and the spleen are par-
ticular—they are Baudelaire's—but they are also representative.
Spandrell is a caricature of the decadence. His analogy between
nights and human beings—"Nights are . . . never interesting till
they're grown up. Round about midnight they reach puberty.

. . . After four they're in full decay," and so on (200)—is a parody of the conventional comparison of literary periods to naturally ordained cycles of time. Huxley even offers Spandrell the conventional final choice of the decadent, in such a way as to make his readers aware of the allusion. In the final phase of Spandrell's life, the text reminds us of the choices that Barbey d'Aurevilly said were open to Baudelaire, to become a Catholic or to kill himself: "What a man!" Rampion is reported to have "mocked" when Spandrell presses him to come to hear the Beethoven. "Ought to join the Church of Rome and have a confessor" (591). But Spandrell, arranging his own death, chooses the other path: it is essential to the novel's critical argument.

Point Counter Point is related to Baudelaire by several threads, however, some finer and more fascinating than those by which Huxley stitches Spandrell into a portrait of "baudelairism" or "decadence." The text often leans heavily on its allusions, using them to fatten thin characters, to complicate dramatic episodes by external reference, and to establish its own attitude toward its material. Cuthbert Arkwright, for instance, who bursts drunkenly into chapter eleven, gains a dimension from Huxley's external reference: "He had an idea that by brawling and behaving offensively, he was defending art against the Philistines. Tipsy, he felt himself arrayed on the side of the angels, of Baudelaire, of Edgar Allan Poe, of De Quincey, against the dull unspiritual mob" (168). In these allusions, Huxley undermines his own hostility to Baudelaire, and reveals the derided subject as a powerful presence in his own mind, shaping the novel. The pub scene, in which Carling gets drunk, furnishes another example: it is offered, mockingly, as an exploration of the *paradis artificiel* that is organized by the pain-observing Spandrell. Carling, whose identity is concealed from us until the end of the episode, is like the women Spandrell so frigidly debauches, wholly under the power of the sadist: he is a soft, pink, pudgy "choir boy" whose weakness is played, cynically. His drinking, like that of the others in the pub in which Spandrell goes slumming, is a mock paradise, artificial and squalid. Huxley presents it, ironically, as a voyage:

Beer flowed, spirits were measured out in little noggins, preciously. In stout, in bitter, in whiskey they bought the equivalents of foreign travel and mystical ecstasy, of poetry

and a week-end with Cleopatra, of big-game hunting and
music. (307)

The voyage, of course, is Baudelaire's central image, multiply
expressive, and the question, "Quand partons-nous pour le bon-
heur?" (I, 655) is the motivation for the many departures that
mark his work, into the artificial paradises, or into the city, or
into the world. Huxley plays on the image here, and then, in-
voking Baudelaire's most famous voyage, mocks the horror:
Spandrell, in a dandy's gesture, pulls out a spotted silk hand-
kerchief. "The choir-boy shuddered and held up his hands. 'But
what a handkerchief!' he exclaimed, 'what a horror!' " (307).
Neither the allusion nor its triviality is accidental, and neither is
insignificant; trivializing and satiric allusion is the first feature
of this novel, in which Huxley's mind moves in a steadily weaving
motion from, as he might have put it, text to pre-text. The voyage
is one of his Baudelairean *motifs*, and he elaborates it with schol-
arly care and with the composer's attention to detail.

The "horror" that Carling feels for Spandrell's handkerchief
is a counter somewhere in the piccolos to a point that belongs
to the double basses. In "Le Voyage," it will be remembered,
Baudelaire's questing poet, one of the "étonnants voyageurs,"
sets sail to discover an essential truth: what he finds—the oasis
of horror in the desert of ennui—Wilde had already mocked
and revered. Huxley makes the oasis and the desert the prin-
ciples of Spandrell's life: the "spleen" passages comprise descrip-
tion of the desert, and the murder and suicide offer him the
oasis. The "horror" is Spandrell's preoccupation: he identifies it
in the first restaurant conversation:

"Like ostriches," said Mary Rampion. "You live like os-
triches."

"And not about revolutions only," said Spandrell. . . .
"About all the important things that happen to be disa-
greeable. There was a time when people didn't go about
pretending that death and sin didn't exist. *Au détour d'un
sentier une charogne infâme*," he quoted. "Baudelaire was the
last poet of the Middle Ages as well as the first modern. *Et*

Quand . . . When do we depart for happiness?
étonnants . . . astonishing travelers.
Au détour . . . there where the path turned, a disgusting corpse.

pourtant," he went on, looking with a smile to Lucy and raising his glass.

> "Et pourtant vous serez semblable à cette ordure,
> A cette horrible infection,
> Etoile de mes yeux, soleil de ma nature,
> Vous, mon ange et ma passion!
>
> Alors, ô ma beauté, dites à la vermine
> Qui vous mangera de baisers . . ."

"My dear Spandrell!" Lucy held up her hand protestingly.
"Really too necrophilous!" said Willie Weaver.
"Always the same hatred of life," Rampion was thinking.
"Different kinds of death—the only alternatives." He looked observantly into Spandrell's face. (181)

The passage, in which Spandrell reveals death as both his passion and his angel, allows the character to speak unmasked: Huxley here provides the "key." But the passage also creates an ironic resonance for a later scene in which an uncooperative corpse is the central player. When Spandrell and Illidge truss the dead Webley, Spandrell, having hoped for "the essential horror" (533), and for the dignity of tragedy, finds that "It was not only not tragic; it was a clownery" (543). The passages describing Webley as corpse undermine the romance of the *charogne:*

> [Spandrell] bent down and moved one of the arms towards the side. It returned, when he let go, half-way to its former position. Like a puppet, Spandrell reflected, with elastic joints. Grotesque rather than terrible; not tragical, but only rather tiresome and even absurd. That was the essential horror—that it was all (even *this*) a kind of bad and tedious jape. (542)

It is the failure of "the essential horror" that drives Spandrell to the conventional exit of the decadent. His last scene is a brilliantly managed composition of borrowings: the absolute transcendence (the "Heaven") of the Beethoven, which comes by way of witty imitation from Baudelaire's "La Musique," gives way to

---

Et pourtant . . . And yet, you will come to resemble that loathsome corruption, o star of my eyes, o sun of my nature, my angel and my passion! Then, o my beauty, tell the vermin which will devour you with kisses . . . (S, 49-50).

Spandrell's decision to plunge to the very bottom of the gulf. Huxley manipulates the Baudelairean antithesis with great cunning: "La Musique" supplies the soaring, sailing, free elevation, and "Le Voyage" provides the plunge into darkness. Spandrell departs to a stage-managed death with an ironical twist at the corners of his mouth: "Enfer ou ceil, qu'importe?"

Point Counter Point, of course, is packed with allusions, references, hints, echoes and plain thefts. It is, as thoroughly as *The Picture of Dorian Gray*, a patchwork. Literary imitation and borrowing comprise a principle of its construction as well as a characteristic of its style, and Baudelaire is not its only secondary author. John Middleton Murry wrote some of the material for Burlap, who, like Spandrell, is a construction of borrowings. When he visits Rampion, for instance, to look at his pictures, he speaks in words that first appeared under Murry's signature: "Life, after all, was the important thing. 'I believe in life.' That was the first article of one's creed" (286). But "one's creed" was Murry's, and Huxley reproduces it here to ridicule it.[26] Nor does Huxley restrict his borrowings to the sort I have been discussing—in which Baudelaire as the model for Spandrell, or Murry as the model for Burlap, or Lawrence as the model for Rampion, write their own lines. When Quarles and Elinor, riding at night in a chauffeur-driven car in India, hit a dog, Huxley reaches into *Passage to India* for his material, and not only for the incident and the location, but also for the theme of the passage, since when the car hits the dog Elinor is meditating on her personal relationship with Philip. She re-enacts Adela Quested.

Baudelaire, however, is different from the other "source characters" in this *roman à clef*, and his differences suggest his special importance. While the others come from Huxley's own time and from his own national culture, the model for Spandrell is a nineteenth-century French poet carried forward by fictional re-creation to a twentieth-century conversation. He represents, in *Point Counter Point*, one of the two major positions on the subject of art in the modern world. Huxley opposes him to Rampion. The character is evidently not intended to convey Huxley's approval of the model—indeed, he suggests the contrary—but he does indicate how solidly Baudelaire had settled into the English tradition since Swinburne had first hailed him.

Enfer . . . Heaven or hell, what does it matter?

Huxley's Baudelaire allusions range widely. The novel in-
cludes not only a full-dress "baudelairism," but also a kind of
allusion intended for close readers of the source. Like Pater,
Huxley provides for more than one kind of audience. His use
of Ary Scheffer's name, in Rampion's insult to Burlap, makes
that clear: after Burlap has failed to approve of his paintings,
Rampion promises him, "Next time you come, I'll have a copy
of Ary Scheffer's 'St. Monica and St. Augustine' for you. That
ought to make you really happy" (288). That painting, though
Huxley does not say so, figures prominently in the *Salon de 1846*,
where it is a touchstone of falseness. It appears in a chapter
titled, "De M. Ary Scheffer et Des Singes du Sentiment" (II,
474). Rampion's insult requires no decoding for a reader of *L'Art
Romantique*, and Huxley most certainly had some of those in mind
when he constructed it. (Burlap himself, for instance, who, as
John Middleton Murry, knew Baudelaire's art criticism very well
indeed.)[27]

There is no doubt that Huxley's intimate audience included
D. H. Lawrence, not only because he appears in the novel, too,
"transfigured" as Mark Rampion, but also because Huxley saw
a good deal of him while he was at work on the book. In January
1928, while he was struggling with "this wretched book," he was
in Switzerland, "with D. H. Lawrence and his wife two minutes
away across the snow in another wooden hut. So that leisure
moments are amusingly filled."[28] *Point Counter Point* was certain
to have been one of their topics of conversation, and it is possible
that some of Huxley's comic or satiric or snide personal and
textual references may have been more open to Lawrence than
to any other reader. It may be, furthermore, that the novel's
conclusion, with which Huxley was struggling, occupied their
talk: Huxley's ending brings Rampion and Spandrell gradually
to a single and direct combat, expanding their initial argument
(in the restaurant) about sex into a contest between life and death
and transcendence and reality. In February 1928, Huxley was
writing that his "bloody novel" was still not finished, and that he
was thinking of going with Lawrence to New Mexico for six
months in the next year.[29] The impact of Lawrence registers
obviously almost everywhere in *Point Counter Point*: his life, art,
and philosophy provide the single stable element in a novel
which, otherwise, is preoccupied with "multiplicity"; and his
views triumph, in the novel's central debate, over those of others.

Lawrence is not irrelevant to consideration of Spandrell, then, since he supplies the views that are championed by Spandrell's antagonist in *Point Counter Point*. Huxley's "transfigurations," his Rampion and his Spandrell, enact a debate whose terms are supplied by Lawrence and Baudelaire, and one may speculate that Huxley's conception of Spandrell had the approval of Lawrence. It is certain that the terms in which Huxley sees Baudelaire are consistent with Lawrence's, and that Spandrell is at every point the antithesis of Rampion. When they are first presented together Rampion is full of light—"The eyes were blue and piercing, and the very fine hair, a little on the reddish side of golden, fluttered up at every moment, every breath of wind, like wisps of brown flame." Spandrell, by contrast, speaks "from the half-darkness outside the little world of pink-tinged lamplight in which their table stood . . . leaning backwards, his chair tilted on its hind legs against the wall" (129). At the end of this novel Spandrell lies dead at the feet of Mark Rampion. (The uniformed British Freemen, hardly relevant to the episode, are merely agents.) Although Huxley mocks the Baudelairean and romantic antitheses—Spandrell's absolutes, good and evil—he resolves his own book into an absolute antagonism, pitting life against death, brightness against darkness, the angel against the demon. In this history, that contest has an exceptional interest: it is a revival of earlier poetic wars, in which Baudelaire was sent out against Tennyson and Wordsworth. In *Point Counter Point* the Victorian Mephistopheles reappears. " 'There, he's the demon again,' thought Rampion. 'He's come to life and he's the demon' " (598).

Huxley's 1929 essay on Baudelaire appeared in *Do What You Will*, the series of "biographies" of what Lawrence called "the grand perverts," for which Huxley took notes while correcting the proofs of *Point Counter Point*. Hailing the idea for this collection in May, 1928, Lawrence put forward some familiar names, among them "Michael Angelo and Leonardo . . . Byron-Baudelaire-Wilde-Proust." In the novel Philip Quarles wondered whether the word "perversion" (one of his aesthetic preoccupations) was meaningless since it imples the existence of a norm, but the norm held nothing problematical for Lawrence, who maintained that the grand perverts "all did the same thing, or tried to: to kick off, or to intellectualise and so utterly falsify the phallic consciousness, which is the basic consciousness, and the thing we mean, in the best sense, by common sense."[30]

The Baudelaire of this collection occupies the middle ground between Spandrell on the one hand and Lawrence's views on the other. Parts of the portrait are duplicated in Spandrell, and its whole argument is to be found in the pages of *Point Counter Point*, as an aspect of content or of treatment. In the novel Rampion is chief among several commentators on Spandrell. In the essay Huxley gathers the various voices into his own, and speaks for himself. The essayist and his "pedagogue pervert," Rampion (564), adopt the same, hostile tone. The essayist, like the pedagogue, mocks: he begins by undermining a claim that the *débauché* is a great philosopher "inasmuch as he pursues an absolute." This, he says, may have been true before Hume, but since then it has been "silly," for "though it may be sublime to pursue the demonstrably unattainable, it is also ridiculous." Though we "may admire" the *débauché*'s "single-mindedness," "we must also laugh at his folly. To pursue the absolute is as demonstrably a waste of time as to speculate on the topography of the invisible portion of the moon." The *débauché*, the satanist, and his inverse the saint, are "mad, all mad; and, however tragical and appalling their insanity may be, madmen are always ridiculous." A satanist is "something of a figure of fun" because of "his partial blindness, his stiffness, his strained and focussed and unwavering fixity of monomaniacal purpose, his inhumanity." Monomaniacal characters, of whom the satanist is one kind and Baudelaire one instance, are distinguished by the absence from their behavior of "normal physical relationship with their fellows and with the world at large." Dostoievsky's *The Possessed* gives a perfect demonstration: "his people do not even eat normally, much less make love, or work, or enjoy nature." What they do instead is "go and commit suicide, or murder, or rape, according to the turn their monomanias happen to have taken." Dostoievsky's horrors, says Huxley, "are tragedies of mental licentiousness. All Dostoievsky's characters . . . have licentious minds, utterly unrestrained by their bodies. They are all emotional onanists, wildly indulging themselves in the void of imagination." All of this is "tragic"; it is also "stupid and grotesque." "If Stavrogin could have gone to bed with women he liked, instead of sleeping, on satanically ascetic principles, with women he detested," much pain and tragedy could have been avoided.

Alternatively, Huxley proposes, he could have laughed at himself: although Baudelaire claims that laughter is satanic, there is "a whole gamut of humorous and unferocious laughter that is entirely and characteristically human" (that is, not satanic). That laughter, present in Chaucer and Burns, might have allowed Baudelaire to see himself not as Satan but as Clootie: then, says Huxley, "he would have been certainly a happier and completer man and perhaps a better because a more comprehensive poet." Lacking a power for non-masochistic sexual relations and the grace of seeing himself as Clootie, Baudelaire turned his cruelties upon himself. He was "above all, a satanist of love," whose cruelties "were directed inwards." Huxley regrets that, since it would have been far better for him (revenging his mother's betrayal) to be cruel to his partners: "For what are a few virginities and a few square inches of tanned cocotte-skin compared with the entire universe?" By redirecting his cruelty, Baudelaire lost everything: "The satanist who is his own victim defaces and defiles for himself the entire universe. And when, like Baudelaire, he happens to be a great poet, he defaces and defiles it for his readers." Huxley's attack employs reiterated qualifying clauses introduced by *although*: although a vain pursuit is sublime, it is also ridiculous; although madness is tragic, it is also ridiculous; although Baudelaire expresses suffering, he might have been therapeutically cured and expressed something quite different. Huxley concedes Baudelaire's importance in the very fervor of his protest, which is against what he sees as orthodox as well as perverse.

It all boils down—or reduces—to Baudelaire's inverted Christianity. (Had it not been inverted, it would have been no more acceptable to Huxley: Burlap provides the opposite case, which is presented with conversational profundity by Rampion in his remark about "St. Anthony and his demons or St. Francis and his half-wits" [563].) You can't be a Satanist without being a "Godist," too, Huxley writes in the essay; and if you are an inverted Godist, you will regard as virtues the Godist's sins, indulging passion in all of the inverted ways. Baudelaire *could* have been saved by a healthy Hellenism—both Huxley and Rampion say so—although nothing could have been more remote from his temperament.

What Huxley gathers together in his essay was divided and distributed among a number of characters in the novel. Spandrell himself thinks in the terms the essay outlines, deriving the existence of God from the existence of evil: "God's best joke, so far as he himself was concerned, was not being there. Simply not there. Neither God nor the devil. For if the devil had been there, God would have been there too" (586). Mary Rampion initiates and pursues the *motif* of grotesqueness: "Like a gargoyle, Mary thought, a gargoyle in a pink boudoir. There was one on Notre Dame in just that attitude, leaning forward with his demon's face between his claws" (131). Quarles outlines in his notebook an attraction to writing about "perverts" or departures from the "norm." But it is given to Rampion to diagnose Spandrell as a "morality-philosophy pervert," to see him in Dostoievsky's terms as "Quite the little Stavrogin," to observe the connection between the satanists and the godists, to specify as yardstick for action "the central norm" and as "perverts" those who depart from it, to assert the moral connection between "perversion" and comedy: "Pardon my saying so, Spandrell; but you really are the most colossal fool. . . . Smiling like all the tragic characters of fiction rolled into one! But it won't do. It doesn't conceal the simple-minded zany underneath" (564). It is Rampion, too, who analyzes the cultural malady from which Spandrell suffers: "You seem to imagine that the cold, modern, civilized lasciviousness is the same as the healthy—what shall I call it?—phallism . . . of the ancients" (165). He also prescribes the cure: "You ought to get married, you know" (131). All of that, of course, is unmistakably Lawrentian, and it is no surprise either that Lawrence wrote to Huxley after the appearance of *Do What You Will* to say that the essay "seemed to me very good. All needs saying, badly."[31]

Lawrence began, like Huxley, disposed to approve of Baudelaire. He wrote in 1910 to Louie Burrows, "I've got Baudelaire's *Fleurs du Mal*—got them for 9d in Charing Cross Rd on Friday: it was a fine capture. I'll read some to you when there is an opportunity. They are better than Verlaine."[32] But *Women in Love*, which records his later view, predicts the Rampion-Spandrell antithesis of *Point Counter Point*. In the chapter called "Gudrun in the Pompadour," Halliday, drunk, reads from a letter of Birkin's to a crowd of what Gerald calls jackasses. The scene, and the letter, pit Birkin against the poet of corruption:

"Oh, I do think these phrases are too absurdly wonderful [says Halliday]. Oh, but don't you think they *are*—they're nearly as good as Jesus. 'And if, Julius, you want this ecstasy of reduction with Minette, you must go on till it is fulfilled. But surely there is in you also, somewhere, the living desire for positive creation, relationships in ultimate faith, when all this process of active corruption, with all its flowers of mud, is transcended, and more or less finished—' I do wonder what the flowers of mud are. Minette, you are a flower of mud."

"Thank you—and what are you?"

"Oh, I'm another, surely, according to this letter! We're all flowers of mud—*Fleurs—hic! du mal*! It's perfectly wonderful, Birkin harrowing Hell—harrowing the Pompadour—*Hic*!"

In 1929, when he wrote the introduction to *Pansies*, Lawrence offered them as an antidote to darker bloom: "This little bunch of fragments is offered as a bunch of *pensées*, anglicé pansies; handful of thoughts. Or, if you will have the other derivation of pansy, from *panser*, to dress or soothe a wound; these are my tender administrations to the mental and emotional wounds we suffer from. Or you can have heartsease if you like, since the modern heart could certainly do with it."[33]

Huxley constructed Spandrell as an inversion of the values Lawrence had preached, and he named him, wittily, to suggest that inversion. Both the essay and the novel insist, in detail and repeatedly, that the character is an inversion of values, an inside-out puritan. (In the novel, Rampion confesses that he is a puritan.) His name continues the theme: a *spandrell*—the word is an architectural term—is the triangular space between the outer curve of an arch and the rectangle framed by the mouldings enclosing it; the adjoining spandrells between two arches would be an inverted arch. Spandrell, Huxley's character, is an inversion of the values with which Will Brangwen invests the cathedral arch in *The Rainbow*. What Lawrence intends by the symbol of the arch, Huxley inverts by the naming of Spandrell. The arch, writes H. M. Daleski, suggests not "unity in diversity, the union of a separate heaven and earth, but the attainment of a 'oneness' that obliterates all distinction . . . 'the timeless ecstasy' of an absolute which is insidiously compelling."[34] That is what Spandrell seeks (since you cannot be a Satanist without being a Godist too), and what he is attempting to persuade Rampion of in the Beethoven, the "*heiliger Dankgesang eines Genesenen an die Gottheit, in der lydischen Tonart* [which] simply must be heard" (591) and whose slow movement is "heaven." Baudelaire, Huxley wrote in his essay, had an idea of the best love as "a purely mental relationship, a conscious interbecoming of two hitherto separate beings."[35] Spandrell's quest for a oneness and a transcendence that were in themselves "anathema" to Lawrence is, like everything else about him, inside out: the spandrell implies the arch. Neither, of course, suits Rampion.

Although Huxley said in his essay that Baudelaire was "the photographic image in negative of a Father of the Church," he casts him in his novel as the shadow of Lawrence; and although he presents Burlap as Spandrell's spiritual opposite, the St. Francis to his St. Anthony, Huxley gives the central debate in his novel, about the nature of art in the modern world, to Spandrell and Rampion. That fact is remarkable: Baudelaire had been dead for fifty years when *Point Counter Point* appeared; yet it is to him, and not to any of his French or English inheritors, that Huxley attributes this key version of modernism. One other fact about Huxley's Baudelaire is remarkable; neither in his novel nor in his essay does he give any very serious attention to what Baudelaire actually wrote. Spandrell is constructed of bits and pieces from the poems and the prose, and the text of *Point Counter Point* is shaped and directed by Huxley's reading of some of the poems, but it is of course not an account of Baudelaire. Following it, the essay in *Do What You Will* is rather a reading of Spandrell than a reading of Baudelaire. This Baudelaire of Huxley, so different from that of most writers I have considered, is nonetheless put to a familiar use: it is an expanded shorthand, a sign of loyalty to a party—this time the party of Lawrence. And the Baudelaire allusion in Lawrence himself has the very quality the historical Baudelaire had described in the passage at the head of this chapter: "il lance le mot: *Pétrus Borel!* et tout est dit. Le jugement est prononcé, l'auteur est foudroyé." In England, Pétrus Borel remained unknown, tucked away in a Swinburne imitation. But "Baudelaire" did not, and *Fleurs— hic!—du Mal!* could constitute the thunderbolt.

*   *   *

Huxley did not attack Baudelaire as the father of the decadents, however, until the 1920's. In the first two decades of the century, during part of which he was making Baudelaire a model for his own work, "baudelairism" was very much alive. English poetry, as C. K. Stead writes, had reached "the lowest point of a long decline": "traditional respect for literature [was] mixed with narrow demands for poetry and novels of a particular, second-rate kind" and poets faced a society in which "literature [was] ignored, except by a tiny minority."[36] "Baudelairism," therefore, fell conveniently to hand. Baudelaire's name, Arthur Symons noted, "(generally mis-spelled) is the journalist's handiest brickbat for hurling at random in the name of respectability."[37] But his name, as Symons did not note, was also the radical poet's handiest brickbat for hurling *at* respectability, and that was a lesson that young poets of the early twentieth century were learning from the later nineteenth. Richard Aldington describes the ease with which, against a background of insular complacency, mention of the model for much of the 'nineties' satanism and eroticism could produce a nervous thrill. He writes of the first literary party he attended in London:

So high-brow was this salon that there was talk of French poetry, and the ladies shivered chastely as they denounced a dreadful man with the mysterious name of Bawdy l'Air. An elderly gentleman in a dinner jacket opined gravely that he was "very Gallic," and the ladies said, "How true!"[38]

Edith Sitwell was, she said, a member of "the most advanced schools."[39] That was true from the beginning of her career: *Wheels* made it clear and *Façade* confirmed it. Except for Hopkins and Yeats, she said, "and with the possible exception of Francis Thompson, the poets writing between the years 1880 and 1900 had little or nothing to recommend them";[40] mere "bad rhetoric" had produced the poetry of the 'nineties. She thought that the "difference between [Keats] and the gentlemen of the 'nineties who said we must have 'Art for Art's sake' is that he is an artist, they were merely house-painters, decorating a flat unliving surface,"[41] and she deplored "the 'eighteen-ninety' taint of affectedness which is so often to be found in young writers."[42] But Edith Sitwell's own modernism is rooted by a thousand small fibres in the later nineteenth century. Her early poetry depends almost entirely on an idea of surfaces that are sharply distinct and even detached from depths; the rhythms of her verse, which are not only musical but often provided by dance, push art's aspiration to the condition of music to a literal conclusion; her

dislocated puppets in their mechanical-toy settings are related
by an extremely close "cousinage," as Baudelaire might have
said—or by "the logic of the imagination," as Wilde might have
put it—to the de-humanized puppets that spring into action
when Dorian Gray leaves his interiors and who inhabit the lurid
world of Wilde's poem "The Harlot's House." Her own convic-
tions about poetry, furthermore, come directly from a tradition
that was once "the most advanced school": she carried it over to
the twenties and thirties. This is not to say that Edith Sitwell was
not genuinely inventive or genuinely "modern," but that her
invention and her modernism take their *point de départ*, as do
Pound's and Eliot's and Joyce's and Huxley's, from a nineteenth-
century inheritance.

Sitwell acknowledged Swinburne, most generously: he seemed
to her to command (in a term familiar to this study) an "impec-
cable virtuosity" and to be "among the greatest masters of his
medium that our race has produced."[43] She first read him at
seventeen, and she admired him throughout her life. When, in
1931, she remembered her first fascination with his work, she
declared her continuing loyalty to him: "The no-longer young
lady was then, and is still, much in love with the poems of Swin-
burne, with Christina Rossetti's 'Goblin Market' and with certain
of the work of slightly older poets, Edgar Allan Poe, Tennyson
and Edward Fitzgerald."[44] Sitwell's poetry positively parades the
effects of her admiration for Swinburne: only poets with "no
subtlety of ear"[45] undervalued him, she said, and in what affects
the ear her poetry issues from his. So, perhaps, does her criti-
cism's preoccupation with "transcendental vowel-technique" and
doubled or jarring consonants. In Sitwell's mythology of herself,
Swinburne has the place of precursor. Her accounts of her flight
to the Isle of Wight to visit his grave are full of significance:

> I was staying in my grandmother Sitwell's house in Bourne-
> mouth, and at 6 o'clock in the morning, I ran away to visit
> Swinburne's grave in the Isle of Wight, taking with me a
> bunch of red roses, a laurel wreath, and a jug of milk; also
> my extremely disagreeable lady's maid.
>   I had a really frightful row with the sexton . . . but poured
> the libation onto the grave, over which bloomed a huge red
> fuschia.
>   When I returned to my grandmother's house there was,

of course, a terrible row, and I found that (in my absence) a man called Losey and his wife had induced her to burn my volume of the 1st Swinburne *Poems and Ballads*, because these would corrupt my mind! (I hadn't the slightest idea of anything wrong in them.)[46]

"At seventeen," her biographer remarks, "she was a very romantic girl."[47] But Edith Sitwell was also a well-read young poet, and she was performing a ritual Swinburne had described in his most widely admired poem:

> I among these, I also, in such station
>   As when the pyre was charred, and piled the sods,
>   And offering to the dead made, and their gods,
> The old mourners had, standing to make libation,
>   I stand, and to the gods and to the dead
>   Do reverence without prayer or praise, and shed
> Offering to these unknown, the gods of gloom,
>   And what of honey and spice my seedlands bear,
>   And what I may of fruits in this chilled air,
> And lay, Orestes-like, across the tomb
>   A curl of severed hair.

By her gesture she made herself part of the dissenting "communion of song" that Swinburne had celebrated in "Ave atque Vale"; and by their action Mr. and Mrs. Losey confirmed her in opposition.

Edith Sitwell took her conception of her role as poet from the later nineteenth century. She *épatait les bourgeois*, of course, and she meant to. She thought, as Wilde had thought in *The Soul of Man under Socialism*, that "Every poet of any importance has been called mad or a liar during his life-time."[48] She saw herself as a revolutionary in taste and in technique, and when she defended her preoccupation with technique she attacked the "belief that poetry should be only a pseudo-philosophy expounding pseudo-scientific ideas" and "the imbecile fallacies that it is better to be good than beautiful, and that technique in poetry is vulgar, in bad form."[49] She longed for former, better times, she said, in which "poetry was regarded as an art, and not as a vehicle for conveying misty moral ideas," and she thought that it was "time that we readmitted what is known as pure poetry."[50] She launched frequent and explosive attacks on "the vulgar," "the pedants," and "all of those persons whose principal pleasure lies in hampering beauty which has any hint of strangeness."[51] She quoted Baudelaire to the effect that "Poetry . . . has no other aim than Herself,"[52] and although she did not approve of the exponents of art for art's sake, their ideas underlie her own: "What a shocking thing it is," she wrote, taking up both Swinburne's subject and his ironic tone, "if you come to think of it, for any workman to be interested in the materials with which he works! Will the old gentlemen, and the young gentlemen, kindly remember these words of William Blake 'Mechanical excellence is the only vehicle of genius' and 'Without innate Neatness of Execution, the Sublime cannot exist.' "[53] Her description of the poems in *Façade* as "*abstract*" patterns in sound, technical experiments, carries into the *annus mirabilis* of the modern period the preoccupations of the 1860's and 1870's: it refuses to entertain non-aesthetic questions and it proclaims the existence of the "laws" of art.[54]

Baudelaire is attached in Sitwell's work both to what she derived from the past, including an English past, and to what she invented for the present. She read him, her brother recalled, along with Swinburne and the others: "How lovely," Sacheverell Sitwell wrote, "to be young and to feel poetry running in your veins!"

> It will be Swinburne or William Morris that she reads: August, or In the Orchard, from *Poems and Ballads*; Anactoria; Golden Wings, or The Blue Closet. Such are poems of pear or apple blossom to be read in the springtime of one's life. But, as well, the Fleurs du Mal darken this paradise, as though with lines of rain. It is poetry of the blood's decline. And her own images begin to form.[55]

Edith Sitwell was introduced to Baudelaire's works—as to Verlaine's and Rimbaud's—by Helen Rootham, who came to Renishaw to be her governess in 1903.[56] Later, Sitwell relied heavily on Arthur Symons for her view of these poets, but in the beginning, four or five years before Eliot read Symons and so began to find his own voice, she caught her enthusiasm from Rootham, herself a poet. Rootham had already lived in France for several years before she came to the Sitwell family, and she had already begun her translation of Rimbaud's *Illuminations*, some of which were to appear later in *Wheels*. When, in 1932, these were published as a book, Edith Sitwell wrote the introduction.

Edith Sitwell's encounter with the French poets defined an enduring note in her modernism: like other modernists, she considered the French and English traditions to have been effectively unified. She would subscribe to *Secession*, she said, "for the purpose of reading its criticism of modernist French works."⁵⁷ That was just after the demise of the Anglo-French Poetry Society, of which Helen Rootham, Edith Sitwell, and Marguerite Bennett were founding members. At meetings of that society, to which Edith Sitwell proposed at one stage to invite as members Bernard Shaw, H. G. Wells, Granville-Barker, Sassoon, W. H. Davies, Gustave Holst, Honegger, Ravel, John Galsworthy, Walter de la Mare, Hugh Walpole and Lady Colefax,⁵⁸ Marguerite Bennett recited works of French poetry, and English poets read their own works. Lytton Strachey's account of one meeting of the group is characteristically snide—"There was an address (very poor)," he wrote to Carrington, "on Rimbaud etc. by an imbecile Frog; then Edith Sitwell appeared, her nose longer than an ant-eater's, and read some of her absurd stuff; then Eliot—very sad and seedy—it made one weep; finally Mrs. Arnold Bennett recited, with waving arms and chanting voice, Baudelaire and Verlaine till everyone was ready to vomit"—but both Edith and Osbert Sitwell took a different view, and both wrote to Marguerite Bennett to congratulate her on her "superb" and "*divinely*" recited Baudelaire.⁵⁹ Sitwell made her devotion to the French poets public in other ways, too: they figure prominently in her *Poet's Notebook*, in her personal anthology, and in her critical work. Nerval, Baudelaire, Mallarmé, Verlaine, and Rimbaud dominate the French section of her anthology, and they appear, with Villon, in *A Book of the Winter*. Among these, she said, she felt the closest personal affinity with Rimbaud, but she reserved her highest poetic praise for Baudelaire: "It is this simultaneity, a kind of water-clearness (into which he fell as into a river) on the verge of death, to which Baudelaire has attained."⁶⁰

Sitwell and her brothers, as John Pearson says, stood, in the poetic wars of the twentieth century, on the side of "left-wing politicians, 'intellectuals,' 'dandy-aesthetes' with Wilde's green carnation still in the button-hole, admirers of experimental poetry and the latest painting from the school of Paris, and the

whole of Bloomsbury."[61] That was to be decidedly and osten-
tatiously modern. But their definitions of their modernism were
not limitingly up to date: "By modern," Edith Sitwell wrote to
Marguerite Bennett, on the subject of programs for The Anglo-
French Poetry Society, "I mean from Baudelaire and Swinburne
onwards."[62] *Wheels*, in which Sitwell expressed her first modern-
ism, reflects her view. Both its contributors and its reviewers saw
it as "Baudelairean," but while the reviewers thought that meant
derivative, the contributors thought it meant modern. The sec-
ond cycle reprinted proudly what *The Morning Post* had said
about the first: " 'Precious,' 'macabre,' 'Baudelairean' are some
of the epithets hurled at [the contributors], for there is nothing
which irritates the hack-critic so much as the appearance of a
new 'school' of poetry engaged in quietly working out its own
conception of the art."[63] "Augustine Rivers," under the same
impression about the newness of the *Wheels* aesthetic, but not
about the quietness of the work, raised Baudelaire as the banner
for his attack on the Squirearchy. In a poem called "The Death
of Mercury," he made it clear that *Wheels* stood for the modern,
the lively, the truthful, and the international.

> Dullness, the Deity, in conclave sat
> With Mediocrity, whose pork-pie hat
> Now flaunts, with intermingled asphodel,
> The homelier herbs that 'Georgians' love so well
> —No Baudelaire flowers now shed exotic scent
> But parsley, garlic sweet, and peppermint.[64]

"Rivers"—Julian Symons suggests that he was Osbert Sitwell, and
every evidence confirms the speculation[65]—goes on to pit *Wheels*
(and its "Baudelaire flowers") against the National muse. "These
Goddesses love England," he writes, where the refrain, "Praise
Squire, Praise Squire," "leaps like fire from every school and
college, / From stately London home or Cotswold Cottage." His
signals are not ambiguous: for *Wheels*, as for Swinburne, Baude-
laire was the ally and emblem of internationalism; he stood for
attack on little England.

   He also stood for truth about the war and against the isolation
of poetry from the conditions of life. "Baudelairean flowers," it
will be recalled, issue not only from evil, but also from death:
"Et le ciel regardait la carcasse superbe / Comme une fleur s'é-
panouir," he wrote in "Une Charogne." His flowers were an

antithesis to "the poetic skylark," which was, for Osbert Sitwell, "symbolic of the great sell-out by the Georgian poets of the Squirearchy," who, during the war, "unforgivably attempted to prettify the slaughter."[66] That corpse, planted in the English garden in the 1860's, sprouts vigorously in some of the war poems in *Wheels*. It is part of an attack on complacency. In "The Beginning" and "The End," Osbert Sitwell contrasts the "chaos of creation"—"golden mist," "clashing colours," "the glowing world"—with an apocalyptic end, in which the only light is "iridescence / As if from off a carrion-fly," a "dim green light" and "faintly phosphorescent glow." In his second poem Sitwell writes that "The air is thick and brings / The tainted subtle sweetness of decay."[67] Iris Tree's poem, "Mouth of the dust I kiss, corruption absolute," makes the "Worm" its principle of non-meaning:

> For you the heart's wild love, beauty, long care,
> Virginity, passionate womanhood, perfected wholeness;
> For you the unborn child that I prepare,—
> You, flabby, boneless, brainless, senseless, soulless.

She, too, contrasts a complacent world, in which we sit, "Cunning in sin," "placid, gay and fat with ease," with "the armies of the world [which] / March doomwards to the rhythm of the drum / Under the thirsting sun." In her poems, as often in the *Wheels* cycles,[68]

> Death holds his state:
> His skeleton hands are filled with scarlet spoil:
> He stands on flaming ramparts, waving high
> The ensign of decay. All his bones are dressed
> With livid roses; all his pillars black
> Are girt in ashen poppies, and on dust
> He raises up his awful golden throne.

In some of the *Wheels* poems, Baudelaire's spleen group contributes to an attempt to explore states of horror, apprehension, and grief. The agonized imagery of *ennui*, which in *Point Counter Point* constitutes Spandrell's satirized inner life, is used here without either satire or self-mockery. These "Cyclists," as the *Wheels* poets dubbed themselves, unlike Huxley in the novel, attached that "stock of imagery" and that conventional analysis of emotional and intellectual dissociation to painfully actual subjects. In her sonnets "Remorse" and "Uneasiness," for instance, Nancy

Cunard draws the walls of the damp room around her to ex-
amine the heightened perception of the *nerveuse*;[69] so does Os-
bert Sitwell in "Black Mass":

> Silence has ceased to be a negative,
> Becomes a thing of substance—fills the room
> And clings like ivy to the listening walls.
> The flickering light flares up—then gutters out.
> The shadows seem to shiver and expand
> To active evil things that breathe and live.[70]

In *Wheels*, that accumulation of evil had a real and particular
reference, and what might have seemed a melodramatic satanism
lent itself to a personal experience that "the poetic skylark" pre-
ferred to ignore. In his phantasmal "Corpse-Day," Osbert Sitwell
writes,[71]

> As a rocket burst
> There fell from it,
> Screaming in horror,
> Hundreds of men,
> Twisted into the likeness of animals
> —Writhing men
> Without feet,
> Without legs,
> Without arms,
> Without faces—. . . .

For him, the imagery of conventional "baudelairism" had an
inescapably objective correlative. This evil, fear, physical cor-
ruption, emotional paralysis and moral horror, which in Huxley's
Spandrell are poses in a ghoulish pantomime, were for some of
the *Wheels* poets redefined by the war. "Baudelairism" was for
them, as T. E. Hulme might have said, the closest point to the
one they were making for, an "already existing method of
expression" from which they had to work toward something
more adequate and natural.[72]

The "Baudelairean flowers" of *Wheels* constitute another his-
torical reversal: Baudelaire, who in England had almost always
seemed, though erroneously, to be the inventor of art for art's
sake, is here made to support a campaign against the separation
of poetry and life. He is enlisted by a group of exceptionally

"aesthetic" writers in opposition to moral complacency. In "Corpse-Day," Osbert Sitwell is outraged:

The earth-cities still rejoiced,
Old, fat men leant out to cheer
From bone-built palaces.
Gold flowed like blood
Through the streets;
Crowds became drunk
On liquor distilled from corpses.

Here Baudelaire becomes the ally of an attack on "those monsters that we hide away / And bury in our self-complacency."[73] That was a new use of him in England, but it was perfectly harmonious with his own intensely moral conception of his art, and it predicted his future in English literature. This moral Baudelaire is closely related to the "Poet and Saint" of Eliot. Osbert Sitwell's monsters of self-complacency evoke the opening accusation of *Les Fleurs du Mal*:

C'est l'Ennui!—l'oeil chargé d'un pleur involontaire,
Il rêve d'échafauds en fumant son houka.
Tu le connais, lecteur, ce monstre délicat,
—Hypocrite lecteur,—mon semblable,—mon frère! (I, 6)

When that delicate monster appears in *The Waste Land* it is again in the context of a surrealist accounting for war dead.

Baudelaire supports Edith Sitwell's modernism in ways that are related to these. She began, like some of the others in *Wheels*, with "baudelairism." It sounds in her earliest poems—"The Mother," "The Drunkard," "The Spider," "Hysterion," and others. Although Sitwell dropped her earliest style quickly, changing from the corporate voice to her own intensely individual speech, she kept Baudelaire with her in both her criticism and her poetry, and she derived some of her central poetic ideas directly, and with astonishing literalness, from what he wrote. For her, as for her brother, he was a moralist; and even more importantly for her he was a poet whose ideas were positively religious.

Baudelaire the moralist appears early in Edith Sitwell's poems.

C'est . . . It is Boredom, *Tedium vitae*, who with an unwilling tear in his eye dreams of gibbets as he smokes his pipe. You know him, Reader, you know that fastidious monster—O hypocritical Reader, my fellow-man and brother! (S, 156).

The "marionnettes" of "Les Petites Vieilles," for instance, are present in her early "Mandoline," where, as in Baudelaire's poem, they issue from frustration and sympathy, and evoke compassion and pathos.

> In the huge house of glass
> Old shadows bent, alas!
> On ebon sticks now pass—
>
> Lean on a shadow boy,
> Creep like a broken toy—
> Wooden and painted joy.[74]

In *I Live Under a Black Sun*, her novel about Swift, Sitwell draws substantially on the *Tableaux Parisiens* to convey the pathos and outrage of life in the impersonal metropolis: and she silently attributes to the fiercely moral Anglo-Irish poet who is her subject the painful perceptions of the modern Frenchman who was one of her masters. One chapter is composed of reminiscences from Baudelaire's Paris poems: the following lines, for instance, shape to his action, vocabulary, and moral vision the city she presents as Swift's London:

> All through the day, under the Bedlam daylight's murderous roar, changing to the enormous Tartarean darkness of a fog, through these deepest circles of Hell all forms of misery loomed and faded, monstrous shapes, their sightless faces turned to the unheeding sky, tapping upon the ground with a hollow noise that seemed to echo down millions of fathoms to the very centre of the ball of the earth. For in this city of universal night, only the blind can see.[75]

That passage alludes to "Les Aveugles"; the following attributes to Swift the experience that is recorded in "Les Sept Vieillards," in which, as Eliot notes in *The Waste Land*, "le spectre en plein jour raccroche le passant!"

> Then the universe of beggars rushed towards them, a sea of rags fluttered about them; as the carriages stopped beside the shops, so brightly lighted in the blackness that the windows seemed fountains of jewels, the beggars, their shapes made monstrous by the changing darkness, huge and menacing, appeared from all sides.

Even when she transforms Swift's London into something arti-
ficial, Sitwell does so by means of Baudelaire's vision. At times,
she writes, "the enormous city seemed of black marble and basalt,
and even the trees were changed to this." In this darkness, "the
palaces appeared even more world-high." In Baudelaire's "Rêve
Parisien," the city of beggars and old women changes to a dream
of metal, marble, and water, all "adamantine" surfaces, as John
Middleton Murry wrote,[76] all cruelly harder than flesh and more
grand: "C'était un palais infini." Swift sees sometimes how "an
elegant figure would shine through this night, circling swiftly as
if it were a swallow, or floating, a black swan, on the wide water-
black marble pavements," as if he had glimpsed the spectacle in
Baudelaire's "Le Cygne."

By these imitations Sitwell attributes to Swift the Baudelairean
view of things, in order at last to associate his disgust and rage
with that of the modern giant. She perceives Baudelaire here as
Lytton Strachey had done in his *Landmarks in French Literature*,
as "the Swift of poetry," and she integrates him, as Swinburne
had done in his *Blake*, with the heroic past of the English tra-
dition. This sub-textual, fictionalized Baudelaire is, like the fig-
ure Strachey described, "concerned almost entirely with the
modern life of Paris and the actual experiences of a disillusioned
soul."[77] For Edith Sitwell, as for her brother, outrage and com-
passion went together, and both here and elsewhere she makes
both of those elements part of her strong creative response to
Baudelaire.

Sitwell's criticism, which is almost always actually about her
own work, is eclectic and repetitive. It wheels round and round
the same questions, answering them over and over again in the
same borrowed voices. A *Poet's Notebook* illustrates her procedure:
it consists of passages anthologized from a wide range of sources,
grouped under headings which convey indirectly a sense of the
principles by which they are grouped. Her own comments on
the quotations, which she calls aphorisms, sometimes draw the
moral, are sometimes only tangentially related to what she
quotes, and sometimes provide a kind of cross-reference to bind
together the whole (so that, for instance, when she quotes Leo-
nardo da Vinci she reminds the reader of her earlier quotation
from Baudelaire).[78] That method, a kind of critical collage, which
operates with only a little more structural rigor in, say, the
"Lecture on Modern Poetry Since 1920," published the same

year as the *Notebook*, makes other writers bear an unusually important part of the burden.[79] Sitwell's position, like Pater's and Wilde's, comes from the varied lights of a galaxy of others.

Sitwell catalogues the figures in her galaxy in the "Lecture on Poetry Since 1920": there she turns to Wagner, Schopenhauer, Cocteau, Roger Fry, Eisenstein, Picasso, Eliot, and Baudelaire. The *Poet's Notebook*, too, places Baudelaire among the moderns: it gives him a central place in current poetic debate, praises him emphatically, and refers to him as to a final authority on poetry. Sitwell quotes him on the beautiful, on the necessity for strict technical discipline, on artistic convention, on the sorcery of words, and on simplicity. She sees his vision as whole and profound, and his incidental critical remarks as among "the most profound lights thrown on the necessities of our time."[80] She borrows from Gautier's 1868 preface to praise his style, his linguistic innovation, his use of polysyllabic words, and his mastery of the alexandrine, and from Cocteau to say that his perfect "welding" of manner and matter produces "(a work of art) 'vegetable and architectural as a banana-tree of Rio.' "[81] She dismisses Rimbaud's criticism of his "flawless and marvelous form"—it was "too ludicrous to be combated"—replying that in him "the forms, though they were not new, are so living, so inherent in the meaning, that form and matter could not be separated. There has never, to my belief, been poetry more actually inherent in the language, and in the form, than that of Baudelaire."[82] Of the first two lines of "L'Invitation au Voyage" (which, in fact, she misquoted in *The Pleasures of Poetry*), she wrote,

> (I do not know of any instance of counterpoint in poetry to compare with this.) [Dryden's *Annus Mirabilis*] has not these beauties, nor has it the strange flutter, as of some magical spray rising from an oar, produced by "à la" after the deep-sea diving of "songe." Those first two lines are among the strangest and most enchanted in all literature.[83]

In 1941, Charles Henri Ford acknowledged Sitwell's admiration for Baudelaire in his dedication to her of *The Mirror of Baudelaire*, which included translations of "Le Voyage," "Le Cygne," and "Voyage à Cythère," in addition to Ford's own "Ballad for Baudelaire," a "Preface" by Paul Eluard, and a drawing by Matisse.[84]

The Baudelaire on whom Sitwell relies, however, is not so

exclusively "modern" in his connections as "The Lecture on Poetry Since 1920" would make him seem. One of the often-present but less visible figures in Sitwell's lexicon of modernism is Arthur Symons: she quotes him in *Aspects of Modern Poetry*, in the "Lecture on Poetry Since 1920," in "Some Notes on My Own Poetry," and, extensively, in her *Poet's Notebook*. There she draws on five of his works: *Blake, The Romantic Movement in English Poetry, Studies in Seven Arts, The Symbolist Movement in Literature*, and *Charles Baudelaire*. If he is not so noticeable in the *Notebook* as some others, that is because he is almost always an intermediary. Sitwell relays what he has to say about Schopenhauer or Verlaine or Villiers—or, more often, she quotes him quoting. He supplies the words of Mallarmé, for instance, in "Notes on the Nature of Poetry," or the comment on Wagner in "On Rhythm." Sometimes he seems to have been the immediate source of words that Sitwell does not attribute to him. She writes, for instance, "Villiers de l'Isle Adam wrote of his own work, *Triboulat [sic] Bonhomet*, that it was 'an enormous and sombre clowning, the colour of the century.' " The quotation—which reappears in "Some Notes on My Own Poetry" to describe "certain poems in *Façade*"—probably comes by way of Symons, who wrote in *The Symbolist Movement* of "Tribulat Bonhomet (which [Villiers] himself defined as *bouffonnerie énorme et sombre, couleur du siècle*)."[85]

Sitwell drew on Symons over a long period and in many contexts. In her 1922 articles in *The New Age*, she describes the symbolist poets in the colorful details he supplied: Nerval, for instance, comes accompanied by his lobster; Villiers enters speaking his famous line, "As for living, our servants will do that for us!"[86] Her *Anthology* and *A Book of the Winter* select from poets he had written on. While Helen Rootham was her first tutor on modern French poetry, Symons was certainly her second, as he was Eliot's and John Gould Fletcher's. *A Poet's Notebook* refers to only two works about Baudelaire, Gautier's preface and Symons's book. It is Symons who provides both Sitwell's translations of Baudelaire and her point of view. That point of view is important, not merely because it makes Sitwell's ultra-modern Baudelaire a very mixed construction, but also because it affects both her poetry and her conception of it.

Although in 1951 Edith Sitwell told John Lehmann that

bouffonnerie . . . enormous clowning, dark, colour of the century.

"Baudelaire is one of the poets whom I think greatest, but I do not know that I have been *influenced* by him,"[87] she took a different view of her development in her 1936 "Auto-Obituary." The early part of her working life, she said there, had been devoted to the attempt to find "a technique suitable to her needs." What she had found, "as far as structure was concerned," was a "development out of the technique used by Christina Rossetti in 'Goblin Market,' and that of Verlaine and Baudelaire; her texture she had learned from wider sources."[88] Although Sitwell's criticism is remarkably unsystematic and eclectic, her poetry is written to uncommonly tight requirements. It is "technical" to a high degree, and its synaesthesthetic technique is, precisely, an extension into practice of Baudelaire's doctrine of *correspondances*. Sitwell's "tradition," as she called it, derives from Baudelaire, and her "development" of it was in the direction suggested by Symons.

Sitwell described the problems of modern poetry in familiar terms: the pressure of the modern, she wrote, was toward the specific, but the myriad specific set itself in opposition to order. The crux of modernism, as she saw it and as she described it in *Aspects of Modern Poetry*, was the reconciliation of that antithesis:

> The modernist artist gives us the great chance of exerting an individuality in seeing. The older beauty, the beauty of the Old Masters, is in the beauty of species and of mass; the new beauty is highly individualized and separate. The modernist artist is not concerned with things in the mass, he is passionately interested in the fulfilling of the destinies of the single individuals that make up the mass—whether those individuals are men, or leaves, or waves of the sea. The great quality of the Old Masters in all the arts is force, used in the scientific sense of the term—the binding together of the molecules of the world. That is partly what makes their sense of design so tremendous. The great quality of the modern masters is an explosive energy—the separating up of the molecules—exploring the possibilities of the atom. This is at once the quality and the danger of pioneer poetry. One technical aim of the more accomplished of the modernist poets is to reconcile this necessity of exploring the possibilities of the atom with the necessity for logical design and form.[89]

But that dilemma hardly differs from Symons's, and it is familiar in Pater: Sitwell has transposed into the language of physics the aesthetic antithesis of "Winckelmann" and the moral opposition of *The Symbolist Movement in Literature*. What she writes is nevertheless true as description: the problem of modern poetry *was* order, the reconciliation of detail and structure. Like Symons and the Imagists, Sitwell saw the conflict as acute in poetry that attempted to render the life of cities; unlike them, she did not see the city material as presenting any special problem. All poetry faced "the almost terrifying *identity* of that idol, the subject,"[90] whether it was about "men, or leaves, or waves of the sea." Realism was no answer: she rejected the "Victorian" desire to "fit in, practically, with ordinary everyday occasions, not to transmute these, but to copy them faithfully,"[91] and, instead, gave to her modern poet a doctrinaire solution: by an act of acute perception she finds out the individuality of the atom, discovering in the process that its uniqueness is not irreconcilable with larger design. Her own poetry, Sitwell writes, is an attempt to "pierce down to the essence of the thing seen, by discovering in it attributes which at first sight appear alien, but which are acutely related—by producing its quintessential colour (sharper, brighter than that seen by an eye grown stale, and by stripping it of all unessential details)."[92] The description might have come from *Gaston de Latour*.

It came more likely from *The Symbolist Movement in Literature* and from Baudelaire's doctrine of "Correspondances." The doctrine, as Symons describes it at length in his book, was designed to deal with just the problems Sitwell had identified as modern: it offered to reconcile atom and design, to provide a "spiritual" significance to each physical detail, to give a priestly, transforming role to the poet, and, in psychological terms, to suggest the idea, which Sitwell admired in Rimbaud, of the mind as the product of the senses. The sonnet itself, which Baudelaire amplifies in prose commentary and links with Swedenborg, offers a validation in nature for the technique of synaesthesia:

Comme de longs échos qui de loin se confondent
Dans une ténébreuse et profonde unité,

Comme . . . Like prolonged echoes which merge far away in an opaque, deep oneness, as vast as darkness, as vast as light, perfumes, sounds, and colours answer to each other (S, 36).

Vaste comme la nuit et comme la clarté,
Les parfums, les couleurs et les sons se répondent. (I, 11)

Sitwell could have read that doctrine in several versions but
Baudelaire and Symons are paramount in her critical writing,
where she attaches it both to Baudelaire and, as he does himself,
to Swedenborg. Her poems give it some of the religious signif-
icance it has in Symons, and, what is much more important to
the poems as poems, they return the idea of *correspondances* as
metaphorically as it was offered in Baudelaire's sonnet.

Sitwell's frequently repeated description of the purpose of her
early poems, which amounts to a statement of her doctrine,
suggests the central place of these ideas in her work. The subject
of many of her early poems, she says, is consciousness:

> Sometimes it is that of a person who has always been blind,
> and who, suddenly endowed with sight, must *learn* to see;
> or it is the cry of that waiting, watching world, where every-
> thing we see is a symbol of something beyond, to the con-
> sciousness that is yet buried in this earth sleep. . . .
>
> Sometimes we find a consciousness awakening from sleep,
> seeing, with a clearer, sharper vision than that of the ordi-
> nary sense dulled with custom—piercing down to the es-
> sence of the thing seen, knowing that the ephemeral six-
> rayed snowflake is the counterpart of the six-rayed crystal
> in its eternity . . . and so guessing at the immense design of
> the world,—at "the correspondences whereby men may
> speak with angels."[93]

Sitwell implicated Baudelaire in practically every side of her
doctrine. She associated him with the search for quintessence:
" 'Pure draughtsmen,' said Baudelaire in *Curiosités Esthétiques*,
'are philosophers and the abstractors of the quintessence.' "[94]
She associated him with "the right kind of simplicity"—that is,
with "a heroic nakedness" and a "return to the savagery of the
senses"—and with " 'the raw elegance of the Lion.' "[95] She also
drew special attention, in *A Poet's Notebook*, to what he had written
in *Fusées* about "the animal of genius," which she reports as
follows: "The poetic idea which disengages itself from the move-
ment, in the lines, would seem to postulate the existence of a
vast being, immense, complicated but of harmonious propor-
tion—an animal full of genius, suffering and sighing all sighs

and all human ambitions."[96] That animal, the "waiting, watching world," is a sentient, suffering transformation of "the six-rayed crystal in its eternity." It is the world to which our dulled senses make us oblivious.

The "animal of genius" recurs everywhere in Sitwell's poems. It serves both her symbolism and, in her early poems, her child-like speech. The conscious, suffering world, which is in Sitwell or in Baudelaire a "temple" and a "forest of symbols," often appears, literally, as an animal. "Sometimes," she wrote, in ex-plication of "Dark Song," "you find a terrible, groping, animal consciousness"; and sometimes, she said about "The Bear," "you get this animal consciousness knowing its own segregation and loneliness—cut off from the outer world by the lack of that higher consciousness which alone can bring us to those corre-spondences, as Swedenborg has said, whereby men may speak with angels."[97] In "Dark Song," the animal consciousness is pain-fully suppressed:

> The fire was furry as a bear
> And the flames purr . . .
> The brown bear rambles in his chain
> Captive to cruel men
> Through the dark and hairy wood.
> The maid sighed, "All my blood
> Is animal. . . ."[98]

And it is the animal of genius that supplies the sense in this poem from *Façade*:

> Jumbo asleep!
> Grey leaves thick-furred
> As his ears, keep
> Conversations blurred.
> Thicker than hide
> Is the trumpeting water;
> Don Pasquito's bride
> And his youngest daughter
> Watch the leaves
> Elephantine grey:
> What is it grieves
> In the torrid day?
> Is it the animal

World that snores
Harsh and inimical
In sleepy pores?[99]

In 1940 Edith Sitwell turned back to this figure to give voice
to the emotions roused by another war. "Still Falls the Rain" links
the suffering of Christ with that of the "blind and weeping bear
whom the keepers beat / On his helpless flesh."[100] Baudelaire
stands behind this fusion of spiritual consciousness and dumb
animal consciousness, both tortured by war, just as he had stood
behind Osbert Sitwell's dismembered men screaming in horror.

Other early poems of Sitwell's embody just as directly the
concepts of immense design and of piercing to the essence that
she associated with Baudelaire's doctrine of *correspondances*. The
cardboard fronts of "Clowns' Houses" stand in front of "Reality"
as mere externality; and several of the early poems describe a
sensory deadness, an imperviousness to the meanings that em-
anate from the spiritual world, embodied in the material. "Ped-
agogues," for instance, has a close connection with Baudelaire's
"Correspondances": it deals with our failure to see, to pierce
down to the essence of the thing seen. It presents in various
metaphors the unintelligibility into which all of nature falls when
faulty perception divorces us from the immediate messages of
material things. The poem presents the material world as lan-
guage:

The air is like a jarring bell
That jangles words it cannot spell.
And black as Fate, the iron trees
Stretch thirstily to catch the breeze.[101]

Language was the connecting element in Baudelaire's sonnet,
too:

La Nature est un temple où de vivants piliers
Laissent parfois sortir de confuses paroles;
L'homme y passe à travers des forêts de symboles
Qui l'observent avec des regards familiers. (I, 11)

La Nature ... Nature is a temple, in which living pillars sometimes utter a
babel of words; man traverses it through forests of symbols, that watch him with
knowing eyes (S, 36).

Sitwell substitutes "iron trees" for living pillars, frustrated communication for meaning, isolation for unity. "Myself in the Merry-Go-Round" makes the same point, and in similar imagery:

> Beneath the heat the trees' sharp hue—
> A ceaseless whirr, metallic-green—
> Sounds like a gimlet shrilling through
> The mind, to reach the dazzling sheen
> Of meanings life can not decide:
> Then words set all awry, and you
> Are left upon the other side.
> Our senses, each a wooden horse
> We paint, till they appear to us
> Like life, and then queer strangers course
> In our place on each Pegasus.[102]

And in "Aubade," as she often explained, Sitwell examines the failure of poor "Jane, Jane, / Tall as a crane" to be sensitive to "this nature, these correspondences in nature, crying from outside."[103]

What Edith Sitwell herself saw as her most important innovation, the "purposeful transfusion from one sense to another,"[104] comes directly from consciousness of the correspondences:

> But one of the principal aims of the new poets is to increase consciousness, and, to do this, we must use all the powers that nature and intelligence and insight and dream and fact have given us. It happens, often, that where the language of one sense is insufficient, we use the language of another. . . . Poets do not want to force their way of seeing on anyone. But they do want to give people their own way of seeing. This enriches life, it adds experience; not only that, it will eventually increase the consciousness of the race.[105]

That technique, which she employed to produce "sharper vision than that of the ordinary sense drilled with custom" and the doctrine from which it sprang were, as Sitwell said in her "Auto-Obituary," a "logical development" from Baudelaire. He provided her with a philosophical and a technical system. It was because he could play upon the "immense clavier des *correspondances!*" it will be recalled, that the splendid traveller of the *Exposition Universelle* was free, and because he had not forgotten "la couleur du ciel, la forme du végétal, le mouvement et l'odeur de l'animalité" (II, 577). The same sensory alertness and the same connecting imagery are central to Sitwell, in whose work what might in the later French or English symbolists have dissipated into theory is preserved solidly as metaphor. In "The Avenue," she borrows the image of the clavier, transforming the keyboard into both a "scale of centuries" and an avenue of black and white, and she gains from the emblem of design a sense of self:

> Meaning comes to bind the whole,
> Fingers separate from thumbs,
> Soon the shapeless tune comes:
> Bestial efforts at man's soul.
> What though notes are false and shrill—
> Black streets tumbling down a hill?
> Fundamentally
> I am you, and you are me—
> Octaves fall as emptily.[106]

Edith Sitwell addressed herself to questions common to most of her contemporaries: everyone considered the problem of "the identity of the object," and almost everyone reached a similar, corresponding reconciliation of detail and pattern. But Sitwell's solution is unlike theirs: she appropriated her theory with little adjustment from the poets of the late nineteenth century: "every touch, sight, sound, smell of the world we live in, has its meaning—is the result of a spiritual state," she announced; and the role of the poet is to "set about interpreting these meanings to us."[107] At an early date she joined her views specifically to those put forward in *The Symbolist Movement in Literature*: "Then, through these likenesses in nature," she writes, "this awakened being guesses, however dimly, that there is a reason, a design, somewhere outside our consciousness." The design, she maintains, makes "death seem less a prison house, and this present world of visual things our brother, instead of an alien."[108] Later in her life Edith Sitwell made her doctrine serve more specifically religious purposes. In 1955 she wrote to Father Philip Caraman that when she was a child she

La couleur . . . the colour of the sky, the shape of plants, the movement and smell of animal life (C, 117).

began to see the patterns of the world, the images of wonder. And I asked myself why those patterns should be repeated— the feather and the fern and rose and acorn in the patterns of frost on the window—pattern after pattern repeated again and again. And even then I knew that this was telling us something. I founded my poetry upon it.[109]

For Edith Sitwell, Baudelaire's *correspondances* justified close attention to poetic technique, provided a reason for cherishing the material world, hallowed the act of perception, and, ultimately, made a base for her religious belief. This use of Baudelaire, which like Squire's and Huxley's, departs from an inherited "decadence," has only its beginnings in common with theirs. Sitwell, who refused to develop the *correspondances* into theory, is nonetheless related by her use of them to the modern theorists: to the Imagists, to Joyce, and to Eliot. Her solidly metaphorical keyboard, which comes straight out of Baudelaire, is related by its intellectual *cousinage* not only to Stephen Daedalus's *epiphany* but also to Joyce's great "chart" for *Ulysses*, not only to the Chopin of "Portrait of a Lady," but also to "the complete consort" of *Four Quartets*.

6

THE IMAGISTS

Lexicon of beautiful is elastic, but
walla-walla not yet poetically possible.

—T. E. Hulme, "Notes on
Language and Style"

For a long time, supported both by Eliot's remark that the Imagists were the *point de repère* of modern poetry and by anthologists of Imagist verse, literary historians took the "modernism" of that English school as given. William Pratt, anthologizing Imagist poems in 1963, adopted Eliot's line: they wrote, he said, "the first 'modern' poems in English." Peter Jones, presenting them anew for Penguin ten years later, said that their ideas "still lie at the centre of our poetic practice."[1] The Imagists themselves, of course, made "modernism" a key element in their platform, and they defined it largely as reaction. T. E. Hulme dismissed virtually the whole of the last century when he named Henley as the single English poet who was "perhaps" a worthwhile model for what he wanted to do,[2] and Richard Aldington voiced a common view with uncommon frankness when he said that "the majority of the poetry of the last century had nothing to do with life and very little to do with poetry . . . except for Browning and a little of Swinburne there was no energy which was not bombast, no rendering of life without an Anglican moral, no aesthetic without aesthetic cant" and when he acknowledged that he was "out to destroy . . . to a certain extent" the reputations of Shelley and Tennyson.[3]

The outpost the Imagists established, however, was nothing like so securely held as historians were for so long willing to believe. Like Murry and Mansfield in *Rhythm*, or the Sitwells and Huxley in *Wheels*, the Imagists named their "modernism" before they knew what it was. Their poetics gather borrowed materials into uneasy equilibrium, and if, as Peter Jones says, we are sometimes struck by the differences between their theories and their practice, that is partly because the materials they borrowed were not always compatible with one another. They did not, however, merely "rummage among a variety of sources," and they were not merely "muddled."[4] They articulated precisely, in both their theories and their poetry, the central conflicts of modern verse. In their theories, they attempted to recover the nineteenth-century synthesis, the accommodating double emphasis of "The School of Giorgione"; in their poetry, they struggled for sincerity, as Hulme defined it: "Each age must have its own special form of expression," he wrote, "and any period that deliberately goes out of it is an age of insincerity" (*FS*, 69). On most important matters, however, the Imagists looked resolutely in two clearly defined and opposed directions: they began by imitating the very models they thought they should reject; they constructed a theory that is based on mutually hostile positions; they cultivated influences that pushed their poetry toward antithetical ideals. These conflicts do not make Imagism any less significant a workshop for modernism—on the contrary, they demonstrate the difficulty of the enterprise and underline the significance of what was achieved—but they do account for the Imagists' failure to accomplish at a stroke what they took to be their chief task, "the reform of poetic style and, above all . . . the assimilation by poetry of modern thought and the complex modern mind."[5] When the Imagists confronted what they came to see as their most important subject matter, the life of great cities, they were paralyzed by their self-contradictions. Aldington's "Xenophilometropolitania," which appeared in the *Egoist* in January, 1914, cover the conflicts with parody, but the "Strange Love," the "foreign" objects of this oddly amorous poetry, emerged as a central problem for the Imagist poets. Aldington's assertion that his "Metropolitania" were "penultimate poetry" was not entirely whimsical.

In all of this, Baudelaire is deeply implicated. He is an aspect of each of the Imagist antitheses—a part of their parentage, an affiliate of their theoretical dilemmas, a model for their precisely defined "modernism." In their work it is possible to observe both the process of his modernizing in England and some of its causes. Moreover, in an account of Baudelaire's shifting English identity, the Imagists are crucial: they redid some of the critical work of Swinburne and Pater, importing massively from modern French writers and so reversing once again the notion that the French could be ignored; they devised a literary classicism which turned the attention of English writers back beyond Mallarmé and Verlaine to the originating double visage of Baudelaire, who carried, as Valéry was to write some time later, his own critic within him; and they articulated a problem for "modernism" that made him seem, inevitably, "the greatest exemplar in *modern* poetry in any language,"[6] as Eliot would put it years later, when all of this Imagist activity had subsided into history.

The Imagists' transactions with French poetry in general and with Baudelaire in particular reflect their characteristic self-contradiction. On the one hand, they placed the French at the heart of their reforming modernism, and for them poets from Villon to Remy de Gourmont represented escape from what they saw as all of that English staleness. But, on the other hand, in rejecting the English mainstream, the Imagists drew heavily on the counter-tradition: their approach to the French was shaped precisely by their English predecessors, and what they sought from their French models was often what had already been domesticated. Although in their later work the Baudelaire who is recognizable as a contributing voice is also recognizably the figure who speaks in *The Waste Land*, in their earlier work he echoes from the 'nineties.

There were powerful reasons for the Imagists' imitations of their predecessors, of course. The poets of the later nineteenth century had neatly prefigured the Imagists' major concerns, proffering the lyric as a corrective to the long Victorian narrative, seeking to purge the language, focussing on "intense" moments, and emphasizing sensation and individuality. Symons's concern for a "revolt from ready-made impressions and conclusions, a revolt from the ready-made of language, from the bondage of traditional form, of a form become rigid," for instance, could settle with smooth consistency into Hulme's "Notes on Language and Style."[7] After the noise of Imagism's opening battles had stilled, its blood relation to the later nineteenth century became clear to some of its members. Pound wrote in 1928 of the "Rapports fr. > eng. via Arthur Symons etc. 1890 Baudelaire, Verlaine, etc." and John Gould Fletcher confessed in 1937 that he and Amy Lowell had agreed from the beginning that there

was nothing . . . particularly new about imagism. It was but a more lyrical, a saner and more intelligible, development of the aesthetic theories of the English Pre-Raphaelite poets, the Parnassians and the symbolists in France.

There *was* something new in Imagism, however, and Harold Monro more accurately described its relationship to the nineteenth century: "We in the twentieth century," he wrote, "are on the tree-tops of the poetic growths represented by the Pre-Raphaelites and the 'Nineties."[8]

T. E. Hulme, who so immoderately dismissed almost all of his English predecessors, was by no means oblivious to complexity and contradiction in the process of literary reform. He said that he had "no reverence for tradition" (*FS*, 68) and that he "started from a standpoint of extreme modernism" (*FS*, 73), but, like Pater, he was fascinated by this fact of transition itself. "Wonder," he said in the conclusion of his essay on "Romanticism and Classicism," "can only be the attitude of a man passing from one stage to another."[9] Like a belated Gautier, delivering a luxurious account of the decomposed language of *Les Fleurs du Mal*, Hulme adopts a violent figure of decay (adding to it the brass knuckles of his misogyny) to represent the present stage in the history of poetic form: "The carcass is dead," he writes, "and all the flies are upon it. Imitative poetry springs up like weeds, and women whimper and whine of you and I alas, and roses, roses all the way. It becomes the expression of sentimentality rather than of virile thought" (*FS*, 69). But Hulme insisted at the same time on the limitations imposed by inheritance: "Just as physically you are not born that abstract entity, man," he wrote, "but the child of particular parents, so you are in matters of literary judgment" (*S*, 123). He observed a similar lag in the development of poetic expression: it was one thing to be in revolt, he suggested, and quite another to produce a new order:

What happens, I take it, is something of this kind: a certain change of direction takes place which begins negatively with a feeling of dissatisfaction with and reaction against existing art. But the new tendency, admitting that it exists, cannot at once find its own appropriate expression. But although the artist feels that he must have done with contemporary means of expression, yet a new and more fitting method is not easily created. Expression is by no means a natural thing. It is an unnatural, artificial and, as it were, external thing which a man has to install himself in before he can manipulate it. . . . A man has first to obtain a foothold in this, so to speak, alien and external world of material expression, at a point near to the one he is making for. He has to utilise some already existing method of expression, and work from that to the one that expresses his own personal conception more accurately and naturally. (*FS*, 116)

For most of the Imagists, the point closest to the one they were making for was the poetry of the 'nineties. Most of them had, after all, grown up on the products of the Aesthetic Movement. Aldington began his career by reading Wilde, whose voice echoes frequently in his poetry, and he conceived for him in youth an admiration he never lost, even though he laced it later with resentment. He edited selections from Wilde and from Pater, and as late as 1950 he produced an anthology of writings of the Aesthetes.[10] Pound's modernism was similarly based, and Aldington complained about that when he reviewed his contributions to *Blast*: "It is not that one wants Mr. Pound to repeat his Provençal feats," he wrote, "to echo the 'nineties—he has done that too much already."[11] Although he always knew what was the last word in Paris, F. S. Flint shaped his own verse to the pattern of the recent English past; and the early work of John Gould Fletcher is devoted exclusively to what Eliot later scorned as the last fashion but one.[12]

Fletcher was not one of the earliest Imagists, but by the time of the *Egoist*'s special number on Imagism, on 1 May 1915, he had established his credentials. In the special number, he reviewed the poems of Amy Lowell, praisingly of course, and his own poems in turn were reviewed by Ferris Greenslet, Amy Lowell's publisher, who found them "in the highest degree vivid, original, and provocative."[13] Pound, too, reviewed Fletcher's early poems, in *The New Freewoman*: he found in them promise of great talent and an admirable French influence, and he urged Harriet Monroe to publish him in *Poetry*.[14] Fletcher continued for some time to enjoy the reputation of an *avant-gardist*: his poems appeared in *The Chapbook* and *Coterie*; Eliot printed his work in *The Criterion*; and the whole of *The Chapbook* for May 1920 was given over to his article on "Some Contemporary American Poets." "In England," says a summary of his life, "he was a leader of the Imagists."[15]

Yet, at this stage in his career, Fletcher's "modernism" was a wholly reflected light. His early poems exemplify the inheritance that was the Imagists' first expression and they identify some of the ways in which Baudelaire was an element in that. Glenn Hughes writes that Fletcher's interest in "the new French poetry, particularly in its wilder manifestations,"[16] developed after his arrival in England, but, in fact, Fletcher, like Eliot, encountered modern French poetry while he was at Harvard, as a consequence of reading the later nineteenth-century English poets. A year after experiencing what he calls in his memoirs "the heady and passing intoxication of Swinburne, Rossetti, and the poets of the nineties," he came upon Symons and so learned of Baudelaire and the French Symbolists, who "held me for unforgettable hours." Baudelaire, Gautier, and Flaubert, translations of whose work he found not in the Harvard Union but in the Boston Public Library, became his models: these could be "read and reread for the sake of their perfect craftsmanship alone, their supreme aesthetic delight, rather than for their social value or for any message of importance they may speak to mankind." In Flaubert's *Trois Contes*, Gautier's *Emaux et Camées*, and "in Baudelaire's incomparable *Fleurs du Mal*," Fletcher found "a world of intense aesthetic sensation." When he came to England in 1913, three years after discovering these poets, he found himself in what now appeared to be the mainstream. "I had rushed headlong via English romanticism and French symbolism into modernity," he remembered.[17]

Shortly after he arrived in London, Fletcher published his first five volumes of verse. These identify his own point of departure. They are virtually handbooks of "baudelairism." Fletcher and Squire, who were to take up opposite sides in the poetic wars of the early twentieth century, set out, though in different countries, from the same texts. Fletcher's books—*Fire and Wine, Fool's Gold, The Book of Nature, The Dominant City* (1911-1912) and *Visions of the Evening*—are enthusiastically and openly derivative. They make *his* tradition their most prominent feature. *Fool's Gold* is dedicated to "Mes 'Poetes [sic] Maudits' " and *The Dominant City* to "The French Poets of To-Day." *Visions of the Evening*, which announces that its author is "a symbol of perverse art," opens with a poem dedicated "To The Immortal Memory of Charles Baudelaire." It takes its imagery and themes from Swinburne:

> Baudelaire, green flower that sways
> Over the morass of misery

Painfully, for days on days,
Till it falls, without a sigh.

Les Fleurs du Mal are a "clarion call, / To the Judgment held on high."[18] The emotional temperature in these poems is elevated, and several of them—"Blasphemy," "Sin," "Revolt," "Midnight Prayer," "The Descent into Hell"—manifest their ancestry in their very titles: it was of course not Fletcher, but Baudelaire, who had become "a symbol of perverse art." And for Fletcher, just after he arrived in London, as for Symons, until the end of his life, Baudelaire, the perverse, *was* the modern poet. When, in *The Dominant City*, Fletcher writes, "Last night I lay disgusted, sick at heart, / Beside a sodden woman of the street: / Who drowsed, oblivious of the dreadful mart, / Her outraged body and her blistered feet,"[19] he is reviving the vocabulary and the iconography of "Une nuit que j'étais près d'une affreuse juive," the thirty-second poem of *Les Fleurs du Mal*, to which the young Squire had been intensely attracted, which he had translated, and which he had subsequently rejected, in middle-aged embarrassment.[20]

Fletcher, like Squire, withdrew his earliest volumes from circulation shortly after they had been published, and so he extended the list of English "Baudelairean" books that had retreated from the public gaze. The books, however, index a well-established convention of Baudelaire borrowings, and what is most important about them in the present context is that their precisely derivative character passed unnoticed by some of Fletcher's most innovating contemporaries. Pound took pains to point out that Fletcher was above all not an imitator: he had faults, Pound said, but these at least were "mostly his own" and they gained him "such distinction as belongs to a man who dares to have his own faults, who prefers his own to those of anyone else." He was, Pound insisted, a man of his time: "I do not think Mr. Fletcher is an imitator, he is influenced, if you like, as all the younger Frenchmen are influenced. If you ask south of the channel *à quoi rêvent les jeunes gens?* you might find that their reveries are not unlike those of Mr. Fletcher."[21]

A similar retrospective rebellion appears in the poems of F. S. Flint, and it is, like Fletcher's, precisely rooted. More than any other Imagist, Flint held the French to be the touchstone of modernity; more than any other Englishman, he was in touch with the French modernists. His works commanded the highest respect of his contemporaries. The Poetry Bookshop published his *Cadences* and advertised his work alongside that of Aldington and Harold Monro; Amy Lowell's Imagist anthologies gave him more space than any other poet save Aldington; *The Egoist, The Anglo-French Review, The English Review, The New Age,* and *Poetry and Drama* published his poems. May Sinclair thought that *Otherworld Cadences* was a landmark in the development of modern poetry; Ford Madox Hueffer found Flint's poems more compelling than those of any other Imagist; and Harold Monro wrote that his sincerity "of thought, originality of mind, and fertility of imagination make his work important to the student of modern poetry."[22]

But Flint's poems, too, like Fletcher's, are striving to be born. "Yet still we are troubled and torn," he might have said with Dowson, "By ennui, spleen and regret."[23] The world of his poems is often a "mephitic hell of dullness and stagnation,"[24] and he frequently seeks to convey a familiar, tormenting *ennui* in figures of enclosure, paralysis, rain, decay, débris, and death. The stock of images comes to him from Baudelaire's *spleen* poems, which document the settling in of solipsism, the imprisonment of the mind. "Silence sings all around me;" Flint writes. "My head is bound with a band; / Outside in the street, a few footsteps; / A clock strikes the hour."[25] The central formal feature of Flint's poetic thought, a characteristic contrast between the deathly solitude of the isolated poet and a dreamed, paradisal escape, comes from the same source, and Flint, like Baudelaire, makes the contrast underline the bitterness of the poet's real circumstances. But while Baudelaire uses it to expose the double nature of the imagination, which turns the poet into a "matelot ivrogne, inventeur d'Amériques / Dont le mirage rend le gouffre plus amer" (I, 130), Flint makes it serve the purposes of his social protest, his anguished attack on what Robert Graves, discussing Aldington, called "the dreariness, obscenity and standardisation . . . [of] the present structure of society."[26] Flint's ironically titled "Unreality," for instance, pits his "dream" ("bloom on the bramble and the wild rose") against the "reality" (a "dull, drab room, in a drab, noisy street") of a degraded world; and his "Once in Autumn," which echoes in its opening line the first stanza of "Une Charogne," establishes a similar contrast for a similar, bitterly critical, effect.[27]

What Richard Aldington took from his predecessors—an idea of the beautiful and an attitude toward the relationship of the poet to society—confirmed him in an idea of aesthetic isolation. He identified himself explicitly with the "aesthetes," as he called them, and throughout his career he defended their causes. He saw Dowson as a heroic example of the "sensitive, almost over-sensitive type of artist" that society cannot tolerate; he attacked "commercial democracy" for its imperviousness to beauty; and he frequently defended poetry against the moralists. "When you find a man whole-heartedly condemning generally every one from Verlaine to Guy-Charles Cros," he wrote, "you can bet your life that that man is an ignoramus who is concealing his ignorance under that easiest of all poses—moral indignation."[28] Often Aldington's early poems show their ancestry proudly. His "Happiness," which is dedicated to "F.S.F.," invokes Dowson in its enumeration of the benefits especially reserved for poets,[29] and his famous "Evening," which is frequently cited as an example of the small perfection sought by the Imagists, borrows its central image—of the moon "With a rag of gauze about her loins"—from Wilde's "Fuite de la Lune."[30] His overriding early theme is that of lost beauty, his dominant tone is lament. Both come to him, filtered through the 'nineties, from Baudelaire and Gautier. In "Beauty Thou Hast Hurt Me Overmuch,"[31] for instance, Aldington takes up the question of "Hymne à la Beauté," and he replies with the answer of "La Beauté" (both of which are quoted above, p. 194. Aldington's borrowings are pointed:

> Where wert thou born
> O thou woe
> That consumest my life?
> Whither comest thou?
>
> Toothed wind of the seas,
> No man knows thy beginning.
> As a bird with strong claws
> Thou woundest me
> O beautiful sorrow.

That borrowed, cruel, Baudelairean beauty was part of Aldington's *English* inheritance.

Although the Imagists may have written the first "modern" poems in English, then, the "already existing method of expression" that they "utilized," as Hulme put it, their own *point de repère*, was the poetry of the 'nineties. Their beginnings constituted for them a limitation they could not ignore: what they derived from the 'nineties bound them to a paralyzing ideal of artistic isolation and an outworn convention of the beautiful. The Imagists' earliest sympathies comprise one element in what came to be their modernist dilemma. Their theories added another. In their attempts to gain a foothold in the "alien and external world of material expression," they became uncommonly theoretical: they are remembered more for their "Rules" than for their verse. Their theories, however, failed in coherence. The Imagists worked earnestly in two directions: Flint was proposing an orthodox, intensely romantic symbolism, a mystical view of poetry which was compatible with the oriental and Greek influences at work in the Imagist group; at the same time, Hulme was arguing for a "classicism," which, while it leaned heavily on French symbolism for some of its terms, was in effect a new realism, a poetic positivism fundamentally at odds with the views Flint had derived from Mallarmé. Imagist theory was the marriage of those two views: "Image from T.E.H.; ism from August, 1912, number of The Poetry Review," Flint wrote in the margin of Eliot's copy of René Taupin's study of the movement.[32] But the theory was a miracle of contradiction, and the strain of its internal conflicts shows in the poetry. Of the first Imagists, only Pound, who came down solidly on the side of "the prose tradition," and H.D., who opted wholeheartedly for the pure poetry, were able to resolve them. In Imagist theory, the double focus of Pater dissolves into mutually excluding viewpoints: the nineteenth-century synthesis fails. But in articulating those conflicts or problems in poetry, the Imagists created a context in which Baudelaire seemed more modern, more usefully a model for modernists, than his great symbolist successors.

One side of the twentieth-century shift in English opinion about Baudelaire is related to the clearly articulated dilemma of the Imagists. They would not have separated their critical from their creative work, of course, since, like Eliot, they saw an adjustment of criticism as the necessary accompaniment of the changes they urged in poetry. "This question of criticism," Aldington wrote in 1914, taking up the nineteenth-century theme four years before Eliot began his major scrutiny of contemporary English criticism, "is of the very essence of our literature":

> It needs constant discussion. A man of parts who could really work out an original, sincere criticism could determine the literary taste of the next twenty years. Ruskin did it in his

time; Pater in his. To-day we either copy these two or weakly
and petulantly react against their ideas.[33]

Aldington was right, and he is here, as he is elsewhere, prophetic.
The man of parts did appear, he did determine the taste of the
next twenty years, and he gained a good deal from what the
Imagists had written. In the meantime, however, the Imagists
made their complaint specific. Pound wrote to Harriet Monroe
that "during my last tortured visit to America I found no writer
and but one reviewer who had any worthy conception of poetry,
The Art."[34] Flint complained bitterly to J. C. Squire that

> English papers are provincial and in the true sense of the
> word illiterate. They understand nothing that comes to them
> first hand, and they accept work only when it has been
> vouched for them by France, or Germany, or Italy, or Ire-
> land. There is in the English papers no conception of lit-
> erature, no liberty of thought, and no ideas. Conceptions
> and forms that are of common acceptance in Paris or Berlin
> or Petrograd are looked at askance here, and, if an English
> poet dares to use them, he is treated with ignorant con-
> tempt.[35]

Like Ford Madox Hueffer, the Imagists thought they knew how
to supply the lack. The remedy was to join "the main literary
stream of the world which flows—and for a hundred years has
flowed—through France alone."[36]

Flint was the chief instrument of that conjunction. He was,
with Hulme, one of the founders of the "School of 1909" and
like the School itself he has been neglected—possibly, as Wallace
Martin suggests, because of Pound's stage-managing remark that
the Imagists were the "descendants of the forgotten school of
1909," possibly because of Flint's paralyzing lack of confidence
in his own work, possibly because of the battle for custody of
the prodigious movement which was carried on between Pound
and the rest[37]—but his contemporaries did not neglect him. Eliot
admired his studies of French poetry and printed his work in
The Criterion, and Hueffer wrote in 1915 that "it is a scandal and
a shame that Mr. Flint is not the head and body of a national
commission for making England understand France . . . that Mr.
Flint should be a power in Paris and unchronicled here."[38] Flint's
importance to his colleagues is unquestionable: Amy Lowell
learned from him about the new French poets; Hulme leaned on

him in his translations of Bergson and Sorel;[39] Pound took instructions from him on how to approach Paris. He was, as René Taupin has said, Imagism's "maître d'école."[40] Aldington mocked him for his busy teacherliness:

> Whenever I meet Mr. Flint I say to him, "Well, I've read the latest thing from Paris you told me about the other day," and he says, "My dear child, did I tell you to read *that* old-fashioned book? However, I'm afraid I can't stop now, because I have six new Fantaisiste authors, two volumes of Apollinaire and thirty-two other books by representatives of sixteen different schools to review by Saturday."[41]

Flint was, furthermore, the first of the Imagists to have any real voice in the press, and he had established his reputation as an authority on modern poetry before joining Hulme's circle. He was made verse critic for *The New Age* in 1908 (when Shaw, Wells, Belloc, Chesterton, and Arnold Bennett were regular contributors) and from the beginning of his work for that paper, he showed the "French device on the pennons of [his] lance."[42] He maintained a platform for presentation of his views on French poetry from then until long after the Imagists had undergone their final transformation into the "Amygists." His influential reviews and articles proliferated through *The New Age*, *The Poetry Review*, *The Chapbook*, and *The Criterion* (which he helped to establish), and between 1916 and 1930 he translated some thirteen works from French, including poems of Verhaeren and Jean de Bosschère. He was widely known as the period's leading critic of French writing. Pound proposed his name, along with those of Joyce, Hueffer, Lawrence, and himself, as possible staff members for a new literary magazine, and he took Flint's work as "Precedent." "That rotten *Poetry and Drama*," he wrote to Harriet Monroe, "established itself solely by Flint's French number which everybody had to get."[43] Flint's article, "the first large article on contemporary stuff," Pound said, in fact caused the demand for the first number of *The Poetry Review* to outrun the supply.[44]

Flint's work was the continual propagation of two causes—*vers libre* (he coined the phrase "unrhymed cadence") and symbolism. His presentation of symbolism centered on the works of contemporary poets—a *Chapbook* article, for instance, informed his readers about Apollinaire, Cocteau, Eluard, Romains, André Spire, Paul Fort, Claudel, and others. That selection, very different from Symons's, was chosen to set the standard of modernity for English verse.

Yet, in spite of his insistence that symbolism was an *avant-garde* force in literature, Flint consciously identified his cause with that of the early symbolists. French verse was dead in 1885, he said: Leconte de Lisle, de Vigny, Banville, Heredia had stultified the alexandrine and "French poets were impelled by an interior necessity to rid their art of the grossness of the sleep that had fallen upon it—to bring it nearer to pure music."[45] Flint felt that he struggled against precisely the abuses which had beset French poetry at the outset of symbolism. In the draft of an article which he did not publish, he wrote, "Nous voulions restaurer l'art d'écrire, qui, en pays anglo-saxons, était tombé à plat, devant le journalisme, dans le ressassement ad nauseam des vieux thèmes, d'un langue poétique désuet, et d'une technique éboulée,"[46] and in a coy but instructive passage of his draft for the article on "Imagisme," he made clear his desire to use French criticism as a model:

> I was delighted that such a thing as the founding of a poetic school in London had been possible. The French device on the pennons of its lances at first shocked my English ear; but a school is a criticism; the language of criticism is, incontestably, French; and French criticism is my special pleasure. . . .[47]

English poetry needed a theory and a practice: like French poetry, as Flint saw it, it would make Mallarmé and Verlaine its masters. In his scathing review of the book of the Poets' Club, *For Christmas MDCCCVIII*, for instance, Flint gave these two as examples of poets who were "pioneers, iconoclasts, craftsmen, and artists who fought for their art."[48] In *The Poetry Review* article he made it plain that Stéphane Mallarmé was the fountainhead and that the poetry that was interesting *now* issued from him. Despite his use of him in his own verse, Flint gave Baudelaire little critical attention, either in that famous article or elsewhere. He was, Flint wrote before quoting "Correspondances" without comment, the "forerunner."[49]

Even though Flint attached symbolism to modern writers, his description of the symbol shares its most important points with

Nous voulions . . . We wanted to restore the art of writing, which, in Anglo-Saxon countries, had fallen flat, in the face of journalism, in the repetition, ad nauseam, of old themes, of obsolete poetic language, and of collapsed technique.

the introduction to *The Symbolist Movement*. For Flint, as for Symons, a symbol was

> . . . a sign used in place of a reality, as in algebra; but the symbolist poet attempts to give you an intuition of the reality itself and of the forces, vague to us, behind it, by a series of images which the imagination seizes and brings together in its effort to insert itself into and express that reality, and to evoke at the same time the infinity of which it is the culminating point in the present. To convey these images, the symbol is necessary, and is a means of expression only.[50]

Symbolism, Flint said in his article on "contemporary stuff," was "really a new way of looking at life." "It sought to suggest infinity by evocation and echo, infinity being an emotion of the poet." "The Romantics," he said, "were content to tell a story, the Parnassians impassibly to describe; but the Symbolist—and all essential poets are symbolists—takes a pure emotion and translates it by eternal images which become symbolical of men's everlasting desires and questionings."[51] For Flint, the essential quality of "essential poetry" is its vagueness: he admired Japanese poetry for the fact that in it

> "the half-said thing is dearest"—the suggestion not the complete picture (one thinks of Stéphane Mallarmé). A word will awaken in [the Japanese], therefore, a whole warp and weft of associations.[52]

His early reviews compound symbolist themes:

> We look on poetry as the highest art . . . poetry, wherein the whole imaginable universe lives—mirrored in the pool of our being, which is stirred by the wind of our emotions— and is expressed in the living beauty of words and symbols and the strange beauty of individuality, which men have imposed on Nature and called Art.[53]

Flint's criticism depends on a distinction between "essential poetry," which deals with pure emotion, and other poetry (mere composition and rhetoric), which is caught up with things. The compiler of an anthology of French poetry, he writes in a review,

> hardly knows the difference between good composition and rhetoric and essential poetry; and so he gives us that intolerable deal of Victor Hugo, most of which is the merest

sublimated rhetoric, and will be one day, I hope, if it is not already, looked upon as fustian. Hugo had enormous power; so has the wind, but the wind has no beauty except as a symbol to a poet, and Hugo was too fond of lashing a sea of things to be quintessential.[54]

For Flint, as for Symons, the "quintessential poet" is "the instrument by which life's most secret musics were reverberated to the infinite."[55]

Those musics echo in other early modern critics—in the earliest work of Middleton Murry, for instance—but only rarely in T. E. Hulme. "Must avoid the word, the Ideal, like a plague," Hulme writes, "for it suggests easy comprehension where there is no easy comprehension" (*FS*, 90). "I will give you an example of the position exactly opposite to the one I take up," he says in his "Lecture on Modern Poetry":

> A reviewer writing in *The Saturday Review* last week spoke of poetry as the means by which the soul soared into higher regions, and as a means of expression by which it became merged into a higher kind of reality. Well, that is the kind of statement that I utterly detest. I want to speak of verse in a plain way as I would of pigs: that is the only honest way. The President told us last week that poetry was akin to religion. It is nothing of the sort. (*FS*, 67)

Hulme was not, as Frank Kermode claims he was, the proponent of a merely updated symbolism:[56] between his views and Flint's there is as great a difference as between the positions of Murry and Eliot, those two genuine antitheses of modern criticism.

Hulme was himself, of course, influenced by the symbolists: by de Gourmont, and by Bergson in particular, whose *Introduction to Metaphysics* (1913) he translated, on whom he wrote several articles, and who, he said, seemed "heaven-sent" to relieve his philosophical nightmares (*FS*, 31). Hulme's description of poetic creation, in which the words create a "separate world, a dome seen in a mist, a thing of terror beyond us, and not of us" (*FS*, 82), would have pleased Flint, as would his Bergsonian assertion that the "function of the artist is to pierce through here and there, accidentally as it were, the veil placed between us and reality by the limitation of our perception engendered by action" (*S*, 147). But the emphasis of his theory is sharply antithetical to Flint's. Evocation and analogy are decidedly not the same procedure, and in every one of his major works Hulme argues that poetry makes its effect by analogy. In the "Notes on Language and Style," he writes that all literary expression "is from *Real to Real* with all the intermediate forms keeping their *real* value" (*FS*, 78). In the essay on "Romanticism and Classicism," he says that

> . . . where the analogy is every bit of it necessary for accurate description . . . when the whole of the analogy is necessary to get out the exact curve of the feeling or thing you want to express—there you seem to me to have the highest verse, even though the subject be trivial and the emotions of the infinite far away. (*S*, 137-38)

In the "Lecture on Modern Poetry," he describes the function of poetry in musical terms, not because of the perfect union in music of form and matter, but because of a "great revolution in music when, for the melody that is one-dimensional music, was substituted harmony which moves in two. Two visual images form what one may call a visual chord. They unite to suggest an image which is different to both" (*FS*, 73). Flint's "quintessential poet" must, like Mallarmé, sweep away one kind of reality in favor of another: Hulme's analogist must have them both.

The distance between Hulme's view and Flint's revealed itself in their first literary confrontation: Flint wrote in his review of the book of the Poets' Club that by comparison with the early heroes of symbolism, "The Poets' Club is death."[57] Hulme replied that Flint was "a belated romantic born out of due time, to carry on the mythical tradition of the poètes maudits."[58] The difference between the two did not vanish when they met. Hulme preserved his scorn for any "attempt to bring in infinity" (*FS*, 98). He threw the whole emphasis of his disapproval onto

> . . . the metaphysic which in defining beauty or the nature of art always drags in the infinite. Particularly in Germany, the land where theories of aesthetics were first created, the romantic aesthetes collated all beauty to an impression of the infinite involved in the identification of our being in absolute spirit. In the least element of beauty we have a total intuition of the whole world. Every artist is a kind of pantheist.

> Now it is quite obvious to anyone who holds this kind of theory that any poetry which confines itself to the finite can

never be of the highest kind. It seems a contradiction in
terms to them. And as in metaphysics you get the last refuge
of a prejudice, so it is now necessary for me to refute this.
(S, 131)

Hulme set out to show that the classical revival he predicted
would have as its "particular weapon" not the imagination but
"fancy": "And in this I imply the superiority of fancy" (S, 117).
The "fundamental quality of verse which constitutes excellence,
which has nothing to do with infinity, with mystery or with emo-
tions," he says—and it is apparent that this is precisely what Flint
would not say—is accuracy: "The great aim is accurate, precise
and definite description" (S, 132). Now, Hulme says, "where you
get this quality exhibited in the realm of the emotions you get
imagination, and . . . where you get this quality exhibited in its
contemplation of finite things you get fancy" (S, 134). It is pre-
cisely in its relationship to finite things, Hulme says, that poetry
differs from prose. In poetry there is always an attempt "to make
you continuously see a physical thing, to prevent you gliding
through an abstract process" (S, 134).

Hulme's "classicism" was not only, nor even primarily, an aes-
thetic theory. It was, like "romanticism," as he saw it, an attitude
"towards the cosmos, towards man . . . [which] gets reflected in
verse" (S, 118-19). But it had its effect for the Imagists in what
Hulme called "the fighting line," the "hurly-burly, the struggle"
(S, 130). To the poets who adopted it, Hulme's theory offered
explicit instructions. It claimed that they could "pierce the veil,"
but that they could do so only by rendering their subject exactly,
by describing and not by suggesting. When art succeeds, Hulme
says, that is because it follows the exact curve of the object it
contemplates:

> You know what I call architect's curves—flat pieces of wood
> with all different kinds of curvature. By a suitable selection
> from these you can draw approximately any curve you like.
> The artist I take to be the man who simply can't bear the
> idea of that "approximately." (S, 132)

You could define art, Hulme says, "as a passionate desire for
accuracy, and the essentially aesthetic emotion as the excitement
which is generated by direct communication" (S, 162-63).

It is important not to allow Hulme's drive for accuracy to be obscured by the symbolist element in his thought. He is clearly not in the line of Flint's, or of Mallarmé's, symbolism. For Mallarmé, Flint's desire to "séparer comme en vue d'attributions différentes le double état de la parole, brut ou immédiat ici, là essentiel" would have seemed the task of the time.[59] Hulme's insistence upon the finite thing in the Eye would have seemed far less sympathetic to the poet who wrote that "Parler n'a trait à la réalité des choses que commercialement: en littérature, cela se contente d'y faire une allusion ou de distraire leur qualité qu'incorporera quelque idée" and who wondered "A quoi bon la merveille de transposer un fait de nature en sa presque disparition vibratoire selon le jeu de la parole, cependant; si ce n'est pour qu'en émane, sans la gêne d'un proche ou concret rappel, la notion pure."[60]

Hulme's ideas became permanently a part of Imagist theory, of course. They infiltrated two of Flint's three "Rules"—"1. Direct treatment of the 'thing,' whether subjective or objective," and "2. To use absolutely no word that did not contribute to the presentation"—and they left their print on Pound's "Don'ts," which proscribe mere description and commend "the definiteness of Dante's presentation."[61] This passion for particularity, however, is in the line of descent from Pater, who wrote in his essay on "Style" that

all language involves translation from inward to outward. In literature, as in all forms of art, there are the absolute and the merely relative or accessory beauties; and precisely in that exact proportion of the term to its purpose is the absolute beauty of style, prose or verse. All the good qualities, the beauties, of verse also, are such, only as precise expression.

In the highest as in the lowliest literature, then, the one indispensable beauty is, after all, truth:—truth to bare fact in the latter, as to some personal sense of fact, diverted

séparer . . . separate as if to allow different attributions the double state of the word, rough or immediate here, there essential.

Parler . . . Speaking does not deal with the reality of things except commercially: in literature, it is sufficient to make an allusion to them, or to separate their quality to embody it in an idea. . . . What use is the marvel of transposing a fact of nature into its almost vibratory disappearance according to the game of the word, however; if it is not so that from it may emanate, without the restriction of an immediate or concrete recall, the pure notion.

somewhat from men's ordinary sense of it, in the former; truth there as accuracy, truth here as expression, that finest and most intimate form of truth, the *vraie vérité*.

Pater maintained steadily what Hulme might have been pleased to have said, that "all art does but consist in the removal of surplusage."[62] His parable about the seashell attempts to discover what the service of the general is to the concrete; Hulme's favorite analogy of the architect's curves represents the relationship between "individual things" and "stock types."

Hulme's alleged "synthesis" is a natural outcome of the encounter of modern French Symbolism and English aesthetics after Pater, an embodiment of Swinburne's dream of a "unified tradition," as though the antithetical positions of *The Renaissance* and *The Symbolist Movement* had been combined into one statement. It constitutes an important stage in a remarkable historical return—the rejection of Symbolism in English poetry—and it prepared indispensably for a rereading of Baudelaire, who appealed to the modern poets precisely by those qualitites of his work which were *not* Symbolist, not an attempt to evoke "la notion pure." Baudelaire (whom Eliot saw as "inevitably the offspring of romanticism, and by his nature the first counter-romantic in poetry")[63] holds Hulme's two emphases together more insistently and with more stability then Hulme does. Even in his essay on Hugo, which may seem to suggest that he saw his *correspondances* as mystical, he makes it clear that *his* system of analogy has always fixed one of its terms firmly in the actual:

> Chez les excellents poètes, il n'y a pas de métaphore, de comparaison ou d'épithète qui ne soit d'une adaptation *mathématiquement exacte dans la circonstance actuelle* [my italics], parce que ces comparaisons, ces métaphores et ces épithètes sont puisées dans l'inépuisable fonds de l'*universelle analogie.*
> . . . (II, 133)

It is his emphasis of the *actual* term of the analogy which makes Baudelaire see "intimité du sujet" as the dominant characteristic of the best works of art and which makes him insist that without

---

Chez . . . In excellent poets, there is no metaphor, comparison, or epithet which is not an adaptation that is mathematically exact in the present circumstances, because these comparisons, metaphors and eptithets are drawn from the inexhaustible mine of universal analogy.

consideration of the objects of transitory experience, "vous tombez forcément dans le vide d'une beauté abstraite et indéfinissable" (II, 695).

Hulme and Flint, as the latter wrote, "se donnaient reciproquement,"[64] and Imagist theory closed upon its central, paralyzing contradiction. From about the time of his meeting with Hulme, Flint's criticism began to give increasing attention to the matter of precise presentation and technical control. His praise of Frost is a far cry from his earlier commendation of Japanese verse: Frost's poetry, he thinks, is characterized by "direct observation of the object and immediate correlation with the emotion." His uncharacteristic criticism of Mallarmé, in a comment on H.D., issues from the same change in his thought:

> [H.D.'s] is the loneliness of a poet who will accept nothing that has not come to her direct, that has not sprung immediately out of her own contemplation; and in this determination, coupled with her ceaseless scrutiny of word and phrase, lurks the greatest danger. For in the creation of beauty and the constant simultaneous criticism of what is created, you can cut too far and produce angularity, or too curiously and produce enigma, which was the fate of Mallarmé.[65]

Flint began to perceive a new problem in poetry: "The riddle the artist always has to answer is, How much shall he give." His praise of H.D. shows his attempt at an answer: Imagism's "precision" will describe the poet's technique; symbolism's "mysteries" will describe the poem's effect. Her work is admirable, Flint says, because "in detail it has the precision of a goldsmith's work, in ultimate effect it is mysterious and only to be comprehended by the imagination." That is Flint's theoretical resolution. In practice, both for him and for Richard Aldington, the "synthesis" proved unworkable.

Aldington's contribution to the early twentieth century's debate about poetic theory and technique is central. Early in his career he set himself against what he saw as a prevailing flatness in verse, and at twenty-two he inspired publication of *Des Imagistes* and became literary editor of *The Egoist*. By 1919 he had

---

vous tombez . . . you inevitably fall into the emptiness of an abstract and indefinable beauty (C, 403).

se donnaient . . . gave themselves reciprocally.

written some of the finest Imagist poems and could count himself among the first English critics to have praised Joyce, Lawrence, Huxley, H.D., and Eliot (as well as the first publisher of some of their works) and possibly the first to have appreciated Proust.[66] His work, both critical and creative, gives as clearly as that of any other poet of his time a view of the struggle to adjust the English tradition to the demand for a "contemporary realism" that was associated with French poetry.

Aldington had followed the 'nineties poets across the channel before he met Pound and Flint. As a student, he was in touch with some modern French poets and with Remy de Gourmont, the most important single channel to the Imagists of the symbolist tradition, and he joined Pound and H.D. "whole-heartedly" because of their awareness of traditions other than the English:

> The Georgians were regional and in love with littleness. They took a little trip for a little week-end to a little cottage where they wrote a little poem on a little theme. Ezra was a citizen of the world, both mentally and in fact. He went off to Paris or Venice with vastly less fuss than a Georgian affronted the perils of the Cotswolds.

Aldington regarded the restoration of full literary commerce between France and England as one of the important accomplishments of the period in which he wrote. Eliot's "greatest service to English literature," he said, was his "insistence that writers could not afford to throw over the European tradition."[67]

While he was literary editor of *The Egoist* (from January 1914 until he went to the front in 1916), Aldington worked for reform on four points, the third of which was "a revolt against our intellectual provincialism."[68] While he was editor, *The Egoist* focussed sharply on French literature: it printed articles on it, side-by-side with the serialized *Portrait of the Artist as a Young Man* and *Tarr*; it announced its intention of printing a column of recent French poetry in each number, published *Poèmes* by André Spire and voiced a hope to "follow up this book with other small collections of new French poetry by the younger poets,"[69] began a series entitled "The French Word in Modern Prose," reviewed recent French books, and, as Aldington said in a review, "hammered at people to read French poetry."[70] By the time Aldington left to fight in France, he had published poems by P. J. Jouve, Paul Fort, Guy-Charles Cros, Jean de Bosschère, Louis Thomas, Charles Grolleau, Remy de Gourmont, André Spire, Stuart Merrill, André Lafon, and others. Furthermore, Aldington himself wrote on "French Authors in the War"; Flint contributed frequently; Pound sent translations; Jean de Bosschère, in a long article on Pound, gave an idea of literary exchange from the other side. Under Aldington, *The Egoist* embodied Swinburne's idea of a unified tradition. When Eliot succeeded him as literary editor, he took up an established editorial theme: "*The Egoist*," he wrote, had "always insisted upon the importance of cross-breeding in poetry, and . . . always welcomed any writer who showed signs of international consciousness."[71]

Like Flint, who dominated the poetry columns of *The New Age*, Aldington came to hold a position of authority regarding French literature. He wrote several articles for *The Anglo-French Review*, which, he said, owing to "the pre-war dislike for 'Gallic' literature . . . had some difficulty in finding English writers who knew anything much about contemporary French work,"[72] and on his return from the war he was made critic of French literature for the *Times Literary Supplement*. He wrote later on "French Periodicals" in *The Criterion* (of which he had become assistant editor in 1921), and he contributed articles to *The Little Review* and *The English Review*. His *Literary Studies and Reviews* (1924) and *French Studies and Reviews* (1926), which reprint some of his articles, give an idea of the range of his interest in French writing. In addition to all of this, he worked seriously at translation from French.

Aldington looked to French literature, as he did to Greek, for help in the definition and practice of his art. Like the other Imagists, he abhorred contemporary English criticism—he thought it was "commercial" or "doctrinaire"[73]—and he felt that however much "people may argue about the respective merits of French and English poetry there can be no doubt that in criticism the French beat us to nothing."[74] The most important and lasting influence in his work—and, indeed, the most consequential *contemporary* French influence on the whole of the Imagist group—was Remy de Gourmont. There is "so great a fascination in his work," Aldington wrote, "whether it be criticism or fiction, philosophic dialogue or prose poem, that whenever he gains a reader it is not for an hour but for life."[75]

Aldington claimed credit for introducing de Gourmont to

English readers. He wrote in 1932 that he had "had to deal with people who knew little and cared less about de Gourmont, while my own enthusiasm for his work was considered as a foolish young man's eccentricity. Now that de Gourmont is famous . . . it is painful to remember how difficult it was to place his articles and to obtain adequate payment for them."[76] Aldington's account exaggerates: by the beginning of the war, Flint, Pound, and Hulme had all felt de Gourmont's influence. But Aldington, who before going to the front had tried to relieve de Gourmont's poverty by translating and selling his work, had good reason for feeling responsible for bringing him to light in England. "It is perhaps not too much to say," Aldington wrote in 1915, "that in his time and generation [de Gourmont] ranks as Sainte-Beuve did in his." He admired especially the *Livres des Masques* and the *Promenades Littéraires*, both apologies for symbolism, and he saw de Gourmont as "the subtlest, the most fascinating, the most modern" of the "living representatives of the great Symbolist school,"[77] invaluable as its chronicler.

In his chronicle, de Gourmont sees himself as a bridge between the symbolist generations—"J'ai vu Henri de Régnier rougir à un compliment discret de Stéphane Mallarmé," he writes, "et c'est lui maintenant qui suscite de telles émotions dans l'âme et sur les joues des jeunes poètes"[78]—and he casts Baudelaire as father to the modern tradition:

> Par [Verlaine et Mallarmé] on descend le long de la montagne triste jusqu'en la cité dolente des *Fleurs du Mal*. Toute la littérature actuelle et surtout celle que l'on appelle symboliste, est baudelairienne, non sans doute par la technique extérieure, mais par la technique interne et spirituelle, par le sens du mystère, par le souci d'écouter ce que disent les choses, par le désir de correspondre, d'âme à âme, avec

J'ai vu . . . I saw Henri de Régnier blush at a discreet compliment from Stéphane Mallarmé, and it is he now who excites such emotions in the soul and on the cheeks of young poets.
Par . . . Through [Verlaine and Mallarmé], we come all the way down the sad mountain to the piteous city of *Les Fleurs du Mal*. All present-day literature, and especially the literature known as symbolist, is baudelairean, not, probably in external technique, but in internal and spiritual technique, in its sense of mystery, in its careful listening to what things say, in its desire to correspond, soul to soul, with the obscure thought scattered throughout the darkness of the world, according to these oft- repeated lines. . . .

l'obscure pensée répandue dans la nuit du monde, selon ces
vers si souvent dits et redits [des "Correspondances"]. . . .[79]

Baudelaire occupies a powerful place in both de Gourmont's
poetry and his criticism,[80] and during the period in which he
was an editor of the *Mercure de France* (from 1895 until his death
in 1915) the periodical published more than thirty articles on
Baudelaire and issued his *Lettres (1841-1866)* (1906) and his
Oeuvres Posthumes (1908) under its imprint. Between 1902 and
1915, the *Mercure*, which many English poets followed scrupu-
lously (Aldington, for instance, went over its old numbers ad-
miringly),[81] developed the view of Baudelaire that would become
current in England toward the end of the second decade of this
century. Its articles were concerned to rescue his reputation, to
show him as a writer of wide appeal, and to present him as
modern. Several of them insisted that he was not (as Flint was
to argue years later) a distant forerunner of symbolism but its
real inventor, more "modern" than Rimbaud; others were con-
cerned to show his importance to writers from his time to theirs:
to Ephraim Mikhael, Verlaine, Francis Carco, Jean Martial, Léon
Dierx.[82] Writing under a pen name in 1901 Remy de Gourmont
said he was "l'un des cinq ou six grands poètes du dix-neuvième
siècle" and admired even more his prose style: "Bien plus que
Gautier, il fut l'impeccable; la fierté froide de son style hautain
et sûr est unique dans la littérature française. Il est le maître par
excellence de tous les esprits qui ne se sont pas laissés contaminer
par le sentimentalisme."[83] One writer claimed that he was the
only critic of his time capable of understanding Ingres,[84] another
that

Les fervents de Baudelaire ne s'en tiennent ni aux *Fleurs
du mal*, ni à ses admirables traductions d'Edgar Poe. Ils se

l'un des . . . one of the five or six great poets of the nineteenth century. . . .
Far more than Gautier, he was the impeccable one; the cold pride of his lofty
and sure style is unique in French literature. He is the master *par excellence* of
all those minds which have not allowed themselves to be contaminated by sen-
timentality.

Les fervents . . . Admirers of Baudelaire do not content themselves with either
Les Fleurs du Mal or the admirable translations of Poe. They delight in the
posthumous works and in those *Curiosités Esthétiques*—as rich in anecdotes as in
ideas—where the artist, voluntarily paradoxical—that goes wihout saying—but
singularly shrewd, reveals and declares his personality in the face of the works
of others.

délectent de ses oeuvres posthumes et de ces *Curiosités esthétiques*—aussi riches d'anecdotes que d'idées—où l'artiste, volontiers paradoxal,—cela va sans dire,—mais singulièrement avisé, révèle et affirme sa personnalité devant les oeuvres d'autrui.[85]

Francis Carco noted that "Il faut arriver à Jarry pour rencontrer, après Baudelaire, un humoriste de haute valeur,"[86] Jean de Gourmont saw his attempt to "faire pénétrer dans ses vers une musique plus secrète et plus savante [que la rime]" as the means by which "il fut le précurseur de la poésie verlainienne, amoureuse de musique et dédaigneuse de la rime riche,"[87] and René Arcos argued that it was his merciless insistence on the value of words that made him, rather than Whitman, the best model for modern poets.[88] Taking up Baudelaire's own point about the critic in the poet, Jean de Gourmont wrote that Baudelaire "possédait une qualité qui manque à la plupart des poètes: un jugement sûr; jugement qu'il exerçait contre son oeuvre propre, et ce qui explique la perfection de cette oeuvre,"[89] and Remy de Gourmont himself praised Baudelaire's technical mastery, founded on the tradition of Boileau and Racine: "Ses poèmes sont composés. Il veut dire quelque chose et il le dit. Ses métaphores sont cohérentes; surtout, elles sont visibles et donnent des visions logiques." "Il y avait autre chose dans les *Fleurs du Mal* qu'un 'frisson nouveau,' " he writes, "il y avait un retour au vers français traditionnel."[90] One critic saw Baudelaire's work as the first "poésie des foules";[91] another, aiming to see him in the symbolist tradition, said, "Transformation des objects extérieurs

Il faut . . . Only with Jarry does one meet, after Baudelaire, a humorist of great value.

faire . . . penetrate his verse with a more secret and subtle music than rhyme . . . he was the precursor of Verlainean poetry, in love with music and scornful of *rime riche*.

possédait . . . possessed a quality lacking in most poets: a sure judgement; a judgement that he exercised on his own work, and that is what explains the perfection of this work.

Ses poèmes . . . His poems are composed. He means to say something and he says it. His metaphors are coherent; especially, they are visible and they produce logical visions. . . . There was something else in *Les Fleurs du Mal* than a "frisson nouveau," there was a return to the traditional French line . . . poetry of crowds.

Transformation . . . Transformation of external objects into symbols, there is the work of Baudelaire's genius in the face of reality! He doesn't see, he transfigures, he metamorphoses. . . .

en symbole, violà le travail du génie de Baudelaire devant la réalité! Il ne voit pas, il transfigure, il métamorphose. . . ."[92] For English poets who read French periodical literature, it would have been difficult to think of Baudelaire as an "offshoot," as Symons had called him, of a past movement: he was, as Jean de Gourmont wrote in 1913 in a comment on Verlaine, "essentiellement l'homme moderne."[93]

For Aldington, Baudelaire was an early enthusiasm and a continuing interest. In the unpublished draft of a review of Eugène Crépet's *Etude Biographique*, which appeared revised in the *TLS* for 18 December, 1919,[94] he writes that he "has sharp memories of the obloquoy [sic] heaped on him for a youthful and injudiciously expressed admiration for the Fleurs du Mal. It appeared that this book was a kind of passport to the lower regions." That may, of course, have been the occasion on which the ladies shivered chastely, but Aldington defied the reproof and cultivated his interest in the French poet. In his review, he remarks on the importance of the publication by the *Mercure de France* of the *Lettres* and by Crès of the *Journaux Intimes*, quotes Remy de Gourmont on Baudelaire's ethics, and judges the book he reviews as "an essential handbook for all Baudelaire enthusiasts." The appearance of several Baudelaire books in the past two years (the work had gone out of copyright in 1917), he suspects, indicates "a revival of interest in the works of that master."

Aldington is more pointed on some matters in the draft of his review than in its printed version. In the draft he is at pains to attack a "deplorable prejudice against a work of genius." In England, he says, "there are many worthy people . . . who look on his work with horror." He sees that as a consequence partly of "heavy British misunderstanding of Baudelaire's preoccupation with ethics" and partly of "the writings of the unspeakable Nordau and . . . the ill-advised translations from pens which were more competent in journalism than in the delicacies of French poetry." Aldington shares the feeling of some of his contemporaries (Eliot and John Middleton Murry, for instance) that Baudelaire's reputation in England had been damaged in the 'nineties, but he writes that it

is not easy to discover what exactly is the attitude of the new generation towards Baudelaire; whether he is still a vital

essentiellement . . . essentially modern man.

force or only one of the innumerable "classics" who are taken
as read without exerting any real influence. In Paris "the
wild men," those who used to write for Les Soirées de Paris
and now produce La Rose Rouge and similar periodicals,
have apparently not much use for Baudelaire. The cult of
the cinema, of negro wood carving and Americanism—
which make up the bizarre formula of the self-styled "avant-
garde"—cannot have very much in common with the Pari-
sian voluptuary of the Second Empire, in spite of his avowed
preference for ladies of colour. Yet it is difficult to see how
an excessive admiration for his chief pupil, Mallarmé, can
exist side by side with a total indifference to Baudelaire. Yet
there certainly exists in France an intelligent appreciation
of Baudelaire's writings. Poetry so nearly perfect in form as
"Les Fleurs du Mal" must always be admired by certain
temperaments.

In Baudelaire's poetry, Aldington sees an antithesis to the poetry
of his own time, and once again the author of Les Fleurs du Mal
is invoked as a corrective to English poets:

In the period vaguely referred to as the "nineties" Baude-
laire was certainly a strong influence in England, an unfor-
tunate influence since the poets ignored the perfection of
his style and produced flowery embroideries on the "scarlet
sin" theme. To-day Baudelaire is scarcely popular in Eng-
land. When the object of a large class of poets is to appear
as childlike and innocent as possible, when people "babble
o' green fields" in little stammering poems, there cannot be
much room for admiration of the sophisticated point of view
and marmoreal construction of lines like [the first four lines
of "La Géante"]. . . .

In his own poetry, as in this unpublished review, Baudelaire
remained, for Aldington, the antithesis of artless innocence. In
the review as it was published, Aldington took out his personal
reminiscence as well as his observations on "heavy British mis-
understanding," and he added a passage underlining what he
saw as the main points. Baudelaire, he said, was an "idealistic
temperament . . . whose yearning for beauty, moral perfection,
for la très-belle, la très-bonne, la très-chère was in sharp conflict
with the realities of a coal-driven civilization." He was also a poet

whose work is marked by "his preoccupation with form, his almost passionate search for the finest method of expression."

The Imagists found some of the innovations urged on them by their studies of modern French poetry compatible with ideas they had already formed or dispositions they had already demonstrated. The *vers-libre* much publicized by Flint, for instance, satisfied a need that English models did not. Hulme said that there

> were certain impressions which I wanted to fix. I read verse to find models, but I could not find any that seemed exactly suitable to express that kind of impression, except perhaps a few jerky rhythms of Henley, until I came to read the French *vers-libre* which seemed to exactly fit the case. (*FS*, 68)

But the Imagists did not so warmly welcome all of their lessons from the French. What they perceived as an obligation to deal with city subjects in their poetry shattered their contemplation of the cool, still beauty of Greek poetry and the stonily static beauty of some of their 'nineties models. When their new obligation was combined with Hulme's emphasis on sensation and direct presentation, it raised a serious conflict for them and came, far more than discussion of verse form or aesthetic questions, near to destroying the work of the poets who felt its force. "Personally," Aldington wrote, "I have long felt that the purely technical question of free verse was subordinate to the reform of poetic style and, above all, to the assimilation by poetry of modern thought and the complex modern mind."[96]

In spite of Henley, Symons, and the whole range of 'nineties poets who had turned to the city for subject matter, the Imagists were by no means certain, at their beginnings, that what they were setting out to do was either desirable or possible. "We can't escape from the spirit of our times," Hulme said in his "Lecture on Modern Poetry" (*FS*, 72), and in his essay on London, Aldington said that he was

> still waiting patiently for the English poet who will do for the aspects of London what Huysmans did for Paris in his *Croquis Parisiens*, and what Jules Romains has done for the psychology of its crowds in his *Puissances de Paris*. Mr. Goldring had a shot at it in his *Streets*, and Mr. Ford Madox

Hueffer, in *The Soul of London*, has written admirable pages
on London, but it is not *tout à fait ça*. . . . It is true that one
or two younger poets have not altogether neglected the ar-
tistic opportunities of London, but somehow they don't quite
"come off"; the Cotswolds are much easier and safer.[97]

For the Imagists, as for Symons, the model for the description
of a city was Paris, the mode entirely French, and the new ob-
ligation clearly associated with Baudelaire. Consider, wrote Al-
dington, what use could be made of London by "a modern Con-
tinental poet who would exploit [it] cunningly to evoke just the
right corner of London, just the right touch of cynicism or
bathos." His attempts and those of his colleagues to deflect the
course of English poetry into that continental modernity were
only moderately successful. In a moment of weariness, he wrote:
"It is perhaps useful to remind oneself that there are many kinds
of excellence even in poetry. I do not think this a good time to
write pastoral poetry, but it is rather a good time to read it. One
cannot live on Baudelaire and James Joyce alone."[98]

When they began to write, the Imagists found themselves con-
fronting Symons's "great problem": "how to be real, true to life,
and yet poetic, true to art."[99] By now the question was debated
on all fronts. This problem of modernism enrolled poets on two
opposing sides: the Georgians seemed "traditional" because they
treated nature; the Imagists seemed "modern" because they
dealt with the town. A reviewer of Flint and Aldington thought
that

> The present epidemic of *vers libres*, of poems about walks
> down the Strand, violent hatreds, railway stations and phys-
> ical dizziness, will presently die down; but it will have intro-
> duced new blood into the veins of poetry and helped to
> avert the risk of that petrifaction that sets in when the treat-
> ment of certain kinds of subjects in traditional forms and
> language comes to be recognised as the only thing a poet
> may legitimately do.
>
> We may therefore welcome such books as those here re-
> viewed, both as symptoms and medicines. . . .[100]

Charles Ricketts thought that the problem was imported, not
really English:

> Unlike the Latins we are not really town people, the best of
> our work is still touched by the country, still full of pleasure

in homely rural things, the exceptions to this rule point to our being influenced by outside movements, impulses of excitement caught for the moment from waves that have their origin in the Mediterranean. Flaubert with his roots in the classical and oriental worlds is unintelligible; so are the "macabre" elements in Poe, Baudelaire, Villiers, all the psychology of towns and old and corrupt civilizations. Gustave Moreau is disliked by Burne-Jones, who is English, understood by Rossetti because he is Italian.[101]

Beauty, however, was under attack. Pound saw room for more than one kind of poetry:

> The cult of beauty is the hygiene, it is sun, air and the sea and rain and the lake bathing. The cult of ugliness, Villon, Baudelaire, Corbière, Beardsley are diagnosis. Flaubert is diagnosis. Satire, if we are to ride this metaphor to staggers, is surgery, insertions and amputations. . . .
> The cult of beauty and the delineation of ugliness are not in mutual opposition.[102]

Others thought that they were: Hueffer for instance wrote, "Upon the face of it, the comfrey under the hedge may seem a safer card to play for the purpose of poetry than the portable zinc dustbin left at dawn for the dustman to take. . . . But it is not really." Hueffer did not argue that only one kind of poetry should exist, but he did make perfectly clear which he thought should be written in his time:

> This is not saying that one should not soak oneself with the Greek traditions; study every fragment of Sappho; delve ages long in the works of Bertran de Born; translate for years like the minnelieder of Walther von der Vogelweide or that we should forget the bardic chants of Patric of the Seven Kingdoms. . . . Let us do anything in the world that will widen our perceptions. We are the heirs of all the ages. But, in the end, I feel fairly assured that the purpose of all these pleasant travails is the right appreciation of such facets of our own Day as God will let us perceive.[103]

For some Imagists, the city presented only a passing problem. H.D., for example, wrote a few poems on the new subject and then ignored it. Fletcher found it a natural development of his earlier interests, and, imitative though it may have been, *The*

Dominant City, which intended to "describe the essence of a mod-
ern city, in terms less reminiscent of Whitman than of Baudelaire
and Verhaeren,"[104] had set him along the path pointed by the
Tableaux Parisiens. But both Flint and Aldington accommodated
their poetry only gradually and with difficulty to what was seen
as the demand of modernity.

For Aldington, the problem was acute. His early work had
worshipped the beautiful and the eternal; the new poetry obliged
him to respect the "real" and the momentary. The conflict is
clear in his essay on Flint:

> "For the modern artist," says Georges Duhamel in one of
> his essays, "there can be only two methods: s'accepter ou
> s'évader." Heaven knows that the temptation is strong to
> evade one's life and surroundings when one is confined
> beneath these sulphurous skies and condemned to gaze un-
> remittingly upon smoky walls, to walk muddy pavements
> and muddier streets; Heaven knows it is a temptation to
> loose one's yearning, to picture the high purple hills of At-
> tica, to re-create in fancy the abrupt cliffs and orange-groves
> of Sorrento, to people one's pages with heroes and gods,
> with impossibly happy and beautiful people.[105]

Aldington concludes that Flint "is strongest and finest when he
accepts." But acceptance was a grim discipline: Aldington's ad-
miration for Flint lay in the fact that he accommodated his verse
to "the very sordidness and greyness which his soul loathes."
Aldington was not prepared to see the city as beautiful: it forced
him to a renunciation. He could only go so far as to say that it
contained "objects of deep interest, if not of beauty." But he
agreed that the romance of ruralism was outmoded and that the
"abstract" offered no refuge—that, he thought, would be "ro-
mantic balderdash." He saw only one way for the modern poet
to avoid sentimentality, artificiality, and irrelevance, a way that
recalls the early Symons: "by rendering the moods, the emotions,
the impressions of a single, sensitized personality confronted by
the phenomena of modern life, and by expressing these moods
accurately, in concrete, precise, racy language."[106]

Hulme's theories comprise a dimension of the conflict. They
demanded vivid treatment of real experience—"sudden ar-
rangement of commonplaces" (*FS*, 93)—and they claimed that
modern poetry "has become definitely and finally introspective

and deals with expression and communication of momentary phases in the poet's mind" (*FS*, 72). Harold Monro noted a connection between the city and the direct presentation of sensory experience in Imagist poems:

> Poets of the Imagist and other kindred modern schools are no longer "visited by the Muses": they are not at home to them. . . . Their minds are obsessed by the Town. They are more concerned effectively to describe their rapid impressions than faithfully to record their abiding sentiments. The passing event and its effect on their minds is everything to them.[107]

Hulme's demand for treatment of "the passing event" seemed incompatible with recording "the abiding sentiment." In the actual writing of poems, the self-contradictions of Imagist theory were unmasked. Aldington saw in Pound the impossible attempt to ride two horses:

> Mr. Pound was the last of the Romantics; when he tried to turn himself into the first of the Realists he unwittingly injured a very delicate poetic sensibility. You cannot be a Realist writing of London, of common people and actual occurrences, like Mr. Ford Madox Hueffer, at the same time that you are a refined Romantic of the type of Mr. Yeats. The two methods of writing are incompatible . . . the endeavour to unite the two methods has been disastrous to Mr. Pound.[108]

Before opting for modernism in his own poetry, Aldington wrote:

> Here is the question: Shall we, or shall we not have "parochialism in art"—or to put it in different words: should artists confine themselves entirely to modern life and to the modern world for their detail as well as for the "spirit" of their works? And here we are up against one of the problems of modern art.

For himself, Aldington wrote, he was "all against the dust-bin and the back-yard and Mr. Potter and all for Daphnis and the Princess of China and Prester John and Pico della Mirandola. But that is because I am a romantic."[109] One of Aldington's "pegs" for criticism was a sentence from Taine: "le laid est beau

peut-être, mais le beau est plus beau"[110]—nevertheless he joined
Flint in the abandonment of the "romantic" for the "real."

Both Flint and Aldington were reluctant moderns. Flint
thought at the beginning of his career that

> There is no poetry in the modern town; great verse and
> fine rhetoric may be made of it—Verhaeren has done so;
> but the world treasures most the simple elemental passions
> married to the forms of beauty which every man knows in
> his heart. The modern poet, who has need of the town,
> because it is the center and fillip of culture, divorces himself
> from the fields and hills and streams of which he has equal
> need; both to be concomitant parts of his daily life; and the
> town itself has no real organic existence—only that of a
> machine. . . .[111]

For Aldington, as late as 1916, the life of the city was "perverted,"
"sordid," "filthy," and could call forth only "disgust or deep sym-
pathy."[112] Both poets developed a characteristic contrast in their
poems between the city's ugliness and the standard of beauty.
Flint set "violets" and "daisies" and "buttercups," and "big, broad
Earth" against a debased city existence.[113] His city destroys:

> Their lamps have been choked,
> And the guttering wick has stunk their souls out,
> Whether they wear gold chains and good leather and cloth,
> Or a greasy cap and torn shoddy.[114]

The poet's sensibility is blighted by the city: he longs to produce
"the great and broad-browed songs of the ever-singing sea," but
he is incapable of such expression "For I have lived in a city, far
from the sea-birds' keen, / And have herded with the sordid, the
low-browed and the mean."[115]

Aldington began his "modernism" with good humor. In Jan-
uary 1914 he published his "Penultimate Poetry—Xenophilo-
metropolitania." His "Elevators" was a fanfare for Pound and
the futurists:

> Come my songs,
> Let us whizz up to the eighteenth floor,
> Let us present our most undignified exterior
> To this mass of indolent superstition,
> To this perverted somnambulistic age;

Let us soar up higher than the eighteenth floor
And consider the delicate delectable monocles
Of the musical virgins of Parnassus:
Pale slaughter beneath purple skies.

The ninth of his series is for Pound alone:

The apparition   of these poems   in a crowd:
White faces   in a black   dead faint.[116]

But Aldington's "Eros and Psyche"[117] allegorizes pure beauty as
a statue standing "in an old dull yard near Camden Town" losing
its character in an environment of filth and flux:

And I peer from a 'bus-top
As we splash through the grease and puddles,
And I glimpse them, huddled against the wall,
Half-hidden under a freight-train's smoke,
And I see the limbs that a Greek slave cut
In some old Italian town,
And I see them growing older
And sadder
And greyer.

In "Whitechapel,"[118] Aldington alternates a vision of the city with
one of nature, making the point that he has no language for his
new subject:

Noise;
Iron hoofs, iron wheels, iron din
Of drays and trams and feet passing;
Iron
Beaten to a vast mad cacophony.

He has, however, inherited a fluent, melodious, graceful speech
for the description of traditional beauty:

In vain the shrill far cry
Of swallows sweeping by;
In vain the silence and green
Of meadows Apriline;
In vain the clear white rain—

Language, like sensation, is brutalized; the poem concludes with
a despairing naming of crude sensations:

Noise, iron, smoke;
Iron, iron, iron.

"Keep present in mind when we look at nature, the curious place of language which is founded on it and *subordinate* to it," Hulme had written. "If only the making and fixing of words had begun in the city stage in the evolution of society and not in the nomadic" (*FS*, 83). Aldington's poetry develops a center of despair for loss of an innocence which is associated with beauty. "Daisy" shows innocence, the kind represented by Thomson's poem of the same name, as girlhood corrupted by the city. Aldington's poem makes its comment on Thomson by means of a sentimental manner directly reminiscent of Symons's "Interruption in Court" and Rossetti's *Found*: "You were my playmate by the sea," he writes, but

> To-day I pass through the streets,
> She who touches my arm and talks with me
> Is—who knows?—Helen of Sparta,
> Dryope, Laodamia. . . .
>
> And there are you
> A whore in Oxford Street.[119]

Aldington's "Defeat" joins Symons's lament for a Beauty which was a "goddess! Lovely, implacable":

> Though our hearts were mad and strong
> With love for you,
> Though we fought for you,
> Though our remnant struggled
> And not one was false,
> We are beaten.
>
> Beauty, for your sake we are lost,
> For you we are crushed,
> Scorn and bitterness are cast at us,
> And fools who hate you
> Are preferred to us.[120]

When Aldington condemned Wilde for his betrayal of art to the philistines, he allotted him at least some praise for seeing the horror of journalistic realism that was to come.

"Some poets," Eliot wrote, "such as Baudelaire, similarly pos-

sessed by the town, turn directly to the littered streets, the squint-
ing slums, the grime and smoke and the viscid human life within
the streets, and find there the centre of intensity."[121] Both Flint
and Aldington did, finally, evolve a language and a style for
treatment of urban subjects, and both came to see a function for
the modern poet which is like that outlined by Baudelaire. Both
ultimately wrote poems which were neither grimly allegorical
nor insignificantly impressionistic. Several of the poems in Flint's
second and third collection, *Cadences* [1915] and *Otherworld Ca-
dences* (1920), turn to the town as to a genuine "centre of inten-
sity." His "Prayer" defines the poet's task and carefully reviews
his options in terms strongly reminiscent of Baudelaire.[122] The
first stanza rejects the Imagists' Hellenism:

> As I walk through the streets,
> I think of the things
> That are given to my friends:
> Myths of old Greece and Egypt,
> Greek flowers, Greek thoughts
> And all that incandescence,
> All that grace,
> Which I refuse.

The second puts aside the romantic alternative:

> If even the orchards of England,
> Its gardens and its woods,
> Its fields and its hills,
> Its rivers and its sea,
> Were mine;
> But they are not.

The third embraces, almost with enthusiasm, the new, limited
conditions of the art:

> But these are nothing.
> Give me the flame, O Gods,
> To light these people with,
> These pavements, this motor traffic,
> These houses, this medley.
>
> Give me the vision,
> And they may live.

That declaration descends from the last lines of "Le Soleil" (which also, it may be recalled, informs the manifesto poem of Symons's *Days and Nights*) and it outlines a performance like that in Baudelaire's magnificent "Projet d'Epilogue":

Anges revêtus d'or, de pourpre et d'hyacinthe,
O vous! soyez témoins que j'ai fait mon devoir
Comme un parfait chimiste et comme une âme sainte.

Car j'ai de chaque chose extrait la quintessence.

Tu m'as donné ta boue et j'en ai fait de l'or. (I, 192)

Like Aldington, Flint retained his nostalgia, but his most famous "image," the swan in his "Easter," is poised in ambiguity, suggesting at once both the destruction of beauty by the city's dirt and the possibility that something splendid and permanent may arise from the drifting filth:

a sheet of sodden newspaper
that, drifting away,
reveals beneath the immaculate white splendour
of its neck and wings
a breast black with scum.[123]

Baudelaire is at the center of Flint's "modern" verse. The opening line of his "London," for instance ("London, my beautiful"), recasts Baudelaire's address to Paris ("Je t'aime, ô ma très belle"), and the poem's conclusion (in which the poet announces his intention to "climb / into the branches / to the moonlit tree-tops" to survey the city) recalls the "Epilogue" to *Les Fleurs du Mal*. In both its opening and its consoling memory of past joys, Flint's "Sadness" suggests "Recueillement," and the last line of Flint's "Courage" echoes the conclusion of "Le Voyage."[124] In his second and third books of poetry, Flint turns insistently, as Aldington said, to "the impressions of a single, sensitized personality confronted by the phenomena of modern life." His "Immortality," "Loneliness," "Beggar," "Accident" aim to provide meaning for the impression, significance for the detail perceived, in precisely the manner of "A une Passante." Even his ambiguous swan, the sign of poetry and beauty blackened by a sheet of journalistic

Anges . . . Angels clad in gold and purple and hyacinth, O you, bear witness that I've fulfilled my task like a perfect alchemist, like a saintly soul: for from each thing I've extracted the quintessence. You gave me your mud and I've turned it into gold (S, 231-32).

prose, has a precise Baudelairean background. It is a close rel-
ative of the emblematical creature of "Le Cygne." In that poem,
which is about loss and urban change ("la forme d'une ville /
Change plus vite, hélas! que le coeur d'un mortel"), Baudelaire
calls to mind "quiconque a perdu ce qui ne se retrouve / Jamais,
jamais" (I, 86-87). It is his swan, displaced from river to street,
which provides the link to contexts and sends the poet off on
his meditation about exiles, his invocation of Ovid and Andro-
mache. That swan, too, wears the filth of the city:

Un cygne qui s'était évadé de sa cage,
Et, de ses pieds palmés frottant le pavé sec,
Sur le sol raboteux traînait son blanc plumage.
Près d'un ruisseau sans eau la bête ouvrant le bec

Baignait nerveusement ses ailes dans la poudre,
Et disait, le coeur plein de son beau lac natal:
"Eau, quand donc pleuvras-tu? quand tonneras-tu, foudre?"
                                                    (I, 86)

Aldington took the same model for his city verse, and history
confers a special interest on the borrowing in his "Interlude."[125]
There, he describes his response to hearing a tune piped in a
London street. The music creates in him a vision of "Gay girls
dancing / in the frozen street," of "Red lips that first were / Red
in Ephesus," but when he rounds a corner he sees that the tune
is piped by a beggar. The vision vanishes and Aldington con-
cludes:

You? Red-nose, piping by the Red-Lion,
You!
Did you bring them!

Here, take my pennies,
Mon semblable, mon frère.

la forme . . . a city's pattern changes, alas, more swiftly than a human heart
(S, 209).
quiconque . . . I think of all those who have lost what they can never, never
hope to find again (S, 211).
Un cygne . . . [I saw] a Swan who had just escaped from his cage. Rubbing the
parched roadway with his webbed feet, he was trailing his white plumes on the
raw ground. Beside a dried-up gutter the poor beast, with gaping beak, was
frantically bathing his wings in the dust, and with his heart full of longing for
his native land, cried out, "O Water, when will you rain down? O lightning, when
will you rage?" (S, 210).

Flint and Aldington were not always successful in their treat-
ment of city subjects: their nostalgia often made them senti-
mental, and their ideological preoccupation with precision did
not protect them from vagueness. But they defined the art to
come. Neither societies nor individuals, W. H. Auden wrote, "can
skip a stage in their development, though they may shorten it.
Whatever its character, the provincial England of 1907, when I
was born, was Tennysonian in outlook, whatever its outlook the
England of 1925 when I went up to Oxford was The Waste Land
in character."[126] It is the achievement of the Imagists that in spite
of a natural disposition toward their traditional subject matter,
toward the "beauty" of the aesthetes and their Greek models,
they articulated the difficulties in the development of modern
poetry. For the wholly successful transformation of urban matter
into poetry, English literature would wait for Aldington's "man
of parts." Aldington's call, at the end of his essay on London,
has specific prophetic and reminiscent interest:

> Who will put down for us the "unanisme" of London, who
> will record for us the "group mind" of its various crowds;
> the drab, discouraged, appalling "soul" of the hastening
> swarm of London's workers, drifting rapidly over the
> bridges to Waterloo and London Bridge . . . the crowd which
> suffers and tramples, pursues its changing illusions, which
> is at once docile and formidable, immensely vital, and a prey
> to death? We need badly an English Jules Romains.[127]

The last section of the first part of *The Waste Land* answers that
question directly, and the conclusion of the *Salon de 1845* puts
it as succinctly:

> Au vent qui soufflera demain nul ne tend l'oreille; et pour-
> tant l'héroïsme *de la vie moderne* nous entoure et nous
> presse.—Nos sentiments vrais nous étouffent assez pour que

Au vent . . . No one is cocking his ear to to-morrow's wind; and yet the heroism
of *modern life* surrounds us and presses upon us. We are quite sufficiently choked
by our true feelings for us to be able to know them. There is no lack of subjects,
nor of colours, to make epics. The painter, the true painter for whom we are
looking, will be he who can snatch its epic quality from the life of today and can
make us see and understand, with brush or with pencil, how great and poetic
we are in our cravats and our patent-leather boots. Next year let us hope that
the true seekers may grant us the extraordinary delight of celebrating the advent
of the *new!* (M, 37).

nous les connaissions.—Ce ne sont ni les sujets ni les couleurs qui manquent aux épopées. Celui-là sera le *peintre*, le vrai peintre, qui saura arracher à la vie actuelle son côté épique, et nous faire voir et comprendre, avec de la couleur ou du dessin, combien nous sommes grands et poétiques dans nos cravates et nos bottes vernies.—Puissent les vrais chercheurs nous donner l'année prochaine cette joie singulière de célébrer l'avènement du *neuf*! (II, 407)

JOHN MIDDLETON MURRY

THE PROBLEM OF SYNTHESIS

John Middleton Murry's early work receives little attention. That is partly because of the excess of praise and blame heaped on him by some of his contemporaries. Disproportionate praise, such as Rayner Heppenstall's in an early "prospectus of Murry's qualifications as leader,"[1] and extraordinarily cruel criticism, such as Huxley's in *Point Counter Point*, dominate discussion of Murry's early years and divert attention from his work to his personal life. The shadow of Lawrence, furthermore, obscures Murry's independent achievement, so that even his great admirer, Richard Rees, who believed him to have been equalled in sophistication only by a very few, such as Valéry, Santayana, and Thomas Mann, saw his role in literature as that of the critic of Lawrence, the one man of his time capable of dealing with the "one great original genius."[2] Modern criticism remembers Murry chiefly in books on Lawrence, and studies of the man himself are often directed by the desire to define the "quality in Murry which appealed to Lawrence."[3] One writer claims that "it would be futile to consider Murry's sense of his own role as a writer without recognizing how deeply it was coloured by the impact of Lawrence."[4] Murry's early work is overpowered also by the sheer volume of his later output; it occupies such a slim fraction of the whole that even for his biographer, attempting to trace the full range of his path meant "bolting the door on a number of side-alleys," of his early literary activity.[5] A number of the *D. H. Lawrence Review* devoted to Murry contains not one article on his work during the period of *Rhythm, Blue Review*, and the *Athenaeum*.[6]

One of the results of this neglect is the notion that Murry was an isolated, peripheral figure. This idea is encouraged by his later personal outpourings and his sometimes astonishing forays into philosophy and politics. These make him seem, as Edward Marsh remarked, "a case apart."[7] Criticism of this later work is bound to consider him a mysterious solitary, "a strange, eccentric, neurotic man."[8] Because of the unsteady pattern of Murry's career, his contribution to literature is usually assessed on grounds of this or that particular critical success: his comments on Shakespeare's metaphor in *The Problem of Style* are seen as a herald to subsequent explorations of Shakespeare's imagery, or his early approval of Eliot, Valéry, Joyce, and Proust is taken as his most substantial critical accomplishment.[9]

Yet Murry's early work is his finest and most influential. Between 1910, when he embraced the "cause" of art, and about 1923, when his search for a "credible religion" became his major interest, he took up the problems of poetry as one intimately involved in their resolution.[10] Only Eliot's or Pound's early critical writings as accurately reflect the concerns of the time, and it is doubtful whether either exercised more influence in the early part of this period. As editor of *Rhythm*, the "organ of Modernism,"[11] and *The Blue Review*, Murry regarded himself as "the self-constituted spokesman" for the "younger generation,"[12] an attitude which he carried into the *Athenaeum*. He became known as a promising poet and novelist and he gained a reputation as "a serious force as a critic."[13] During the period of his editorship of the *Athenaeum*, he presided, with a few others, over what Eliot called "the high summer of literary journalism in London in my lifetime," a summer which produced, among other things, most of the essays of *The Sacred Wood*.[14] The range, excellence, and originality of some of Murry's work during the period is remarkable. He wrote on many of the concerns of his time—Hegel, Bergson, the French poets, the Russian novelists, the Russian ballet, primitive art—and on the relation of twentieth-century English poetry to its own tradition. His essays show the evolution of some of the period's most characteristic critical concepts; his contribution to the debate over romanticism and classicism accurately accounts for some of the attitudes and aspirations of his time and identifies its parentage; his long career as a reviewer of French literature and as an admirer of Russian literature makes him, along with the Imagists and others, partly responsible for the characteristic "cosmopolitanism" of his time.

Murry has a place in this study for three closely related reasons. His critical theory, at the time of his greatest strength, when

he seemed to his contemporaries to be a distinguishing feature
in the landscape of modernism, has major, nourishing roots in
Baudelaire's criticism: Murry's conception of the problem of
style is as Baudelairean as Pater's. Then, between 1910 and 1931,
Murry gave an intense critical attention to Baudelaire, publishing
five essays on his life and work. These, three of which were
extremely influential, distinguish sharply between the figure they
propose as the "modern" Baudelaire and the figure they deride
as the fabrication of the nineteenth century. They comprise a
radically new English reading, at once a demonstration of the
modernist transformation of the Baudelaire myth and a contri-
bution to it. (It is very likely because Murry gave Baudelaire such
a sustained and close critical attention, attributing to him both
literary and moral importance, that Huxley gave Burlap and
Spandrell such an intimate, though antithetical, relation to one
another in *Point Counter Point.*) And, finally, Murry's early crit-
icism exemplifies the shift in attitude about symbolism that is
both a major development of the modern period and an aspect
of Baudelaire's renewed importance in England. In Murry's ear-
liest work, symbolism *is* modernism; but before he had ended
his earliest explorations, Murry had begun to reject an exclusive
emphasis on the inward and the sugestive and to assert the value
in literature of what seemed to him to be the outward and the
rational. By 1922, when he lectured in Oxford on *The Problem
of Style*, Murry had re-achieved the nineteenth-century synthesis
of the world and the self.

Murry began his literary career as a result of his heady en-
counter, in the summer of 1909, with Paris art circles. He had
gone to Paris to hear Bergson and to acquire enough fluency in
French to read the symbolists, with whom he was still "trying to
grapple,"[15] and this trip and others altered his plan to enlist in
the Civil Service. He wrote to Philip Landon in 1911 that in Paris
he had heard art "worshipped" and watched "sacrifices made
for it" and that the experience had "given me myself an end to
live for—which will be a life of Art as far as I can make it so."[16]
Murry divided his time in Paris between the Café d'Harcourt
("the Bohemian . . . *d'Harcourt*," Arthur Symons had written,
"where art is loved, but with something of haste")[17] where, as a
solitary, he experienced "Life," and the Closerie des Lilas "where
the left-bank *littérateurs* foregathered round Paul Fort."[18] On
another trip to Paris at Christmas of the next year, he met "most

of the leading French men of letters," including Valéry and Charles du Bos, who "became his friends and lifelong admirers,"[19] and John Duncan Fergusson, the Scottish "Fauve," whose influence on him he describes in his autobiography.

Murry's experiences in Paris had both immediate and lasting consequences. On his return, he abandoned his academic work and devoted himself exclusively to the cause of Art. *Rhythm*, which he conceived in Paris in discussions with Fergusson, was established in 1911 as the English arm of an international movement of which Murry was to be the resident *chef d'école*. He was also launched on a distinguished career as a critic of French literature. His earliest published work was an article on Verhaeren. He wrote on French works in *Rhythm* and later in the *Athenaeum* and elsewhere, and in 1914 Bruce Richmond made him reviewer of French literature for the *Times Literary Supplement*. By 1916 he felt that he was "well established" as a reviewer of French literature and that when he wrote on that subject "I had something to say, and I said it well."[20] When he went back to Paris in 1922 Murry was already known to French writers as "the 'presenter' of Proust and Gide to the English public."[21] When Rayner Heppenstall catalogued Murry's library he noted that it "lacked nothing in English and French, old or new, and there were affectionately inscribed copies of works by Paul Valéry and others."[22]

There are three stages in the influence of French writers on Murry's work. His very early critical views, advanced in the first few numbers of *Rhythm*, are an amalgam of Bergsonism and aestheticism. In about 1913, when he had begun to reject some of the tenets of symbolist doctrine and to look for a critical theory which would take account of the rational processes in literature, Murry turned to the pre-symbolist French writers of the nineteenth century. At about this time, he writes, he experienced "a very complete surrender to Stendhal," who seemed to him to be "the greatest novelist who ever wrote."[23] About the same time, and throughout the period of his finest criticism, Murry admired and used other French writers—de Gourmont, Flaubert, and Baudelaire. Later, after about 1923, when his criticism began explicitly to consider ethical questions as primary, he rejected the French writers on grounds that they were over-conscious and excessively "aesthetic," and he turned enthusiastically to the Russians, whom he had admired for many years.

During his early period, Murry focussed his attention chiefly
on modern poetry, which, he felt, "like the modern consciousness
of which it is the epitome, seems to stand irresolute at a crossways
with no signpost."²⁴ He aimed to provide a signpost: his work,
from his earliest article, is characterized by its search for an all-
embracing critical theory. His first two articles in *Rhythm* con-
front, as Malcolm Bradbury notes, two of the period's most im-
portant aesthetic theorists, Bergson and Croce.²⁵ *Rhythm* itself
was plainly intended to be a doctrinaire publication, concerned
not only to publish particular works but also to impose upon its
time a theory of art. Murry's first two articles are remarkable
for their lack of reference to specific works. His need to gen-
eralize was so strong that there is a sense in which it is true to
say that he approached every artist as though approaching a
critic, and every work for an implied critical theory. For Murry,
a "revival of criticism" seemed "the only way of salvation" for
literature,²⁶ and the construction of literary principles for mod-
ern poetry seemed a necessary and creative act: "A presentiment
that our poetic values are chaotic is widespread; we are uncom-
fortable with it, and there is, we believe, a genuine desire that
a standard should be once more created and applied."²⁷ Murry's
need to account theoretically for the difference between a gro-
cer's bill and a song by Sappho²⁸ partly explains his swift passage,
in his early years, from one theory to another. He needed a
theory which would provide criteria for criticism rather than
rationalization for practice: in this he was, as Eliot wrote, "first
and foremost" a critic.²⁹

Murry's sudden shifts in critical theory were animated by his
single-minded attention to the problem of the conflict between
"intellection" and "sensation" as means of poetic knowledge, and
to an attempt to avoid the "two parallel dangers" that it pre-
sents.³⁰ The problem, central to Pater, Symons, and the Imagists,
is firmly associated with the late symbolist renaissance which is
linked with Bergson, and it underlies Eliot's and Murry's debate
over romanticism and classicism. It was always compelling for
Murry, whose criticism wholeheartedly espoused now one side
and now the other. For him, the problem dissolved into a series
of analogous conflicts: in his very early work he saw it as the
opposition of "reason" and "mysticism," later as that of "reason"
and "emotion," of an "aesthetic" and "moral" view of art, and
of "realism" and "romanticism."³¹ His criticism can be seen as

the long development of the position represented by his article "Towards a Synthesis."[32] Although he rejected Bergson's theories long before he engaged Eliot in the dispute over "intuition," the French philosopher colored his whole literary career, not only by suggesting that the solution to the problem lay in positing a synthetic faculty over and above the opposing two, but also in providing the poles between which Murry's criticism moved. It was the desire to resolve the series of conflicts that drew Murry to Baudelaire and Stendhal: they seemed to him to offer a means to "triangulate" modern literature from a point on the boundary between these two sets of opposing values.[33] The period of their strongest influence, from about 1918 to about 1923, was Murry's best period, yet it represents no more than a tenuous phase in his development. *The Problem of Style* (1922) gave indications that Murry had definitively chosen his position, and by 1927 he proclaimed himself to be "on the side of intuition," a genuine antithesis to Eliot's option for the side of "intelligence."[34]

Murry's appropriation of Bergson's theories was enthusiastic and naive. He went to Paris to hear Bergson and while he did not in the event attend the lectures, he read *L'Evolution Créatrice* and wrote his essay "Art and Philosophy" in his praise. The essay is, as Murry's biographer writes, "immature . . . diffuse, hortatory, seeking to make up by emphasis for all that it lacks in definition,"[35] but it shows Murry associating with Bergson themes familiar in Hulme: that language is conventional and in need of reform; that truth in art consists in the direct rendering of sensation; that poetry is the most intense form of concentration; that the poet must attend to what is "essential." For Murry, Bergson's theories represented a release from the rigid philosophies which "are but barren jugglings with worthless counters"; "intuition" offered liberation from "the crude opposition of subject and object." In an excess of admiration he wrote that Bergson was "the final word in aesthetic." According to Murry, intuition ratifies the intellect: it can be seen as "heightened reason"— (Pater and Arnold echo here)—and so can allow the dubious proposition that "Philosophy is the greatest art because art is the greatest philosophy." Murry's Bergsonian notion of a new, synthetic faculty predicts his later idea of "synthesis." Here, it establishes its own doubleness: the "ordinary" occupies a different plane from the "essential," and the poet's vision is a familiar "moment's lifting of the veil, a chord caught and remembered

from the vast world music, less or more, yet always another bond
between us and the great divinity immanent in the world."[36]
Bergson, who seemed revolutionary enough to be "the final
word," was, of course, as Guy Michaud writes, in the mainstream
of existing symbolist thought. His synthesis, as Murry would
discover later, was unreliable:

> Bergson invitait l'homme à regarder en soi, à découvrir les
> données immédiates de la conscience, et, reprenant en l'ex-
> plicant le processus baudelairien, demandait à cette con-
> science "de s'isoler du monde extérieur," et, par un vigou-
> reux effort d'abstraction, de redevenir elle-même.[37]

For the moment, however, Murry saw the doctrine of intuition
not as an invitation to isolation from the external world, but as
a means of recognizing the object.

It is curious that *Rhythm*'s symbolist orientation is not acknowl-
edged. John Gross asserts that the magazine's modernism was
"a vague aspiration rather than a distinct doctrine," and Malcolm
Bradbury, while arguing that its insistence on the unity of the
arts contributed importantly to "the linked movements of mod-
ernism in England," regards its direction as "vague."[38] Yet the
dominance of a symbolist outlook in *Rhythm* is evident from its
earliest number, and no magazine in England at the time of its
launching was more doctrinaire. Murry had, after all, spent his
first year in Oxford supporting Michael Sadler's and Frederick
Goodyear's efforts to "win Oxford for the Symbolists,"[39] and the
"Aims and Ideals" of *Rhythm*'s first number announce its sym-
bolist goal of providing art "which shall have its roots below the
surface, and be the rhythmical echo of the life with which it is
in touch." While Murry put forward Bergson's views, Michael
Sadler, who edited the paper with Murry until Katherine Mans-
field replaced him in 1912, discussed the relevance to Fauvism
of the "psychological problem of the possibility of hearing colour,
seeing sound, touching rhythms, and so forth." Sadler saw Mal-
larmé's poetry as analogous to Kandinsky's painting and argued
that both arts, side by side, can "strive . . . for the new ideal. For
the anti-naturalism of the two methods is the same."[40] Murry

---

Bergson . . . Bergson invited man to look inside himself, to discover the im-
mediate data of consciousness, and, taking up again and explaining the baude-
lairean process, asked this consciousness "to isolate itself from the exterior world,"
and, by a vigorous effort of abstraction, to become itself again.

and Mansfield defined "rhythm" itself as the demand that "the artist shall have seen the ultimate through the externals . . . [as] an inevitable and infallible directness of vision."⁴¹ *Rhythm* was inextricably, ostentatiously linked with France: while Fergusson, who edited the art side of the magazine from Paris, sent works by Picasso, George Banks, Derain, Henri Maugin, and others, Murry included a French-language contribution in almost every number. From its second year of publication *Rhythm* included a regular "Lettre de France," written alternately by Francis Carco and Tristan Derème, both confirmed Bergsonians and determined modernists. Derème wrote that

> il apparait nettement que la situation poétique est actuellement dominée par les représentants de ce lyrisme qui a ses sources dans les livres de Charles Baudelaire, de Paul Verlaine, de Stéphane Mallarmé et de Tristan Corbière. Il n'est pas un poème de valeur à notre époque qui ne se ressente de l'atmosphère qu'ont crée Rimbaud, Laforgue, Samain, Moréas, Rodenbach, Guérin parmi les morts et, parmi les vivants, MM. Francis Jammes, Paul Fort, Henri de Régnier, Emile Verhaeren, Stuart Merrill, Vielé-Griffin, Gustave Kahn et le Maurice Maeterlinck des *Serres Chaudes*.⁴²

The list could have been Flint's, and the paternity of Baudelaire is not in doubt: only, it should be noted, it is "lyricism" he is said to have fathered, and music, rather than poetic revolution.

Murry, however, saw the doctrine he brought from Paris as entirely revolutionary: "To say that art is revolutionary is to say that it is art." For Murry, modernism meant opposition to what had gone before, and, in particular, it meant scorn for the generation of the 'nineties. *Rhythm* declared one of its chief goals to be replacement of a "narrow aestheticism, cramping and choking itself," by an art that "strikes deeper, that touches a profounder reality."⁴³ And yet the degree to which Murry's modern symbolism was shaded by that aestheticism is evident both in his

il apparait . . . it seems clear that the poetic situation is at the moment dominated by representatives of the lyricism that has its sources in the books of Charles Baudelaire, Paul Verlaine, Stéphane Mallarmé and Tristan Corbière. There is not a single poem of value in our time which does not manifest the atmosphere created by Rimbaud, Laforgue, Samain, Moréas, Rodenbach, Guerin, among the dead, and, among the living, Francis Jammes, Paul Fort, Henri de Régnier, Emile Verhaeren, Stuart Merrill, Vielé-Griffin, Gustave Kahn and the Maurice Maeterlinck of the *Serres Chaudes*.

work and in his letters to Landon. He wrote that he had "come
to see and see clearly how living and quivering a thing is Art"
and that "L'Art pour L'Art has a different but a much more real
meaning now to my soul."⁴⁴ The notion of "rhythm," which came
to mean "the distinctive element in all the arts," can be seen as
an up-dated substitute for "beauty" in this revolutionary rhet-
oric, and *Rhythm*'s insistence on the "exclusive freemasonry of
artists . . . against the bourgeois" does not distinguish the journal
from the products of the 'nineties. At the beginning of his career,
Murry frequented Dan Ryder's bookshop in search of "Life,"⁴⁵
and he is remembered by Anne Estelle Rice as affecting a good
measure of dandyism:

> "The Tigers" was a name John Middleton Murry and Kath-
> erine Mansfield gave themselves, but I am not sure of its
> origin. It had some connection with flouting the conventions
> and "The Tigers" used to go down the Strand in cowboy
> shirts and a swaggering gait *pour épater les bourgeois.*⁴⁶

Murry's essay "Art and Philosophy" took its tone from the move-
ment it opposed: the letter of his doctrine came from Bergson,
its spirit from the *fin-de-siècle*. "Art," Murry writes, "is beyond
creeds, for it is the creed itself. It comes to birth in irreligion
and is nurtured in amorality."⁴⁷ The scandalous, tenuous par-
adoxes, and the subversive claim, qualify Murry's modernity.

The contents of *Rhythm*, particularly of its early numbers, re-
flect a double disposition which characterizes the young "mod-
ernists" and which Murry shares. It was "the first literary peri-
odical to come directly out of that new mood of artistic euphoria
and commitment to artistic change that immediately preceded
the First World War," yet Murry conceived it as " 'The Yellow
Book' of the modern movement."⁴⁸ It was "emphatically, ag-
gressively cosmopolitan, aiming directly at those who had been
excited, the winter before, by the first Post-Impressionist exhi-
bition at the Grafton Gallery," and Murry calculated its success
from the fact that "most of the prominent writers of the younger
generation had gathered round it";⁴⁹ yet the poetry and prose
it printed was bred by the 'nineties. Arthur Crossthwaite's fre-
quent contributions, for example, were distilled from the *fin-de-
siècle*. His verse concentrates on the moment at which "the quiv-
ering senses reel / And sink in a passionless dream" and his prose
poems cull their themes from a tired stock:

A mortal sickness creeps over the heart. Ennui hangs heavy, narcotic, as opium-fumes in the air. To fight against it, to strike blindly is but to sink back into the grim eddy, the foul colour of decay—a colour that deadens, an ennui that strangles and kills.[50]

The magazine includes a generous share of attenuated satanism—Crossthwaite's "Three Eclogues," Francis Coutts's "The Guardian Demon," John Harvey's "In the Cool of the Evening." Other poems—W. A. Orton's "Nocturne," Margaret Sackville's "Le Voyage en Cythère—the Return," and some of Murry's own (his "Life," for instance)—aim, as at least one of those titles advertises, at a familiar "baudelairism."[51] For a magazine devoted to the new optimism, *Rhythm* exhibits an uncommon amount of torment. William Davies compounds an extraordinary mixture of the 'nineties themes and the new Georgian revival of nature—

> Now how could I, with gold to spare,
> Who know the harlot's arms, and wine,
> Sit in this green field all alone,
> If Nature was not truly mine.[52]

Holbrook Jackson's "Plea for Revolt in Attitude" claims liberty for the new art in the old tone: "Art must not preach, it must not teach, it must express, it must fulfill its own conditions of technique, it must, in short, be art, separate, ornamental, and complete in itself."[53] Out of the midst of this monotony of imitation Laurence Binyon proclaimed: "Slowly we have emerged from the nineteenth century. We are breathing a different air. We are no longer *fin-de-siècle*. We are being changed, and the world with us."[54]

Both doctrinaire symbolism and the old aestheticism left permanent marks on Murry's mind: the former advanced him on the path to his romantic synthesis and the latter foreshadowed his more complex view of the moral superiority of the great artist. But he began to draw away from symbolism shortly after publishing his essay on Bergson. The motive of his disenchantment is evident as early as the second number of *Rhythm*. Here he found Croce's aesthetic inadequate because of its "maze of subjectivity" and its failure to allow for "a definitely intellectual process" in art. Already he opposed the idea, which he found in Croce, of the intellectual faculty as "generically different"

from intuition.[55] By December 1911 he no longer considered
Bergson's "intuition" to be a solution to what he had earlier called
"the crude opposition of subject and object." In an article on
Hegel he wrote that

> this refusal to accept the conception of the universal as iden-
> tity in difference, as concrete, . . . brings us to the position
> of scepticism or mysticism in which we cannot rest. Bergson,
> like Kant, has made a false abstraction. Thought is not,
> unless violently isolated, essentially static or mathematical.

Murry's position has been drastically altered: what we must have,
he thinks, is "that conception of reason itself as a living and
developing form of mental activity to which we must always
return from the barren wastes of scepticism and the meaningless
ecstasy of mysticism."[56] By May 1913 he thought Bergson had
failed totally:

> "Instinct" or "Intuition" is no panacea for the realities of
> life. The intellect and the desires of the intellect are as potent
> and as valuable to their possessor as instinct and the blind
> impulses of instinct. It has not been given to M. Bergson in
> the twentieth century to solve the difficulties and quiet the
> groanings of St. Paul.[57]

As Murry rejected Bergson he turned away from symbolism
in poetry. In June 1913 he announced, as well as Bergson's
failure, that "young French writers of to-day have completely
broken with Symbolism" and that the movement had been de-
stroyed by its assumptions: "It is true," he wrote, "that any ev-
olution from the artistic position taken up by Mallarmé was of
itself doomed to sterility." Symbolism, which he later linked with
the "Yellow Book" and the art-for-art's-sake movement, had led
to an "anarchy and cosmopolitanism" which could be remedied
only by a "classical revival."[58] The remark is not so surprising as
over-simplification of Murry's debate with Eliot would make it
seem: his admiration in June 1913 for the *Action Française* is not
typical of him, but his concern to balance the virtues of "ro-
manticism" and "classicism" would characterize his criticism from
this time until *The Problem of Style*. Only later did he make *The
Adelphi* the ground of romanticism's last stand: in 1920 he wrote
that he was "almost impelled to declare" that Irving Babbitt's
Rousseau and Romanticism was "the only book of criticism worthy

the name which has appeared in English in the twentieth century."[59]

Murry's reaction against a loosely defined tradition of symbolism prompted him to adjust his aesthetic judgments. Verlaine seemed to him now "an almost perfect specimen of the minor poet" whose faults issued from his lack of respect for the rational faculty:

> He is, in the main, a mere vehicle for emotions. They pass through him, he knows not why or whence; they leave him, and they leave nothing behind them, not so much as a particle made immune or resistant. . . . The great poet grows from strength to strength. Verlaine did not. All that finally remained of his emotions was a vague memory, sufficient only to blunt their keen edge when they came to him again. Instead of having conviction added to them, their freshness was taken away.[60]

During this second phase in his criticism, Murry's consistent emphasis fell onto discipline and mental toughness. In his second article on Hegel, written nine years after the first, he reiterated the point with which he had despatched Bergson: "Hegel's emphasis on the essential rationality of art is as necessary in 1920 as it was in 1820, and his diagnosis of the romantic disease of originality has more than a little aptness to some poetic manifestations of the present day."[61]

Murry's abandonment of his early symbolist doctrine, complete by 1913, coincided with two other important events. In that year he underwent his "very complete surrender" to Stendhal, and when he went to Paris he was made a reviewer of French books for the *Times Literary Supplement*. Both events were fruitful: just when his criticism was maintaining that an adequate aesthetic must take account of the rational, Murry worked on the great pre-symbolist writers. Between 1913 and 1922 he wrote on Stendhal, Flaubert, Baudelaire, Amiel. His own criticism was nourished by them: in that, Murry was claiming the very ground on which Pater had constructed *The Renaissance*.

Murry wrote five articles on Baudelaire.[62] The first, "The Influence of Baudelaire," appeared in the *Literary Supplement* to the fourteenth number of *Rhythm*, in March 1913. The second, "Baudelaire," appeared in the *Athenaeum* (of which Murry was then editor) in two parts, on 22 and 29 October 1920. The third, a revised and expanded version of the second, appeared as "Baudelaire and Decadence" in the *Times Literary Supplement* for 7 April 1921. This essay, reprinted in both *Countries of the Mind* (1922) and *John Clare and Other Studies* (1950), was among the most important modern English essays on Baudelaire. Murry's last two articles were short pieces in the *Times Literary Supplement*, on "Baudelaire's Letters," a review of Symons's translation of the poet's letters to his mother, and on "Baudelaire as Hero," a review of Lewis Paget Shanks's book on the poet. The first three of Murry's articles comprise a series that perfectly exemplifies the stages in the French poet's modernization in England. Murry began with an assault on the notion that Baudelaire was the exclusive property in England of the aesthetes; he went on to a point-by-point refutation of a description of Baudelaire as decadent in the usual sense; and he concluded that in both achievement and character Baudelaire ought to be associated with a group of modern moralists which includes Dostoevsky, Nietzsche, and Stendhal. The articles are transition pieces, heralding the new view of the poet but preoccupied by the old, aiming to detach him from old contexts and to see him in his splendid isolation as the author of *Les Fleurs du Mal*, but taking as their chief tactic a discussion of the very "decadence" they seek to dispose of. They chart both the revision of Baudelaire's reputation in England and the confident emergence of a new generation in criticism. Murry sifts his inheritance, deciding what to carry forward and what to leave behind. Baudelaire, he concludes, is decidedly current.

In the first of these articles, Murry claims the right to revalue the works of the past according to the standards of the present, and he finds the past all wrong. Baudelaire barely resembles the poets with whom he has most frequently been compared, Murry writes; the elements of sadism and eroticism in his work have received far too much emphasis; both of the rough, received views of him—the one that finds him titillatingly subversive because of his "decadence" and the one that finds him trivial and insincere because of his "decadence"—must be rejected. Baudelaire, Murry writes in *Rhythm*, sketching an argument that he would elaborate eight years later in his own *Athenaeum* and in Bruce Richmond's *Times Literary Supplement*, wrote poems that were unaffected products of his personal moral struggle, "the concrete expression of the Baudelairian spirit."

Murry's first, 1913 article was prompted by a remarkable (and widely reviewed) publication of the same year, G. Turquet-Milnes's book, *The Influence of Baudelaire in France and England*, which details the progress in literature, painting, and music of the "Baudelaire Spirit." It sees Baudelaire as one of the originators and the best example of an attitude in art which it analyzes as follows:

1. The faculty of self-analysis and self-torment in love.
2. Pursuit of lust mingling with it a kind of sacrilegious pleasure. Pursuit of sensation at any cost, with its inevitable consequences: perversity and madness on the one hand, mysticism on the other;—creation of a new language.
3. Moral anarchy, overwhelming pessimism, and terrible solitude of the soul.[63]

The antecedents of that description are immediately apparent: Gautier's preface to the *Fleurs du Mal* of 1868 is one, Symons's "Decadent Movement in Literature" another. *The Influence of Baudelaire in France and England* turns into official history precisely the view of Baudelaire that Murry was keen to dispose of. In Turquet-Milnes's book, one attitude is perfected; in Murry's article, a new one begins to gather shape.

Murry rejects the idea of the "Baudelaire Spirit" on two grounds. One is that it fails to describe Baudelaire; the other is that it fails to describe literary history. Turquet-Milnes, he says, shares a version of one of Matthew Arnold's "strangest critical delusions," the idea of "the Zeitgeist as a person," and so commits the mistake that

. . . personifies the mental attitude of a generation in a particular person, and, forgetting that the particular person owes his symbolic significance to the existence of a number of disparate individuals, tends to treat them as his dependents. . . . A particular artist may well be the most eminent and most gifted of a number of artists who possess a certain community of mental attitude. It may be, for instance, critically convenient even to call a certain period of English literature the Shakespearean age; but it must never be forgotten that such terms are nothing more than a kind of critical shorthand. In the end we must consider the individ-

uality as more significant than the community; and the uni-
versal as possessing its real existence only in the particular.

Murry's article aims to undo the symbolism, to dissociate the
individual from his reputation, and then, having cut the portrait
out of its canvas, to provide a new background. This is a revision
of literary history. Once we have seen Baudelaire's "great indi-
viduality," Murry implies, we shall see that criticism that asso-
ciates him with Turquet-Milnes's "curious congerie of writers
and artists"—"Swinburne, Arthur O'Shaugnessy, Oscar Wilde,
Arthur Machen, George Moore, Richard Middleton, Alfred
Douglas and Aubrey Beardsley"—is simply in error.

In an argument intended to retrieve Baudelaire for "the
younger generation," Murry sweeps away decades of English
poetry. *His* tradition will include Baudelaire—who has certainly
had "a line of lineal descendants" in France, and whose influence
is even now apparent in "one of the most interesting of the
younger French literary movements, that of the 'Fantaisistes' "—
but it will not include Swinburne or Wilde or any members of
that brotherhood. English aestheticism and the poetry of the
'nineties, he says, "derive from sources very different from
Baudelaire. The true line of descent is English and insular, from
Ruskin through Walter Pater":

> We should never have heard so much of the so-called French
> influence upon our literature of the nineties if Oscar Wilde
> had not been able to take advantage of the abysmal igno-
> rance of French literature then prevailing. Wilde treated
> the French as a professional secret, a privately printed book
> of pornography. . . . The mere idea of Wilde understanding
> Baudelaire, or Verlaine, or Laforgue or Mallarmé is some-
> thing ludicrous.

In response to Turquet-Milnes's claim that Swinburne can be
understood only in the light of the "Baudelaire Spirit" (and in
anticipation of Eliot's comparison of Baudelaire and Symons),
Murry argues that there is a "world of difference" between
Baudelaire and his English imitators:

> We believe,—and this is what the difference really amounts
> to—when Baudelaire writes of some strange emotion, that
> he really experienced it, and we feel it again. . . . But Swin-
> burne's "Roses and raptures of vice"—. . . . We never believe

Swinburne's sensations. We always believe Baudelaire. Baudelaire's matter and manner always fit. Swinburne's never. And if this is true of Swinburne, it is a thousand times more true of Wilde.

Murry subscribes to Laforgue's remark that in Baudelaire "there is never a wrong fold in the impressions with which he clothes himself. He is always courteous with ugliness. He behaves well," and he draws the obvious and dismissing contrast: "The English Baudelairians," he says, "never behave." This is the voice of the "organ of modernism" announcing a break in the continuity of the English tradition. (The terms of the announcement, however, and its assumption of the aesthetic primacy of form, constitute the triumph of the very writers Murry dismisses. It was the "unbelievable" Swinburne who had written of form as the one adorable thing in the world, and the "insular" Pater who had derived his formal aesthetic from Baudelaire.)

Murry returned to Baudelaire during his best and busiest period as a literary critic, with his weighty two-part *Athenaeum* article of 22 and 29 October 1920, which was a review,[64] and its revised, even longer, version as the leading article in the *Times Literary Supplement* of 7 April 1921. Four years before that he had published his first major critical work, *Dostoevsky*; in the same year he published two collections of essays, *The Evolution of an Intellectual* and *Aspects of Literature*; and within a year he had administered his consequential, cutting attack on the Georgians[65] and delivered his Oxford Lectures on *The Problem of Style*. Now when Murry wrote on Baudelaire he spoke not as a romantic undergraduate attempting to win Oxford for the symbolists by burning the books of the past, but as a well-respected critic and editor.

In these articles, Murry puts the idea of decadence under the knife. The word, he says, has been "more prolific of literary misunderstandings in the last half century" than perhaps any other. In the general mind, "to be decadent is to be impure, immoral, or, in the now more frequent and really more damaging phrase, to be 'unhealthy.' " ("Healthy we cannot call it, and healthy it does not wish to be considered," Symons had said of the decadent movement.) Writers of the nineteenth century who were branded "decadent," Murry writes, suffered from the label, and Baudelaire, "who was the first and greatest of the line, suffered most and deserved it least." Murry rejects absolutely the popular understanding of the word, which is useful to him only when it refers to periods of social or literary transition or to works produced in such periods. "It may be true," he says, "though it remains to be proved, that the literatures of all periods of decadence have certain elements in common; it is certainly untrue that the literature of such a period is necessarily inferior as literature." Baudelaire, Murry writes, "is the poet of an historical decadence; he is not in any useful sense of the word a decadent poet."

Murry's description of Baudelaire is a systematic refutation of what he took to be the received view. Sex and genetics provide his vocabulary of praise: Baudelaire, we are told, was "strong, masculine, deliberate, classical; not a puny successor of great men, but the heroic founder of a line." Practically nothing in his work issues from weakness: its occasional admitted perversity is "the least important, the least relevant, and, to the unbiased reader, the least noticeable of its qualities"; its driving impulse was not a "predilection" but a "conviction"; he is "not a poet of weak nerves, but of strong convictions." Decadence is indeed a central consideration in his work, but not because he was one of its tainted products. He was, by contrast, its *critic*:

> Baudelaire was convinced that the age in which he lived was a decadence, and we who know it not only by his own passionate protest against it, but by Balzac's romantic anatomy of its corruption, must acquiesce in his conviction. . . . It was the age of rampant industrialism and violent and abortive revolution; of the hideous and uncontrolled eruption of the great cities; of the squalor of a victorious materialism. Against this tyranny Baudelaire conceived it his duty to protest, not merely by the poetic utterance of cries of revolt but by the actual conduct of his life.

Murry's profoundly moral Baudelaire (who heralds Eliot's) is "the deliberate and determined poet of an attitude to life to which we cannot refuse the epithet heroic."

Baudelaire's heroism, as Murry sees it, consists in his superb integrity, in his ability to hold together both sides of the antitheses that plague Murry's own thought, and in his refusal to isolate his art. "As an artist," Murry writes, "Baudelaire works from a single centre; his attitude to life and his attitude to art lend each other aid and confirmation." The contrast between this view and, say, Symons's or Aldington's—in which the implacable baudelairean beauty is chillily remote from life—is marked, and Murry's view of Baudelaire links him not with Swinburne and the others but with Mérimée, Stendhal, Nietzsche, and Dostoevsky, "intellectual romantics" whose "disciplined and contemptuous" romanticism is characteristically modern. The romanticism Murry ascribes to these writers has no important ties to the French Romantic Movement, but is "rather a kind of sublimated realism, . . . romantic in its aspiration away from the *bourgeois* society which it loathed, realistic in its determination to accept the facts as they were." Baudelaire embodies this attitude of revolt in his dandy, whom Murry sees as "an ideal of human beauty" that enabled Baudelaire to achieve his "chief distinction," his "successful and undeviating effort to translate his ethical attitude towards life into a purely poetical gesture."

Baudelaire's *revised* dandy, the dandy as Murry describes him, is barely recognizable as the figure who inspired Wilde, Beardsley, and Beerbohm on nature and cosmetics, and who fuelled the long argument that art was splendidly separate from the sordid practicalities of ethics. This dandy has only an antithetical relation to the figure Yeats cast as the type of the sensuous man or to the author of the assertion that "No artist has ethical sympathies."[66] He has, on the contrary, an unusually strong sense of the moral implications of his actions; he is an intellectual rather than a sensualist, so that mere hedonism would be for him an abject defeat; and his "essential trait" is an asceticism that Murry sees as "almost monastic." Being above all self-conscious, he judges his own actions neither by a received idea of virtue nor by a superficial admiration of novelty, but by the evidence they give of the strength of his will. Nothing in Baudelaire, Murry writes, corresponds to "the fantastic naughtiness of the legend." The dandy is a kind of existential prop, a role that allowed Baudelaire to express a single attitude in both his life and his art. It was his means of finding "an equivalent in pure poetry to his detestation of the world and his defiance of the powers that ordained it." The *Intimate Journals* make clear the poet's single center: "And how unexpected to those who persist, like Mr. Arthur Symons in his recent study, in seeing in Baudelaire only a Swinburnian singer of 'strange sins,' will this be."

Murry sees the mental and moral qualities of the dandy reproduced as the hard, disciplined style of the poetry. Baudelaire could have been a confessional poet, he writes, "pouring out his wounded soul in lyrical *cris de coeur*." Instead, he chose to master the alexandrine as no other French poet has done. The texture of his verse is "adamantine," "metallic"; the work is marked by its "astringency, terseness, hardness, impenetrability." For Baudelaire, Murry writes, poetry is "a process of definition, a making concrete and particular of vague emotions and perceptions, an activity of concentration." Indeed, it was desire for concreteness that produced one of the most characteristic traits of his work, its "crystallisation of the image" or "exacerbation of the image," which conveys a special, heightened effect.

This Baudelaire is not recognizable as the smoky father of the symbolists: he might have been created by Pound as a model for the Imagists or described by Eliot as the "greatest exemplar in *modern* poetry in any language"; and he has some of his major characteristics in common with the later Baudelaire of Walter Benjamin. Murry precedes Eliot in naming Baudelaire as a poet for "our time," and he describes some of the qualities for which Eliot would commend Baudelaire to the modern poets. His idea of a crystallized or exacerbated image, for instance, which has important consequences in *The Problem of Style*, is Eliot's later imagery of "the *first intensity*."[67] Murry's essays adjust the critical myth: they bring the discussion of decadence full circle so that now, once again, when Baudelaire is said to be a "decadent" poet, then "decadence" is made to mean revolt, heroism, modernism. "Baudelaire," Murry writes, "was a great poet of a decadence. In other words, he was a great modern poet; for the decadence which shaped him by compelling him to revolt against it was the 'civilisation of industrial progress' which has endured from his day to our own."

But if Murry's essays on Baudelaire constitute an unusually concise record of a present reshaping its past, they also reveal a present defining itself in relation to the past it recreates. They have a special place in his work. The dandy, as a dramatized representation of the integrity of life and art, is a hero Murry needed, though he could not keep him for long, and the essays show Murry working out some of the central positions of the manifesto of his critical maturity, *The Problem of Style* (1922). That work is Murry's most important, a statement of the ripened views of the earlier "spokesman for the younger generation," his last formulation of the delicate "synthesis" of aesthetic and moral concerns, which, very shortly afterward, he would abandon. Before turning to it, however, I want to show how Murry had much earlier learned to shape his utterances on behalf of the young with material borrowed from Baudelaire's critical writings.

Murry was, very briefly and very early in his career, art critic for *The Westminster Gazette*. Later (between 1919 and 1921) he contributed a group of articles on art to the *Nation* and the *Athenaeum*. His art criticism is all fashionably French: English painters, Murry said, were crippled by "amateurishness," lacking a sense, natural to the French, of the *métier*. He praised Roger Fry for being "the most active mediator between French painting and our own,"[68] Sickert for having "bathed pretty deep in the undefiled well of French painting of the 'eighties." He had no doubt that "The modern painter *must* learn from France," and it is clear from what he wrote that he thought that the modern critic of painting must do that, too.[69] To turn to French art, of course, was to turn almost automatically to the criticism of Baudelaire, by then recognized, as Camille Mauclair wrote, as "notre plus grand critique d'art français, esthéticien visionnaire autant que sagace," a writer who had "tout prévu de notre temps."[70]

Murry's article on Augustus John shows how specific was his debt.[71] John's vices, as Murry names them, are precisely those of Baudelaire's villains—of Horace Vernet, Charlet, or Troyon. Murry casts himself as the critic of a decadent age, attacking the taste of his time, the commercialism of contemporary art, fashionable "modernity," and the destructive collusion which exists between a fashionable public and a fashionable painter. The attack is rich in borrowed scorn: like Vernet, who fulfills a "mission officielle" and who is "cet artiste éminément national," John is "the painter by warrant" of his time, "typical of the age"; like Vernet, who is a sort of "vaudevilliste," John is the creator of a "cabaret" (II, 469-70). Vernet is satirized as a man "qui habit un pays artificiel dont les acteurs et les coulisses sont fait du même carton; [et qui] règne en maître dans son royaume de parade et de divertissements" (II, 472), and John as the creator of newsprint cut-outs:

notre plus . . . our greatest French art critic, an esthetician as visionary as he was wise . . . had foreseen everything about our time.

mission . . . official mission . . . eminently national artist . . . he inhabits an artificial country, where the actors and the scenery are all made of cardboard, but he reigns supreme in his kingdom of parade and entertainment (C, 88, 86, 90).

Instead of a conference room, I entered a cabaret. Straight from the novels of Mrs. Elinor Glyn, straight from the cover of the sensational story magazine, they came. *L'Implacable Sizka* was there, and *Fumeuse d'Opium*. There was absinthe and maiden-blush and jazz. There was the frilly lady coming out of the egg-shell, *les Soeurs Glad-Eye*, a podgy impresario, a few bored soldiers . . . a Rajah, Mr. Bernard Shaw . . . four fancy-dress Arabs. . . .

Baudelaire detests Vernet for his facile realism, which is the antithesis of imaginative art, the betrayal of vision by mere technique: he detests him because "il est né *coiffé*, et que l'art est pour lui chose claire et facile," because he substitutes "le *chic* au dessin, le charivari à la couleur et les épisodes à l'unité" (II, 470). The *chic*, Baudelaire says, is "absence de modèle et de nature . . . l'abus de la mémoire" (II, 468). That is the core of Murry's objection to John, who, he says, perverts his imagination with superficial observations:

This is a shop-window age, when it is taken for granted that everything a man has is written on his front door, if it has not been already shouted through his own private megaphone. Why should Mr. John look inside or listen longer? He, too, has lost the habit. His sitters push their individual idiosyncrasies under his eye, and he hastens to combine his with theirs and dash the mixture onto the canvas.

John has entered into a debasing agreement with his public, he has been "submerged, overwhelmed and saturated" by his time, and both the artist and his public share the shame: "Every little helps in the race. The ladies prove their modernity by getting Mr. John to paint them; and he proves his by the way he paints them. No wonder everybody is satisfied." Both John's offensiveness and the tone of Murry's offendedness echo Baudelaire on Charlet: "C'est un homme très artificiel qui s'est mis à imiter les idées du temps. Il a décalqué l'opinion, il a découpé son intelligence sur la mode. Le public était vraiment son *patron*" (II, 548).

il est . . . for being born with a *caul* and because art for him is as clear as glass . . . *chic* for drawing, a medley for colour, and episodes for unity . . . painting without reference to a model or to nature . . . the abuse of memory (C, 88, 86).

C'est . . . He is a very artificial man, who had the idea of imitating the popular ideas of the day. He took a carbon copy of public opinion. He modelled himself on fashion. The public, really, was his dressmaker's pattern (C, 214).

That article lashes the age, and it takes its satiric attitude from Baudelaire; and it also shows how firmly Murry had taken hold of a view of the imagination and of its relation to technique that he had encountered in Baudelaire. In "The War Pictures at the Royal Academy,"[72] he deals with basic Baudelairean issues, taking up almost entirely a distinction, which appears in the *Salon* of 1846, of three kinds of drawing, "exacts ou bêtes, physionomiques et imaginés." Baudelaire distinguishes the three on grounds of their relation to their subject:

> Le premier est négatif, incorrect à force de réalité, naturel, mais saugrenu; le second est un dessin naturaliste, mais idéalisé, dessin d'un génie qui sait choisir, arranger, corriger, deviner, gourmander la nature; enfin le troisième, qui est le plus noble et le plus étrange, peut négliger la nature; il en représente une autre, analogue à l'esprit et au tempérament de l'auteur. (II, 434)

That very distinction appears in Murry's article, supplying him with the major grounds for his judgments. He divides the painters in the exhibition into three kinds—those who "were concerned to make a faithful record of the material event," those "who sought to create art out of the material event," and those "who have wrestled with the expression of the event in the mind." The work of the first kind of painter may be accurate, Murry says, but untrue: good professional draughtsmen are useful, but "they never saw any dead men. As a truthful record of war, Mr. Sassoon's poems are worth the whole five hundred of them." The work of the second sort of painter is second-order art, in which the untransformed material remains dominant. But the work of the third kind of painter is the product of "the haunting imaginative vision" and a "dominant motive," and, while it may sometimes fail in technique (as, in Murry's view, some of Nash's work does), it is superior to the other two kinds of painting because it transforms its material to feed an over-riding and complete personal vision.

exactes . . . the exact or stupid style, the physiognomical and the imaginative. The first is negative and inaccurate, by its slavish copying, natural but absurd; the second is a naturalist style, but idealized, the style of a genius who knows how to select, organize his subject, how to correct, divine, scold nature; and lastly the third style, which is the noblest and the strangest, can afford to neglect nature; it depicts another nature, which reflects the mind and the temperament of the artist (C, 67-68).

That hierarchical distinction of kinds of art on grounds of the relation of the artist to his subject is basic to Murry's scheme of judgment, and it entails another consideration to which he returns as a central preoccupation in his criticism of painting and sculpture, that of the relation of technique to vision. Success in technique alone, Murry writes, is insignificant—"A talent is only an instrument"—and artists like John, a "skillful painter" who is too lazy to attempt to impose his vision on reality, command no respect from this young critic, for whom mere "skill" was too much like mere (old-fashioned) "aesthetics." All of the artists of whom Murry approves make technical mastery subservient to imaginative strength. Eric Gill was "a stone-carver of unusual probity, not unusual imaginative power," he wrote, but Gaudier-Brzeska made a flawless technique the servant of his vision, and Epstein was the "real thing" because of the "intense and definite impression" his work makes.[73] The imaginative artist Murry admires is possessed of strong individuality on the one hand and of speedy execution on the other. Sickert, whom he thought the best contemporary English painter, commanded both qualities: the speed of his execution was the consequence of his fidelity to his vision. And Gaudier was so absorbed in his imagined reality that his very works were "more truly the chips which flew from his chisel as he trued the foundation out of the living rock for the temple to be, than things with a complete and final purpose of their own."

Murry found every one of those critical concerns, as well as the scourging tone of some of his pieces, in Baudelaire's critical writing. Baudelaire saw technical mastery as essential—"Il n'y a pas de hasard dans l'art, non plus qu'en mécanique" (II, 432)—but for him the essential creative act lay elsewhere. Although he admired the craftsmanship and color of Robert Fleury, for instance, he saw him as a painter of second order because of his lack of "génie involontaire" (II, 363), and he condemned Ingres for an over-attention to technique. For Baudelaire, the great painter was a "mélange admirable de science,—c'est-à-dire, un peintre complet,—et de naïveté, c'est-à-dire un homme complet"

Il n'y a . . . There is no such thing as chance in art any more than in mechanics (C, 65).
génie . . . involuntary genius.
mélange . . . an admirable mixture of knowledge—that is to say a complete painter—and naïveté—that is to say a complete man" (C, 68).

(II, 435), so that Delacroix, who was coldly determined to find means for expressing passion, was his ideal. In both Delacroix and Guys, speed was essential, but it was speed at the service of vision: "Si une exécution très nette est nécessaire, c'est pour que le langage du rêve soit très nettement traduit; qu'elle soit très rapide, c'est pour que rien ne se perde de l'impression extraordinaire qui accompagnait la conception" (II, 625). So far, Murry's aesthetic is Baudelaire's.

The borrowing goes one step further. Baudelaire sees the artist's individuality as fundamental to his conception, the dominant motive, as Murry would call it, of his technique, and it is his idea of individualities (both that of the artist and that of the subject) that determines his position on the ideal in art. A portrait is a model complicated by the artist, he writes, and the aim to be attained in art is "l'individu redressé par l'individu, reconstruit et rendu par le pinceau ou le ciseau à l'éclatante verité de son harmonie native" (II, 456). Murry's reflections on the subject take up the idea: the "lasting excellence" of some of Epstein's work, for instance, will be the result of his ability to "catch the equipoise of correspondence between the physical and the spiritual in his models at moments."[74] That is Baudelairean; but even more so is Murry's essay on Fry. Baudelaire's most famous passage on the relation of the model and the ideal appears in his *Salon* of 1846:

La circonférence, idéal de la ligne courbe, est comparable à une figure analogue composée d'une infinité de lignes

Si une . . . If a very neat execution is necessary, that is so that the language of dreams may be very clearly translated; if it should be very quick, that is to ensure that nothing is lost of the extraordinary impression that accompanied the birth of the idea (C, 304).

l'individu . . . the individual modified by the individual, rebuilt and restored by brush or chisel to the dazzling truth of its own essential harmony (C, 78).

La circonférence . . . The circumference, which is the ideal of the curve, is comparable to an analogous figure composed of an infinite number of straight lines and destined to merge with the ideal circumference, its interior angles becoming ever more obtuse.

But since no perfect circumference exists, the absolute ideal is a piece of nonsense. The exclusive taste for simplification leads the fathead sort of artist to repeated imitations of the same type. Poets, artists, and the whole human race would be most unhappy, if the ideal, that absurdity, nay impossibility, were to be discovered. What would each of us do thereafter with his poor ego, his broken line? (C, 76-77).

droites, qui doit se confondre avec elle, les angles intérieurs
s'obtusant de plus en plus.

Mais comme il n'y a pas de circonférence parfaite, l'idéal
absolu est une bêtise. . . . Les poètes, les artistes et toute la
race humaine seraient bien malheureux, si l'idéal, cette ab-
surdité, cette impossibilité, était trouvé. Qu'est-ce que cha-
cun ferait désormais de son pauvre *moi*,—de sa ligne brisée?
(II, 455)

Murry picks up this analogy and drops it into his essay on Fry:

Pure art, quintessential art, is an abstraction like the perfect
circle of the mathematician; it is a will-o'-the-wisp which men
may spend their lives pursuing, but in vain. And it is, es-
sentially and historically, a romantic abstraction. . . .[75]

The positions Murry outlines in his "amateurish" essays on
art—where the borrowed bones of his developing aesthetic are
prominent—are basic to the more sophisticated *Problem of Style*.
When they made their way from the early essays to the lectures,
Baudelaire's ideas gained—not for the first and not for the last
time, as Swinburne might have put it—a voice in an important
work of English criticism. Murry gave the lectures in Oxford at
the invitation of Sir Walter Raleigh in 1921; they were printed
in 1922; they have been reprinted widely since.

The *Problem of Style* is based on the series of oppositions that
is evident throughout Murry's criticism, and it outlines an aes-
thetic that aims at resolving them. The object of Murry's inquiry
is not style in some of its usual senses, as he makes clear at the
outset, ridding himself of the obligation to confine himself to
style as "technique of exposition" or style as "personal idiosyn-
crasy." He focuses instead on style as "the highest achievement
of literature," and he tells us what that is: it is a "complete fusion
of the personal and the universal . . . the complete realization
of a universal significance in a personal and particular expres-
sion."[76] Style in this sense is "equipoise," balance, the meeting-
point of perfectly equal antithetical forces—Murry's true syn-
thesis. A work possessing what he calls "absolute style" is not
only particular and universal, personal and impersonal, but also
realistic and romantic, a product of emotion supported by in-
tellect, the outcome of vision supported by technique. Murry's
"style" is a kind of theoretical fantasy, a name for the composite

virtues of achieved art as they were dreamed by a generation which had come to see the bodilessness of Symbolism. Murry's "absolute style" implies his own theory of "the psychology of literary creation,"[77] his outline of a theory of the imagination, but it also addresses issues that are raised by Yeats and Eliot and Pound and Sitwell and the others. When he lectured in Oxford, Murry really was a "spokesman": *The Problem of Style* is very much a voice of its time.

Murry's idea of "absolute style" owes much to Wordsworth and Coleridge: its belief that "the source of style is to be found in a strong and decisive original emotion" (*PS*, 15) in a person of "more than ordinary sensitiveness" (*PS*, 26), for instance, and its dependence on the idea that great poetry is the direct expression of a coherence in the poet's sum of experience. And though he had earlier said that the *Biographia Literaria* was sometimes confusing and prolix, Murry also thought that every one of the four points that Coleridge makes characteristic of early poetic genius deserves "to be called back to the mind again and again."[78] One of these points serves Murry's argument and he quotes it in *The Problem of Style*:

> ... images, however beautiful, however faithfully copied from nature, and as accurately represented in words, do not of themselves characterize the poet. They become proofs of original genius only so far as they are modified by a predominant passion, or by associated thoughts or images awakened by that passion. (*PS*, 40)

The passage contributes to Murry's own account of the psychology of the poet and to his remarks on metaphor. It supports his determination to show on the one hand that the creative act is not a "rational process" (*PS*, 29)—Wordsworth, he says, seems to place excessive emphasis on "the part played by thought" (*PS*, 28)—and to deny on the other that it is the product of mere random impressionism or bare emotional response. The poet's expression, he concludes, is shaped by a "coherent emotional nucleus" which is formed by the long accumulation of extraordinarily rich sense experience and a "predominantly emotional" inner life (*PS*, 26-29).

Murry's description of the "coherent emotional nucleus" of the great poet goes beyond suggestions he took from Wordsworth and Coleridge. This "nucleus," he says, should not be called the writer's "philosophy" (since that implies his merely intellectual bias), but it could be called his "attitude." It is not identical with the spontaneous emotion he feels at the moment of making the poem, nor is it merely the necessary outcome of an accumulation of his raw experience: it is "the element which determines [the poet's] mode of experience and gives unity to his work as a whole." This "attitude" is really a "large and complex emotional conviction" (*PS*, 29-30). Here again, Murry makes "conviction" function as the synthesis of the warring faculties: it is both "philosophy" and emotional response. "The thought that plays a part in literature," Murry writes, "is systematized emotion, emotion become habitual till it attains the dignity of conviction" (*PS*, 74). It is his "self-consistent" attitude that dominates the poet's creative acts: he chooses his plots, metaphors, images, to serve "in the office of a prism" (*PS*, 34), to concentrate and direct the complexity of his conviction into a single statement.

   It is already remarkable to what extent Murry's "psychology of literary creation" is carried forward from his carefully revised work on Baudelaire, the poet of heroic integrity, whose art issued, not from "weak nerves," but from "strong convictions," and whose dandy, it will be remembered, the dramatization of the poet's integrity, made possible his "successful and undeviating effort to translate his ethical attitude towards life into a purely poetic gesture." In *The Problem of Style*, Baudelaire supports Murry's remarks in point after point. (That Murry had him very much in mind from the beginning of the work appears in his opening remarks: after claiming that criticism's perpetual problem is its vague language, he launches into analysis of the word "decadence.")

   It is Baudelaire who supplies Murry with the lines (from *Fusées*) out of which he extracts his description both of the creative act and of the "highest style." These lines appear more than once in *The Problem of Style* in Murry's own translation:

> In certain states of the soul . . . the profound significance of life is revealed completely in the spectacle, however commonplace, that is before one's eyes: it becomes the symbol of this significance. (*PS*, 27-28)

Murry had been drawn to those lines before. In his *Athenaeum* article, they support his notion of the strength with which Baudelaire had maintained his "vision of life": the lines describe, he says, the act that produces the highest poetry: "This perception of the quality of life, concentrated and manifested in a single incident, is the method and the gift of the great poet. To attain to it calls for a rare singleness of purpose."[79] In his *TLS* article the same lines conclude his claim that Baudelaire's "unremitting exercise of will in transforming his keen emotions is a poetic achievement that makes a single and profound impression upon our minds." They are the magnetic center of *The Problem of Style*. The fusion of past experience and present spectacle that they describe *is*, in Murry's view, the creative act. He rephrases his description of this act from time to time in his book, but it always points back to those lines as the center: the ideal poet, he says, will "let a completely adequate structure form in his mind . . . wait for the emergence of the incident, real, historical, or invented, which he will recognize, by the vividness and depth of his own emotion, as peculiarly his own, and as the perfect symbol of all the emotion latent in himself" (*PS*, 107). This process, Murry writes, can be described as a "crystallization," the process of "condensing your emotion upon the cause, which becomes the symbol" (*PS*, 131). The image, Murry says in a note, is an "unconscious memory" of his other French master, Stendhal (*PS*, 147); but it is also to be found in Pater, and by 1919 Eliot had exploited it fully in "Tradition and the Individual Talent."[80] Murry's "highest style" is the achievement of that same act: it is "a combination of the maximum of personality with the maximum of impersonality; on the one hand it is a concentration of peculiar and personal emotion, on the other it is a complete projection of this personal emotion into the created thing" (*PS*, 35).

Murry says that he aims to identify "the distinguishing mark of the writer of the highest rank" (*PS*, 98). It appears from *The Problem of Style* that this mark is the faculty for "crystallization," the faculty for "enlarging and refining . . . impressions until they comprehend life as a whole" (*PS*, 98). In the great poet, individual experiences will crystallize immediately and accumulate to a "store of perceptions" (*PS*, 99), a "vast vocabulary of symbols on which to draw" (*PS*, 97). The great artist comes to his experience armed by his past with a supply of symbols which are "stored up, waiting . . . to be employed in the crystallization of some more comprehensive and recondite perception" (*PS*, 99).

If the description of the poet's mind irresistibly evokes Eliot's most famous essay of 1919, then that is a comment on the closeness of Eliot's views to Baudelaire's, since Murry's language here, no less than elsewhere in his book, comes mainly from him. "Ce qu'il y a de plus fort dans les batailles avec l'idéal, c'est une belle imagination disposant d'un immense magasin d'observations" (II, 622), he writes in the *Salon* of 1859, and his comments on Gautier's poetic power (quoted above, pp. 92-93) make a relevant comparison. Gautier's style, it will be remembered, consists not only of his unerring knowledge of the language, but also of his "immense intelligence inée de la *correspondance* et du symbolisme universels, ce répertoire de toute métaphore," and those two faculties empower him to "définir l'attitude mystérieuse que les objets de la création tiennent devant le regard de l'homme" (II, 117). Art, Baudelaire writes, is "une mnémotechnie du beau" (II, 455).

The appeasing aesthetic of *The Problem of Style* dismantles the antitheses of Murry's criticism. It calls truce to the conflict between reason and emotion by making both of those into elements of a faculty to which both are subordinate; it resolves the polarities between "personal" and "impersonal" literature, between "realism" and "romanticism," by arguing that all literature is produced by the same kind of creative act, the same originating fusion. Murry argues against Coleridge: when "crystallization," a complex fusing in the poet's mind of his past and the moment, is seen to be the characteristic act of creation, then all forms of literary creation are essentially the same, and "personal literature" is of no higher order than "impersonal literature." In lyric poetry the fusing act joins a personal emotion to a personal expression: this is "the primary form of crystallization" (*PS*, 105). But the production of other forms of literature is the same: incidents of historical, actual, or imaginary life rise before the imagination and become the symbol of the emotion of which they are the cause. Crystallization, then, is found also in "the articulation of more complex works of literature, where, like the

Ce qu'il . . . a fine imagination with an immense store of observed data at its disposal is the strongest combination of all in an artist's battles with the ideal (C, 300).

immense . . . profound and innate understanding of universal correspondence and symbolism, that repository of metaphor . . . define the mysterious attitude that all created objects present as men look at them (C, 272).

more subtle form of crystallization which is manifested in met-
aphor, it is accessory to another crystallization, of a large and
structural kind" (PS, 105). When this is seen to be true it is clear
that so-called "objective" literature is no less personal than so-
called "personal" literature. Murry writes that "the notion that
the objective writer is 'a mere voice' is fantastic: the plot is his,
the incidents are his, the characters are his. By concealing himself
the objective writer is a giant" (PS, 41). Realism and romanticism
are spuriously distinct categories: great writers are always those
who have "accumulated a harmonized experience to guide them
in the choice of a congruous plot, [and] . . . it is merely the
accident of occasion that makes one a realist and the other a
romantic; and, for this reason, many of the greatest writers—I
had very nearly said all the greatest writers—are both" (PS, 31-
32). By carrying the literary arguments into a psychological dis-
cussion, Murry has banished, to his own temporary satisfaction
at least, the "crude opposition of subject and object"; by insisting
on describing the act of literary creation, he has managed to be
at once moral and aesthetic. Murry settled his post-symbolist
accounts with lavish borrowings from Baudelaire. His reconcil-
ing aesthetic returns to the pre-symbolist balances, and the
"giant" he admires, the hidden "objective" writer, is identified
by echo as the Balzac whom Baudelaire described in lines Swin-
burne translated, Wilde borrowed, and Symons quoted.[81]

The Problem of Style, like the rest of Murry's work, draws on a
wide range of sources—Stendhal, de Gourmont, Coleridge,
Wordsworth, among others. One of its major creditors is Pater,
who joins Baudelaire, not for the first time, as precursor. While
it was Baudelaire who provided Murry with his description of
"absolute style," it was likely Pater who supplied the term: "In
literature, as in all forms of art," he writes, in his own approach
to what he called "the problem of style," "there are the absolute
and the merely relative or accessory beauties; and precisely in
that exact proportion of the term to its purpose is the absolute
beauty of style, prose or verse."[82] In a work attached both by its
title and by its key term to what Pater wrote, Murry also adopts
his conception of criticism: if it is the poet's duty to look for "an
incident that shall be completely congruous to his harmonized
experience of life," it is the critic's duty to find a quotation from
his author "that shall be completely congruous to his harmonized
experience of the author's work." In this, Murry says, the critic

"has become—in all but name—a creative artist in miniature himself" (*PS*, 34).

Baudelaire, like Stendhal, was useful to Murry until about 1924. After that, the syntheses that these two French writers supported began to crumble. His developing preference for a strictly moral criticism, already evident by 1918, came, at about the time of the launching of the *Adelphi*, to seem incompatible with any purely aesthetic interest. In his early years, Murry believed with Baudelaire and Stendhal that "la peinture n'est que de la morale construite" (II, 419), but like them he took "morale" in its widest sense of "character" or "attitude to life." After 1922, moral art meant for Murry art that was narrowly relevant to living, and moral criticism seemed to him the antithesis of aesthetic criticism. The French masters of his earlier work now seemed to represent a wholly unhealthy influence on English writing. He began to think that French art was "founded on a quite modern and one-sided emphasis on a single, formal element in literature: an exaltation of what Pater called the qualities of mind at the cost of what he thought the more precious qualities of soul." Murry now believed that Russian literature, which he said was "absolutely permeated, saturated through and through, with a sense of the problem of conduct," was the healthier influence. "It has done more than any other single influence," he writes, "to diminish the prestige of the French conception of literary art."[83] While the French concentrated on the way of saying the thing, Murry writes, the Russians concentrated on the thing said:

> The problem they are tormented by is the problem of conduct: the question that is always present to their mind is: How shall we live? and the spirit in which they approach it is one that can only be described as a spirit of complete loyalty to humanity.

Stendhal, who had once seemed to Murry the greatest novelist who ever lived, was now overshadowed by Dostoevsky, whose books "so far exceeded Stendhal's capacities that they cannot be compared."[84] When he reviewed Baudelaire's letters to his mother, in 1928, Murry saw the French poet with diminished

la peinture . . . Painting is essentially a system of moral values made visible! (C, 51).

sympathy: what had seemed heroic seven years earlier now seemed merely "sordid misery";[85] when he returned to him, in his 1931 review of Shanks's book, he gave a spiritless version of his idea of dandyism. Proust and Joyce, judged by Murry's new criterion, were "essentially . . . nothing." "They have talent," Murry writes, "buckets of it, but talent—what's the use of talent except to help you to say something of importance for life?"[86] From a point in his career which corresponds roughly with the launching of the *Adelphi*—which was, Richard Rees wrote, "not a literary gesture" but "an *act* of adherence to the doctrine, as he understood it, of Lawrence's *Aaron's Rod* and *Fantasia of the Unconscious*"[87]—Murry's criticism throws aesthetic questions to the wind.

T. S. ELIOT

"POET AND SAINT . . ."

Eliot is both the object and the analyst of Baudelaire's influence, and his claims for Baudelaire's importance both to his own work and to his time have drawn copious attention.[1] Baudelaire's voice sounds in his poetry almost from the beginning, and it remains a defining note through all the stages of his maturity. Only Dante figures with so much power in what he wrote. Moreover, Eliot made Baudelaire a central figure in his criticism, citing him frequently in the years between *The Love Song of J. Alfred Prufrock* and *Ash Wednesday,* naming him explicitly as progenitor, proposing him as the modern master of the poetic procedure he called "wit," advancing his claims as "a great poet, a great landmark in poetry . . . the greatest exemplar in *modern* poetry in any language."[2] When, later in his career, Eliot came to write the history of modern poetry, it was the history of a poetic "influence"—the word appears prominently in his account—the outline of a "tradition" derived from Baudelaire's perception, appreciation, and absorption of Poe.[3] When Eliot recognized Baudelaire as *his* "brother," he confirmed the change in the direction of the main current of the English tradition that Swinburne had initiated, and he enshrined in official history the much-altered "ideal order" that Swinburne had foreseen. In Eliot, the Victorian "Mephistopheles" becomes a "saint," the subversive undergoes its final transformation into the canonical.

Like Swinburne, Eliot made no secret of his affiliation of Baudelaire, though it would not be fair to say that he "advertised" it. He did, however, draw attention to it. *The Waste Land* not only quotes him—"V. Baudelaire," Eliot advises in his note, "Preface to *Fleurs du Mal*"—but also documents an allusion. Eliot's procedure is significant. His note instructs his reader to compare the "Unreal City" of line sixty with the "Fourmillante

cité" of "Les Sept Vieillards." The note would be as usefully
appended to *Little Gidding*, where that arresting Baudelairean
"spectre" reappears, but here it is intended to alert the reader
to Eliot's method, the creation of what in "Tradition and the
Individual Talent" he calls a "new compound," and to identify,
together with the other notes, his poem's line of descent. Eliot's
notes, like the picture gallery in *Dorian Gray* or the wall of por-
traits in *Gaston de Latour*, suggest his poem's genetic make-up.
Eliot's concern with "influence" did not begin with his lecture
"From Poe to Valéry" nor with the notes to *The Waste Land*,
though both confirm it.

Eliot's version of the history of modernism constitutes a re-
markable cultural "swerve": he made his own poetic develop-
ment paradigmatic; he made it commonplace to say, in an ac-
count of modern English poetry, that it derived from the French;
he made it fashionable to trace the line of descent of the moderns
from the English metaphysical poets, through the nineteenth-
century French, and back to the English modernists. Eliot's
preoccupation with "influence"—that is, his conception of lit-
erary history as a "handing down" and his vision of literary
creation as wisely managed inheritance—enabled him to draft
an account that omits not only Tennyson but also Morris and
Swinburne and Pater and Symons and the whole range of poets
of the 'nineties, those very writers who had labored to make
available the tradition from which, now, Eliot excluded them.
"The kind of poetry that I needed, to teach me the use of my
own voice," he wrote in his late essay on Yeats, "did not exist in
English at all; it was only to be found in French."[4] In his 1944
article in *La France Libre* Eliot wrote, and in the language of the
precursor, "Si je n'avais [pas] découvert Baudelaire, et toute la
poésie qui découle de Baudelaire . . . je ne crois pas que j'aurais
jamais pu écrire."[5]

But Eliot's use of Baudelaire has much in common with Swin-
burne's: it is itself part of his English inheritance. Like Swin-
burne, he used Baudelaire partly as a defense against a mere
"timid or blind adherence" to the English tradition.[6] Baudelaire
served to establish an idea of difference. But that use required
of him a remarkable act of dissociation. Pound praised Eliot for

---

Si je . . . If I hadn't discovered Baudelaire, and all the poetry that springs from
him . . . I do not believe that I would ever have been able to write.

having "actually trained himself *and* modernized himself *on his own*,"[7] but in fact Eliot modernized himself, as Pound did, in the study of nineteenth-century models. His *Poems Written in Early Youth* chronicle the speed with which the updating took place, and what is most remarkable about Eliot's swift attainment of his earliest poetic voice is that it depends upon conventions that *seemed* continental but *were* wholly established in English poetry. Eliot read the major instrument of his modernization, *The Symbolist Movement in Literature*, in 1908,[8] and his poems registered its effect immediately. The "divine" "flowers of life" and the "wild roses" of 1907 give way to the "fragrance of decay" and to the petals "fanged and red / With hideous streak and stain" of 1908; and the "Song" of the next year concludes with the question, "Have you no brighter tropic flowers / With scarlet life, for me?" The "Nocturne" and the "Humouresque (After J. Laforgue)" confirm a narrower choice of direction, but *The Symbolist Movement* left its own mark, as well as that of Laforgue, on Eliot's early work, and the assertion that "T. S. Eliot's verse was conceived in Paris and inspired by Mallarmé and Laforgue"[9] needs to be nuanced. In the essay in which he found the "Autre Complainte de Lord Pierrot," Eliot also read this:

> And [Laforgue] sees, not only as an imposition, but as a conquest, the possibilities for art which come from the sickly modern being, with his clothes, his nerves: the mere fact that he flowers from the soil of his epoch.
>
> It is an art of the nerves, this art of Laforgue, and it is what all art would tend towards if we followed our nerves on all their journeys. There is in it all the restlessness of modern life, the haste to escape from whatever weighs too heavily on the liberty of the moment, that capricious liberty which demands only room enough to hurry itself weary. It is distressingly conscious of the unhappiness of mortality, but it plays, somewhat uneasily, at a disdainful indifference. And it is out of these elements of caprice, fear, contempt, linked together by an embracing laughter, that it makes its existence.[10]

Not only the major themes of "Prufrock" but also some of its imagery lie ready in that passage, and yet the "modernism" it describes is that of *Days and Nights* or *London Nights*, the modernism of Symons's review of Meredith and Henley. The effect

on Eliot's poetry of the impressionist critic whose poetry he was
at one stage careful not to disparage[11] is probably more impor-
tant than has been imagined. It may have been in Symons's essay
on "Modernity in Verse," for instance, which was included in
Studies in Two Literatures, that Eliot encountered these stanzas
from Henley's "The Operation":[12]

> You are carried in a basket,
>   Like a carcass from the shambles,
>   To the theatre, a cockpit
>   Where they stretch you on a table.
>
> Then they bid you close your eyelids,
>   And they mask you with a napkin,
>   And the anaesthetic reaches
>   Hot and subtle through your being.
>
> And you gasp and reel and shudder
>   In a rushing, swaying rapture,
>   While the voices at your elbow
>   Fade—receding—fainter—farther.
> . . . .
> Then the lights grow fast and furious,
>   And you hear a noise of waters,
>   And you wrestle, blind and dizzy,
>   In an agony of effort,
>
> Till a sudden lull accepts you,
>   And you sound an utter darkness . . .
>   And awaken . . . with a struggle . . .
>   On a hushed, attentive audience.

In those stanzas, there is a strong suggestion of the opening and
the closing imagery of *Prufrock.* The "Preludes" enforce the
point: while they confirm Eliot's early disposition toward an im-
agist method, they also identify his attraction to the subject mat-
ter of "modernism" as Symons had defined it. The third, for
instance, is strikingly like Symons's "In Bohemia," not in its
means of presenting details, but in its choice of them.[13] Eliot's
admiration for the *Sacre du Printemps* signals the unity of his aim
with that of some of his English predecessors: it seemed, he
wrote, "to transform the rhythm of the steppes into the scream
of the motor horn, the rattle of machinery, the grind of wheels,

the beating of iron and steel, the roar of the underground railway, and the other barbaric cries of modern life; and to transform these despairing noises into music."[14] Eliot achieves the adjustment of manner to matter that Symons and the Imagists aimed at, and the mood, manner, and furnishings of his early verse suggest how much he learned from them. His yellow fog may have come from St. Louis, but Wilde shrewdly indicated its aesthetic genesis: "Where," he says, "if not from the Impressionists, do we get those wonderful brown fogs that come creeping down our streets, blurring the gas-lamps and changing the houses into monstrous shadows?"[15] The streets, the nerves (as in the unpublished "First Caprice in North Cambridge"),[16] the pathological moments (as in "Hysteria," for instance), and a conception of poetry as analysis of those nerves and moments—these characteristics give Eliot's early work its most prominent features in common with later nineteenth-century English poetry. The themes and images to which he turned in an attempt to discover his first voice were part of an already internalized French influence. The title of his unpublished "Fourth Caprice" shows his veneering technique: it began as "Fourth Caprice in North Cambridge," but he changed its title in manuscript, and moved the caprice from North Cambridge to Montparnasse. In fact several of the poems in the "Notebook" that is in the Berg Collection amplify what we know about Eliot's relation, as a young poet, to "the immediate generation before us."[17] They gather together *impressions*; they watch the effects of sensations on nerves. The daffodils of his "Easter: Sensations in April," for instance, come from a much-altered English romantic tradition in which poetry is not the product of "tranquillity" but of the *"Genus irritabile vatum!"*

In Eliot's early poetry, a disposition toward those subjects comes together with a quite conventional or an already established use of Baudelaire. His poems on "modern" subjects or "pathological" moments invoke Baudelaire in a manner reminiscent of Symons or Swinburne, or, sometimes, of the early manner of the Sitwells. Eliot told E.J.H. Greene that when he read Baudelaire for the first time in 1907 or 1908, the poems had made a "great impact" upon him, but that they were too powerful and that he had to put them aside for some time.[18] The mark of his reading remains, however, linking his early poems more closely to some of Symons's than to his own later work. In *The Symbolist Movement*, Symons wrote that "Baudelaire, in whom the spirit is always an uneasy guest at the orgy of life, had a certain theory of Realism which tortures many of his poems into strange, metallic shapes, and fills them with imitative odours, and disturbs them with a too deliberate rhetoric of the flesh."[19] Eliot included in his "Circe's Palace" elements of "Un Voyage à Cythère" (which he later used to much greater effect) as well as suggestions of the poem which Francis Scarfe reproves him for calling the "Préface" to *Les Fleurs du Mal*, that from which the last line of "The Burial of the Dead" is taken.[20] Eliot dresses the visit to Circe in the kind of imagery sensational tradition associated with Baudelaire (the carnivorous flowers mentioned above), and he gives the animals of his second stanza a clear "cousinage" with the extraordinary bestiary in "Au Lecteur." Eliot writes, "Panthers rise from their lairs / In the forest which thickens below, / Along the garden stairs / The sluggish python lies."[21] Baudelaire had developed a more lavish catalogue: "Mais parmi les chacals, les panthères, les lices, / Les singes, les scorpions, les vautours, les serpents . . ." (I, 6). The unpublished poems, too, lay bare their roots. "Embarquement pour Cythère" claims a subject Baudelaire had exploited for horror, but in this early treatment of it Eliot is merely "aesthetic." His "Paysage Triste" focuses, like so many poems of Symons's and several of the early poems of Flint and Aldington, on the subject matter of "A une Passante"; and "Burnt Dancer" describes a figure whose origin lies in Baudelaire's comparison, in "Hymne à la Beauté" (I, 25), of the blinded moth and the lover, and it addresses its subject in a French refrain. The unpublished poems are of course multiply connected, and they look both forward and back. One element in their pre-history, though he is also an element that Eliot would carry forward into the future, is Baudelaire, and it is a Baudelaire we recognize. Some of Eliot's later poems, too, associate Baudelaire with a conventional subject matter. D.E.S. Maxwell points out a general and Francis Scarfe a specific use of Baudelaire in "Rhapsody on a Windy Night," for instance, a poem in which Helen Gardner sees "rather 'literary' horror in certain images, which recall self-consciously decadent poetry," and in which the paper roses and the used eau-de-cologne along

---

Mais parmi . . . But among the jackals, panthers, bitch-hounds, monkeys, scorpions, vultures, snakes . . . (S, 155).

with the chestnuts in the streets and the female smells evoke the 'nineties.[22]

Even in his earliest poems, Eliot's attitude toward this inheritance is ambivalent. From the beginning he depends upon a technique of ironic reversal, sweeping away the accumulated images and sensations of his "First Caprice in North Cambridge," for instance, with a weary dismissal. That is recognizably the strategy of "Conversation Galante," which he included in *Prufrock and Other Observations*, or of "Preludes." His "Fourth Caprice," too, shifts its tone radically in its last line, utterly undermining what it had begun by taking very seriously indeed. These early ironic reversals are the germ of Eliot's characteristic conclusion, though in *Portrait of a Lady, Prufrock*, and *The Waste Land*, the terms of the reversal are exchanged. There, it is not feeling that is undercut by sudden irony, but insistent, nervous, self-conscious irony that is undercut by the sudden expression of feeling. In these earliest poems, the ironic reversal is the product of Eliot's ambivalence toward his literary inheritance. His matter is that of "the immediate generation before"; his ironic reversal dismisses it (so enacting, by its reconsideration, the temporal relation of the poet to his predecessors).

By the time he came to write *The Waste Land*, Eliot had abandoned his early voice. Even so, the drafts of the poem embody his ambivalence toward the later nineteenth century. On the one hand, Eliot writes under its influence; on the other, he assembles its characteristics into a satiric portrait. The drafts indicate the degree of his concern—and Pound's—for the poem's modernity. Pound chides him more than once for insufficient care on this point: he brackets the lines of "A Game of Chess" which describe the "sylvan scene" and notes beside them, "1921"; the "closed carriage" of the same section provokes him to write "1880" beside it, and "Why this Blot on Scutchen / between 1922 & Lil."[23] If Eliot was working to get away from Laforgue, Pound was working to keep him centered in 1921.[24] Still, *The Waste Land* drafts confirm the importance to Eliot of the *English* nineteenth century. Two passages of manuscript in particular suggest the possibility that Tiresias came to Eliot as a modification of the impressionist "eye." One is the poem from which the finished work retained the lines beginning "A woman drew her long black hair out tight"; the other is the apostrophe to London, which Pound described as "B‑ll‑S" and cancelled entirely.[25] Mrs. Eliot judges from the handwriting that the first poem dates from "about 1914 or even earlier";[26] the second passage is not distinguished in date from the main part of the poem. The first has obvious similarities with "Prufrock": it shows a speaker in progress through a street whose mode of existence is sometimes ambiguous and sometimes internal. The speaker suffers; the street mirrors his suffering. The "violet air," the "sullen sunbaked houses," the "wrinkled road which twists and winds and guesses," and the subsequent deformed interior landscape are made to convey his feeling. He serves to unite them; they suggest him. Although the poem can be seen as a sketch for "Prufrock," the points at which Eliot departed from his sketch are telling. In "Prufrock," he hits on two distancing devices which change entirely the speaker's relationship to the reader. One is to name his character; the other is the pronominal conceit, the ambiguously floating "you" that David Ward examines closely.[27] In the earlier poem, the "I" brings the reader, in the impressionist manner, flat up against the material described, while in "Prufrock," the "you" confers a distance.

The second impressionist passage in *The Waste Land* drafts is explicitly so. Eliot writes that the swarming life which London breeds and kills, itself "unconscious," "lives in the awareness of the observing eye."

Phantasmal gnomes, burrowing in brick and stone and steel!
Some minds, aberrant from the normal equipoise

. . . .
Record the motions of these pavement toys
And trace the cryptogram that may be curled
Within these faint perceptions of the noise,
Of the movement, and the lights!

The "observing eye" of this passage is specifically related to Baudelaire's poetry and to Symons's. In the drafts, these lines lie between the "Unreal City" passage and the introduction of Tiresias and the typist and the clerk. They constitute a gloss on the function of Tiresias, a gloss subsequently transferred to the "Notes," where Eliot made his famous claim that "What Tiresias *sees*, in fact, is the substance of the poem." This "observing eye," which links the scene with the seer, conferring life on it by means of his "awareness" and "faint perceptions," enacts the impressionism of Symons's city verses, and Eliot describes the act in

Baudelaire's language. (See below, pp. 342-43.) The passage, which suggests both what Eliot found vital in the "city poetry" that preceded his and what alterations to that he effected by his "mythic" ordering, exemplifies *The Waste Land*'s historical doubleness and shows its author in his already characteristic position between two worlds.

Eliot made his historical ambivalence clear long before he published *The Waste Land*, of course. *Prufrock* carries seriously into modern English verse a portrait derived from Gautier's preface to *Les Fleurs du Mal*. "L'action chez lui s'arrête," Gautier writes of Baudelaire the poet. "Il ne vit plus; il est le spectateur de la vie. Toute sensation lui devient motif d'analyse. Involontairement il se dédouble et, faute d'autre sujet, devient l'espion de lui-même. S'il manque de cadavre, il s'étend sur la dalle de marbre noir, et, par un prodige fréquent en littérature, il enfonce le scalpel dans son propre coeur."[28] But Eliot joins Chaplin to this self-scrutinizing decadent, and *Prufrock* strains toward caricature, relying for its grotesqueness on literary mockery, an art of sinking in poetry that is the product not merely of the character's self-deflating reflex but also of the poet's sharply focussed satire. Prufrock's sadly comic sexual terror, for instance, expressing itself as an imagination of the chilling decapitation, tracks its way back to its heroic and Biblical sources by means of a fashionable thread laid through the contrived corridors of literary history by Beardsley and Wilde and Mallarmé and Flaubert—not to mention Strauss—so that Prufrock's anxiety reduces for mockery an impeccably decadent ancestry. And in "Portrait of a Lady," which was written at about the same time as "Rhapsody on a Windy Night," Eliot performs a complicated double dissection of *fin-de-siècle* sensibilities. The "lady" who is the poem's initial subject, the chief actor in a scene that seems to have arranged itself, is as over-wrought and self-savoring as Wilde's Gilbert, who tells Ernest:

> After playing Chopin, I feel as if I had been weeping over sins that I had never committed, and mourning over tragedies that were not my own. Music always seems to me to produce that effect. It creates for one a past of which one has been ignorant, and fills one with a sense of sorrows that have been hidden from one's tears. I can fancy a man who

Il ne vit . . . translated above, p. 177.

had led a perfectly commonplace life, hearng by chance
some curious piece of music, and suddenly discovering that
his soul, without his being conscious of it, had passed
through terrible experiences, and known fearful joys, or
wild romantic loves, or great renunciations.[29]

But by the end of the poem, Eliot has redirected his satire,
exposing as a mere "aesthete" the chilly, self-absorbed "I" of the
poem, who is frozen into a carefully artful picture, "sitting pen
in hand" on an "Afternoon grey and smoky, evening yellow and
rose." In the manuscript version of *Portrait of a Lady* that is in
the Notebook in the Berg Collection, the poem is headed not by
its present epigraph, but by this line from the last scene of Web-
ster's *White Devil*: "I have caught / An everlasting cold."

While some passages of the draft *Waste Land* indicate the still
powerful hold on Eliot's practice of the poetry of the later nine-
teenth century, the opening lines of "A Game of Chess" and the
proposed opening for "The Fire Sermon" show his fullest car-
icature of its left-over manifestations. The two passages embody
the two sides of the Baudelairean or decadent woman, pitting
her artificiality against her nature. The "strange synthetic per-
fumes" of the first passage, which survived Pound's surgery,
present a familiar topos of the decadence and join this passage
of *The Waste Land* to Baudelaire's and Wilde's and Beerbohm's
reflections on the cosmetic, though, like Thomas Mann in *Death
in Venice*, Eliot is here concerned to show the streaks in the paint,
and this version of Salomé's toilette gives way under the pressure
of nature. In the proposed opening of "The Fire Sermon,"[30]
Eliot reiterates the antithesis in some crude details—"Fresca slips
softly to the needful stool, / Where the pathetic tale of Richard-
son / Eases her labour till the deed is done"—but here his target
is both the woman and the literary generation she represents.
The character is compiled from the affectations of the 'eighties
and 'nineties: her literary world includes Rossetti, Symonds, Pa-
ter, Vernon Lee; her social surroundings give occasion to drop
the name of the Marquess of Queensbury, famous as the enemy
of Wilde; her own poems (since her artificiality is her pretense
to literature) reflect a conventional mood of spleen, and her
critics, blind to the existence of their own *Zeitgeist*, allow that
"her style is quite her own," and judge them by the aesthetic

canon of personality. Fresca's style, artificial, is inevitably the woman.

The Waste Land, of course, *is* a "modern" poem, the expression, in spite of Eliot's now-famous disclaimer, of a time—and both the time and its expression are profoundly different from the time and the expression of the poets with whom I have been comparing Eliot's work. But originality "is by no means a simple idea in the criticism of poetry. True originality is merely development; and if it is right development it may appear in the end so *inevitable* that we almost come to the point of view of denying all 'original' virtue to the poet."[31] While *The Waste Land* drafts reveal debts, they also reveal magnificent development. And they show Eliot's wholly personal appropriation of Baudelaire. The impressionist passage discussed above, for instance, amplifies what we know of the way Baudelaire influenced the making of *The Waste Land*.[32] It makes more sense of the note in which Eliot invites comparison of his "Unreal City" with the first lines of "Les Sept Vieillards" than the finished poem does, and so makes us reconsider the character of "Unreal City" as it now stands, alone. In the apostrophe to London, Eliot seems to have written with "Les Sept Vieillards" (I, 87-88) and also "Les Petites Vieilles" (I, 89-91), from which he quotes in his 1921 essay on Dryden, before him. The first line of that passage, for instance, simply translates the adjective from "Fourmillante cité, cité pleine de rêves"; but the atmosphere of Baudelaire's line is appropriated more successfully in Eliot's repeated "O City, City." The "jerky motions of these huddled toys" aims at the effect of Baudelaire's "monstres disloqués" who "trottent, tout pareils à des marionnettes" in "Les Petites Vieilles." The inhabitants of Eliot's London are "dazed," "half stunned," "knowing little what they think, and much less what they feel"; Baudelaire's old women "dansent, sans vouloir danser, pauvre sonnettes / Qù se pend un Démon sans pitié!" Eliot's are "bound upon the wheel"; Baudelaire's are under "la griffe effroyable de Dieu." Substituting "Phantasmal" for "Spectral" in his draft, Eliot merely exchanges one word of Baudelaire's for another. The impressionist eye and the cryp-

---

Fourmillante . . . O swarming city, city full of dreams (S, 193).
monstres . . . disjointed freaks . . . trot like puppets (S, 193, 196).
dansent . . . though they don't intend to, they do a kind of jig, like puny bells swung by a merciless demon (S, 196).
la griffe . . . God's terrible claw (S, 200).

togram have their general and specific sources in Baudelaire, who in "Les Petites Vieilles," explains that the relationship between the perceiver and the perceived is an imaginative one:

Mais moi, moi qui de loin tendrement vous surveille,
L'oeil inquiet, fixé sur vos pas incertains,
Tout comme si j'étais votre père, ô merveille!
Je goûte à votre insu des plaisirs clandestins:

Je vois s'épanouir vos passions novices;
Sombres ou lumineux, je vis vos jours perdus;
Mon coeur multiplié jouit de tous vos vices!
Mon âme resplendit de toutes vos vertus!

Again in "Les Veuves," Baudelaire writes that "Un oeil expérimenté . . . déchiffre toute de suite les innombrables légendes de l'amour trompé" (I, 292). Eliot agreed to cancel his city passage, but not before he had worked it through three different states, and not before its imprint had been unmistakably set on other, surviving, passages of his poem.

The proposed opening for "Death by Water," a passage which summons an impressive number of literary voyages, has a first line modelled on that of "Le Voyage."[33] In his 1921 essay on "The Metaphysical Poets," Eliot praised and quoted the first stanza of Baudelaire's poem, which was to echo again in the setting-out of his own "Animula,"[34] and in the voyaging and the lamplight evening of East Coker:

Pour l'enfant, amoureux de cartes et d'estampes,
L'univers est égal à son vaste appétit.
Ah! que le monde est grand à la clarté des lampes!
Aux yeux du souvenir que le monde est petit!

Baudelaire and Racine, he said in the essay, were the "greatest two masters of diction," "the greatest two psychologists, the most

Mais moi . . . But I, who watch you tenderly from afar, with my uneasy eye fixed on your tottering steps, as though (what next!) I were your father—unknown to you I enjoy secret pleasures: I watch your untutored passions flower, and dark or bright, I relive your vanished days; my manifold heart delights in all your vices, and my soul resplends with all your virtues (S, 200).

Un oeil . . . The experienced eye . . . at once deciphers innumerable histories of cheated love . . . (S, 201-202).

Pour . . . For the child in love with maps and prints, the universe matches his vast appetite. Ah, how big the world is, in the lamplight; but how small, viewed through the eyes of memory! (S, 182).

curious explorers of the soul."[35] Not only the first line—"the
sailor, attentive to the chart or to the sheets"—but also the three
quatrains that were to open "Death by Water" demonstrate again
the close knitting of Eliot's criticism to his poetry, recalling in
their movement as well as in their subject matter Baudelaire's
great voyage poem. And when the *Waste Land* manuscript pas-
sage dissipates its form into the prosey second part, it recalls the
flat reply to eager questioners of Baudelaire's voyagers:

> Dites, qu'avez-vous vu?
>
> "Nous avons vu des astres
> Et des flots; nous avons vu des sables aussi;
> Et, malgré bien des chocs et d'imprévus désastres,
> Nous nous sommes souvent ennuyés, comme ici."

In the dream vision which is the center of the passage, Baude-
laire's "Le Voyage" joins itself to *Heart of Darkness*:

> . . . no one dared
> To look into anothers face, or speak
> In the horror of the illimitable scream
> Of a whole world about us.
> . . . .
> . . . I was
> Frightened beyond fear, horrified past horror, calm. . . .

"Amer savoir, celui qu'on tire du voyage," Baudelaire had writ-
ten:

> Le monde, monotone et petit, aujourd'hui,
> Hier, demain, toujours, nous fait voir notre image:
> Une oasis d'horreur dans un désert d'ennui!

In the lines that suggest the Sirens and Clarence's dream, "Le
Voyage" merges with the other Baudelairean voyage in which
Eliot found, as E.J.H. Greene first noted,[36] some of the landscape
of the waste land. The "fore cross-trees," like the "gibet à trois
branches" of "Un Voyage à Cythère" (I, 117-19), ought to be
associated with erotic pleasure; instead, they convey horror. The

Dites . . . Tell us, what have you seen? We have seen stars and waves, and
deserts also, and despite many an alarm and many an unforeseen disaster, we
were often bored, just as we are here (S, 185).
Amer savoir . . . Bitter the knowledge we draw from voyaging! Monotonous
and mean, today, yesterday, tomorrow, always, the world shows us our own
image—an oasis of horror in a desert of tedium (S, 188).

suppression of this part of "Death by Water" removes to a more distant plane of awareness Eliot's conflation of the sea-voyage and sexual adventure. It also deprives of some of its original context (though not to its disadvantage) the splendid and mysterious passage in "What the Thunder Said" in which the ship and the heart are seen together. Those lines, which recall the astonishing lift into lyric of the end of "Prufrock," are one of Eliot's most controlled and masterly uses of Baudelaire. The "Voyage à Cythère" opens with these lines:

> Mon coeur, comme un oiseau, voltigeait tout joyeux
> Et planait librement à l'entour des cordages;
> Le navire roulait sous un ciel sans nuages,
> Comme un ange enivré d'un soleil radieux.

One manuscript version of these lines reads:

> Damyata. the wind was fair, and the boat responded
> Gaily, to the hand expert with sail and wheel.
> The sea was calm, and your heart responded
> Gaily, when invited, beating responsive
> To controlling hands.[37]

The lines, though in a bitterly ironic context in both poems, give a glimpse of the "sublimation of passion" that Eliot admired in Baudelaire and that Grover Smith suggests as a forming motive in "Ash Wednesday."[38]

Pound wrote to Harriet Monroe,

> And—dieu le sait—there are few enough people on this stupid little island who know anything beyond Verlaine and Beaudelaire [sic]—neither of whom is the least use, pedagogically, I mean. They beget imitation and one can learn nothing from them. Whereas Gautier and de Gourmont carry forward the art itself, and the only way one can imitate them is by making more profound your knowledge of the very marrow of art.[39]

Eliot learned from Gautier and especially from de Gourmont. Pound, on the other hand, did not learn from Baudelaire, and Eliot noted that as one of the limitations of his criticism:

Mon coeur . . . My heart was soaring gaily as a bird and hovering untrammelled round the rigging; the ship sailed on beneath a cloudless sky, like an angel enraptured by the dazzling sun (S, 97).

... Pound performed a great service ... for the English-speaking reader in emphasising the greatness of Villon. He was quick to appreciate the originality of Laforgue and Corbière. He showed a discriminating taste among the minor poets of the "Symbolist Movement." But he ignores Mallarmé; he is uninterested in Baudelaire; and to his interest such poets as Malherbe and La Fontaine are irrelevant.[40]

To ignore Baudelaire was, in Eliot's view, to ignore the greatest French poet.[41] He could be imitated; he could also be of "pedagogical use." Eliot's poetry shows both. What began as an element of Eliot's debt to the later nineteenth century developed into a characteristic element of his modernism. Baudelaire's influence on *The Waste Land* was a major force enabling Eliot—through Pound—to cast the other ancestral ghosts which had haunted its early versions.

*   *   *

Baudelaire is no less present in Eliot's criticism than in his poetry. Here, too, Eliot aligns himself in relation to the nineteenth century on the one hand and to modernism on the other. Later in his career, Eliot repudiated criticism that evaluated art primarily on grounds of its representation of its own time,[42] but in his early years in London he shared with Pound and others the desire to reflect, to criticize, and to prescribe for the place and age. He praised Pound's poems on modern subjects (though later he changed his mind about them)[43] and he wrote in his first "London Letter" that he intended there "to construct such a portrait of the time as might seem in my power."[44] The development of a properly local art implied for him, as for many of his contemporaries, the shaking off of forms of thought and speech that were not authentic expressions of the time. If Eliot seems obsessed at this stage in his career with nationality, he was equally preoccupied with modernity, measuring its degrees with ironic precision: "To-day," he wrote in the *Dial*, Shaw "is perhaps an important elder man of letters in a sense in which Mr. Hardy is not. Hardy represents to us a still earlier generation not by his date of birth but by his type of mind. He is of the day before yesterday, whilst Shaw is of a to-day that is only this evening."[45] In matters of language and thought, Eliot aimed to detach his time from the nineteenth century. The "twentieth century is still the nineteenth," he wrote in 1921, "although it may in time acquire its own character."[46] His early criticism is aimed at furthering that acquisition.

Pound wrote on the typescript of The Waste Land that, as Eliot was referring to London, to say "cautious critics" was tautological.[47] By that time, Eliot had left no room to doubt his sympathy with the remark. He had sifted through the critical inheritance of the immediate past and found it all unsatisfactory. An icy voice has arisen, Murry wrote in a Times Literary Supplement leading article, a voice we respect, to tell us that there is reviewing but no criticism.[48] Everybody knows, Eliot wrote in the Athenaeum, where Murry kept him company in his continuing complaint, that "the amount of good literary criticism in English is negligible."[49] The nineteenth century offered, he said, no model: Coleridge was "certainly the greatest of English critics, and in a sense the last,"[50] and even he was too little a critic and too much a man of letters; Pater did not count;[51] Swinburne was ultimately "an appreciator and not a critic";[52] and Arnold himself, as Eliot saw him mirrored in Clive Bell, was "not precisely a critic, but the Sunday afternoon preacher to a small select public."[53] Eliot's contemporaries, under his steady gaze, showed each a defect: Edward Thomas was "distinctly a 'literary' man; a man with a taste for books, rather than a critic in the serious French way";[54] Alice Meynell had "not the single critical motive" but was "an amateur of letters" who "has not in the end criticized the author at all";[55] Charles Whibley, who had "some other equipoise of his own," had not "the balance of the critic";[56] Robert Lynd never "quite dares to treat a book austerely by criteria of art and of art alone."[57]

Eliot did not hesitate to diagnose the fault in criticism as endemic: the English critic had an "essentially uncritical" conception of literature as "an institution—accepted, that is to say, with the same gravity as the establishments of Church and State."[58] It was not "that the critical faculty is wholly lacking to the English mind, but that our interest is seldom wholly in good literature, or in the goodness of anything as literature."[59] Although he took care not to be indiscriminate—he saw it as a fault of Englishmen to have an "uncritical admiration (in the present age) for France"[60]—Eliot measured English criticism against French. It was a "commonplace," he said, "that the French surpass us in every kind of critical writing. They are assumed to have devel-

oped standards and the skill in dissociation to a degree quite
unknown in this country."[61] *The Sacred Wood* scrutinizes this com-
monplace and agrees with it, describing criticism in terms of
national virtues and national failings: the Americans, Babbitt
and More, derived their merit from the French and their final
inadequacy from their transatlantic outlook. "The French influ-
ence is traceable in their devotion to ideas and their interest in
problems of art and life as problems which exist and can be
handled apart from their relations to the critic's private tem-
perament."[62]

All of this was revolutionary, but of course it was not new. By
1889, praise of French literary art at the expense of English
seemed trite to Dowden, who said wearily in a Taylorian lecture
that we could all grow the flowers since we had all got the seed.[63]
Eliot was aware of the reduplication: "what makes Arnold seem
all the more remarkable is, that if he were our exact contem-
porary, he would find all his labour to perform again."[64] But
Eliot justified the labor on grounds of the familiar tyranny of
"the solid and eternal Podsnap himself . . . the insurgent middle
class, Mr. Monro's General Reading Public."[65] The two central
clauses of his complaint against criticism measure his inheritance
from the aesthetic writers. He insists both that art must be con-
sidered in artistic terms and that the quality of art reflects directly
the quality of criticism. It is the present state of English criticism,
he says, that makes Pound's verse inaccessible to English readers:
"The absence of leisure, the pressure of political interest have
tended to blunt critical discrimination and obscure the truth that
only what is well written is good literature."[66] And "because we
have never learned to criticize Keats, Shelley, and Wordsworth
(poets of assured though modest merit), Keats, Shelley, and
Wordsworth punish us from their graves with the annual scourge
of the Georgian Anthology."[67] French criticism provided a guide
precisely because it was pure, it had a "skill of dissociation," it
was able to treat art as art. These points comprise the frequently
reiterated critical message of Pound, the Imagists, Murry, and
the Sitwells. But they are also central to Swinburne, Pater, Wilde,
and Symons. "Believe me, Ernest," Wilde's Gilbert had said,
"there is no fine art without self-consciousness, and self-con-
sciousness and the critical spirit are one";[68] and Swinburne had
complained in his essay on Baudelaire of failure to remember

"that a poet's business is presumably to write good verses, and by no means to redeem the age and remould society."[69]

Eliot's desire to impose on criticism the clarity of the language of philosophy and the systematic order of science, however, distinguishes the tone and attitude of his criticism from that of nineteenth-century critics from Swinburne to Symons. Wilde, following and enlarging on Pater, wanted to judge literature by the evidence it gave of a created egotism.[70] That emphasis on personality was anathema to Eliot—he could not, he said in 1932, accept any theory "which is erected upon purely individual-psychological foundations"[71]—and to avoid the abuses he thought it led to, he withdrew into the philosophic language and scientific metaphor characteristic of his early criticism. But his efforts to force criticism into objectivity often rely on refocussing or redirecting critical ideas that were part of the English tradition. Eliot stiffened the language, created the "icy voice," and brought to a number of texts an acute and disciplined perception, but in its broadest outlines and in a surprising number of its specific points, his criticism is clearly and deeply indebted to that of which Baudelaire had been an important element since Pater.

Eliot's early criticism sometimes echoes Pater ironically. In the essay on George Wyndham, for instance, he writes that there "must probably be conceded to history a few 'many-sided' men. Perhaps Leonardo da Vinci was such."[72] In "Tradition and the Individual Talent," he writes, "It is in this depersonalisation that art may be said to approach the condition of science."[73] He refers to "the pattern of Sainte-Beuve's carpet,"[74] and later he writes that "the poet aspires to the condition of the music-hall comedian."[75] In direct confrontation with him, Eliot dismisses Pater archly. "We should be thankful," he wrote in "Hamlet and His Problems," "that Walter Pater did not fix his attention on this play."[76] In the essay on Dryden, he dismisses a judgment of Pater's as "cheap journalism."[77] At this early stage, Eliot has hardly a kind word for any of Pater's work, though he ventures in an *Egoist* article that Pater, "if he had had a better English style, and been more interested in what he wrote about," might have produced some criticism.[78] By 1924, however, he saw Pater, with Arnold, Newman, and Bradley, differently: "in the gradual dissolution of nineteenth-century ideas and ideals, theirs are amongst the names which carry the most promise of future power."[79]

Even in passages in which he recommends wiping the critical
slate clean, Eliot reveals his important proximity to Pater. The
following comment, from an article of 1918, will illustrate:

> The work of the critic is almost wholly comprehended in
> the "complementary activities" of comparison and analysis.
> The one activity implies the other; and together they pro-
> vide the only way of asserting standards and of isolating a
> writer's peculiar merits. In the dogmatic, or lazy, mind com-
> parison is supplied by judgment, analysis replaced by ap-
> preciation. Judgment and appreciation are merely tolerable
> avocations, no part of the critic's serious business. If the
> critic has performed his laboratory work well, his under-
> standing will be evidence of appreciation; but his work is by
> the intelligence not the emotions. The judgment also will
> take place in the reader's mind, not in the critic's explicit
> statement. When he judges or appreciates he simply (per-
> haps from a legitimate compulsion to spare time or thought)
> is missing out a link in the exposition.[80]

But Pater's "Preface" to *The Renaissance*, one of the documents
most obviously liable to the charge of a too-emotional appreci-
ation, is strikingly close to Eliot in what it requires of criticism:

> the function of the aesthetic critic is to distinguish, to ana-
> lyse, and separate from its adjuncts, the virtue by which a
> picture, a landscape, a fair personality in life or in a book,
> produces this special impression of beauty or pleasure, to
> indicate what the source of that impression is, and under
> what conditions it is experienced. His end is reached when
> he has disengaged that virtue, and noted it, as a chemist
> notes some natural element, for himself and others. . . .[81]

Like Pater, Eliot demands the exclusion from aesthetic delib-
erations of extra-aesthetic matters, and his insistence upon that
point makes his early criticism uncommonly negative: he tells us
again and again what are *not* aesthetic matters and who is *not* a
critic, but he comes very little closer to defining his "pure" crit-
icism than saying that criticism is pure which does not serve
uncritical purposes or consider matters not properly aesthetic.
His description of critical practice, however, suggests Pater's
"Preface" in its style as well as in what it urges:

To bring the poet back to life—the great, the perennial, task
of criticism—is in this case to squeeze the drops of the es-
sence of two or three poems; even confining ourselves to
these, we may find some precious liquor unknown to the
present age. Not to determine rank, but to isolate this qual-
ity, is the critical labour.[82]

In his early criticism, Eliot can be seen devising a number of
ideas and concepts which provide the structure for much of his
subsequent work. These do not comprise a critical system, but
they outline the critic's preoccupations, the centers of value
around which his thought moves, or, to use his notorious met-
aphor, the filaments upon which the crystals develop. His view
of the emotion proper to art, for instance, is one; his idea of
"point of view" is another. During the early years Eliot constructs
his thought on the relation of criticism to creation, the process
of poetic creation, the relationship of the temporal and the eter-
nal in a work of art, the duty of the poet toward language, the
struggle of the specific to prevail over the general. Those centers
of preoccupation reflect the consanguinity of his work and Pa-
ter's, and of Baudelaire's.

It is precisely in opposition to a kind of criticism descended
from Pater that Eliot outlines his view of emotion in art and
criticism. He makes two telling points against impressionist crit-
icism: one is that "we do not find the impressions of another
person, however sensitive, very significant"; the other is that pure
impressionism is impossible, since the "moment you try to put
the impressions into words, you either begin to analyse and con-
struct, to 'ériger en lois,' or you begin to create something else."
The fault of impressionist critics is that they do both of these
things, and so the proper function of criticism, which is the first,
is made impure by the second. They are most often a version
of the sentimental person, the incomplete artist "in whom a work
of art arouses all sorts of emotions which have nothing to do
with that work of art whatever, but are accidents of personal
association."[83] They fail to recognize what Eliot calls elsewhere
"the data of criticism," the emotion proper to the aesthetic ex-
perience. On Coleridge, who represents a different fault but the
same consequence, Eliot comments that "a literary critic should
have no emotions except those immediately provoked by a work
of art—and these (as I have already hinted) are, when valid,

perhaps not to be called emotions at all."[84] Eliot's "perfect critic" will be neither (in de Gourmont's terms) a "sensitif" nor an "abstrait," both of whom impurify criticism by introducing extraneous emotion, but a "free mind," an independent "intelligence."

What is especially interesting about this is that Eliot corrects Symons, the impressionist critic, with ideas that had themselves shaped impressionist criticism. The "Perfect Critic" is a close relative of the aesthetic critic of the "Preface" to *The Renaissance.* The quotation from de Gourmont that heads the first part of "The Perfect Critic" suggests the degree to which the essay is based on the view it opposes. The phrase, also appropriated by Pound and Murry, is partly an apology for impressionist criticism: "Eriger en lois ses impressions personelles, c'est le grand effort d'un homme s'il est sincère." That is a version of Baudelaire's desire to "transformer ma volupté en connaissance" and it is close to the response of Pater's aesthetic critic to the "influence he feels, and wishes to explain, by analysing and reducing it to its elements."[85] Like Baudelaire's comment, and Pater's, de Gourmont's holds in balance the two elements of impression and reflection, makes the act of criticism include them both. Eliot underlines the "lois" of de Gourmont's dictum, and so corrects Symons's criticism with a text from Symons's early correspondent and with the double disposition of the critical tradition he sees Symons representing. More than that, Eliot judges Symons, "the critical successor of Pater," by criteria which are those of Pater's own work. His comments on improper emotion are clearly a complaint against utility in art, consistent with the complaints he lodges against English criticism in general, and they are related to, but not the same as, the idea of a purely aesthetic emotion. Eliot does not postulate "an aesthetic emotion," but he does maintain that emotion in art is modified into something fundamentally different from its real-life equivalent:

> A poet like M. de Bosschère is an intellectual by his obstinate refusal to adulterate his poetic emotions with human emotions. Instead of refining ordinary human emotion (and I do not mean tepid human emotion, but human however intense—in the crude living state) he aims direct at emotions of art.[86]

That insistence on the necessary distinction between emotion in life and emotion in art is closely related to Pater's comments, in

"The School of Giorgione," on the matter and the art of Legros. Furthermore, Eliot's description of the faculty that distinguishes the "perfect critic," Aristotle's "universal intelligence," develops precisely the antithesis of Pater's "Preface" between a dogmatic criticism and a correctly aesthetic criticism. Aristotle, Eliot writes, had no "impure desires" to satisfy, no need to make art serve other ends:

> in whatever sphere of interest, he looked solely and stead-
> fastly at the object; in his short and broken treatise he pro-
> vides an eternal example—not of laws, or even of method,
> for there is no method except to be very intelligent, but of
> intelligence itself swiftly operating the analysis of sensation
> to the point of principle and definition.[87]

Aristotle is an antidote for the dogmatic criticism descended from Horace and Boileau, for criticism which is merely "unfinished analysis." The "free intelligence," of which, Eliot wrote in the *Egoist*, "an important function is the discernment of exactly what, and how much, we feel in any given situation,"[88] is a faculty like that cultivated by Pater's critic. It is unbound by rules and it is capable of distinguishing what is *in* the object. It neither sets out from nor concludes with precepts; it regards sensations as the data of criticism.

Eliot's chief requirement of a work of criticism, as of a work of art—that it should have a distinct "point of view"—is not remote from the question at issue here. In great criticism, Eliot says, there must be analysis and comparison, and there must also be "a subject and a personal point of view to hold the book together."[89] That is a characteristic of the greater and the lesser French critics. Eliot does not define it, but he distinguishes it both from a purely affective response and from a purely intellectual one. It is a personal characteristic, more important than impersonal ideas. Conrad, for instance, "has no ideas, but he has a point of view, a 'world,' " and James, of course, "is like the best French critics in maintaining a point of view, a view-point untouched by the parasite idea."[90] The "point of view" holds together precisely the elements of the de Gourmont phrase which heads the essay on Symons, as Eliot's comments on "The Lesson of Baudelaire" show: "Baudelaire," Eliot says, aimed, with "more intellect" than the Romantics "*plus* intensity, and without much help from his predecessors, to arrive at a point of view toward good and evil."[91] Of Bertrand Russell, Eliot writes: he "can be accepted by his own test of a man of science as one who has invented a new method . . . he is also a philosopher who has invented a new point of view; and a new point of view is style."[92] If the best work is to be informed by a personal quality that combines intellect and feeling and that can be called style, neither Wilde's created egoism nor the late romantic valuation of personality seems any longer remote.

Although Eliot thought it crucial that criticism and creation should not be confused with one another, he insisted that the "critical genius is inseparable from the creative," and he judged critical and creative works by some of the same canons.[93] (He looked in both for the distinct "point of view," for instance.) He took care to dissociate his interest in their relationship from the interest of Symons and of Pater (whose criticism, he said in 1920, was "etiolated creation"),[94] but his consideration of the question led him at one stage to a dangerous exaggeration of the nineteenth-century desire for creative criticism and ultimately to a reversal of that to a demand for critical creation.

In "A Brief Treatise on the Criticism of Poetry" Eliot wrote that if " 'critical journalism' is an activity quite apart from creative activity, if critics are a race apart from artists who hold the artist's destiny in their hands, both criticism and art perish."[95] At the same time, he expressed a view which, if followed, could rush both to as swift a destruction: the only criticism useful to poets, he said, is the criticism of poets. Because the proper matter of criticism is technique, Remy de Gourmont, for instance, "could not have been a critic" unless he had also been a poet:

> The critic is interested in technique—technique in the widest sense. You cannot understand a book on mathematics unless you are actively, not merely passively, a mathematician, unless you can perform operations, not merely follow them. And you cannot understand the technique of poetry unless you are to some extent capable of performing this operation. Only the person who is working on words in that way can understand their values. The philosopher who works a mathematical or physical theory into his system is certainly "criticising" the theory; but to the mathematician or physicist, occupied in further extending his theory, this philosophy is not of much use. And to the poet only the criticism of poets is useful.[96]

That is a dangerously extreme relative of the view that criticism should be creative, and it leads Eliot to some questionable decrees, as, for instance, his remark that "if you hold the opinion that Swinburne was a very great poet, you can hardly deny him the title of a great critic."[97] The claim is an extension of that of the aesthetic "purity" of criticism: "technique" is incontestably a question proper to poetry. Eliot has argued criticism into a position of the greatest importance (without it art cannot survive) but he has banished it to a remote kingdom (to be useful it must be as specialized as physics). He was not always so extreme. "The Function of Criticism," in which he recants the claim that only criticism by poets will do, takes up the position of Swinburne and Baudelaire:

> Matthew Arnold distinguishes far too bluntly, it seems to me, between the two activities: he overlooks the capital importance of criticism in the work of creation itself. Probably, indeed, the larger part of the labour of an author in composing his work is critical labour; the labour of sifting, combining, constructing, expunging, correcting, testing: this frightful toil is as much critical as creative. I maintain even that the criticism employed by a trained and skilled writer on his own work is the most vital, the highest kind of criticism: and (as I think I have said before) that some creative writers are superior to others solely because their critical faculty is superior.[98]

Eliot did not change this view: in *The Use of Poetry and the Use of Criticism* he affirmed the "significant relation between the best poetry and the best criticism of the same period" and that "To ask 'what is poetry?' is to posit the critical function."[99] His insistence on that significant relation clearly benefits from the work of the later nineteenth century: not only from Arnold, but also from the controversial tradition of Swinburne and Pater and Wilde.

So crucial did the relationship between the two activities seem to Eliot at the beginning of his career that he derived from it his idea of "critical poetry,"[100] turning the witty reversal of Wilde into a practical aesthetic. The essay on Henry James indicates the iconoclastic line his thought was taking in 1918. James's best quality as a novelist is his critical faculty: "He was a critic who preyed not upon ideas, but upon living beings. It is criticism

which is in a very high sense creative."[101] The work of Haw-
thorne—who had what no one else in Boston had, "the firmness,
the true coldness, the hard coldness of the genuine artist"—was
"truly a criticism."[102] In an essay on "Beyle and Balzac," Eliot
amplified his view that, as he wrote a year later in Lewis's *Tyro*,
imagination and criticism "are one."[103] Imagination, he says in
"Beyle and Balzac," is not responsible for hazy vision, for ro-
manticizing *ambiance*. It is not separate from observation but, in
the great artist, "it becomes a fine and delicate tool for an op-
eration on the sensible world." It is, like criticism, analysis:

> It is this intensity, precisely, and consequent discontent
> with the inevitable inadequacy of actual living to the pas-
> sionate capacity, which drove them to art and to analysis.
> The surface of existence coagulates into lumps which look
> like important simple feelings, which are identified by names
> as feelings, which the patient analyst disintegrates into more
> complex and trifling, but ultimately, if he goes far enough,
> into various canalizations of something again simple, terri-
> ble, and unknown.[104]

The critical faculty here is clearly not merely the necessary part-
ner of the creative faculty, nor even the poet's ability to perform
"the labour of sifting, combining, constructing, expunging, cor-
recting, testing": it is the most important element of creation
itself. It is, like the "point of view," both a unifying and a dis-
tancing faculty: it involves thought and sensation, it includes an
ethical dimension, and so it embraces the whole sensibility of the
artist. It allows, though, for no confusion between the artist and
his material; indeed, it sets him against his material, as we shall
see later. For the moment, it is sufficient to note that in the
development of his view of poetry (or in description of the typical
viewpoint of his own poetry), Eliot continues a line of thought
which descends from Pater and Baudelaire.

One further point in common between Eliot and those nine-
teenth-century writers is to be found at the heart of his view of
poetry. For him, as for Pater and Baudelaire, the question of
what poetry ought to do is not only a question of practical crit-
icism. "You can never draw the line between aesthetic criticism
and moral and social criticism," one of his "voices" said, "you
cannot draw a line between criticism and metaphysics."[105] His
thesis on Bradley involved him directly in the question central

to symbolist thought, that of the nature of subjectivity and objectivity, and Bradley's view, like that of Bergson, makes a response to the question which is entirely compatible with orthodox symbolist views. As Kenner notes, Bradley thought that "the dichotomy of observer and observed is [nothing] but a late and clumsy abstraction, of limited usefulness, crassly misrepresenting the process of knowing,"[106] and that "feeling," as Eliot wrote in his thesis, is " 'the general condition before distinctions and relations have been developed, and where as yet neither any subject nor object exists.' "[107] But where Bradley merely doubts that there is ever a stage at which experience is "merely immediate" (that is, unanalyzed, nonrelational), Eliot positively asserts that there is not: "There is no absolute point of view from which real and ideal can be finally separated and labelled."[108] The monist, Eliot explains, often holds that experience is the adjective of the subject (*my* experience), the pluralist that experience is what is experienced (objects in the world). But both, Eliot says, are constructions *from* experience, both are "as ideal as atoms." "In short," he says, "we can only discuss experience from one side and then from the other, correcting these partial views."[109] Bradley's "wholes," as Kenner says, can be the basis for an idea about "the dissociation of sensibility."[110] But Eliot's remarks retain the dichotomy: "We do not find feeling without thought, or presentation without reflection: we find both feeling and thought, presentation, redintegration and abstraction, all at a lower stage," while we find "in our own knowing exactly the same constituents, in a clearer and more apprehensible form."[111] That is the basis for a double statement about the way we know: knowing is one action, but it calls upon two faculties. The writer of the thesis maintains two points of view, each partial, each corrective of each. This provides the basis for an ironic poetry: if it makes reasonable the view that Prufrock *is* his experience, feeling with thought, presentation with reflection, it also makes reasonable the mutually correcting points of view of, say, the "Conversation Galante" or "The Portrait of a Lady," poems written before Eliot worked on Bradley. Eliot does not dispense with analysis but, on the contrary, makes it the necessary companion of feeling: "There is no greater mistake than to think that feeling and thought are exclusive—that those beings which think most and best are not also those capable of the most feeling."[112] Neither point of view is absolute:

A toothache, or a violent passion, is not necessarily dimin-
ished by our knowledge of its causes, its character, its im-
portance or insignificance. To say that one part of the mind
suffers and another part reflects upon the suffering is per-
haps to talk in fictions. But we know that these highly-or-
ganized beings who are able to objectify their passions, and
as passive spectators to contemplate their joys and torments,
are also those who suffer and enjoy the most keenly.[113]

Criticism is thus an indispensable part of creation; imagination
and criticism are thus one.

We are now on familiar ground. Pater's probings into the
relationship of the real and the ideal, and the importance of that
relationship to art, comprise an early blow in criticism against
the "false distinction" between subject and object, but they do
not, like Bergson's, posit a synthetic faculty over and above the
faculties of intellection and sensation. Pater insists that both fac-
ulties are a part of the process of knowing and that this is a fact
of first relevance to art. From the point of view of the reader/
spectator, it means that the experience of the poem is not iden-
tical with experience of what the poem is about; from the point
of view of the critic, it means the best art is that which most
perfectly fuses its matter with its form; from the point of view
of the practicing artist, it means fidelity to the concrete, the stuff
of sensation.

Eliot's view of what poetry ought to do is not that of the
symbolism of, say, Arthur Symons. His early criticism is involved
directly in the question which Symons described as a body-spirit
dualism—although Eliot considers it in language more like Pa-
ter's. He takes a stiff attitude, for instance, toward the "slightly
veiled and resonant abstractions . . . of Swinburne, or the moss-
iness of Mallarmé," but admires Pound because his verse is "al-
ways definite and concrete, because he has always a definite
emotion behind it."[114] He writes of the "laboured opacity" of
Mallarmé and attributes everything good in Verlaine to Rim-
baud's influence.[115] In the *Egoist* he writes that one of the ways
"by which contemporary verse has tried to escape the rhetorical,
the abstract, the moralizing, to recover (for that is its purpose)
the accents of direct speech, is to concentrate its attention upon
trivial or accidental or commonplace objects." He admires
Donne's "bracelet of bright hair" in which

the feeling and the material symbol preserve exactly their proper proportions. A poet of morbidly keen sensibilities but weak will might become absorbed in the hair to the exclusion of the original association which made it significant; a poet of imaginative or reflective power more than emotional power would endow the hair with ghostly or moralistic meaning. Donne sees the thing as it is.[116]

The "thing as it is" means, of course, the thing as Eliot believes it to be. In Bosschère, Eliot finds the same proportion: "there are none of these sidelong glances; he is directly in front of his object; it occupies the fovea."[117] For Eliot in his early years, art is grounded in the real. He admires Dostoevsky by contrast to Balzac precisely because of the place of the concrete in the former's art:

No one will deny to Dostoevsky an imagination at least equal to Balzac's; some of the things he tells are even more unimaginable. But the Imagination is utterly different, and put to utterly different uses. If you examine some of Dostoevsky's most successful, most imaginative "flights," you find them to be projections, continuations, of the actual, the observed: the final scene of the "Idiot," the hallucinations at the beginning of the same book and in "Crime and Punishment," even (what is more questionable) the interview of Ivan Karamazov with the Devil—Dostoevsky's point of departure is always a human brain in a human environment, and the "aura" is simply the continuation of the quotidian experience of the brain into seldom explored extremities of torture. Because most people are too unconscious of their own suffering to suffer much, this continuation appears fantastic. But Dostoevsky begins with the real world, as Beyle does; he only pursues reality farther in a certain direction. In Balzac the fantastic element is of another sort: it is not an extension of reality, it is an atmosphere thrown upon reality direct from the personality of the writer. We cannot look *at* it, as we can look at anything in Dostoevsky; we can only see things *in* it, we are plunged into it ourselves. . . .[118]

The point is that Eliot always wants the object to carry the feeling: and if that desire links him to the Imagists, it distinguishes him sharply from Symons or early Yeats. It also connects his view of modern poetry with that in *Gaston de Latour*.

Eliot's concern for the object is related to what he takes to be the material of poetry. The greatest artists, like Dostoevsky, perform an operation upon a "quotidian" reality: the material of art, Eliot says, is always actual life. It was Shakespeare's business, for instance, "to express the greatest emotional intensity of his time, based on whatever his time happened to think."[119] Similarly, Baudelaire's achievement was his ability to heighten to universality the quotidian environment of the modern city. Eliot, as we have seen, took seriously his own obligation to deal with his time. Yet his concern for the local in time and space went together with concern for the permanent and the universal. The 1919 essay on Charles Whibley notes as that critic's major shortcoming his inability to "detect unerringly the transition from work of eternal intensity to work that is merely beautiful, and from work that is beautiful to work that is merely charming." It is essential that a critic be able "not only to saturate himself in the spirit and the fashion of a time—the local flavor—but also to separate himself suddenly from it in appreciation of the highest creative work."[120] The paradox that a "great poet, in writing himself, writes his time" occupied Eliot throughout his critical career: in 1940, for instance, he made the analogous point that Yeats, "in becoming more Irish . . . became at the same time universal."[121] The historical sense itself, he wrote in "Tradition and the Individual Talent," is "a sense of the timeless as well as of the temporal and of the timeless and of the temporal together."[122]

The conflation of those two interests (in a poem's intensity and in its permanence) is familiar. Gaston de Latour's Ronsard performs the action that Eliot requires of the best poetry. Eliot's distinction between "eternal intensity" and "mere beauty" leads directly to his elevation of Baudelaire as "the greatest exemplar in *modern* poetry" "not merely in the use of imagery of common life, not merely in the use of imagery of the sordid life of a great metropolis, but in the elevation of such imagery to the *first intensity*—presenting it as it is, and yet making it represent something much more than itself."[123] Gaston's Ronsard, "transforming his own age and the world about him, presenting its everyday touch, the very trick one knew it by," did exactly that; and, furthermore, Pater's essay on Wordsworth substitutes for the more superficial distinction between "fancy" and "imagination," precisely what Eliot thought Whibley was unaware of,

> a far deeper and more vital distinction, with which indeed all true criticism more or less directly has to do, the distinction, namely, between higher and lower degrees of intensity in the poet's perception of his subject, and in his concentration of himself upon his work.[124]

Eliot's concern for the temporal and the timeless comes to him from the same source as Pater's. In the essay on Dryden (1921), he writes:

> Our valuation of poetry, in short, depends upon several considerations, upon the permanent and upon the mutable and upon the transitory. When we try to isolate the essentially poetic, we bring our pursuit in the end to something insignificant; our standards vary with every poet whom we consider.[125]

In the *Salon de 1846*, to which Eliot is indebted for other things, Baudelaire writes:

> Toutes les beautés contiennent, comme tous les phénomènes possibles, quelque chose d'éternel et quelque chose de transitoire,—d'absolu et de particulier. La beauté absolue et éternelle n'existe pas, ou plutôt elle n'est qu'une abstraction écremée à la surface générale des beautés diverses. (II, 493)

In a *Criterion* "Commentary" in 1932, Eliot used the word Baudelaire used in his more famous statement about the transitory and the eternal: "It is certainly not the artist's business to be wholly aware of the 'elements' of permanent and transitory in his own work. . . ."[126] In the first Charles Eliot Norton Lecture, he wrote that "the study of criticism, not as a sequence of random conjectures, but as readaptation, may also help us to draw some conclusions as to what is permanent or eternal in poetry, and what is merely the expression of the spirit of an age."[127]

Toutes . . . All forms of beauty, like all possible phenomena, have within them something eternal and something transitory—an absolute and a particular element. Absolute and eternal beauty does not exist, or rather it is nothing but an abstract notion, creamed off from the general surface of different types of beauty (C, 104-105).

An aesthetic view which holds together those two opposed "elements" must account for the transformation of one into the other. Pater's does, as we have seen: in Ronsard, as in Wordsworth,

> when the really poetical motive worked at all, it united, with absolute justice, the word and the idea; each, in the imaginative flame, becoming inseparably one with the other, by that fusion of matter and form, which is the characteristic of the highest poetical expression.

The instrument of the fusion is "that sort of creative language which carries the reality of what it depicts, directly, to the consciousness."[128] The proximity of Eliot's views to Pater's on this question can be measured in a comparison of the "objective correlative" (with its concern for the "exact equivalence" of sensory experience and evoked emotion) and Pater's comment on the choice of "one word for the one thing":

> One seems to detect the influence of a philosophic idea there—the idea of a natural economy, of some pre-existent adaptation, between a relative, somewhere in the world of thought, and its correlative, somewhere in the world of language—both alike, rather, somewhere in the mind of the artist, desiderative, expectant, inventive—meeting each other with the readiness of "soul and body reunited," in Blake's rapturous design. . . .[129]

Like Pater, Eliot found Baudelaire of extraordinary relevance in resolving the question of the relationship of the two elements of poetry. The important essays of 1921 turn insistently around the issue of fusing disparate elements in poetry, or transmuting the matter of poetry into what is permanent. The essay on Marvell strives to identify wit; that on Dryden considers "the transformation of the ridiculous into poetry";[130] "The Metaphysical Poets" discusses the "heterogeneity of material compelled into unity."[131] In those essays, Eliot is concerned with the quality of language, the element of surprise, and the precision of image. The essay on Marvell, which assumes that suggestiveness is a quality of "true poetry," develops an important contrast between Marvell and William Morris. Marvell's verses "have the suggestiveness of true poetry; and the verses of Morris, which are nothing if not an attempt to suggest, really suggest nothing; and we are inclined to infer that the suggestiveness is the aura around a bright clear centre, that you cannot have the aura alone." Marvell's "bright, hard precision" contrasts with the "mistiness" and "vagueness" of Morris;[132] the essay on Dryden, in a passage quoted below, makes the point again.[133] Baudelaire is present explicitly in Eliot's mind throughout his deliberations on these matters, and in each case he represents the fusion of opposites. On the one hand, "of the magniloquence, the deliberate exploitation of the possibilities of magnificence in language which Milton used and abused, there is also use and even abuse in the poetry of Baudelaire."[134] On the other hand, the "sort of wit" Eliot wanted to identify was to be found in Gautier and in Baudelaire and Laforgue. And it is Baudelaire who most splendidly exemplifies the ability to "make the ridiculous, or the trivial, great."[135] Baudelaire is thus implicated not only in Eliot's poetry but also in his conception of poetry.

The Baudelaire who moves so ubiquitously and so powerfully in Eliot's work has much in common with those earlier versions that I have been examining in the works of other English writers from Swinburne. He is to a considerable extent a traditional figure, and he is a connection, as Eliot suggested later in his career, between the generations of English poets. When Eliot took him up, he must have recognized him; and the value that he found in him both for his own poetry and for his own criticism, must have been partly that of the powerful role he had already played in the debate about modernism in English poetry. Like Swinburne—and Pater and Wilde and the others—Eliot had repudiations to make, and though, ironically, what he needed to repudiate were these very writers, his means of repudiation had been devised by them. Like Swinburne, he used the French tradition to fence with the English; and, like him, he saw Baudelaire as the best representative of the modern French writers.

But Eliot's use of Baudelaire's criticism is as personal as his use of the poetry, and *The Waste Land* drafts make it possible to look closely at a moment in which Eliot draws poetic sustenance from Baudelaire's criticism. The material Eliot sent to John Quinn provides reasons and rewards for an examination of his reading and writing during the difficult year in which *The Waste Land* took shape. The poem he published brought to a head the movement of his writing from boredom to horror; the poem he began with, however, touched both the boredom and the horror with a comic spirit that links *The Waste Land* with his earlier poetry and Aristophanic fragments, and which is shown by his critical writing of 1921 to have drawn support from Baudelaire.

Between the time he told Quinn—on 5 November 1919[136]—that he wanted to get to work on his new poem, and the year after its publication, Eliot's critical writing diminished drastically. During 1918 and 1919 he had written prodigiously, piling up more than fifty articles. In 1921, by contrast, he wrote only nine. Of these, four were the chatty "London Letters" for *Dial*. The remarkable "Notes on Current Letters" appeared that spring in the first number of Wyndham Lewis's *Tyro*; "Prose and Verse" was written in April for the *Chapbook* debate on that topical subject. Only the superb *Times Literary Supplement* articles on Marvell, Dryden, and the metaphysical poets, which I have just discussed, were at all formal.[137] All these essays share four converging centers of interest: they continue Eliot's icy review of contemporary criticism, launch his attempt to re-evaluate the standing of seventeenth-century poets on the basis of their fusion of the disparate elements in poetry, declare his interest in comedy—and give evidence of the close attention with which he was reading Baudelaire. The focus on comedy narrows Eliot's concerns of 1918 and 1919: what he then saw as issues central to the discussion of poetry in general, he now saw as central to the discussion of comedy.

The *Tyro* article alone provides sufficient caution against seeing those interests as unrelated or even separate from one another. The general heading of the page—"Notes on Current Letters"—claims relevance to contemporary matters, although the page names not one contemporary English writer. It has the diagnostic and prescriptive tone: it describes disease and it claims, with more defiant muscle than Meredith's essay, that comedy is the specific. The page includes, under its general title, a short, abrasive article entitled "The Romantic Englishman, the Comic Spirit, and the Function of Criticism," and a provocative, blunt note called "The Lesson of Baudelaire." Those threads may seem to be dissimilar, but Eliot draws them into a tight knot. The lesson he proposes in the first "Note" is one he acknowledges, tangentially, in the second. The Romantic Englishman, Eliot says, "is in a bad way." He expires for want of a "myth," a corporately held moral character:

Sir Tunbelly Clumsy, Sir Giles Overreach, Squire Western, and Sir Sampson Legend, who was lately so competently revived by Mr. Byford at the Phoenix, are different contributions by distinguished mythmakers to the chief myth which the Englishman has built about himself. The myth that a man makes has transformations according as he sees himself as hero or villain, as young or old, but it is essentially the same myth; Tom Jones is not the same person, but he is the same myth, as Squire Western; Midshipman Easy is part of the same myth; Falstaff is elevated above the myth to dwell on Olympus, more than a national character. Tennyson's broad-shouldered genial Englishman is a cousin of Tunbelly Clumsy; and Mr. Chesterton, when he drinks a glass of beer (if he does drink beer), and Mr. Squire, when he plays a game of cricket (if he does play cricket), contribute their little bit. This myth has seldom been opposed or emulated; Byron, a great mythmaker did, it is true, set up the Giaour, a myth for the whole of Europe. But in our time, barren of myths—when in France there is no successor to the *honnête homme qui ne se pique de rien*, and René, and the dandy, but only a deliberate school of mythopoeic nihilism— in our time the English myth is pitiably diminished. There is that degenerate descendant, the modern John Bull, the John Bull who usually alternates with Britannia in the cartoons of *Punch*, a John Bull composed of Podsnap and Bottomley. And John Bull becomes less and less a force. . . .

The myth, Eliot says in this article, is supplied by the imagination and it has a crucial relationship to the actual. The characters of the "serious" stage of the time, he says, fail to give it because they are all abstraction—they are made of abstract qualities and "we are supposed to respond [to them] with the proper abstract emotions." But the performers of music hall and cinema—Eliot names Little Tich and Chaplin, among others—can give the myth a "partial realization," can do, partly, what the seventeenth-century theater did. The "myth," by contrast with the pale abstractions of the serious stage, is derived from the actual: "it is a point of view, transmuted to importance; it is made by the transformation of the actual by imaginative genius." The serious stage of the time, Eliot says, satisfies nothing, but the myth satisfies Englishmen "with a craving for the ideal": "Man desires to see

himself on the stage, more admirable, more forceful, more vil-
lainous, more comical, more despicable—and much more else—
than he actually is." The relationship of the purging myth to the
actual is the important thing, and Eliot describes it in paradoxes
appropriate to a member of what he called elsewhere the "in-
teresting and energetic race" of Tyros:[138] "The myth is based
upon reality, but does not alter it." The relationship is that of
comic transformation. It is a moral relationship, because the
myth is a measuring standard, and it is criticism, because it shows
"life in the light of the imagination." "The myth is imagination
and it is also criticism," Eliot says, "and the two are one." In this
consideration of the comic spirit, Eliot is dead serious: the music
hall and the cinema can do what the serious stage cannot. They
can supply what he calls a "criticism of humanity" and so they
can enable him to say that "What is sometimes called 'vulgarity'
is . . . one thing that has not been vulgarised." The famous "Lon-
don Letter" comment on Marie Lloyd makes exactly the same
points. In "giving expression to the life of [her] audience," Eliot
says, "in raising it to a kind of art," she performed a moral
function.[139] The morality and the criticism of the kind of comedy
Eliot approves here come from the tension between the "ideal"
and the "actual," from the transmuted point of view. " 'Vol-
pone,' " Eliot says in the "Notes," "does not merely show that
wickedness is punished; it criticises humanity by intensifying
wickedness." The article on "The Lesson of Baudelaire," which
has no apparent relationship to the note on the comic spirit,
generalizes the point. Eliot comments on developments in Paris:

> Whatever value there may be in Dada depends upon the
> extent to which it is a moral criticism of French literature
> and French life. All first-rate poetry is occupied with mo-
> rality: this is the lesson of Baudelaire. More than any poet
> of his time, Baudelaire was aware of what most mattered:
> the problem of good and evil. What gives the French Sev-
> enteenth Century literature its solidity is the fact that it had
> its morals, that it had a coherent point of view. Romanticism
> endeavoured to form another Morals. . . . But they have not
> sufficient coherence. . . . Baudelaire . . . aimed . . . to arrive
> at a point of view toward good and evil.

During this year Eliot made very similar pedagogical use of
Baudelaire and of the music hall. In the "London Letter" for

June, Eliot returns to discussion of the national character of the comic and, as in the *Tyro* "Notes," sees the attraction of the comic in its clash of opposites. In Lancashire music-hall, the confrontation is that between a strong performer and a strong audience. (In terms of the "Notes," that would be the fruitful conflict of the "ideal" and the "real.") "The Lancashire comedian," he says, "is at his best when . . . making a direct set, pitting himself, against a suitable audience." In what he called the "fierce talent" of Nellie Wallace, Eliot sees exemplified the "mordant, ferocious, and personal" Lancashire wit. The comedy of revue performers, he says, has a different quality, an "element of *bizarrerie*." Ethel Levey, for instance, shows "an extremely modern type of beauty. Hers is not broad farce, but a fascinating inhuman grotesquerie. . . . It is not a comedy of mirth." Having done with music-hall, Eliot turns to caricature. He distinguishes two kinds: one is serious and traditional; one is merely funny. Bateman's work, he says, is both: sometimes "his drawings descend to the pure and insignificant funniness without seriousness which appeals to the readers of *Punch*; while others continue the best tradition from Rowlandson and Cruikshank. They have some of the old English ferocity." Wyndham Lewis, whom Eliot contrasts approvingly with Bateman, aims consciously and deliberately "to restore this peculiarly English caricature and to unite it with serious work in paint." In all of these remarks, Eliot makes it perfectly clear that he takes the comic seriously; that, in fact, he sees comedy as only insignificantly related to what is funny; that he considers it to represent "an extremely modern type of beauty"; and that he sees in comedy a vital relationship between the real and the transmuted.

That these comments are related to Eliot's reading of Baudelaire is clear, but in the June "London Letter" he more explicitly yokes his interest in the comic to his interest in Baudelaire. He opens his remarks on caricature with these lines from *De L'Essence du Rire*, an essay, he says, "(*qui vaut bien celui de Bergson*)": "Pour trouver du comique féroce et très féroce, il faut passer la Manche et visiter les royaumes brumeux du spleen . . . le signe distinctif de ce genre de comique était la violence." Nellie Wallace, Lancashire wit, Cruikshank, Rowlandson, Hogarth, and Wyndham

Pour trouver . . . To find the ferocious and ultra-ferocious comic, we must cross the Channel and pay a visit to the misty kingdoms of the spleen (C, 154).

Lewis thus embody the national comic spirit defined from across the Channel by Baudelaire. But Eliot's reflections on the comic have more in common with Baudelaire's than merely those borrowed and acknowledged adjectives. In *Le Rire*, Baudelaire considers together both caricature and theatrical comedy and he sees them in the light of his "point of view toward good and evil." Eliot's distinction between the idealizing art of the music-hall (the "Notes") and the bizarre or grotesque art of the revue, for instance, as well as his reproof of Bateman for slipping into the "insignificant," have interesting equivalents in Baudelaire's essay. *Le Rire* distinguishes "le comique absolu" (the fantastic, the grotesque, which shows "créations fabuleuses, les êtres dont la raison, la légitimation ne peut pas être tirée du code du sens commun") and the "comique ordinaire, que j'appellerai comique significatif" (II, 535). The distinction is based upon consideration of the relationship of the comic art to the actual:

> Le comique significatif est un langage plus clair, plus facile à comprendre pour le vulgaire, et surtout plus facile à analyser, son élément étant visiblement double: l'art et l'idée morale; mais le comique absolu, se rapprochant beaucoup plus de la nature, se présente sous une espèce *une*, et qui veut être saisie par intuition. (II, 535-36)

The significant comic artist is an idealizer: "Le comique est, au point de vue artistique, une imitation; le grotesque, une création. Le comique est une imitation mêlée d'une certaine faculté créatrice, c'est-à-dire d'une idéalité artistique" (II, 535). It is the significant comic which he associates with both France and England, though the English version of it is intensified into the ferocity we have seen him describe: "En exagérant et poussant aux dernières limites les conséquences du comique significatif,

créations . . . fabulous creations, beings for whose existence no explanation drawn from ordinary common sense is possible (C, 151).
Le comique . . . The significative comic speaks a language that is clearer, easier for the common man to understand, and especially easier to analyse, its element being obviously double: art and the moral idea; but the absolute comic, coming as it does much closer to nature, appears as a unity that must be grasped intuitively (C, 152).
Le comique est . . . From the artistic point of view, the comic is an imitation; the grotesque, a creation. The comic is an imitation mixed with a certain degree of creative capacity, or, in other words, of artistic ideality (C, 151).
En exagérant . . . By exaggerating the consequences of the significative comic and driving them to their extreme limit, we get the ferocious comic (C, 153-54).

on obtient le comique féroce . . ." (II, 537). The significant comic
is analogous to "l'école littéraire intéressée" (literature of in-
volvement) and the absolute comic to "l'école de l'art pour l'art"
(II, 535); the latter, Baudelaire says, is the purer. Significant
comedy, which comprises the moral element, is closely linked to
the actual.

Those Baudelairean considerations of the comic were prob-
ably not new to Eliot in 1921. He told E.J.H. Greene that he had
taken up Baudelaire for the second time in 1919 or 1920 (he
had forgotten which) and that he had not put him down again
until 1930.[140] There is reason to think that the earlier of these
dates is the more accurate. Eliot's essay on Ben Jonson, published
as the leading article in the *TLS* for 13 November 1919 (the
month of his earliest reference to *The Waste Land*), shows him
thinking about comic modes in terms suggestive of the essay
from which he quotes in his reflections on caricature. The essay
on Jonson is preeminently concerned with questions of *genre*.
Normal classifications of tragedy and comedy, Eliot says, are
adequate to a dramatic literature of "more rigid form and treat-
ment," but they cannot describe a drama as varied as the Eliz-
abethan. In discussion of a passage from *Catiline*, Eliot turns
over the terms: the scene he considers is "no more comedy than
it is tragedy, and the 'satire' is merely a medium for the essential
emotion." The following passage considers Jonson's "satiric
comedy":

> Jonson's drama is only incidentally satire, because it is only
> incidentally a criticism upon the actual world. It is not satire
> in the way in which the work of Swift or the work of Molière
> may be called satire: that is, it does not find its source in
> any precise emotional attitude or precise intellectual criti-
> cism of the actual world. It is satire perhaps as the work of
> Rabelais is satire; certainly not more so. The important thing
> is that if fiction can be divided into creative fiction and crit-
> ical fiction, Jonson's is creative. . . . Certainly, one sense in
> which the term "critical" may be applied to fiction is a sense
> in which the term might be used of a method antithetical
> to Jonson's. It is the method of "Education Sentimentale."
> The characters of Jonson, of Shakespeare, perhaps of all
> the greatest drama, are drawn in positive and simple out-
> lines. They may be filled in. . . . But Frédéric Moreau is not
> made in that way. He is constructed partly by negative def-

inition, built up by a great number of observations. We can-
not isolate him from the environment in which we find him;
it may be an environment which is or can be universalized;
nevertheless it, and the figure in it, consist of very many
observed particular facts, the actual world. Without this
world the figure dissolves. The ruling faculty is a critical
perception, a commentary upon experienced feeling and
sensation. If this is true of Flaubert, it is true in a higher
degree of Molière than of Jonson. The broad farcical lines
of Molière may seem to be the same drawing as Jonson's.
But Molière—say in Alceste or Monsieur Jourdain—is crit-
icising the actual; the reference to the actual world is more
direct. And having a more tenuous reference, the work of
Jonson is much less directly satirical.[141]

That passage displays some of Eliot's recently enunciated ideas
on creativity and criticism (compare, for instance, the essay on
Henry James),[142] and it contains a description of the method of
"Prufrock" ("constructed partly by negative definition, built up
by a great number of observations"), but its chief interest in the
present context is its relationship to Baudelaire's essay on laugh-
ter. For one thing, the distinction Eliot is making here is the one
he makes in his reflections upon music-hall comedy, that between
a comedy based on the actual and one not directly so based. That
recalls the distinction made in Baudelaire's essay, and so, inter-
estingly, do Eliot's illustrations. Rabelais and Jonson, he says,
brush the borders of satire, but because of their distant relation
to the actual they are not dominantly satiric. In the description
of French comedy that directly precedes his comment upon the
ferocious English kind, Baudelaire writes: "Rabelais, qui est le
grand maître français en grotesque [that is, in absolute comic],
garde au milieu de ses plus énormes fantaisies quelque chose
d'utile et de raisonnable." Molière, Eliot says, like the earlier
Frenchman, uses both kinds of comedy, but in reverse propor-
tion. Baudelaire writes: "En France . . . le comique est générale-

Rabelais . . . Rabelais, who is the great French master of the grotesque, even
in the midst of his most colossal fantasies preserves a semblance of the useful
and the reasonable (C, 154).

En France . . . In France . . . the comic is usually significative comic. Molière
was the highest French expression of this type . . . too little read, unfortunately,
and too rarely performed, amongst others those of the *Malade imaginaire* and
the *Bourgeois Gentilhomme* (C, 154).

ment significatif. Molière fut dans ce genre la meilleure expres-
sion française," but he adds that it is in Molière that one finds
French examples of the absolute comic, particularly in some
pieces that are "malheureusement trop peu lus et trop peu joués,
entre autres ceux du *Malade imaginaire* et du *Bourgeois gentil-
homme*" (II, 537).

The point so far is this: that in the period during which he
did most of the work on *The Waste Land*, Eliot was preoccupied
with the nature of comedy and its various kinds, and that his
thinking on the subject was sparked and fuelled by his reading
of Baudelaire (whose widely recognized contribution to Eliot's
long poem is the provision of imagery for the boredom and the
horror). Two of the preoccupations of 1921, Baudelaire and the
comic, consistently join in Eliot's criticism. They necessarily in-
volve the third, his concern with the function of criticism, because
comedy, as Eliot sees it, *is* criticism. The more literary essays on
Marvell, Dryden, and the metaphysical poets, which appeared
in the *Times Literary Supplement* that year, show the degree to
which some of the same considerations bore upon Eliot's in-
spection of those poets.

Little Tich is quite a different case from Andrew Marvell, but
the "point of view" of their critic is consistent. There are obvious
similarities between Eliot's description of what is best in Lan-
cashire wit and his attempt to fix that quality in metaphysical
poetry for which he finds no adequate word in the modern
critical lexicon and for which he revives the term "wit." The sort
of wit he wants to identify, Eliot writes, is "this alliance of levity
and seriousness (by which the seriousness is intensified)." It is
always more than mere funniness, though it is clearly connected
with what is funny. Dryden, like Bateman, sometimes forgets
the point: "In Dryden wit becomes almost fun, and thereby loses
some contact with reality; becomes pure fun, which French wit
almost never is." What prevents the wit of these poets from
descending into mere funniness is its character of criticism: "it
implies a constant inspection and criticism of experience."[143]
And, like the "significant comic" of Baudelaire, the wit of the
metaphysical poets involves some idealization: Eliot admires Dry-
den's "unique merit . . . in his ability to make the small into the
great, the prosaic into the poetic, the trivial into the magnificent."
Because he can do that, Dryden is "much nearer to the master
of comic creation than to Pope. As in Jonson, the effect is far

from laughter; the comic is the material, the result is poetry."
Eliot's use of Baudelaire as a bench-mark for wit is well known:
the passage needs repetition here only to show its perfect com-
patibility with his other associations of comedy and *le roi des poètes*.
In the essay on Dryden, he writes:

> Nor is Dryden unchallenged in his supreme ability to
> make the ridiculous, or the trivial, great.
>> *Avez-vous observé que maints cercueils de vielles*
>> *Sont presque aussi petits que celui d'un enfant?*
> Those lines are the work of a man whose verse is as mag-
> nificent as Dryden's, and who could see profounder possi-
> bilities in wit, and in violently joined images, than ever were
> in Dryden's mind.[144]

Eliot mentions Baudelaire in every one of his publications of
1921 except two of the "London Letters," and in each case he
mentions him as able to hold the trivial and the great together
in one statement.

Eliot gave other indications, while he was constructing *The
Waste Land*, of his interest in the comic. He wrote to Quinn that
he had seen the "latter part" of *Ulysses* and found it "truly mag-
nificent," and the drafts of his poem show the mark of Joyce's
work.[145] In the letter in which he queried a number of Pound's
criticisms, Eliot noted that he was "Trying to read Aristophane."
Pound's reply indicates that in spite of depression and illness
Eliot was still concerned with a comic work that had occupied
him since Harvard: Pound told him to "forward the 'Bolo' to
Joyce if you think it won't unhinge his somewhat sabbatarian
mind," though, he added, "On the hole he might be saved the
shock, shaved the sock."[146] Bernard Bergonzi speculates that
"Bolo" includes the "excellent bits of scholarly ribaldry" that
Lewis failed to print in *Blast*, possibly because of his fastidious-
ness about word-endings. His conclusion that "Eliot's talent for
light verse was later directed into more universally acceptable
channels with *Old Possum's Book of Practical Cats*"[147] probably over-
estimates the lightness with which Eliot was handling the comic
in the year of *The Waste Land*'s composition.

The Waste Land drafts reflect his serious interest in the comic.

Avez-vous . . . Have you ever noticed that many old women's coffins are almost
as small as little children's? (S, 197).

Three important sections of the manuscript and one of the longer appended poems, "The Death of the Duchess," none of which was included in the first edition, show his attempt to incorporate his version of the comic spirit into his vision of the horror. The passages do not "descend to the pure and insignificant funniness without seriousness which appeals to readers of Punch"; they have the ferocity of the traditional English comic. They show how in the process of revision Eliot's poem was steered away from a particular close connection with "the actual." They present man and woman "more forceful, more comical, more despicable"; they aim at the transmutation of the actual which Eliot saw as the distinguishing mark of the best comedy.

Eliot's concern with the transmutation of the actual is explicit in the three stanzas which open the deleted sea-passage. (The first is cited above, p. 344.) The others continue:

> Even the drunken ruffian who descends
> Illicit backstreet stairs, to reappear,
> For the derision of his sober friends,
> Staggering, or limping with a comic gonorrhea,
>
> From his trade with wind and sea and snow, as they
> Are, he is, with "much seen and much endured,"
> Foolish, impersonal, innocent or gay,
> Liking to be shaved, combed, scented, manucured.[148]

The opening four lines of the passage suggest "Le Voyage," as we have seen. The second and third stanzas recall "Le Vin des Chiffonniers," a poem in which Baudelaire is similarly occupied with the transmutation of a detail of street life:

> Souvent, à la clarté rouge d'un réverbère
> Dont le vent bat la flamme et tourmente le verre,
> Au coeur d'un vieux faubourg, labyrinthe fangeux
> Où l'humanité grouille en ferments orageux,
>
> On voit un chiffonnier qui vient, hochant la tête,
> Butant, et se cognant aux murs comme un poète,

Souvent . . . Often, in the red glare of a streetlamp, with the wind flailing its flame and racking the glass panes, in the heart of some old suburb, a slimy labyrinth in which mankind seethes in tempestuous ferments, you'll see a ragpicker coming along, wagging his head, stumbling and banging himself against the walls like a poet, and, heedless of the stool-pigeons, his thralls, unburden his heart of his world-shaking intentions (S, 95).

Et, sans prendre souci des mouchards, ses sujets,
Épanche tout son coeur en glorieux projets. (I, 106)

In his introduction to the *Intimate Journals*, Eliot quotes four of
those lines to illustrate his claim that Baudelaire "gave new pos-
sibilities to poetry in a new stock of imagery of contemporary
life"; they introduce, he says, "something new, and something
universal in modern life." He goes on to make his famous com-
ment upon Baudelaire:

> It is not merely in the use of imagery of common life, not
> merely in the use of imagery of the sordid life of a great
> metropolis, but in the elevation of such imagery to the *first
> intensity*—presenting it as it is, and yet making it represent
> something much more than itself—that Baudelaire has cre-
> ated a mode of release and expression for other men.[149]

Eliot's admiration of this quality in Baudelaire reminds us that
the echo in his deleted sea-passage is not insignificant, since he
intends here to turn even that "ridiculous or trivial" gonorrhea
into something great. Transformation is the subject of the verses,
which, detached by a row of asterisks as well as by their form
from the body of the sea-passage, serve as a kind of instruction
to the reader. In a passage " 'rather inspired' " by the Ulysses
Canto of the *Inferno* and "influenced by Tennyson's *Ulysses*"[150]—
and which invites comparison with Homer himself, with *Le Vo-
yage*, *Heart of Darkness*, and *The Ancient Mariner*, to name a few—
Eliot is concerned to transmute to importance an oily watercask
and a putrid stench of canned baked beans. He counts on the
mythic parallel and the allusions to bestow significance. In "The
Death of the Duchess"[151] he aims to universalize the particular
by different means, simply pluralizing it into the general. Part
I tells us twice that it describes the "inhabitants of Hampstead,"
and it begins four of its first nine lines with "They," substituting
places for persons and movement for actions. Having given that
easily generalized life as his subject, Eliot shifts abruptly to the
"you and me" who will occupy the main body of the poem, which
in Part II moves increasingly into the intimate imaginings of a
speaker who comes to resemble Prufrock (as Pound noted) and
the speaker of Browning's "My Last Duchess," as Pound may
not have noticed. Both passages evidence a fiercely comic inten-
tion. In the first, Eliot sets the ordinarily heroic against the em-

phatically trivial; in the second, he sets the eternal *ennui* of the inhabitants of Hampstead against a jarring jingle.[152]

Eliot's comic drawing is clearest in the other two major cancellations in the drafts. The opening section of "The Burial of the Dead,"[153] cancelled by Eliot himself, has obvious affinities with *Ulysses* (which Mr. Donavan, little Ben Levin the tailor, Steve, and the final walk at sunrise may be intended to convey), and it recounts an odyssey which is a clear parallel to the deleted opening of "Death by Water." Its protagonist lists, with a mechanical energy, the events of a night out which include drink, food, cigars, a show, a brothel, a brush with the law, and more than one kind of violence. He finds it all terribly funny, and Eliot intended him at various stages to have "a good laugh" or "a couple of laughs" or a "real" laugh. Indeed, the passage is packed with matter for raucous laughter: old Tom, boiled to the eyes, blind; a foot in the drum and didn't the girl squeal; a manipulated madam, an intimidated policeman; and Mr. Donavan, who told the girls to cheer up and then put his foot through the window; not to mention the music and the show. Of course, it is not funny; but it is a grotesque representation of its protagonist's idea of what is funny. (Nor did Myrtle think it was funny, who intended to give it all up and retire to a farm; but little Ben Levin the tailor, who had read George Meredith, *he* probably knew about the comic spirit.) The passage is caricature, and it is Hogarthian, fierce, but its clichés remain untransformed. It has not the shaping refrain of the pub scene in "A Game of Chess," nor the parodic point of view of the verses about Fresca, nor the observing eye of the passage about the typist and the clerk. It is, like so many other parts of the poem, an exercise in comic deformation (consider Trixie and Stella, for instance, those two mutilated romantic heroines), but it does not succeed, in Eliot's terms, in idealizing the actual it describes. If it had, *The Waste Land* could have opened with the sound of hollow laughter. "The light of Athene over the head of Achilles illuminates the birth of Greek Tragedy," Meredith tells us. "But Comedy rolled in shouting under the divine protection of the Son of the Wine-jar."[154]

The proposed opening for "The Fire Sermon" succeeds,[155] as the other does not, in extracting its matter from cliché. If Marie Lloyd's comedy depended upon knowing exactly what a middle-aged char would have in her handbag, this piece of wit depends upon knowing exactly what a *mondaine* would have in her mind.

Fresca's sensibility is, like the character of Frédéric Moreau, built up by a great number of observations, and it cannot be separated from its environment. The ruling faculty here, as in the method Eliot describes in the essay on Jonson, is "a critical perception, a commentary upon experienced feeling and sensation." Fresca's language, her gestures, her habits are all as precise as the polished tray or the soothing chocolate. The passage is a neat pair to the cancelled opening of "The Burial of the Dead," detailing in mockingly fastidious couplets the intimate life of the "more sinned against than sinning" protagonist. The rough social, sexual, and physical life of old Tom's friend, rendered in slice-of-life detail, balances the precious social, sexual, and biological life of Fresca. He drinks a bottle of fizz with old Tom and old Jane, listens to Mrs. Fay sing, and wheedles a meal out of Myrtle; she sips soothing chocolate, dips for pathos into Richardson, and sends evidence of a carefully worked-up *ennui* to a friend. "For varying forms, one definition's right," Eliot writes in this section, "Unreal emotions, and real appetite." Pound complained about the verse and ultimately drew a line through the whole scene, thus disposing of a passage in which Eliot's comic transmutation succeeded, in which are audible both "the rattle of the bones" and "the chuckle spread from ear to ear."

What distinguishes the Fresca passage and "The Death of the Duchess" from the unsuccessful opening to "The Burial of the Dead" is a tension in the first two between the subject and the treatment. In the elaborately conceited imagery of "The Death of the Duchess," Eliot forces interest out of the boredom; in the passage about Fresca the form, like the Lancashire comic, makes a direct set, pits itself against, its subject. In the opening section of "The Burial of the Dead," only the dimly audible Odyssean allusions suggest a perspective from which to judge the rowdy wanderer. It seems likely that Eliot was aiming to incorporate a myth of a different kind: the point of view derived from the actual, which is in itself a criticism.

The removal of the opening lines of "The Burial of the Dead" and the Fresca passage considerably alters the architecture of the whole. The poem would, with their inclusion, have moved toward the encounter of the typist and the clerk by way of descriptions of both the raw brutality of a swaggering male character and of the etiolated sensibility of a self-deceiving female. Tiresias would thus have seen the caricatured sexes joined in the mechanical coupling which remains in the poem, and the convergence would seriously have changed the impression, given in the first edition, of "a centre of gravity nowhere explicitly located."[156] Furthermore, what is in the finished poem extremely general until the lovely woman stoops to folly was, in the drafts, much more specific. The sexual despair of the revised poem detaches itself gradually from the generalized desolation, while in the manuscript version it was announced immediately in the visit of the too-drunk man to the motherly prostitute. The larger engagement with the actual in the manuscript version of the poem had another effect: what the first edition finds analogies for in all of the dimensions of time, the unrevised version rooted more firmly in the contemporary.

The revised poem does not, of course, abandon the comic spirit. What the systematic revisions did to the poem, however, was to shift the balance: the poem as it came finally to be structured confines the treatment of the actual, but it does not eliminate it. In the pub scene, the nerves scene, and the typist's agon, Eliot is clearly working with the same kind of material he uses in the cancelled sections of the drafts. The revisions trim that material and surround it with the more generalized and mythic. In the published poem, what is specific and actual is made exemplary and illustrative—and to the degree that the revisions tipped the poem toward the mythic they tipped it away from its comic material.

In a lecture given soon after the publication of *The Waste Land* drafts, Helen Gardner noted that in the two great works of 1922, *The Waste Land* and *Ulysses*, "The comic acceptance of the conditions of life in this world and the tragic acceptance confront each other."[157] The drafts of *The Waste Land* give reason to think that that confrontation was a near thing. Furthermore, considered in the light of his critical writing of 1921, they reveal one of Eliot's most important Baudelairean lessons: in his essay on *Le Rire*, Baudelaire summarizes his "propositions principales, qui sont comme une espèce de théorie du rire."

Le rire est satanique, il est donc profondément humain. Il est dans l'homme la conséquence de l'idée de sa propre

propositions . . . principal propositions which form a kind of theory of laughter. Laughter is satanic; it is therefore profoundly human. In man it is the consequence of his idea of his own superiority; and in fact, since laughter is essentially human it is essentially contradictory, that is to say it is at one and the same time a sign of infinite greatness and of infinite wretchedness (C, 147-48).

supériorité; et, en effet, comme le rire est essentiellement humain, il est essentiellement contradictoire, c'est-à-dire qu'il est à la fois signe d'une grandeur infinie et d'une misère infinie. . . . (II, 532)

Laughter, Baudelaire says, issues from the double nature of man, from "l'accident d'une chute ancienne" (II, 528). While the pared-down version of *The Waste Land* finds other forms for the deleted satanic laughter of the original opening section and concentrates a stronger light on its universalized bony chuckle and on its universalized calling of time on the garrulous and the backbiting, it makes no less insistent than does the first version of the poem the link between the comic and the damnable. One lesson of Baudelaire, which is reflected in *The Waste Land*, is that the comic represents one means of arriving at "a point of view toward good and evil."

*   *   *

Eliot wrote three essays on Baudelaire: "The Lesson of Baudelaire" (1921), " 'Poet and Saint . . .' " (1927), which was a review of Arthur Symons's *Baudelaire: Prose and Poetry*, and the introduction to Christopher Isherwood's translation of *Les Journaux Intimes* (1930).[158] He also wrote four pieces in which Baudelaire figures importantly, although not solely: a review of Peter Quennell's *Baudelaire and the Symbolists*,[159] the lecture *From Poe to Valéry* (1946), and introductions to Joseph Chiari's *Contemporary French Poetry* (1952) and *Symbolism from Poe to Valéry* (1956). The two kinds of work have precisely antithetical purposes: in the essays, Eliot aims, explicitly, to "distinguish the man from his influence . . . to detach him from the associations of those English poets who first admired him";[160] in the other pieces, he attaches Baudelaire to what *he* sees as his influence and places him in what *he* sees as his tradition. The essays, which issue from the period of Eliot's closest attention to Baudelaire, are plainly personal, and they show the intense relevance to Eliot's own poetry of the Frenchman whom he was casting as originator. The other pieces—except the review of Quennell's book, which is in some ways a preliminary to the introduction to the *Journaux Intimes*—are more distant, the retriangulating backward glance of the literary historian. Together, the essays and the other pieces ef-

l'accident . . . the accident of an ancient fall (C, 143).

fected an astonishing appropriation and revision. They made it seem to most readers, as to Bernard Bergonzi, that this much commented-on, translated, interpreted, and imitated French poet owed his English reputation almost entirely to Eliot's attention;[161] they made it seem, as to William Chace, that this nineteenth-century Frenchman, genuinely the *semblable* of the modern English-American writer, could "figure darkly as a comrade to [Eliot's] own figures of great passive suffering and tortured knowledge";[162] and they made it as orthodox and ordinary in England as it had by now become in France to derive the history of modern poetry from *Les Fleurs du Mal*. What Eliot wrote on Baudelaire has a commanding place in the identifying myth of modernism.

From the beginning, Eliot's Baudelaire essays are iconoclastic, aiming at precise reversals of the received view. They make the "godfather as it were of the modern fleshly school," the poet who had symbolized the aesthetic attack on utilitarianism, into a "lesson"—the didacticism is of course pointed—that art is not for art's sake. "All first-rate poetry is occupied with morality: this is the lesson of Baudelaire," Eliot writes in his *Tyro* essay, in which he yokes Baudelaire together with Dada, brings him intensely up to date, and makes him the standard for judgment of the modern. Eliot's earliest argument—that technique and morals are knitted into one knot—is basic to all of his Baudelaire essays, and it leads him, in all of them, to an act of dissociation. In his first essay he dismisses both "the academic poets of to-day (Georgian et caetera)" and "the poets who consider themselves most opposed to Georgianism, and who know a little French." One group is morally and technically timid, the other morally superficial, capable of imagining "the Last Judgement only as a lavish display of Bengal lights." But Eliot's Baudelaire is distinct from all of these, as he is distinct from the Romantics of both France and England, standing in isolation as a kind of "deformed Dante" (Eliot borrows the phrase from Barbey d'Aurevilly), who "aimed with more intellect *plus* intensity, and without much help from his predecessors, to arrive at a point of view toward good and evil." The opening phrase of Eliot's second essay on Baudelaire, his review of Symons's translations, is telling: "First," he writes, "I must protest."

Protest is Eliot's instrument of definition. In "Poet and Saint . . . ," continuing the dissociation that he had begun in his *Tyro* article, he identifies the line of descent of Baudelaire's translator, opposing that to the poet's own. Symons, Eliot writes, derives from Wilde, is related to Lionel Johnson, has connections with Huysmans, suggests "the remoter spectre of Pater," and is grounded in Swinburne. These, he says, are the poets of "vice." Baudelaire's connections, however, were not with Huysmans and the decadents, but with wholly different generations:

> The important fact about Baudelaire is that he was essentially a Christian, born out of his due time, and a classicist, born out of his due time. In his verse technique, he is nearer to Racine than to Mr Symons; in his sensibility, he is near to Dante and not without a sympathy with Tertullian.

And, since "we are nearer to Racine than is Mr Symons," Baudelaire is connected to us. "Baudelaire as he is now understood," Eliot writes, "*notre* Baudelaire," is sharply distinct from the Baudelaire of the nineteenth century. In his last essay, the introduction to the *Intimate Journals*, Eliot develops the same contrast, shifting Baudelaire from an association with Swinburne, by whom, he says, it was his "misfortune to be first and extravagantly advertised," into alliance with T. E. Hulme, of whose doctrine of Original Sin he "would have approved."

Eliot's reversals are of course intentional: this Baudelaire opposes art for art's sake and the isolation of the aesthetic. "He was a great poet; he was a great critic. And he was also a man with a profound attitude toward life."[163] In his review of Peter Quennell's book, Eliot pushes the point:

> The difficulty is that the minor men can be wholly, and even more than generously, confined within what can beyond question be called literary criticism; whereas any adequate criticism of Baudelaire must inevitably lead the critic outside of *literary* criticism. For it will not do to label Baudelaire; he is not merely, or in my opinion even primarily, the *artist*.
> . . .

The "legacy and lesson" of Baudelaire, Eliot says in the "Introduction," comes from his conduct of his life, his attitude to himself, and from the fact that he is "a greater man than was imagined, though perhaps not such a perfect poet." The "true claim of Baudelaire as an artist is not that he found a superficial form, but that he was searching for a form of life."

It is Baudelaire's concern with "the real problem of good and evil" that is the thread through Eliot's three essays. In the first, Eliot sees it as the product of personal struggle: he aimed "without much help from his predecessors, to arrive at a point of view toward good and evil." In "Poet and Saint . . . ," he admires what Du Bos called Baudelaire's "incoercible besoin de prière au sein même de l'incredulité." Baudelaire was, he writes, "*naturaliter* Christian": "And being the kind of Christian that he was, born when he was, he had to discover Christianity for himself. In this pursuit he was alone in the solitude which is only known to great saints." Bernard Bergonzi sees in "Journey of the Magi" and "A Song for Simeon" a reflection of "something of Eliot's spiritual struggle," but he thinks that the prose work on religious subjects, except the 1931 essay on Pascal, is "rarely of more than secondary interest." The 1927 essay on Baudelaire, with its emphasis on prayer "au sein même de l'incredulité," contradicts that judgment, linking Baudelaire closely to Eliot, who, Bergonzi reports, said that he held his beliefs "with a scepticism which I never even hope to be quite rid of."[164] The language of the final essay on Baudelaire, the introduction to the *Intimate Journals*, joins it firmly to the imagery of "Journey of the Magi" and "East Coker." Baudelaire's significance, Eliot writes, is his "theological innocence":

He is discovering Christianity for himself; he is not assuming it as a fashion or weighing social or political reasons, or any other accidents. He is beginning, in a way, at the beginning; and being a discoverer, is not altogether certain what he is exploring and to what it leads; he might almost be said to be making again, as one man, the effort of hundreds of generations. His Christianity is rudimentary or embryonic. . . . His business was not to practise Christianity, but—what was much more important for this time—to assert its *necessity*.

Baudelaire's solitude separates him from most of his contemporaries, not only from Swinburne, Wilde, and Symons, but also from Whitman and Tennyson, whose "satisfaction" Eliot compared to Baudelaire's dissatisfaction in a comment in 1926. " 'Leaves of Grass,' " he said, "appeared in 1856, 'Les Fleurs du

incoercible . . . uncoercible need of prayer even at the heart of unbelief.

mal' in 1857: could any age have produced more heterogeneous leaves and flowers? The contrasts should be noted." Whitman and Tennyson showed a quality of "self-righteousness," he said, which was connected with the fact that both were "conservative, rather than reactionary or revolutionary; that is to say, they believed explicitly in progress, and believed implicitly that progress consists in things remaining much as they are." Baudelaire, on the other hand, "was a disagreeable person who was rarely satisfied with anything: *je m'ennuie en France*, he wrote, *où tout le monde ressemble à Voltaire*."[165] For Whitman "there was no chasm between the real and the ideal, such as opened before the horrified eyes of Baudelaire." Tennyson, Eliot wrote later, had also avoided the horror:

> ... Tennyson faced neither the darkness nor the light, in his later years. The genius, the technical power, persisted to the end, but the spirit had surrendered. A gloomier end than that of Baudelaire: Tennyson had no *singulier avertissement*. And having turned aside from the journey through the dark night, to become the surface flatterer of his own time, he has been rewarded with the despite of an age that succeeds his own in shallowness.[166]

Baudelaire's character of discoverer included his capacity to look into the dark, and so in "all his humiliating traffic with other beings, he walked secure in this high vocation, that he was capable of a damnation denied to the politicians and the newspaper editors of Paris." The unity of that paradox—"it is better . . . to do evil than to do nothing"—with the Heraclitean paradox of the *Four Quartets*, is clear.

Eliot's Baudelaire essays gather together some of his other concerns of the time. They probe, for instance, the question of Baudelaire's "classicism" (and, in their shifts of emphasis, reflect Eliot's own changing position). The first essay hints that Baudelaire must be seen as a correction to the romantics; the second claims unequivocally that he was "a classicist, born out of his due time"; the review qualifies that judgment, but it calls Quennell's chapter on Baudelaire "the first of a sequence of studies in the post-mortem of Romanticism, and in the insurgence of something which can hardly be called classicism, but which may de-

je m'ennuie . . . I am bored in France, where everybody is like Voltaire.

cently be called Counter-Romanticism"; the "Introduction" sees Baudelaire as inevitably "the offspring of romanticism, and by his nature the first counter-romantic in poetry," a poet who because of the time in which he wrote could not be a " 'classical' poet except in tendency." The tendency, however, was important. Baudelaire represented remarkably a collocation of values which Eliot associated elsewhere with Maurras, Hulme and others. Baudelaire made clear in his *Journals* and elsewhere that he believed with de Maistre that "toutes les institutions imaginables reposent sur une idée réligieuse, ou ne font que passer."[167] "Il n'y a de gouvernement raisonnable et assuré que l'aristocratique," he wrote (I, 684). "La vraie civilisation," Eliot quoted, "n'est pas dans le gaz, ni dans la vapeur, ni dans les tables tournantes. Elle est dans la diminution des traces du péché originel."[168] In Baudelaire, Eliot found the very dispositions he had announced as his own in the preface to *For Lancelot Andrewes*.

Eliot's views of Baudelaire were not new. In France, Baudelaire's reputation had long been established. Remy de Gourmont had argued for many of the points Eliot made; Mauclair had insisted that he was now free of his reputation;[169] Banville had defended his romanticism by arguing that when he wrote there were only two "classes" in literature and the arts, there was "d'une part, les romantiques, et de l'autre, les imbéciles,"[170] and Valéry had given his important lecture on the "Situation de Baudelaire."[171] He had become the property of modern writers: editions of his poems had been prefaced by Henri de Régnier, Apollinaire, André Gide, Gustave Kahn.[172] In 1921, the year Eliot wrote his first short note on Baudelaire, André Fontainas published an article which predicts some of Eliot's conclusions of 1927 and 1930. "Qu'est-ce qui fait que Baudelaire, mort quatre ans à peine après Alfred de Vigny, avant Lamartine, avant Leconte de Lisle, nous est un maître, un guide, un conseiller, un ami plus proche, plus sensible, plus essentiel, plus présent . . . ?"[173]

toutes . . . all imaginable institutions rest on a religious idea or they pass away. . . . There is no reasonable and sure government but the aristocratic. . . . True civilization lies not in gas nor in steam nor in spiritualist séances. It lies in the diminution of the traces of original sin.

d'une part . . . on one side the romantics and on the other the imbeciles.

Qu'est-ce qui . . . How is it that Baudelaire, dead hardly four years after Alfred de Vigny, before Lamartine, before Leconte de Lisle, is for us a master, guide, and counsellor, a closer, more sensitive, more essential, more present friend . . . ?

Nor were all of Eliot's points new in England. In 1909, James Huneker's articles on Baudelaire were published in London: they put Baudelaire forward as a great poet and a great critic, the "first of the 'Moderns' and the last of the Romantics."[174] In 1913, *Blackwood's Magazine* reviewed Turquet Milnes's book on Baudelaire's influence. The "legend of Baudelaire," it said, "has done his fame an irreparable injury." He stood in glorious solitude, a writer who "would have been at home . . . in what is called the Silver Age of Rome. He would have been equally at home, we think, with Marlowe, and Webster, and Cyril Tourneur." [175] In 1924, the American journal *The Fugitive* published an article which linked modernism with the first edition of *Les Fleurs du Mal.*[176]

Still, it is not possible to overestimate the importance of Eliot's articles. They comprised, as Eliot intended them to, a reversal of received opinion. "In England," Peter Quennell wrote after the publication of " 'Poet and Saint . . . ,' " "Mr. T. S. Eliot's critical judgements enjoy a considerable and deserved weight."[177] Like Murry, Eliot aimed to detach Baudelaire from his reputation. In his review of Quennell's book he wrote that Symons had "fumbled" Baudelaire badly,[178] and his attack upon Symons's view of Baudelaire does not need description here. Baudelaire, Eliot said, "*notre* Baudelaire," was not to be found in "the Swinburnian violet-coloured London fog of the 'nineties."[179] Baudelaire, said the greatest living English poet, was "the greatest exemplar in *modern* poetry in any language,"[180] a poet for "our time."

Peter Quennell's article and one published in *Poetry* in 1933 suggest how effectively Eliot had detached Baudelaire from the 'nineties. Quennell wrote that after the publication (in 1917) of Baudelaire's letters to his mother,

> it was necessary to dismiss a conception of the poet hitherto obtaining. . . . We were obliged to strip his image bare of the rather tawdry rags and tatters in which Swinburne's magnificent rhetoric had swaddled it. Our previous conception, the "strange, sad brother," Satanic dandy or frigidly preoccupied amateur of Vice, aghast, yet delightfully stimulated by the imminence of that horrific capital V, must be remodelled afresh. But, since modes of literary thought are as slow to germinate as they are sometimes quick to fade, it is now, during the last few years, that his restored portrait

shows the first signs of assuming a distinct and novel shape.[181]

Zabel's article in *Poetry* took up the theme: in England, it said, Arthur Symons's sensational and vitiating translations had enveloped Baudelaire's reputation in

the fumes of vagrancy and disease, of elaborate and luxuriating spiritual masochism, of every moral violence that presaged the day of *A Rebours, Dorian Gray, Une Saison en Enfer*, and the deepening nihilism of sensation and disgust.[182]

Eliot, Quennell wrote, had set to work "refurbishing our mental portrait."[183] Zabel, referring to Eliot's remarks about the *poésie des départs*, drew from him all of the major points of his article. Not every critic of Baudelaire agreed with Eliot, but most from now on took him as the critic to whom the dialogue must be addressed, an authority or antagonist. Quennell suggests, for instance, that "we shall be as ill-advised if we entitle [Baudelaire] Christian Saint like Mr. Eliot, as if, like Mr. Arthur Symons, we write him down Diabolist and dilettante of the Black Art."[184] An article in *Scrutiny* accused Baudelaire of irresponsible writing and declined to accept the idea "that, because he frequently mentions the devil, he was not only a Christian, but a sort of Christian ascetic."[185] But Eliot's articles gave the *coup de grâce* to the old view. Baudelaire had been borne out of his due time: "If it is true that the Nineteenth Century belonged to Baudelaire," Zabel wrote in *Poetry*, "there is all the evidence of critical enthusiasm, scholarship, and even popularity to show that he himself belongs to the Twentieth."[186] He had not only become a part of the mainstream of the English tradition; he had deflected it to himself. Re-enacting the retrospection of a Huysmans or a de Gourmont, tracking the modern back to its beginnings, Eliot wrote: "I look back to the dead year 1908; and I observe with satisfaction that it is now taken for granted that the current of French poetry which sprang from Baudelaire is one which has, in these twenty-one years, affected all English poetry that matters."[187]

* * *

It is this newly canonized Baudelaire, now wholly absorbed into English poetry, fiction, and criticism, and recently reconciled to the orthodoxies of classicism, conservatism and Catholicism, who is commemorated in *Four Quartets*. Here, the *semblable* of *The Waste Land* appears again as a "double"; here he is once more summoned by allusion as "familiar." But the Baudelaire who is present in *Four Quartets* is part of an altered pattern, and in this poem Eliot takes up again some of his own central Baudelaire borrowings to locate them in the new design and to shape them to the new meaning. The voyage motif of *East Coker*, for instance: it is multiply connected here, as in *The Waste Land*, resonant with echoes from the whole range of European literature. But it is also connected specifically, by allusion, with "Le Voyage," and in particular with the first stanza of that poem, to which Eliot had been drawn in his essay on the metaphysical poets, which he had imitated in the drafts of *The Waste Land*, and to which he had turned again, according to D.E.S. Maxwell, in "Animula."[188] Eliot's last version of the lines initiates the final section of *East Coker*:[189]

> Home is where one starts from. As we grow older
> The world becomes stranger, the pattern more complicated
> . . . .
> There is a time for the evening under starlight,
> A time for the evening under lamplight
> (The evening with the photograph album).

In the section that is launched by his last recasting of the lines which had lead to a vision of the horror in both *Heart of Darkness* and *The Waste Land*, Eliot radically revises Baudelaire's ideas both of exploration and of newness, defining one now as the movement to union and communion and the other as the discovery of "a lifetime burning in every moment." In *East Coker*, Eliot turns his initial imagery of travel into an imagery of exploration and sea-voyage, ending with a beginning and moving to "a deeper communion" to discover the new. For Eliot, Baudelaire's voyage motif, and especially the beginning and the end of "Le Voyage," was a permanent possession of the imagination, as Robert Lowell intended, perhaps, to acknowledge when he dedicated his "imitation" of "Le Voyage" to Eliot.[190] Baudelaire was, Eliot said in his essay on the metaphysical poets, a "curious explorer." In the "Introduction" to Isherwood's translation of the *Intimate Journals*, he wrote: "He is beginning, in a way, at the beginning; and being a discoverer, is not altogether certain what he is exploring and to what it leads." Baudelaire's explorations support one vision in *The Waste Land* and quite another in *Four Quartets*, yet in his transfigurations of the pattern, Eliot keeps him current.

Baudelaire is most directly invoked in the "familiar compound ghost" passage of "Little Gidding." Here, Eliot identifies his brotherhood, but he does so in such a way as to indicate his departures from his own past, summoning Baudelaire, along with the many others in the "compound," in a passage which itself enacts the poem's proposition that retrospection changes the pattern. "Between three districts whence the smoke arose," he writes, "I met one walking. . . ."

> So I assumed a double part, and cried
> And heard another's voice cry: "What! are *you* here?"

In that doubly voiced cry, which both dramatizes poetic influence and exemplies the carefully measured allusions that are under his control in his last poem, Eliot brings his Baudelaire into the new present. In *The Waste Land*, he had directed his readers to Baudelaire by quotation and footnotes; here, by a layering of allusion, he sets his own earlier work between himself and his source, and these lines join Baudelaire to Dante as a powerful "master" by means of an internal echoing within Eliot's own whole work. The hailing lines of "Little Gidding," which occur in the section of the poem that treats the theme of the literary resurrection of the dead, carefully reconstruct the lines at the end of "The Burial of the Dead." They recall them in almost every vital point of figure and vocabulary: it is at the crepuscular time, in both poems, that the poet and the double meet; it is in a hellish and specifically Dantesque location that the meetings take place; the poet and the double are, in both cases, soldiers of a sort; and the direct address of both passages is, unusually, rendered in dramatic speech. In this passage of "Little Gidding," Eliot revises Eliot:

> There I saw one I knew, and stopped him, crying, "Stetson!
> "You who were with me in the ships at Mylae!
> "That corpse you planted last year in your garden,
> "Has it begun to sprout? Will it bloom this year?
> . . . .
> "You! hypocrite lecteur!—mon semblable,—mon frère!"

In *The Waste Land*, Eliot presses his allusions to their source, citing Baudelaire both at the beginning and at the end of the "Unreal City" passage of "The Burial of the Dead." In his first note, he actually quotes from "Les Sept Vieillards," so drawing out of Baudelaire's poem precisely the action of his own, that of the ghostly encounter in the street. In "Little Gidding," however, he grafts the Baudelairean, "*modern*," street encounter onto the Dantesque pattern by means of a self-reference that both preserves the old and changes it. While the crepuscular encounter of *The Waste Land* takes its tone partly from the tradition Eliot inherited from the nineteenth-century English poets, the meeting in "Little Gidding" takes its tone from a much wider tradition. The corpse whose sprouting and blooming is heralded in "The Burial of the Dead" is part of the "cousinage" of the "carcasse superbe / Comme une fleur" (I, 31), which attracted so much attention in the late nineteenth century; but the doubling in "Little Gidding" takes its tone from the *Inferno*. Eliot's Baudelaire changed with him.

When Swinburne introduced Baudelaire to English readers, he made it plain that the Frenchman was, like Blake, a member of "the Church of Rebels" and that his wine of communion was the *vinum daemonum*. Now, eighty years later, Eliot joined Baudelaire to his pilgrimage to the royalist church of the community at Little Gidding. But Eliot's last invocation of his brother gives him much in common with Swinburne, since the "familiar compound ghost" section of "Little Gidding" is, of course, a hailing and a farewell—"a kind of valediction." It was by just such an act that Swinburne had begun Baudelaire's history in the English tradition.

   carcasse . . . proud carcass . . . like a flower (S, 48).

NOTES

INTRODUCTION

1. When quotations in this "Introduction" appear elsewhere in the text, I have left documentation for the fuller discussion.

2. Swift, *A Tale of a Tub*, III, in *Prose Works*, ed. Herbert Davis (Oxford, 1939-1968), I, 57.

3. I am grateful to Professor Cecil Y. Lang for pointing this out to me.

4. See Shirley Neuman, "*Heart of Darkness*, Virginia Woolf and the Spectre of Domination," in *Virginia Woolf: New Critical Essays*, ed. P. Clements and I. Grundy (London, 1983), pp. 57-76.

5. Ian Watt sees Baudelaire's "Correspondances" as well as the title of his book in *Heart of Darkness* (*Conrad in the Nineteenth Century*, London, 1980, pp. 200, 225). But he is surely a specific source of the design of the novel, which relies on him, as Eliot might put it, not only for its plan but also for a good deal of its incidental symbolism. Marlow's early remark is an imitation ("Now when I was a little chap I had a passion for maps. I would look for hours at South America, or Africa, or Australia, and lose myself in all the glories of exploration ... [but now] The glamour's off"). So, of course, is his discovery of "the horror" in "the most unexciting contest you can imagine." Conrad plays throughout with Baudelairean sources: his description of the "undersized railway-truck lying there on its back with its wheels in the air," looking "as dead as the carcass of some animal," suggests parody of "Une Charogne," a poem that was much in the English air by the time of composition of *Heart of Darkness* (*Youth, A Narrative and Two Other Stories* [London, 1923], pp. 52, 150, 63).

CHAPTER 1

1. *Essais sur les Modernes* (Paris, 1960; repr. 1964), p. 7.

2. Baudelaire, *Correspondance*, texte etabli, présenté et annoté par Claude Pichois, avec la collaboration de Jean Ziegler, 2 vols. (Paris, 1973), II, 299-300, 396. Baudelaire's letter to his mother is dated 3 June 1863, the one to Whistler 10 October 1863. The full text of his letter to Swinburne is also printed in Swinburne, *Letters*, ed. Cecil Y. Lang, 6 vols. (New Haven, 1960), I, 87-88.

3. Swinburne, *Letters*, I, 164, and see also III, 201; *William Blake, A Critical Essay* (London, 1868), reprinted in Swinburne, *Complete Works*, ed. Sir Edmund Gosse and Thomas James Wise, 20 vols. (London, 1926), XVI, 138. See Georges Lafourcade, *Swinburne, A Literary Biography* (London, 1932), pp. 110-11.

4. *Letters*, IV, 19.

5. Starkie, *From Gautier to Eliot, The Influence of France on English Literature, 1851-1939* (London, 1960, new ed. 1962), p. 43. See Lafourcade, *Swinburne*, p. 194.

6. *Letters*, III, 243.

7. "Ave atque Vale," *Poems and Ballads, Second Series* (London, 1878), pp. 71-83; reprinted in *Works*, III, 44-59.

8. Rossetti, *Swinburne's Poems and Ballads, A Criticism* (London, 1866), p. 46; Buchanan, *The Fleshly School of Poetry and Other Phenomena of the Day* (London, 1872), p. 19.

9. Georges Lafourcade, *La Jeunesse de Swinburne* (1837-1867), two vols. (Paris, Oxford, 1928), I, 243-44; Taine quoted by Edmund Gosse, *The Life of Algernon Charles Swinburne* (London, 1917), p. 202. See also James Douglas, "Swinburne and his Circle," *Bookman*, 36, 213 (June 1909), 117-23; F. Delattre, "A.-C. Swinburne et la France," *Revue des Cours et Conférences*, I (28 Feb. 1926), 548-67.

10. Francis Adams, *Essays in Modernity* (London, 1899), p. 141; G. Turquet-Milnes, *The Influence of Baudelaire in France and England* (London, 1913), p. 222; Arthur Symons, "Algernon Charles Swinburne: with Some Unpublished Letters," *Fortnightly Review*, 101, n.s. (May 1917), 798.

11. Gosse, *Life*, p. 89; G.-Jean Aubry, "Baudelaire et Swinburne," *Mercure de France*, 124, 466 (16 Nov. 1917), 272.

12. *Swinburne and Baudelaire* [The Zaharoff Lecture] (Oxford, 1930), p. 15; *Swinburne* (London, 1926), p. 10.

13. Murry, "The Influence of Baudelaire," *Rhythm*, 14 (March 1913), xxvi; Eliot, " 'Poet and Saint . . . ,' " *Dial*, 82, 5 (May 1927), 426. This essay was revised and reprinted as "Baudelaire in Our Time" in *For Lancelot Andrewes* (1928).

14. Introduction to Baudelaire, *Intimate Journals*, trans. Ch. Isherwood (London, 1930), p. 7. Reprinted as "Baudelaire," in *Selected Essays* (1932).

15. "Charles Baudelaire: Les Fleurs du Mal," *Spectator*, 6 Sept. 1862, pp. 998-1000; Gosse, *Portraits and Sketches* (London, 1912), p. 5. Swinburne's article was reprinted in *Les Fleurs du Mal and Other Studies*, ed. Edmund Gosse (London, 1913), pp. 3-18, in *Works*, XIII, 417-27, and in Clyde K. Hyder, ed., *Swinburne as Critic* (London and Boston, 1972), pp. 27-36. Hereafter I shall refer to the article parenthetically in my text as (*CB*).

16. Eliot, " 'Poet and Saint . . . ,' " p. 429.

17. "Matthew Arnold's New Poems," *Works*, XV, 64.

18. *A Study of Shakespeare*, second edition (London, 1880), p. 137n.; reprinted in *Works*, XI, 99n.

19. [Unsigned], *"Poems and Ballads.* By Algernon Charles Swinburne," *Athenaeum*, 2023 (Aug. 4, 1866), 137-38; "Thomas Maitland," "The Fleshly School of Poetry," *Contemporary Review*, 18 (Oct. 1871), 334-50. Buchanan, "The Monkey and the Microscope," in *St. Paul's Magazine*, August 1872. Quoted by Thomas J. Wise in Swinburne, *Works*, XX, 111.

20. George Meredith, letter of 1861, in *Swinburne: The Critical Heritage*, ed. Clyde K. Hyder (New York, 1970), p. 124.

21. A. E. Housman, "Swinburne," *Cornhill*, 1061 (Autumn 1969), 384; W. M. Rossetti, *Swinburne's Poems and Ballads, A Criticism*, pp. 30-31, 33.

22. Alice Meynell, "Swinburne's Lyrical Poetry," *Dublin Review*, 145, 290 (July 1909), 179; Robert Nye, *A Choice of Swinburne's Verse* (London, 1973), pp. 16-18.

23. Paul Bourget, *Essais de Psychologie Contemporaine* (Paris, first pub. 1883, repr. 1887), p. viii.

24. Nicolson, *Swinburne*, p. 21. Robert Nye (op.cit.) cites Nicolson as the author of the idea, but in fact it derives from William Michael Rossetti's *Criticism*: ". . . the largest and most fundamental of all the influences acting upon Swinburne is the artistic, or . . . the literary, and . . . his poetry is literary poetry of the intensest kind" (p. 34). George Bernard Shaw restated it on the occasion of Swinburne's death: "Now it happens that Swinburne, who seemed incapable of receiving any stimulus from the life around him, was highly susceptible to literary impressions" (*Bookman*, June 1909, p. 129).

25. T. S. Eliot, "Swinburne as Poet," *The Sacred Wood* (London, 1920; 7th ed., 1950, repr. 1953), p. 149.

26. Nicolson, *Swinburne*, pp. 13-14.

27. Starkie, *From Gautier to Eliot*, p. 43.

28 Gosse, *Life*, p. 41.

29. Quoted in Baudelaire, *Oeuvres Complètes*, texte établi, presenté et annoté par Claude Pichois, 2 vols. (Paris, 1975), I, 1182. See pp. 1176-1224, "Le Procès des 'Fleurs du Mal.' " See also Louis Barthou, *Autour de Baudelaire* (Paris, 1917), George Brosset et Claude Schmidt, *Le Procès des Fleurs du Mal ou L'Affaire Charles Baudelaire* (Genève, 1947), Enid Starkie, *Baudelaire* (London, 1957), pp. 307-27, and Jacques Hamelin, *La Réhabilitation Judiciaire de Baudelaire* (Paris, 1952).

30. Jacques Crépet, in *Les Fleurs du Mal* (Paris, 1922; repr. 1930), p. 364.

31. Reprinted in Baudelaire, *Oeuvres Complètes* (cited above, note 29), I, 812. Whenever possible I use this edition and refer to it in the text by volume and page number.

32. Baudelaire, *Oeuvres Complètes*, Préface, Présentation et Notes de Marcel A. Ruff (Paris, 1968), p. 20.

33. Edward J. H. Greene, *T. S. Eliot et la France* (Paris, 1951), p. 18.

34. See Swinburne, *New Writings, or Miscellanea Nova et Curiosa* . . . , ed. Cecil Y. Lang (Syracuse, New York, 1964), p. 225.

35. *Letters*, II, 139.

36. Gosse (*Life*, p. 90n.) reports this incorrectly. See Sotheby, Wilkinson, and Hodge, *Catalogue of the Library of Algernon Charles Swinburne, Esq.* (London, 1916), pp. 3-4; D. G. Rossetti, *Letters*, ed. O. Doughty and J. R. Wahl, 4 vols. (Oxford, 1965-67), II, 529-30.

37. Baudelaire's influence on Swinburne's *Poems and Ballads* has been much discussed. See, among others, Paul de Reul, *L'Oeuvre de Swinburne* (Brussels, 1922), pp. 191-99; F. Delattre, "A.-C. Swinburne et la France," *Revue des Cours et Conférences*, I (28 Feb. 1926), 554-58; Georges Lafourcade, "Swinburne et Baudelaire, Etude sur *Ave Atque Vale* suivie d'une traduction en vers du poème," *Revue Anglo-Américaine*, I, 3 (Février, 1924), 183-96, and *La Jeunesse de Swinburne (1837-1867)*, two vols. (Paris, Oxford, 1928); Nicolson, *Swinburne and Baudelaire*, pp. 11-12; Enid Starkie, *From Gautier to Eliot*, pp. 45-47; Anne Walder, *Swinburne's Flowers of Evil: Baudelaire's Influence on Poems and Ballads, First Series*, Acta Universitatis Upsaliensis, Studia Anglistica Upsaliensia (Uppsala, 1976); Jerome McGann, *Swinburne, An Experiment in Criticism* (Chicago & London, 1972); David G. Riede, *Swinburne, A Study in Romantic Mythmaking* (Charlottesville, Virginia, 1978); David A. Cooke, "The Content and Meaning of Swinburne's 'Anactoria,' " *Victorian Poetry*, 9 (1971), 77-93.

38. *Letters*, I, 201.

39. *William Blake, Works*, XVI, 138.

40. *A Study of Shakespeare, Works*, XI, 99n.

41. *Blake, Works*, XVI, 138.

42. Lafourcade, *La Jeunesse de Swinburne*, I, 200-201; Gosse, *Life*, pp. 237-38.

43. *Letters*, III, 115.

44. *August Vacquerie par Swinburne* (Paris, Michel Lévy Frères, 1875).

45. *Letters*, II, 59.

46. Poèmes et Ballades [trans. into French prose by Gabriel Mourey]. Notes sur Swinburne par Guy de Maupassant (Paris, 1891); *Laus Veneris, Poème de Swinburne*, trans. Francis Vielé-Griffin (Paris, 1923).

47. Christophe Campos, *The View of France From Arnold to Bloomsbury* (London, 1965), p. 53.

48. *Royal Literary Fund. Report of the Anniversary* . . . (London, 1866), pp. 17-27.

49. T. S. Eliot, "Contemporanea," *Egoist*, 5, 6 (June/July 1918), p. 84.

50. *Letters*, I, 164.

51. Valéry, "La Situation de Baudelaire," *Oeuvres Complètes*, ed. Jean Hytier, 2 vols. (Paris, 1957), I, 598-613.

52. *Letters*, III, 34-35; see also II, 369-70.

53. *Letters*, III, 134.

54. "Charles Baudelaire," *Fortnightly Review*, 18 n.s. (1 Oct. 1875), pp. 500-18.

55. Baudelaire, *Correspondance*, II, 324-26.

56. *Works*, XVI, 81.

57. Quoted in *New Writings by Swinburne*, ed. C. Y. Lang, p. 225.

58. Cf. T. S. Eliot, "Preface to the 1928 Edition," *The Sacred Wood* (cited above, note 25), p. viii.

59. *Works*, XVI, 60-61. See especially Robert L. Peters, *The Crowns of Apollo. Swinburne's Principles of Literature and Art. A Study in Victorian Criticism and Aesthetics* (Detroit, 1965), pp. 95-108, and Jerome McGann, *Swinburne, An Experiment in Criticism* (Chicago, 1972), pp. 50-60.

60. Gautier, *Mademoiselle de Maupin* (Paris, 1835; ed. A. Boschot, 1966), p. 23; *Albertus* (Paris, 1832; repr. 1930), pp. 8-9. For another view, see Ruth Z. Temple, *The Critic's Alchemy, A Study of the Introduction of French Symbolism into England* (New Haven, Conn., 1953), pp. 83, 86ff.

61. *Works*, XVI, 133.

62. *Study of Shakespeare, Works*, XI, 4.

63. *Works*, XVI, [51]. Further references are given parenthetically in the text.

64. Riede, *Swinburne*, p. 14.

65. *Letters*, II, 370.

66. See Riede, *Swinburne*, p. 14; Lafourcade, *Swinburne*, p. 194.

67. As quoted by Swinburne. See also *Oeuvres Complètes*, II, 793.

68. *Works*, XVI, 132-40.

69. Quoted above, p. 33.

70. The passage in *Notes Nouvelles Sur Edgar Poe* is as follows:

Mais il est une autre hérésie, qui, grâce à l'hypocrisie, à la lourdeur et à la bassesse des esprits, est bien plus redoutable et a des chances de durée plus grandes,—une erreur qui a la vie plus dure,—je veux parler de l'hérésie de l'*enseignement*, laquelle comprend comme corollaires inévitables l'hérésie de la *passion*, de la *vérité* et de la *morale*.

Mais il est . . . But there is yet another heresy, which, thanks to the hypocrisy, the dullness and the meanness of our minds, is far more dangerous, and has greater chances of lasting—an error far harder to kill; I refer to the heresy of didacticism, which includes, as inevitable corollaries, the heresies of passion, of truth and morality. A whole crowd of people imagine that the aim of poetry is some sort of lesson, that its duty is to fortify conscience, or to perfect social behaviour, or even, finally, to demonstrate something or other that is useful. Edgar Poe claims that the Americans, particularly, have fostered this heterodox notion; alas! there is no need to go as far as Boston to come upon the heresy in question. Here, in this very place, we are besieged by it, and every day it batters a hole in the ramparts of true poetry. If we will even briefly look into ourselves, question our souls, bring to mind our moments of enthusiasm, poetry will be seen to have no other aim but itself; it can have no other, and no poem will be as great, as noble, so truly worthy of the name "poem" as the one written for no purpose other than the pleasure of writing a poem. (C, 203)

Une foule de gens se figurent que le but de la poésie est un en-
seignement quelconque, qu'elle doit tantôt fortifier la conscience,
tantôt perfectionner les moeurs, tantôt enfin *démontrer* quoi que ce
soit d'utile. Edgar Poe prétend que les Américains ont spécialement
patronné cette idée hétérodoxe; hélas! il n'est pas besoin d'aller
jusqu'à Boston pour rencontrer l'hérésie en question. Ici même,
elle nous assiège, et tous les jours elle bat en brèche la véritable
poésie. La poésie, pour peu qu'on veuille descendre en soi-même,
interroger son âme, rappeler ses souvenirs d'enthousiasme, n'a pas
d'autre but qu'elle-même; elle ne peut pas en avoir d'autre, et aucun
poème ne sera si grand, si noble, si véritablement digne du nom
du poème, que celui qui aura été écrit uniquement pour le plaisir
d'écrire un poème. (II, 333)

71. *Works*, XVI, 138.
72. Riede, *Swinburne*, p. 170. See also McGann, *An Experiment in Crit-
icism*, pp. 292-312.
73. *Correspondance*, II, 98; *Oeuvres Complètes*, II, 321.
74. "The Monomaniac's Tragedy, and Other Poems," *New Writings*,
ed. Lang, pp. 81-87.
75. "Les Amours Etiques. Par Félicien Cossu," *New Writings*, pp. 88-
96; "Les Abîmes. Par Ernest Clouët," *New Writings*, pp. 97-102.
76. *New Writings*, p. 218; see also pp. 218-20.
77. *New Writings*, pp. 232-36.
78. Lang, *New Writings*, p. 225.
79. *New Writings*, p. 225.
80. *New Writings*, p. 112.
81. "Notes on Poems and Reviews," in *Swinburne Replies*, ed. Clyde
Kenneth Hyder (Syracuse, 1966), p. 30.
82. See *A Year's Letters*, ed. Francis Jacques Sypher (New York, 1974),
pp. xx-xxxii, and *Lesbia Brandon*, ed. Randolph Hughes (London, 1952),
pp. 193ff.
83. *Poems and Ballads, Second Series* (London, 1878), p. 97; reprinted
in *Works*, III, 60.
84. *A Year's Letters*, p. 155. In the following discussion, I give references
to this work parenthetically in the text, usually simply by number, where
necessary using the abbreviation *AYL*.
85. Oliver Elton, *Modern Studies* (London, 1907), p. 208.
86. *A Study of Shakespeare*, *Works*, XI, 99-100n. Since the passage reap-
pears in the history of English appropriations of Baudelaire, I quote it
here:

I have many a time been astonished that to pass for an observer
should be Balzac's great popular title to fame. To me it had always
seemed that it was his chief merit to be a visionary, and a passionate
visionary. All his characters are gifted with the ardour of life which
animated himself. All his fictions are as deeply coloured as dreams.

From the highest of the aristocracy to the lowest of the mob, all the actors in his *Human Comedy* are keener after living, more active and cunning in their struggles, more staunch in endurance of misfortune, more ravenous in their enjoyment, more angelic in devotion, than the comedy of the real world shows them to us. In a word, every one in Balzac, down to the very scullions, has genius. Every mind is a weapon loaded to the muzzle with will. It is actually Balzac himself. And as all the beings of the outer world presented themselves to his mind's eye in strong relief and with a telling expression, he has given a convulsive action to his figures; he has blackened their shadows and intensified their lights. Besides, his prodigious love of detail, the outcome of an immoderate ambition to see everything, to bring everything to sight, to guess everything, to make others guess everything, obliged him to set down more forcibly the principal lines, so as to preserve the perspective of the whole. He reminds me sometimes of those etchers who are never satisfied with the biting-in of their outlines, and transform into very ravines the main scratches of the plate. From this astonishing natural disposition of mind wonderful results have been produced. But this disposition is generally defined as Balzac's great fault. More properly speaking, it is exactly his great distinctive quality. But who can boast of being so happily gifted, and of being able to apply a method which may permit him to invest—and that with a sure hand—what is purely trivial with splendour and imperial purple? Who can do this? Now, he who does not, to speak the truth, does no great thing.

Fragments of this passage appear unacknowledged in Wilde (see below, p. 145, and Arthur Symons quotes it entirely, attributing it to Swinburne, in "A Study of Charles Baudelaire," *London Quarterly Review*, 206 (Oct. 1918), 187-88. It surfaces also in John Middleton Murry (see below, p. 329.

87. *Letters*, I, 224.

88. See Lafourcade, *La Jeunesse de Swinburne*, II, 307, and Randolph Hughes in *Lesbia Brandon*, p. 393.

89. See Hughes, "The Frustrate Masterpiece *or* The Fine Art of Suppression" in *Lesbia Brandon*, pp. 193-272.

90. "Under the Microscope," in *Swinburne Replies*, p. 60.

91. Edmund Wilson, *The Novels of A. C. Swinburne*, pp. 27, 37.

92. *Letters*, II, 282.

93. "In Memory of Barry Cornwall," "Memorial Verses on the Death of Théophile Gautier," "Théophile Gautier," *Works*, III, 64, 150, 53.

94. McGann, p. 298; Eliot, "Tradition and the Individual Talent," *Selected Essays* (London, 1932, 3rd ed. 1951, repr. 1972), p. 14.

95. Charles Baudelaire, *Les Fleurs du Mal*, Précédées d'une notice par Théophile Gautier (Paris, 1868), pp. 29, 20.

96. "Portraits littéraires: Charles Baudelaire" appeared in *L'Univers*

Illustré on 7, 14, 21, 28 March and 4, 11, 18 April 1868. "Cette notice, datée dans le journal [de Gautier] du 20 février 1868, reparut la même année en tête des *Fleurs du mal*, tome premier des *Oeuvres complètes* de Charles Baudelaire. En 1875, elle est entrée aussi dans le volume de Théophile Gautier: *Portraits et Souvenirs littéraires*." Charles de Lovenjoul, le Vicomte de Spoelberch de Lovenjoul, *Histoire des oeuvres de Théophile Gautier*, 2 vols. (Paris, 1887), II, 353-54.

97. *Letters*, I, 164.

98. "Charles Baudelaire," in *Les Poètes Français*, ed. Eugène Crépet, 4 vols. (Paris, 1862), IV, 597, 595.

99. Swinburne, "Dedicatory Epistle," in *Swinburne Replies*, p. 91. See C. K. Hyder, *Swinburne's Literary Career and Fame* (Durham, N.C., 1933), pp. 51-71.

100. Morley, "Mr. Swinburne's New Poems," *Saturday Review*, 22, 562 (4 Aug. 1866), 145-47 (see Hyder, *Career and Fame*, p. 275n.); [Buchanan], "*Poems and Ballads*. By Algernon Charles Swinburne," *Athenaeum*, 2023 (4 Aug. 1866), 137; [Unsigned], *London Review*, 13 (4 Aug. 1866), 130-31, cited here from *Swinburne, The Critical Heritage*, p. 37.

101. "Immorality in Authorship," *Fortnightly Review*, 6, 33 (15 Sept. 1866), 289-300.

102. In the following discussion, references to this work (in Hyder, *Swinburne Replies*) are given parenthetically in the text.

103. "Under the Microscope," in *Swinburne Replies*, p. 61.

104. *Poems and Ballads. A Criticism*, pp. 42, 46-47.

105. "Under the Microscope," *Swinburne Replies*, p. 36.

106. It also included Deschamps' verses, "Sur *Les Fleurs du Mal*: à Quelques Censeurs."

107. Vol. 80, pp. 769-75.

108. *Varieties in Prose*, 3 vols. (London, 1893), III [177]; *William Allingham, A Diary*, ed. H. Allingham and D. Radford (London, 1907), p. 331.

109. "Julio," *Poems* (London and Brighton, 1870), pp. 175-79. See also Joseph Sykes, *Selected Works*, 3 vols. (London, 1853 and 1855). I am grateful to Dr. John Stokes of the University of Warwick for making me aware of Julio's poem.

110. "Baudelaire," *Belgravia*, 15 (Oct. 1871), 438-52. A shorter, more moderate article by Stigand had been published in Boston three years earlier, as translated from the *Revue National*. In this, Stigand writes that while the poet must be regarded as a "moral curiosity," he is also "in matter of form of prose or sense . . . one of the masters of the present time." (*Every Saturday* [Boston], 4 [26 Oct. 1867], 528-32.)

111. [Unsigned], "*Poems and Ballads*. By Algernon Charles Swin-

Cette notice . . . This notice, dated in Gautier's journal as 20 February, 1868, appeared again at the head of *Les Fleurs du Mal*, volume one of Charles Baudelaire's *Oeuvres complètes*. In 1875, it also went into Gautier's book, *Portraits et Souvenirs littéraires*.

NOTES TO PAGES 69 - 78

burne," *Athenaeum*, 2023 (4 Aug. 1866), 137-38; Robert Buchanan, "Immorality in Authorship" (cited above, note 101), pp. 289-300: "Thomas Maitland," "The Fleshly School of Poetry," *Contemporary Review*, 18 (Oct. 1871), 334-50; *The Fleshly School of Poetry and Other Phenomena of the Day* (1872).

112. "Under the Microscope," in *Swinburne Replies*, pp. 35-87. In the following discussion, references are given in the text.

113. Eliot, "Baudelaire," *Selected Essays* (London, 1932, 3rd ed. 1951, repr. 1972), p. 429.

114. "The Poems of Dante Gabriel Rossetti," *Works*, XV, 23.

115. "Tennyson and Musset," *Works*, XIV, 314-15.

116. Hyder, *Career and Fame*, p. 175.

117. "Anglo-Scotus," "The Fleshly School of Poets," *The Christian World*, 7 July 1876, p. 454. The attribution is Harriet Jay's in *Robert Buchanan* (London, 1903; repr. N.Y., 1970), pp. 164-65.

118. E.W.G., "Mr. Swinburne's Essays," *Examiner*, 12 June 1875, p. 666.

119. [Unsigned], "Mr. Swinburne on Christianity," *Saturday Review*, 81, 2108 (21 March 1896), p. 297.

120. Gosse, *Life*, p. 89.

121. See above, note 86.

CHAPTER 2

1. [Unsigned], "Poems by William Morris," *Westminster Review* 34, 2 (n.s.) (1 Oct. 1868), 300.

2. *Marius the Epicurean. His Sensations and Ideas*, 2 vols. (London, 1885), I, 105.

3. See "A typescript of Pater's reading taken from the *Librarian's Book* in the Taylorian Institute, Oxford." Taken by W. A. Ward, 1963. Arch III D. 41, Taylorian Library. Also Billie Andrew Inman, *Walter Pater's Reading: A Bibliography of His Library Borrowings and Literary References, 1858-1873* (New York and London, 1981).

4. William Sharp, *Papers Critical and Reminiscent*, Selected and arranged by Mrs. William Sharp (London, 1912), p. 201; William Rothenstein, *Men and Memories, Recollections*, 2 vols. (London, 1931), I, 139; George Moore, *Avowals* (London, 1919), p. 205.

5. "Mr. Pater's Essays," *Fortnightly Review*, 76 n.s. (1 April 1873), 469-77.

6. "M. Lemaître's Serenus, and Other Tales," *Macmillan's Magazine*, 58, 337 (Nov. 1887), 71; "Prosper Mérimée," *Fortnightly Review*, 48 n.s. (1 Dec. 1890), 852-64; *Marius*, I, 65; "A Poet with Something to Say," *Uncollected Essays* (Portland, Maine, 1903), p. 83. (First published *Pall Mall Gazette*, 49 [23 March 1889], 3.)

7. Pater, *Letters*, ed. Lawrence Evans (Oxford, 1970), p. 120.

8. Richard Ellmann, *Eminent Domain* (New York, 1967), p. 8.

9. J. A. Symonds, review of *The Renaissance*, *Academy* 4 (15 March 1873), 103-105, reprinted in R. M. Seiler, ed., *Walter Pater, The Critical Heritage* (London, 1980), pp. 57-61; Arthur Symons, review of *Imaginary Portraits*, *Time* 6 (Aug. 1887), 157-62, reprinted in *Critical Heritage*, pp. 175-82.

10. Enid Starkie, *From Gautier to Eliot*, pp. 51-57; René Wellek, *History of Modern Criticism: 1750-1950*. IV: *The Later Nineteenth Century* (London, 1966), p. 388; Sir Kenneth Clark, Introduction and Notes to Pater, *The Renaissance* (London, 1961), p. 22n.; G. C. Monsman, *Pater's Portraits, Mythic Pattern in the Fiction of Walter Pater* (Baltimore, 1967), p. 47.

11. Ruth C. Child, *The Aesthetic of Walter Pater* (New York, 1940; repr. 1969), pp. 13, 18.

12. Pater, *Appreciations, With an Essay on Style* (London, 1889), p. 34; John Payne, *Intaglios, Sonnets* (London, 1871), p. 9; Swinburne, "Simeon Solomon: Notes on his 'Vision of Love' and Other Studies," *Works*, XV, 456. (The essay was first published in *Dark Blue*, 1871.)

13. D'Hangest, *Walter Pater, L'Homme et l'Oeuvre*, 2 vols. (Paris, 1961), I, 125. See also I, 349-51. John J. Conlon, *Walter Pater and the French Tradition* (Lewisburg, London and Toronto, 1982), p. 85.

14. G. C. Monsman, *Walter Pater's Art of Autobiography* (New Haven and London, 1980), pp. 137-66; and see below, pp. 101ff.; Walter Pater, *The Renaissance*, ed. Donald L. Hill (Berkeley, Los Angeles, London, 1980); Inman, cited above, note 3.

15. Houghton b MS 1150 (23). Described by Samuel Wright, *A Bibliography of the Writings of Walter H. Pater* (Folkestone, Kent, 1975), p. 147: "[Miscellaneous brief notes] A. MS (unsigned); [n.p., n.d.] 1 folder."

16. Pater, *Studies in the History of the Renaissance* (London, 1873), pp. 187-88. In subsequent editions, the work was called *The Renaissance, Studies in Art and Poetry*. I refer to it in subsequent notes as *Renaissance*, indicating the date of the edition when other than the first. When it is possible to refer to the first edition, I give page numbers parenthetically in the text. Donald Hill prints the 1893 text of the *Renaissance* in his edition, and he gives variant readings, pp. 207-75.

17. Houghton b MS 1150 (23). Described above, note 15.

18. Harold Bloom and Lionel Trilling, "Walter Pater," in *The Oxford Anthology of English Literature*, ed. Frank Kermode and John Hollander, 2 vols. (New York, 1973), II, 1097-98.

19. David Newsome, *On the Edge of Paradise. A. C. Benson: The Diarist* (London, 1980), p. 192: "Benjamin Jowett had gained possession of certain compromising letters which he had threatened Pater he would publish should he ever think of standing for university office." See also Robert Seiler, "Walter Pater Studies: 1970-1980," in Philip Dodd, ed., *Walter Pater: An Imaginative Sense of Fact* (London, 1981), p. 87.

20. Symons, *A Study of Walter Pater* (London, 1932), p. 69; Benson, *Walter Pater* (London, 1906), p. 23.

21. *Gaston de Latour, An Unfinished Romance* (London, 1896), p. 87.

22. Houghton Library b MS Eng 1150 (13). Described by Samuel Wright, *A Bibliography*, p. 145: "["English Literature"] A. MS (unsigned); [n.p., n.d.] 34s. (38 p.)."

23. See Pater, *Letters*, pp. xxxviii-xxxix, 11-12.

24. Swinburne, *Letters*, II, 240-41. Watts-Dunton remarked to Rothenstein that "Swinburne of course invented [Pater]" (*Men and Memories*, I, 232).

25. 9 December [1872]. *Letters*, p. 12.

26. "Notes on Poems and Reviews," *Swinburne Replies*, p. 18.

27. *Works*, XVI, 136.

28. *Renaissance*, 1877, p. 7.

29. *Swinburne Replies*, pp. 26, 27.

30. Cited above, note 1.

31. Samuel Wright, *A Bibliography*, p. 3.

32. *Works*, XVI, 137.

33. Saintsbury's essay ("Charles Baudelaire," *Fortnightly Review*, 18 n.s. [1 Oct. 1875], 500-18) produced a skirmish in the correspondence columns of *The Nation* that was brought to an end by Henry James's condescending essay, "Charles Baudelaire" (*Nation*, 22 [27 April, 1876], 279-82). James's essay was reprinted in *French Poets and Novelists* (London, 1878), pp. 72-83. Saintsbury's was reprinted in his *Collected Essays and Papers* (London, 1924), in whose "Preface" he dates his interest in Baudelaire as very early: "It was in 1866 that a friend, at my request, brought me from Paris the second edition of the *Fleurs du Mal*. (Mr. Andrew Lang long afterwards gave me the first, which I still have.)" In the year in which James's essay was reprinted in London, Baudelaire also figured in Edward Dowden's *Studies in Literature*. Saintsbury recommended him as a model; James said he was superficial, puerile, and immature; and Dowden presented him as the analyst of modern life. In the few years following publication of *The Renaissance* the Baudelaire debate continued to be heated.

34. "Romanticism," *Macmillan's Magazine*, 35 (Nov. 1876), 64-70; "Prosper Mérimée" (cited above, note 6), reprinted in *Miscellaneous Studies* (London, 1895), pp. 1-29; *Gaston de Latour* (cited above, note 21), pp. 60-90. Since, in the immediately following discussion, I refer only to this chapter, I shall make no further references to this text. G. C. Monsman makes Pater's reference to "flowers of evil" central in his argument that *Gaston* "concerned itself with the 'disentangling' of the 'dubious, double root' of beauty and evil," and he takes it to mean, as I do, that "Baudelaire is for Pater what Ronsard is for Gaston." (*Walter Pater's Art of Autobiography*, pp. 137-38.)

35. *Miscellaneous Studies*, p. 21.

36. *Works*, XVI, 85. And see above, pp. 39-40.

37. Ellen Moers, *The Dandy, Brummell to Beerbohm* (London, 1960), p. 271.

38. Claude Pichois et François Ruchon, *Iconographie de Charles Baude-*

laire (Genève, 1960), p. 50. The editors report a "curious confusion" relating to this portrait: it appeared in a Belgian journal as the picture of a famous murderer, Léon Peltzer. The editors of the new journal, hoping for great and rapid success, wanted to publish Peltzer's photograph in their first number. Unable to get the real thing, they cut Baudelaire's portrait out of the third edition of *Les Fleurs du Mal*: " 'Un illustrateur reproduisit le dessin, et le lendemain, tout le Brabant croyait contempler les terribles traits du Plista du jour.' "

39. The lecture, as I have noted above (note 6), appeared first in *The Fortnightly Review* for 1 December 1890, pp. 852-64. It was also printed in *Littell's Living Age* (Boston), 73, 2429 (17 Jan. 1891), 131-39; in *Miscellaneous Studies* (London, 1895), pp. 1-29; and in *Studies in European Literature: Being the Taylorian Lectures 1889-1899* (Oxford, 1900). See Wright, *A Bibliography*, pp. 41-42. I have quoted from the *Fortnightly Review*.

40. See below, pp. 120ff.

41. The phrase is also Stendhal's, as Pater notes when he uses it of Arthur Symons in "A Poet with Something to Say" (cited above, note 6), p. 80.

42. Michael Holquist, "The Politics of Representation," in *Allegory and Representation: Selected Papers from the English Institute, 1979-80*, ed. Stephen J. Greenblatt (Baltimore and London, 1981), p. 182.

43. See Pater, *Letters*, ed. Lawrence Evans (Oxford, 1970), pp. xxvii, 8n. Also *The Renaissance*, ed. Hill, pp. 384-85, and Hayden Ward, "The 'Paper in MS.': A Problem in Establishing the Chronology of Pater's Composition" in *Walter Pater: An Imaginative Sense of Fact*, pp. 81-83.

44. *The Renaissance* (London, 1888), p. 246.

45. "Poems by William Morris" (cited above, note 1), pp. 302, 301; *Appreciations*, p. 215. See Inman, pp. 190-92.

46. *Plato and Platonism, A Series of Lectures* (London, 1893), p. 245.

47. "Coleridge's Writings," *Westminster Review*, 29, 1 n.s. (1 Jan. 1866), p. 107.

48. "Coleridge's Writings," p. 107.

49. *Oeuvres Complètes*, II, 417-19.

50. Margaret Gilman, *Baudelaire the Critic* (New York, 1943), p. 6.

51. "Poems by William Morris," p. 309.

52. P. 311.

53. See *Letters*, pp. 7-9.

54. See Donald Hill, ed., *Renaissance*, pp. 384-85.

55. See below, pp. 119-20.

56. *Studies in Seven Arts* (London, 1906), p. 301.

57. *The Raw and the Cooked: Introduction to a Science of Mythology*: I. Translated from the French by John and Doreen Weightman. First published in French in Paris in 1964 (New York and Evanston, 1969), pp. 1-32.

58. I quote from "The School of Giorgione" as it was published in

The Fortnightly Review, 130 n.s. (1 Oct. 1877), 526-38. See Hill, ed., *Renaissance*, pp. 102-22, and textual notes, pp. 236-43.

59. Swinburne, *New Writings* (cited above, Chapter I, note 34), p. 48. Hill, *Renaissance*, p. 385, points out the precise relevance to this claim of Pater's subject matter: "By insisting throughout his essay on the strictly artistic interests and traditions of the Venetian painters, Pater sets his own aesthetic view against the moral one of Ruskin, who had attacked 'the pestilent art of the Renaissance' on moral grounds in *The Stones of Venice* (1851-1853) and other writings."

60. D'Hangest, *Walter Pater, L'Homme et l'Oeuvre*, I, 349, n. 8. See also Conlon, *Walter Pater and the French Tradition*, pp. 90-94.

61. P. 388.

62. D'Hangest, *Walter Pater*, I, 350 n. 27; *Oeuvres Complètes*, II, 791.

63. See Walter Pater, *The Renaissance*. Introduction and notes by Kenneth Clark (1961), pp. 20-23. Pater's debt here is specific: he remolds Baudelaire's prose. But Baudelaire is often to be found conflating the arts or asserting their aspirations to the condition of one another. See *Oeuvres Complètes*, II, 423, for only one example.

64. Hill, ed., *Renaissance*, p. 440.

65. The image suggests Baudelaire's "Les Phares," and it recalls the title of the "tradition" poem of Ernest Clouet. (See above, p. 44).

66. "Romanticism" (cited above, note 34), pp. 64-70. All references to this article are to this version of it.

67. Pater shared his interest in Stendhal with Baudelaire, who cited him frequently and plagiarized from him on important occasions. See Margaret Gilman, "Baudelaire and Stendhal," *PMLA*, 54, 1 (March 1939), 288-96. The point has relevance not only to the essay on "Romanticism," but also to the "Preface" to *The Renaissance*, in which Pater draws on Baudelaire's *Salon de 1846*. This is one of the works in which Baudelaire both plagiarizes from Stendhal and cites him. Ward's list of Pater's borrowings from the Library of the Taylor Institute shows that Pater returned copies of the *Histoire de la Peinture en Italie* (the work from which Baudelaire borrows in his *Salons* and elsewhere) and *Chroniques Italiennes*, in June, 1873. It is tempting to speculate that Pater may have borrowed these works of Stendhal (he had borrowed none before) because Baudelaire had cited them. (Pater's "Preface," not yet revised in November, 1872, was published in February, 1873.) Ward's list also shows that Pater returned "Stendhal, Oeuvres, 2 vols." on a date unspecified between January 1872 and June 1873.

68. See Billie Andrew Inman, *Walter Pater's Reading* (cited above, note 3), p. 190, and Hill, ed., *Renaissance*, pp. 371-72.

69. See Inman, p. xxv.

70. "Amiel's 'Journal Intime' " [first published, unsigned, in *The Guardian*, 41, 2102 (17 March 1886), pp. 406-407], *Essays from the Guardian* (London, 1896), pp. 32-33. Pater writes that Amiel "was meant, if people ever are meant for special lines of activity, for the best sort of

criticism, the imaginative criticism; that criticism which is itself a kind of construction, or creation, as it penetrates, through the given literary or artistic product, into the mental and inner constitution of the producer, shaping his work."

71. See Monsman, *Walter Pater's Art of Autobiography* (cited above, note 14), p. 5.

72. Hugh Kenner, "The Possum in the Cave," in *Allegory and Representation*, ed. Greenblatt (cited above, note 42), p. 140; Samuel Hynes, "Pound and the Prose Tradition," in *Edwardian Occasions* (London, 1972), p. 129.

73. *Plato and Platonism* (cited above, note 46), p. 137. In the following discussion, references to this edition are given parenthetically in the text.

74. "The Poems of William Morris," p. 309.

75. "Coleridge's Writings" (cited above, note 47), p. 122.

76. *Renaissance*, p. 177.

77. First published *Fortnightly Review*, 15, n.s. (April 1874), pp. 456-65; cited here from *Appreciations*, p. 41.

78. *Appreciations*, pp. 41-42.

79. *Appreciations*, pp. 45-46.

80. *Appreciations*, pp. 46-47.

81. "Imaginary Portraits I. The Child in the House," *Macmillan's Magazine*, 38 (Aug. 1878), p. 318.

82. *Appreciations*, p. 15.

83. P. 259.

84. *Gaston de Latour*, p. 68.

85. "Walter Pater Studies: 1970-1980," *Walter Pater: An Imaginative Sense of Fact* (cited above, note 43), p. 87.

86. Monsman, *Walter Pater* (Boston, 1977), pp. 16ff.

87. *Stephen Hero* (New York, 1944; repr. 1963), p. 78.

88. "Coleridge's Writings," p. 107; "A Few Don'ts by an Imagiste," *Poetry*, 1, 6 (March 1913), 200.

89. F. S. Flint, "Imagisme," *Poetry*, 1, 6, 199.

90. "Style," *Appreciations*, p. 16.

CHAPTER 3

1. *The Artist as Critic. Critical Writings of Oscar Wilde*, ed. Richard Ellmann (New York, 1968, repr. 1969), p. x.

2. "The Decay of Lying," *The Artist as Critic*, p. 307. Further references to this dialogue are to this edition.

3. Ludwig Wittgenstein, *Philosophical Investigations*, trans. G.E.M. Anscombe (Oxford, 1953, third ed., 1967), p. 193e.

4. "The Truth of Masks," *The Artist as Critic*, p. 432. Further references to this essay are to this edition.

5. "The Decay of Lying," p. 312.

6. Cf. *Oeuvres Complètes*, II, 115; quoted by Wilde, "The English Renaissance of Art," *Miscellanies*, ed. Robert Ross (London, 1908), p. 255.

7. "A Few Maxims for the Instruction of the Over-Educated," in *Letters*, ed. Rupert Hart-Davis (London, 1962), p. 870; cf. *Oeuvres Complètes*, II, 494.

8. "Dinner and Dishes," *The Artist as Critic*, p. 21. First published *Pall Mall Gazette*, 41, 6236 (7 March 1885) 5.

9. *Impressions of America*, ed. with an introduction by Stuart Mason (Sunderland, 1906), p. 34.

10. "The Relation of Dress to Art. A Note in Black and White on Mr. Whistler's Lecture," *The Artist as Critic*, p. 17. (First published *Pall Mall Gazette*, 41, 6230 (28 Feb. 1885), 4.) Cf. "The Truth of Masks," *The Artist as Critic*, p. 430: "The value of black is hardly appreciated. . . . And this is curious, considering the general colour of the dress of a century in which, as Baudelaire says, 'Nous célébrons tous quelque enterrement.' . . . In modern plays the black frock coat of the hero becomes important in itself, and should be given a suitable background." Cf. *Oeuvres Complètes*, II, 494-96, in which Baudelaire supplies the idea Wilde cites and links it to dandyism and to the beauty of evil.

11. *The Artist as Critic*, p. 168; *Letters*, p. 185.

12. Sir Henry Newbolt, *My World as in My Time, Memoirs* (London, 1932), pp. 96-97; Bloom, *The Anxiety of Influence, A Theory of Poetry* (London, Oxford, New York, 1975; first pub. 1973), p. 6. For a detailed account of Wilde's borrowings in the poems, see Averil Gardner, " 'Literary Petty Larceny': Plagiarism in Oscar Wilde's Early Poetry," *English Studies in Canada*, 8, 1 (March 1982), 49-61.

13. *The Picture of Dorian Gray*, ed. with an introduction by Isobel Murray (London, 1974), p. 156.

14. *Letters*, p. 304.

15. George Moore, *Hail and Farewell, Ave, Salve, Vale*, ed. Richard Cave (Gerrards Cross, 1976), p. 679, n. 30.

16. On Beardsley's drawings, see below, pp. 179-80.

17. *Letters*, p. 180.

18. "Mr. Swinburne's Last Volume," *The Artist as Critic*, p. 146. First published *Pall Mall Gazette*, 49, 7574 (27 June 1889), 3; W. B. Yeats, *Autobiographies* (London, 1955, repr. 1977), p. 130; *A Critic in Pall Mall* (London, 1919), p. 205; *Letters*, p. 264.

19. *Letters*, p. 460.

20. "The Soul of Man under Socialism," *The Artist as Critic*, p. 272. First published *Fortnightly Review*, 49, 290 (Feb. 1891), 292-319.

21. Reported by Hesketh Pearson, *The Life of Oscar Wilde* (London, 1946), p. 210.

22. *The Artist as Critic*, pp. 29-30, 298-99. Cf. Swinburne, *A Study of Shakespeare*, quoted below. In "The Decay of Lying," Wilde changed "distinction" to "difference," and so softened the echo of Swinburne. Stanley Weintraub observes, "Frugally, he reused some of the

lines from the review in *The Decay of Lying*, adding to them a sentence linking his observations to a theme of the essay: 'Balzac is no more of a realist than Holbein was' " (Weintraub, ed., *Literary Criticism of Oscar Wilde* [Lincoln, Nebraska, 1968], p. xxx). Wilde was even more frugal than Weintraub suggests, and the linking sentence is out of Baudelaire. "I have many a time been astonished that to pass for an observer should be Balzac's great popular title to fame" (Swinburne's translation).

23. *The Artist as Critic*, pp. 393, 391; *The Picture of Dorian Gray*, p. 142.

24. "The Critic as Artist," *The Artist as Critic*, pp. 378-79. Further references to this dialogue are to this edition.

25. "The Critic as Artist," p. 393.

26. II, 78-79. Prose translation here by Francis Scarfe in Baudelaire, *Selected Verse*, Translated, introduced, and edited by Francis Scarfe (London, 1961), pp. 159-60.

27. "The Grosvenor Gallery 1877," *Miscellanies*, p. 23. (First published *Dublin University Magazine*, July 1877.)

28. Wilde, "L'Envoi" in Rennell Rodd, *Rose Leaf and Apple Leaf* (Philadelphia, 1882), p. 11.

29. *Rose Leaf and Apple Leaf*, pp. 15, 12-13, 26.

30. "The Critic as Artist," pp. 368-69, 367.

31. "The Critic as Artist," pp. 364, 355.

32. *The Artist as Critic*, pp. ix-x.

33. *Letters*, p. 471.

34. *Miscellanies*, p. 274.

35. "The Critic as Artist," p. 393.

36. "The Critic as Artist," p. 365.

37. "The Decay of Lying," pp. 313-14.

38. H. Montgomery Hyde, *Famous Trials, Seventh Series: Oscar Wilde* (London, 1962), p. 109.

39. "The English Renaissance," *Miscellanies*, p. 262. The square brackets are not mine.

40. See above, pp. 120ff.

41. *Miscellanies*, pp. 243-44.

42. *Renaissance* (1873), pp. 2, xi.

43. "The Critic as Artist," p. 351.

44. "The Decay of Lying," p. 294.

45. P. 301.

46. Pp. 290-91.

47. *Letters*, p. 520.

48. Cf. John Middleton Murry, below, pp. 315-18.

49. Cited above, note 6.

50. *The Picture of Dorian Gray*, p. 47.

51. "The Decay of Lying," p. 309.

52. "The Decay of Lying," p. 291.

53. Pp. 302, 303.

54. Pp. 294-95.

55. P. 301.
56. P. 344.
57. P. 359.
58. *Dorian Gray*, p. [xxxiii]. "The Critic as Artist," p. 371.
59. "The Critic as Artist," pp. 369, 370.
60. P. 359.
61. "The Critic as Artist," p. 368.
62. P. 125.
63. "The Critic as Artist," p. 370.
64. P. 382.
65. *The Picture of Dorian Gray*, p. 130. In the following discussion I give page references parenthetically in the text.
66. "The Critic as Artist," p. 378.
67. *Oscar Wilde: Art and Egotism* (London, 1977), p. 113, quoted from *Letters*, p. 352. Compare Christopher Nassaar, who sees "the yellow book" as a combination of Pater and Huysmans (*Into the Demon Universe, A Literary Exploration of Oscar Wilde* [New Haven and London, 1974], p. 55). I cannot agree with Nassaar that "The two major influences on the English decadent movement were Pater's *The Renaissance* (1873) and Joris-Karl Huysmans's *A Rebours* (1884)." Pater's overwhelming influence is evident, but Huysmans is only one of several continental influences, and I think that he is less significant than Baudelaire.
68. "Introduction" to her edition of *Dorian Gray*, pp. xx-xxvi, and "Oscar Wilde's Absorption of 'Influences': The Case History of Chuang Tzu," *Durham University Journal*, 64, 1 (N.S. 33, 1), Dec. 1971, pp. 1-13. The article also discusses briefly Baudelaire's influence on Wilde's dandyism, but it concludes with the suggestion that Wilde "was protected by the very large number of his 'sources' from undue influence by any" (p. 13).
69. See Richard Ellmann, "Overtures to Wilde's Salomé," *Tri-Quarterly*, 15 (Spring, 1969), pp. 45-65.
70. Shewan, *Art and Egotism*, p. 123.
71. J.-K. Huysmans, *A Rebours*. Chronologie, introduction, et archives de l'oeuvre par Pierre Waldner (Paris, 1978), pp. 176-77.
72. Pp. 177-78.
73. *The Artist as Critic*, p. 15. First published *Pall Mall Gazette*, 41, 6224 (21 Feb. 1885), 1-2.
74. P. 210.
75. P. 213.
76. P. 214.
77. Quoted by Ellen Moers, *The Dandy*, p. 300.
78. Quoted in the following discussion from Wilde, *Complete Works*, with an Introduction by Vyvyan Holland. New edition (first pub. London and Glasgow, 1948; new ed. 1966, repr. 1971), pp. 791-801.
79. *Letters*, p. 435.
80. Hesketh Pearson, *The Life of Oscar Wilde*, pp. 170-71.

81. Cf. Christopher Nassaar, *Into the Demon Universe*, p. 46. Nassaar sees Sibyl Vane as the allegorical antithesis to Lord Henry Wotton: "serene and untouched by any knowledge of evil," she "represents the Hellenic ideal." Elsewhere, he writes that Basil Hallward "expounds a theory of art straight out of Pater's essay on Leonardo" (40). It will be apparent in what I have written above that I disagree on both counts.

82. George Moore, *A Drama in Muslin, A Realistic Novel*, with an Introduction by A. Norman Jeffares (Gerrards Cross, 1981), pp. 32-33.

83. Cf. Christopher Nassaar, *Into the Demon Universe*, who sees *Dorian Gray* as one step on the way to Wilde's open celebration of "demonism" as a "true religion" (86). In my view, the text does not justify so extravagant a reading.

84. Lionel Johnson, *Complete Poems*, ed. Iain Fletcher (London, 1953), pp. 246-47. Fletcher's translation (which I have used) is on pp. 386-87. Johnson wrote:

> Amat avidus amores
> Miros, miros carpit flores
>   Saevus pulchritudine:
> Quanto anima nigrescit,
> Tanto facies splendescit,
>   Mendax, sed quam splendide!

85. Cf. John Stokes, *Oscar Wilde* (London, 1978), p. 31.

86. Baudelaire, *Les Fleurs du Mal*. Précédés d'une notice par Théophile Gautier (Paris, 1868), p. 12.

87. Pp. 31-32.

88. See above, p. 96.

89. *Les Fleurs du Mal* (1868), p. 2.

90. Pp. 3-4, 10.

91. "English Renaissance," *Miscellanies*, p. 255.

92. See R. A. Walker, *The Best of Beardsley* (London, 1948), plate 10, plate 11. In "The Toilette of Salomé. I," the bookshelf includes *Fleurs du Mal* and Zola, *La Terre*, with other illegible titles; in "The Toilette of Salomé. II," *Les Fleurs du Mal* do not appear, and *La Terre* is replaced by *Nana*. The second bookshelf also includes *Les Fêtes Galantes, Marquis de Sade, Manon Lescaut*, and *The Golden Ass*. See also Simon Wilson, *Beardsley* (Oxford, 1976), p. 11: "This drawing was suppressed by John Lane, the publisher of *Salomé*, on the grounds of indecency. The main objection, apparently, was the pubic hair and just perceptible tumescence of the boy on the Japanese stool, but Beardsley introduced a number of other provocative features. . . ." Wilson numbers *Les Fleurs du Mal* among the provocative features. Sir Kenneth Clark, in *The Best of Aubrey Beardsley* (London, 1979), p. 22, says that Beardsley "seems to have read *Les Fleurs du mal*, for he gave a copy to Sir William Rothenstein, but in general he was uninfluenced by any near contemporaries, except Wagner." Raymond Furness, *Wagner and Literature* (Manchester,

1982), p. 38, differs: *"Venus and Tannhäuser* took Baudelaire's poem 'La Géante' to grotesque extremes of pornotopia."

93. *Into the Demon Universe*, p. 92.

94. *Letters*, p. 466.

95. *Art and Egotism*, p. 150.

96. *A Study of Oscar Wilde* (London, 1930), p. 43.

97. Rothenstein, *Men and Memories*, I, 90; Sherard, *The Story of an Unhappy Friendship* (London, 1902), pp. 46-47.

98. See *The Real Oscar Wilde* (London, 1916), pp. 251-52; *The Life of Oscar Wilde* (London, 1906), pp. 238-40; *The Story of an Unhappy Friendship*, pp. 45-48.

99. *Oscar Wilde* (Paris, 1927), pp. 22-23.

100. Shanks, "Oscar Wilde," *London Mercury*, 9, 57 (July, 1924), p. 281; Jackson, *The Eighteen Nineties* (London, 1913), p. 99.

101. *Oscar Wilde and the Yellow 'Nineties* (New York, 1940), p. 110.

102. *The Religion of Beauty*, ed. Aldington (London, 1950), p. 27.

103. Wilde, *Selected Works, With Twelve Unpublished Letters*, ed. Aldington (London, 1946), pp. 25-26.

104. "An Improbable Life," *New Yorker*, 39, 3 (9 Mar. 1963), p. 176.

105. *Degeneration*, translated from the Second Edition of the German Work (London, 1895), pp. [vii], 322, 285.

106. *Letters*, pp. 458, 461.

107. André Gide, *Oscar Wilde*, trans. Bernard Frechtman (London, 1951), p. 15.

108. *Story of an Unhappy Friendship*, pp. 43-44.

109. *Letters*, pp. 490, 480.

CHAPTER 4

1. *London Nights* (London, 1895; second edition, revised 1897), p. xiii.

2. *Silhouettes* (London, 1892; second edition, revised and enlarged, 1896), p. xiii-xiv.

3. *London Nights* (1897), p. xiii.

4. "Editorial Note," *Savoy*, II (April 1896), p. [5].

5. Russell M. Goldfarb, "Arthur Symons' Decadent Poetry," *Victorian Poetry*, 1, 3 (Aug. 1963), 231-34.

6. *Silhouettes* (1896), p. xv.

7. "The Soul of Man under Socialism," *The Artist as Critic*, p. 272.

8. *Studies in Two Literatures* (London, 1897), pp. 188-89.

9. *Studies in Seven Arts* (London, 1906), p. 108.

10. *Studies in Two Literatures*, pp. 232-33, 203.

11. *Studies in Two Literatures*, pp. 239, 196, 192.

12. *The Symbolist Movement in Literature* (London, 1899), p. 111.

13. "A Note on W. S. Blunt," *Café Royal and Other Essays* [London, 1923], p. 49.

14. *Studies in Two Literatures*, pp. 188-201.

15. T. S. Eliot, "Ulysses, Order, and Myth," *Dial*, 75, 5 (Nov. 1932), 483.

16. *Studies in Two Literatures*, p. 189.

17. "The Decadent Movement in Literature," *Harper's New Monthly Magazine*, 87, 522 (Nov. 1893), 859.

18. "The Decadent Movement in Literature," p. 859.

19. *Studies in Seven Arts*, p. 139.

20. *Studies in Two Literatures*, p. 191.

21. *London, A Book of Aspects* (London, 1909), pp. 50-51.

22. *Wanderings* (London, 1931), p. 216.

23. *Marius*, II, 19; "A Poet with Something to Say," *Uncollected Essays*, p. 85.

24. *London, A Book of Aspects*, p. 59.

25. "On the Genius of Degas," *From Toulouse-Lautrec to Rodin* (London, 1929), p. 118; *Studies in Two Literatures*, p. 233.

26. See Claude Pichois et François Ruchon, *Iconographie de Charles Baudelaire* (Genève, 1960), pp. 119-20, and plate 117.

27. This poem echoes in Symons's work more than once: in *Images of Good and Evil* (1899) he alludes to it sardonically:

> I am the torch, she saith, and what to me
> If the moth die of me? I am the flame
> Of Beauty, and I burn that all may see
> Beauty, and I have neither joy nor shame,
> But live with that clear life of perfect fire
> Which is to men the death of their desire.

Since she is "Modern Beauty," she lacks lovers: "Still am I / The torch, but where's the moth that still dares die?" (pp. 118-19).

28. T. S. Eliot, "Introduction" to Baudelaire, *Intimate Journals* (trans. Isherwood), p. 17.

29. R. Lhombreaud, *Arthur Symons, A Critical Biography* (London, 1963), p. 29; *Days and Nights*, pp. 84-89.

30. "The Paris of the Second Empire in Baudelaire," completed in 1938, first pub. 1967-68, repr. in Charles Baudelaire, *A Lyric Poet in the Era of High Capitalism*, trans. Harry Zohn (London, 1983), p. 38. Compare Eliot in the drafts of *The Waste Land*. (See below, pp. 338-40.)

31. "A Note on W. S. Blunt," *Café Royal and Other Essays*, pp. 51-52.

32. *Studies in Seven Arts*, pp. 136-37.

33. See above, p. 12. Several of Symons's critics have noted these or other borrowings. See, e.g., Wendell Harris, "Innocent Decadence: The Poetry of the *Savoy*," *PMLA*, 77, 5 (Dec. 1962), 635.

34. *Silhouettes* (1896), p. 30; *OC*, I, 92.

35. *Savoy*, V (Sept. 1896), 55-56; *OC*, I, 89-91.

36. *Savoy*, I (Jan. 1896), 149-50; *OC*, I, 129-34.

37. *London Nights* (London, 1895), p. 66.

38. Villiers de l'Isle-Adam, *Claire Lenoir*, trans. Symons (New York, 1925), p. xx.

39. *Images of Good and Evil*, pp. 68, 71.

40. Lhombreaud, p. 34; "The Decadent Movement," p. 866.

41. *Studies in Two Literatures*, pp. vii-viii.

42. P. [viii].

43. Coleridge, *Biographia Literaria*, introduction by Symons [1906], p. [vii].

44. *The Romantic Movement in English Poetry*, p. 14.

45. *The Purgatory of Dante Alighieri*, trans. C. L. Shadwell. Introduction by Pater (1892), p. xviii.

46. See Lhombreaud, pp. 166-67.

47. See below, pp. 265, 334-35; Edward Thomas, *Maurice Maeterlinck* (London, 1911), p. ix; Thomas Hardy, *Literary Notebooks*, II.

48. *The Symbolist Movement in Literature*, ed. Richard Ellmann (New York, 1958), p. viii. On the essays in the book, and for a discussion of Symons's attitude toward Baudelaire, see Ruth Z. Temple, *The Critic's Alchemy*, pp. 153-73.

49. *The Symbolist Movement in Literature* (1899), p. 6.

50. Eliot, " 'Poet and Saint . . .' " (cited above, p. 390, n. 13).

51. Ellmann, *The Symbolist Movement in Literature*, p. vii.

52. Quoted by Lhombreaud, p. 141.

53. Under the title of "The Decadent Movement in Literature," *Savoy*, VIII (Dec. 1896), 93; "Walter Pater, Some Characteristics," pp. [33]-41.

54. "Walter Pater, Some Characteristics," pp. 34, 35. This article became the introduction to *Portraits Imaginaires*, trans. George Knopff (Paris [1899]).

55. Barbara Charlesworth, *Dark Passages: The Decadent Consciousness in Victorian Literature* (Madison & Milwaukee, 1965), p. 97.

56. *The Symbolist Movement in Literature*, p. 6.

57. *Renaissance* (1873), pp. 208-12; *The Symbolist Movement in Literature* (1899), pp. [171]-75.

58. See Ellmann, *The Symbolist Movement in Literature* (1958), p. xii; Lhombreaud, pp. 132-35; John M. Munro, "Arthur Symons and W. B. Yeats: The Quest for Compromise," *Dalhousie Review*, 45, 2 (Summer 1965), 137-52.

59. Arnold B. Sklare, "Arthur Symons: An Appreciation of the Critic of Literature," *Journal of Aesthetics*, 9, 4 (1951), 316-22.

60. "Arthur Symons and W. B. Yeats . . . ," p. 143.

61. *Autobiographies*, p. 373; *The Symbolist Movement in Literature* (1899), p. 10.

62. *Renaissance* (1873), pp. xi, 15.

63. *The Symbolist Movement in Literature*, pp. 10, 35.

64. *The Symbolist Movement in Literature*, pp. 34, 31, 33.

65. *The Symbolist Movement in Literature*, pp. 4, 51, 136.

66. *Dante Gabriel Rossetti* (London, [1910]), p. 33; cf. *OC*, II, 425.

67. *The Symbolist Movement in Literature*, p. 35.
68. *The Symbolist Movement in Literature*, p. 129; *OC*, II, 791.
69. *The Symbolist Movement in Literature*, p. 8.
70. *The Critic's Alchemy*, p. 133.
71. *The Symbolist Movement in Literature*, p. 85.
72. *The Symbolist Movement in Literature*, p. 44.
73. P. 60. Cf. Yeats, "The recoil from scientific naturalism has created in our day the movement the French call *symboliste*, which, beginning with the memorable 'Axel,' by Villiers de l'Isle-Adam, has added to drama a new kind of romance. . . . This movement, and in art more especially, has proved so consonant with a change in the times, in the desires of our hearts grown weary with material circumstance, that it has begun to touch even the great public" (*Savoy*, III [July 1896], 41).
74. *The Symbolist Movement in Literature*, p. [41].
75. *The Symbolist Movement in Literature*, p. 91.
76. *Spiritual Adventures* (London, 1905), p. 169.
77. *Spiritual Adventures*, pp. 160-61, 154, 110-11.
78. *Cities* (1903), p. v.
79. Lhombreaud, p. 187.
80. "Balzac," *Studies in Prose and Verse* (London, [1904]), pp. 5-6. First published in *Fortnightly Review* (May 1899), 745-57.
81. *London, A Book of Aspects*, p. 59.
82. Pater, *Letters*, pp. 79-80. Quoted by Lhombreaud, p. 43.
83. *Spiritual Adventures*, p. 49. ("A Prelude to Life," the first chapter of *Spiritual Adventures*, was probably written about 1895. See Lhombreaud, p. 309n.)
84. Quoted here from *Figures of Several Centuries* (London, 1916), pp. 311-12. Here, the essay is dated 1906. It actually appeared first in 1907: "Baudelaire in His Letters," *Saturday Review*, 103 (26 Jan. 1907), pp. 107-108. (I am grateful for this information to Professor L. W. Markert.)
85. *Studies in Seven Arts*, pp. 18, 15, 188, 136, 139.
86. *Cities*, p. v.
87. *Spiritual Adventures*, p. 152. First published as "Peter Waydelin's Experiment," *Lippincott's Monthly Magazine* (Feb. 1904), 219-29.
88. *Spiritual Adventures*, p. 53.
89. *London, A Book of Aspects*, pp. 22, 48.
90. *London*, p. 14; *OC*, I, 85-87.
91. *London*, pp. 66-73; *OC*, I, 296.
92. Lhombreaud, p. 322n.; *Wanderings*, pp. 169, 216-17.
93. "Charles Baudelaire," *English Review*, 26 (Jan. 1918), 49-55; "A Study of Charles Baudelaire," *London Quarterly Review*, 260 (Oct. 1918), pp. 178-88; "Baudelaire and His Letters," *English Review*, 28 (May 1919), 376-86 (also in *North American Review*, 210, 776 [Sept. 1919], pp. 379-87).
94. Lhombreaud, pp. 301, 257.

95. See "Baudelaire and Decadence," *TLS*, 1003 (7 April 1921), 217, and below, pp. 315ff.

96. *From Toulouse-Lautrec to Rodin*, p. 66: the passage is repeated in Pierre Louys, *The Woman and the Puppet*, translated with an introduction by Symons (London, 1935), p. 19.

97. Lhombreaud, p. 323n.

98. *Charles Baudelaire, A Study*, pp. 99, 101-102. "Symons also had in his library an unpublished manuscript of Baudelaire, a review of Janin's *Le Gâteau des rois*. His copy of *Les Fleurs du mal*, which he described in his *Baudelaire* as one of the very rare on Holland paper, was actually one of those on ordinary paper." Information from Professor W. T. Bandy.

CHAPTER 5

1. *Charles Baudelaire* (Paris, 1917), pp. viii, ix.

2. "Charles Baudelaire," *Fortnightly Review*, 18 n.s. (1 Oct. 1875), pp. 500-18.

3. *The Beardsley Period* (London, 1925), pp. 61-62.

4. Stanford, *Poets of the 'Nineties* (London, 1965), p. 41.

5. Cf. *Oeuvres Complètes*, II, 472.

6. "Poet and Saint . . . ," *Dial*, 82, 5 (May 1927), p. 430.

7. *Landmarks in French Literature* (London, 1912; repr. 1923), p. 222.

8. Symons, "Charles Baudelaire," *The English Review*, 26 (Jan. 1918), 49; Yeats, *A Vision* (London, 1925, second ed. 1937, repr. 1962), p. 129.

9. *Trio: Dissertations on Some Aspects of National Genius* (London, 1938), pp. 101-102.

10. J. C. Squire, *The Honeysuckle and the Bee* (London, 1937), pp. 198-99.

11. *Poems and Baudelaire Flowers*, pp. 9, 28-29, 33.

12. "Baudelaire," *Books Reviewed* (London, 1922), pp. 39-45. (First published as "Baudelaire as a Literary Artist," *Living Age*, 19 March 1921.)

13. Published by the Limited Editions Club, New York.

14. Cf. D. H. Lawrence, below, p. 237.

15. "Editorial Notes," *London Mercury*, 1, 2 (Dec. 1919), pp. 130-31.

16. Aldington, [Review of] "Blast," *The Egoist*, 1, 14 (15 July 1914), p. 272.

17. *Letters*, ed. Grover Smith (London, 1969), p. 64.

18. "Accidie," *On the Margin, Notes and Essays* (London, 1923), pp. 18-25; "Baudelaire," *Do What You Will* (London, 1929), pp. 171-202.

19. [T. S. Eliot], "The Post-Georgians," *Athenaeum* (11 April 1919), p. 171.

20. R. Z. Temple, "Aldous Huxley et la littérature française," *Revue de littérature comparée*, 19 (Jan.-March 1939), 65-110. See also James S. Patty, "Baudelaire and Aldous Huxley," *South Atlantic Bulletin*, 33, 4

(Nov. 1969), pp. 5-8; and Derek P. Scales, *Aldous Huxley and French Literature*, Australian Humanities Research Council Monograph Number 13 (Sydney, 1969).

21. *Letters*, p. 282.

22. *Letters*, p. 308. He writes to Valéry: "En le traduisant Mallarmé a transfiguré 'The Raven' à peu près comme Beethoven a transfiguré dans ses grandes variations la valse de Diabelli."

23. See Scales, p. 87. A photograph of the death mask is printed in Enid Starkie, *Baudelaire*, facing p. 512.

24. *Point Counter Point* (London, 1928), p. 132. Further references to the novel will be to this edition and will be given parenthetically in the text.

25. See Scales, pp. 87-90.

26. Cf. Murry, "The Cause of it All," *Adelphi* 1,1 (June 1923), p. 5: "We believe in life. Just that. And to reach that belief, to hold it firm and unshakable, has been no easy matter for some of us. We have paid for it. Good!"

27. See below, pp. 318-24.

28. *Letters*, p. 294.

29. *Letters*, p. 295.

30. D. H. Lawrence, *Collected Letters*, ed. Harry T. Moore, 2 vols. (London, 1962, repr. 1965), [ii], 1049.

31. D. H. Lawrence, *Letters*, ed. Aldous Huxley (London, 1932), p. 834.

32. D. H. Lawrence, *Letters*, ed. James T. Boulton (Cambridge, 1979), I, 179.

33. *Women in Love*. With an Introduction by Richard Aldington (London, 1921, repr. 1966), p. 375. *Pansies, Poems* (Bandol, 1929), p. [iii].

34. H. R. Daleski, *The Forked Flame, A Study of D. H. Lawrence* (London, 1965), p. 102. See Lawrence, *The Rainbow*. With an Introduction by Richard Aldington (London, 1915; new ed. 1955, repr. 1968), pp. 194-207.

35. *Do What You Will*, p. 189.

36. *The New Poetic* (London, 1964), pp. 54, 49.

37. *Figures of Several Centuries*, p. 310.

38. "Farewell to Europe," *Atlantic Monthly*, 166, 4 (Oct. 1940), 517.

39. "A Few Remarks on Sitwellism," *Time and Tide*, 9, 14 (6 April 1928), 332.

40. *Aspects of Modern Poetry* (London, 1934), p. 13.

41. "Modern Poetry," *Time and Tide*, 9, 13 (30 March 1928), 308.

42. "New Publications," *Sackbut*, 2, 11 (June 1922), 35.

43. *Edith Sitwell's Anthology* (London, 1940), pp. 152-53.

44. *The Pleasures of Poetry* (London, 1930), 3 vols., III, 4.

45. *Edith Sitwell's Anthology*, p. 153.

46. *Selected Letters*, ed. John Lehmann and Derek Parker (London,

1970), p. 252. See also pp. 104, 198, and cf. *The Pleasures of Poetry*, III, 3-4.

47. Victoria Glendinning, *Edith Sitwell, A Unicorn Among Lions* (London, 1981), p. 34.

48. "A Few Remarks on Sitwellism," p. 333.

49. *Aspects of Modern Poetry*, p. 142; "Readers and Writers," *New Age*, 31, 18 (31 Aug. 1922), 222.

50. *Aspects of Modern Poetry*, p. 141.

51. "Readers and Writers," *New Age*, 31, 15 (10 Aug. 1922), 184.

52. Arthur Rimbaud, *Prose Poems from Les Illuminations*, trans. Helen Rootham, with an introductory essay by Edith Sitwell (London, 1932), p. 47.

53. "Lecture on Poetry Since 1920," *Life and Letters To-Day*, 39, 75 (Nov. 1943), 74-75.

54. "Some Notes on My Own Poetry," *Collected Poems* (London, 1957, repr. 1965), p. xvi.

55. Sacheverell Sitwell, *Sacred and Profane Love* (London, 1940), p. 41.

56. John Pearson, *Façades, Edith, Osbert, and Sacheverell Sitwell* (London, 1978), pp. 54-55.

57. "Readers and Writers," *New Age*, 31, 21 (21 Sept. 1922), 261.

58. Pearson, *Façades*, pp. 166-67.

59. See Pearson, *Façades*, pp. 166-68; Glendinning, *Edith Sitwell*, pp. 65-70.

60. *A Poet's Notebook* (London, 1943), p. 55.

61. Pearson, *Façades*, p. 145.

62. Quoted by Glendinning, *Edith Sitwell*, p. 67.

63. *Wheels*, 1917, p. 106.

64. *Wheels*, 1921, p. 57.

65. "Miss Edith Sitwell have and had and heard," *London Magazine*, 4, 8 (Nov. 1964), 57. Cf. also "The Jolly Old Squire or Way-Down in Georgia," *Chapbook*, 29 (Sept. 1922), 13-24.

66. Pearson, *Façades*, p. 151.

67. *Wheels* I (1916), pp. 9-12.

68. *Wheels* I, pp. 60-61.

69. *Wheels* I, pp. 32-33.

70. *Wheels* I, p. 27.

71. *Wheels* IV (1919), pp. 9-11.

72. "Modern Art I: The Grafton Gallery," *Further Speculations*, ed. Sam Hynes (Minneapolis, 1955), p. 116.

73. *Wheels*, I, 25.

74. *Collected Poems*, pp. 4-5. Cf. *Oeuvres Complètes*, I, 89-91.

75. *I Live Under a Black Sun* (London, 1937), pp. 154-55.

76. See below, p. 318.

77. *Landmarks in French Literature*, p. 223.

78. *A Poet's Notebook*, p. 39.

79. *Life and Letters To-Day*, 39, 75 (Nov. 1943), pp. 70-97.

80. *A Poet's Notebook*, pp. v, 55.

81. *A Poet's Notebook*, p. 55.

82. "Introductory Essay," in Rimbaud, *Illuminations*, pp. 28-29.

83. *The Pleasures of Poetry*, I, 45-46. Sitwell printed, "Mon ange, ma soeur, / Songe à la douceur"; Baudelaire wrote, "Mon enfant, ma soeur." As Victoria Glendinning reports, the incident produced "a hell of a row" in the TLS (*Edith Sitwell*, pp. 146-47).

84. *The Mirror of Baudelaire*, ed. Charles Henri Ford, with a Preface by Paul Eluard and a drawing by Henri Matisse (Norfolk, Connecticut, 1941).

85. *A Poet's Notebook*, p. 14; *Collected Poems*, p. xvii; *The Symbolist Movement in Literature*, p. 59.

86. 31, 12 (20 July 1922), 148; 31, 10 (6 July 1922), 120. Cf. *The Symbolist Movement*, pp. 15, 56.

87. *Selected Letters*, p. 175.

88. "Auto-Obituary III—'The Late Miss Sitwell,' " *Listener*, 16, 394 (29 July 1936), pp. 191-92.

89. *Aspects of Modern Poetry*, pp. 186-87.

90. *A Poet's Notebook*, p. 13.

91. *Aspects of Modern Poetry*, pp. 10-11.

92. *Taken Care Of, An Autobiography* (London, 1965), p. 49.

93. *Trio*, pp. 165-66.

94. "In Praise of Jean Cocteau," *London Magazine*, 3, 2 (Feb. 1956), 14.

95. *A Poet's Notebook*, p. v.

96. *A Poet's Notebook*, p. 4.

97. "A Few Remarks on Sitwellism," p. 333.

98. *Collected Poems*, p. 149.

99. *Collected Poems*, p. 119.

100. *Collected Poems*, p. 273.

101. *Collected Poems*, p. 165.

102. *Collected Poems*, pp. 170-71.

103. "A Few Remarks on Sitwellism," p. 332.

104. "On My Poetry," in *Orpheus: A Symposium of the Arts*, ed. John Lehmann, 2 (London, 1949), 103.

105. "Modern Poetry," *Time and Tide*, IX, 13, 308.

106. *Collected Poems*, p. 9.

107. "New Publications," *Sackbut*, 3, 1 (Aug. 1922), 32.

108. "A Few Remarks on Sitwellism," p. 332.

109. *Selected Letters*, p. 195.

CHAPTER 6

1. T. S. Eliot, *American Literature and the American Language* (St. Louis, Mo., 1953), reprinted in *To Criticize the Critic and Other Writings* (London,

1965), p. 58; William Pratt, ed., *The Imagist Poem* (New York, 1963), p. 8; Peter Jones, ed., *Imagist Poetry* (London, 1972), p. 14.

2. T. E. Hulme, *Further Speculations*, ed. Sam Hynes (Minneapolis, 1955), p. 68. In this chapter, further references to this work will be given in the text and its title abbreviated as *FS*.

3. Richard Aldington, "Reviews," *Egoist*, 1, 13 (1 July 1914), 247; "A Note on Free Verse in England," *Egoist* 1, 18 (15 Sept. 1914), 352.

4. J. B. Harmer, *Victory in Limbo, Imagism 1908-1917* (London, 1975), p. 146.

5. Aldington, "A Note on Free Verse," *Chapbook*, 40 (1925), 36.

6. "Introduction" to Baudelaire, *Intimate Journals* (London, 1930), p. 18. (*Selected Essays*, p. 426.)

7. Symons, "The Decadent Movement in Literature," p. 859.

8. Pound, *Letters 1907-1941* (New York, 1950), p. 216. I have corrected Pound's "1980." Fletcher, *Life is My Song* (New York, 1937), p. 222; [Monro], "Literature in 1922: A Survey," *Chapbook*, 23 (Jan. 1923), 13.

9. *Speculations, Essays on Humanism and the Philosophy of Art*, ed. Herbert Read (1924; second ed. 1936), p. 140. In this chapter, further references to this work will be given in the text and its title abbreviated as *S*.

10. Oscar Wilde, *Selected Works* (London, 1946); Walter Pater, *Selected Works* (London, 1948); *The Religion of Beauty, Selections from the Aesthetes* (London, 1950).

11. Aldington, "Blast," *Egoist*, 1, 14 (15 July 1914), 273.

12. [Unsigned], "The Post-Georgians," *Athenaeum*, 4641 (11 April 1919), 171-72. The attribution is Donald Gallup's (*T. S. Eliot, A Bibliography* [London, 1969], p. 203).

13. "The Poetry of John Gould Fletcher," *Egoist*, 2, 5 (May 1915), 73.

14. "In Metre," *New Freewoman*, 1, 7 (15 Sept. 1913), 131-32; Pound, *Letters*, p. 59.

15. James D. Hart, *The Oxford Companion to American Literature*, Fourth Edition (New York, 1965, repr. 1971), p. [282].

16. *Imagism and the Imagists* (Stanford and London, 1931), p. 126.

17. *Life is My Song*, pp. 16, 21-22, 245.

18. *Visions of the Evening* (London, 1913), pp. 21, 1-2.

19. "Song of a Night," *The Dominant City*, p. 19.

20. See above, p. 221-25.

21. "In Metre," p. 132.

22. Sinclair, "The Poems of F. S. Flint," *English Review*, 32 (Jan. 1921), 6-18; Hueffer, "Literary Portraits—XXXV, Les Jeunes and 'Des Imagistes,' " *Outlook*, 33, 849 (9 May 1914), 636, 653; Monro, "A Bibliography of Modern Poetry," *Chapbook*, 12 (June 1920), 16.

23. Ernest Dowson, *Poetical Works*, ed. Desmond Flower (London, 1934, third ed. 1967), p. 158.

24. *In the Net of the Stars* (London, 1909), p. 13.

25. *Otherworld Cadences* (London, 1920), p. 44.

26. Robert Graves, *Contemporary Techniques of Poetry* (London, 1925), p. 18.

27. *In the Net of the Stars*, p. 18; Wallace Martin, *The New Age Under Orage, Chapters in English Cultural History* (Manchester and New York, 1967), p. 165.

28. "Some Reflections on Ernest Dowson," *Egoist*, 2, 3 (1 March 1915), 41.

29. *Egoist*, 3, 2 (1 Feb. 1916), 26.

30. *Images* [1919], p. 35.

31. *Images (1910-1915)* [1915], p. 6.

32. René Taupin, *L'Influence du Symbolisme Français sur la Poésie Américaine* (de *1910 à 1920*) (Paris, 1929). The marginal comment is on p. 83. The book is in the Henry W. and Albert A. Berg Collection, The New York Public Library. Its inscriptions indicate that it was given by Taupin to Eliot and by Eliot to Flint.

33. "The Prose of Frederick Manning," *Egoist*, 1, 19 (Oct. 1914), 375.

34. *Letters*, p. 9.

35. Christopher Middleton, "Documents on Imagism from the Papers of F. S. Flint," *The Review* (Oxford), 15 (April 1965), 46.

36. *Thus to Revisit, Some Reminiscences* (London, 1921), p. 28.

37. *The New Age After Orage*, p. 145. Pound made the remark in his *Ripostes, Whereto are Appended the Complete Poetical Works of T. E. Hulme, With a Prefatory Note* (London, 1912), p. 59.

38. "A Jubilee," *Outlook*, 36, 910 (10 July 1915), 47.

39. The Humanities Research Center, University of Texas, has letters from Hulme to Flint which make clear the fact of Hulme's dependence upon Flint for the translations.

40. Taupin, *L'Influence du Symbolisme Français* . . . , p. 129; cf. Le Roy C. Breunig, "F. S. Flint, Imagism's 'Maître d'Ecole,' " *Comparative Literature*, 4, 2 (Spring 1952), 118-36.

41. "Some Recent French Poems," *Egoist*, 1, 12 (15 June 1914), 221.

42. Middleton, "Papers of F. S. Flint," p. 36.

43. *Letters*, pp. 34, 35.

44. Joy Grant, *Harold Monro and The Poetry Bookshop* (London, 1967), p. 47.

45. "Contemporary French Poetry," *Poetry Review*, 1, 8 (Aug. 1912), pp. 357-58.

46. Middleton, "Papers of F. S. Flint," pp. 44-45. The transcript is correct.

47. "Papers of F. S. Flint," p. 36.

48. "Recent Verse," *New Age*, 4, 16 (11 Feb. 1909), 327.

49. *Poetry Review*, 1, 8, 356.

50. *Poetry Review*, 1, 8, 357.

51. "Verse," *New Age*, 5, 23 (30 Sept. 1909), 412.

52. "Recent Verse," *New Age*, 3, 11 (11 July 1908), 212.

53. "Recent Verse," *New Age*, 4, 16 (11 Feb. 1909), 327.

54. *New Age*, 5, 23, 412.

55. "Contemporary French Poetry," *Poetry Review*, 1, 8, 361.

56. *Romantic Image* (London, 1957; repr. 1961), pp. 121, 129.

57. "Recent Verse," *New Age*, 4, 16 (11 Feb. 1909), 327.

58. "Belated Romanticism" [letter to the Editor], *New Age*, 4, 17 (18 Feb. 1909), 350.

59. Mallarmé, *Oeuvres Complètes* (Paris, 1945; repr. 1970), p. 368.

60. Mallarmé, *Oeuvres Complètes*, pp. 366, 368.

61. "Imagisme," *Poetry*, 1, 6 (March 1913), 199; "A Few Don'ts by an Imagiste," *Poetry*, 1, 6, 203, 205.

62. *Appreciations*, pp. 31-32, 16.

63. "Introduction" to Baudelaire, *Intimate Journals*, trans. C. Isherwood, p. 16.

64. Marginal comment in Berg Collection copy of Taupin, *L'Influence du Symbolisme Français . . . ,*" p. 128.

65. "*A Boy's Will* by Robert Frost," *Poetry and Drama*, 1, 2 (June 1913), 250; "The Poetry of H. D.," *Egoist*, 2, 5 (1 May 1915), 73.

66. "Farewell to Europe," *Atlantic Monthly*, 166, 3-6 (Sept. 1940 to Dec. 1940), 657; F.-J. Temple in *Richard Aldington: An Intimate Portrait*, ed. Alistair Kershaw and F.-J. Temple (Carbondale, Ill., 1965), p. 141.

67. "Farewell to Europe," pp. 521, 656.

68. "Loose Leaves," *Egoist*, 2, 6 (1 June 1915), 98.

69. *Egoist*, 2, 12 (1 Dec. 1915), 195.

70. "New Poetry," *Egoist*, 2, 6 (1 June 1915), 89.

71. "Contemporanea," *Egoist*, 5, 6 (June/July 1918), 84.

72. "Farewell to Europe," pp. 653-54.

73. "A Young American Poet," *Little Review*, 2, 1 (March 1915), 22.

74. "Some Reflections on Ernest Dowson," p. 41.

75. "Remy de Gourmont," *Little Review*, 2, 3 (May 1915), 10.

76. Gourmont, *Selections*, Chosen and trans. Aldington (London, 1932), p. 7.

77. *Little Review*, 2, 3, 11.

78. *Promenades Littéraires (Quatrième Série)* (Paris, 1912; 8th ed., 1920), p. 5.

79. *Le Livre des Masques* (Paris, 1896; 15th ed., 1923), pp. 57-58.

80. See Glenn S. Burne, *Remy de Gourmont, His Ideas and Influence in England and America* (Carbondale, Ill., 1963), p. 104.

81. "Some Reflections on Ernest Dowson," p. 41.

82. Marcel Coulon, "Le Symbolisme d'Ephraim Mikhael," 101 (1 Nov. 1913), 497; Ernest Raynaud, "Considérations sur Paul Verlaine," 95 (16 Jan. 1912), 277; Georges Duhamel [review of *Au Vent Crispé du Matin*], 105 (16 Sept. 1913), 378; Georges Duhamel, "Les Poèmes," 106 (16 Nov. 1913), 365; Henri Dérieux, "L'Oeuvre de Léon Dierx," 95 (16 Jan. 1912), 226.

83. R. de Bury [Remy de Gourmont], "Les Journaux," 40 (Oct. 1901), 226. I am grateful to Professor W. T. Bandy for the identification.

84. Varcollier, "Lettres Inédites de M. Ingres," 91 (1 May 1911), 7.

85. Jean Giraud, "Georges Catlin, le 'cornac des sauvages,' et Charles Baudelaire," 107 (6 Nov. 1914), 875.

86. "Réflexions sur l'Humour," 110 (1 July 1914), 56.

87. "Littérature," 61 (15 April 1907), 724.

88. "A Propos de Quelques Poètes Modernes," 105 (16 Oct. 1913), 696-713. "Et j'aborderai tout de suite un des points importants de cette étude. BAUDELAIRE OU WALT WHITMAN?" (p. 697).

89. "Littérature," 66 (15 April 1907), 722.

90. "Baudelaire et le Songe d'Athalie," 56 (1 July 1905), p. 25.

91. Ernest Raynaud, "Considérations sur Paul Verlaine," p. 277.

92. Gilbert Maire, "Un Essai de Classification des 'Fleurs du Mal' et son Utilité Pour la Critique," 65 (15 Jan. 1907), 265.

93. "Littérature," 104 (1 Aug. 1913), 604.

94. The draft is entitled, "A Note on Baudelaire To-day." (Charles Baudelaire, Etude Biographique par Eugène Crépet. Paris. Messein. 5 fr.) It is MS Orioli, 9, Misc. 2, at the Humanities Research Center, University of Texas. It was published, anonymously, as "Notes on Baudelaire," *TLS*, 935 (18 Dec. 1919), 762. For this last fact, I am indebted to Professor W. T. Bandy.

95. Baudelaire, *Lettres, 1841-1866* (first published 1906; repr. 1915); *Journaux Intimes*, ed. Ad. van Bever (Paris, 1919).

96. "A Note on Free Verse," *Chapbook*, 40 (1925), 36.

97. *Sphere*, 80, 1045 (31 Jan. 1920), 128.

98. *Literary Studies and Reviews* (1924), p. 239.

99. *Studies in Two Literatures*, p. 232.

100. [Unsigned], "Experiments," *New Statesman*, 6, 155 (25 March 1916), pp. 599-600.

101. [To Robert Ross], June 1918, in *Robert Ross Friend of Friends*, ed. Margaret Ross (London, 1952), p. 332.

102. "The Serious Artist," *New Freewoman*, 1, 9 (15 Oct. 1913), 162.

103. "The Poet's Eye," *New Freewoman*, 1, 6 (1 Sept. 1913), 109.

104. *Life is My Song*, p. 53.

105. "The Poetry of F. S. Flint," *Egoist*, 2, 5 (1 May 1915), 80.

106. "The Poetry of F. S. Flint," p. 80.

107. "The Imagists Discussed," *Egoist*, 2, 5 (1 May 1915), 78.

108. "The Poetry of Ezra Pound," *Egoist*, 2, 5 (1 May 1915), 71.

109. "Parochialism in Art," *Egoist*, 1, 23 (1 Dec. 1914), 443.

110. "Two Poets," *Egoist*, 1, 22 (16 Nov. 1914), 422.

111. "Verse," *New Age*, 6, 10 (6 Jan. 1910), 234.

112. "The Little Demon," *Egoist*, 3, 5 (1 May 1916), 65-66.

113. "Simplicity," *In the Net of the Stars*, pp. 32-33.

114. "Otherworld," *Otherworld Cadences*, pp. 8-9.

115. "Palinode," *In the Net of the Stars*, pp. 14-15.

116. *Egoist*, 1, 2 (15 Jan. 1914), 36.

117. *Images* [1919], p. 42.

118. *Images* [1919], p. 51.

119. *Images* [1919], p. 49.

120. *Complete Poems* (London, 1958), pp. 111-13.

121. Harold Monro, *Collected Poems*, ed. Alida Monro, with a biographical sketch by F. S. Flint and a critical note by T. S. Eliot (London, 1933), p. xv.

122. *Otherworld Cadences*, p. 28.

123. *Cadences*, p. 25.

124. *Cadences*, pp. 22, 12, 19.

125. *Images* (1910-1915) [1915], p. 24.

126. "A Literary Transference," *Southern Review*, 6, 1 (1940), 83.

127. *Sphere*, 80, 1045, 128.

CHAPTER 7

1. *Middleton Murry: A Study in Excellent Normality* (London, 1934), p. 16.

2. "Politics of a Mystic," *D. H. Lawrence Review*, 2, 1 (Spring 1969), 24; *A Theory of My Time, An Essay in Didactic Reminiscence* (London, 1963), p. 24.

3. Ernest G. Griffin, *John Middleton Murry* (New York, 1969), p. 21.

4. John Gross, *The Rise and Fall of the Man of Letters* (London, 1969), p. 246.

5. F. A. Lea, *The Life of John Middleton Murry* (London, 1959), p. [x].

6. 2, 1 (Spring 1969).

7. *A Number of People* (London, 1939), p. 225.

8. C. G. Thayer, "Murry's *Shakespeare*," *D. H. Lawrence Review*, 2, 1, 47.

9. See Gross, *The Rise and Fall of the Man of Letters*, p. 250 and Griffin, *John Middleton Murry*, p. 43.

10. Lea, *Life*, p. 157.

11. G. P. Lilley, *A Bibliography of John Middleton Murry* (London, 1974), p. 7.

12. *Blue Review*, I, 3 (July 1913), 164.

13. [Unsigned], "The Things We Are," *Saturday Review*, 133, 3468 (15 April 1922), 397.

14. "Foreword" to Murry, *Katherine Mansfield and Other Literary Studies* (London, 1959), p. ix.

15. Murry, *Between Two Worlds* (London, 1935), p. 121.

16. Quoted by Lea, *Life*, p. 20.

17. *Symbolist Movement in Literature*, p. 124.

18. *Between Two Worlds*, p. 129.

19. Lea, *Life*, p. 89.

20. *Between Two Worlds*, pp. 420, 430.

21. Lea, *Life*, p. 89.

22. Heppenstall, *Four Absentees* (London, 1960), p. 67.

23. *Between Two Worlds*, pp. 259, 255. See Griffin, *John Middleton Murry*, pp. 71-73 for a discussion of Murry's interest in Stendhal.

24. "Gerard Manley Hopkins," *Athenaeum*, 4649 (6 June 1919), 425.

25. " 'Rhythm' and 'The Blue Review,' " *TLS*, 3452 (25 April 1968), 423.

26. "The Condition of English Literature," *Athenaeum*, 4697 (7 May 1920), 598.

27. "Poetry and Criticism," *Athenaeum*, 4691 (26 March 1920), 408.

28. "The Aesthetic of Benedetto Croce," *Rhythm*, 1, 1 (Autumn 1911), 13.

29. "Forward" to *Katherine Mansfield and Other Literary Studies*, p. viii.

30. A. G. Lehmann, *The Symbolist Aesthetic in France 1885-1895* (Oxford, 1950; second ed., 1968), p. 81.

31. See "Art and Philosophy," *Rhythm*, 1, 1 (Summer 1911), 9-12; cf. *The Problem of Style*; and see below, pp. 324ff.

32. *Criterion*, 5, 3 (June 1927), pp. 294-313.

33. "Critical Interest," *Athenaeum*, 4686 (20 Feb. 1920), 234.

34. Murry, "Towards a Synthesis," *Criterion*, 5, 3, 294-313; Eliot, "Mr. Middleton Murry's Synthesis," *Criterion*, 6, 4 (Oct. 1927), 342-43.

35. Lea, *Life*, pp. 22-23.

36. "Art and Philosophy," *Rhythm*, 1, 1, 9-12.

37. *Le Message Poétique du Symbolisme* (Paris, 1947), p. 487.

38. *The Rise and Fall of the Man of Letters*, p. 246; *TLS*, 3452, p. 423.

39. Lea, *Life*, p. 18.

40. *Rhythm*, 1, 1, 36, 26.

41. "The Meaning of Rhythm," *Rhythm*, 2, 5 (June 1912), 19.

42. "Lettres de France: II, Esquisse de la Poésie Française Actuelle," *Rhythm*, 2, 3 (Aug. 1912), 114. The transcript is corrected.

43. *Rhythm*, 1, 1, 11; 1, 1, 36.

44. To P. Landon, Jan. 1911, quoted by Lea, *Life*, p. 20.

45. *Between Two Worlds*, pp. 156, 154, 174.

46. "Memories of Katherine Mansfield," *Adam International Review*, 300 (1965), p. 79.

47. *Rhythm*, 1, 1, 10.

48. Malcolm Bradbury, *TLS*, 3452, p. 423; *Between Two Worlds*, p. 157.

49. Lea, *Life*, p. 27; *Between Two Worlds*, p. 238.

50. "Songe d'Eté," *Rhythm*, 1, 1, 13; "Ennui," *Rhythm*, 1, 1, 22.

51. *Rhythm*, 1, 2 (Autumn 1911), 22-25, 8, 15; 2, 4 (Sept. 1912), 161; 2, 9 (Oct. 1912), 214-17; 1, 3 (Winter 1911), 17.

52. "The Two Lives," *Rhythm*, 2, 3 (Aug. 1912), 84.

53. *Rhythm*, 1, 3 (Winter 1911), 6.

54. "The Return to Poetry," *Rhythm*, 1, 4 (Spring 1912), 1.

55. *Rhythm*, 1, 2, 13.

56. "The Importance of Hegel to Modern Thought," *New Age*, 10, 9, n.s. (28 Dec. 1911), 204-205.

57. "French Books," *Blue Review*, 1, 1 (May 1913), 60.

58. *Blue Review*, 1, 2, 134, 138.

59. "The Cry in the Wilderness," *Athenaeum*, 4687 (27 Feb. 1920), 267.

60. "Verlaine," *Nation and Athenaeum*, 29, 2 (9 April 1921), 64.

61. "Hegel and Modern Criticism," *Nation*, 26, 24 (13 March 1920), 814.

62. "The Influence of Baudelaire," *Rhythm Literary Supplement*, 14 (March 1913), xxiii-xxvii; "Baudelaire," *Athenaeum*, 4721 (22 Oct. 1920), 564-65 and *Athenaeum*, 4722 (29 Oct. 1920), 596-97; "Baudelaire and Decadence," *TLS*, 1003 (7 April 1921), 217-18; "Baudelaire's Letters," *TLS*, 1360 (23 Feb. 1928), 126; "Baudelaire as Hero," *TLS*, 1536 (9 July 1931), 543. This last attribution is G. P. Lilley's (*John Middleton Murry*, p. 125).

63. Quoted by Murry, *Rhythm*, 14, xxv; Turquet-Milnes, p. 17.

64. A review of Ad Van Bever's edition of *Les Fleurs du Mal, Le Spleen de Paris, Journaux Intimes*.

65. "A Poet of the Moon," *Athenaeum*, 4710 (6 Aug. 1920), 169-70.

66. Wilde, "Preface" to *The Picture of Dorian Gray*, ed. Murray, p. [xxxiii].

67. In "Introduction" to Baudelaire, *Intimate Journals*, trans. C. Isherwood (1930), p. 18. Walter Benjamin sees this same quality as "a kind of mimesis of death" (*Baudelaire, A Lyric Poet in the Era of High Capitalism*, p. 83).

68. "Young English Painting," *Nation*, 28, 5 (30 Oct. 1920), 161-62.

69. "Mr. Walter Sickert's Paintings," *Nation*, 27, 17 (24 July 1920), 526; "English Painting and French Influence," *Nation*, 26, 18 (31 Jan. 1920), 600.

70. "Une Maladie Artistique: 'La Manie du Décoratif,' " *Anglo-French Review*, 4, 3 (Oct. 1920), 265.

71. "The Modernity of Mr. Augustus John," *Nation*, 26, 23 (6 March 1920), 770-71.

72. *Nation*, 26, 12 (20 Dec. 1919), 419-20.

73. "Epstein's Christ," *Nation*, 26, 20 (14 Feb. 1920), 669; "Henri Gaudier-Brzeska," *Nation*, 23, 10 (8 June 1918), 254.

74. "Epstein's Christ," p. 670.

75. "Mr. Fry among the Architects," *Nation and Athenaeum*, 29, 22 (27 Aug. 1921), 776.

76. *The Problem of Style* (London, 1922, 8th impression, 1952), p. 8. Further references to this work are given parenthetically in the text and abbreviated as *PS*.

77. *Countries of the Mind* (London, 1922), pp. 3-4.

78. "Coleridge's Criticism," *Athenaeum*, 4694 (16 April 1920), 504.

79. *Athenaeum*, 4722, p. 597.

80. See, for instance, *Renaissance* (1873), p. x, and compare Eliot and Pater, *Appreciations*, p. 27.

81. See below, pp. 394-95, and above, p. 145.

82. *Appreciations*, p. 31.

83. *Discoveries, Essays in Literary Criticism* (London, 1924), pp. 47-48.

84. "The Journeyman," "Novels and Thought-Adventures," *Adelphi*, 1, 6 (Nov. 1923), 532.

85. "Baudelaire's Letters" [review of *The Letters of Charles Baudelaire to His Mother (1833-1866)*, Translated by Arthur Symons], *TLS*, 1360 (23 Feb. 1928), 126.

86. "Novels and Thought-Adventures," p. 536.

87. In Murry, *Selected Criticism*, chosen and introduced by Rees (London, 1960), p. ix.

CHAPTER 8

1. See especially René Taupin, *L'Influence du Symbolisme Français* . . . , pp. 211-40; E.J.H. Greene, *T. S. Eliot et la France* (Paris, 1951); Wallace Fowlie, "Baudelaire and Eliot: Interpreters of Their Age," *Sewanee Review*, 74,1 (Jan.-March 1966), 293-309, repr. as *T. S. Eliot. The Man and His Work*, ed. Allen Tate (London, 1967); Nicole Ward, " 'Fourmillante Cité': Baudelaire and *The Waste Land*," in *The Waste Land in Different Voices*, ed. A. D. Moody (London, 1974), pp. 87-104; Francis Scarfe, "Eliot and Nineteenth-Century French Poetry," in *Eliot in Perspective, A Symposium*, ed. Graham Martin (New York, 1970), pp. 45-61; J. A. Beery, "The Relevance of Baudelaire to T. S. Eliot's *The Waste Land*," *Susquehanna University Studies*, 7, 5 (1966), 283-302; Sister M. Cecilia Carey, "Baudelaire's Influence on 'The Waste Land,' " *Renascence* (Milwaukee, Wisconsin), 14, 4 (1962), pp. 185-92, 198; R. Galand, "T. S. Eliot and the Impact of Baudelaire," *Yale French Studies*, 6 (1950), 27-34; Nelly Stéphane, "T. S. Eliot et Baudelaire," *Europe*, Année 45, No. 456-457 (April/May 1967), 244-46; A. K. Weatherhead, "Baudelaire in Eliot's *Ash Wednesday IV*," *ELN*, 2, 4 (June 1965), 288-89; K. Weinberg, *T. S. Eliot and Charles Baudelaire* (*Studies in General and Comparative Literature*, 5) (The Hague, 1969).

2. "John Dryden," *TLS*, 1012 (9 June 1921), 362; "Introduction" to Baudelaire, *Intimate Journals* (trans. Isherwood), p. 18.

3. "From Poe to Valéry," A lecture delivered at the Library of Congress, Washington, on Friday, November 19, 1948. Repr. in *To Criticize the Critic and Other Writings* (London, 1965), pp. 27-42.

4. *On Poetry and Poets* (London, 1957; repr. 1969), p. 252.

5. "What France Means to You," *La France Libre*, 8, 44 (15 June 1944), 94.

6. "Tradition and the Individual Talent," *Egoist*, 6, 4 (Sept. 1919), p. 55. Reprinted in *The Sacred Wood* (1920) and *Selected Essays* (1932).

7. Pound, *Letters*, p. 40.

8. "*Baudelaire and the Symbolists*. Five Essays. By Peter Quennell," *Criterion*, 9, 35 (Jan. 1930), 357.

9. *Poems Written in Early Youth* (London, 1967), pp. 18, 24, 25, 26, 28; Christophe Campos, *The View of France from Arnold to Bloomsbury* (London, 1965), p. 6.

10. *The Symbolist Movement in Literature*, p. 111.

11. "The Perfect Critic [I]," *Athenaeum*, 4706 (9 July 1920), 41; but cf. " 'Poet and Saint . . . ,' " *Dial*, 82, 5 (May 1927), [424]-31. "The Perfect Critic [I]" and "The Perfect Critic II" appear also in *The Sacred Wood*.

12. Quoted in *Studies in Two Literatures*, pp. 192-93.

13. *Silhouettes* (1896), p. 23.

14. "London Letter," *Dial*, 71, 4 (Oct. 1921), 453.

15. *Artist as Critic*, p. 312.

16. In "The Notebook" which is in the Berg Collection of the New York Public Library. The Notebook and its contents are described by Donald Gallup, "The 'Lost' Manuscripts of T. S. Eliot," *TLS*, 3480 (7 Nov. 1968), 1238-40.

17. "Tradition and the Individual Talent," *Egoist*, 6, 4, 55.

18. *T. S. Eliot et la France*, p. 18.

19. *The Symbolist Movement in Literature*, p. 6.

20. Scarfe, "Eliot and Nineteenth-Century French Poetry," p. 51: "Here, Eliot spoils Baudelaire's line (the last) by giving a line of thirteen syllables, and also gives his own punctuation, while, in his note, saying it is from the preface to *Les Fleurs du mal* when it is from 'Au Lecteur,' which is not strictly a preface." The point is trivial, since the "Au Lecteur" of the first edition of *FM* was the "Préface" of the "definitive edition" of 1868. Eliot's use of "Preface" perhaps indicates which edition he was using in about 1921.

21. *Poems Written in Early Youth*, p. 26.

22. D.E.S. Maxwell, *The Poetry of T. S. Eliot* (London, 1952), p. 60; Francis Scarfe, *op.cit.*, p. 50; Helen Gardner, *The Art of T. S. Eliot* (London, 1949), p. 81.

23. *The Waste Land, a Facsimile and Transcript of the Original Drafts Including the Annotations of Ezra Pound*, ed. Valerie Eliot (London, 1971), p. [10], [12]. (This edition hereafter cited as *TWLMS*.)

24. Pound, *Letters*, p. 161.

25. *TWLMS*, pp. [112]-[114], p. [30]. The second passage is shown in MS on p. [36].

26. *TWLMS*, p. 130.

27. David Ward, *T. S. Eliot, Between Two Worlds* (London, 1973).

28. Gautier in Baudelaire, *Les Fleurs du Mal* (Paris, 1868), p. 12. Gautier's preface was now translated into English. (Théophile Gautier, *Charles Baudelaire, His Life, Translated into English, with Selections from his Poems, "Little Poems in Prose," and Letters . . .* , by Guy Thorne [London, 1915].)

29. *Artist as Critic*, p. 343.

30. *TWLMS*, pp. [22]-29.

31. Eliot, in Ezra Pound, *Selected Poems*, ed. with an Introduction by Eliot (London, 1928), pp. x-xi.

32. *TWLMS*, p. [36].

33. *TWLMS*, pp. [54]-61; *Oeuvres Complètes*, I, 129-34.

34. Maxwell, *The Poetry of T. S. Eliot*, p. 73.

35. *TLS*, 1031 (20 Oct. 1921), p. 670. Reprinted in *Selected Essays*.

36. *T. S. Eliot et la France*, pp. 122-23.

37. *TWLMS*, p. [78].

38. "Poet and Saint . . . ," p. 429; *T. S. Eliot's Poetry and Plays* (1956; 8th impression, 1968), p. 157.

39. Pound, *Letters*, p. 23.

40. Pound, *Literary Essays*, ed. Eliot (1954), p. xiv.

41. "Introduction" to Pound, *Selected Poems*, p. viii.

42. *The Use of Poetry and the Use of Criticism* (London, 1933), p. 25.

43. *Ezra Pound, His Metric and Poetry* (New York, 1917) [i.e., 1918. See Donald Gallup, *T. S. Eliot, A Bibliography* (London, 1969), p. 24], pp. 16-17; "Introduction" to Pound, *Selected Poems*, p. xiii.

44. *Dial*, 70, 4 (April 1921), [448].

45. "London Letter," *Dial*, 71, 4 (Oct. 1921), 454.

46. "John Dryden," *TLS*, 1012 (9 June 1921), [361]. Reprinted in *Selected Essays*.

47. *TWLMS*, p. [26].

48. "The Function of Criticism," *TLS*, 956 (13 May 1920), 289; cf. *Aspects of Literature*, p. 2.

49. "Criticism in England," *Athenaeum*, 4650 (13 June 1919), 456-57.

50. "The Perfect Critic [I]," p. 40.

51. "A Brief Treatise on the Criticism of Poetry," *Chapbook*, 2, 9 (March 1920), 2.

52. "Swinburne and the Elizabethans," *Athenaeum*, 4664 (19 Sept. 1919), 909. Reprinted, with some changes, in *The Sacred Wood*.

53. "Shorter Notices," *Egoist*, 5, 6 (June/July 1918), 87.

54. "Short Reviews," *Egoist*, 4, 11 (Dec. 1917), 173.

55. "Professional, or . . . ," *Egoist*, 5, 4 (April 1918), 61.

56. "The Local Flavour," *Athenaeum*, 4676 (12 Dec. 1919), 1332. Reprinted in *The Sacred Wood*.

57. "Criticism in England," p. 456.

58. *The Sacred Wood* (London, [1920]; Second ed. 1928), p. 40.

59. "A Note on Ezra Pound," *To-Day*, 4, 19 (Sept. 1918), 3.

60. "In Memory of Henry James," *Egoist*, 5, 1 (Jan. 1918), 2.

61. "Studies in Contemporary Criticism II," *Egoist*, 5, 10 (Nov./Dec. 1918), 131.

62. *Sacred Wood*, p. 39.

63. E. Dowden, "Literary Criticism in France," in *Studies in European Literature, The Taylorian Lectures 1889-1899* (Oxford, 1900), p. 3.

64. *Sacred Wood*, p. xi.

65. "London Letter," *Dial*, 70, 4 (Apr. 1921), 450.

66. "A Note on Ezra Pound," *To-Day*, 4, 19, 3.
67. "Observations," *Egoist*, 5, 5 (May 1918), 69.
68. *Artist as Critic*, p. 356.
69. *Spectator*, 6 Sept. 1862, p. 998.
70. *The Artist as Critic*, p. 342.
71. *The Use of Poetry and the Use of Criticism*, p. 17.
72. "A Romantic Patrician," *Athenaeum*, 4644 (2 May 1919), 265-67. Reprinted in *The Sacred Wood* as "A Romantic Aristocrat."
73. *Egoist*, 6, 4 (Sept. 1919), 55. Reprinted in *The Sacred Wood*.
74. "A Brief Treatise on the Criticism of Poetry," *Chapbook*, 2, 9, 2.
75. *The Use of Poetry and the Use of Criticism*, p. 32.
76. *Athenaeum*, 4665 (26 Sept. 1919), 940. Reprinted in *The Sacred Wood*.
77. *TLS*, 1012, [361].
78. "Observations," p. 70.
79. "A Commentary," *Criterion*, 3, 9 (Oct. 1924), [1].
80. "Studies in Contemporary Criticism I," *Egoist*, 5, 9 (Oct. 1918), 113.
81. *The Renaissance*, p. ix.
82. "Andrew Marvell," *TLS*, 1002 (31 March 1921), [201].
83. "The Perfect Critic [I]," p. 41.
84. "The Perfect Critic II," p. 103.
85. See above, pp. 114ff.
86. "Reflections on Contemporary Poetry," *Egoist*, 4, 9 (Oct. 1917), 133.
87. "The Perfect Critic II," p. 103.
88. "Reflections on Contemporary Poetry," *Egoist*, 4, 10 (Nov. 1917), 151.
89. "Criticism in England," p. 457. *Points of View* is the title John Hayward gave to his selection of Eliot's critical writing (London, 1941).
90. "Kipling Redivivus," *Athenaeum*, 4645 (9 May 1919), 297-98; "In Memory of Henry James," p. 2.
91. "The Lesson of Baudelaire," *Tyro*, I [Spring 1921], [4].
92. "Style and Thought," *Nation*, 22, 25 (23 March 1918), 770.
93. "A Brief Treatise on the Criticism of Poetry," *Chapbook*, 2, 9, 1.
94. "A Brief Treatise," p. 2.
95. "A Brief Treatise," p. 9.
96. "A Brief Treatise," p. 3.
97. *Sacred Wood*, p. 24.
98. "The Function of Criticism," *Criterion*, 2, 5 (Oct. 1923), 38.
99. *The Use of Poetry and the Use of Criticism*, pp. 30, 20.
100. *The Use of Poetry and the Use of Criticism*, p. 30.
101. "In Memory of Henry James," pp. 1-2.
102. "American Literature," *Athenaeum*, 4643 (25 April 1919), 236-37.

103. "The Romantic Englishman, the Comic Spirit and the Function of Criticism," *Tyro*, I [Spring 1921], [4].

104. *Athenaeum*, 4648 (30 May 1919), 392-93.

105. John Dryden, *Of Dramatick Poesie, An Essay*. Preceded by a *Dialogue on Poetic Drama by T. S. Eliot* (London, 1928), p. xxiii.

106. Hugh Kenner, *The Invisible Poet* (London, 1960; repr. 1965), p. 42.

107. *Knowledge and Experience in the Philosophy of F. H. Bradley* (London, 1964), p. 16.

108. *Knowledge and Experience*, p. 18.

109. *Knowledge and Experience*, p. 19.

110. Kenner, pp. 45-46.

111. *Knowledge and Experience*, p. 17.

112. *Knowledge and Experience*, p. 18.

113. *Knowledge and Experience*, p. 23.

114. *Ezra Pound, His Metric and Poetry*, (New York, 1917 [i.e., 1918]), p. 13.

115. "The Borderline of Prose," *New Statesman*, 9, 215 (19 May 1917), 158.

116. "Reflections on Contemporary Poetry," *Egoist*, 4, 8 (Sept. 1917), 118.

117. "Reflections on Contemporary Poetry," *Egoist*, 4, 9 (Oct. 1917), 133.

118. "Beyle and Balzac," p. 392.

119. *Shakespeare and the Stoicism of Seneca*, An Address read before the Shakespeare Association, 18 March 1927. Reprinted in *Selected Essays*, p. 137.

120. "The Local Flavour," *Athenaeum*, 4676, p. 1333.

121. "Shakespeare and the Stoicism of Seneca," *Selected Essays*, p. 137; "Yeats," *On Poetry and Poets*, p. 256.

122. "Tradition and the Individual Talent [I]," p. 55.

123. "Introduction" to Baudelaire, *Intimate Journals*, p. 18.

124. *Gaston de Latour*, p. 71; "Wordsworth," *Appreciations*, p. 37.

125. *TLS*, 1012, [361].

126. "A Commentary," *Criterion*, 11, 45 (July 1932), 679.

127. *The Use of Poetry and the Use of Criticism*, p. 27.

128. "Wordsworth," *Appreciations*, p. 57.

129. "Hamlet and His Problems," p. 941; "Style," *Appreciations*, p. 27.

130. *TLS*, 1012, [361].

131. *TLS*, 1031, [669].

132. *TLS*, 1002, 202.

133. Below, p. 372.

134. *TLS*, 1002, [201].

135. "John Dryden," p. 362.

136. *TWLMS*, pp. xvii-xviii.

137. "London Letter," *Dial*, 70, 4 (April 1921), [448]-53; 70, 6 (June

1921), pp. [686]-91; 71, 2 (Aug. 1921), [213]-17; 71, 4 (Oct. 1921), [452]-55; *Tyro*, I [Spring 1921], [4]; *Chapbook*, 22 (April 1921), 3-10; *TLS*, 1002, [201]-202; 1012, [361]-62; 1031, [669]-70.

138. "London Letter," *Dial*, 70, 6 (June 1921), 689.

139. "London Letter," *Dial*, 73, 6 (Dec. 1922), 660-61.

140. Greene, *T. S. Eliot et la France*, pp. 108-109.

141. *TLS*, 930 (13 Nov. 1919), [637].

142. *Egoist*, 6, 1 (Jan. 1918), 1-2.

143. *TLS*, 1002, [201]-202.

144. *TLS*, 1012, 362.

145. *TWLMS*, p. xx.

146. Pound, *Letters*, p. 171.

147. Bernard Bergonzi, *T. S. Eliot* (London, 1972), p. 31.

148. *TWLMS*, p. [54].

149. Pp. 17-18.

150. *TWLMS*, p. 128.

151. *TWLMS*, pp. [104]-107.

152. *TWLMS*, pp. [58], ll. 48-51; p. [104], ll. 10-13.

153. *TWLMS*, p. [4].

154. "On the Idea of Comedy and of the Uses of the Comic Spirit," *Works*, Memorial Edition, XXIII (London, 1910), p. 5.

155. *TWLMS*, pp. [22], [26]-29.

156. Kenner, *The Invisible Poet*, p. 126.

157. *The Waste Land 1972. The Adamson Lecture*, 3rd May 1972, University of Manchester (Manchester, 1972), p. 25.

158. "The Lesson of Baudelaire," *Tyro*, I [Spring 1921], [4]; " 'Poet and Saint . . . ,' " *Dial*, 82, 5 (May 1927), [424]-31, reprinted with some changes as "Baudelaire in Our Time" in *For Lancelot Andrewes* (1928), and in *Essays Ancient and Modern* (1936); "Introduction" to Baudelaire, *Intimate Journals*, trans. C. Isherwood (1930), pp. 7-26 (included, somewhat changed, in *Selected Essays* [1932] as "Baudelaire").

159. *Criterion*, 9, 35 (Jan. 1930), 59.

160. *Intimate Journals*, p. 7.

161. *T. S. Eliot*, pp. 71-72.

162. *The Political Identities of Ezra Pound and T. S. Eliot* (Stanford, 1973), p. 149.

163. " 'Poet and Saint . . . ,' " p. 430.

164. *T. S. Eliot*, p. 113.

165. "Whitman and Tennyson," *Nation and Athenaeum*, 40, 11 (18 Dec. 1926), 426.

166. "In Memoriam," *Essays Ancient and Modern* (London, 1936), pp. 189-90.

167. De Maistre, quoted by Eliot in "A Commentary," *Criterion*, 13, 51 (Jan. 1934), p. 273.

168. *Intimate Journals*, p. 24.

169. See above, pp. 218-19.

170. Baudelaire, *Les Fleurs du Mal.* Introduction by Banville (Paris, 1917), p. ix.

171. Valéry, *Oeuvres Complètes*, I, 598-613. The lecture was given in February, 1924.

172. Régnier, Gide, Apollinaire, Kahn (Paris, 1917).

173. "Baudelaire," *Mercure de France*, 147, 547 (1 April 1921), 14.

174. *Egoists, A Book of Supermen* (London, 1909), p. 90.

175. [Unsigned], "Musings without Method," *Blackwood's Magazine*, 649 (March 1913), 413-14.

176. A[llen] T[ate], "One Escape from the Dilemma," *Fugitive*, 3, 2 (April 1924), 34-36.

177. "Baudelaire," *Life and Letters*, 1, 2 (July 1928), 133.

178. *Criterion*, 9, 35, 357.

179. " 'Poet and Saint . . . ,' " pp. 428-29.

180. *Intimate Journals*, p. 18.

181. *Life and Letters*, 1, 2, 133.

182. M. D. Z[abel], "Baudelaire," *Poetry*, 43, 1 (Oct. 1933), 38-39.

183. *Life and Letters*, 1, 2, 133.

184. *Life and Letters*, 1, 2, 135.

185. James Smith, "Baudelaire," *Scrutiny*, 7, 2 (Sept. 1938), 145.

186. "Baudelaire," p. 38.

187. *Criterion*, 9, 35, 359.

188. See above, note 34.

189. Quotations from Eliot's poems, in the following pages, are from *Collected Poems, 1909-1962* (London, 1963; repr. 1970).

190. Robert Lowell, "The Voyage (For T.S. Eliot)," *Imitations* (London, 1962), p. 66.

INDEX

abstraction in art, 31, 118-23
Action Française, 310
Adelphi, 310, 330, 331
aesthetic criticism, 31-33, 36-40, 47-49, 68, 104-16, 121, 123, 147-51, 157-62, 165, 198-200, 319-24, 328-30, 346-63
aesthetic emotion, 118, 352
Aesthetic Movement, 264. *See also* art for art's sake
Aldington, Richard, 5, 140, 187, 225, 260, 264, 267-70, 279-82, 285-87, 290-92, 295, 337, 412n33, 412n34, 417n76; and Baudelaire, 239, 285-87, 297, 418n94; on the city in modern poetry, 288, 290, 291, 292, 297; on criticism, 269-70, 285; on Flint, 290; on London, 298; and the *Mercure de France*, 283; and the 'nineties, 280, 285, 296; on Pound, 291; and Remy de Gourmont, 281-82; review of Crépet's *Etude Biographique*, 285-87, 418n94; translations from French, 281; on Wilde, 181-82, 264
—WORKS: "Beauty Thou Hast Hurt Me Overmuch," 268; "Daisy," 294; "Defeat," 294; "Eros and Psyche," 293; "French Authors in the War," 281; *French Studies and Reviews*, 281; "Happiness," 268; "Interlude," 297; *Literary Studies and Reviews*, 281; "Penultimate Poetry—Xenophilometropolitania," 261, 292-93; "White Chapel," 293-94
allegory, 49-54, 88-92, 103, 134-35, 162-71, 196
Allingham, William, 5, 64, 68, 96, 219

allusion, 7, 180; in Aldington, 268, 292-93, 297; in Conrad, 6-7, 389n5; in Eliot, 7, 332-33, 337-38, 342-45, 373-74, 386-88; in George Moore, 7; in Huxley, 227-32, 237; in Lawrence, 6-7; in Pater, 80-81, 86, 87-104, 131, 137-38, 191; in Swinburne, 33, 37, 38, 49, 52, 53-54, 61; in Symons, 192-95, 203-205, 408n27; in Wilde, 141-43, 145-46, 152-53, 157, 166-67, 171
Amiel, 131, 311
Anglo-French Poetry Society, 243, 244
Anglo-French Review, 266, 281
Apollinaire, Guillaume [*pseud.*], 271, 383, 428n172
Aristophanes, 372
Aristotle, 162, 353
Arnold, Matthew, 14, 22, 105, 162, 305, 313, 347, 348, 349, 355
Art, 18
art for art's sake, 16, 26, 28, 32, 38, 42, 47, 75, 85-86, 102, 103, 118, 222, 239, 310
artificiality. *See* nature and art
Asselineau, Charles, 19, 64, 65, 67, 73, 96
Athenaeum, 216, 225, 300, 301, 303, 312, 315, 319, 326, 347, 420n24
Auden, W. H., 5, 181, 182, 298

Babbitt, Irving, 310-11, 348
Bacon, Francis, 138
Balzac, Honoré de, 46, 47, 49, 50, 51, 53, 127, 156, 158, 181, 210, 212, 329, 359, 403-404n22; *La Fille aux Yeux d'Or*, 46; *Les Illusions Perdues*, 145

Library of Congress Cataloging in Publication Data

CLEMENTS, PATRICIA.
BAUDELAIRE & THE ENGLISH TRADITION.

BIBLIOGRAPHY: P.
INCLUDES INDEX.
1. ENGLISH POETRY—20TH CENTURY—HISTORY AND
CRITICISM.   2. MODERNISM (LITERATURE)   3. BAUDELAIRE,
CHARLES, 1821-1867—INFLUENCE.   4. ENGLISH LITERATURE—
19TH CENTURY—HISTORY AND CRITICISM.   I. TITLE.
II. TITLE: BAUDELAIRE AND THE ENGLISH TRADITION.

PR605.M63C58 1985   821'.009'1   85-42681
ISBN 0-691-06649-3 (ALK. PAPER)